Principles and Methods of Test Construction

About the Editors

Karl Schweizer, PhD, is a Professor in the Department of Psychology at Goethe University Frankfurt, Germany. He received his PhD from the University of Freiburg and was a faculty member there and at the University of Tübingen. His research interests focus on assessment, cognitive-differential psychology, psychological statistics, and research methods. He has served on the Executive Committee of the European Association of Psychological Assessment and was editor of *European Journal of Psychological Assessment*.

Christine DiStefano, PhD, is an Associate Professor of Educational Measurement in the College of Education at the University of South Carolina. Her research interests are in validity, survey construction, structural equation modeling with categorical data, and classification.

Acknowledgments

We would like to acknowledge the support of people who were important for the success of this book. We are grateful to the editor of the book series, Dr. Anastasia Efklides of Thessaloniki University, and the evaluation committee, which included Dr. Tuulia Ortner of Salzburg University and Dr. Willibald Ruch of Zurich University. Furthermore, we would like to thank Rob Dimbleby, who served as the representative of the publisher. We would like to acknowledge the invaluable contribution of the authors of the chapters who invested their expertise, time, and effort in providing state-of-the-art manuscripts. Chris wishes to thank George, Nora, and Fred for their unending support.

Psychological Assessment – Science and Practice

Each volume in the series *Psychological Assessment – Science and Practice* presents the state-of-the-art of assessment in a particular domain of psychology, with regard to theory, research, and practical applications. Editors and contributors are leading authorities in their respective fields. Each volume discusses, in a reader-friendly manner, critical issues and developments in assessment, as well as well-known and novel assessment tools. The series is an ideal educational resource for researchers, teachers, and students of assessment, as well as practitioners.

Psychological Assessment – Science and Practice is edited with the support of the European Association of Psychological Assessment (EAPA).

Psychological Assessment – Science and Practice, Vol. 3

Principles and Methods of Test Construction

Standards and Recent Advances

Edited by

Karl Schweizer and Christine DiStefano

Library of Congress Cataloging in Publication information for the print version of this book is available via the Library of Congress Marc Database under the LC Control Number 2016930840

Library and Archives Canada Cataloguing in Publication
   Principles and methods of test construction : standards and recent advances / edited by Karl Schweizer and Christine DiStefano.

(Psychological assessment--science and practice ; vol. 3)
Includes bibliographical references and index.
Issued in print and electronic formats.
ISBN 978-0-88937-449-2 (paperback).--ISBN 978-1-61676-449-4 (pdf).--ISBN 978-1-61334-449-1 (epub)

   1. Psychological tests--Design and construction. 2. Psychometrics.
I. Schweizer, Karl, 1951-, author, editor II. DiStefano, Christine, 1969-, author, editor
III. Series: Psychological assessment--science and practice ; v. 3

BF176.P75 2016   150.28'7   C2016-900441-4
                                          C2016-900442-2

© 2016 by Hogrefe Publishing
http://www.hogrefe.com

PUBLISHING OFFICES
USA: Hogrefe Publishing Corporation, 38 Chauncy Street, Suite 1002, Boston, MA 02111
              Phone (866) 823-4726, Fax (617) 354-6875; E-mail customerservice@hogrefe.com
EUROPE: Hogrefe Publishing GmbH, Merkelstr. 3, 37085 Göttingen, Germany
              Phone +49 551 99950-0, Fax +49 551 99950-111; E-mail publishing@hogrefe.com

SALES & DISTRIBUTION
USA: Hogrefe Publishing, Customer Services Department,
              30 Amberwood Parkway, Ashland, OH 44805
              Phone (800) 228-3749, Fax (419) 281-6883; E-mail customerservice@hogrefe.com
UK: Hogrefe Publishing, c/o Marston Book Services Ltd., 160 Eastern Ave., Milton Park,
              Abingdon, OX14 4SB, UK
              Phone +44 1235 465577, Fax +44 1235 465556; E-mail direct.orders@marston.co.uk
EUROPE: Hogrefe Publishing, Merkelstr. 3, 37085 Göttingen, Germany
              Phone +49 551 99950-0, Fax +49 551 99950-111; E-mail publishing@hogrefe.com

OTHER OFFICES
CANADA: Hogrefe Publishing, 660 Eglinton Ave. East, Suite 119-514, Toronto, Ontario, M4G 2K2
SWITZERLAND: Hogrefe Publishing, Länggass-Strasse 76, CH-3000 Bern 9

Hogrefe Publishing
Incorporated and registered in the Commonwealth of Massachusetts, USA, and in Göttingen, Lower Saxony, Germany

Printed and bound in Germany

ISBN 978-0-88937-449-2 (print) • ISBN 978-1-61676-449-4 (PDF) • ISBN 978-1-61334-449-1 (EPUB)
http://doi.org/10.1027/00449-000

Table of Contents

Part VI: Topics of Special Relevance

Part I

Introduction

Chapter 1

Introduction

Karl Schweizer[1] and Christine DiStefano[2]

[1]Department of Psychology, Goethe University Frankfurt, Germany
[2]Department of Educational Studies, University of South Carolina, USA

During the past 10–20 years, the methodology used to develop and to administer tests has experienced a number of substantial advancements. However, many of these advancements are dispersed across numerous outlets, such as journal articles, conference papers, or presentation materials. A major motivation for undertaking this book project was to collect knowledge concerning advancements in test construction, to provide information about the current practices, and to disseminate information about recent advances. We hope that in this way we may equip researchers and students with sufficient knowledge to successfully execute test construction projects, rather than learning of advancements through unfavorable interactions with discussants, editors, or journal reviewers. So, to us (and hopefully also to the readers), it appears to be valuable to collect information about the state of the art in test construction. The selection of the chapters is the result of our perceptions regarding advancements in test construction as well as issues that may benefit from further elaboration.

The first section provides a platform to examine and strengthen the role of the underlying theory when designing tests. The standards that govern test construction are explored to provide readers with information about the history and evolution of the guidelines that regulate best practices. Also included are chapters that discuss a modern test theory approach toward designing new measures according to a theory base and the study of the associated psychometric properties. Both the factor analytic and the item response theory (IRT) frameworks are provided.

The second section considers features related to item format and test presentation. A variety of item formats are examined to assist researchers with best practices for writing items for cognitive or affective measures. Discussion includes both formats that are more traditional (e.g., multiple choice) as well as newer formats that incorporate technological advances into items, producing a more interactive testing experience for examinees. Also, computerized and online assessments provide favorable preconditions for the increased utilization of adaptive testing. Online assessment has become more and more important for research as the Internet provides the opportunity of accessing large samples without a personal contact or a visit to a central location, such as a laboratory, career center, or testing site, needed. Thus, it is necessary to understand the possibilities as well as the potential pitfalls and shortcomings of this type of assessment. Moreover, adaptive testing shows a number of advantages that generally require fewer items to achieve a precise measurement of latent constructs with a shorter time commitment; such advantages need to be balanced against the challenges that online testing poses.

The third section discusses features related to model testing and selection, primarily from the structural equation modeling framework. Recent advancements have seen the rise of alternative estimators to deal with issues often encountered in test construction, such as analysis of nonnormally distributed observed level data or analysis and/or ordered categorical data. The chapters included provide information regarding selection of an estimation technique that can accommodate the characteristics of the collected data. Further, model selection and reporting of model-data fit information has been a controversial topic for many years and, in a way, has created insecurity of what constitutes best practice.

Group-specific biases of psychological measures have become a concern because of public sensitivity and, therefore, demand an especially exhaustive treatment. The fourth section provides information regarding statistical methods that enable the identification of group-specific bias. These chapters discuss differential item functioning, originating from the IRT framework, as well as multiple group testing from the structural modeling framework. The use of these methods can be helpful in evaluating the general appropriateness of the items selected or the differences in conceptualization of latent variables for relevant subgroups of a population.

The fifth section of the book discusses topics of special relevance. For example, test construction assuming one latent source gives rise to the expectation of one underlying dimension. This preferred model has stimulated the construction of measures showing a high degree of homogeneity, but may impose a structure that is not appropriate for the construction of measures representing intermediate or even higher-order constructs. The elaboration of the bifactor model may provide a method for researchers to consider. Also, since the publication of the seminal work by Campbell and Fiske it is known that the true variance characterizing a measure may be inflated by a contribution of the observational method. More recent research suggests that the presence of method effects in survey data is more likely than its absence. Chapters describing modern techniques for conducting multitrait–multimethod research as well as examination of method effects due to position effects are included. Another challenge is the creation of abridged scales or screeners, as short forms of instruments are increasingly common owing to testing expenses in terms of time and cost. Methods for creating both abridged forms and screening instruments are provided in this section.

Part II

Major Approaches to Test Construction

Chapter 2

The Use of Standards in Test Development

Fons J. R. van de Vijver

Department of Culture Studies, Tilburg University, The Netherlands

The present chapter deals with the question of the use of standards in test development. The best known example of such standards are the "Standards for Educational and Psychological Testing" published by the American Educational Research Association, the American Psychological Association, and the national Council on Measurement in Education (American Educational Research Association, American Psychological Association, & National Council on Measurement in Education, 2014). The latest version, published in 2014, has just been released. This version updated earlier editions of the standards. For example, the 1999 publication of the standards was an update of the 1985 edition (http://www.teststandards.org/history. htm), which mainly covered the groundwork of test development, grounded in classical statistics, such as classical test theory (Lord & Novick, 1968). At that time it was the most comprehensive overview of do's and don'ts in test development. The 1999 version was updated to recognize the following (American Psychological Association, 2013):

> Changes in federal law and measurement trends affecting validity; testing individuals with disabilities or different linguistic backgrounds; and new types of tests as well as new uses of existing tests. The Standards is written for the professional and for the educated layperson and addresses professional and technical issues of test development and use in education, psychology and employment.

Changes from 1999 to the current standards are discussed in this chapter. The Standards, as they are usually referred to, were originally meant for the American market of test users, test developers, and policy makers. However, since the Standards were so comprehensive and similar standards were not formulated in many other countries, the book became an authoritative source in the area of test development.

The aforementioned quotation reflects important characteristics of many standards. First, they are compiled on a voluntary basis. Also, they provide links with the recent developments and psychometrics so as to ensure their scientific soundness and up-to-date nature. Finally, standards are influenced by various developments in science and society. Psychology is not unique in its attempts to enhance the quality of its services by implementing standards. The ISO (International Organization for Standardization; http://www.iso.org/iso/home/about.htm) is the world's largest developer of voluntary international standards. In this organization, "a standard is a document that provides requirements, specifications, guidelines or characteristics that can be used consistently to ensure that materials, products, processes and services are fit for their purpose" (http://www.iso.org/iso/home/standards.htm). Since 1947, almost 20,000 standards have been developed, covering almost all aspects of technology and business. ISO certification has become an important hallmark of quality. Psychology as a discipline does not have the highly formalized systems of service delivery and quality checks as implemented in the ISO Standards. Still, the same underlying reasoning of enhancing quality by agreeing on standardized procedures can be found in psychology.

Since the launch of the Standards for Educational and Psychological Testing in 1955, many more standards have been developed. The present chapter gives an overview of recent advances in the development of standards in the domain of psychological assessment. It is impossible to review all aspects of the standards presented here. Therefore, I present the contents of standards in tables and deal with other aspects in the main text. I focus on various sets of standards that have been proposed in the last 20 years so as to accommodate new target groups and new modes of administration. Furthermore, I move outside of the realm of psychological and educational testing where the standards were originally developed. More specifically, I describe guidelines that were designed for international testing, notably dealing with translations and adaptations, standards for computer-based and Internet testing, standards for test use, and standards for quality control. Conclusions are drawn in the last section.

Two caveats are needed on terminology. The first is the distinction between educational and psychological testing. This distinction is made more in the American literature than in the European literature, in which the two types of assessment are often considered together. I follow here the European tradition and refer to testing and assessment as involving both educational and psychological instruments. Second, the literature uses two related concepts to refer to desirable features of psychological assessment: standards and guidelines. There is a subtle, yet essential, difference between the two. Standards typically have a prescriptive meaning. Standards describe prerequisites of instruments and their administration needed to ensure valid outcomes of the assessment process. Guidelines, on the other hand, are typically less prescriptive and are formulated as aspired or best practices. The distinction between these aspects seems to be easy to make. In practice, the distinction can be fuzzy as the terms are not always used from the perspective of this difference. Some guidelines are prescriptions, while some standards describe recommendable practices.

The Standards for Educational and Psychological Testing

The Standards for Educational and Psychological Testing are an initiative of the American Educational Research Association (AERA), the American Psychological Association (APA), and the National Council on Measurement in Education (NCME). The Standards for Educational and Psychological Testing have been very influential in psychology and education; the latest version, the fifth revision, was launched in 2014 (a description of the changes in this version was made by Plake & Wise, 2014). The history of the standards has clearly shown that defining norms regarding development, administration, and interpretation of tests helps to advance the quality of the field of assessment. References in the literature to the Standards for Educational and Psychological Testing are numerous (see, e.g., http://teststandards.org/files/Standards_citations_Jan_2010.pdf) and to the best of my knowledge, their reception has not been controversial. The standards are meant to provide criteria for the evaluation of tests, testing practices, and the effects of test use (AERA, APA, & NCME, 2014). The standards are not meant to influence policy, but they can provide recommendations on how psychometrics can be used to underline policy decisions. For instance, rather than prescribing which minimum cutoff score should be established for an admission test, the standards can help to identify conditions that are critical for determining cutoff scores.

The Standards for Educational and Psychological Testing cover three domains (see Table 2.1). The description of each domain starts with a general presentation of the context. Important concepts are defined and an overview of the main issues in the domain is presented.

Table 2.1. Overview of topics covered in 1999 Standards for Educational and Psychological Testing (American Educational Research Association, American Psychological Association, & National Council on Measurement in Education, 2014)

(a) Aim and domains covered	
Aim	To promote the sound and ethical use of tests and to provide a basis for evaluating the quality of testing practices
Domains covered	1. Foundations 2. Operations 3. Testing Applications

(b) Guidelines

Part I. Foundations

1. Validity
2. Reliability/precision and errors of measurement
3. Fairness in testing

Part II. Operations

1. Test design and development
2. Scores, scales, norms, score linking, and cut scores
3. Test administration, scoring, reporting, and interpretation
4. Supporting documentation for tests
5. The rights and responsibilities of test takers
6. The rights and responsibilities of test users

Part III. Testing Applications

1. Psychological testing and assessment
2. Workplace testing and credentialing
3. Educational testing and assessment
4. Uses of tests for program evaluation, policy studies and accountability

Source: http://www.apa.org/science/programs/testing/standards.aspx

The first part of the Standards for Educational and Psychological Testing, called Foundations, refers to the core business of psychometrics: test construction, evaluation, and documentation. Validity, viewed as pivotal in the psychological assessment process, refers to the degree to which evidence and theory support the interpretations of test scores entailed by proposed uses of tests (AERA, APA, & NCME, 2014). Thus, the standards describe how validity evidence can be obtained. The standards emphasize the need for finding validity evidence, specifying intended test use, and for clearly stating the recommended interpretation and use of test scores. The common theme of norms in the validity section of the standards is that it is incumbent on the user to provide validity evidence and to refrain from making untested assumptions about test use. The chapter on reliability, referring to consistency when a testing procedure is repeated, emphasizes the need for standardized administration procedures so as to increase reliability. The chapter describes various approaches to reliability, such as classical test theory with its internal consistency coefficients, standard errors, and interrater agreement (e.g., Lord & Novick, 1968), item response theory (e.g., Van der Linden & Hambleton, 1997) with its test information functions, and generalizability theory (e.g., Webb, 1991) with its multiple ways of computing reliability. The remaining chapters of the first section deal with test development and revision, scales, norms, administration scoring, and documentation. The standards mentioned there provide an excellent overview of commendable practices in these domains.

The next section is called Operations. The section is a major revision of the previous (1999) version. An important aspect of the section is fairness. Issues of fairness are salient aspects of assessment in all multicultural societies. Where in the 1999 version there was an emphasis on fairness for various subgroups in society that could be adversely affected by the use of psychological tests, such as women, members of specific ethnic groups, or people from the LGBT community, the 2015 version takes a broader perspective.

A measure is fair if it is free from bias. The conceptualization that is used in the standards is borrowed from the literature on item bias (usually labeled *differential item functioning*; Van de Vijver & Leung, 1997). An item is said to be biased if individuals from different groups (e.g., different genders, age groups, or ethnic groups) with the same standing on the latent trait that is being assessed do not have the same expected scores on the item. A strong aspect of this definition is that it is supported by many statistical procedures to identify this bias, such as analysis of variance, regression analysis, exploratory and confirmatory factor analysis, and contingency table analyses (see Van de Vijver & Leung, 1997; Zumbo, 2007). The weak spot of this definition is its emphasis on item-related sources of bias. In my experience, important sources of cross-cultural differences in scores that are not related to the target construct that is measured are usually not item based but instrument based. For example, there are large cross-cultural differences in response styles, such as social desirability (Van Hemert, Van de Vijver, Poortinga, & Georgas, 2002). Vieluf, Kuenther, and Van de Vijver (2013) analyzed the 2008 TALIS data on teacher self-efficacy. At country level, significant positive correlations were found between self-efficacy and job satisfaction; in addition, teacher self-efficacy was related to collectivism, modesty, and extremity scoring. It was concluded that mean score differences between 23 countries were strongly influenced by extremity scoring. Such response styles challenge the validity of cross-cultural comparisons in personality and attitude assessments, among many other domains. However, statistical procedures to identify item bias will typically not pick up cross-cultural differences in response styles, as the latter tend to have a global rather than item-specific influence on the assessment process.

Another problem with the chapter on operations is its focus on instrument characteristics. There are useful standards describing how to validate measures in each group and how to examine the identity of the meaning of test scores; however, there is no description of which group characteristics could impact bias. Examples are previous test exposure, response styles, education, and various other background variables that tend to differ across target groups, notably in the assessment of ethnic groups. Similarly, in the chapter on the assessment of individuals of diverse linguistic backgrounds, the description of the problem and the Standards for Educational and Psychological Testing do not refer to specific groups or acculturation issues, but only to recommendations to be cautious and to present evidence about the validity of the measure. Apart from these qualms, the chapter on fairness describes many valuable procedures to achieve equitable treatment among all test takers.

The third part of the Standards for Educational and Psychological Testing, called Testing Applications, describes issues in testing applications, such as work place testing and credentialing. The Standards in this part are based on a rich experience of psychological assessment in many different domains and a keen awareness of the legal issues accompanying psychological assessment. There is also a chapter on specific issues in educational assessment.

The Standards for Educational and Psychological Testing are the most elaborate standards available in the field of psychology and education. It is a major strength of these standards that many experts have been involved in the process of writing standards and providing feedback on earlier versions. As a consequence, the standards integrate theoretical and practical insights in the assessment process. The quality of the standards is so high that it is easy to appreciate why they have become so influential. In their quest for quality, the authors have attempted to be inclusive and exhaustive in many ways. For example, in the chapter on reliability, various theoretical perspectives on the concepts are presented, emphasizing common themes rather than highlighting differences between approaches. The quest has also been beneficial from another perspective. The Standards for Educational and Psychological Testing have influenced testing practices and have served as a template in many countries. Many standards that have been formulated are relevant in various countries. Notably the first part, dealing with test construction, evaluation, and documentation, has many standards that are widely applicable. The part on fairness also has a broad applicability, even though particular issues related to fairness may be country specific as the diversity of countries differs in nature. The part on testing applications is also widely applicable, although there are aspects such as credentialing that are relatively more important in a country with much high-stakes testing, such as the US, than in other parts of the world.

Plake and Wise (2014) warn against possible misuse and misinterpretation of the standards. Their description is interesting as their recommendations go beyond the standards. The first aspect they mention is that the standards are meant to provide professional guidelines and are not meant to be applied in a literal fashion. Professional judgment, based on solid scientific insights, should undergird any decision about the application of the standards. Furthermore, the authors emphasize that there is no authority to enforce or guard applications of the standards, which implies that any claim about compliance with the standards should be checked. Finally, the standards cover a rapidly evolving field; as a consequence, older versions may no longer apply and elements of the current version may also need modification in the near or distant future. In short, the standards should be used judiciously and should not be used as a detailed guide of what (not) to do.

Guidelines for International Testing

In 1992 the International Test Commission (ITC; http://www.intestcom.org) took the initiative to set up a project to develop guidelines for international assessment; an updated version was published in 2010. Various international psychological associations participated in the project: European Association of Psychological Assessment, European Test Publishers Group, International Association for Cross-Cultural Psychology, International Association of Applied Psychology, International Association for the Evaluation of Educational Achievement, International Language Testing Association, and International Union of Psychological Science. The idea behind development of the Guidelines for International Testing was the perceived need to attend to issues of quality during the process of translating and adapting tests. In those days there was a continually growing body of international studies and there was no agreement as to the criteria for evaluating quality standards regarding reliability, validity, sampling procedures, and translation procedures that apply to such studies (Hambleton, 1994, 2001; Gregoire & Hambleton, 2009; Hambleton, Yu, & Slater, 1999; Van de Vijver & Hambleton, 1996). The criteria that were taken to apply to these international tests adhered to the standard psychometric practice, as described earlier, as well as implementing checks to assess the quality of the translations. These criteria were greatly expanded by the ITC Guidelines.

The most common translation check was the use of the so-called back-translation procedure (Brislin, 1970). Such a procedure consists of three steps. In the first, an instrument is translated from a source language to a target language, followed in the second step by an independent back translation. In the final step, the source and back-translated versions are compared. If the two instruments are identical or do not deviate in any major respect, the translation is taken to be adequate. If the two versions are not identical, some adjudication is needed, which usually takes place through interactions between the researcher and one or more translators. The main advantage of this widely applicable procedure is that the researcher does not need to have knowledge of the target language. However, in the 1990s it had already become clear that the procedure also has some disadvantages. For example, the most important quality criterion is the correspondence between the original and back-translated version. This favors translations that stay very close to the original source (literal translations). Such translations often do not have the natural flow and clarity of the original version. Notably if the original text includes metaphorical expressions (e.g., "I feel blue"), close translations are near impossible and back translations are almost never identical to the original text. Various new procedures have been proposed for translating instruments (Harkness, 2003), such as the comparison of multiple, independent forward translations, followed by an adjudication procedure to select the best translation. Also, a committee approach has been advocated. A group of experts, usually combining linguistic, cultural, and psychological knowledge of the target construct, jointly prepare a translation. The main advantage of such an approach is the balanced treatment of various perspectives that are relevant in the translation process. Whereas translations in the past were mainly viewed as involving linguistic aspects, the zeitgeist of the 1990s brought forth the idea that translating requires multiple types of expertise and that a good translation must try to do justice to psychological, linguistic, and cultural considerations. One of the most significant changes created by this new way of thinking has been the introduction of the term *adaptation* (Hambleton, Merenda, & Spielberger, 2005); subsequently, the term *translation* is used less frequently nowadays. Compared with the old procedures, adaptations tend to be more tailored to the specific cultural context in which the instrument will be applied.

These ITC Guidelines for International Testing are not the only ones that have been developed in the domain of test adaptations. Another example is Comparative Survey Design and Implementation (http://ccsg.isr.umich.edu/archive/pdf/fullguide061108.pdf). The group behind this initiative has developed an extensive set of guidelines concerning how to develop and implement cross-cultural surveys. There are various topics in the guidelines about Comparative Survey Design and Implementation that are minimally covered or not covered under ITC guidelines, such as costs, ethics considerations, sample design, and harmonizing data (e.g., converting socioeconomic status data based on country-specific indicators to a common metric). These Comparative Survey Design and Implementation Guidelines have been written from the perspective of large-scale international reviews, such as the International Social Survey Programme (http://www.issp.org). Where psychological and educational guidelines are often somewhat more focused on statistical procedures to ascertain equivalence, these survey guidelines focus more on design and implementation issues. Therefore, these are a valuable addition to psychological and educational guidelines.

The Guidelines for International Testing are presented in Table 2.2. It is significant that the guidelines start with recommendations regarding the context. Thus, rather than opening with specific recommendations, the guidelines start with the notion that is considered to be crucial in developing adaptations: It is important to study the context in which this study will take place and try to minimize the relevant yet confounding cross-cultural differences in the background variables as much as possible. This recommendation does not primarily refer to psychometric concentrations or to procedures to prepare translations, but emphasizes the need to take the linguistic and cultural context seriously. The second recommendation that deals with a description of the context of the study in general argues that we cannot simply assume that constructs or instruments work the same way in all cultures, and that this should be empirically demonstrated.

Table 2.2. International Test Commission Guidelines for Translating and Adapting Tests (version January 2010)

(a) Aim and domains covered	
Aim	"The objective was to produce a detailed set of guidelines for adapting psychological and educational tests for use in various different linguistic and cultural contexts" (ITC, nd)
Domains covered	1. Cultural context 2. Technicalities of instrument development and adaptation 3. Test administration 4. Documentation and interpretation

(b) Guidelines

Context

C.1 Effects of cultural differences which are not relevant or important to the main purposes of the study should be minimized to the extent possible.

C.2 The amount of overlap in the construct measured by the test or instrument in the populations of interest should be assessed.

Test Development and Adaptation

D.1 Test developers/publishers should insure that the adaptation process takes full account of linguistic and cultural differences among the populations for whom adapted versions of the test or instrument are intended.

D.2 Test developers/publishers should provide evidence that the language use in the directions, rubrics, and items themselves as well as in the handbook are appropriate for all cultural and language populations for whom the test or instrument is intended.

D.3 Test developers/publishers should provide evidence that the choice of testing techniques, item formats, test conventions, and procedures are familiar to all intended populations.

D.4 Test developers/publishers should provide evidence that item content and stimulus materials are familiar to all intended populations.

D.5 Test developers/publishers should implement systematic judgmental evidence, both linguistic and psychological, to improve the accuracy of the adaptation process and compile evidence on the equivalence of all language versions.

D.6 Test developers/publishers should ensure that the data collection design permits the use of appropriate statistical techniques to establish item equivalence between the different language versions of the test or instrument.

D.7 Test developers/publishers should apply appropriate statistical techniques to (1) establish the equivalence of the different versions of the test or instrument, and (2) identify problematic components or aspects of the test or instrument which may be inadequate to one or more of the intended populations.

D.8 Test developers/publishers should provide information on the evaluation of validity in all target populations for whom the adapted versions are intended.

D.9 Test developers/publishers should provide statistical evidence of the equivalence of questions for all intended populations.

D.10 Non-equivalent questions between versions intended for different populations should not be used in preparing a common scale or in comparing these populations. However, they may be useful in enhancing content validity of scores reported for each population separately.

Administration

A.1 Test developers and administrators should try to anticipate the types of problems that can be expected, and take appropriate actions to remedy these problems through the preparation of appropriate materials and instructions.

Table 2.2. contiued

> A.2 Test administrators should be sensitive to a number of factors related to the stimulus materials, administration procedures, and response modes that can moderate the validity of the inferences drawn from the scores.
>
> A.3 Those aspects of the environment that influence the administration of a test or instrument should be made as similar as possible across populations of interest.
>
> A.4 Test administration instructions should be in the source and target languages to minimize the influence of unwanted sources of variation across populations.
>
> A.5 The test manual should specify all aspects of the administration that require scrutiny in a new cultural context.
>
> A.6 The administrator should be unobtrusive and the administrator-examinee interaction should be minimized. Explicit rules that are described in the manual for administration should be followed.
>
> Documentation/Score Interpretations
>
> I.1 When a test or instrument is adapted for use in another population, documentation of the changes should be provided, along with evidence of the equivalence.
>
> I.2 Score differences among samples of populations administered the test or instrument should not be taken at face value. The researcher has the responsibility to substantiate the differences with other empirical evidence.
>
> I.3 Comparisons across populations can only be made at the level of invariance that has been established for the scale on which scores are reported.
>
> I.4 The test developer should provide specific information on the ways in which the socio-cultural and ecological contexts of the populations might affect performance, and should suggest procedures to account for these effects in the interpretation of results.

Source: International Test Commission at http://www.intestcom.org/upload/sitefiles/40.pdf

These context guidelines describe the framework from which the other guidelines have been derived. This second type of guideline refers to test development and adaptation. These form the core of the adaptation guidelines, as they describe the do's and don'ts in designing new instruments. There are some recurring themes in these guidelines. The first is the need to take full cognizance of the cultural and linguistic context of the study. The second is the need to combine adequate instrument design with appropriate statistical analysis. A good test adaptation starts from a conceptual analysis of the underlying construct(s), including an analysis of the applicability of the construct and its measure in the new cultural context. These theoretical considerations, which may result in smaller or larger changes of the stimuli so as to increase their cultural fit, should be complemented by cognitive interviews (Miller, 2003), pilot studies, or field trials in which the appropriateness of the new instrument is tested. In the next stage, statistical evidence should be accumulated to demonstrate the adequacy of the instrument in the new cultural context. If a comparative study is conducted in the quantitative stage, evidence should be collected to test that the instrument measures the same construct in each culture by demonstrating invariance (Van de Vijver & Leung, 1997; Vandenberg & Lance, 2000).

Administration Guidelines deal with issues arising in implementing the instrument in the new cultural context, including the need to keep the ambient conditions of testing as similar as possible across cultures, the need to standardize test instructions and administrations, and the need to minimize the influence of the test administrator on the test outcome. Some of these aspects tend not to be influential in applications of an instrument within a single cultural group, but experience shows that these factors can contribute to unwanted score differences in cross-cultural applications.

The last set of Guidelines for International Testing deal with documentation and score interpretations. The guidelines in this section refer to the need to clearly document all the adaptations that were implemented, the reasons for the adaptations, as well as a description of the potential influence of these adaptations on scores. In short, these guidelines express the frequently observed need to describe and document the changes of the original instrument in the adaptation process and to provide evidence for the validity of these procedures.

The Guidelines for International Testing have been used in many studies. Special sections of the *European Journal of Psychological Assessment* (Van de Vijver, 1999) and the *International Journal of Testing* (Gregoire & Hambleton, 2009) were devoted to test adaptations and the ITC Guidelines for International Testing. The guidelines have introduced a new way of thinking about translations. Several decades ago, translation studies usually dealt with Western-developed instruments that had to be exported outside of their context of development. The original, usually English, instrument was then the template and the Western data served as frame of reference. The procedure of translating and back translating worked well when the implicit ideal of the translation was a close rendering of the original. Statistical analyses were then conducted to establish whether the constructs that were observed were the same as previously found in Western regions. However, this template for conducting translation studies is less and less adequate for modern studies. It is increasingly appreciated that maximizing the similarity of an instrument to the version that works well in Western populations may not be the best possible way of maximizing the validity of an instrument in a new cultural context. Maximizing the cross-cultural validity and maximizing the similarity of instruments do not always produce the same results. The ITC Guidelines for International Testing no longer represent the conventional template but emphasize the cultural appropriateness of instruments in the new cultural context.

Guidelines for Computer-Based and Internet Testing

The development of guidelines for computer-based and Internet testing can be seen against the backdrop of important developments in information technology of the last decades, which made it technically possible to use new devices, such as personal computers, laptops, smartphones, handheld devices, and tablets. In the 1980s and 1990s, there was an emphasis on what was technically possible in terms of computer-based testing and on whether computer-based and paper-and-pencil administration yield assessments of the same underlying construct(s). More recently, this situation has changed in that many new devices have become available, most clients have experience in working with information technology devices (thereby presumably reducing differential exposure to computers as an unwanted source of performance differences), and Internet connections have become widely available. The Guidelines for Computer-Based and Internet Testing should be seen as an attempt to professionalize and standardize practices in Internet-based assessment. Internet-based assessment is no longer the playground of a small group of geeks, but it has become an essential tool for notably large testing agencies.

The International Test Commission (2005, 2006; Coyne, 2006; Coyne & Bartram, 2006) has developed guidelines for Internet-based assessment. The Guidelines for Computer-Based and Internet Testing are targeted at three groups. In the first part are test users, such as test purchasing managers, proctors surveying test administrations, and professionals who formulate reports, draw inferences, and provide advice to clients on the basis of test results (e.g., counselors). The second group comprises test developers who need to combine substantive knowledge of the construct measured, psychometric expertise, cultural and linguistic expertise (in line with the test adaptation guidelines described previously), and technical knowledge to decide on the implementation of Internet-based tests. Test publishers are the third group. They need to have knowledge of the legal structure in a country regarding Internet-based assessment, provide a platform for administration of instruments, interpretation of scores, and communication of test results. The Guidelines for Computer-Based and Internet Testing refer to several domains; within each domain, related yet distinct guidelines are formulated for the users, developers, and publishers of tests.

The working group that prepared the Guidelines for Computer-Based and Internet Testing was focusing on four domains. The first involves questions related to technology, such as the requirements for the hardware and software of computer-based test delivery. The second refers to the quality of the testing materials as well as the quality of the assessment process. The third refers to control regarding the delivery of tests, test-taker authentication, and prior practice. Finally, Internet-based assessment comes with various security issues, such as the avoidance of uncontrolled dissemination of items, data protection, and confidentiality.

The Guidelines for Computer-Based and Internet Testing are presented in Table 2.3. An important theme in the guidelines is related to technical aspects. For example, good Internet-based test delivery requires the use of good browsers, the control of the appearance of the instrument's graphical user interface on different types of displays, robustness of the administration process against system failures and loss of Internet connection, and modifications for disabled persons. In addition, country-specific regulations may require adaptations of standard procedures. A second theme refers to quality issues; an example is the establishment and documentation of psychometric characteristics, notably reliability and validity. There are also some specific quality issues with regard to computer-based assessment. If an instrument has been converted from a paper-and-pencil version to the computer, evidence should be presented that the two versions are equivalent and function in the same way. Also, it is relatively common nowadays to employ adaptive procedures in large-scale assessment (van der Linden & Glas, 2000). Such procedures have distinct advantages in that they minimize assessment time and minimize exposure of items to clients, thereby reducing the problem of item dissemination in the target population. However, there is a need to explain the scoring procedure of such adaptive tests so that test takers have at least some understanding of the way in which their test score was computed. When working with clients, individual differences related to computer experience may arise that could have an adverse impact. This concept, drawing from multicultural assessment, refers to group differences in performance that are unrelated to the target construct. Differential computer experience could lead to adverse impact in heterogeneous populations.

Compared with conventional assessment based on the interaction of a tester and test taker, the supervision of computer-based testing can take several forms. The first is called *open mode*; in such an assessment procedure there is no direct human supervision required. The computer monitors the item responses of the test taker. The second is the *controlled mode*. This mode is slightly different in that the test is made available only to known test takers, and the administration is unsupervised. The third mode is called the *supervised mode*. Test users have to log on a candidate and confirm that the testing was administered and completed correctly. The last mode, the managed mode, is most similar to conventional testing. A high level of human supervision is used and control over test-taking conditions is required to ensure authenticity and security of administration as well as to minimize cheating. The administration mode has implications for various issues, including privacy and data security.

Table 2.3. Outline of Guidelines for Computer-Based and Internet Testing

(a) Aim and domains covered	
Aim	To produce a set of internationally developed and recognized guidelines that highlight good practice issues in computer-based (CBT) and Internet-delivered testing To raise awareness among all stakeholders in the testing process of what constitutes good practice.
Domains covered	Technology – ensuring that the technical aspects of CBT/Internet testing are considered, especially in relation to the hardware and software required to run the testing. Quality – ensuring and assuring the quality of testing and test materials and ensuring good practice throughout the testing process. Control – controlling the delivery of tests, test-taker authentication and prior practice. Security – security of the testing materials, privacy, data protection and confidentiality.

(b) Guidelines
1. Give due regard to technological issues in computer-based (CBT) and Internet testing

a. Give consideration to hardware and software requirements
   b. Take account of the robustness of the CBT/Internet test
   c. Consider human factors issues in the presentation of material via computer or the Internet
   d. Consider reasonable adjustments to the technical features of the test for candidates with disabilities
   e. Provide help, information, and practice items within the CBT/Internet test

2. Attend to quality issues in CBT and Internet testing

a. Ensure knowledge, competence and appropriate use of CBT/Internet testing
   b. Consider the psychometric qualities of the CBT/Internet test
   c. Where the CBT/Internet test has been developed from a paper and pencil version, ensure that there is evidence of equivalence
   d. Score and analyze CBT/Internet testing results accurately
   e. Interpret results appropriately and provide appropriate feedback
   f. Consider equality of access for all groups

3. Provide appropriate levels of control over CBT and Internet testing

a. Detail the level of control over the test conditions
   b. Detail the appropriate control over the supervision of the testing
   c. Give due consideration to controlling prior practice and item exposure
   d. Give consideration to control over test-taker's authenticity and cheating

4. Make appropriate provision for security and safeguarding privacy in CBT and Internet testing

a. Take account of the security of test materials
   b. Consider the security of test-taker's data transferred over the Internet
   c. Maintain the confidentiality of test-taker results

Source: International Test Commission at http://www.intestcom.org/Downloads/ITC%20Guidelines%20on%20Computer%20-%20version%202005%20approved.pdf

Software developers are often confronted with pirating. Notably in the early years of computer-based testing, there was a similar problem with copyright infringements of psychological tests. These infringements could take place at a relatively small scale, when testing agencies use public-domain instruments for commercial purposes or when these agencies computerize existing paper-and-pencil tests without paying rights to the owner. Also, some countries do not recognize international copyright laws, which implies that test publishers have no legal ground in these countries to combat pirating. Although these infringements still occur, many large-scale testing agencies have implemented security measures to prevent illegal copying of their testing materials.

The Guidelines for Computer-Based and Internet Testing are important for all stakeholders in the assessment process (test takers, users, developers, and publishers). Like other guidelines, they are intended to enhance levels of professionalism and to standardize ways of developing and administering tests. The guidelines can help to make computer-based assessment more transparent for all parties.

Guidelines for Test Use

The ITC Guidelines for Test Use (Bartram 2002; International Test Commission, 2000, 2001) involve the fair and ethically responsible use of tests. The target group are test developers, publishers, users, clients, and significant others, such as parents, and policy makers. The work is based on experiences obtained with the compilation of guidelines for test adaptations, as described previously, and on work by various national associations on responsible test use, such as work by the Australian Psychological Society, the British Psychological Society, and the Canadian Psychological Association. All these associations have developed guidelines to promote professional test use in their countries (e.g., http://www.psychology.org.au/Assets/Files/using_psychological_tests_ethical_guidelines.pdf).

Although the Guidelines for Test Use primarily refer to test use, the report in which the guidelines are described pays much attention to the skills that are required to make all the necessary judgments and decisions that will eventually lead to ethically responsible test use. To start with, the test user should have relevant declarative knowledge, including knowledge of basic psychometric principles and procedures, a good grasp of the technical requirements of tests (e.g., reliability), sufficient knowledge of measurement to enable the proper understanding of test results, as well as understanding of the relevant theories and models of the constructs tested. This knowledge is necessary to properly inform the choice of tests and the interpretation of test results; and knowledge of the tests and the test suppliers relevant to one's area of practice is also important. Instrumental knowledge and skills include (a) knowledge and skills relating to specific assessment procedures or instruments and (b) knowledge of and practitioner skills associated with using those tests that are within one's repertoire of assessment tools. General personal task-related skills include the performance of relevant activities such as test administration, reporting, and the provision of feedback to test takers and other clients, necessary oral and written communication skills, and interpersonal skills needed for the proper management of the assessment process. Contextual knowledge and skills refer to knowing when and when not to use tests, knowing how to integrate testing with other less formal components of the assessment situation, and knowledge of professional, legal, and ethics issues. Task management skills involve knowledge of codes of conduct and good practice relating to the use of tests, test data, and the provision of feedback, as well as knowledge of the social, cultural, and political context. Finally, contingency management skills refer to knowing how to deal with problems, difficulties, and breakdowns in routine, knowing how to deal with a test taker's questions during test administration, and knowing how to deal with situations in which there is the potential for test misuse. An important aspect in these skills is the understanding of local context. Even though many of the guidelines that have been proposed may have a broad applicability, the report warns against a one-size-fits-all approach and argues that all guidelines have to be interpreted against the backdrop of the local situation.

The Guidelines for Test Use are presented in Table 2.4. The guidelines strike a balance between various considerations that are relevant for the quality of assessment, such as standardization, preparedness to deal with contingencies, the need to stick to standardized procedures where possible and to be flexible when needed as well as to comply with the recommendations of the test manual, to be fair and accessible for the test takers, and to analyze test results in a competent, meticulous manner, etc. In short, the test user should have a very complete and accurate insight into all the relevant factors that could have a bearing on test performance and understand which of these recommendations should be applied at any moment in the assessment process.

Table 2.4. Guidelines for test use

(a) Aim and domains covered	
Aim	The long-term aim of this project includes the production of a set of guidelines that relate to the competencies (knowledge, skills, abilities and other personal characteristics) needed by test users. These competencies are specified in terms of assessable performance criteria. These criteria provide the basis for developing specifications of the evidence of competence that would be expected from someone seeking qualification as a test user. Such competencies need to cover such issues as: • Professional and ethical standards in testing; • Rights of the test taker and other parties involved in the testing process; • Choice and evaluation of alternative tests; • Test administration, scoring, and interpretation; and • Report writing and feedback.
Domains covered	Responsibility for ethical test use Good practice in the use of tests Regulating the supply and availability of tests and information about tests.
(b) Guidelines	
1. Responsibility for ethical test use	

  a. Act in a professional and ethical manner
  b. Ensure they have the competence to use tests
  c. Take responsibility for their use of tests
  d. Ensure that test materials are kept securely
  e. Ensure that test results are treated confidentially

2. Follow good practice in the use of tests

  a. Evaluate the potential utility of testing in an assessment situation
  b. Choose technically sound tests appropriate for the situation
  c. Give due consideration to issues of fairness in testing
  d. Make necessary preparations for the testing session
  e. Administer the tests properly
  f. Score and analyze test results accurately
  g. Interpret results appropriately
  h. Communicate the results clearly and accurately to relevant others
  i. Review the appropriateness of the test and its use

Source: International Test Commission at http://www.intestcom.org/upload/sitefiles/41.pdf

Although the Guidelines for Test Use are detailed as can be seen in Table 2.4, it is important to note that these guidelines can never be sufficiently comprehensive to deal with all contingencies in practical situations. Therefore, the guidelines can also be read as an instruction to use a specific mindset by the test user to achieve fair and ethically responsible test use. In cases where the Guidelines for Test Use do not provide a clear solution for a given problem, it is not difficult to generalize the type of reasoning behind the guidelines and to apply the reasoning to the problem at hand.

Standards for Quality Control

Quality control has received a lot of attention in the past few decades. The ITC has developed a list of guidelines to support the quality control of assessment processes (International Test Commission, 2011). Quality control is defined as (International Test Commission, 2011):

A formal systematic process designed to help ensure that high quality standards are maintained at all stages of scoring, test analysis, and reporting of test results, and to thereby minimize error and enhance measurement reliability. (p. 6).

The development of quality control guidelines fits in a schema in which quality assurance procedures have been applied in many services and industries. These procedures have a strong tendency to break down complex processes in smaller units and to describe procedural steps to ensure quality in these smaller units. The ITC Quality Control Guidelines also adopt this approach. One of the main advantages of these approaches is their transparency. It transforms the process of quality control from an implicit and, presumably, intuitive process to a set of steps that can be described, are applicable, and are independent of the person adopting the procedures.

These Standards for Quality Control can be seen as a companion to the Test Use Guidelines, described earlier. The perspective of the Quality Control Guidelines is not test development. These guidelines apply to the processes *after* the development of the test when the test has entered the stage of administration. The main domain of application of the Standards for Quality Control can be found in large-scale assessment procedures, such as university entry examinations, language assessments prior to studies abroad, and educational tests at specified time points in the curriculum, such as final exams. In many cases, these assessments are high-stakes and have a major influence on the lives of test takers, as test results may imply that test takers are admitted or not admitted to specific schools, are recognized as a licensed professional, or are entitled to receive services. Ensuring a high quality of assessment and ensuring identical administrations for all test takers are important elements in this process. However, the Standards for Quality Control also apply to assessment in smaller testing agencies. Some of the specified standards may be less relevant when fewer clients are assessed, but basic principles of quality control must be applied to any assessment process, regardless of the number of test takers involved. Whereas various standards have been developed with educational assessment as the primary frame of reference, the Standards for Quality Control also apply to job interviews, clinical intakes, and assessment centers. In general, these standards apply to all types of psychological assessment.

The Standards for Quality Control start with general principles, followed by step-by-step working guidelines. The former are more contextual guidelines, such as verifying quality control standards, whereas the latter involve detailed instructions about scoring and reporting test results. This sequence of first describing global guidelines, followed by more specific guidelines, is present in all ITC Guidelines. Compared with the other guidelines that have been developed by the ITC, the Standards for Quality Control are more specific and refer more to necessary steps to be followed than to more general recommendations.

The numerous standards, described in Table 2.5, entail distinct perspectives on the quality control process. Some standards have a managerial background and require the person responsible for the quality control to have a bird's eye view of the whole process. For example, the first standard refers to the need to determine which quality control standards are currently in use in the organization, while the second standard refers to the need to ensure that quality control procedures are in place before the start of any test administration. Other standards have a more psychometric background. For example, there is a standard that specifies that the standard setting model should be defined and described, while another standard specifies the need to compute item analyses (Sireci, 2013). A third type of standard refers to operational procedures. For example, there is a standard that specifies the need to record seat numbers while another refers to procedures to deal with suspected cheaters.

Table 2.5. Standards for quality control

(a) Aim and domains covered	
Aim	The quality control (QC) guidelines presented below are intended to increase the efficiency, precision and accuracy of the scoring, analysis, and reporting (SAR) process of testing. They have a twofold function: They can be used on their own, as specific guidelines for quality control in scoring, test analysis and score reporting; and they can also be regarded and used as an extension of specific parts of the ITC International-al Guidelines for Test Use (2000).
Domains covered	1. Verifying quality control standards currently in use 2. Basic preparations and agreements between persons involved 3. Resources 4. Demands and expectations of stakeholders 5. Professional staff and working atmosphere 6. Independent monitoring of quality control procedures 7. Documenting and reporting mistakes

(b) Guidelines

1. Verifying quality control standards currently in use

a. Determine what quality control guidelines currently exist for tests in your organization or in your country. If necessary, formulate test-specific quality control procedures before the test is administered. Review, update and modify guidelines whenever changes in the process are made, and also from time to time as a routine check.
b. Ensure that adequate quality control procedures are in place before administering the test.
c. When dealing with a new test, consider performing a trial, a pilot simulation for the whole SAR process. Where no pilot has been performed, treat the first administration as a trial run and be ready to make improvements before subsequent test administrations.
d. Create test-specific standards for each test, in cases where they do not yet exist.
e. Create test-specific standards for each new test at the time of its construction.

2. Basic preparations and agreements between persons involved

a. Identify all the stakeholders in the testing process and agree who is responsible for decision making with respect to the different parts of the testing process.
b. Determine and state the purpose or purposes of test use (e.g., selection, measuring achievement, research).
c. Agree on the timetable for the SAR process.
d. Establish the best means of communication between persons or teams (where more than one team is involved), for example, the best way to convey relevant information from one team to another, or to transmit detailed descriptions (test structure, test key, etc.) from the test development team to the test analysis team.
e. Establish the best means for communicating with the client about the testing process.
f. Decide on methods for transferring assessment data to those responsible for the SAR process, for example, data obtained using an optical reader or scanner for paper & pencil tests, or electronically obtained data for computerized tests.
g. Define the weights to be used for the subtests (when they are used) and provide the rationale for choices made. One should also be ready to modify the weights after receiving the data, but this should be done only in accordance with the theory and the test purpose.
h. Agree upon scoring instructions, that is, on the number of credits to be given for each correctly answered item, and decide how to deal with wrong answers. One should also be ready to modify the instructions after receiving the data.
i. Choose a scoring scale and determine the range of scale points.
j. Decide how to deal with missing data (e.g., cases where test takers have overlooked an item or mistakenly skipped a line when shading in answers, or cases where an assessor either forgets to assess a specific test taker or does so in a nonstandardized manner with no possibility of repeating the assessment)
k. Define and describe the equating model, design and sample sizes needed if the scores of different test versions must be put on the same scale, as well as the equating methods used.
l. Define and describe the standard setting model, and the design and sample sizes needed if standard setting procedures are used.

Table 2.5. continued

m. Agree upon the degree of detail with which scores should be reported to the test takers and institutions involved, and what additional information regarding score distributions and score use should be delivered.
n. Determine which specific individuals, bodies or institutions should receive test results, ensuring compliance with legal constraints regarding data privacy
o. Determine whether reports can or should provide other personal information (e.g., whether the test content was modified, how many items were completed, what accommodations for disabilities were offered).
p. Agree upon the level of documentation needed for the whole process.
q. Agree upon the level of replication effort to be allocated to critical processes (e.g., raw-to-scale conversion tables).

3. Resources

a. Confirm that there are adequate resources (cost, time and personnel) available for efficient and appropriate scoring, test analysis and reporting of scores.
b. Check available backup for each resource (e.g., if the equating specialist cannot do the equating, determine who will do it instead; or if the answer-sheet scanner is out of order, locate an alternate scanner).
c. Be aware of timing problems that can occur if backups are used. Consider contingency plans to cover the unexpected absence of key personnel.
d. Allocate tasks to appropriate members of the team: Who will take care of test scoring, analysis, and reporting of test scores? Who is in charge of the whole process? The professionals in charge of testing must determine, for example, whether the individuals involved in each step of the process have the skills needed for the work they are to carry out; they must also specify requirements and specifications, and define level of process automation.
e. Determine the necessary time resources: establish a timetable for each step in the SAR process. The deadline for finalizing the process and reporting the scores should be realistic.
f. Determine the necessary software, computer and network resources: copyrighted and custom-developed software, laptops, personal computers, main frames, disk space, server space, bandwidth analysis, and so forth.
g. Determine the necessary workspace resources – is there a sufficiently large work area (with enough rooms, tables, chairs, etc.) for all staff and test takers?
h. Determine the steps needed to keep the data safe and secure electronically.
i. Ensure that any additional equipment needed (e.g., hand scoring key, calculators) is available.

4. Demands and expectations of stakeholders

a. Where appropriate, formulate the agreement between the parties involved – stakeholders, vendors, test takers, clients, and others – in consultation with the professionals responsible for scoring, equating and reporting. Be aware that changes are made in the contract from time to time.
b. Agree upon who has final responsibility and authority to decide how to proceed when problems occur and how to resolve them.
c. Decide in advance on the process for dealing with cases where a mistake is discovered after scores have been released.
d. Provide test takers with the opportunity to question the correctness of proposed answers and to challenge their scores, or provide test takers with an opportunity to raise issues and ensure that these are addressed.
e. Have a document that can be used to defend the scoring of each item that appears on the test.

5. Professional staff and working atmosphere

a. Avoid unreasonable pressure on individuals for speed of performance.
b. Avoid excessive work hours.
c. Try to cultivate a meticulous, attention-to-detail work approach (especially with regard to error prevention), but one that is also relaxed. A calm but purposeful working atmosphere is most effective in maintaining high standards.
d. Support staff by providing professional development and training, and in some cases also personal growth and social skills training, (for example, opportunities for staff to participate in system testing based on previous year data preparatory to processing current year data.)

6. Independent monitoring of quality control procedures

7. Documenting and reporting mistakes

a. All those involved in the testing process should follow agreed procedures regarding the documentation of activities and of errors or issues that arise.

Table 2.5. continued

b. Agree in advance which member of staff is responsible for each stage.

c. Document all activities. Use standard check sheets to show that each process has been carried out and checked off accordingly.

d. Document in detail all mistakes or errors (regardless of whether the cause is already known), beginning with the nature of the mistake, who discovered it and when, what are/were the implications, and what steps have been/will be taken to deal with it. Also document cases in which mistakes were discovered before any harm was done.

e. Advise other professionals of mistakes in an appropriate and timely manner, sometimes in a special meeting devoted to error prevention.

f. Document how to prevent future mistakes or errors.

Source: International Test Commission at http://www.intestcom.org/upload/sitefiles/qcguidelines.pdf

What is particularly striking in these Standards for Quality Control is their comprehensiveness. The author of the Standards for Quality Control has extensive experience and large-scale testing and has everyday experience with managing a complicated test process. Many colleagues who provided feedback on earlier versions have a similar professional background. The Standards for Quality Control are the joint efforts of these colleagues. There is always some arbitrariness as to which recommendations will make it to a standard. It is not difficult to envision conditions in which more standards would need to be added or in which some of the specified standards are less relevant. In addition, it is quite clear that the Standards for Quality Control also have an implicit message to convey. Readers who have digested all the standards will be keenly aware of the underlying type of thinking, thereby making it easier to evaluate the adequacy of these guidelines in their specific professional and cultural context.

Conclusion: The Use of Guidelines and Standards in Test Development

Standards and guidelines for assessment are always developed in a specific zeitgeist. They are typically meant to enhance levels of professionalism, to increase transparency, and to make the profession more accountable. There have even been attempts by the European Federation of Psychologists' Associations (EFPA; http://www.efpa.eu/) to systematize test evaluations by designing a standardized inventory for evaluating psychological instruments (Muñiz & Bartram, 2007). Standards and guidelines are an appropriate way for a profession to communicate to its members as well as to the public what is considered to be recommended in the size and practice of assessment. The description of the standards and guidelines usually starts with a description of context followed by general standards, followed by specific-purpose guidelines. This order helps to convey an important implicit meaning of standards. Users will appreciate that it is impossible to define standards for all contingencies. Therefore, standards and guidelines in a profession do not only describe best practices, but they also identify ways of thinking about desirable features of the assessment process. Professionals involved in the assessment process, such as test developers, publishers, and users, will usually find it easy to determine which standards are particularly relevant and where the standards could be complemented in specific cases. In other words, standards and guidelines do not only describe recommended practices, they also teach users a specific way of thinking about the assessment process. The latter is important because rigid applications of standards and guidelines are counterproductive when they become a straitjacket by not considering contextual conditions. Notably in countries in which psychology is emerging as a discipline, it would be unrealistic to assume that standards and guidelines can be fully implemented. The context of assessment is not conducive to such an implementation. This is not to say that quality considerations are not important, but to emphasize that we should be aware of what can be achieved under difficult assessment conditions. However, even in such difficult conditions, standards and guidelines can be used to define the way forward. It should be noted that standards are usually set up to enhance quality, not to rigidify the assessment process.

In the last few decades quality assurance has become increasingly important in society. Our psychological services, of which assessment is presumably the most important, have been influenced by this perceived need to ensure quality. This trend is expected to continue. Forty years ago there was no need for a description of recommended practices in test adaptations. In those days, such adaptations were the work of a few specialists. However, increased internationalization has changed psychology as a profession (Van de Vijver, 2013). Standards are a useful way to keep up with such developments. The rapid rise of standards and guidelines in the last few decades will undoubtedly continue. It can be expected that the development stage will be followed by an implementation stage. It is clear in my view that standards and guidelines are here to stay. Hopefully, this chapter contributes to the knowledge and usage of standards and guidelines in all aspects of the assessment process.

References

American Educational Research Association, American Psychological Association, & National Council on Measurement in Education. (2014). *Standards for educational and psychological testing*. Washington, DC: American Educational Research Association.

American Psychological Association. (2013). *The Standards for Educational and Psychological Testing*. Retrieved from http://www.apa.org/science/programs/testing/standards.aspx

Bartram, D. (2002). International guidelines for test use. *International Journal of Testing, 1*, 2001.

Brislin, R. W. (1970). Back-translation for cross-cultural research. *Journal of Cross-Cultural Psychology, 1*, 185–216. http://doi.org/10.1177/135910457000100301

Coyne, I. (2006). International guidelines on computer-based and internet-delivered testing. *International Journal of Testing, 6*, 143–171. http://doi.org/10.1207/s15327574ijt0602_4

Coyne, I., & Bartram, D. (2006). Design and development of the ITC Guidelines on Computer-Based and Internet-Delivered Testing. *International Journal of Testing, 6*, 133–142. http://doi.org/10.1207/s15327574ijt0602_1

Gregoire, J., & Hambleton, R. K. (2009). Advances in test adaptation research: A special issue. *International Journal of Testing, 9*, 75–77. http://doi.org/10.1080/15305050902880678

Hambleton, R. K. (1994). Guidelines for adapting educational and psychological tests: A progress report. *European Journal of Psychological Assessment, 10*, 229–244.

Hambleton, R. K. (2001). The next generation of the ITC test translation and adaptation guidelines. *European Journal of Psychological Assessment, 17*, 164–172. http://doi.org/10.1027//1015-5759.17.3.164

Hambleton, R. K., Merenda, P. F., & Spielberger, C. D. (Eds.). (2005). *Adapting educational tests and psychological tests for cross-cultural assessment*. Mahwah, NJ: Erlbaum.

Hambleton, R. K., Yu, J., & Slater, S. C. (1999). Field test of the ITC guidelines for adapting educational and psychological tests. *European Journal of Psychological Assessment, 15*, 270–276. http://doi.org/10.1027//1015-5759.15.3.270

Harkness, J. A. (2003). Questionnaire translation. In J. A. Harkness, F. J. R. Van de Vijver, & P. P. Mohler (Eds.), *Cross-cultural survey methods* (pp. 35–56). Hoboken, NJ: Wiley.

International Test Commission. (2000). *International guidelines for test use*. Retrieved from http://www.intestcom.org.

International Test Commission. (2001). International guidelines on test use. *International Journal of Testing, 1*, 95–114.

International Test Commission. (2005). *ITC guidelines on computer-based and internet delivered testing.* Retrieved from http://www.intestcom.org

International Test Commission. (2006). International Guidelines on computer-based and Internet-delivered testing. *International Journal of Testing, 6*, 143–172. http://doi.org/10.1207/s15327574ijt0602_4

International Test Commission. (2011). *ITC Guidelines for quality control in scoring, test analysis, and reporting of test scores.* Retrieved from http://www.intestcom.org

Lord, F. M., & Novick, M. R. (1968). *Statistical theories of mental test scores.* Reading, MA: Addison-Wesley.

Miller, K. (2003). Conducting cognitive interviews to understand question-response limitations. *American Journal of Health Behavior, 27*(Suppl. 3), S264–S272. http://doi.org/10.5993/AJHB.27.1.s3.10

Muñiz, J., & Bartram, D. (2007). Improving international tests and testing. *European Psychologist, 12*, 206–219. http://doi.org/10.1027/1016-9040.12.3.206

Plake, B. S., & Wise, L. L. (2014). What is the role and importance of the revised AERA, APA, NCME standards for educational and psychological testing? *Educational Measurement: Issues and Practice, 33*(4), 4–12. http://doi.org/10.1111/emip.12045

Sireci, S. G. (2013). Standard setting in an international context: Introduction to the special issue. *International Journal of Testing, 13*, 2–3. http://dx.doi.org/10.1080/15305058.2013.744659 http://doi.org/10.1080/15305058.2013.744659

Van de Vijver, F. J. R. (1999). Testing the ITC Guidelines for adapting educational and psychological tests. *European Journal of Psychological Assessment, 15*, 257. http://doi.org/10.1027//1015-5759.15.3.257

Van de Vijver, F. J. R. (2013). Contributions of internationalization to psychology: Toward a global and inclusive discipline. *American Psychologist, 68*, 761–770. http://doi.org/10.1037/a0033762

Van de Vijver, F. J. R., & Hambleton, R. K. (1996). Translating tests: Some practical guidelines. *European Psychologist, 1*, 89–99. http://doi.org/10.1027/1016-9040.1.2.89

Van de Vijver, F. J. R., & Leung, K. (1997). *Methods and data analysis for cross-cultural research.* Newbury Park, CA: Sage.

Van der Linden, W. J., & Hambleton, R. K. (Eds.) (1997). *Handbook of modern item response theory.* New York, NY: Springer. http://doi.org/10.1007/978-1-4757-2691-6

Van Hemert, D. A., Van de Vijver, F. J. R., Poortinga, Y. H., & Georgas, J. (2002). Structural and functional equivalence of the Eysenck Personality Questionnaire within and between countries. *Personality and Individual Differences, 33*, 1229–1249. http://doi.org/10.1016/S0191-8869(02)00007-7

Vandenberg, R. J., & Lance, C. E. (2000). A review and synthesis of the measurement invariance literature: Suggestions, practices, and recommendations for organizational research. *Organizational Research Methods, 2*, 4–69. http://doi.org/10.1177/109442810031002

Vieluf, S., Kuenther, M., & Van de Vijver, F. J. R. (2013). Teacher self-efficacy in cross-cultural perspective. *Teaching and Teacher Education, 35*, 92–103. http://doi.org/10.1016/j.tate.2013.05.006

Webb, N. M. (1991). *Generalizability theory: A primer.* Thousand Oaks, CA: Sage.

Zumbo, B. D. (2007). Three generations of DIF analyses: Considering where it has been, where it is now, and where it is going. *Language Assessment Quarterly, 4*, 223–233. http://doi.org/10.1080/15434300701375832

Chapter 3

Using Factor Analysis in Test Construction

Deborah L. Bandalos[1] and Jerusha J. Gerstner[2]

[1]Department of Graduate Psychology, James Madison University, Harrisonburg, VA, USA
[2]Marriott Corporation, Washington DC, USA

Exploratory and confirmatory factor analytic methods are two of the most widely used procedures in the scale development process. For example, in a recent review of 75 articles reporting on the development of new or revised scales in the educational and psychological research literature, 77% used one or both of these methods (Gerstner & Bandalos, 2013). In this chapter we first review the basic concepts of exploratory and confirmatory factor analysis. We then discuss current recommendations for the use of both exploratory factor analysis (EFA) and confirmatory factor analysis (CFA) taken from commonly used textbooks and from articles on these topics. In the remainder of this chapter we discuss the conceptual and statistical bases for EFA and CFA, practical considerations in using the methods, and ways in which both EFA and CFA can be used to improve the scale development process. Finally, we illustrate these topics with an example.

Review of Basic Concepts

Factor analysis, both exploratory and confirmatory, allows researchers to explicate a model that underlies the observed correlations or covariances among scores on a set of variables. In essence, these methods answer the question, "Why are these scores correlated in the way we observe?" In factor analysis, the answer to this question is that the scores are correlated due to a common cause: the factor(s). The diagram in Figure 3.1 represents such a model in which there are six item (or variable scores) (in this chapter, we use the terms item and variable somewhat interchangeably) labeled $X_1 - X_6$; two factors, F_1 and F_2; and six error terms, one for each item score. The two factors are correlated, as indicated by the curved arrow between them.

Note that single-headed arrows run *from* the factors *to* the item scores (Xs). This means that, according to the factor analytic model, variation in the factors results in variation in the item scores. For example, if the item scores were measures of respondents' underlying levels of depression and the factors represented two aspects of depression, such as somatic and physical complaints, an increase (or decrease) in level of depression is posited to result in a corresponding increase (or decrease) in the level of the item response. This is, in fact, why researchers take an interest in answers to items on a scale; they are thought to be a window into respondents' levels of some attribute of interest. The same is the case with achievement or aptitude tests, or any measurements that are used in an attempt to capture an unobservable entity, or construct, such as creativity or motivation.

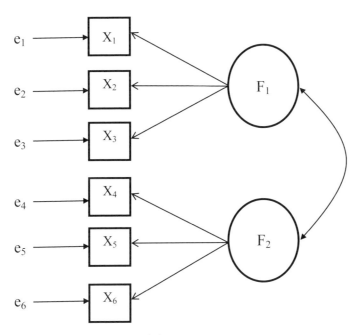

Figure 3.1. Hypothetical 2-factor model.

There is an additional influence on each of the items: an error component (a term cannot be an influence). This component is a residual in the sense that it captures the variation in an item score that is not explained through the item's relationship with the factor. In EFA, the residual components are typically called *uniquenesses*, because they represent the unique, or idiosyncratic, variation in the score. Although well-developed items of the same construct should be highly correlated, they should not be perfectly correlated. Thus even items developed to measure the same construct will have some unique variation, because items are typically written to tap into slightly different aspects of the construct of interest. This results in some lack of correlation among the items, which is reflected in the error, or uniqueness component. Having said this, the uniqueness also captures random error, or lack of reliability, in the items. The residual component is therefore a combination of specific, or unique, and random error.

A factor model such as that depicted in Figure 3.1 gives rise to the mathematical model for factor analysis:

$$X_{iv} = w_{v1}F_{1i} + w_{v2}F_{2i} + ... + w_{vf}F_{fi} + w_{vu}U_{iv} \tag{1}$$

where X_{iv} is the score of person i on variable v, w_{vf} is the weight, or loading, of variable v on factor f (i.e., factor loading), F_{fi} is the score on factor f of person i, w_{vu} is the weight of variable v on the error component, or uniqueness, and U_{iv} is the score of person i on the unique factor for variable v. The same equation holds for CFA, although the terms w, F, and U are usually replaced with λ, ξ (or η), and δ (or ε).

Equation 1 represents the score on an item (X) of one person. However, as we noted previously, factor analysis is a methodology for studying the relationships among variable scores; thus, individual's scores on the Xs are collected across all items and respondents and the relationships between variables are summarized for the set of respondents in the form of a correlation or covariance matrix. This correlation or covariance matrix of the variable scores is typically analyzed instead of the raw data. The model of Equation 1 results in the following matrix equation:

$$\Sigma_X = \Lambda \, \Phi \, \Lambda' + \Theta_\delta \qquad (2)$$

Here, Σ_x is the matrix of correlations or covariances among the items, Λ is a v by f matrix of factor loadings, Φ is an f by f matrix of correlations or covariances among the factors, and Θ_δ is a v by v matrix of the variables' unique variances. As can be seen from Figure 3.1, the uniquenesses are assumed to be uncorrelated, making Θ_δ a diagonal matrix. From Equation 2 it can be seen that the correlations or covariances among item scores can be decomposed into components due to the factor, represented by Λ, to the correlations or covariances among the factors, or Φ, and to error (Θ_δ).

Factor analysis can thus be seen as a method of modeling the covariation among a set of observed variable scores as a function of one or more latent variables or factors, the correlations among these factors, and error. Here, we use the term latent variable to refer to an unobservable but theoretically defensible entity, such as intelligence, self-efficacy, or creativity. These variables are considered to be latent in the sense that they are not directly observable (see Bollen, 2002, for a more detailed discussion of latent variables). The purpose of factor analysis is to assist researchers in identifying and/or understanding the nature of the latent variables underlying the items of interest. Technically, these descriptions exclude component analysis, which is a method for reducing the dimensionality of a set of observed variables through the creation of an optimum number of weighted composites. In this chapter, we confine discussion to factor, and not component, models.

Differentiating EFA and CFA

As their names imply, one difference between exploratory and confirmatory factor analyses lies in the manner in which they are used. However, although the exploratory/confirmatory distinction is often treated as a dichotomy, in practice it is more of a continuum. Any statistical analysis can be used in a manner that is more exploratory or more confirmatory, and despite their nomenclature, the same is true of EFA and CFA. For example, researchers employing EFA often have strong theory to support a particular factor model, with hypotheses about the number of factors, the variables that should load on these, and even the level of correlation among the factors. On the other hand, a researcher may have limited or conflicting theory or evidence to support a particular factor model. The first situation represents a more confirmatory use of EFA and the second a more exploratory use. Having said this, CFA does represent a more confirmatory approach because it allows researchers to specify, or restrict, more aspects of the model than in EFA. In addition, CFA more easily allows for tests of the hypothesized model, both as a whole and of specific parameters, such as factor loadings or correlations/covariances.

However, it is precisely because of the restrictive nature of the typical CFA model that it may be best to use EFA for situations in which little previous research and/or theory exists to guide specification of the factor model. This is because specification of a CFA model requires the researcher to indicate not only which variables load on each factor, but also which do not. Typically, a simplified model structure in which variables load only on one factor is specified. If such a model does not hold, it can result in a serious misfit of the model to the data. In such situations the researcher would likely attempt to determine a more appropriate structure. Within the CFA approach there are so many options for respecification of parameters that the researcher could easily be led down an unprofitable path. Particularly during the beginning stages of scale construction, variables often display an annoying tendency to load onto more than one factor, or to fail to load on the factor for which they are written. Such tendencies can be difficult to detect from the output of a typical CFA, but are readily apparent from any EFA output.

A final reason to use EFA in the beginning stages of scale construction is that the exploration of different models, as is recommended under the EFA paradigm, may reveal interesting and conceptually plausible structures that can help the researcher to more thoroughly explore the nature of the construct of interest. As a general guideline, therefore, we recommend that EFA be used for situations in which the variables to be analyzed are either newly developed or have not previously been analyzed together, or when the theoretical basis for the factor analysis model (i.e., number of factors, level of correlation among factors) is weak. In such situations, it is not possible to specify the model a priori in sufficient detail to conduct a CFA.

This is not to say that CFA cannot also be a powerful tool in the scale development process. On the contrary, if theory is sufficiently strong and/or previous EFAs have supported a particular structure for the variables, this structure should be subjected to the more rigorous model testing available through CFA. Thus, at later stages of scale development, after item analyses have been conducted, and when the structure through which the variables and factors are related is sufficiently well-understood, the CFA model has several advantages over that of EFA. These include the ability to completely specify all aspects of the model, such as which variables load (and do not load) on each factor, and the ability to statistically test both the overall fit of the model to the data and the significance of model parameter estimates. In the context of testing parameter estimates, however, we hasten to point out that the typical practice of claiming statistical support for a factor model on the basis of statistically significant loadings is not justified. This is because a finding of statistical significance simply means that the factor loading is not zero, which represents a standard so low as to be meaningless. At the very least, factor loadings should be greater than zero; more typically these would be expected to be much higher. As an aside, we point out that it is possible to use SEM software to constrain loadings to any value and thus obtain tests that parameter estimates differ from any constant.

Finally, researchers should keep in mind that scale development is an iterative process. During this process items may be rewritten or discarded on the basis of information provided by item analyses as well as EFA and CFA results. Given this, it is likely that researchers will determine that EFA is appropriate at some points in the process and CFA at other points. For example, if several items have been rewritten and the researcher is not sure whether the factor structure has changed as a result of these revisions, an EFA may be most appropriate. CFA may be implemented later on in the process, when researchers are satisfied they have found a fairly stable factor structure.

Conceptual Principles and Statistical Assumptions

Need for Theoretical Grounding in EFA and CFA

Many of the decisions made in EFA are, to some degree, subjective (e.g., determining the number of factors; interpreting factors) and are made, at least in part, on the basis of theory. Given this, it is crucial for researchers using EFA techniques to be thoroughly familiar with theories and previous research regarding the construct of interest. Of course, for researchers developing scales, it goes without saying that such familiarity would be necessary. Although some researchers are uncomfortable with EFA methods for the very reason that their implementation involves a degree of subjectivity, it must be kept in mind that EFA is not, in general, an inferential technique in which strict hypothesis testing practices are used. Instead, EFA is, as its name implies, an exploratory method, the purpose of which is to investigate plausible factor structures for the variables. Although statistical tests can provide information about the plausibility of structures from a purely mathematical point of view, in order to be useful data structures must also be plausible from a theoretical point of view. Thus, in EFA the theoretical basis of the model is arguably at least as important as the statistical assumptions. One example of the need for theory is the common situation in which researchers find either more or fewer factors than anticipated. These situations are known as over- and underfactoring, respectively, and the latter is generally considered to be a greater problem than the former (Fabrigar, Wegener, MacCallum, & Strahan, 1999). The reason is that when too many factors are extracted, it is typically the case that the last of the factors is loaded by only one or two variables, and even these loadings are often quite weak. It is therefore fairly straightforward to detect overfactoring. Of course, factors having only one or two loadings are not necessarily the result of overfactoring. Such factors could represent important aspects of the construct being measured for which there are not sufficient items. However, determining whether or not a weak factor is potentially useful or simply an artifact of overfactoring would require a reliance on theory.

Within the CFA paradigm, a solid grounding in the theory of the construct being measured is equally as important as in EFA. In fact, given that confirmatory analyses require the researcher to specify every aspect of the factor model a priori, some researchers argue that a thorough theoretical background is even more critical in CFA than in EFA (Bandalos & Finney, 2010). In addition to being needed for model specification, theory also comes into play when interpreting the results of confirmatory analyses. In particular, researchers conducting confirmatory analyses can request so-called *modification indexes* (MIs) that indicate parameters that could be included to improve model fit. Researchers can also calculate correlation residuals to examine misfit in the model. These are calculated as the difference between the observed and model-implied correlations. For ease of interpretation, these residuals are typically placed on either a correlation metric, ranging from −1 to 1 (so-called *correlation residuals*) or on a z-score metric (so-called *standardized residuals*). Although the use of such indexes, and in particular of MIs, is not without controversy (e.g., Hutchinson, 1998; MacCallum, Roznowski, & Necowitz, 1992), it seems clear that they are used by at least some researchers. Even if the suggested parameters are not added to the model, researchers may examine the MIs or residuals in an attempt to better understand model lack of fit.

In the context of scale development, both MIs and residuals can yield useful information about the nature of the relationships among variables. However, this information must be considered carefully, and in light of theory about the construct being measured. This is because a lack of model fit can be the result of quite different underlying structures. For example, MIs frequently indicate that correlated measurement errors between pairs of variables should be added. Similarly, large correlation residuals for some covariance elements are often interpreted as suggesting shared measurement errors. However, the apparent need for shared measurement errors results from many sources, including shared method effects, wording similarities among items, serial order effects, or the need for additional factors that tap into a subarea of the construct. Thus, correlated measurement errors may be either substantive or artifactual, and researchers must rely on theory to determine which explanation is most reasonable.

MIs or residuals suggesting that certain variables be allowed to cross-load can be due to the same artifactual or substantive influences as those resulting in suggestions for correlated measurement errors. On the other hand, these can also indicate that the variable is more factorially complex than had been supposed. In the latter case, researchers must decide whether it is reasonable to allow variables to load on more than one factor. It may be the case that the construct is itself complex, and/or is measured by multiple correlated subscales. In this case it may be reasonable to suppose that some of the variables measuring the construct will also be complex. In fact, it could be argued that factorially complex variables are necessary for measuring multifaceted constructs. On the other hand, factors based on such complex variables can be difficult to interpret, and may also complicate scoring and reporting of subscales. Again, the researchers' best course of action in such situations is to make use of theory in determining the most judicious solution.

Statistical Assumptions of EFA and CFA

Exploratory Factor Analysis

Variable Distributions

As noted previously, most EFA estimation methods are not based on strict assumptions about the nature of the variables to be analyzed and their distributions. This is because EFA methods do not typically involve inferential testing of parameters or of the model as a whole (although such tests are possible if an estimation method such as maximum likelihood (ML) is used (see McDonald, 1999, pp. 169–170). However, this should not be taken to imply that variable distributions do not affect the results obtained from EFA. On the contrary, it has been known for some time that variables with similar levels of skew and/or kurtosis can form artifactual factors, known as *difficulty factors* (e.g., McDonald & Ahlawat, 1974). This occurs because similarly distributed variables are more highly correlated with each other than with differently distributed variables, given that all else is equal. The severity of this problem increases with the level of nonnormality. If variable distributions are not severely nonnormal (i.e., values of skewness and kurtosis are less than |2.0|, although some authors suggest kurtosis can be as high as 7.0), distortion should not be serious enough to distort results. However, nonnormally distributed variables can result in the retention of meaningless difficulty factors, unless researchers can correctly identify these as being due to distributional artifacts. This is one reason that authors such as Nunnally and Bernstein (1994; see also Bernstein & Teng, 1989) argue against the use of individual items in EFA, preferring the analysis of scales or subscales. These authors point out that items are more subject to distributional artifacts than are scales or subscales.

Because EFA estimation is typically based on analysis of Pearson Product-Moment (PPM) correlation matrices, violations of the assumptions underlying PPM correlations can result in bias of EFA parameters. More specifically, continuity of variable distributions and a linear relationship between the variables and factors are necessary to obtain accurate results. These assumptions are violated if data are coarsely categorized (i.e., if scoring is dichotomous or ordinal in nature), with bias increasing as the number of response categories decreases. With five or more ordered categories bias should be minimal, but for variables with fewer categories the analysis of the PPM correlation matrix can produce biased estimates of factor loadings and correlations. This bias results from the fact that PPM correlations cannot completely capture the nonlinear relationship resulting from the regression of a binary or ordinal variable on a continuous factor. Because of this, researchers working with data based on fewer than five response categories should consider using item response theory (IRT, see Chapter 4) in lieu of EFA, as IRT methods were designed specifically for modeling relationships among such variables. Alternatively, so-called categorical least squares (cat-LS) estimation has been found to perform well with coarsely categorized data (see Finney & DiStefano, 2014, or Chapter 8 of this volume).

Sample Size

Recent studies (Hogarty, Hines, Kromrey, Ferron, & Mumford, 2005; MacCallum, Widaman, Zhang, & Hong, 1999, 2001; Velicer & Fava, 1998) have shown that the sample size needed to obtain accurate estimates of factor loading coefficients depends on the level of communality of the variables, the number of variables per factor, and the interaction of these two characteristics. A variable's communality represents the amount of variance in the variable that is accounted for by the factors, and is calculated as the sum (across all factors) of the variable's squared loadings. Thus, variables with higher loadings and/or with loadings on more factors have higher communalities. These findings call into question earlier rules of thumb suggesting that the needed sample size was an increasing function of only the number of variables. The studies by MacCallum et al. and by Hogarty et al. suggest that the accuracy of recovery of known loading coefficient values increases with sample size, communality level, and the number of variables per factor. Thus, contrary to previous rules of thumb, recovery was actually better for large than for small numbers of variables per factor (assuming all else was equal). However, if communalities were high (averaging .7), the number of variables per factor had little effect on recovery. The studies cited here suggest that samples of 100 may be sufficient to obtain accurate estimates for solutions with three factors, if the factors are measured by at least three to four variables each and variable communalities are between .6 and .8. However, it should be noted that this level of communality implies an average loading of at least .77, assuming variables load on only one factor. In most social science applications, loadings are often well below this level and much larger samples would be needed. For example, MacCallum et al. go on to state that if communalities are lower than .5 (which would still imply an average loading of .71), sample sizes of at least 300 would be needed. Larger sample sizes are also needed if there are more factors. If there were seven factors rather than three, a sample size of 500 would be needed to obtain accurate parameter estimates in a situation with communalities less than .5 and three to four variables per factor.

Estimation Methods

Estimation in EFA (and in CFA) involves fitting the so-called implied covariance matrix $\widehat{\Sigma}$, which is a function of the model parameters, as shown in Equation 2, to the observed covariance matrix of the variables, S. The difference between S and $\widehat{\Sigma}$ forms the basis of a discrepancy function. This function is analogous to the least squares criterion in regression in that it forms the basis of the quantity that is minimized during the estimation process. The parameter estimates that yield the minimum value of the discrepancy function are taken as the final estimates. There are many discrepancy functions, based on different assumptions which lead to different ways of weighting the S - $\widehat{\Sigma}$ discrepancies. Although a full discussion of estimation methods is beyond the scope of this chapter (but see Chapter 8 of this volume), we briefly introduce findings from a study by Briggs and MacCallum (2003) because of its potential relevance to the use of EFA in scale development studies.

Briggs and MacCallum (2003) have shown that two commonly used discrepancy functions, those based on maximum likelihood (ML) estimation and on ordinary least squares (OLS) estimation, can yield estimates of loading coefficients that are quite different. As they explain, ML estimation is based on the assumptions that the factor model holds exactly in the population and that any error is the result of sampling error. The implication of this assumption is that ML estimation will allow more discrepancy in the fit of small than of large correlations, resulting in better estimation of the latter. This is because small correlations have more sampling error than large correlations, and are therefore expected to fluctuate more around their population values. Put another way, ML weights discrepancies involving large correlations more heavily than those involving small correlations, because the latter are allowed more sampling error. The upshot of this is that factors with low loadings may not be estimated well in ML because they are based on relatively smaller correlations. OLS, on the other hand, does not weight discrepancies involving small and large correlations differentially, but rather weights all discrepancies equally. OLS should therefore result in better recovery of factors with low loadings. These differences between ML and OLS should be most apparent when the model does not fit perfectly in the population (as is typical), and/or when sample size is small. Briggs and MacCallum conducted a simulation study to determine the degree to which their theoretically derived hypotheses were borne out, and found that OLS did result in better recovery of known factor loadings than did ML when the sample size was small (100) and when the model was misspecified.

These findings are pertinent to the use of EFA in scale development because in the early stages of scale development, poorer items that would exhibit lower correlations with other items may not yet have been screened out. In addition, models estimated at early stages of scale development may well be misspecified, as researchers may not yet fully comprehend the structure underlying the items. If such conditions are likely, or if the sample size available is small (100 or fewer) researchers should consider the use of OLS rather than ML estimation.

Confirmatory Factor Analysis

In contrast to the case with EFA, CFA estimation methods are based on strong assumptions regarding the nature of the data being analyzed. These assumptions have to do with the normality of variable distributions, the linearity of the relationships between factors and variables, and the independence of observations, In addition, the sample size used must be large enough for the asymptotic properties of commonly used estimators to accrue (see Chapter 8, this volume). With regard to the latter point, the sample size recommendations discussed in the context of EFA also apply to CFA, so these will not be repeated here. However, we briefly discuss the assumptions regarding variable distributions and linearity as they apply to CFA.

Variable Distributions

Most commonly used estimation methods in CFA are based on the assumption that the variables being analyzed are multivariate-normally distributed, and violations of this assumption can result in underestimates of standard errors and overestimates of the chi-square value. Univariate normality of the individual variable distributions is a necessary but not a sufficient condition for multivariate normality. Multivariate normality is typically assessed by calculation of Mardia's (1970) kappa. DeCarlo (1997) provides macros for computing Mardia's kappa and a variety of other measures of multivariate normality using the SAS and SPSS programs. Values of Mardia's kappa of less than 3.0 have been suggested as acceptable departures from normality, although interpretation depends on the specific version of kappa being used. Although most structural equation modeling programs compute a version of this index, the specific formula used differs across programs. For example, the *EQS* program provides a centered version of Mardia's kappa which is computed as kappa − E(kappa), where E(kappa) is equal to $p \times (p + 2)$, and p is the number of variables. Because there are several variations on Mardia's original formula, researchers should check the documentation of the program being used to determine how to interpret the particular version provided. If it is determined that data are not multivariate-normally distributed, researchers may opt to use an estimation method that is robust to such violations (see Chapter 8 in this volume). We urge scale developers to routinely investigate the normality of their data, as violations can result in bias in standard errors and fit index values, the severity of which increases with increasingly nonnormality.

Linearity

As with EFA, the scales of the observed variables can affect results. Specifically, coarsely categorized scales such as those based on the commonly used Likert-type format violate the normal-theory CFA assumption of linearity of the relationship between the factors and variables. As noted previously, variables whose measurement scale consists of only a few categories can, at best, only approximate linear relationships with the corresponding factors. As the number of categories increases, this approximation improves. Because of this, most simulation studies (Bandalos, 2014; Beaducel & Herzberg, 2006; Flora & Curran, 2004; Green, Akey, Fleming, Hershberger, & Marquis, 1997; Rhemtulla, Brousseau-Liard, & Savalei, 2012) have found that little bias occurs for scales with five or more categories. For data based on fewer than five categories, categorical least squares estimation methods are available and we recommend these be used instead of the more commonly used maximum likelihood (ML) methods in such situations. Estimation methods for CFA (and for structural equation models more broadly) are discussed thoroughly in Chapter 8 of this volume so we do not discuss them in detail here. Briefly, however, these methods are based on analysis of matrices of polychoric correlations, which more accurately capture the nonlinear relationships among coarsely categorized variables. Although parameter estimates obtained from this approach should be unbiased, standard errors will be negatively biased and chi-square values will be positively biased. Because of this, a specialized weight matrix is typically applied to adjust these values.

Independence of Observations

Respondents are assumed to be randomly sampled from a single population, which should result in *independent observations*. A simple example of a situation in which observations would not be independent is that in which one respondent copies the answers of another. More generally, however, responses may lack independence due to use of a sampling design, such as *stratification* or *multistage sampling*. Stratified samples are those in which elements of the population of interest are divided into categories, or *strata*, and a random sample of a given size is selected from each stratum. For example, a researcher may stratify on the basis of ethnicity in order to ensure that sufficient numbers of respondents from each ethnic group are obtained. Multistage sampling is often used as a strategy to obtain samples that are representative of a geographically diverse population without the need to sample every geographical area. As the name implies, such sampling takes place in stages. At the first stage, broad geographic regions such as the northwestern, mideastern, and southeastern parts of the country might be sampled from among all possible regions. From these, specific districts or counties would be randomly selected. At even further stages, specific towns, cities, or rural areas may be selected. At the final stage, individual respondents are randomly selected from the specified areas. This technique is often used in educational research, with schools being randomly selected from school districts, classrooms selected from schools, and students selected from classrooms. In both stratified and multistage sampling, respondents from the same sampling unit (i.e., stratum or classroom) likely respond in a more similar fashion than respondents from different sampling units. This introduces dependencies in the resulting data that are not accounted for by the factor model and will result in underestimation of parameter standard errors if it is not taken into account through special estimation methods (see Stapleton, 2013, for more information on this topic).

Practical Considerations in the Use of EFA and CFA in Scale Development

How should the results of EFA and CFA be used in the scale development process? Many of the results obtained from both EFA and CFA, such as factor loadings and correlations, are essentially the same, and would be interpreted in the same manner. Given this, we devote most of this section to a general discussion of the interpretation and use of results in both EFA and CFA. However, there are several issues that arise in one method and not the other, and we devote separate sections to these. Specifically, in EFA researchers often find that either more or fewer factors than anticipated emerge. In such situations, researchers must determine why this occurred and what action to take. In CFA, researchers may obtain so-called modification indexes (MIs) and/or standardized or correlation residuals and base model modifications on these. As is well-known, the cavalier addition (or deletion) of parameters without a well thought-out theoretical justification can be risky (e.g., Hutchinson, 1998; MacCallum et al., 1992). However, our feeling is that, when used carefully, both MIs and residuals can aid in understanding the nature of the relationships among the variables of interest. In the following sections we discuss these issues in more detail. We end the section with a discussion of considerations common to both EFA and CFA.

Implications of Obtaining More Factors Than Anticipated

Although most EFA software packages allow researchers to specify the number of factors to be extracted a priori, researchers often use some combination of theory and other criteria to determine the number of factors. A full discussion of methods for determining the number of factors is outside the scope of this chapter, but methods that have been found to perform most accurately in simulations include parallel analysis, the minimum average partial (MAP) method, the comparison data technique, and the Hull method (Lorenzo-Seva, Timmerman, & Kiers, 2011; Ruscio & Roche, 2012; Velicer, Eaton, & Fava, 2000; Zwick & Velicer, 1986). Researchers often have some sense, based on the theory of the construct and/or previous research, of the number of factors that should emerge. Even so, it is not uncommon for researchers to find that statistical criteria favor selection of a model with more factors than were anticipated. This can occur for several reasons. It is possible that one or more of the factors is based on similarities in item distributions rather than on similarities in item content. This can be ascertained by reviewing descriptive statistics for the items. Another possibility is that of method effects, which can arise due to similarities in wording or of the type of item used. For example, in cognitive testing it is sometimes found that multiple-choice and essay items tend to form separate factors. Or, affective items that are negatively worded may tend to cluster together. Method effects are the subject of Chapter 15 in this volume, so we do not discuss them further here except to say that these can often be detected by reviewing the wording of the items, or the methods used to collect the data. A finding of more factors than anticipated can also occur because a set of items thought to be unidimensional is not. That is, a factor may consist of one or more related, but distinct subfactors. Researchers should be able to determine whether this is the case by examining the items on the separate factors for any similarity in content. If it is determined that subfactors exist, the researcher must then make a judgment regarding the utility of such subfactors. In some cases, the researcher may determine that such factors are too narrow, and are not likely to be useful in the context for which the scale is being developed. In other cases, the researcher may feel that the subfactors represent important aspects of the construct that should be studied further. In the latter case, it may be necessary to develop more items in order to fully measure these subfactors.

Implications of Obtaining Fewer Factors Than Anticipated

A finding of fewer factors than anticipated may indicate that aspects of the construct that were thought to be distinguishable are not. If this is the case, it may require the researcher to rethink the theory on which the original hypothesis about the number of factors was based. Alternatively, it may be the case that the expected separate factors exist, but that the items developed to tap into these factors are not pure measures of them. If this is the case, it seems likely that the items will have cross-loadings on a related factor or factors. Such items could be rewritten in an attempt to create more focused measures of the subfactor of interest. A related possibility is that there are not sufficient items to bring out the particular aspect of the factor. In this case, more items would have to be developed.

Interpreting Cross-Loadings

One situation in which items might cross-load was alluded to above; the items are not sufficiently pure measures of the factor for which they were intended. Of course, it may also be the case that the intended factor is simply not distinguishable from a related factor, with the result that items load on both factors. In the latter case, indistinguishable factors could simply be collapsed. Even though a structure in which items load cleanly onto only one factor is the goal of many factor analysts, it is not wrong, in a factor analytic sense, for items to cross-load. Such cross-loadings simply indicate that items share variance with more than one factor. If the factors represent relatively broad constructs, this should not be surprising, because such constructs may be based on sets of related content. A lack of cross-loadings is appealing in terms of interpretation, because factors with cleanly loading items can be interpreted in a less ambiguous manner. However, it is important to note that such clarity may be obtained at the cost of creating overly narrow measures. If the construct is itself narrowly defined, this is appropriate, but if the construct is complex, it is not. We point out in passing that, although Thurstone's (1947) simple structure criteria are often cited in support of the elimination of cross-loading items, Thurstone himself does not seem to have considered the absence of cross-loading items to be the most important aspect of simple structure, placing it last in his list of five criteria.

Finding a Lack of Model Fit

In addition to the usual model parameter estimates (factor loadings, etc.), researchers conducting CFAs obtain tests of the fit of the specified factor model to the data. Both inferential tests, such as the chi-square test of goodness of fit, and descriptive indexes such as the standardized root mean square error residual (SRMR) and the comparative fit index (CFI) are typically reported for these analyses. Discussion of the formulation and interpretation of these indexes is beyond the scope of this chapter, but are discussed in detail in Chapter 9 of this volume. It is not uncommon for researchers to find that their hypothesized model fails to fit. When this occurs, researchers must choose between reporting the hypothesized model and its associated lack of fit or attempting to modify the model to obtain a better fit to the data. As discussed in a previous section, researchers choosing the latter strategy often rely on so-called modification indexes, and/or on model residuals. Modification of models on the basis of such measures has been the subject of much controversy, most of which stems from the fact that modifying one's model in a post hoc fashion violates the research principle of specifying hypotheses before conducting statistical testing. As a consequence of this violation, the probability values associated with statistical tests are no longer accurate. In addition to these concerns, researchers studying the efficacy of MIs in leading researchers to the true model have found their performance to be quite spotty (Hutchinson, 1998; MacCallum, 1986; MacCallum et al., 1992; Silvia & MacCallum, 1988). Hutchinson studied the performance of MIs in the context of CFA, so her findings are particularly relevant here, although her results are somewhat disheartening. Hutchinson found that the percentages of true model recovery ranged from 19 to 98% when the sample size was 400 or less. Similarly, MacCallum (1986) found that adding parameters based on MIs did not lead to the true model much of the time. When using MIs to modify a model, the chances of identifying the true or population model are enhanced as (1) sample size increases, (2) the number of misspecified parameters in the model decreases, and, (3) the originally specified model is closer to the true model. Points 2 and 3, in particular, are of concern to those developing scales because it is often the case in that enterprise that several iterations of item writing/revising and data analysis are required before an acceptable model is found. In such cases, the initial model is often far from perfect, and many item revisions and reformulations of the factor structure may be needed before an adequate fit is obtained.

In spite of the issues noted above, we do feel that careful use of MIs or other model modification information can help those developing scales to better understand the nature of the relationships among items. The key is that information from MIs must be interpreted in light of the relevant theory. That is, researchers should use their theoretical knowledge of the construct to understand why modifications are being suggested. For example, measurement error covariances for pairs of items are often indicated by MIs as possible additions to the model. Such error covariances occur because the pair of items covary more than can be accounted for by the model. This could be due to: similarity in the distribution of the two items, use of similar or identical wording or phraseology, redundancy in the content of the two items, the need for an additional factor, the presence of a method effect that influences both items, the fact that the factor is multidimensional and the items both tap into more than one dimension, or simply the fact that the items appear next to each other on the page or screen when administered. Of these, some effects can be eliminated through careful item writing or by revisions to the items or administration method. Use of similar or identical wording in different items should be avoided, because it can induce respondents to provide answers that are more similar than they might otherwise have been. In the same vein, if upon careful inspection items are found to be redundant, one should be dropped. Method factors, such as those stimulated by the fact that sets of items are negatively worded or are susceptible to social desirability effects, are discussed in Chapter 15. With regard to item order, we have found that measurement error covariances can result from contiguously placed items, and that random ordering of items via computer administration can reduce or eliminate these effects (Bandalos & Coleman, 2012).

The remaining two sources of measurement error covariances, the need for an additional factor and the multidimensional nature of a factor, clearly have theoretical implications. The need for an additional factor is suggested for situations in which several pairs of items exhibit error covariances and these items appear to represent a specific content area or aspect of the construct. If the researcher considers the possible factor to be of importance theoretically, and to be interpretable in a meaningful way, the factor model should be reconfigured to accommodate the new factor. It may also be necessary to write additional items in order to fully measure the factor. On the other hand, the researcher may decide it makes theoretical sense for the factor to be multidimensional. In this case the researcher must be able to make a reasonable argument, based on theory, that the observed error covariances stem from the additional dimensionality of the factor. In both of these cases, interpretation of measurement error covariances in light of theory has the potential to enhance understanding of the construct. For this reason, we do not advocate a wholesale prohibition of the use of residuals and/or MIs, as do some. Instead, we feel that researchers may profitably use these indexes as a source of information that might, when used in conjunction with theory, further their understanding of the construct.

Validity Implications of EFA/CFA Results

Researchers often use EFA/CFA results to support arguments for the validity of inferences made on the basis of their scales. EFA and CFA results can support claims of measurement validity in several ways. In EFA, researchers can either request a particular number of factors, or can use one of a variety of methods to determine the number of factors that is best supported by the data. In the latter case, obtaining the hypothesized number of factors is an indication that the hypothesized dimensionality of the scale is supported. Of course, such a claim is only supported if the nature and items loading on each factor is in agreement with what was hypothesized. The second way in which EFA/CFA results can support a validity argument is through the pattern and/or magnitude of the loadings. If the anticipated number of factors is obtained, and the hypothesized variables are found to load on each, this does support validity arguments regarding both the dimensionality of the construct and the nature of its components. However, as Benson (1998) points out, the results of a factor analysis do not necessarily provide plausible information about what is being measured by a factor. This is because, although the nature of factors can be inferred from the content of the items loading on them, commonalities among the items are also driven by the processes involved in responding to them. As noted previously, in educational testing it is commonly found that items based on the same format, such as multiple choice, tend to share more variance with each other than with items based on another format, such as essay or short answer. In psychological testing, loadings can reflect shared variance due to similarities in wording, or shared susceptibility to response styles. Items that are negatively worded often share more variance with each other than with items that are positively worded, and many studies have found that such items tend to form artifactual factors (e.g., Barnette, 2000; Lai, 1994; Marsh, 1986; Motl, Conroy, & Horan, 2000; Pilotte & Gable, 1990). Similarly, items may share variance because they are influenced to the same extent by socially desirable responding. These possibilities should be kept in mind when interpreting the results of an EFA. In the context of CFA, such effects will result in a lack of fit of the model, because items with shared variance due to response processes tend to be more highly correlated than can be accounted for by the factor model. As mentioned in the previous section, these sources of lack of fit may be identified through the use of modification indexes or residuals, and are usually manifested as measurement error covariances.

Determining a Cut-Off Value for Salient Loadings

One practical aspect of deciphering the pattern of loadings is that of determining a threshold at which a loading is considered to be meaningful. It is common to use values such as 0.30 or 0.40 as for this purpose, and in our review of the literature (Gestner & Bandalos, 2013), we found that the median cutoff was 0.40 with a range of 0.32 to 0.78. Although such thresholds are, to some degree, arbitrary, it does seem reasonable to choose a higher threshold for situations in which variables are known or expected to be more highly correlated. For example, items on scales measuring narrowly defined constructs will typically have high loadings, because such items will tend to be highly correlated. Conversely, broadly defined scales will likely exhibit lower loadings. We feel it is important that researchers establish thresholds for salient loadings a priori, based on such theoretical considerations. Failure to do so may lead to self-serving choices, such as, setting a loading threshold of .35 after observing that a number of variables have cross-loadings around 0.32.

In the context of CFA, researchers sometimes argue that a finding of statistically significant loading estimates supports the validity of the scale. However, this form of evidence is weak, at best, as it simply means that the loading is likely not zero in the population. At the very least, one would hope that the loadings of variables on their hypothesized factors would not be zero. We therefore feel that such evidence can only be disconfirmatory in nature. That is, a finding of statistically significant loading estimates does little to advance one's validity argument, but a finding of nonsignificant loadings certainly throws doubt on it. A more comprehensive validity argument would involve specifying, based on theory, which variables are hypothesized to load at high, low, and intermediate levels. Obtained results that are consistent with these predictions would constitute much stronger evidence in support of proposed score interpretations than do the usual blanket statements that validity is supported because the obtained factor structure is loosely similar to what was expected.

A final way in which one's validity argument can be tested in the context of either EFA or CFA is to include so-called marker variables in the analysis along with the scale items. Marker variables can be any observed variable that ought, theoretically, to have a specified relationship (positive, negative, or zero) with one or more of the factors of interest. For example, if a researcher hypothesizes that intelligence should not be related to creativity, a measure of intelligence could be included in a factor analysis of creativity items. A finding that the intelligence measure did not load with any of the creativity items would support the hypothesis. In some cases, the marker variable is a measure of the construct of interest that is considered to be purer or more direct than the items on the scale. For instance, a researcher developing a measure of anxiety could obtain a physiological measure such as respondents' adrenaline levels when under stress, and include this in the factor analysis of the anxiety items. To the extent that the physiological measure loaded on the anticipated anxiety factor(s), the argument that the items can be interpreted as measures of anxiety is strengthened. In EFA, the marker variable(s) would simply be included in the analysis and the pattern of loadings examined to determine whether the marker loaded as expected. For CFA, the hypothesized pattern of loadings for the marker variables would be specified in advance, as part of the factor model. The magnitude of the marker variable loading(s) could then be examined to determine if these conformed to expectations.

Using EFA/CFA Results in Scale Revision

As noted previously, scale development is an iterative process in which the researcher may go through several cycles of item writing, analyses (including EFA and/or CFA) and item revision. Scale revisions are often based on the results of item-total correlations, alpha-if-item-deleted values, and information from EFA and/or CFA. Both low loadings and cross-loadings are often cited as reasons for item deletion. Such practices are not entirely unreasonable, because items with low loadings are arguably not related to the other items on the scale, while those with cross-loadings may not constitute pure measures of the construct of interest. However, as noted previously, constructs may be complex in nature, implying a need for complex items to more fully capture their nuances. In such situations, the deletion of cross-loading items may simplify the factor structure at the expense of the validity of the scale. Similarly, the desirability of deleting items on the basis of low loadings depends on the desired nature of the scale. As Cronbach and Meehl (1955) pointed out 60 years ago, high inter-item correlations, such as those that would yield scales in which all items have high loadings, only support validity inferences if they are theoretically warranted. Researchers should keep in mind that scales based on highly correlated items will be quite narrowly focused. In some cases, this is desirable. For example, items on scales designed to measures respondents' attitudes about a specific topic or within a limited context would be expected to correlate very highly. However, correlations of items on scales that are more broad-based will likely vary more. The point is that decisions to delete items on the basis of low or cross-loadings should take into account the context of the scale. Finally, it should be noted that factor loadings are functions of item correlations, and in small samples these can be quite unstable. We therefore recommend against making decisions regarding the deletion or retention of items based on only one sample of data, particularly if the sample is small in size. A better strategy, in our view, is to note items that perform poorly in a single sample of data and re-examine their performance when a new set of data is available. If their performance is similarly poor in the second sample, researchers can have more confidence in any subsequent decisions to remove them.

Example

To illustrate the role EFA and CFA can have in the scale development process, we provide an example from a recent revision of an existing instrument, the Scale of Ethnocultural Empathy (SEE; Wang et al., 2003). Although this example is based on a scale revision rather than the development of a scale, we feel that it nonetheless illustrates many of the points made in this chapter. The scale developers originally examined the scale using CFA based on item parcels. As the practice of analyzing item parcels is problematic (Bandalos, 2002; Bandalos & Finney, 2001), we were interested in whether the structure would replicate with an independent sample when analyses were conducted at the item level. We evaluated the scale's structure using EFA and then CFA on separate samples of students from a midsized, mid-Atlantic university. The SEE contains 31 items that are posited to represent 4 factors: Acceptance of Cultural Differences (ACD), Empathic Perspective Taking (EPT), Empathic Awareness (EA), and Empathic Feeling and Expression (EFE; see Table A1 in Appendix A).

EFA

We began by examining the factor structure of the SEE with EFA, using a sample of 848 students. We estimated the EFA models with the M*plus* statistical software in order to obtain MIs and residuals that might suggest reasons for any model lack of fit, as well as to obtain fit indexes to compare fit across different models. Because there was not strong theoretical support for the authors' proposed 4-factor solution (the original theory suggested 3-factors;

Ridley & Lingle, 1996) we first used EFA to examine the scale dimensionality. Based on the results of previous studies, values of the fit indices, and results of parallel analysis, we decided to examine factor solutions ranging from 1 to 7. Mplus syntax for this analysis is shown in Appendix B.

Comparing Across EFA Models

Prior to estimating the models, we decided that a cutoff of 0.30 would be used to determine salient loadings. We chose this value because previous research on the scale did not indicate that correlations among the variables were particularly high. Given this, we expected most loadings to be moderate, so a higher cut-off value did not seem warranted. We compared all seven solutions on the basis of (a) interpretability relative to the theory on which the scale was based, (b) degree to which the items had strong loadings on a factor, (c) degree to which items cross-loaded, and (d) whether each factor had at least four saliently loading items. The latter criterion was implemented because researchers recommend that factors have at least three items (Kline, 2011). The 7-factor solution exhibited patterns of loadings that did not appear to align with theory. In addition, this solution results in three items with cross-loadings and four items that failed to load on any factor. We therefore did not consider the 7-factor solution further. Results for the other six solutions are displayed in Table 3.1.

We determined that the 4-factor model, shown in Figure 3.2, was most interpretable. In addition, as can be seen from the results in Table 3.1, this solution exhibited many desirable characteristics based on our criteria. Specifically, this solution had the fewest items that did not load on a factor (1), as well as the fewest items that loaded on more than one factor (1). In addition, all factors in this solution had at least four items with loadings of 0.30 or above. Finally, this solution was most in line with the theoretical model specified by the authors of the original scale. Although the 4-factor solution was deemed to be the best of those we investigated, the results of our EFAs did suggest some problems with specific items. For instance, Item 2 did not exhibit a salient loading on any of the four factors in this solution, or in any of the other solutions. Our results also suggested that Item 29 may be measuring Acceptance of Cultural Differences (ACD) rather than Empathic Perspective Taking (EPT), as the scale authors had originally hypothesized. We inspected the item content and felt that this change in representation was supported.

CFA

We followed up the exploratory analyses with CFAs estimated on a new sample of 994 students from the same university as the first sample. We estimated the 4-factor model we had judged to be most acceptable based on the previous EFA. Given the previously noted issues with Items 2 and 29, we estimated two additional models. In the first of these, we specified that Item 29 should load on the ACD factor instead of on the EPT factor on which it was originally specified to load. In the second additional model Item 29 remained on the ACD factor and we also removed Item 2 from the analysis. This was done because Item 2 failed to load on any factor in our EFA. The CFA syntax for the 4-factor model is displayed in Appendix C

Table 3.1. Factors to which items were assigned across solutions

Wang et al. Subscale	Item number[a]	6-Factor solution	5-Factor solution	4-Factor solution	3-Factor solution	2-Factor solution	1-Factor solution
EPT	2	0	0	0	0	0	0
EPT	4	2	2	2	2	2	0
EPT	6	2	2	2	2	2	0
EPT	19	2	2	2	2	2	1
EPT	28	2	2	2/3	2	2	1
EPT	31	2	2	2	2	2	0
ACD	1	3	3	3	3	1	1
ACD	10	3	3	3	3	1	1
EPT	29	3	3	3	3	1	1
ACD	5	3	3	3	3	1	1
ACD	8	3	3	3	3	1	1
ACD	27	3	3	3	3	1	1
EA	7	4	4	4	1	0	1
EA	20	4	4	4	1	1	1
EA	24	4	4	4	1	1	1
EA	25	4	4	4	1	1	1
EFE	16	5	5	1	1	1	1
EFE	21	5	5	1	1/3	1	1
EFE	30	5	5	1	1	1	1
EFE	12	1/6	1	1	1	1/2	1
EFE	22	6	1	1	1	1	1
EFE	23	6	1	1	1	1	1
EFE	26	6	1	1	1	1	1
EFE	11	1	0	1	0	1	1
EFE	13	1	1	1	1	1	1
EFE	14	1	1	1	1	1	1
EFE	15	1	1	1	1/3	1	1
EFE	3	1	0	1	1	1	1
EFE	17	0	0	1	1/3	1	1
EFE	18	0	1	1	1	1/2	1
EFE	9	1	0	1	3	1	1
Number of items	with cross loadings	1	0	1	3	2	0
	not loading on a factor	3	5	1	2	2	4
Number of factors	with < 4 items loading[b]	2	1	0	0	0	0

Note. EPT = Empathic Perspective Taking; ACD = Acceptance of Cultural Differences; EA = Empathic Aware-ness; EFE = Empathic Feeling and Expression. In every column, a value of 0 indicates the item did not load on any factor with a loading > |.30|. Lines designate the division of factors in the 6-factor solution.
[a]Item numbers correspond to those from Wang et al. (2003). [b]Cross-loading items were not included as an item loading on a factor.

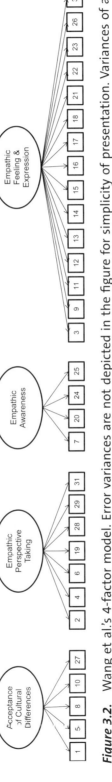

Figure 3.2. Wang et al.'s 4-factor model. Error variances are not depicted in the figure for simplicity of presentation. Variances of all factors were set to a value of 1.0 to scale the factors.

Comparing Across CFA Models

When examining the various models, we first considered model fit. Because our data were multivariate-nonnormally distributed, we implemented the Satorra-Bentler adjustment (termed MLM in Mplus) to obtain the robust chi-square, CFI, and RMSEA values, in addition to the SRMR (see Table 3.2 for fit indices). However, we also considered values of modification indexes and correlation residuals in an effort to understand specific reasons for any model misfit. Wang et al.'s (2003) original 4-factor model did not fit the data well, as indicated by both the fit indexes and by the fact that 60 correlation residuals (out of a total 465 correlations) were greater than an absolute value of .10. The models allowing Item 29 to load on the ACD factor and dropping Item 2 both yielded better fit than the original model; however, there were still many areas of misfit. Inspection of the residuals and modification indexes indicated some possible reasons for this lack of fit. Because we did not create the original scale and lacked theoretical knowledge of the attribute being measured, we did not implement any further changes to the model. However, we discuss these below to illustrate possible changes that might be implemented in the process of developing a scale.

Table 3.2. Fit indices for the various tested models

Model	M-L χ^2	S-B χ^2	df	Robust CFI	Robust RMSEA	SRMR
1. Four-factor model[a]	2791.10*	2218.36*	428	.82	.065	.067
2. EFA-suggested models						
A. Switch Item 29	2612.81*	2076.84*	428	.84	.062	.061
B. Removed Item 2	2468.69*	1955.45*	399	.84	.063	.059

Note. N = 994. Robust CFI = robust comparative fit index; Robust RMSEA = robust root mean square error of approximation; SRMR = standardized root mean square residual. [a] Corresponds to Figure 3.1.
* $p < .001$

Other Possible Scale Modifications

As noted previously, scale development is an iterative process, and items are often revised or dropped on the basis of information obtained from EFA and/or CFA. Researchers may also use such information to revise the factor structure. For example, two scales that appear to be measuring the same thing, based on similarity of content, high factor correlations, or both, may be collapsed into a single scale. Or, a scale that appears to be tapping into more than one aspect of the construct may be split into two or more subscales. In the latter case, it may be necessary to write additional items in order to flesh out the subscales, because there may not be a sufficient number of items to fully measure these. In our analysis of the SEE, we examined the correlation residuals and modification indexes for clues about possible changes to the factor structure. These suggested that some items may share variability due to item wording. For example, within the Empathic Feeling and Expression (EFE) factor there appeared to be two sets of items that shared variance beyond that accounted for by the factor. Items 16, 21, and 30 all included the word racist (e.g., Item 16 reads "I rarely think about the impact of a racist or ethnic joke on the feelings of people who are targeted"), whereas Items 12, 22, 23, and 26 included the word *share* (e.g., Item 12 reads "I *share* the anger of those who face injustice because of their racial and ethnic backgrounds").

Although we originally interpreted these results as being due to the presence of wording similarities among the items, upon reflection we felt that there could be a more substantive interpretation. Specifically, the four items that contained the word *share* (Items 12, 22, 23, and 26) appear to reflect feelings of a more personal nature than the other items. These four items may tap into an emotional connection to the feelings of those from ethnic or racial groups other than one's own that the other items do not. Items 16, 21, and 30 all refer to one's reactions to hearing racist jokes or statements, and may tap into specific feelings about such encounters. When items share variability beyond that due to their relationship to the substantive factor, it is important that the possibility of such substantive factors be considered. Although it may be the case that this variability is due simply to wording similarities, a second possibility is that the items represent unique aspects of the construct that should be considered. If subject matter experts deem these areas of the construct important to measure separately, it may be useful to write more items to address these aspects of EFE in order to model these as separate factors. On the other hand, if subject matter experts feel the excess variation is simply due to a nuisance factor, such as wording, then it may be useful to reword the items. As a final alternative, if the scale developers determine that there are enough items to cover the breadth of the construct without including these items they could be removed from the scale.

Summary

Factor analysis methods posit that the covariation in a set of items is due to one or more underlying factors. Factors account for the shared variance among items, whereas variance due to random measurement error and to the unique component of an item are modeled as error variance. Although, as their names imply, EFA is typically used in a more exploratory fashion and CFA in a more confirmatory fashion, the exploratory/confirmatory distinction is not a strict dichotomy. Applications of both methods can vary along a continuum from exploratory to confirmatory, with most analyses lying somewhere in between. Because of the iterative nature of scale development, it is common to use both EFA and CFA at different points in the process of developing and revising items. In this chapter, we have discussed how the results of factor analytic studies can be used to provide information regarding both the quality of individual items and of the factor structure as a whole. The magnitude of an item's loading on a posited factor and the absence of any cross-loadings are typically taken as evidence that an item is a solid indicator of its factor. Although this is generally a reasonable inference, we have pointed out exceptions to such a rule. With regard to quality of the overall factor structure, both EFA and CFA can provide information about the need for respecification of a posited factor model. For example, results obtained from factor analytic studies may suggest that more or fewer factors are needed. More factors may be suggested if items share variance due to wording or other artifacts, whereas a high degree of overlap among factors may suggest that some factors could be combined. As with most decisions made in the process of scale development, decisions about item revision or deletion and factor structure should be based on theoretical considerations. Although the results of statistical analyses can and should inform such decisions, statistical information should not usurp the role of theory, or of the researcher's knowledge of the construct.

References

Bandalos, D. L. (2002). The effects of item parceling on goodness-of-fit and parameter estimate bias in structural equation modeling. *Structural Equation Modeling: A Multidisciplinary Journal, 9*(1), 78–102. http://doi.org/10.1207/S15328007SEM0901_5

Bandalos, D. L. (2014). Relative performance of categorical diagonally weighted least squares and robust maximum likelihood estimation. *Structural Equation Modeling, 21*, 102–116. http://doi.org/10.1080/10705511.2014.859510

Bandalos, D. L., & Coleman, C. (2012, October). *The company you keep: The effect of serial order on correlated residuals*. Presented at the annual meeting of the Society for Multivariate Experimental Psychology, Vancouver, BC.

Bandalos, D. L., & Finney, S. J. (2001). Item parceling issues in structural equation modeling. In G. A. Marcoulides & R. E. Schumacker (Eds.), *New developments and techniques in structural equation modeling* (pp. 269–296). Hillsdale, NJ: Lawrence Erlbaum.

Bandalos, D. L., & Finney, S. J. (2010). Factor analysis: Exploratory and confirmatory. In G. R. Hancock & R. O. Mueller (Eds.), *The reviewer's guide to quantitative methods in the social sciences* (pp. 93–114). New York, NY: Routledge.

Barnette, J. (2000). Effects of stem and Likert response option reversals on survey internal consistency: If you feel the need, there is a better alternative to using those negatively worded stems. *Educational and Psychological Measurement, 60*, 361–370. http://doi.org/10.1177/00131640021970592

Beauducel, A., & Herzberg, P. Y. (2006). On the performance of maximum likelihood versus mean and variance adjusted weighted least squares estimation in CFA. *Structural Equation Modeling, 13*, 186–203. http://doi.org/10.1207/s15328007sem1302_2

Benson, J. (1998). Developing a strong program of construct validation: A test anxiety example. *Educational Measurement: Issues and Practice, 17*, 10–17. http://doi.org/10.1111/j.1745-3992.1998.tb00616.x

Bernstein, I. H., & Teng, G. (1989). Factoring items and factoring scales are different: Spurious evidence for multidimensionality due to item categorization. *Psychological Bulletin, 105*, 467–477. http://doi.org/10.1037/0033-2909.105.3.467

Bollen, K. A. (2002). Latent variables in psychology and the social sciences. *Annual Review of Psychology, 53*, 605–634. http://doi.org/10.1146/annurev.psych.53.100901.135239

Briggs, N. E., & MacCallum, R. C. (2003). Recovery of weak common factors by maximum likelihood and ordinary least squares estimation. *Multivariate Behavioral Research, 38*, 25–56. http://doi.org/10.1207/S15327906MBR3801_2

Cronbach, L. J., & Meehl, P. E. (1955). Construct validity in psychological tests. *Psychological Bulletin, 52*, 281–302. http://doi.org/10.1037/h0040957

DeCarlo, L. (1997). On the meaning and use of kurtosis. *Psychological Methods, 2*, 292–307. http://doi.org/10.1037/1082-989X.2.3.292

Fabrigar, L. R., Wegener, D. T., MacCallum, R. C., & Strahan, E. J. (1999). Evaluating the use of exploratory factor analysis in psychological research. *Psychological Methods, 4*(3), 272–299. http://doi.org/10.1037/1082-989X.4.3.272

Finney, S. J., & DiStefano, C. (2014). Nonnormal and categorical data in structural equation modeling. In G. R. Hancock & R. O. Mueller (Eds.). *A second course in structural equation modeling* (2nd ed., pp. 439–492). Charlotte, NC: Information Age.

Flora, D. B., & Curran, P. J. (2004). An empirical evaluation of alternative methods of estimation for confirmatory factor analysis with ordinal data. *Psychological Methods, 9*, 466–491. http://doi.org/10.1037/1082-989X.9.4.466

Gerstner, J. J., & Bandalos, D. L. (2013, May). *An evaluation of the use of exploratory factor analysis in scale development*. Poster presented at the annual meeting of the Association for Psychological Science, Washington, DC.

Green, S. B., Akey, T. M., Fleming, K. K., Hershberger, S. L., & Marquis, J. G. (1997). Effect of the number of scale points on chi-square fit indices in confirmatory factor analysis. *Structural Equation Modeling, 4*, 108–120. http://doi.org/10.1080/10705519709540064

Hogarty, K. Y., Hines, C. V., Kromrey, J. D., Ferron, J. M., & Mumford, K. R. (2005). The quality of factor solutions in exploratory factor analysis: The influence of sample size, communality, and overdetermination. *Educational and Psychological Measurement, 65*, 202–226. http://doi.org/10.1177/0013164404267287

Hutchinson, S. R. (1998). The stability of post hoc model modifications in confirmatory factor analysis models. *Journal of Experimental Education, 66*, 361–380. http://doi.org/10.1080/00220979809601406

Kline, R. B. (2011). *Principles and practice of structural equation modeling* (3rd ed.). New York, NY: Guilford.

Lai, J. (1994). Differential predictive power of the positively versus the negatively worded items of the Life Orientation Test. *Psychological Reports, 75*, 1507–1515. http://doi.org/10.2466/pr0.1994. 75.3f.1507

Lorenzo-Seva, U., Timmerman, M. E., & Kiers, H. A. L. (2011). The Hull method for selecting the number of common factors. *Multivariate Behavioral Research, 46*(2), 340–364. http://doi.org/10.1080/0 0273171.2011.564527

MacCallum, R. (1986). Specification searches in covariance structure modeling. *Psychological Bulletin, 100*(1), 107–120. http://doi.org/10.1037/0033-2909.100.1.107

MacCallum, R. C., Roznowski, M., & Necowitz, L.B. (1992). Model modifications in covariance structure analysis: The problem of capitalization on chance. *Psychological Bulletin, 111*(3), 490–504. http:// doi.org/10.1037/0033-2909.111.3.490

MacCallum, R. C., Widaman, K. F., & Hong, S. (2001). Sample size in factor analysis: The role of model error. *Multivariate Behavioral Research, 36*, 611–637.

MacCallum, R. C., Widaman, K. F., Zhang, S., & Hong, S. (1999). Sample size in factor analysis. *Psychological Methods, 4*, 84–99. http://doi.org/10.1037/1082-989X.4.1.84

Mardia, K. V. (1970). Measures of multivariate skewness and kurtosis with applications. *Biometrika, 57*, 519–530. http://doi.org/10.1093/biomet/57.3.519

Marsh, H. (1986). Negative item bias in ratings scales for preadolescent children: A cognitive-developmental phenomenon. *Developmental Psychology, 22*, 37–49. http://doi.org/10.1037/0012-1649.22.1.37

McDonald, R. P. (1999). *Test theory: A unified treatment*. Mahwah, NJ: Lawrence Erlbaum.

McDonald, R. P., & Ahlawat, K. S. (1974). Difficulty factors in binary data. *British Journal of Mathematical and Statistical Psychology, 27*, 82–99 http://doi.org/10.1111/j.2044-8317.1974.tb00530.x

Motl, R., Conroy, D., & Horan, P. (2000). The Social Physique Anxiety Scale: An example of the potential consequence of negatively worded items in factorial validity studies. *Journal of Applied Measurement, 1*, 327–345.

Nunnally, J. C., & Bernstein, I. H. (1994). *Psychometric theory* (3rd ed.). New York, NY: McGraw-Hill.

Pilotte, W., & Gable, R. (1990). The impact of positive and negative item stems on the validity of a computer anxiety scale. *Educational and Psychological Measurement, 50*, 603–610. http://doi. org/10.1177/0013164490503016

Ridley, C. R., & Lingle, D. W. (1996). Cultural empathy in multicultural counseling: A multidimensional process model. In P. B. Pedersen, J. G. Draguns, W. J. Lonner, & J. E. Trimble (Eds.), *Counseling across cultures* (4th ed., pp. 21–46). Thousand Oaks, CA: Sage Publications.

Rhemtulla, M., Brousseau-Liard, P. E., & Savalei, V. (2012). When can categorical variables be treated as continuous? A comparison of robust continuous and categorical SEM estimation methods under suboptimal conditions. *Psychological Methods, 17*, 354–373. http://doi.org/10.1037/a0029315

Ruscio, J., & Roche, B. (2012). Determining the number of factors to retain in an exploratory factor analysis using comparison data of known factorial structure. *Psychological Assessment, 24*(2), 282–292. http://doi.org/10.1037/a0025697

Silvia, E. S. M., & MacCallum, R. C. (1988). Some factors affecting the success of specification searches in covariance structure modeling. *Multivariate Behavioral Research, 23*, 297–326. http://doi. org/10.1207/s15327906mbr2303_2

Stapleton, L. M. (2013). Multilevel structural equation modeling with complex sample data. In G. R. Hancock & R. O. Mueller (Eds.), *Structural equation modeling: A second course* (pp. 521–562). Charlotte, NC: Information Age Publishing.

Thurstone, L. L. (1947). *Multiple–factor analysis: A development and expansion of the vectors of mind*. Chicago, IL: University of Chicago Press.

Velicer, W. F., & Fava, J. L. (1998). Effects of variable and subject sampling on factor pattern recovery. *Psychological Methods, 3*, 231–251. http://doi.org/10.1037/1082-989X.3.2.231

Velicer, W. F., Eaton, C. A., & Fava, J. L. (2000). Construct explication through factor or component analysis: A review and evaluation of alternative procedures for determining the number of factors or components. In R. D. Goffin & E. Helmes (Eds.), *Problems and solutions in human assessment: Honoring Douglas N. Jackson at seventy* (pp. 41–71). New York, NY: Kluwer Academic/Plenum.

Zwick, W. R., & Velicer, W. F. (1986). Comparison of five rules for determining the number of compo-
    nents to retain. *Psychological Bulletin, 99*(3), 432–442. http://doi.org/10.1037/0033-2909.99.3.432

Wang, Y., Davidson, M. M., Yakushko, O. F., Bielstein, H. B., Tan, J. A., & Bleier, J. K. (2003). The scale
    of ethnocultural empathy: Development, validation, and reliability. *Journal of Counseling Psychol-
    ogy, 50*(2), 221–234. http://doi.org/10.1037/0022-0167.50.2.221

Appendix A

Table A1. The Scale of Ethnocultural Empathy (SEE; Wang et al., 2003)

Item number	Wang et al. Subscale	Item
1	ACD	I feel annoyed when people do not speak standard English.
2	EPT	I don't know a lot of information about important social and political events of racial and ethnic groups other than my own.
3	EFE	I am touched by movies or books about discrimination issues faced by racial or ethnic groups other than my own.
4	EPT	I know what it feels like to be the only person of a certain race or ethnicity in a group of people.
5	ACD	I get impatient when communicating with people from other racial or ethnic backgrounds, regardless of how well they speak English.
6	EPT	I can relate to the frustration that some people feel about having fewer opportunities due to their racial or ethnic backgrounds.
7	EA	I am aware of institutional barriers (e.g., restricted opportunities for job promotion) that discriminate against racial or ethnic groups other than my own.
8	ACD	I don't understand why people of different racial or ethnic backgrounds enjoy wearing traditional clothing.
9	EFE	I seek opportunities to speak with individuals of other racial or ethnic backgrounds about their experiences.
10	ACD	I feel irritated when people of different racial or ethnic backgrounds speak their language around me.
11	EFE	When I know my friends are treated unfairly because of their racial or ethnic backgrounds, I speak up for them.
12	EFE	I share the anger of those who face injustice because of their racial and ethnic backgrounds.
13	EFE	When I interact with people from other racial or ethnic backgrounds, I show my appreciation of their cultural norms.
14	EFE	I feel supportive of people of other racial or ethnic groups, if I feel they are being taken advantage of.
15	EFE	I get disturbed when other people experience misfortunes due to their racial or ethnic backgrounds.
16	EFE	I rarely think about the impact of a racist or ethnic joke on the feelings of people who are targeted.
17	EFE	I am not likely to participate in events that promote equal rights for people of all racial and ethnic backgrounds.
18	EFE	I express my concern about discrimination to people from other racial or ethnic groups.
19	EPT	It is easy for me to understand what it would feel like to be a person of another racial or ethnic background other than my own.

Table A1. continued

Item number	Wang et al. Subscale	Item
20	EA	I can see how other racial or ethnic groups are systematically oppressed in our society.
21	EFE	I don't care if people make racist statements against other racial or ethnic groups.
22	EFE	When I see people who come from a different racial or ethnic background succeed in the public arena, I share their pride.
23	EFE	When other people struggle with racial or ethnic oppression, I share their frustration.
24	EA	I recognize that the media often portrays people based on racial or ethnic stereotypes.
25	EA	I am aware of how society differentially treats racial or ethnic groups other than my own.
26	EFE	I share the anger of people who are victims of hate crimes (e.g., intentional violence because of race or ethnicity).
27	ACD	I do not understand why people want to keep their indigenous racial or ethnic cultural traditions instead of trying to fit into the mainstream.
28	EPT	It is difficult for me to put myself in the shoes of someone who is racially and/or ethnically different from me.
29	EPT	I feel uncomfortable when I am around a significant number of people who are racially/ethnically different than me.
30	EFE	When I hear people make racist jokes, I tell them I am offended even though they are not referring to my racial or ethnic group.
31	EPT	It is difficult for me to relate to stories in which people talk about racial or ethnic discrimination they experience in their day to day lives.

Appendix B

Mplus syntax for EFA models with 1–7 factors

```
TITLE: EFA;

DATA:
 FILE IS "C:\…\Documents\efa.dat";
 FORMAT IS free;

!!Note: the lines above provide the location of an external data
file in free format that contains item-level responses.

VARIABLE:
 NAMES ARE id i1-i31;

!!Note: the lines above indicate the number of variables and
their names.

ANALYSIS:
 ESTIMATOR=MLM;
 TYPE = EFA 1 7;
 ROTATION = promax;
!! Note: the lines above specify use of the MLM (adjusted ML)
estimator. TYPE = EFA 1 7 indicates that factor solutions based
on 1,2,3…7 factors should be obtained. ROTATION = promax speci-
fies the promax (oblique) rotation method.
```

Appendix C

Mplus syntax for the 4-factor model

```
TITLE: Wang et al.'s Original Model

DATA:
file is "C:\...\Example\cfa.dat"
format is free;

VARIABLE:
names are i1-i31;

ANALYSIS:
ESTIMATOR IS MLM;

MODEL:

 efe by i3 i9 i11 i12 i13 i14 i15 i16 i17 i18 i21 i22 i23 i26
 i30;
 ept by i2 i4 i6 i19 i28 i29 i31;
 acd by i1 i5 i8 i10 i27;
 ea by i7 i20 i24 i25;
!! Note: the lines above specify which items load on which factor.

[efe@0 ept@0 acd@0 ea@0];
!! Note: in CFA it is common to estimate the "mean structure."
The mean structure for a CFA model consists of estimates of the
item intercepts and factor means. Mplus automatically estimates
the intercept terms for each item. The mean of each factor can
also be estimated, but here we have set each factor mean to be
equal to zero. This will cause the item intercepts to be equal
to the observed mean of the item.


OUTPUT: residual standardized modindices;

!!Note: the statement above requests the standardized solution
as well as information on residuals and modification.
```

Chapter 4

Item Response Theory as a Framework for Test Construction

Lale Khorramdel and Matthias von Davier

Educational Testing Service, Princeton, NJ, USA

Introduction

Test construction refers to a process in which tasks are selected based on their association with a psychological construct and are arranged into an instrument that can be administered under standardized conditions. The association between task and trait is typically determined by means of both interpretive (content) and statistical criteria. Domain experts determine what type of tasks can potentially be useful to elicit information, and statistical methods are used to determine the strength of association between observed task responses and the construct that the test is intended to measure.

Classical Test Theory and Item Response Theory in a Nutshell

This introduction provides an integrated description of the assumptions used in classical test theory (CTT; e.g., Novick, 1966) and item response theory (IRT; e.g., Lord & Novick, 1968). Assume there is a population P of persons, and that a person v from this population generates values on K random variables X_k for $k = 1\ldots K$. Let X_{vk} denote the k-th random variable for test-taker v and assume that this variable has finite expectation and variance. Assume that this random variable can be repeatedly observed and denote

$$x_{vkt}, \text{ with } t = 1,2,\ldots \tag{1}$$

the repeated realizations of test k for person v and replicate t.

Classical Test Theory

CTT defines the true score of person v on test k as

$$T_{vk} = E_t(x_{vk*}). \tag{2}$$

This is the (unobserved) expected value over repeated draws from X_{vk}. For each replication t, an error term can be defined as follows

$$e_{vkt} = x_{vkt} - T_{vk} \tag{3}$$

Obviously, e_{vkt} is unknown since T_{vk} is unknown. Note that $E_t(e_{vk*}) = 0$ (see also Novick, 1966) and that $V_t(e_{vk*}) = V_t(x_{vk*})$. The correlation $\rho(e_{vk*}, x_{vk*}) = 1$ due to the linearity between observed score replications and associated error term for a given person v. By definition, the true score T_{vk} of person v on test k is the expected score and hence a constant for this person over replications of the random experiment.

Let us now assume that persons are sampled from the population P. Following Novick (1966), let X_{*k}, X_{*g} denote the random variables for the case of a randomly selected person generating a single score x_{*k} and x_{*g} on tests k and g, respectively. We will drop the *replicate index* from now on and use x_{*k} instead of x_{*k*} since we typically observe only a single value for each person. The discussion of independent replications is needed here only to define the unobserved true score $T_{*k} = E_t(x_{*k*})$ that plays a central role in CTT. Correspondingly, let T_{*k}, T_{*g} and E_{*k}, E_{*g} denote the true-score and error variables for the two tests, respectively. Then, we can write

$$e_{*k} = x_{*k} - t_{*k} \text{ and } e_{*g} = x_{*g} - t_{*g}. \tag{4}$$

Novick (1966) states that the following equalities can be derived based on the assumptions made so far:

$$E(e_{*k}) = 0, \tag{5}$$

$$COV(e_{*k}, t_{*k}) = 0, \tag{6}$$

$$COV(e_{*k}, e_{*g}) = 0. \tag{7}$$

While Equations 5 and 6 are implied, it turns out that additional assumptions are needed (Zimmerman & Williams, 1977) in order to obtain Equation 7. Lord and Novick (1968) add an assumption as a precondition to Equation 7 that observed scores are independently distributed given true scores, which makes Equation 7 a simple corollary. Why this assumption is needed can be seen by a simple counterexample: If we consider three observed scores X_{*1}, X_{*2}, X_{*3} with

$$X_{*3} = X_{*1} + X_{*2} \tag{8}$$

we have

$$e_{*3} = X_{*1} + X_{*2} - T_{*1} - T_{*2} = e_{*1} + e_{*2} \tag{9}$$

and some simple algebra shows that

$$COV(e_{*1}, e_{*3}) - COV(e_{*1}, e_{*2}) = V(e_{*1}) > 0 \tag{10}$$

in this case. This result violates Equation 7 and shows that dependent observed scores (for example scores obtained from tests that share some items) may not be advisable.

Note that Equation 6 can be utilized to derive the well-known variance decomposition of CTT, one of the central building blocks of defining the reliability of a test in CTT. We can write

$$V(X_{*k}) = V(T_{*k}) + V(E_{*k}) \tag{11}$$

and use this result to define

$$Rel(X_{*k}) = \frac{V(T_{*k})}{V(T_{*k}) + V(E_{*k})}. \tag{12}$$

So far, no assumptions have been made about how the observed score variables X_{*k}, X_{*g} for the $k = 1,...,K$ tests are obtained. Note that T_{*k}, T_{*g} and E_{*k}, E_{*g} are all unobserved. In order to make inferences about the T_{*k} and E_{*k}, some additional assumptions are helpful. We started the section assuming $k = 1,...,K$ tests with observed scores for each person, and for a randomly chosen person we defined random variables $X_{*1}, \ldots, X_{*K}$.

If there are tests for which the same true score can be assumed, for example two tests designed to measure the same skills, using very similar task materials, for some $g, k \in \{1...K\}$ one may assume

$$X_{vk} = T_v + E_{vk} \text{ and } X_{vg} = T_v + E_{vg} \text{ for all } v, \text{ and } V(E_{*g}) = V(E_{*k}). \tag{13}$$

In many practical applications, the observed score variable X_{*k} of test form k is based on administering a number of tasks with binary outcomes $Y_{*ki} \in \{0,1\}$, for $i = 1, \ldots, I_k$, to a random sample of persons from P. Then, the observed score X_{*k} is often obtained as the sum of these binary outcomes

$$X_{*k} = \sum_{i=1}^{I_k} w_i Y_{*ki} = T_{*k} + E_{*k}, \tag{14}$$

and similarly for X_{*g}. In many applications of CTT, item weights are chosen to be uniform, e.g., $w_i = 1$ or $w_i = (I_k)^{-1}$. The Y_{*ki} and Y_{*gi} are sometimes carefully selected to make assumption (Equation 13) plausible. In that case we can use the two sets of binary variables and their associated score variables interchangeably, i.e., they can be viewed as *parallel tests* in CTT.

Using the definition of observed score X_{*g} based on binary item scores Y_{*ki} as in Equation 14 with $i = 1$leads to a sum score that is a discrete random variable

$$S_{*k} = \sum_{i=1}^{I_k} Y_{*ki} = T_{*k} + E_{*k} \in \{0, \ldots I_k\}. \tag{15}$$

CTT decomposes this bounded, integer-valued variable $S_{*k} \in \{0, \ldots I_k\}$ into two real-valued components, the unobserved expectation T_{*k} and the error term E_{*k}. Holland and Hoskens (2002) explain that CTT can be viewed as a first-order (mean and variance) approximation to a general version of IRT. The next section discusses the approach IRT takes to model the individual binary responses Y_{*ki} directly. This involves assumptions how the probability of these responses is associated with the target of inferences, an unobserved person variable. Hambleton and Jones (1993) speak of CTT as a weak model since the assumptions made are more easily met than the assumptions made in IRT, which they call a strong model. However, while CTT does not make explicit assumptions how the individual response variables Y_{*ki} are related to the target of inference, there are a number of implicit assumptions made in CTT. One is shown in Equation 15, namely that the unweighted sum of item scores is accepted as the appropriate aggregate, instead of estimating optimal scoring weights (Lord, 1980; McDonald, 1968; Thissen, Nelson, Rosa, & McLeod, 2001), for the parameters shown in Equation 14. In addition, there are assumptions that are made when looking at item-total covariance $COV(S_{*k}$, $Y_{*ki})$ terms or item-total correlations to select items. Also estimates of reliability such as Cronbach's (1951) alpha or the Kuder and Richardson (1937) formula's KR20 and KR21 are based on the idea that not only S_{*k} but also each item-level variable Y_{*ki} should be related to T_{*k} in systematic ways (e.g., Sijtsma, 2009).

Item Response Theory

IRT specifies a model for the statistical dependency of the item-level variables Y_{*ki} on a person variable θ. In many applications we will deal with tests consisting of discrete units, often with binary outcomes, where $y_{vki} = 1$ may represents the event that person v solves (or endorsed) item i on test k, and $y_{vki} = 0$ represents the complement. Instead of a linear decomposition, IRT utilizes an approach that models the probability of these responses. More specifically, IRT assumes a model

$$P(Y_{*ki} = 1|\theta) \tag{16}$$

for all $i = 1, \ldots, I_k$. While the person variable θ is not based on expected scores, the above expression immediately enables the production of a *true-score-like* variable

$$T_{*k}(\theta_v) = \sum_{i=1}^{I_k} P(Y_{*ki} = 1|\theta_v) \tag{17}$$

for a randomly drawn person with trait level θ_v. This function is also known as the test characteristic curve.

Instead of aggregating binary variables Y_{*ki} into a sum score (Equation 14) with prespecified weights w_i, IRT utilizes the item functions $P(Y_{*ki} = 1|\theta)$ with estimated parameters (see below) and the vector of response variables $(Y_{*ki}, \ldots, Y_{*kI_k})$ as a basis to make inferences about the unobserved person variable θ.

While there are also IRT models for items with nominal and polytomous outcomes (for many of which assigning category scores for the different outcomes and summation as in Equation 14 is less obvious), as well as models with multiple person variables, we will only discuss models for binary responses. For information about this topic the reader is referred to the edited volume(s) by van der Linden and Hambleton (1997, 2014) describing a wide variety of available IRT models, and to Fischer and Molenaar (1995) and von Davier and Carstensen (2007) for a discussion of Rasch models for various types of observed responses and extensions of the latent variable space to multilevel, multiple-population models and multidimensional θ variables.

The assumptions many IRT models for binary data are based on can be summarized as follows: IRT assumes a unidimensional person variable (Equation 18), monotonicity of response probabilities in this variable (Equation 19), and conditional independence (Equation 20) given the person variable. More formally, it is customary to assume

$$\theta \in \mathbb{R}, \text{ i.e., the random variable is unidimensional,} \tag{18}$$

$$\text{for all } i: P(y_i|\theta_1) < P(y_i|\theta_2) \text{ if } \theta_1 < \theta_2, \tag{19}$$

$$P(y_1, \ldots, y_K|\theta) = \prod_{i=1}^{K} P(y_i|\theta). \tag{20}$$

Parametric IRT models assume a specific functional form of the conditional response probabilities $P(y_i|\theta)$ while for the Rasch model (Rasch, 1960) the only additional requirement involves the assumption that the total score is a sufficient statistics (e.g., Fischer, 2007; Fischer & Molenaar, 1995) for θ:

$$P(y_1, \ldots, y_K|S, \theta) = P(y_1, \ldots, y_K|S) \text{ with } S = \sum_{i=1}^{K} v_i. \tag{21}$$

The Rasch model is sometimes also referred to as one parameter logistic model, however it is not to be confused with the OPLM (Verhelst & Glas, 1995) that, spelled out, shares the same name. Commonly applied examples of IRT models include the one, two and three parameter logistic (1PL, 2PL, 3PL) models (Lord & Novick, 1968). The conditional response probability for these can be written as

$$P(y_i = 1|\theta) = c_i + (1 - c_i)\frac{\exp(a_i(\theta - b_i))}{1 + \exp(a_i(\theta - b_i))}. \qquad (22)$$

The a_i, b_i, c_i are real-valued parameters that can either be fixed or estimated. In the 3PL, all of these are estimated for all items $i = 1, \ldots, I_k$, while in the 2PL model, it is assumed that $c_i = 0$, and the Rasch model is obtained by fixing $a_i = 1$ in addition. The 2PL, 3PL and the Rasch model provide a statistical model for the conditional distribution of binary $y_1, \ldots, y_K$ and allow inferences about θ given the observed vector of responses on these observed item variables. This can be done by assuming a distribution $\varphi(\cdot)$ for the person variable θ, for example a standard normal distribution and by forming the marginal distribution

$$p(y_1, \ldots, y_K) = \int p(y_1, \ldots, y_K|\theta)\varphi(\theta)d\theta. \qquad (23)$$

For a sample of $v = 1, \ldots, N$ respondents with observed responses $y_{v1}, \ldots, y_{vK}$ on the binary variables, maximum likelihood methods can be used to obtain estimates of the a_i, b_i, c_i (or some of these for the 2PL and the Rasch model). Subsequently, a proficiency estimate $\hat{\theta}_v$ for each observed response vector $y_{v1}, \ldots, y_{vK}$ can be generated using either maximum likelihood, weighted, maximum likelihood, or Bayesian estimators.

In recent years, general families of statistical models have been developed that include many of the more frequently used IRT models as special cases. In addition, these modeling families can be used to derive extensions of IRT models, or to combine IRT models for binary responses with models for ordinal, multinomial, or continuous variables, and include covariates or multilevel structures in the model (e.g., De Boeck & Wilson, 2004; Moustaki & Knott, 2000; Rijmen, Jeon, von Davier, & Rabe-Hesketh, 2013; Skrondal & Rabe-Hesketh, 2004; von Davier, 2008).

There are many other IRT-based models one may wish to apply under certain circumstances. As a general rule, however, the Rasch model and the 2PL model, or their counterparts, can cover a wide range of applications. The Rasch and the 2PL model can be extended to item responses that are scored in more than two categories; they can be modeled with so-called polytomous or ordinal IRT models. The partial credit model (PCM; Masters, 1982) generalizes the Rasch model to a model for more than two response categories, while the generalized partial credit model (GPCM; Muraki, 1992) generalizes the 2PL model to ordered multicategory data. Apart from one application of the GPCM, Rasch model and 2PL are the two we will use in the examples; therefore, we discuss these below in some more detail.

The Rasch Model

One of the most prominent IRT models is the *Rasch model* or *one-parameter logistic model* (1PL model) for dichotomous data (e.g., Rasch, 1960; for an overview of the model, estimation methods, and model tests see von Davier, in press). The Rasch model postulates that the probability of a response y_i to item i by respondent v depends on two parameters: the difficulty of the item b_i and the respondent's ability or trait level (person variable) θ;

$$P(y_i = 1|\theta) = \frac{\exp(\theta - b_i)}{1 + \exp(\theta - b_i)}. \qquad (24)$$

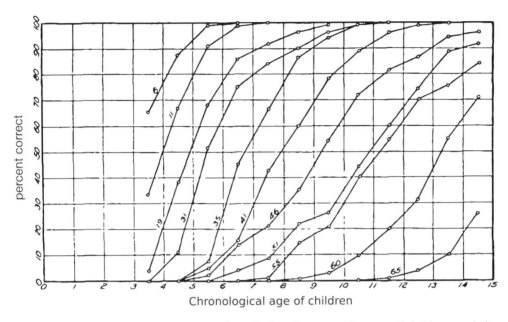

Figure 4.1. Empirical ICCs showing the relation between the age of children and the percent correct for a certain item (Thurstone, 1925).

The probability of a positive response (e.g., solving an item) is strict monotonic increasing in θ and decreasing in b_i. This functional relationship can be displayed by an item characteristic curve (ICC). Figure 4.1 provides an example of empirically found ICCs showing the relation between the age of children and the percent correct for a certain set of items (Thurstone, 1925; see also Lord, 1980, for similar plots). Figure 4.2 illustrates how a model-based approximation of these empirically observed associations can be visualized. The ICC in Figure 4.2 is based on the Rasch model. If a respondent's ability or trait level matches the item difficulty, a probability of .50 for a correct response is obtained, shown at the inflection point of the ICC. This point can be interpreted as the threshold at which a person is as likely to pass as to fail the item.

The formal structure of the Rasch model permits algebraic separation of the person and item parameters (the person parameter can be eliminated during the estimation of item parameters). The reason behind this parameter separability is that both the item parameter b_i and the person parameter θ have simple *sufficient statistics* in the Rasch model. More specifically, a person total score contains all information about the respondent's trait level (see Equation 21), and the item total score contains all information about the item.

Another consequence of parameter separability due to the existence of the simple sufficient statistics is what Rasch (1960) called *specific objectivity,* or specific objective comparisons: Comparison between individuals can be made independent of which particular items each person has taken, and the comparison between two items is independent of which person responded to them. This feature of the Rasch model presents an advantage over other models that can hardly be overstated (von Davier, in press): The Rasch model allows looking at differences of test taker abilities based on potentially completely different sets of tasks, provided that the task characteristics have been obtained in a comprehensive analysis across all test forms together, and that the Rasch model can be shown to provide an adequate statistical fit to

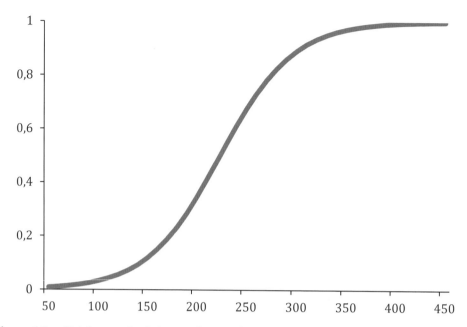

Figure 4.2. Strict monotonic increasing ICC based on the Rasch model.

the observed response data. Similar comparisons are possible with more general IRT models as well. However, the simplicity of the direct calculation of ability or trait differences is facilitated by the separability of parameters in the Rasch model and a few variants of the model (e.g., Haberman, 2006; Verhelst & Glas, 1995; von Davier & Rost, 1995).

The Two-Parameter Logistic Model

The two-parameter logistic model (Birnbaum, 1957, 1968) is a generalization of the Rasch model. Like the Rasch model, the 2PL model assumes that the probability for response y_i to item i by respondent v depends on the difference between the respondent's trait level θ and the difficulty of the item b_i. In addition, the 2PL model postulates that for every item, the association between this difference and the response probability depends on an additional item discrimination parameter a_i:

$$P(y_i = 1|\theta) = \frac{\exp\big(a_i(\theta - b_i)\big)}{1 + \exp\big(a_i(\theta - b_i)\big)}. \tag{25}$$

The probability of a positive response (e.g., solving an item) is strict monotonic increasing in θ and decreasing in b_i. The item discrimination parameter a_i, sometimes scaled by a constant ($D = 1.7$), characterizes how fast the probability of solving the item approaches 1 with increasing trait level θ when compared to other items. In other words, the model accounts for the possibility that item responses are not equally strongly related to the latent trait. The discrimination parameter a_i describes how well an item discriminates between examinees with different trait levels. The 2PL, just as the Rasch model and other models of IRT, greatly facilitates incomplete designs and multiple test forms in a much more straightforward way than methods of classical test theory can. All international large-scale studies (such as the Programme for

International Student Assessment, or PISA, or the Programme for the International Assessment of Adult Competencies, or PIAAC) use IRT or versions of the Rasch model for linking up to 20 (or more) test forms in a single language, and linking up to 100 language versions, as well as linking over multiple assessment cycles (e.g., Yamamoto, Khorramdel, & von Davier, 2013; Mazzeo & von Davier, 2013; Oliveri & von Davier, 2011, 2014; Yamamoto & Mazzeo, 1992). This may lead to models that contain 100 different language versions, with 13 or more test forms nested within these languages. A linking or equating for this many test forms would be a rather tedious undertaking.

In the following sections, we will review a couple of approaches to evaluate the assumptions made in IRT models. Then we focus on IRT as a practical tool for test analysis and test construction. We will use the Rasch model, the 2PL model and the Generalized Partial Credit Model (GPCM) in examples that work through some aspects of test development. We will address issues around violations of the assumptions made and how to address these violations in a practical setting.

Model and Item Fit Measures

One major advantage of IRT is that the assumptions made can be tested by means of goodness-of-fit measures (e.g., Andersen, 1973; Glas, 2007; Glas & Verhelst, 1995, Gilula & Haberman, 1994; Martin-Löf, 1973) as well as measures specific to item fit (e.g., Haberman, Sinharay, & Chon, 2013; Orlando & Thissen, 2000, 2003; Rost & von Davier, 1994) or person fit (e.g., von Davier & Molenaar, 2003). Several methods can be used to decide whether an IRT model fits a dataset based on a specific item pool in a certain population of respondents. Due to the different formal structures and assumptions of IRT models, different methods of detecting misfit have to be used. These methods can be divided into those which test the model fit for the whole item pool and those which show the fit for each single item (item-fit statistics). If a global model test rejects an IRT model for a dataset, the item-fit statistics may be used to determine if this misfit is due to a small or large number of items. If the misfit is due to only a few items and the item pool is large enough, those items may be excluded in order to obtain model fit for the remaining item pool. The Rasch model allows defining certain global model tests that utilize features such as the availability of simple sufficient statistics due to its formal structure.

Glas (2007), Glas and Verhelst (1995), Kubinger (1989), and von Davier (in press) give an overview of global model tests for the Rasch model such as the Andersen's likelihood ratio test (Andersen, 1973) and the Martin-Löf test (Martin-Löf, 1973), as well as item-fit statistics like the Fischer–Scheiblechner z-test (Fischer & Scheiblechner, 1970), the item Q-index (Rost & von Davier, 1994) and item-fit evaluations such as the graphical model test suggested by Rasch (1960). These models and item-fit measures are illustrated below.

Andersen's conditional likelihood ratio test is a significance test based on the assumption of specific objective comparisons that implies item parameters can be consistently estimated in subsamples drawn from a population where the Rasch model applics. It tests if the observed data can be described more accurately with multiple sets of model parameters estimated in different subsamples than with parameters estimated using the whole sample. The sample is typically divided into subsamples by using internal criteria such as the raw score or ability (or trait) levels, or external criteria such as gender, age, or educational level. Then parameter estimates are generated for the total sample and, additionally, for the two subsamples. The asymptotically chi-square distributed test statistic χ^2 is defined as follows:

$$\chi^2 = -2\ln\left(\frac{L_0}{cL_1 * cL_2}\right) \tag{26}$$

with $df = (k_1 - 1 + k_2 - 1) - (k_0 - 1)$ where L_0 is the likelihood in the total sample, and cL_1 and cL_2 are the conditional likelihoods in the two subsamples 1 and 2; k_0 is the number of items in the total sample, and k_1 and k_2 are the number of items in subsample 1 and 2.

If the test statistic exceeds a critical value given by the chi-square distribution, an a priori specified level of uncertainty, and the degrees of freedom specified above, the item parameter estimates of the different groups are considered to differ significantly and the hypothesis of equal parameter estimates has to be rejected. The likelihood ratio test is sensitive to the sample sizes. A small sample size below 200 for testing the fit of the Rasch model may not provide sufficient power to detect deviations from the Rasch model, while the test will almost surely be significant in very large samples even if graphical inspection seems to indicate the parameters are virtually identical.

The Martin-Löf conditional likelihood ratio test, often called *the Martin-Löf test* (Martin-Löf, 1973), is a significance test aimed at determining whether two sets of items form a one-dimensional (or Rasch) scale. Thus, this statistic focuses on the assumption of unidimensionality. The item pool of interest is split into two or more subsets by hypothesis, and a likelihood ratio test is computed comparing the respondents' scores in these subsets of items. The statistic can be defined as follows, assuming that r_1 and r_2 denote the responses (scores) to the two item sets k_1 and k_2, and n_r the number of respondents who responded to the items:

$$Z = -2\ln\left\{\frac{L_{\hat{\sigma}}}{L_{\hat{\sigma}_1} \cdot L_{\hat{\sigma}_2}} \cdot \frac{\prod_{r=0}^{k}\left(\frac{n_r}{n}\right)^{n_r}}{\prod_{r_1=0}^{k_1}\prod_{r_2=0}^{k_2}\left(\frac{n_{r_1 r_2}}{n}\right)^{n_{r_1 r_2}}}\right\} \tag{27}$$

$L_{\hat{\sigma}}$ represents the likelihood for the whole test with k items, $L_{\hat{\sigma}_1}$ and $L_{\hat{\sigma}_2}$ as the likelihoods for the two item sets, and $n_{r_1 r_2}$ the number of respondents with score r_1 and r_2 in the two item sets. If the items form a Rasch scale, the statistic defined in Equation 6 is asymptotically χ^2-distributed with $df = k_1 k_2 - 1$.

The Martin-Löf test and Andersen's likelihood ratio test have a similar structure. However, the Andersen test uses parameter estimates of two different subsamples of respondents, testing the homogeneity of the population by looking at invariance in subsamples defined by certain grouping variables. The Martin-Löf test is based on parameter estimates from two different sets of items and assumes that the subscores (r_1, r_2) from these two item sets are sufficient, rather than the total score $r = r_1 + r_2$. Therefore, the Martin-Löf test addresses whether the set of items is homogeneous, or whether there are different subsets that can be identified as Rasch homogeneous subscales.

The Fischer–Scheiblechner z-test offers an item-based statistic to test the fit of the Rasch model for individual items. By using this approach, it can be decided which items to exclude from the item pool to improve model fit of the remaining scale. The test statistic for the parameter estimation $\hat{\sigma}$ for i items and two defined subsamples of respondents l and s is defined as:

$$z_i = \frac{\hat{\sigma}_i^l - \hat{\sigma}_i^s}{\sqrt{\frac{1}{I_i^l} + \frac{1}{I_i^s}}} \tag{28}$$

with I_i^l and I_i^s as the ith diagonal element of the information matrix, which is the matrix of the second partial derivative of the conditional likelihood function for the subsamples l and s. A similar statistic can be based on the Wald test (see Glas & Verhelst, 1995).

Rost and von Davier (1994) describe an item-fit test that is based on the conditional maximum likelihood framework. This so-called item-Q test statistic can be shown to be approximately normally distributed and can be used to check whether an item follows the mode-based ICC for the dichotomous Rasch model, as well as a variety of polytomous Rasch models.

Rasch (1960) suggested a graphical model test that is not a statistical test but can be used to examine the relationship of item parameters obtained from different samples. It involves item difficulty parameters that were estimated separately for two (or more) samples of respondents and plotted in a graph, and the scatter plot is evaluated against the 45-degree line. This type of graphical display shows whether the rank order of item parameters, as well as the relations between item parameters, are equal for all subsamples (if item parameters align with or are close to the 45-degree line) or not (item parameters coordinates located far from the 45-degree line). The latter would indicate that items are functioning differently for subsamples of respondents and, therefore, indicate a deviation from a model that assumes invariance across subpopulations. As mentioned above, the sample can be divided with regard to internal criteria (e.g., the median or mean of the test score) or external criteria (e.g., age, gender, educational level, immigrant status, etc.).

All of the above mentioned model and item-fit measures are based on the assumption of specific objective comparisons and thus are mainly useful for testing the fit of the Rasch model. Those fit statistics that work with parameter estimates in different subsamples also offer the possibility to test a set of items for differential item functioning (DIF).

For IRT models that do not provide the feature of specific objective comparisons, such as the 2PL and 3PL models, other item-fit statistics can be used to test the fit of the model for each single item such as the root mean squared deviation (RMSD) and the mean deviation (MD).

Both the root mean squared deviation (RMSD) and the mean deviation (MD) are measures to quantify the magnitude and direction of the shift of the observed data from the estimated ICC for each single item. While MD measure is most sensitive to the deviations of observed item difficulty parameters from the estimated ICC, the RMSD measure is sensitive to the deviations of both the observed item difficulty parameters and item slope parameters.

The RMSD indicates the absolute differences between two ICCs. It is computed by squaring the deviations, multiplying the proficiency distribution as weights, and then taking the square root of the total sum. The RMSD is always between 0 and 1 and can be defined as:

$$RMSD = \sqrt{\int \left(P_o(\theta) - P_e(\theta)\right)^2 f(\theta)d\theta} \qquad (29)$$

with $P_o(\theta)$ as the observed proportion of correct responses at θ and $Pe = P(\theta|\beta_i, \alpha_i)$ as the conditional probability.

The MD is the weighted sum of differences between two ICCs. It linearly relates to the proportion of correct responses. The MD is always between -1 and 1 and can be defined as:

$$MD = \int \left(P_o(\theta) - P_e(\theta)\right)f(\theta)d\theta. \qquad (30)$$

The definition shows that a negative value for MD indicates an item that is on average (over the distribution of the skill to be measured) harder than what the model indicates. A positive MD, in turn, indicates an item that is easier on average than what the model predicts.

Poorly fitting ICCs are usually revealed using a RMSD > 0.1 criterion where a value of 0 indicates no discrepancy (in other words, a perfect fit of the model). Depending on the aim of the IRT calibration, other criteria might be chosen (e.g., RMSD > 0.15 or RMSD > 0.2).

To test which IRT model fits an item pool best, model-fit indices such as the AIC (Akaike, 1974) and the BIC (Schwarz, 1978) can be calculated for each model and compared to each other, although, these model-fit indices provide no information on whether a model itself fits an item pool. Both AIC and BIC use the maximum likelihood value (L) of a model, the number of estimated model parameters (k), and the sample size:

$$AIC = -2\ln(L) + 2k \tag{31}$$

$$BIC = -2\ln(L) + \ln(N)k \tag{32}$$

While the number of model parameters in the AIC is weighted with 2, the BIC uses the logarithm of the sample size (N) as weight, thus with a stronger penalty than the AIC if $\ln(N) > 2$. Beyond the AIC and BIC, other information criteria have been developed on the basis of these two. An overview of these developments can be found, for example, in Burnham and Anderson (2004). Note that the application of some of these criteria to assessing model fit to clustered data (for example students nested in schools) requires some additional considerations (e.g., Jones, 2011).

The usefulness of the goodness-of-fit tests and the model and item-fit measures is illustrated in the following sections by means of three different examples of how IRT-based methods can guide test construction and test application.

Item and Model Selection With IRT

In general, two goals of test construction can be identified: fitting a scale by selecting items that agree with a certain IRT model (item or test calibration) versus finding an IRT model that fits a certain scale containing a given set of items.

To achieve a homogeneous set of items (in terms of unidimensionality) for which the IRT model of interest fits, the above listed model tests and item-fit measures can be used to guide stepwise item exclusion in order to eliminate items that do not seem to elicit data that agree with the underlying assumptions about the latent trait. If there is a homogeneous item pool that exhibits appropriate model fit and the item pool is large enough, the next step should be selection of the most suitable items with regard to the target of inference. Items may be selected relative to the expected ability (or trait) distribution of the population so that items at the appropriate difficulty level and item discrimination (slope) may be chosen to develop a scale that is suitable for the population for which the test is intended. If, for example, an ability test is intended to best differentiate between respondents in the high ability range, items with average to high difficulties will more likely be selected. If an ability test is intended for differentiating between respondents in the lower ability range, items of lower difficulty would be chosen.

Finally, tests that are intended to discriminate between respondents of different ability levels should be based on a variety of items with a broad range of difficulty parameters. The Fisher information (e.g., Edgeworth, 1908; Efron & Hinkley, 1978) can be used to determine the measurement accuracy in different ability ranges (Baker, 2001). In the case of a 2PL model, items with the highest discrimination parameters can be selected if the goal is to discriminate between persons in a narrow ability range, or items that discriminate over a larger range of abilities can be selected. The estimated discrimination parameter may also be selected as a criterion for choosing items or eliminating them completely from consideration, for example if there is indication that an item does not relate to the ability variable of interest.

If the aim is not to calibrate an item pool with regard to a certain model but to explore a dataset or evaluate an already calibrated item pool for a new population, model-fit indices and item-fit measures can be used to test different IRT models against each other to find the most suitable model.

The process of item and model fitting can contain different combinations of these strategies and depends on the goal of the test construction or the evaluation of an existing instrument. The following description of strategies provides a distinction between some major approaches to constructing or evaluating scales with IRT:

- *Strategy 1: Item selection for test construction* (strategy of fitting the data to the model). One IRT model is chosen a priori, and items that do not fit this model are excluded until satisfactory model fit for the remaining subset of items is obtained. This generates a homogeneous item pool at the cost of many items potentially being removed from the scale. Another approach would be to reorganize the item pool into different scales based on existing theories or hypothesis using appropriate methods to test the homogeneity of item subsets in order to fit a certain model.

- *Strategy 2: Model selection for fitting item-response data* (strategy of fitting a model to the data). Different IRT models are tested against each other (without reducing the item pool) until a model is found that describes the data best.

- *Strategy 3: Fitting data from additional populations* to an IRT model (strategy of revealing similarities and differences in different populations). The fit of an already IRT-calibrated item pool is evaluated for a new population under this strategy, or a test has to be fitted to or explored with regard to multiple populations (e.g., different cultural or language groups). The aim may be to examine additional populations with respect to mean or variance of the variable measured with the test. An important part of this strategy involves ensuring that the test is a reliable and valid instrument in these additional populations. An important prerequisite is that the majority of the items fit the same IRT model, and with the same parameters as in the initial population(s). This ensures that measurement invariance holds, while it is not necessary to assume that invariance with respect to the ability (or trait) distribution is given. Under this strategy, more lenient approaches allow that a few items could still be excluded, while the main goal remains to evaluate the fit of the overall item pool, explore the data, and find potential reasons in case of model or item misfit (such as technical problems that occurred during the test administration, or translation issues).

All of these strategies need, of course, appropriate sample sizes to avoid selection bias and may be combined with an additional selection/separation process if it is determined that the original item pool was not well fitting either the a priori selected model (Strategy 1) or any of the multiple IRT models (Strategy 2). Under this modification, the set of items may be rearranged in different subsets (based on hypothesis about meaningful item subsets; see Strategy 1) to obtain better model fit without excluding (too many) items. This second approach may split the original set of items into much smaller sets of short scales that fit a certain IRT model. Extensions of this approach to multidimensional models for item response data are discussed in Reckase (2009) as well as chapters in van der Linden and Hambleton (1997, 2014) and in von Davier and Carstensen (2007). Along the same lines, additional strategies may be applied to identify additional subpopulations if the IRT model fails to fit the data in the total sample, which may in this case be considered a sample that is composed of a mixture of subsamples originating from different populations. Rost and von Davier (1995), Rost and Langeheine (1997) and von Davier and Rost (in press) give an overview of IRT-based methods for test construction that utilize this approach.

In the following, three examples are presented to illustrate the different strategies of utilizing IRT methods for test construction or evaluation of an existing item pool scaled with IRT. The first example focuses on item selection for the construction of a reading test by excluding misfitting items from the item pool (Strategy 1); this example also gives an outlook of using the alternative Strategy 2. The second example uses data from a personality questionnaire to illustrate the reorganization of items to obtain model fit (Strategy 1). A third example shows the evaluation of item fit for new and multiple populations using the method of fixed item parameter linking (Strategy 3). The examples might not be based on optimal data (e.g., the sample sizes in Example 2 is rather small resulting in low test power) and are only used to illustrate how to use certain IRT-based strategies within test construction (without claiming completeness).

Example 1: Item Selection (Optimizing Homogeneity) and Model Selection

The aim of the following example was to construct a computer-based test to measure reading ability for fourth-grade students. The data used for the calibration of the 57 items come from 1,294 Austrian students between the age of 9 and 10 who were tested in 2007 (male: 50.1%, female: 49.9%, German as first language: $n = 77.7\%$, another language as first language: 22.3%). The IRT model applied for this purpose was the Rasch model and the following model tests and item fit measures were used to select items:
- Andersen's likelihood ratio test (Andersen, 1973);
- Fischer–Scheiblechner z-test (Fischer & Scheiblechner, 1970); and
- Graphical model test.

The R-package *eRm* (Mair & Hatzinger, 2007a, 2007b) was used for the analyses. The sample was split according to the internal criterion *median of the test score* (beneath vs. above the median score) and the two external criteria *gender* and *first language* (German vs. another). Model and item fit were evaluated for all three split criteria. In the following, the process of item selection will be illustrated using the median split criterion only.

The fit of the Rasch model was tested using the Andersen likelihood ratio test (LRT); for the critical χ^2 – value $\alpha = 1\%$ was used. If the empirical χ^2 – value is larger than the critical χ^2 – value, the test result is assumed to be significant. As the Andersen LRT showed to be significant (Table 4.1), it was decided to exclude items until the remaining item pool did not show misfit with regard to all relevant split criteria. To maintain as many items as possible, the item exclusion was done in a stepwise process. To decide which items to exclude, the results of the Fischer–Scheiblechner z-test (Table 4.2) as well as graphical model tests (Figures 4.3, 4.4, 4.5) were considered. For illustration, the results for the median split are given in Table 4.1 and Table 4.2. In a first step, the three items with the highest z-values were excluded. The same items show clear deviations in the graphical model test (Figure 4.3). As the Andersen LRT was still significant after this exclusion, more items were excluded in five additional steps. A total of 10 items (17.5% of the item pool) had to be excluded until the Andersen LRT showed a nonsignificant result (see Table 4.1 and Figure 4.5), while the graphical model test already looks satisfactory after exclusion of the first three items (see Figure 4.4). Because the item pool is large enough and 17.5% of misfitting items are still a rather small amount, it was decided to exclude the 10 items from the item pool.

Table 4.1. Results of the Andersen likelihood ratio test (LRT)

	All items	−3 Items	−5 Items	−7 Items	−9 Items	−10 Items
χ^2_{emp}	189.69	101.59	87.49	77.49	73.99	60.89
df	56	53	51	49	47	46
$\chi^2_{crit}(\alpha = 1\%)$	83.51	79.84	77.39	74.92	72.44	71.20
sign. at $\alpha = 1\%$	sign.	sign.	sign.	sign.	sign.	Not sign.

Table 4.2. Results of the Fischer–Scheiblechner z-test

Item ID	All items	−3 Items	−5 Items	−7 Items	−9 Items	−10 Items
20	2.194	2.745				
22	−2.405	−2.436	−2.178	−2.078	−2.983	
30	1.824	2.197	2.018	1.612	1.635	1.603
35	0.942	1.155	1.332	1.345	1.007	0.926
36	5.287					
41	0.386	0.937	1.216	1.346	0.527	0.277
42	−0.697	−0.681	−0.451	0.255	0.178	0.162
43	0.254	1.119	1.480	1.189	1.102	1.066
46	−0.686	−0.214	−0.172	−0.004	−0.044	−0.447
49	1.598	1.458	1.790	1.639	2.250	1.919
50	−2.261	−1.588	−1.438	−1.458	−1.449	−1.498
53	−1.479	−0.679	−0.464	0.043	0.354	0.015
54	−2.475	−1.919	−1.740	−1.557	−1.921	−1.684
57	0.082	0.789	0.903	0.919	1.078	1.074
58	2.278	2.724				
60	0.192	0.706	0.187	0.257	0.733	0.254
62	−0.313	−0.401	0.198	0.292	0.727	0.775
63	2.033	2.086	2.703			
65	−0.200	1.029	0.960	0.768	0.691	0.675
122	−0.944	−0.340	−0.590	−0.809	−1.363	−1.271
126	−0.669	−0.294	−0.117	0.196	0.218	0.206
127	−1.314	−0.931	−0.820	−0.942	−0.791	−0.697
128	1.839	2.082	1.283	1.807	2.073	2.152
129	−1.336	−1.254	−0.832	−0.652	−1.396	−1.063
130	−0.496	0.013	0.127	0.038	−0.477	−0.475
131	−2.313	−1.803	−0.887	−1.759	−1.746	−1.796
132	−1.785	−1.965	−2.163	−2.191	−2.157	−2.264
134	−1.112	−0.800	−0.250	−0.851	−0.278	−0.373
135	0.073	1.014	0.848	0.739	1.110	1.052
138	−1.738	−1.371	−1.401	−1.413	−0.961	−1.322
145	−0.314	0.547	0.459	0.012	0.422	0.368
147	−0.160	0.350	0.474	0.326	0.872	1.26

Table 4.2. continued

Item ID	All items	−3 Items	−5 Items	−7 Items	−9 Items	−10 Items
156	1.220	1.519	1.653	1.806	1.319	1.433
162	1.769	1.922	2.144	2.274		
165	0.781	1.565	1.683	1.799	1.151	1.094
166	4.238					
167	−1.593	−1.760	−1.785	−1.703	−1.876	−1.465
169	−2.430	−2.124	−2.071	−2.284		
171	−0.183	0.175	0.571	0.119	0.047	0.037
178	−1.499	−1.560	−1.358	−1.023	−1.613	−2.225
179	1.915	1.927	1.537	1.676	1.738	1.684
183	−2.701	−2.413	−2.601			
184	0.903	0.769	1.135	1.479	2.012	1.457
185	−0.567	0.000	−0.088	−0.626	−0.599	−0.697
192	−1.856	−1.505	−1.235	−1.113	−1.209	−0.996
193	−1.333	−0.881	−0.967	−0.953	−1.250	−1.284
194	−1.425	−0.402	−0.132	−0.007	−0.211	−0.869
195	−1.314	−1.072	−0.973	−0.999	−0.843	−0.89
196	−0.466	−0.395	−0.104	−0.242	−0.011	−0.298
198	0.174	−0.179	0.400	0.515	0.454	0.57
202	4.844					
203	0.485	0.625	0.940	1.311	1.189	1.157
204	0.870	1.200	0.728	0.401	0.585	0.666
206	−0.730	−0.663	−1.009	−1.061	−1.025	−1.142
210	−0.895	−0.489	−0.405	−0.139	−0.225	−0.261
212	−1.945	−1.413	−1.670	−1.381	−1.122	−0.794
216	0.428	0.649	0.866	0.565	0.793	0.805

For the strategy of item exclusion, until model fit is obtained, the item pool has to be large enough. This strategy leads to shorter tests so that the final item selection may provide less reliable measures than originally intended. If the goal is to retain as many items as possible, Strategy 2 (model selection to fit the data) might be considered instead.

Excursus

This example also shows that even if the graphical model test does not provide indication of any obvious outliers, the Andersen LRT might still be significant and vice versa (in the case of a nonsignificant LRT, items can still be excluded based on the graphical model test to ensure the quality of the item pool). Thus, it is advisable to use different item-fit measures to evaluate the test quality as well as additional item information such as the average difficulty, percent of correct responses, item content, and so on.

Moreover, different split criteria should be considered when applying the Andersen LRT. In this example we only illustrated one (median of the test score), while three criteria were used

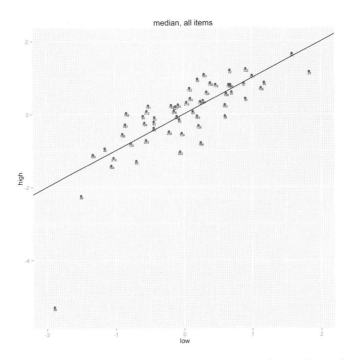

Figure 4.3. Graphical model test for the whole item pool; the median of the test score was used as split criterion.

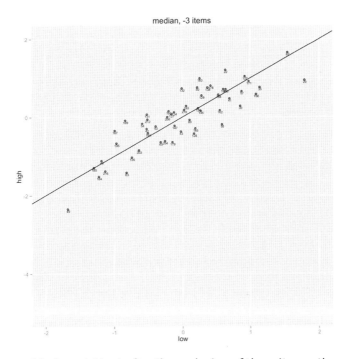

Figure 4.4. Graphical model test after the exclusion of three items; the median of the test score was used as split criterion.

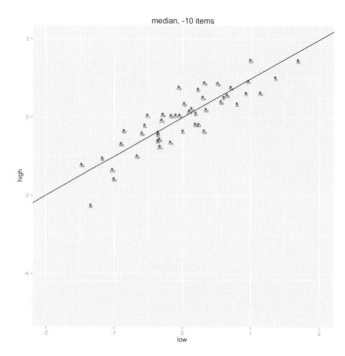

Figure 4.5. Graphical model test after the exclusion of 10 items; the median of the test score was used as split criterion.

in the original test construction (median of the test score, gender, first language). Split criteria should be chosen with regard to the purpose of the test, that is, they should be meaningful in that regard. For the same data, the Andersen LRT can be significant relative to one split criterion and nonsignificant with respect to another. Experience shows that median of the test score tends to be the most rigorous split criterion. It appears that items should only be excluded if they are the reason for significant LRT results with respect to those split criteria that are most relevant to the types of inferences one wishes to make with the test.

There is no universal rule that can be applied in test construction; the decisions made depend on the goal of the test construction, the target population and area of application (e.g., low stakes versus high stakes assessment). Fundamentally, test construction aims at maximizing the potential of the test to be a valid measure of the construct domain that allows for making statements about test takers with respect to future behavior relative to the domain. As an example, if an admissions test is to be constructed to select applicants to become jet pilots, we would ideally like to be able to split the test construction sample into two groups, one that finished flight school and one that did not. Because we often cannot wait that long, we may split the sample by means of median test performance based on an old test that is known to be valid, or by means of a proxy – maybe performance on a flight simulator – or some other variable that is easier to collect than waiting three years to see whether students finish or drop out of flight school. We may be more willing to delete items that violate the difficulty equivalency based on this proxy rather than based on a split criterion that is less related to successful completion of flight school.

In an additional step of quality assurance, a validation of results could be conducted using an additional sample (cross validation). For this, the data from an additional sample would be used to test if the selected and calibrated item set shows no significant deviations from model fit as well. If the original sample size is large, the sample could be split into two or three sub-samples, which are used for calibration and cross validation. A cross validation for the current example showed a significant Andersen LRT for the split criterion median (χ^2_{emp} = 82.59, df = 46, χ^2_{ecrit} = 71.20) but nonsignificant results for the other split criteria.

There can be different reasons for model misfit of an IRT calibrated item pool in an additional population. Example 3 addresses such a case and discusses potential reasons.

Outlook on Strategy 2

An alternative to excluding misfitting items would be to apply Strategy 2 where different IRT models are tested to check which of these models fits the data without any selection or dele-tion of items. In the example above, one could reasonably assume that the 2PL model could provide better model fit without the need to drop items from the pool. However, this may mean that we retain items that do not fit the Rasch model, even though these generate responses that are not related to the trait we wish to measure. In other words, while selecting a more general model is certainly an option that should be considered any time a more restrictive model does not fit the data, this strategy comes at a price. We may be able to fit the data, but we may at the same time include items in a test that are not necessarily strongly related to the target of infer-ence. If the item pool is large enough, selecting items (Strategy 1) might be the better choice, while Strategy 2 is generally be preferred if the item pool is not large and the exclusion of items would reduce the reliability of the measure below acceptable levels.

Table 4.3 shows results of estimating the 2PL model and comparing the results against the Ra-sch model using the (minimum) AIC (Akaike, 1974) as well as the (minimum) BIC (Schwarz, 1978). The software *mdltm* (von Davier, 2005) for multidimensional discrete latent traits mod-els was used to generate these results. In this example, the 2PL model fits the data better than the Rasch model when looking at the AIC, while the Rasch model would be preferred when looking at the BIC.

Table 4.3. Model fit indices for the Rasch model and the 2PL model

	Rasch model	2PL model
AIC	22606.79	22431.28
BIC	22921.88	23035.64

To gain some more insight into the fit of the 2PL model, additional information can be gleaned from item-fit measures such as the RMSD and MD. In this example, results show no item mis-fit in the 2PL model using a RMSD > 0.1 as well as a MD < –0.1 or MD > 0.1 criterion. When looking at the Rasch model, only one item appears to be deviant using the same criteria: item 58 with RMSD = 0.1197. An additional option is to look at the item difficulties and item slopes to evaluate the quality of items. One item shows a negative slope parameter in the 2PL model, item 36 (slope: –0.61); the same item showed to be most deviant in the Rasch model with re-gard to the z-test. A negative slope could indicate that the coding of the item is incorrect or that a technical problem has occurred regarding the computer-based testing platform. This item is also extremely difficult and should probably be excluded from the scale no matter whether the Rasch model or the 2PL model is estimated. The other items show positive slope parameters in the 2PL model, but some of them are very low (below 0.5) indicating that these items do not discriminate well between respondents. This is the case for items 36, 58, 166, and 202 (these items were also flagged as deviant in the Rasch model regarding the z-test).

In the process of data analysis, these items could either be excluded from the 2PL model to improve model fit, or another, yet more general, model could be tested against the 2PL model. This example shows that the different strategies mentioned above can be combined and that different fit statistics and item information should be taken into consideration when evaluating the quality and dimensionality of a test or item pool.

Example 2: Item/Scale (Re-)Organization and Model Selection for Fitting the Data

The second example illustrates the use of the Martin-Löf test to help reorganize items into homogeneous item subscales for which the Rasch model can be fitted. The data come from a study using a pilot version of the Viennese Study-Qualification Personality Inventory 2 (WSP-2 pilot; cf. Khorramdel, 2014). The items of this questionnaire are designed to assess the constructs *organization, working styles and working behavior, motivation, frustration tolerance, social competence, emotional competence, self-perception,* and *perceived cognitive ability,* which in turn consist of a total of 26 subscales. The data come from 352 Austrian and German university students tested in 2013 and 2014 who responded to the WSP-2 pilot (mean age: 23.62 years, male: 27.8%, female: 72.2%). We used two subscales for these analyses, consisting of 25 items out of a total of 332 items that were piloted for the 26 subscales of the WSP-2. The R-package *eRm* (Mair & Hatzinger, 2007a, 2007b) was used for all analyses presented here.

The aim of the study was to scale the constructs of the WSP-2 pilot using the Rasch model. For the current example, we took two (out of five) subscales of the construct "working styles and working behavior" to illustrate the use of the Martin-Löf test. The subscales used are *accuracy* and *independence*. The hypothesis was that, together with the three other subscales, these scales could be combined into one general scale called working styles and working behavior. On the other hand, it was hypothesized that these two subscales may measure two separate variables because some individuals may show an accurate working style but still need a lot of help from others (without being independent). The following IRT analyses are designed to test these two assumptions. We used the Martin-Löf test (Martin-Löf, 1973) to test whether the two subscales form one Rasch scale or whether they have to be treated as two separate scales. Table 4.4 shows the results of the Martin-Löf test with critical χ^2 – value of $\alpha = 1\%$. If the empirical χ^2 – value is larger than the critical χ^2 – value the test result is assumed to be significant.

Table 4.4. Results of the Martin-Löf test to test if two subscales Accuracy and Independence form one Rasch scale

Scale	Subscales	Martin-Löf LRT	
Working Styles and Working Behavior	Accuracy (14 items)	χ^2_{emp}	219.48*
	Versus independence	df	153
	(11 items)	$\chi^2_{crit}(\alpha = 1\%)$	196.61

Note: * = significant result

The Martin-Löf test (Table 4.4) shows a significant result; thus, we conclude it is not appropriate to combine the two subscales into one Rasch homogeneous scale. To further illustrate the consequences of this result, a Rasch model was estimated for both subscales combined in a single Rasch model (see Table 4.5), and for the two subscales separately (see Table 4.6). The fit of the Rasch model was examined using the Andersen likelihood ratio test, with the median test score as a split criterion. A critical χ^2 – value of $\alpha = 1\%$ was used. In addition, the fit of individual items to the Rasch model was examined using the Fischer–Scheiblechner z-test.

Table 4.5. Results of the Andersen LRT using the median test score split criterion for fitting the Rasch model to items of the subscales Accuracy and Independence combined together into one scale

Accuracy and independence combined into one scale		Andersen LRT
All items (25 items)	χ^2_{emp}	241.15*
	df	24
	$\chi^2_{crit}(\alpha = 1\%)$	42.98
After exclusion of 5 items (20 items)	χ^2_{emp}	34.53
	df	19
	$\chi^2_{crit}(\alpha = 1\%)$	36.19

Note. * = significant test results at the α = 1% level

Table 4.6. Results of the Andersen LRT using the median test score split criterion for fitting the Rasch model to the two subscales treated as separate independent scales

(Sub)Scale			Andersen LRT
Accuracy	All items (14 items)	χ^2_{emp}	319.57*
		df	13
		$\chi^2_{crit}(\alpha = 1\%)$	27.69
Accuracy	After exclusion of 3 items (11 items)	χ^2_{emp}	22.25
		df	10
		$\chi^2_{crit}(\alpha = 1\%)$	23.21
Independence	All items (11 items)	χ^2_{emp}	6.504
		df	10
		$\chi^2_{crit}(\alpha = 1\%)$	21.67

Note. * = significant test results at the α = 1% level

Table 4.5 and Table 4.6 show a nonsignificant LRT for the combined subscales only after exclusion of five items. These items were chosen based on the Fischer–Scheiblechner z-test and removed from the item pool, while only three items had to be excluded from the subscale Accuracy and no items from the subscale Independence if they are treated as separate scales. Given that fewer items had to be excluded in the latter case and the hypothesis that these scales are measuring somewhat distinct facets of the construct, we conclude that the two subscales should be treated as separate scales. This also agrees with the findings that led to the final WSP-2 form (Khorramdel, 2014).

Fixed Item Parameter Linking and Concurrent Calibration

Very often tests are being used not only in a single study but are administered in a number of samples drawn from multiple populations. One important example is the use of subsets of items to link across several assessment cycles. Another is the use of the same test, translated into multiple languages, and administered in international large-scale assessment studies (ILSA) such as PISA, PIAAC, Trends in International Mathematics and Science Study, or Progress in International Reading Literacy Study. In the following, two methods that are useful when dealing with multiple populations are described: fixed item parameter linking and concurrent calibration.

The method of *fixed item parameter linking* can be useful when evaluating an already IRT-calibrated item pool with regard to new populations. Item parameters that were obtained from a previous calibration are treated as fixed constants in subsequent calibrations on additional populations. In contrast to the fixed parameters method that aims at validating an already calibrated item pool in additional population(s), item parameters in the *concurrent calibration* are not fixed to certain values but are estimated freely while constrained to be the same across two or more samples. The goal of these types of analyses is a determination whether the same set of item parameters can be assumed to hold across multiple populations. However, we should point out that for all practical purposes, fixed item parameters are based on a previous sample, so that the evaluation of model-data fit, and particularly the assessment of how many parameters were estimated to achieve fit, is nontrivial in this case. This concerns concurrent calibration to a lesser extent, since here all parameters for all items are re-estimated.

If items are identified for which the assumption of a common item parameter does not hold, remedial action has to be taken. There are two common approaches: Either, these items are removed from the new samples while retained in the original calibration, or these items are split, that is, an item that appears to function differently in different populations is no longer considered a linked item. These types of misfit can be encountered if item content becomes more mainstream over time so that a formerly difficult item appears to become easier, or if items have been translated into multiple target languages, with some deviations from translation and adaptation guidelines resulting in an item being harder (or easier) in a certain language version.

While the ideal situation would be one where all items function the same across all populations targeted by the assessment, a more realistic expectation should be that most IRT parameters can be assumed to stay the same, while a few items may function differently in a few countries. By applying an approach that starts with the most restrictive model assuming all items to be equal, we can work on this from the perspective of model parsimony. Only in those item-by-country or item-by-population cases that can be shown to produce substantial deviations from the common item function we apply an approach that splits off this item-by-group instance from the remainder of all the other populations. This strategy results in a model that retains as many common item parameters across all populations as possible while at the same time maximizing model-data fit. The following example illustrates the utility of the fixed item parameter linking approach and the concurrent calibration with data from an ILSA.

Example 3: Evaluating the Item Fit for Additional Populations

ILSAs are usually operated by conducting a field test, which is used for item selection and to provide a trial run as far as operational and technical procedures of test administration for participating countries, followed by a main study. The data from the main study are then used in international studies to compare different countries or groups, and for further (national) studies within a country or group.

The ILSA illustrated in this example consists of two different rounds of data collections, with a larger group of countries being assessed first, followed by a smaller set of countries in subsequent years. Three cognitive domains – literacy/reading, numeracy/mathematics, and problem solving – were assessed. Data was collected from more than 5,000 respondents in more than 20 countries in round-1 of the data collection. In round-2, the same item pool used in the main study of round-1 was tested in fewer than 10 additional countries. Before applying the same item pool for an upcoming main study to form a comparable scale across countries participating in round-1 and round-2, a field test for round-2 countries was conducted to ensure procedures were followed in test administration and to evaluate the item fit for the new countries. This was necessary because adding countries to international assessments usually requires translations of all test material and to provide countries the opportunity to align their procedures of test administration with the international standards applied in round-1. Figure 4.6 illustrates the relation between the field test and main study in round-1 and round-2.

The main goal of the field test data collection in round-2 was to evaluate possible item misfit, which could be due to translation issues or technical problems during test administration in either the paper- or computer-based assessment, or could be due to the application of scoring issues in different countries. Item misfit relative to a previously calibrated item pool can be understood as differences in item functioning between round-1 and round-2. Ideally, no items should be excluded (the main study of round-1 and round-2 should contain the same item pool) to make round-1 and round-2 as comparable as possible, and item misfit should be explored in order to improve the test administration and scoring for the main study in round-2. The item calibration methods were based on multiple group IRT models that allow items to discriminate differently: the 2PL for dichotomous items and the GPCM for polytomous items. The scaling was carried out separately for each of the three cognitive domains.

In the round-2 field test, 150 items distributed across the three cognitive domains were administered to more than 10,000 respondents from multiple countries. Analyses were carried out for each of these countries to be able to identify possible item-by-country and item-by-language interactions. This was done by estimating multiple-group IRT models using a mixture

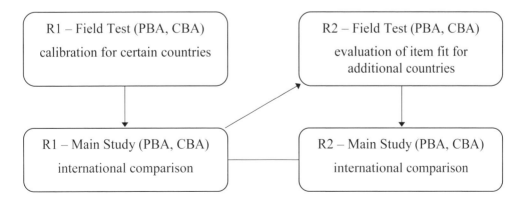

Figure 4.6.   ILSA design for round-1 and round-2.
            PBA = paper-based assessment. CBA = computer-based assessment.

of normal population distributions (one for each group) where item parameters were generally constrained to be equal across groups with a unique mean and variance for each group. For the analyses, the software *mdltm* (von Davier, 2005) for multidimensional discrete latent traits models was used.

The IRT analyses had two different goals. First, the comparability between the round-1 main study and the round-2 field test had to be examined (method of *fixed item parameter linking*). To be able to identify issues around comparable item fit between round-1 and round-2, the item parameters for all items in the field test of round-2 were fixed to the item parameters obtained from the main study in round-1; we refer to them as common item parameters. Second, the comparability across the different participating countries had to be examined in order to be able to provide a test that allows fair comparisons across participating countries (method of *concurrent calibration*; see next section). For this, all item parameters were constrained to be equal across participating countries in a first step.

Overall model fit was evaluated using AIC (Akaike, 1974) and BIC (Schwarz, 1978). To identify misfitting items, the MD and the RMSD were calculated for all item-by-country pairs. Poorly fitting items were flagged using an RMSD and MD > 0.2 or < –0.2 criterion. This rather lenient criterion was applied to account for the fact that the field test is not designed to be a representative sample, has a smaller sample size than the main study, and is basically a tool to identify major operability issues. Items not exhibiting appropriate fit using a common (fixed) item parameter received a unique item parameter. If multiple countries shared the same deviation from the round-1 parameter, subgroup specific parameters were estimated. Identification of poor fitting items and the replacement of common item parameters with unique parameters used an algorithm that detects and flags patterns of misfit. The IRT analyses with common and unique item parameters were conducted simultaneously for all groups. Through the use of common item parameters across countries in the case of concurrent calibration, or through the use of common round-1 parameters, respectively, it was ensured that all estimated item parameters (common and unique) were located on the same scale and comparisons could be made across participating countries.

Comparability Between Round-1 and Round-2

Item fit was evaluated separately for CBAs and PBAs. In general, the round-1 item parameters fit well when applied to the round-2 data; misfit was found for only a few items-by-country pairs. In addition, the results of the assessment of misfit regarding those items that showed technical difficulties were shared with item developers and programmers to remediate the issues for the round-2 main study the CBA, in the domain of literacy/reading, a proportion of 91.2% of round-1 item parameters was retained. The number was even higher, 93.7%, if we do not account for deviations that were caused by technical issues of the computer-based testing platform that affected data collection in some countries on a few isolated items. For the CBA data on numeracy/mathematics items, the proportion of retained round-1 item parameters was 94.3%, or 94.8% if we do not account for deviations based on technical issues. For the domain of problem solving, we found more need to account for technical issues: While 90.5% of parameters were based on round-1, this number increased to 97.6% when disregarding deviations based on technical issues. Note that overall this is a success story because about 95% of the items were functioning as expected on the computer platform.

For the PBA data, in the literacy/reading domains, 93.6% of items were retained from the round-1 parameters. As for the numeracy/mathematics item, the proportion was 97.2%

Given that the percentage of retained item parameters from the previous data collection exceeded 95% on average, we conclude for this example that the link between round-1 and round-2 can be established, and assessment results from both rounds can be reported on the same dimension.

Improving Overall Model Fit by Allowing the Estimation of Unique Item Parameters

The aim of the field test is to reveal possible problems with items (such as technical issues or translation errors) for the purpose of fixing them for the main study. But if item misfit occurs in the main study, model fit can be improved by allowing estimation of unique item parameters for certain items in certain countries or groups of countries. In the case of the field test for round-2 overall model-data fit (by estimating all three domains in one multidimensional model but as separate dimensions) was improved by allowing the estimation of unique item parameters for 121 out of 2988 (4%) item-by-country pairs across all three domains. The model fit is illustrated in Table 4.7; the lower the AIC and BIC, the better the model fit.

Table 4.7. Model fit indices for the round-2 field test data before and after allowing for the estimation of unique item parameters

	Initial model: All item parameters are common (fixed)	Final model: Unique item parameters for 4% item-by-country pairs
AIC	309872.9	300019.8
BIC	311058.8	302303.7

Comparability Across Countries

Using the fixed parameter approach is suitable if the subsequent data collections are not representative, or contain too little data, to allow independent estimation. If the sample(s) collected in subsequent rounds are as large as, or larger than in previous data collections, a different approach should be considered. A more sophisticated method of examining the fit of an IRT model for multiple populations is using a comprehensive analysis of all the data at once. As pointed out above, this is commonly referred to as concurrent calibration, and it has the advantage that no assumptions are made about the parameters in terms of which ones are the correct estimates. In the case of fixed parameter evaluation, one set of item difficulties (and discrimination parameters) obtained from analyzing a certain sample is considered fixed and known (but not necessary as true), while the fit of the new data relative to this set of fixed parameters is evaluated. This is different in concurrent calibrations using IRT models, where the data from multiple samples is combined into a single analysis, and the fit of the model to this combined *multiple group* dataset is evaluated (Mazzeo & von Davier, 2008; von Davier & von Davier, 2007; Xu & von Davier, 2008; Yamamoto & Mazzeo, 1992).

In contrast to the fixed parameters method, which aims to extend the validity of an already calibrated item pool to additional population(s), item parameters are not fixed to certain values in the concurrent calibration but estimated freely. Still, item parameters are constrained to be equal across groups, but jointly estimated across all groups. Items with misfit, that is, those that exceed the threshold on item fit statistics such as RMSD and MD, are assumed to work differently across groups. After the main study data for round-2 are collected, this would be the appropriate approach. While the field test data provided an evidence base that allows evaluation of technical difficulties and to identify potential item-by-country deviations for remediation, the main test data collection will provide a sufficiently large independently collected set of cases for the best venue of action to establish a common, valid, international IRT scale for this large scale assessment program.

Outlook

IRT has become popular in test construction, especially in large-scale educational assessment, and has grown in use with the advent of greater computing power. In many of the largest assessment programs conducted around the world, IRT is used to establish scales, optimize item selection, and ensure the linking of scales across assessment cycles and across diverse populations. The scales in these assessments are aimed at measuring skills and cognitive domains such as reading, scientific literacy, and mathematics and to provide internationally comparable information.

While the work to support this goal uses IRT methodologies as an integral part, it is important to understand that these assessments will need elaborate methods to assess model data fit as well as procedures aided by powerful methods of fit diagnostics. A rigorous application of any significance test to evaluate a model (be it IRT or another approach) will lead to rejection if samples are large enough. The methods presented here are suitable to diagnose where a model fails in the case of one that assumes 100% of item parameters to be the same across complex samples collected across multiple modes of assessments in a wide variety of educational systems. The methods presented here show how the data can be used to improve a model, to relax assumptions where necessary, and finally arrive at a scale that either retains most of the items or a set of international test booklets and country parameters that agree to 95% or more with the set of parameters used in all other countries.

Note that the use of IRT does not end with the assessment of skills and proficiencies: IRT methodologies are being successfully applied to the analysis of psychological scales such as those designed to measure interests, attitudes, and personality domains like the Big 5 (Costa & McCrae, 1992). Nowadays, IRT methods are widely applied and can provide tools to analyze very complex assessment designs and individualized test forms such as the ones administered in computer adaptive testing.

Parameter estimation methods for IRT-based models once suffered from limitations of computing power. That is no longer the case. The lack of computing power in the past often led to reliance on methods with stronger assumptions, or on approaches that preaggregated the data or only used subsamples of respondents or items. This is no longer necessary. In addition, user-friendly software is available for many operating systems, and IRT as well as Rasch modeling software with graphical user interfaces have been around for more than two decades now (e.g., von Davier, 1994, in press).

To guide users, numerous methods exist to evaluate the fit of IRT models and single items. Some of them are illustrated in this chapter. Many more can be found in overview chapters that focus specifically on certain types of fit diagnostics (e.g., chapters in van der Linden & Hambleton, 1997, 2014).

References

Andersen, E. B. (1973). A goodness of fit test for the Rasch model. *Psychometrika, 38*, 123–140. http://doi.org/10.1007/BF02291180

Akaike, H. (1974). A new look at the statistical model identification. *IEEE Transactions on Automatic Control, 19*, 716–723. http://doi.org/10.1109/TAC.1974.1100705

Baker, F. (2001). *The basics of item response theory*. College Park, MD: ERIC Clearinghouse on Assessment and Evaluation, University of Maryland. Retrieved from http://echo.edres.org:8080/irt/baker/

Birnbaum, A. (1957). *On the estimation of mental ability (Series Report No. 15)*. Randolph Air Force Base, TX: USAF School of Aviation Medicine.

Birnbaum, A. (1968). Some latent trait models and their use in inferring an examinee's ability. In F. M. Lord & M. R. Novick (Eds.), *Statistical theories of mental test scores*. Reading, MA: Addison-Wesley.

Burnham, K. P., & Anderson, D. R. (2004). Multimodel inference: Understanding AIC and BIC in model selection. *Sociological Methods and Research, 33*, 261–304. http://doi.org/10.1177/0049124104268644

Costa, P. T., Jr., & McCrae, R. R. (1992). *Revised NEO Personality Inventory (NEO-PI-R) and NEO Five-Factor Inventory (NEO-FFI) manual*. Odessa, FL: Psychological Assessment Resources.

Cronbach, L. J. (1951). Coefficient alpha and the internal structure of tests. *Psychometrika, 16*, 297–334. http://doi.org/10.1007/BF02310555

De Boeck, P., & Wilson, M. (Eds.). (2004). *Explanatory item response models: A generalized linear and nonlinear approach*. New York, NY: Springer. http://doi.org/10.1007/978-1-4757-3990-9

Edgeworth, F. Y. (1908). On the probable errors of frequency-constants. *Journal of the Royal Statistical Society, 71*, 499–512. http://doi.org/10.2307/2339461

Efron, B., & Hinkley, D. V. (1978). Assessing the accuracy of the maximum likelihood estimator: Observed versus expected fisher information. *Biometrika, 65*, 457–482. http://doi.org/10.1093/biomet/65.3.457

Fischer, G. H. (2007). Rasch models. In C. R. Rao & S. Sinharay (Eds.), *Psychometrics: Handbook of statistics* (*Vol. 26*, pp. 515–585). Amsterdam, The Netherlands: Elsevier.

Fischer, G. H., & Molenaar, I. W. (Eds.). (1995). *Rasch models: Foundations, recent developments, and applications*. New York, NY: Springer.

Fischer, G. H., & Scheiblechner, H. H. (1970). Algorithmen und Programme für das probabilistische Testnodell von Rasch. [Algorithms and programs for Rasch's probabilistic test model]. *Psychologische Beiträge, 12*, 23–51.

Gilula, Z., & Haberman, S. J. (1994). Conditional log-linear models for analyzing categorical panel data. *Journal of the American Statistical Association, 89*, 645–656. http://doi.org/10.1080/01621459.1994.10476789

Glas, C. A. W. (2007). Testing generalized Rasch models. In M. von Davier & C. H. Carstensen (Eds.), *Multivariate and mixture distribution Rasch models: Extensions and applications* (pp. 37–55). New York, NY: Springer.

Glas, C. A. W., & Verhelst, N. D. (1995). Testing the Rasch model. In G. H. Fischer & I. W. Molenaar (Eds.), *Rasch models: Foundations, recent developments, and applications* (pp. 69–95). New York, NY: Springer.

Haberman, S. J. (2006). *Joint and conditional estimation for implicit models for tests with polytomous item scores* (Research Report No. RR-06-03). Princeton, NJ: Educational Testing Service.

Haberman, S. J., Sinharay, S., & Chon, K. H. (2013). Assessing item fit for unidimensional item response theory models using residuals from estimated item response functions. *Psychometrika, 78*, 417–440. http://doi.org/10.1007/s11336-012-9305-1

Hambleton, R. K., & Jones, R. W. (1993). Comparison of classical test theory and item response theory and their applications to test development. *Educational Measurement: Issues and Practice, 12*, 38–47. http://doi.org/10.1111/j.1745-3992.1993.tb00543.x

Holland, P. W., & Hoskens, M. (2002). *Classical test theory as a first-order item response theory: Application to true-score prediction from a possibly nonparallel test* (Research Report No. RR-02-20). Princeton, NJ: Educational Testing Service.

Jones, R. H. (2011). Bayesian information criterion for longitudinal and clustered data. *Statistics in Medicine, 30*, 3050–3056. http://doi.org/10.1002/sim.4323

Khorramdel, L. (2014). *WSP-2 – Wiener Studieneignungs-Persönlichkeitsinventar 2* [Viennese Study-Qualification Personality Inventory 2]. Mödling, Austria: Schuhfried GmbH.

Kubinger, K. D. (1989). Aktueller Stand und kritische Würdigung der Probabilistischen Testtheorie [Current status and critical appreciation of probabilistic test theory]. In K. D. Kubinger (Ed.), *Moderne Test Theorie* [Modern test theory] (pp. 19–83), Weinheim, Germany: Beltz.

Kuder, G. F., & Richardson, M. W. (1937). The theory of estimation of test reliability. *Psychometrika, 2*, 151–160. http://doi.org/10.1007/BF02288391

Lord, F. M. (1980). *Applications of item response theory to practical testing problems*. Mahwah, NJ: Erlbaum.

Lord, F. M. & Novick, M. R. (Eds.). (1968). *Statistical theories of mental test scores*. Reading, MA: Addison-Wesley.

Mair, P., & Hatzinger, R. (2007a). *eRm: Extended Rasch modeling. R package (Version 0.9.7)* [Computer software]. Retrieved from http://cran.r-project.org/

Mair, P., & Hatzinger, R. (2007b). CML based estimation of extended Rasch models with the package in R. *Psychology Science* [later: Psychology Science Quarterly], *49*, 26–43.

Martin-Löf, P. (1973). *Statistika modeler. Anteckningar fran seminarier lasaret 1969-70, utarbetade av Rolf Sundberg. Obetydligt ändrat nytryck, Oktober 1973* [Statistical models. Notes from seminars in the academic year 1969–1970, with the assistance of Rolf Sundberg. Slightly modified reprint, October 1973]. Stockholm, Sweden: Institutet för Försakringsmatematik och Matematisk Statistisk vid Stockholms Universitet.

Masters, G. N. (1982). A Rasch model for partial credit scoring. *Psychometrika, 47*, 149–174. http://doi.org/10.1007/BF02296272

Mazzeo, J., & von Davier, M. (2008). *Review of the Programme for International Student Assessment (PISA) Test design: Recommendations for fostering stability in assessment results*. Retrieved from https://edsurveys.rti.org/pisa/documents/mazzeopisa_test_designreview_6_1_09.pdf

Mazzeo, J., & von Davier, M. (2013). Linking scales in international large-scale assessments. In L. Rutkowski, M. von Davier, & D. Rutkowski (Eds.), *A handbook of international large-scale assessment: Background, technical issues, and methods of data analysis* (pp. 229–258). London, UK: Chapman Hall/CRC Press.

McDonald, R. P. (1968). A unified treatment of the weighting problem. *Psychometrika, 33*, 351–381. http://doi.org/10.1007/BF02289330

Moustaki, I. & Knott, M. (2000). Generalised latent trait models. *Psychometrika, 65*, 391–411. http://doi.org/10.1007/BF02296153

Muraki, E. (1992). A generalized partial credit model: Application of an EM algorithm. *Applied Psychological Measurement, 16*, 159–177. http://doi.org/10.1177/014662169201600206

Novick, M. R. (1966). The axioms and principal results of classical test theory. *Journal of Mathematical Psychology, 3*, 1–18. http://doi.org/10.1016/0022-2496(66)90002-2

Oliveri, M. E., & von Davier, M. (2011). Investigation of model fit and score scale comparability in international assessments. *Psychological Test and Assessment Modeling, 53*, 315–333.

Oliveri, M. E., & von Davier, M. (2014). Toward increasing fairness in score scale calibrations employed in international large-scale assessments. *International Journal of Testing, 14*, 1–21. http://doi.org/10.1080/15305058.2013.825265

Orlando, M., & Thissen, D. (2000). New item fit indices for dichotomous item response theory models. *Applied Psychological Measurement, 24*, 50–64. http://doi.org/10.1177/01466216000241003

Orlando, M., & Thissen, D. (2003). Further investigation of the performance of S-X2: An item fit index for use with dichotomous item response theory models. *Applied Psychological Measurement, 27*, 289–298. http://doi.org/10.1177/0146621603027004004

Rasch, G. (1960). *Probabilistic models for some intelligence and attainment tests*. Copenhagen, Denmark: Nielsen & Lydiche.

Reckase, M. D. (2009). *Multidimensional item response theory*. New York, NY: Springer. http://doi.org/10.1007/978-0-387-89976 3

Rijmen, F., Jeon, M., von Davier, M., & Rabe-Hesketh, S. (2013). A general psychometric approach for educational survey assessments: Flexible statistical models and efficient estimation methods. In D. Rutkowski, M. von Davier, & D. Rutkowski (Eds.), *A handbook of international large-scale assessment: Background, technical issues, and methods of data analysis*. London, UK: Chapman Hall/CRC Press.

Rost, J., & Langeheine, R. (1997). A guide through latent structure models for categorical data. In J. Rost & R. Langeheine (Eds.), *Applications of latent trait and latent class models in the social sciences* (pp. 13–37). Muenster, Germany: Waxmann. Retrieved from http://mail.ipn.uni-kiel.de/aktuell/buecher/rostbuch/c01.pdf

Rost, J., & von Davier, M. (1994). A conditional item fit index for Rasch models. *Applied Psychological Measurement, 18*, 171–182. http://doi.org/10.1177/014662169401800206

Rost, J., & von Davier, M. (1995). Mixture distribution Rasch models. In G. H. Fischer & I. W. Molenaar (Eds.), *Rasch models: Foundations, recent developments, and applications* (pp. 257–268). New York, NY: Springer.

Schwarz, G. (1978). Estimating the dimension of a model. *Annals of Statistics, 6*, 461–464. http://doi.org/10.1214/aos/1176344136

Sijtsma, K. (2009). On the use, the misuse, and the very limited usefulness of Cronbach's alpha. *Psychometrika, 74*, 107–120. http://doi.org/10.1007/s11336-008-9101-0

Skrondal, A., & Rabe-Hesketh, S. (2004). *Generalized latent variable modeling: multilevel, longitudinal and structural equation models*. Boca Raton, FL: Chapman & Hall/CRC. http://doi.org/10.1201/9780203489437

Thissen, D., Nelson, L., Rosa, K., & McLeod, L. D. (2001). Item response theory for items scored in more than two categories. In D. Thissen & H. Wainer (Eds.), *Test scoring* (pp. 141–186). Mahwah, NJ: Erlbaum.

Thurstone, L. L. (1925). A method of scaling psychological and educational tests. *Journal of Educational Psychology, 16*, 433–451. http://doi.org/10.1037/h0073357

van der Linden, W. J., & Hambleton, R. K. (1997). Item response theory: Brief history, common models, and extensions. In W. J. van der Linden & R. K. Hambleton (Eds.), *Handbook of modern item response theory* (pp. 1–28). New York, NY: Springer.

van der Linden, W. J., & Hambleton, R. K. (Eds.). (2014). *Handbook of modern item response theory. Models (Vol. 1*, 2nd ed.). New York, NY: Springer.

Verhelst, N. D., & Glas, C. A. W., (1995). The one parameter logistic model. In G. H. Fischer & I. W. Molenaar (Eds.), *Rasch models: Foundations, recent developments, and applications* (pp. 215–238). New York, NY: Springer.

von Davier, M. (1994). *WINMIRA (A Windows program for analyses with the Rasch model, with the latent class analysis and with the mixed Rasch model)* [Computer software]. Kiel, Germany: Institute for Science Education.

von Davier, M. (2005). *A general diagnostic model applied to language testing data (Research Report No. RR-05-16)*. Princeton, NJ: Educational Testing Service.

von Davier, M. (2008). A general diagnostic model applied to language testing data. *British Journal of Mathematical and Statistical Psychology, 61*, 287–307. http://doi.org/10.1348/000711007X193957

von Davier, M. (in press). The Rasch model. In W. J. van der Linden & R. K. Hambleton (Eds.), *Handbook of modern item response theory* (2nd ed., *Vol. 1*, pp.). New York, NY: Springer.

von Davier, M., & Carstensen, C. H. (Eds.). (2007). *Multivariate and mixture distribution Rasch models: Extensions and applications*. New York, NY: Springer. http://doi.org/10.1007/978-0-387-49839-3

von Davier, M., & Molenaar, I. W. (2003). A person-fit index for polytomous Rasch models, latent class models, and their mixture generalizations. *Psychometrika, 68*, 213–228. http://doi.org/10.1007/BF02294798

von Davier, M., & Rost, J. (1995). Polytomous mixed Rasch models. In G. H. Fischer & I. W. Molenaar (Eds.), *Rasch models: Foundations, recent developments, and applications* (pp. 371–382). New York, NY: Springer.

von Davier, M., & Rost, J. (in press). Logistic mixture-distribution response models. In W. J. van der Linden & R. K. Hambleton (Eds.), *Handbook of modern item response theory* (2nd ed., *Vol. 1*, pp.). New York, NY: Springer.

von Davier, M., & von Davier, A. (2007). A unified approach to IRT Scale linkage and scale transformations. *Methodology, 3*, 115–124. http://doi.org/10.1027/1614-2241.3.3.115

Xu, X., & von Davier, M. (2008). *Linking with the general diagnostic model (Research Report No. RR-08-08)*. Princeton, NJ: Educational Testing Service.

Yamamoto, K., & Mazzeo, J. (1992). Item response theory scale linkage in NAEP. *Journal of Educational Statistics, 17*, 155–173. http://doi.org/10.3102/10769986017002155

Yamamoto, K., Khorramdel, L., & von Davier, M. (2013). Scaling PIAAC cognitive data. In *Technical Report of the Survey of Adult Skills (PIAAC)* (pp. 406–438). Retrieved from http://www.oecd.org/site/piaac/_Technical%20Report_17OCT13.pdf

Zimmerman, D. W., & Williams, R. H. (1977). The theory of test validity and correlated errors of measurement. *Journal of Mathematical Psychology, 16*, 135–152. http://doi.org/10.1016/0022-2496(77)90063-3

Part III
Item Formats and Test Presentation

Chapter 5

Item Types, Response Formats, and Consequences for Statistical Investigations

Robert L. Johnson[1] and Grant B. Morgan[2]

[1]Department of Educational Studies, University of South Carolina, Columbia, SC, USA
[2]Department of Educational Psychology, Baylor University, Waco, TX, USA

Introduction

In the United States what it means to be *tested* has undergone significant changes since the 1980s. With the advent of computer-based testing, credentialing examinations have been broadened to include variations of multiple-choice items, referred to as technology-enhanced items. In nursing, for example, licensure examinations present nursing candidates with test items that require the candidates to analyze information provided in exhibit tabs (e.g., patient history, laboratory results, prescriptions) to answer an item (Wendt, Kenny, & Brown, 2010). The United States Medical Licensing Examination™, a three-part licensure test, includes multiple-choice items and a performance-based assessment (Federation of State Medical Boards of the United States & National Board of Medical Examiners, 2013). In the performance assessment, medical students engage in history taking and physical examination of a standardized patient to demonstrate the ability of the examinees (i.e., medical students) to gather information from patients, perform physical examinations, and communicate their findings to patients and colleagues.

In education, the Partnership for the Assessment of Readiness for College and Careers (PARCC) and the Smarter Balanced Assessment Consortium (Smarter Balanced), two large-scale testing consortia in the United Sates, develop testing systems that engage students in the full range of item formats: multiple-choice, technology-enhanced, constructed-response, extended constructed-response, and performance based (Doorey, 2012). This chapter reviews the item formats that are being used in credentialing examinations (i.e., licensure and certification) and student achievement tests, presents guidelines for writing the various types of items, and examines issues related to the statistical investigations of data from these various item formats.

Item Types and Response Formats

Item types currently used in educational testing programs and by credentialing boards include multiple-choice/multiple-selection, technology-enhanced, short constructed-response/extended constructed-response, and performance tasks. Table 5.1 presents a summary of the various item formats used in testing programs, provides a description of each item type, and lists the form of scoring typically used with each type of item.

Table 5.1. Types of items and response formats

Format	Description	Scoring
Multiple-choice	An item stem that consists of one or more introductory sentences and interpretive material and a list of options (i.e., multiple distractors and a single correct choice).	Dichotomous
Multiple-selection	A type of multiple-choice item with multiple correct choices	Dichotomous or polytomous
Technology-enhanced	An item or task that consists of a stem/prompt with one or more introductory sentences and interpretive material. Uses computer interactive features such as drag and drop, highlighting, hot spots, simulations.	Dichotomous or polytomous
Short constructed-response	A task that requires a brief written or oral response in the form of a single word, phrase, sentence, number, or set of numbers. Technology-enhanced, short constructed-response items may use automated scoring.	Polytomous
Extended constructed-response	A task that requires an elaborated written or oral response that includes explanations or reasoning. Technology-enhanced versions may use automated scoring.	Polytomous
Performance task	A response demand (i.e., stem or prompt) that elicits an elaborated written, physical, or oral response from examinees.	Polytomous

Multiple-Choice/Multiple-Selection Items

Likely the most widely used assessment type in education and licensure examinations, the multiple-choice item consists of a stem and response options (see Figure 5.1). The stem is the question to which the examinees respond and consists of one or more introductory sentences. The stem includes any interpretive material (e.g., graph, diagram, literary text) that is required for answering the question. The stem is followed by a list of options (i.e., multiple distractors and a single correct choice). These items generally are scored dichotomously.

The multiple-selection item takes the same form as the multiple-choice item; however, the options include multiple distractors and multiple correct choices (see Figure 5.2). This type of item can be scored dichotomously (i.e., 0 or 1) or polytomously (e.g., 0, 1, 2, 3). For example, the intent is for some of the selected-response items in the Smarter Balanced English language arts assessment to include multiple correct answers and contribute more than one point to the examinee's score (Measured Progress & Educational Testing Services [ETS], 2012a).

Technology-Enhanced Items

Features of technology-enhanced items that test developers should consider include (a) examinee response modes, (b) stimulus materials, (c) input devices, and (d) scoring (Measured Progress & ETS, 2012d; Parshall, Davey, & Pashley, 2000; Sireci & Zenisky, 2006). Response modes include multiple-choice (choosing one correct answer), multiple-selection (choosing multiple correct answers), fill-in-the-blank, highlighting, inserting text, drag and drop, and graphic organizers (Sireci & Zenisky, 2006; Wendt & Harmes, 2009; Wendt et al., 2010; Zenisky & Sireci, 2002). Stimulus materials include animations, interactive and static graphics, embedded audio clips (see Figure 5.3),

Use the photograph below to answer the question.

15.   Which of the following is **MOST** emphasized in the artwork?

A. Balance

B*. Contrast

C. Proportion

D. Shape

A: 12%; B: 33%; C: 17%; D: 35% (3% of students did not answer)

$p = .33$; $r_{bis} = .16$

Figure 5.1. Sample multiple-choice visual arts item from the South Carolina Arts Assessment Program (SCAAP) item bank of archived items. Response option B is the correct response as denoted by the asterisk (*). Item statistics are provided beneath the response options. Reprinted with permission.

Joseph wants to create a landscape with an orange sunset.

Which colors should he mix? (Select all that apply.)

A. Black

B. Blue

C. Red

D. Yellow

Figure 5.2. Example of a multiple-selection item.

Read this first.

Click the play button to listen to the audio. As you listen, read the journal entry below about people exploring an island far away. Then do the task.

When we first arrived on the island, we saw mountains and fields with lots of colorful flowers and large, strange-looking trees. There were no people. No humans had ever been here before. The first animal we saw was so tall that it had to bend down to eat the leaves off the treetops . . .

Imagine that you are one of the people exploring this remote island. Write a story that begins where the journal entry ends.

Figure 5.3.   Example of a technology-enhanced item that incorporates an audio clip into the writing prompt.
Source: National Center for Education Statistics, 2012.

and interactive video (Pearson, 2012; Wendt & Harmes, 2009). Input devices include the mouse, keyboard, touch screens, light pens, joysticks, and speech recognition software (Parshall et al., 2000; Sireci & Zenisky, 2006). Scoring requires consideration of whether an item has a limited set of options from which examinees will select, the development of scoring rubrics for constructed-response items, the determination of the number of scoring levels an item can support, and specification of the features of the response that will be scored.

The content and the cognitive process that are the focus of the technology-enhanced item determine the response mode and stimulus materials. For example, if examinees are to complete a music improvisation after listening to an audio clip of a beginning beat, the content is their understanding of improvisation and the cognitive process is to analyze the music passage. In terms of technology enhancement, the technology presents audio for the initial beat and the possible improvisations for the options.

The scoring of technology-enhanced items can be dichotomous or polytomous. Automated scoring is used with selected-response items that are technology-enhanced, whereas, constructed-response items that are technology-enhanced use automated or human scoring.

Short Constructed-Response/Extended Constructed-Response Items

A short constructed-response item consists of a prompt or stem to which an examinee responds with a brief written or oral response that might take the form of a single word, phrase, sentence, number, or set of numbers. In contrast, extended constructed-response tasks require a written or oral response that provides more elaboration and explanation of reasoning (Measured Progress & ETS, 2012b).

For short and extended constructed-response items, examinee responses are typically scored with analytic or holistic scoring rubrics. When responses are scored with analytic rubrics, raters evaluate and assign scores to examinee performance along several dimensions, such as ideas, organization, style, and conventions, with each dimension scored on a 4-point or 6-point scale (Johnson, Penny, & Gordon, 2009). Each score point represents a performance level and provides a detailed description of the performance at each level. For example, the highest performance level of the content/development dimension of a rubric might be described as:
* Presents a clear central idea about the topic;
* Fully develops the central idea with specific, relevant details; and
* Sustains focus on central idea throughout the writing (South Carolina State Department of Education, 2008).

Holistic scoring requires raters to consider the dimensions collectively to assign one score that reflects the quality of performance. For the constructed-response items in its English language arts assessment, the Smarter Balanced consortium planned to use a 2-point or a 3-point holistic rubric. (Measured Progress & ETS, 2012c). Smarter Balanced plans included automated scoring when possible and use some human rating for validation (Measured Progress & ETS, 2012b).

Performance Tasks

A performance task consists of a prompt or stem that elicits the performance and a response demand that requires an examinee to produce a written, physical, or oral response. One use of this item type is to assess examinees' ability to produce a written or oral response that integrates knowledge and skills across content areas (Measured Progress & ETS, 2012c). Smarter Balanced planned for its performance tasks to consist of three basic components: stimulus presentation, information processing, and scorable product or performance. The component of information processing involves examinees in interactions with stimulus materials and the content. Examples include note taking, data generation, and other activities that enhance the students' understanding of the stimulus content or the assignment. When scoring student work, the intent is to use multiple scoring rubrics that are consistent with the primary content claims and targets identified by the task developer. Either analytic or holistic rubrics may be used for scoring.

Item-Writing Guidelines

Item-writing guidelines contribute to the clarity of the task that examinees are to complete in responding to an item or prompt. Such a function serves to reduce the influence of construct irrelevant variance on examinees' scores and the misinterpretation of those scores. (Construct irrelevant variance is the variability of a test score that is due to some factor other than the construct the examination is intended to measure, such as reading demands influencing mathematics or science scores.) Typically those guidelines are presented separately by item type (e.g., selected-response; performance task); however, such a presentation obscures the common elements of items and tasks and the issues that must be addressed in their development. We first present guidelines that are relevant to writing across item types and then address item-writing guidelines specific to selected-response, technology-enhanced, and constructed-response items, including performance tasks.

Item-Writing Guidelines for All Item Types

The guidelines in Table 5.2 address issues relevant to the full range of item formats. Issues to consider include item writers, content, and cognitive processes, item format, item and task qualities, conventions of language, and sensitivity and fairness.

Table 5.2. Item-writing guidelines for all item types

Item writers should ...
• Be subject-matter specialists or practitioners in the field.
• Be diverse in representation of various cultures, social backgrounds, and ethnic and gender groups.
The content and cognitive processes in the item should ...
• Align with the skills in the test specifications.
• Be important knowledge, skills, and abilities.
The selection of the item format should be informed by ...
• The ability of the item format to assess the content and cognitive process.
• The cost of the development, scoring, and ongoing calibration of items.
Qualities to consider in the development of items/tasks include ...
• Establishing real-world contexts.
• Engaging examinees at higher cognitive levels (e.g., analysis, evaluation) through the use of content-relevant stimulus materials that are new to the examinees.
• Controlling for ancillary knowledge and skills (e.g., reading demands in a social studies achievement test) that might introduce construct irrelevant variance.
Items/tasks should be written to follow language conventions as related to ...
• Mechanics, grammar, style, and clarity.
Sensitivity and fairness should be addressed by ...
• Writing items that are free of words and content that would be regarded as offensive, controversial, or negative.
• Balancing representation with respect to culture, gender, and ethnicity.
• Avoiding stereotyping of gender and ethnic groups.

Summarized from Baiker, 1993; Downing, 2006; Hopkins, 1998; Johnson, Penny, & Gordon, 2009; Measured Progress & ETS, 2012b; Moreno, Martinez, & Muniz, 2006.

Item Writers

We list first guidelines about the item writers to reflect their importance to test development. Item writers should be experts in their field and should be representative of different cultures, social backgrounds, and ethnic or gender groups. In a discussion about performance tasks, Bond, Moss, and Carr (1996) noted that experts from varied cultural backgrounds and gender or ethnic groups "will probably vary substantially in their opinions about ... what performance tasks should be included" (p. 120). Such representation also serves to assure that the wording and context of items and tasks are relevant to all examinee groups.

Content and Cognitive Processes

The next cluster of guidelines in Table 5.2 describes the content and cognitive processes that item writers should consider as they develop items and tasks. For example, items and tasks should focus on the content and cognitive skills listed in the test specifications. Item writing for the assessments for the Smarter Balanced and PARCC focus on the English language arts and mathematics skills specified in the Common Core Standards. In 2010, the standards were adopted in the US by 45 states and the District of Columbia. These standards specify the important content for students in kindergarten through 12th grade (National Governors Association Center for Best Practices & Council of Chief State School Officers, 2010).

For a licensure or certification examination, such as the National Council Licensure Examination for Registered Nurses (NCLEX-RN®), a practice analysis identifies the importance and frequency in which nursing activities are performed (Wendt et al., 2010). The knowledge, skills, and abilities (KSAs) associated with these activities become the content assessed in the examination.

Cognitive process skills are also assessed in education and licensure examinations. Bloom's taxonomy (Bloom, Engelhart, Furst, Hill, & Krathwohl, 1956) and the Revised Bloom's taxonomy (Anderson & Krathwohl, 2001) guide the development of items for the nursing exam (Wendt, 2003). The revised Bloom's taxonomy lists a cognitive process dimension and knowledge dimension. The cognitive process dimension derives from the original taxonomy and lists the following processes:
- Remember – retrieve knowledge from memory;
- Understand – construct meaning from communications;
- Apply – implement a procedure in a given situation;
- Analyze – break material into its parts and determine how parts relate to one another and an overall structure;
- Evaluate – make judgments based on criteria; and
- Create – bring elements together to form a new pattern or structure.

The knowledge dimension is composed of:
- Factual knowledge – of discrete, basic elements associated with a discipline;
- Conceptual knowledge – of interrelationships among the basic elements within more complex, organized knowledge forms;
- Procedural knowledge – of a series or sequence of steps, methods, or techniques to be completed to do something and criteria for when to use such; and
- Meta-cognitive knowledge – of cognition and self-awareness of one's own cognition (Anderson & Krathwohl, 2001).

Items and tasks are written to assess the knowledge and cognitive process at the intersection of the two dimensions. For example, items that require examinees to balance chemical equations by applying the law of conservation of matter involve examinees in the application (cognitive dimension) and procedural form of knowledge. This example also shows how the taxonomy can help to write items at different difficulty levels and to ensure that test developers include items at a range of difficulty levels.

Additional taxonomies that may be used with test construction include the New Taxonomy of Marzano (2001) and the Depth of Knowledge framework of Webb (2006). Both taxonomies overlap considerably with the original and revised Bloom's taxonomies.

In training item writers it should be stressed that if the purpose of an assessment is to assess important KSAs, then items should not focus on trivia nor should items be tricky. Both practices are likely to introduce construct irrelevant variance in that examinee scores will not be related to their deep understanding of important content or KSAs.

Item Format

After identifying the content and cognitive levels to be assessed, then the item writer should consider the format of the item or task. The question is, "Should the item be selected-response (SR), technology-enhanced (TE), short constructed-response (SCR), extended constructed-response (ECR), or a performance task?" To answer the first question, you might start by asking another question: "Can the content and cognitive process be assessed by using multiple-choice or is a more complex item format required?" Smarter Balanced provided guidelines that technology-enhanced items and tasks are appropriate when they can provide information that could not be as reliably obtained from selected-response or constructed-response items (Measured Progress & ETS, 2012b). They noted that performance tasks will better serve to assess such areas as depth of understanding and research skills than will selected- or constructed-response items. Thus, in preparing to write an item or task, the item writer should consider each of the item formats, beginning with selected-response, moving to short or extended constructed-response, progressing to technology-enhanced, and culminating with a performance task.

The answer to the question about item type is also informed by considering the depth of understanding associated with the item content and cognitive strategy. When accompanied by static stimulus materials (e.g., graphs, literary passages, reproductions of historical documents), the selected-response format can assess examinees' ability to analyze or evaluate information. However, it is much more of a challenge to write selected-response items to assess examinees' ability to complete a procedure. For example, a nurse's ability to perform an intubation (i.e., the introduction of a tube into the trachea in preparation for administering anesthesia) may be an important skill to test.

In considering the use of the technology-enhanced format and the costs associated with development of this type of item, Smarter Balanced (Measured Progress & ETS, 2012b) wrote:

> Technology-Enhanced items will take advantage of drag-and-drop, hot spot, drawing, graphing, gridded-response items ... and simulation technologies, along with the use of online tools to measure content that was previously not assessed or was assessed through constructed response item formats requiring more elaborate scoring procedures. (p. 29)

Constructed-response items and performance tasks have the potential to engage examinees at all levels of cognitive complexity. With constructed-response and performance tasks, it is possible to assess examinees' ability to organize information and integrate ideas from multiple sources. In terms of performance tasks, the Smarter Balanced Assessment Consortium (Measured Progress & ETS, 2012c) stated:

> A key component of college and career readiness is the ability to integrate knowledge and skills across multiple content standards. Smarter Balanced will address this ability through performance tasks because it cannot be adequately assessed with selected-response or constructed-response items. (p. 1)

However, if responses are not machine scorable, then scoring adds costs to the assessment and increases the amount of time required to complete scoring.

Item and Task Qualities

To the extent possible, items should be framed within a real-world context so that examinees are engaged and so that they learn their skills and knowledge are valuable in the world beyond the classroom. Context can be established through the use of stimuli, such as text-based scenarios, images of medical charts, or political cartoons. Recall that in the nursing licensure examinations, the developers created a real world context by use of technology-enhanced items that present examinees with a question and provide exhibit tabs with relevant information, such as the patient's history, laboratory results, and prescriptions (Wendt et al., 2010). The use of such stimulus materials requires that item writers reference the materials needed in the item and stipulate the resources needed to answer the items. The stimulus materials must be new to the examinee or the task may require only memory and not analysis and synthesis of the task information. For example, in the field of law, Lenel (1990) advised against the Bar exam's use of actual court cases if the intent was to assess reasoning rather than recall of facts.

Item writers should also consider any ancillary KSAs that the items or tasks might require of examinees. Ancillary skills include those KSAs that are required for task success but potentially introduce construct irrelevant variance to examinees' scores (Haertel & Linn, 1996). For example, reading demands in a social studies achievement test might contribute unrelated variability to examinees' score; thus, items should not require advanced reading skills (unless measuring literacy skills). Smarter Balanced stipulated that text readability/complexity should be at least one grade below grade level for nonreading items and tasks (Measured Progress & ETS, 2012b). In addition, the directions for performance tasks were to provide the definitions of specialized terminology and vocabulary that examinees were not expected to know (Measured Progress & ETS, 2012c). The Smarter Balanced item writing guidelines for performance tasks also required item writers to avoid dense text. The guidelines suggested the use of bullets and tables to present the directions, requirements, and needed information.

A concern about the technology-enhanced items is whether examinees' scores will be influenced by their ancillary skills related to using computers. In a study of items for a nursing examination, Wendt and Harmes (2009) reported that statistical properties of items presented in both technology-enhanced and text-only format were generally similar. However, when the statistical properties of items differed, the technology-based items did better than text-based items in discriminating between low scoring examinees and high scoring examinees. The authors did not conjecture the reason for the higher discrimination associated with the technology-enhanced items.

Conventions of Language

Adhering to the conventions cluster of guidelines will support examinees in understanding what the item or task is asking them to do. Mechanics, grammar, and style address the essentials in writing items that clearly communicate what is expected of an examinee.

Sensitivity and Fairness

Items and tasks should be free of words and content that would be regarded by examinees as offensive, controversial, or negative (Johnson et al., 2009; Measured Progress & ETS, 2012a). When depicting people in stimulus materials, such as video clips, historical documents, and photographs, the materials should include people of various cultural, ethnic, and gender groups. To avoid portraying stereotypes, item developers should attend to the depiction of ethnic, gender, and other groups in activities, behaviors, dress, environment, professions, language, and family structures (Baiker, 1993). Those depictions should not promote stereotypes nor convey negative messages about those portrayed in the stimulus material.

Item-Writing Guidelines for Selected-Response Formats

In preparing to write selected-response items, an item writer should review the guidelines in the previous section (Table 5.2). Guidelines specific to the use of selected-response items are listed in Table 5.3.

Table 5.3. Item-writing guidelines for selected-response items

Stems for a multiple-choice items should ...
- Include the question and stimulus material in the stem.
- Have the omission at the end, or near the end, of the stem for incomplete items.
- Be phrased positively and use *NOT* sparingly.

Options for a multiple-choice items should ...
- Be three or more, including the correct answer(s) and plausible distractors.
- Be conceptually similar or answers that are typically given by examinees with partial knowledge.
- Have answer options that do not overlap.
- Not give clues to the right answer (e.g., repeating words in the stem and the correct response, grammar clues, qualifiers, patterns in answers, lengthy correct answer choices).
- Use *none of the above* with caution and avoid *all of the above*.
- Be listed one per line, unless all options fit on one line.
- Be arranged in a logical order (e.g., alphabetically, numerically, chronologically, short to long).
- Be formatted such that
  - When the stem is an incomplete statement, then the options should begin with a lower case – unless the first word is a proper noun – and the stem should end with the appropriate punctuation mark (e.g., period).
  - When the question is a complete statement, then the options begin with a capital and have no punctuation at the end. If the options are complete sentences, then capitalize and punctuate as appropriate for each sentence.

Summarized from Downing, 2006; Hopkins, 1998; Measured Progress & ETS, 2012b; Moreno et al., 2006.

Stems

In writing multiple-choice items, of importance is for the stem to contain any relevant directions, the question, and the stimulus material. The item can be written as a question or an incomplete statement. For incomplete statements, the convention is for the omission or blank to be at the end of the stem. Generally it is advised to word the stem positively and avoid negative phrasing. For example, the word *NOT* should be used sparingly. Negatively phrased items may introduce measurement bias related to the wording used and impact the measurement of the domain under study (see Chapter 15 of this volume). If the writer must use *NOT*, or some other negative term (e.g., *NEVER*), then he or she should use all caps to emphasize the term to clarify the item demands for the examinee.

Writing Options

In a meta-analysis of research spanning 80 years, Rodriguez (2005) reported that psychometric qualities of an examination will be optimal when multiple-choice items have three well-written options. The options should be conceptually similar or answers typically given by examinees with partial knowledge in order to determine those misconceptions that must be addressed in the curriculum. For example, if an item asked about figurative language, then the options should be forms of figurative language, such as metaphor, simile, personification, and hyperbole. Options should not be a mix of types of figurative language and parts of speech (e.g., noun, verb, adjective).

Item options must be mutually exclusive; if options overlap the correct answer will be ambiguous. An example would be if a question asked when toddlers typically begin to walk. Options that overlap include 9–12 months, 12–15 months, and 14–16 months. If 12–15 months is the correct answer, then all the options contain part of the right answer. The overlapping options likely introduce some construct irrelevant variance to examinees' scores.

Drasgow and Mattern (2006) noted that a common criticism of multiple-choice items is that an examinee who has not mastered the material can guess the answer. The effect of guessing, however, can be greatly reduced if item writers do not provide inadvertent clues to the right answer. Common types of clues are:
- Repetition of words in the item stem and the correct response;
- Grammar clues (e.g., use of *an* at the end of a stem and only one option that begins with a vowel);
- Qualifiers (e.g., all, none);
- Patterns in option answers (e.g., a,a,b,b,c,c); and
- Length (i.e., the correct option is often the longest).

The *all of the above* option actually provides clues to the answer. For example, if for a 5-option item an examinee knows two options are correct, then she can ignore the other options and mark *all of the above*. So, the *all of the above* option only required partial knowledge for the examinee to answer the item correctly. *None of the above* is sometimes used with mathematics items that involve calculations. It should be used with caution because an examinee might surmise that two options for an item are incorrect and then be able to use this partial knowledge to answer the question. If *all of the above* and *none of the above* options are used, then they should be used when they are the correct option in some items and when they are a distractor in other items. This practice will help item writers to avoid the tendency to include these options only when they are the correct answer.

Options should be listed one per line – unless all options fit on one line – and arranged in a logical order (e.g., alphabetically, numerically, chronologically, length of options). They should be formatted such that when the question is an incomplete statement, then the options should begin with a lower case – unless the first word is a proper noun – and the stem should end with the appropriate punctuation mark (e.g., period). When the question is a complete statement, then the options begin with a capital and have no punctuation at the end. If the options are complete sentences, then capitalize and punctuate as appropriate for each sentence.

Item-Writing Guidelines for Technology-Enhanced Items

In preparing to write technology-enhanced items, the general item-writing guidelines in Table 5.2 and the multiple-choice specific guidelines in Table 5.3 should be reviewed. Guidelines specific to technology-enhanced items are shown in Table 5.4. The first guideline requires the item writer to consider the interaction (e.g., produce a geometric shape, highlight a block of text) that the examinee must engage in to produce a response. The development of the item requires the specification of any technology-enabled or technology-enhanced stimulus materials (e.g., video clip) needed for the stem/prompt or the answer options. Also required is the specification of the technology-enhanced response format (e.g., insert text, fill-in the blank). The stem/prompt directions should state the input device that the examinee uses in responding. Formatting of an item involves placing the stem/prompt at the top of the frame (e.g., computer screen) and answer options or a free-response text box at the bottom of the frame. In another format, the stem/prompt is in the left side of the frame and the answer options or free-response text boxes on the right side.

Table 5.4. Item-writing guidelines for technology-enhanced items

In writing a technology-enhanced item ...
• Determine the interaction that a student performs to produce a response that provides evidence about the content and cognitive process that are the focus of the item. • Identify any required technology-enabled stimulus materials (e.g., music passage, video clips) required. • Identify the technology-enhanced response format (e.g., drag and drop, highlight) required. • Determine the input device (e.g., mouse, keyboard) required for the item. • Format the item with the stem/prompt at the top of the page, followed by the answer options or freeresponse text boxes. An alternative format is to place the stem/prompt on the left and the answer options/text boxes on the right.

Summarized from Measured Progress & ETS, 2012d; Zenisky & Sireci, 2002.

Item-Writing Guidelines for Constructed-Response and Performance Tasks

Again, the item-writing guidelines presented for all item types (Table 5.2) should be considered in developing constructed-response and performance tasks. Considerable resources are required in the development and scoring of constructed-response items. In addition, examinees commit considerable resources in responding to essay prompts and performance tasks. So a first guideline to consider is whether the task will be meaningful to examinees (see Table 5.5).

Table 5.5. Item-writing guidelines for constructed-response and performance tasks

Constructed-response and performance tasks should...
• Be meaningful to examinees. • Engage examinees in the integration of knowledge and complex cognitive skills across multiple content standards or strands within a content area. • Allow for multiple approaches to completion of the task. • Allow for multiple points of view and interpretations.
In writing a performance task ... • Review the content and cognitive process that are the focus of the tasks and select the most appropriate task format (i.e., process or product). • Specify the audience for the response. • Consider the degree of structure. • Require examinee-initiated planning, management of information and ideas, and interaction with other materials.
Making the response expectations clear to examinees includes ... • Incorporating scaffolds into the task to clarify the task expectations for examinees. • Preparing directions with an overview of the task, briefly describing steps that examinees are to complete. The overview should give examinees knowledge of the scorable products or performances to be created. • Providing rubrics with criteria consistent with the task demands.

Summarized from Johnson, Penny, & Gordon, 2009; Measured Progress & ETS, 2012c.

As well as being meaningful, tasks should engage examinees in the integration of knowledge and complex cognitive skills across multiple content standards or strands within a content area (Measured Progress & ETS, 2012c). Performance tasks should be written to elicit complex cognitive capacities such as research skills, complex analysis, and identification/providing of relevant evidence. The task should allow examinees to demonstrate important knowledge and skills, including those that address 21st-century skills such as critical thinking and problem solving (Partnership for 21st Century Skills, 2009).

Performance tasks should allow for multiple approaches in completion of the task. In addition they should allow for multiple points of view and interpretations. With many correct answers possible, the scoring guides described earlier play a critical role in controlling for error in rating.

In preparing to write a task, a first step is to review the content and cognitive processes that are the focus and determine if the response format should be a process or a product. Smarter Balanced adopted the view that such tasks engage examinees in the production of extended responses, such as oral presentations and exhibitions. The prompt, or task directions, should specify the audience for the response. An example is provided in the credentialing examination for orthotists and prosthetists, professionals who develop devices for patients with disabling conditions of the limbs and spine. In this performance task, examinees (i.e., candidates for credentialing) demonstrate their practical abilities in a patient model interaction (American Board for Certification in Orthotics, Prosthetics, and Pedorthics, 2013). In this instance, the patient is the audience.

In determining the degree of structure to bring to the task, consider the following issues:
* Topic – Will the task/topic be specified or will the examinee determine the focus?
* Response format – Will you stipulate whether the task will focus on process or product?
* Time – Will you specify the length of time the examinee has to respond to the task?
* Resources – Will you specify the resources (e.g., Internet, calculator, word-processing software, video camera) that examinees may use? (Khattri, Reeve, & Kane, 1998).

Smarter Balanced indicated that performance tasks require examinee-initiated planning, management of information and ideas, and interaction with other materials. This quality appears consistent with the idea that performance tasks require students to organize their ideas and to integrate information across content standards.

Making the response expectations clear for examinees can be achieved by preparing scaffolds (e.g., planning tools such as concept maps) to frame the task. In addition, if the task directions provide an overview of the task and steps in completing the task, such an overview will contribute to the clarity of the task expectations. Rubrics that will be used to score the task can make clear the aspects of the performance that will be scored.

Examining Test Data

To this point, we have identified and described the development of various item formats, which is a crucial step in order to craft an instrument that will yield the data necessary for answering one's research questions of interest. A next step in the development of test items is piloting or field testing the items and examining the psychometric properties of the test data.

Pilot Testing Items

The purpose of the pilot test is to provide data for review of the psychometric qualities of test items and a scale. These analyses provide information that test developers can use for quality control and test construction. Piloting the test allows test developers to examine items to determine, for example, if some items are so difficult that almost none of the examinees answered an item correctly or so easy that almost all examinees answered it correctly. Items that are easier than expected, or harder than expected, might be flawed and require additional scrutiny to determine if they require additional revision (Livingston, 2006).

In terms of test construction, one use of data from a pilot test is to complete analyses that will inform the development of the statistical specifications for an examination. For example, the difficulty of a test that rank orders examinees, such as a college entrance exam, is considered appropriate if the target population can answer correctly 50–60% of the items (Wendler & Walker, 2006). Thus, the difficulty of items should be around .50 (i.e., 50% of examinees answered the item correctly) with some harder and some easier items to provide information about examinees who have mastered the content and those who have not mastered the content, respectively. In the following sections, we provide a more detailed treatment of the statistical analyses used in the review of items and scales.

Descriptive Statistical Analyses

After collecting responses to a set of items, researchers should first examine the data descriptively. When developing sets of items, researchers commonly wish to assess examinees' position along a continuum as represented by a total score. Therefore, items are developed that have different target difficulty levels. Item analysis can provide support for whether or not the target difficulties were realized. Descriptive analysis not only provides information about the item characteristics but also helps researchers identify potential errors, such as those related to data entry and/or scoring, and whether respondents omitted certain items. The presence of these types of errors may adversely affect the quality of decisions made about the items and should therefore be corrected before proceeding with item analysis.

Dichotomous data are very common in educational and psychological research. In educational assessment, for example, each student's response to a test item can be scored as correct (coded as "1") or incorrect (coded as "0"). Thus, dichotomously scored data can be obtained from any form of selected-response items (e.g., multiple-choice, true/false, matching) or certain forms of constructed-response, such as short answer (see Table 5.1). In certain areas of psychological research, respondents are asked to indicate whether a description provided by an item accurately describes himself or herself. On these items, someone may respond "Yes" (coded as "1") if he or she believes the item content is accurate or "No" (coded as "0") if he or she does not believe the item content is accurate.

Whereas dichotomous data take on only one of two possible values, polytomous data can assume more than two values. In educational settings, one might observe polytomous data in a set of scores of student essays that were graded with, for example, a 6-point rubric. Thus, a student whose essay was very poor would be scored very low (e.g., 1), and a student whose essay was excellent would be scored very high (e.g., 6). Polytomous data in psychological research might be observed in a set of responses to survey items that use, say, a four-point (i.e., Likert-type) response scale that assigns a response of *strongly disagree* a 1, *disagree* a 2, *agree* a 3, and *strongly agree* a 4.

After item responses are collected, one should first generate a frequency table for each item to examine the distribution of the scores for each item. Frequency tables are easily generated and are intuitively understood by nontechnical audiences. Where meaningful, descriptive information, such as item mean/standard deviation values or the probability of examinees responding correctly to an item, may be computed.

Item Analyses

Test developers routinely complete item analyses to examine the characteristics of the items included in the data collection instrument. Two common item characteristics in the classical test theory framework are item difficulty and discrimination. Item difficulty refers to the item mean and is typically denoted p. When item responses are dichotomously scored, the item mean corresponds to the proportion of examinees who answered the item correctly. Thus, items with higher means are easier than items with lower means because higher item means indicate that a larger proportion of examinees answered the item correctly. Items to which everyone ($p = 1.0$) or no one ($p = 0.0$) answered correctly provide no information about examinees because it results in either a 1 being added to every examinee's observed score if p is 1.0, or a 0 being added to every examinee's observed score if p is 0.0. More information is provided by items with difficulty estimates between about 0.4 and 0.6, though it may be prudent to include easier or harder items depending on the purpose of the assessment. For polytomous data, the item difficulty may range from the minimum possible score to the maximum possible score for an item. The item mean can also be adjusted for polytomous data to fix the minimum to zero and maximum to one by dividing the computed item mean by the range of possible scores.

Item discrimination generally refers to the ability of an item to distinguish between those examinees with higher ability and those with lower ability. Researchers can use the score on the test as a proxy for ability because a researcher cannot know an examinee's true ability. In practice, item discrimination is commonly estimated by the correlation between the responses to an individual item with the sum score on the rest of the test. This correlation is often called the item-to-total correlation. It is important to note that the sum score should not include the item under investigation. This requires a new sum score to be computed when each item is examined.

Ideally, examinees who answer an item correctly will have higher sum scores on the rest of the test, and those examinees who answer an item incorrectly will have lower sum scores on the rest of the test. Thus, the item-to-total correlation should be positive for the correct answer, and values above 0.2 are generally considered acceptable. Two specific correlation coefficients that are used for estimating the item-to-total correlation with dichotomous data are the point-biserial (r_{pbis}) and biserial (r_{bis}) correlations. The point-biserial correlation expresses the relationship between a dichotomous variable and continuous variable. The biserial correlation expresses the relationship between the underlying continuous distribution that has been dichotomized by an item and a continuous observed variable. The biserial correlation is based in part on the point-biserial, and it always larger than the point-biserial.

Another estimate of discrimination is the D index, which is computed as the difference between the p values of the high-scoring examinees and the low-scoring examinees. The classification of the high- and low-scoring examinees is determined by those scoring in some specified percentiles. The upper and lower 27% are commonly used for determining these groups. For example, the high scoring examinees are those examinees scoring at the 73rd percentile or higher, and the low scoring examinees are those examinees scoring at the 27th percentile or lower.

The preceding analysis can be conducted for the correct answer as well as for each of the distractors although the range of desired values of difficulty and discrimination differs for distractors. Item difficulty for distractors is the proportion of examinees that selected each incorrect response option. This is an important item characteristic to assess. Recall that distractors should be plausible options and are ideally based on possible examinee misconceptions.

Incorrect response options that are infrequently chosen are ineffective distractors and needlessly increase the reading load for examinees. The inclusion of implausible distractors may artificially make items too easy. As for discrimination of the distractors, there is mixed support in the literature for estimating the point-biserial correlation between distractors and the sum score (Attali & Fraenkel, 2000; Haladyna, 2004). On the one hand, when the correct response is included in the distractor analysis, the correlation between a given distractor and sum score is attenuated. On the other hand, if the correct answer is excluded from the distractor analysis, the effective sample size is reduced, and this effect is strengthened for easier items. Attali and Fraenkel (2000) proposed an adjusted point-biserial correlation to be used when examining distractor discrimination, but its use appears rare among testing programs. Should a researcher compute distractor discrimination, the estimates should be nonpositive.

Examining Associations Between Items

After examining item difficulty and discrimination, one should next explore the strength of association between the items. Sets of items developed to measure the same underlying construct should return similar responses, and the similarity can be expressed with a correlation coefficient. A matrix of inter-item correlations can be used for examining the dimensionality of the set of item responses. Review of the correlation matrix reveals the extent to which the responses to each pair of items are associated.

The Pearson product-moment correlation coefficient (PPM) is very commonly used as an index of the strength and direction of the association between two variables. The correlation between two dichotomous variables is the phi (Φ) coefficient. Due to the restricted variance in dichotomous data, Φ is likely to have a restricted range (i.e., have limits less than |1|). The PPM can be used for reporting the correlation between polytomous item responses also, but studies have shown that PPM tends to underestimate the correlation between polytomous variables because polytomous data do not often meet the normality assumption required for PPM (Bollen & Barb, 1981). Thus, PPM is not recommended for expressing the relationship between polytomous variables.

Alternatively, the polychoric correlation coefficient may be used when normally distributed variables are assumed to underlie the item. The polychoric correlation expresses the association between the underlying continuous variables that were categorized by the item responses. Ideally the inter-item correlations for items measuring the same construct should be positive. Interested readers should see Chapter 8 in this volume for more detailed treatment of analysis with categorical data.

Examining Scales (Sets of Items)

Following descriptive analysis of the items individually, researchers should next consider scale-level analysis, where a scale is defined as a set of items. Examining the characteristics of scales is a crucial step before proceeding to analysis involving latent variables. The following considerations are applicable to both dichotomous and polytomous data.

The following analysis is based on classical test theory (CTT), which posits that any given test score consists of two parts: (a) the person's actual value on the latent construct, and (b) measurement error. Under CTT, the person's actual value on the latent construct is called the true score, and CTT is commonly expressed as:

$$X_j = T_j + E_j, \tag{1}$$

where X_j is the observed score for person j, T_j is the true score of person j, and E_j is the error included in the observed score for person j. The observed score is computed as the sum of the item responses. Ideally, the observed score, X, for a given person will have very little error, which means that the observed score is strongly reflective of the person's true score. It is assumed that for any given administration of an instrument, the observed score may be slightly higher or slightly lower than the true score, and over repeated administrations, the true score is the expected value of the observed scores. This also implies that the expected value of the errors over many administrations is zero.

The reliability of an instrument can be conceptualized as the correlation between the observed scores and true scores and can be expressed as the ratio of true score variability to observed variability. The reliability coefficient can be expressed as:

$$\rho_{X,T} = \frac{\sigma_T^2}{\sigma_X^2} = \frac{\sigma_T^2}{\sigma_T^2 + \sigma_E^2}. \tag{2}$$

Unfortunately, it is not possible to know a person's true score, therefore, under CTT, reliability is typically thought of as the correlation between two parallel tests measuring the same construct.

Reliability can be estimated from scores of one or more administrations of an instrument. When the same instrument is administered twice, reliability can be estimated with the PPM correlation between the two sets of scores. This type of reliability is called test-retest reliability. When equivalent forms of an instrument are administered to the same group of examinees, reliability can be estimated with the Pearson correlation between the two sets of scores. This type of reliability is called parallel forms reliability.

Reliability estimated from a single administration of an instrument is generally referred to as internal consistency, and there are multiple ways to estimate internal consistency. When an instrument is administered only once, one might create two sets of scores by dividing the responses into halves, and then estimate reliability as the Pearson correlation between the scores on the two halves. This type of reliability is called split-half reliability. A consideration with this approach is that the reliability estimate needs to be adjusted using the Spearman–Brown prophecy formula because the length of the instrument was artificially divided in half. There are many ways a set of scores could be divided in half, and each configuration will provide a slightly different reliability estimate. If someone were interested in estimating the average of all split halves, then she or he could estimate coefficient alpha (Cronbach, 1951). Alpha is based on the ratio of inter-item covariances to total score variance.

Alternatively, if one fit a single factor model to the data collected from a single administration, then the loading and residual variance estimates could be used to estimate omega (McDonald, 1999). As noted by McDonald (1999), specific variance cannot be distinguished from random error variance if the instrument is administered only once. Omega is the ratio of the true score variability to the total variability of the outcome variables. Therefore, it seeks to identify the variability in the data that is due to the common factor. It can be expressed as:

$$\omega = \frac{\sigma_T^2}{\upsilon_Y^2} = \frac{(\sum \lambda_i)^2}{(\sum \lambda_i)^2 + \sum \psi_i^2} \tag{3}$$

where λ_i is the factor loading of the ith item and ψ_i^2 is the residual variance of the ith item. It should also be noted that both alpha and omega can be computed based on a polychoric cor-

relation matrix if the observed variables are ordinal categories with underlying normal distribution (Gadermann, Guhn, & Zumbo, 2012).

Applied Example

To demonstrate the analyses discussed in this chapter, we provide an item analysis of a visual arts
assessment used as a part of the South Carolina Arts Assessment Program (SCAAP). The data
presented here were collected from one form of the visual arts administration. Responses were
collected from 2,071 students. The form contained 45 multiple-choice items that were scored as
correct or incorrect. Figure 5.1 shows an example of a visual arts item from the item bank.

Before analyzing the data, the responses were first screened to ensure that all options had
plausible values. All items on the assessment included four response options, labeled *A, B, C,*
or *D,* so we made certain that responses consisted of these four values. The assessment was
administered in computer-based format so no data entry problems were expected. Regardless,
it is always advisable to perform appropriate data screening and clean the data as needed.

First, we computed a sum score for each of the examinees. Each correct response was coded
as "1," and each incorrect response was coded as "0." Therefore, the sum score represents the
number of items each examinee answered correctly, and the range of possible scores were
from 0 to 45. The average observed sum score was 25.9 ($SD = 8.0$) with a minimum score of
7 and maximum score of 45. We also estimated reliability using coefficient alpha and omega
based on the polychoric correlation matrix. The estimated alpha was .90 and estimated omega
was .92, which were both considered acceptable.

Next, we computed the item difficulty and discrimination estimates (i.e., D, r_{pbis}, r_{bis}). Table 5.6
includes the item difficulty and discrimination estimates for the first five items. Of these items,
Item 1 was the least difficult ($p = .82$) because 82% of the examinees answered it correctly, and
Item 2 was the most difficult ($p = .64$) because 64% of the examinees answered it correctly.
Each of these items shows an acceptable level of item difficulty although Item 1 is very near
the threshold for being too easy. The item shown in Figure 5.1 was relatively difficult, with
only 33% of the examinees correctly identifying item B, *contrast,* as the correct answer.

According to the biserial correlations, in Table 5.6 the most discriminating item is Item 5
($r_{bis} = .58$), and the least discriminating item is Item 4 ($r_{bis} = .42$). Although Item 4 is the least
discriminating of these five items, all five have very good discrimination. The lower bound of
acceptable discrimination is .2, but ideally the discrimination will be as high as possible. For
the discrimination estimates, the item under investigation was excluded from the sum score.
For example, the point-biserial correlation reported for Item 1 expressed the correlation between the responses to Item 1 and the sum of the scores on Items 2 through 45. For the item in
Figure 5.1, the discrimination index was .16.

Table 5.6. Item difficulty and discrimination estimates for SCAAP items

Item	Difficulty (p)	D index	Point-biserial correlation (r_{pbis})	Biserial correlation (r_{bis})
1	.82	0.31	0.31	0.46
2	.64	0.50	0.42	0.54
3	.73	0.40	0.37	0.50
4	.67	0.36	0.32	0.42
5	.78	0.42	0.41	0.58

Next, we evaluated the distractors by first examining the frequency with which examinees selected each response. Table 5.7 includes the proportion of examinees who selected each response option. For Item 1, *B* was the popular incorrect response option. Options A and C were rarely chosen. Option A was only chosen by 1% of the examinees, which indicates that option A was viewed as an implausible answer choice by the majority of examinees and should probably be revised or replaced by another, better answer choice. For the item in Figure 5.1, the proportion of examinees selecting each distractor was .12 for A, .17 for C, and .35 for D. Thus, all the distractors were viable.

Table 5.7. Proportion of examinees by response option for SCAAP items

Item	Item response			
	A	B	C	D
1	0.01	0.13	0.04	0.82[a]
2	0.06	0.18	0.13	0.64[a]
3	0.11	0.10	0.73[a]	0.06
4	0.11	0.67[a]	0.08	0.14
5	0.78[a]	0.12	0.05	0.05

Note. [a] = Correct answer.

We also computed the discrimination index (D) for each distractor (see Table 5.8). Each distractor had a negative discrimination estimate, which indicates that the lower scoring examinees tended to select the incorrect responses more frequently than the higher scoring examinees. This is a desirable pattern for distractors to follow.

Table 5.8. Discrimination index (D) by response option for SCAAP items

Item	A	B	C	D
1	−0.02	−0.23	−0.07	0.31[a]
2	−0.12	−0.28	−0.15	0.50[a]
3	−0.14	−0.16	0.40[a]	−0.14
4	−0.19	0.36[a]	−0.12	−0.11
5	0.40[a]	−0.29	−0.10	−0.06

Note. [a] = Correct answer.

The analysis demonstrated here is meant to be a first step in investigating the psychometric properties of the instrument that should be done before estimating more complex models (e.g., item response, Rasch, or factor analytic models). Based on the more complex latent variable models, ability estimates that take the item characteristics into account can be generated for each of the examinees. Under CTT, each item is given equal weight in the sum score calculation. Through the use of latent variable models, examinee ability estimates take into account each item's characteristics. Furthermore, the analysis provided here assumes only one underlying construct. The data may be submitted to a latent variable analysis to assess the extent to which this assumption is tenable.

Although the analyses discussed here are relatively intuitive, the major disadvantage of these analyses is that they are both sample- and test-dependent. That is, if the same items were administered to a different group of examinees, the item characteristics estimates would likely be different. Similarly, if the same examinees were given a different set of items, their computed sum scores would likely be different. Latent variable models are far less dependent on the characteristics of the sample data. Again, the analyses discussed here represent only the first step of the examination of item and test performance.

References

American Board for Certification in Orthotics, Prosthetics, and Pedorthics. (2013). *Orthotist and prosthetist*. Retrieved from http://www.abcop.org/

Anderson, L., & Krathwohl, D. (Eds.). (2001). *A taxonomy for learning, teaching, and assessing: A revision of Bloom's taxonomy of educational objectives* (abr. ed.). New York, NY: Longman.

Attali, Y. & Fraenkel, T., (2000). The point-biserial as a discrimination index for distractors in multiple-choice items: Deficiencies in usage and an alternative. *Journal of Educational Measurement, 37*(1), 77–86. http://doi.org/10.1111/j.1745-3984.2000.tb01077.x

Baiker, K. (1993). *Reflecting diversity: Multicultural guidelines for educational publishing professionals*. New York, NY: Macmillan-McGraw Hill.

Bloom, B., Engelhart, M., Furst, E., Hill, W., & Krathwohl, D. (1956). *Taxonomy of educational objectives: Handbook I: Cognitive domain*. New York, NY: David McKay Company.

Bollen, K. A., & Barb, K. H. (1981). Pearson's r and coarsely categorized measures. *American Sociological Review, 46*, 232–239.

Bond, L., Moss, P., & Carr, P. (1996). Fairness in large-scale performance assessment. In G. Phillips (Ed.), *Technical issues in large scale performance assessment* (pp. 117–140). Washington, DC: National Center for Education Statistics.

Cronbach, L. (1951). Coefficient alpha and the internal structure of tests. *Psychometrika, 16*, 297–334. http://doi.org/10.1007/BF02310555

Doorey, N. (2012). Coming soon: How two common core assessment consortia were created – and how they compare. *Educational Leadership, 70*(4), 28–34.

Downing, S. (2006). Selected-response item formats in test development. In S. Downing & T. Haladyna (Eds.), *Handbook of test development* (pp. 287–301). Mahwah, NJ: Lawrence Erlbaum.

Drasgow, F., & Mattern, K. (2006). New tests and new items: Opportunities and issues. In D. Bartram & R. Hambleton, *Computer-based testing and the Internet: Issues and advances* (pp. 59–75). Chichester, UK: John Wiley & Sons.

Federation of State Medical Boards of the United States (FSMB) & National Board of Medical Examiners (NBME). (2013). *United States medical licensure examination step 2: CK*. Retrieved from http://www.usmle.org/

Gadermann, A. M., Guhn, M., & Zumbo, B. D. (2012). Estimating ordinal reliability for Likert-type and ordinal item response data: A conceptual, empirical, and practical guide. *Practical Assessment, Research & Evaluation, 17*(3). Retrieved from http://pareonline.net/getvn.asp?v=17&n=3

Haertel, E., & Linn, R. (1996). Comparability. In G. Phillips (Ed.), *Technical issues in large scale performance assessment* (pp. 59–78). Washington, DC: National Center for Education Statistics.

Haladyna, T. (2004). *Developing and validating multiple-choice test items* (4th ed.). Hillsdale, NJ: Lawrence Erlbaum Associates.

Hopkins, K. (1998). *Educational and psychological measurement and evaluation* (8th ed.). Needham Heights, MA: Allyn and Bacon.

Johnson, R., Penny, J., & Gordon, B. (2009). *Assessing performance: Developing, scoring, and validating performance tasks*. New York, NY: Guilford Publications.

Khattri, N., Reeve, A., & Kane, M. (1998). *Principles and practices of performance assessment*. Mahwah, NJ: Lawrence Erlbaum Associates.

Lenel, J. (1990). The essay examination part II: Construction of the essay examination. *The Bar Examiner, 59*(2), 40–43.

Livingston, S. (2006). Item analysis. In S. Downing & T. Haladyna (Eds.) *Handbook of test development* (pp. 421–441). Mahwah, NJ: Lawrence Erlbaum Associates.

Marzano, R. J. (2001). *Designing a new taxonomy of educational objectives*. Thousand Oaks, CA: Corwin Press.

McDonald, R. P. (1999). *Test theory: A unified treatment*. Mahwah, NJ: Lawrence Erlbaum Associates.

Measured Progress & Educational Testing Services. (2012a). *Smarter Balanced Assessment Consortium: English language arts item and task specifications*. Retrieved from http://www.smarterbalanced.org/

Measured Progress & Educational Testing Services. (2012b). *Smarter Balanced Assessment Consortium: General item specifications*. Retrieved from http://www.smarterbalanced.org/

Measured Progress & Educational Testing Services. (2012c). *Smarter Balanced Assessment Consortium: Performance task specifications*. Retrieved from http://www.smarterbalanced.org/

Measured Progress & Educational Testing Services. (2012d). *Smarter Balanced Assessment Consortium: Technology-enhanced items guidelines*. Retrieved from http://www.smarterbalanced.org/

Moreno, R., Martinez, R., & Muniz, J. (2006). New guidelines for developing multiple-choice items. *Methodology, 2*(2), 65–72. http://doi.org/10.1027/1614-2241.2.2.65

National Center for Education Statistics. (2012). *Writing 2011: National assessment of educational progress at grades 8 and 12*. Retrieved from http://nces.ed.gov/nationsreportcard/pdf/main2011/2012470.pdf

National Governors Association Center for Best Practices & Council of Chief State School Officers. (2010). *Common core state standards*. Washington, DC: Authors. Retrieved from http://www.corestandards.org/thestandards

Parshall, C., Davey, T., & Pashley, P. (2000). Innovative item types for computerized testing. In W. van der Linden & G. Glas (Eds.), *Computerized adaptive testing: Theory and practice* (pp. 129–148). Boston, MA: Kluwer Academic Publishers.

Partnership for 21st Century Skills. (2009). *P21 framework definitions*. Retrieved from http://www.p21.org/

Pearson. (2012). *PARCC item development*. Retrieved from http://www.parcconline.org/

Rodriguez, M. (2005). Three options are optimal for multiple-choice items: A meta-analysis of 80 years of research. *Educational Measurement: Issues and Practice, 24*(2), 3–13. http://doi.org/10.1111/j.1745-3992.2005.00006.x

Sireci, S., & Zenisky, A., (2006). Innovative item formats in computer-based testing: In pursuit of improved construct representation. In S. Downing & T. Haladyna (Eds.), *Handbook of test development* (pp. 329–347). Mahwah, NJ: Lawrence Erlbaum.

South Carolina Department of Education. (2008). *Extended response scoring rubric: Grades 3–8*. Columbia, SC: Author.

Webb, N. (2006). Identifying content for student achievement tests. In S. Downing & T. Haladyna (Eds.), *Handbook of test development* (pp. 155–180). Mahwah, NJ: Lawrence Erlbaum.

Wendler, C. & Walker, M. (2006). Practical issues in designing and maintaining multiple test forms for large-scale programs. In S. Downing & T. Haladyna (Eds.) *Handbook of test development* (pp. 421–441). Mahwah, NJ: Lawrence Erlbaum Associates.

Wendt, A. (2003). The NCLEX-RN® examination: Charting the course of nursing practice. *Nurse Educator, 28*(6), 276–280.

Wendt, A., & Harmes, J. (2009). Developing and evaluating innovative items for the NCLEX: Part 2, Item characteristics and cognitive processing. *Nurse Educator, 34*(3), 109–113. http://doi.org/10.1097/NNE.0b013e3181990849

Wendt, A., Kenny, L., & Brown, K. (2010). Keeping the NCLEX-RN current. *Nurse Educator, 35*(1), 1–3. http://doi.org/10.1097/NNE.0b013e3181c41fce

Zenisky, A. & Sireci, S. (2002). Technological innovations in large-scale assessment. *Applied Measurement in Education, 15*(4), 337–362. http://doi.org/10.1207/S15324818AME1504_02

Chapter 6
Adaptive Testing

Klaus D. Kubinger

Faculty of Psychology, University of Vienna, Austria

Introduction

At first the concept of *adaptive testing* seems to be self-explanatory. For instance, one could think of the case where the test instructions require breaking off the test administration after too many incorrectly responded items; of course, this approach of testing is somehow adaptive. However, in its strict sense, adaptive testing is a *terminus technicus* within psychometrics. That is, it is strictly conditioned on models of item response theory (IRT): Basically, the optimal item selection occurs on the basis of the examinee's performance on preceding items and of model specifications determining the probability of this examinee responding correctly to every one of the items.

One can credit the development of adaptive testing within psychometrics to several shortcomings of conventional testing, where every examinee is administered the same items in the same sequence, usually ordered by difficulty. Although adaptive testing would also be suitable for personality questionnaires (see Walter, 2010), we restrict our considerations in the following to the items of achievement tests. There are five objections to conventional (so-called fixed item) testing.

The Number of Actually Informative Items Per Examinee

Typically, an achievement test (e.g., subtest of any intelligence test battery) is aimed at testing a broad age group, and consequently it needs to capture a large continuum of the respective ability dimension to be measured. This means that there must be very easy items as well as very difficult items. Take as an example the following two fictitious items (modeled on items of a published test): "Which day follows Sunday?" and "How long is the circumference of the globe?" This broad range of item difficulties requires a relatively large number of items, say 30 to 40. Completing such a long (sub-)test presupposes a great deal of willingness on the part of the examinee; however, only a small portion of this item pool is informative and of diagnostic use. This is true because, for many items, the examiner knows almost certainly in advance whether the examinee in question will respond correctly to the item or not. Many items are either too easy or too difficult for this examinee. Hence, administration of these items hardly results in new information for the examiner. Only a relatively small number of items are actually informative in the sense that the examiner is unsure whether the examinee will or will not respond correctly to them. From the point of view of the examiner, both outcomes are almost equally likely for those items. Therefore, it seems uneconomical to administer items that are obviously too easy or too difficult to a certain examinee.

Bear in mind that, indeed, there were early attempts by Binet, and to some extent even by Wechsler, not to administer items that would be inappropriate given the examinee's age or his/her level of performance on preceding items. In these approaches, however, omitted items are scored as having being responded to either correctly (if the item is assumed to be too easy for the examinee) or incorrectly (if the item is assumed to be too difficult for the examinee). However, as IRT demonstrates, by definition there is never a probability of one for mastering any (even extremely easy) item for any examinee, and there is never a probability of zero for mastering any (even extremely difficult) item. Thus, these early approaches of dealing with almost noninformative items fail to satisfy. See, for instance, Hohensinn and Kubinger (2011), who demonstrate most illustratively how much the measurement of ability is biased when late items that are not administered are scored automatically as incorrect responses.

Measurement Error at Very High or Very Low Ability Levels

In practical single-case consulting, measurement at extreme ability levels is the norm rather than the exception: only on comparatively rare occasions is psychological assessment needed for persons with average ability. Now, when it is important to differentiate reliably between examinees of similar high or low levels of ability, the few actually informative items given with conventional testing do not provide an adequate level of accuracy. This problem is exacerbated by the fact that item difficulties are usually distributed in a peaked manner, leading to even fewer informative items at the relevant (extreme) levels of difficulty. In fact, such tests offer very few different scores for persons within a homogeneous class of peers (or the like). Hence, the de facto shortness of the test causes dramatic errors of measurement, because large chance effects are quite likely.

Examinee's Achievement Motivation Due to Ascending Item Difficulties

Traditionally, the items of a test are (more or less strictly) administered from the easiest to the most difficult. The original reason might have been to provide some warm-up items for the examinee, and perhaps there was an intention to break off test administration when an examinee failed at several easier items. However, (too many) too easy items at the very beginning of a test might discourage people with moderate or high ability levels; on the other hand, many people will be frustrated at the end of a test, whether there is a criterion for abandoning the administration or not, because having just a low or moderate level of ability makes their chances of success extremely small.

Bear in mind that test batteries conceptualized accordingly almost always begin a new subtest with an examinee's achievement motivation at the level of high frustration.

Interpretation of a Test Battery's Profile

Because of the very low accuracy of measurement due to very few actually informative items, interpretation of an examinee's profile of results across all subtests of a test battery is hardly possible: If one takes into account the confidence intervals based on the expected error of measurement of each subtest, then these confidence intervals become so large that they all overlap for nearly every examinee. That is, no strengths and weaknesses across the profile of results will be identified.

Crediting Only Partially Correctly Responded Items or Rewarding Quickly Given Correct Responses With a Bonus

Owing to the relatively limited informative character of the items explained in the previous section, test authors often prefer multicategorical scoring instead of dichotomous scoring rules (correct vs. incorrect). That is, either items that have been responded to correctly very quickly earn a bonus (e.g., two points instead of one point) or even only partially correctly responded items earn some gratification (e.g., an incorrect response scores no points, a completely correct response scores two points, and a partially correct response scores one point). However, as IRT shows, developing a test that properly fits multicategorical models (i.e., accommodating polytomous data) is a much greater challenge than developing a test that fits a dichotomous model (above all the Rasch model; see, for instance, Kubinger, 2009a).

For the aforementioned reasons, an alternative testing strategy is needed. The starting point of this strategy must be not just to administer the same items to every examinee, but also to present only those items that suit the individual level of ability of the given examinee. The sample of items of a (large) item pool must be selected accordingly. This means that the choice of each successive item (or small cluster of items) to be administered during testing must be dynamically and individually determined (i.e., adapted) with respect to the performance of the examinee up to that point. In short, adaptive testing involves selecting optimal items for a given examinee due to his/her performance on preceding items. In doing so, an item is optimal when its psychometric characteristics (quantified by so-called item parameters, above all the item difficulty parameter) correspond to the examinee's level of ability (quantified by a so-called ability parameter, estimated on the basis of all completed items up to that point). As discussed, this correspondence makes the item informative. In the best and most simple case, the probability of a correct item response is .50: Whether the examinee in question responds correctly to that item or not is equivalent to the situation of tossing a coin; the result is not at all predictable.

Of course, one could present items in this fashion without knowing any item parameter, for instance, just by ranking the items' difficulties more ore less intuitively. That is, if an examinee fails to respond correctly to some moderately difficult item, then the examiner could offer him/her a much easier item next; at the very end, the examiner would not have administered (many) very difficult or very easy items. But operating in this way, outside of the IRT framework, would rule out any fair comparison of the performance of examinees who worked on (partially) different items. Obviously, the number of correctly responded items fails to serve for a fair comparison, as one examinee could respond correctly to a relatively large number of rather easy items while another responds correctly to fewer items but of greater difficulty. Only IRT-immanent comparisons are feasibly fair.

Basics of Adaptive Testing: IRT

We restrict our considerations for reasons of simplicity to items of achievement tests that score any response of an examinee either as correct or as incorrect. For this case, the inventory of pertinent models is represented best by the so-called 3PL model (three-[item-]parameter logistic model; Birnbaum, 1968). This model postulates a specific probabilistic function between the response category, on the one hand, and the examinee's ability (i.e., person) parameter and the item's parameters, on the other hand. The model equation then is as follows:

$$P\left(1 \mid \xi_v; \sigma_i, \alpha_i, \beta_i\right) = \frac{\beta_i + e^{\alpha_i(\xi_v - \sigma_i)}}{1 + e^{\alpha_i(\xi_v - \sigma_i)}} \qquad (1)$$

This model contains the ability parameter ξ_v of examinee v and the item parameters σ_i, α_i, and β_i of item i; the first of the latter is the item difficulty parameter, the second the item discrimination parameter, and the third the item guessing parameter. In this model, the probability P for examinee v responding correctly to item i ("1") depends in a logistic way on all these parameters. Looking at the most important special case of this model, that is all $\alpha_i = 1$ (for every $i = 1, 2, \ldots,$ k) and all $\beta_i = 0$ (for every $i = 1, 2, \ldots, k$) – leading to the Rasch model (Rasch, 1960/1980) or 1PL [parameter-logistic] model –, illustrates very simply the meaning of the ability parameter ξ_v and the item difficulty parameter σ_i:

$$P\left(+\mid \xi_v, \sigma_i\right) = \frac{e^{\xi_v - \sigma_i}}{1 + e^{\xi_v - \sigma_i}} \qquad (2)$$

If the ability parameter ξ_v goes to ∞, then (given that σ_i is not ∞) the probability of responding correctly to the item tends to 1; if the ability parameter ξ_v tends to $-\infty$, then (given that σ_i is not $-\infty$) the probability of responding correctly to the item tends to 0. That is, the larger ξ_v, the higher the level of examinee v's ability. Conversely, if the difficulty parameter σ_i tends to ∞, then (given that ξ_v is not ∞) the probability of responding correctly to the item tends to 0; if the difficulty parameter σ_i tends to $-\infty$, then (given that ξ_v is not $-\infty$) the probability of responding correctly to the item tends to 1. That is, the larger σ_i, the more difficult item i is.

The item discrimination parameter α_i in the 3PL model refers to different discrimination powers of items with the same difficulty parameter. That is, for instance, two examinees with slightly different ability parameters may not differ in their probabilities of responding correctly to the same extent for two different but equally difficult items (see Figure 6.1). The larger α_i, the better an item can discriminate between the two examinees. The item guessing parameter β_i quantifies in particular for multiple-choice items the phenomenon of lucky guessing, that is, even an examinee with an ability parameter $\xi_v = -\infty$ has a chance larger than zero of responding correctly to the item (see Figure 6.1). Hence, $\beta_i \geq 0$. The model with some $\alpha_i > 1$, but all $\beta_i = 0$, is called the 2PL model (Birnbaum, 1968); obviously the 3PL model in Equation 1 implies some $\alpha_i > 1$ and some $\beta_i > 0$. The model with all $\alpha_i = 1$, but some $\beta_i > 0$, is called difficulty-plus-guessing-PL model (Kubinger & Draxler, 2006).

Since, of all the mentioned models, only the Rasch model allows for specific objective comparisons of examinees (as well as of items), we will restrict the following text to this model. Specific objective comparisons (Rasch, 1960/1980; but see also Scheiblechner, 2009) imply measurements that put subjects (or objects) in empirically adequate relationships to one another independent of which other subjects (or objects) have ever been or will be under consideration. This property of the Rasch model ensures that there are means of testing the model: based on empirical data, the hypothesis of whether the model holds for a certain item

---

1   Actually, Birnbaum (1968) used the symbol θ instead of ξ, b instead of σ, a instead of α, and c instead of β; as, however, in statistics Greek symbols are traditionally used for parameters (e.g., Rasch, Kubinger, Yanagida 2011), his denotations are inconsistent. We use in the following Georg Rasch's original denotation ξ (see Rasch, 1960/1980), and – although Rasch initially used either ε or δ – according to Gerhard Fischer's pioneering book (Fischer, 1974) the symbol σ.

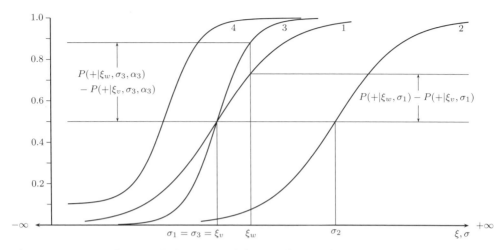

Figure 6.1. Item characteristic curves of the Rasch model, the 2PL, and the 3PL model. The curves represent the probability of responding correctly to item *i* dependent on the item difficulty parameter σ_i and the ability parameter ξ_v of any examinee *v*. Only Items 1 and 2 conform to the Rasch model. Both these items along with Item 3 fit the 2PL model; however, due to an item discrimination parameter $\alpha_3 > \alpha_1 = \alpha_2$, the latter item discriminates better, for example, between examinee *v* and *w* with ability parameters ξ_v and ξ_w – although $\sigma_1 = \sigma_3$. Finally, all four items as a pool fit the 3PL model, although Item 4 additionally depends on an item guessing parameter $\beta_4 > 0$.

pool can be tested. This goes beyond pertinent goodness-of-fit indices, which only indicate the extent to which the data can be explained by the model. The most well-known model test is Andersen's likelihood ratio test (for some standards of testing the Rasch model, see, e.g., Kubinger, 2005).

In fact, adaptive testing can occur only after item calibrations according to the given IRT model have taken place and not-fitting items have been deleted. The resulting item parameter estimations – in the best case based on a very large sample – are then considered to be the true item parameters themselves. Thus, in the statistical sense, all the items are seen as definite levels of a fixed factor and their characteristics (e.g., difficulties) are actually quantified by fixed parameters, not random variables.

Principles of Tailored Testing

The most effective type of adaptive testing is tailored testing: After each administered item, the most informative next item is provided for each examinee, personally. Although there are several suggestions on how to start tailored testing, there is one approach that is, for didactical reasons, most plausible. This approach involves beginning with an item whose difficulty parameter equals the median of the difficulty parameters of all items. If the examinee responds correctly to this item, he/she is presented with the most difficult item next, otherwise with the easiest one. By this means, it is most likely that the examinee has correctly responded to one of the first two items and has failed to response correctly to the other. This allows for an estimation of the initial ability parameter of the examinee (see, however, the approach of Warm, 1989, which allows for even earlier ability parameter estimations). In the worst but rare case, more than two items are needed in order to get finite parameter estimations: bear in mind that the ability parameter of an examinee who responds correctly to all items is estimated as ∞, and that the ability of an examinee who responds to no item correctly is estimated as $-\infty$ (again, however, see the approach of Warm, 1989, as well as several Bayes approaches presupposing a specific ability parameter distribution within the population in question; see van der Linden & Pashley, 2010).

Afterward, the most informative item can be chosen as follows. According to the mathematical definition of *information* in general (*information in the sample*; see the theory of maximum likelihood estimation by R.A. Fisher, e.g., Lord & Novick, 1968), in the case of IRT information leads to (see Fischer, 1974):

$$I_i(v) = \frac{\left[P_i'(+\,|\,v)\right]^2}{P(+\,|\,i,v)\cdot P(-\,|\,i,v)} \tag{3}$$

– that is, item i's information $I_i(v)$ is just a function of examinee v, in fact, of the probability of examinee v responding correctly to item i, $P(+\,|\,i,\,v)$, and, redundantly, of the probability of him/her failing to respond correctly to item i, $P(-\,|\,i,\,v)$. If $P(+\,|\,i,\,v) = P_i(+\,|\,v)$ is considered as a function of v itself, then $P_i'(+\,|\,v)$ is its first deviation. Actually, in the case of the Rasch model, $I_i(v)$ results at the very end as

$$I_i(v) = P\!\left(+\,\big|\,\xi_v,\sigma_i\right)\cdot P\!\left(-\,\big|\,\xi_v,\sigma_i\right) = \frac{e^{\xi_v-\sigma_i}}{1+e^{\xi_v-\sigma_i}}\cdot\frac{1}{1+e^{\xi_v-\sigma_i}} \tag{4}$$

Obviously, information reaches a maximum for $P(+\,|\,\xi_v,\,\sigma_i)\cdot P(-\,|\,\xi_v,\,\sigma_i) = \frac{1}{2}\cdot\frac{1}{2} = .25$. This result means that item difficulty σ_i must equal ξ_v. In fact, the same is true for the 2PL model, but not for the 3PL model (see Birnbaum, 1968) and the difficulty-plus-guessing-PL model; for both of these models, the item information is maximal for some $\xi_v > \sigma_i$.

To summarize, as soon as there is a finite ability parameter estimation $\hat{\xi}_v$ for examinee v, tailored testing involves looking for the maximally informative item (using $\hat{\xi}_v$ instead of ξ_v in Equations 3 and 4, respectively) that is to be administered next. After administration of this item, a (more accurate) ability parameter estimation can be established and the procedure repeated. The question of interest then is when to finish with that procedure's repetitions.

Obviously, this tailored testing technique requires ongoing computer calculations while the test is administered. For this reason, tailored testing is sometimes called *computerized adaptive testing* (CAT). However, *computer-assisted testing* suffices for this technique, as the examinee (e.g., a very young child or a very old person) does not need to be tested on a computer; the test examiner only needs to refer first to a computer before he/she can present the appropriate item by paper and pencil.

Principles of Branched Testing

A minor (but in comparison with conventional testing nevertheless quite) effective kind of adaptive testing is so-called branched testing – or multistage testing. Thereby the items are clustered in advance according to some intended cluster averages of item difficulty parameters and their ranges (or standard deviations): After each administered cluster of items, the optimally informative next item cluster is presented to the examinee in question. The optimally informative next item cluster is also determined in advance. As a consequence, an ability parameter estimation is not needed after each administered item (cluster), nor must any item's information $I_i(v)$ be calculated during testing. Hence, branched testing is more manageable than tailored testing if computerized test administration is not feasible. This is because all ability parameter estimations can be done in advance as well and do not necessarily have to be carried out during test administration. Ability parameter estimation for all possible combinations of administered item clusters and all the respective numbers of correctly responded items must be performed only once, before testing the first examinee. Bear in mind that the number of possible combinations of administered item clusters in branched testing is rather strictly limited, while the number of combinations of administered items in tailored testing, given the usual large item pool, comes rather close to an unfeasible size (see the problem of full enumeration, e.g., in Rasch, Kubinger & Yanagida, 2011). Therefore, tailored testing necessarily involves computer-assisted test administration, as emphasized before; branched testing does not.

In branched testing, the number of items in each cluster is preferably larger than one but should not exceed five or six. In addition to item cluster size, it is also necessary to determine how many stages the test will include and how differentiated the branching from one stage (item cluster) to the next stage (item cluster) will be. If there is an ability level grouping based on prior information (e.g., the examinee's age), it is important to decide how many starting item clusters shall be used at the first testing stage. Figure 6.2 gives an example of a 60-item pool

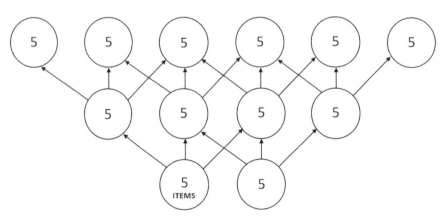

Figure 6.2.   An example of a branched testing design. There are two starting clusters, three stages, and item clusters of five items each. Imagine the item clusters ordered from left to right from the easiest to the most difficult (e.g., as concerns the mean item difficulty parameter), and imagine item clusters in a line from bottom to top as almost equally difficult. A three-way branching is shown: if the examinee has responded correctly to at most one item in the first or second stage, then he/she is presented with an easier item cluster next; if he/she has responded correctly to at least four items, then a more difficult item cluster is administered next, but if he/she responds correctly to two or three items (roughly half of the items), then an item cluster is administered that matches the (mean) item difficulty of the preceding item cluster. In all, each examinee is tested with 15 items.

divided into clusters of five items, using two starting clusters and a three-way branching; there are three stages for each examinee.

Specific Questions and Problems of Adaptive Testing

Although adaptive testing always assumes a given IRT-calibrated item pool, we will not go into detail as concerns item parameter estimation (for an excellent overview, see Baker & Kim, 2004). The following section considers only a specific problem of item difficulty parameter estimation in the case of adaptive testing. However, as concerns the estimation of ability parameters and calculation of the respective standard errors of estimation, we go into more depth.

The primary aim is to estimate an ability parameter for a certain examinee after he/she has completed at least two items, responding correctly to one and failing to respond correctly to the other. Here the maximum likelihood estimation approach is of use. The model-specific likelihood of the actual data is deduced given the fixed item parameters (see previous section). Using $\hat{\xi}_v$ as the estimation of ξ_v, that likelihood's first derivative (as a function of $\hat{\xi}_v$) must be set to zero in order to find an extremum (maximum). For instance, under the Rasch model, the likelihood in question is

$$L_v = \prod_{i=f_1(v)}^{f_{k_v}(v)} \left(\frac{e^{(\hat{\xi}_v - \sigma_i)}}{1 + e^{(\hat{\xi}_v - \sigma_i)}} \right)^{x_{vi}} \cdot \left(\frac{1}{1 + e^{(\hat{\xi}_v - \sigma_i)}} \right)^{1 - x_{vi}} \tag{5}$$

with $x_{vi} = 1$ if examinee v has correctly responded to item i and $x_{vi} = 0$ if v did not; $f_1(v), f_2(v), \dots$ $f_{k_v}(v)$ are the labels of the k_v items administered to examinee v. Numerical mathematics delivers several algorithms for iterative solutions of the extremum problem; for practical application, we recommend the R-package PP (person parameter estimation; Reif, 2012), which serves for 1-, 2-, and 3PL models and suits the frame of the R philosophy by offering open source and being under peer supervision.

Once the parameter estimation $\hat{\xi}_v$ is obtained, the optimal informative next item (cluster) is determined in the manner described previously – in the case of the Rasch model and tailored testing, this means looking for the item whose item difficulty parameter σ_i is nearest to $\hat{\xi}_v$. Bear in mind that branched testing could happen similarly, but the design of branching and the allocation of items to item clusters has, so far, been done rather intuitively. Although long ago Kubinger and Wild (1989) demonstrated that certain alternatives of a given design would lead to a higher accuracy of measurement, no algorithm for arranging the items in order to achieve the highest (expected) measurement accuracy has yet been established. Of course, fully enumerating the items (see, again, Rasch et al., 2011) and then embedding the resulting clusters in several concurrent designs of branching would work.

Given an estimation $\hat{\xi}_{v(k)}$ after k tailored administered items, the next estimation $\hat{\xi}_{v(k+1)} = \hat{\xi}_v$ is to be calculated accordingly, and so on. However, some criterion is needed to determine when the test administration should be stopped. In addition to criteria based on practical restrictions due to (1) the reasonability of test duration, (2) the number of remaining items, and (3) the availability of items with an item difficulty parameter appropriately fitting the current ability parameter estimation, there are two statistical criteria: (a) an irrelevant difference of two succeeding ability parameter estimations $\hat{\xi}_{v(k)}$ and $\hat{\xi}_{v(k+1)}$, or (b) a standard error of estimation that is lower than a given target value. While (2) and (3) correlate to some extent and both refer to an insufficient item pool, (1) defines some maximal number of items to administer. Criterion

(a) might also be met simply because the item pool is insufficient. Hence, only criterion (b) satisfies in a fundamental way, although it, too, could fail to be met because of an insufficient item pool.

As concerns the standard error of estimation, once more the theory of maximum likelihood estimation of R. A. Fisher applies, as does his definition of information (in the sample). The reciprocal of the information $I_i(v)$ given in Equations 3 and 4, summarized over all items administered to examinee v, constitutes the variance of the error of (maximum likelihood) estimation. With respect to the Rasch model, this leads to the following standard error of estimation $S(\hat{\xi}_v)$:

$$S(\hat{\xi}_v) = \sqrt{\dfrac{1}{\displaystyle\sum_{i=f_1(v)}^{f_{k_v}(v)} I_i(v)}} = \left[\sum_{i=f_1(v)}^{f_{k_v}(v)} \dfrac{e^{\hat{\xi}_v - \sigma_i}}{1 + e^{\hat{\xi}_v - \sigma_i}} \cdot \dfrac{1}{1 + e^{\hat{\xi}_v - \sigma_i}}\right]^{-\frac{1}{2}} \tag{6}$$

Again, the R-package PP (Reif, 2012) is recommend here for practical application. Beyond its role as a criterion for breaking off test administration, the standard error of estimation $S(\hat{\xi}_v)$ can serve to calculate a confidence interval

$$\xi_v^{1,2} = \hat{\xi}_v \pm z_{\alpha/2} \cdot S(\hat{\xi}_v) \tag{7}$$

with $z_{\alpha/2}$ as the $\alpha/2$-quantile of the normal distribution and α as the confidence coefficient, that is, the probability for the correctness of the conclusion that ξ_v lies within that interval.

Comparison of Test Performance of Different Examinees Tested by Different Items

Obviously, using Equation 5, any examinees can be compared with respect to their test performances in a fair manner. No matter which items each examinee has processed, the estimation of his/her ability parameter is the same. Take, for instance, an examinee v who responds correctly to Item 1 and Item 9, but not to Item 5. In this case, ability parameter estimation is given by

$$L_v = \prod_{i=f_1(v)}^{f_{k_v}(v)} \left(\dfrac{e^{(\hat{\xi}_v - \sigma_i)}}{1 + e^{(\hat{\xi}_v - \sigma_i)}}\right)^{x_{vi}} \cdot \left(\dfrac{1}{1 + e^{(\hat{\xi}_v - \sigma_i)}}\right)^{1 - x_{vi}} =$$

$$P\left(1^+, 5^-, 9^+ \middle| \hat{\xi}_v; \sigma_1, \sigma_5, \sigma_9\right) = \dfrac{e^{\hat{\xi}_v - \sigma_1}}{1 + e^{\hat{\xi}_v - \sigma_1}} \cdot \dfrac{1}{1 + e^{\hat{\xi}_v - \sigma_5}} \cdot \dfrac{e^{\hat{\xi}_v - \sigma_9}}{1 + e^{\hat{\xi}_v - \sigma_9}} = max \tag{8}$$

Another examinee w, responding correctly to Items 2 and 3, but not to Item 4, would have an analogous ability parameter estimate $\hat{\xi}_w$. The distance between $\hat{\xi}_w$ and $\hat{\xi}_v$ discloses differences on the target ability dimension in an interval-scaled manner. Using the standard error of estimation of Equation 6 – or 7, applied one-sided twice – would even offer a test of whether the two examinees differ significantly.

Precondition: There Are No Item Position Effects

As already emphasized, the approach of adaptive testing depends on a given IRT-calibrated item pool. If the items do not fit the model in question, in particular if the item pool (significantly) contradicts the Rasch model, then the indicated ability parameter estimation is absolutely inadequate. In the worst case, the items, as a pool, do not measure the same ability, and therefore unidimensional measurement of ξ fails. In the best case, only differential item functioning (DIF; for an excellent overview, see Teresi et al., 2009) takes place, meaning that a few items handicap some particular subpopulations of examinees. In any of these cases, serious measurement through either conventional or adaptive testing is not possible.

Even if there is a proper IRT-calibrated item pool, however, it is also necessary to test whether the model in question holds for the item pool in general or only for a certain sequence of administered items. Of course, adaptive testing is completely compromised if the difficulty parameter σ_i of an item changes depending on the item's position in the administered test sequence: if σ_1 changes to $\sigma_1^* = \sigma_1 + c$ when the item is administered at position x instead of position y ($x \neq y$), then all of Equation 8 changes as well. A fair comparison of different examinees' test performances becomes impossible in such cases, because there are no fixed item difficulty parameters at all. Even if two examinees have been tested using the same items, their scores become incomparable as soon as the items are administered at different positions. Kubinger (2009b) showed how an item pool can best be tested in regard to item position effects by using the LLTM (linear logistic test model; Fischer, 1973). Hohensinn, Kubinger, Reif, Schleicher, and Khorramdel (2011) applied this approach and illustrated that there are, in fact, psychological and educational tests that disclose generalized model conformity of an item pool (although their analysis is applied to large-scale assessment, this also assumes position-independent item difficulty parameters).

In short: the quality of an adaptive test must always be evaluated by making sure there are no existing item position effects.

Superiority of Adaptive Testing Over Conventional Testing

In addition to the thought-provoking paper of Weiss (1982), early support for the superiority of adaptive testing is given in an overview by Bloxom (1989). With a focus on accuracy of measurement (reliability) and mostly based on simulation studies, one was able to show that adaptive testing either reached an accuracy equivalent to that of conventional testing using substantially fewer items or measured much more accurately using the same number of items. In the following, we provide an empirical example (see Kubinger, 1987) based on 53 Rasch model-calibrated items. In sum, normalized to zero, the item difficulty parameters ranged from –7.0 to 6.0, following a rather peaked distribution with a standard deviation of 3.5. The focus of the investigation was the ability continuum between $-5.0 \leq \xi \leq 5.0$, specifically all the values in this range at 0.25 intervals (see Figure 6.3). For each ability parameter, the following five procedures were applied:

(1) Using ξ_v instead of $\hat{\xi}_v$ in Equation 6, the standard error of estimation $\Sigma(\xi_v)$ was calculated under the assumption that all the 53 items were conventionally administered (see Graph a in Figure 6.3).

(2) In all, 300 simulated participants with ability parameter ξ_v were created and tailored tested. That is, using a random number generator and Equation 2 (Rasch model), the responses of simulee v to 15 adaptively administered items $f_1(v), f_2(v), \ldots f_{15}(v)$, were simulated as either being correct or incorrect. The resulting estimation $\hat{\xi}_v$ of each of the 300 simulees was then used in Equation 6 in order to ascertain the standard error of estimation $S(\hat{\xi}_v)$. Finally, the mean of all these standard errors was computed (see Graph b in Figure 6.3).

(3) Using ξ_v instead of $\hat{\xi}_v$ in Equation 6, the standard error of estimation $\Sigma(\xi_v)$ was calculated assuming conventional administration of only 15 items whose difficulty parameters formed a peaked distribution in the interval $-5.0 \leq \xi \leq 5.0$ (see Graph c in Figure 6.3).

(4) Using ξ_v instead of $\hat{\xi}_v$ in Equation 6, the standard error of estimation $\Sigma(\xi_v)$ was calculated assuming conventional administration of only 15 items whose difficulty parameters were equally distributed in the interval $-5.0 \leq \xi \leq 5.0$ (see Graph d in Figure 6.3).

(5) Referring to the branched testing design of Figure 6.2 and using ξ_v instead of $\hat{\xi}_v$ in Equation 6, the standard error of estimation $\Sigma(\xi_v)$ was calculated for each possible combination of three item clusters (altogether 15 items). Computing their weighted average resulted in an expected standard error of estimation $E(\xi_v)$. The weights were chosen as the Rasch model probabilities that any examinee with ability parameter ξ_v would work on the specific combination of item clusters under consideration (for the exact equation, see Kubinger & Wild, 1989). As there were two starting clusters, two separate analyses were performed (see Graph e_1 and e_2 in Figure 6.3; note that curve e_1 starting from approximately $\xi_v > 3.0$ constitutes a decision for the wrong starting cluster, and the same is true for curve e_2 starting from approximately $\xi_v < -3.0$).

Figure 6.3 discloses that conventional testing with almost four times as many items administered results in smaller standard errors of estimation than tailored testing, although the differences are not overwhelming (bear in mind that psychological assessment is very often applied

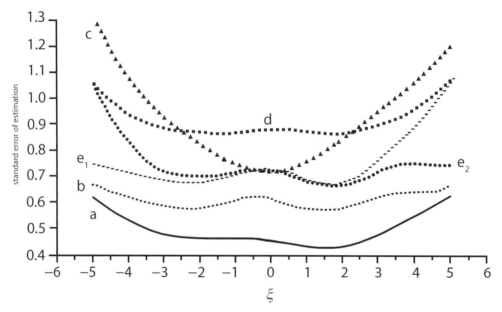

Figure 6.3. The (actual, estimated, or expected) standard error of estimation for five different testing procedures using an arbitrarily chosen empirically given item pool of 53 items whose difficulty parameters followed a peaked distribution: (a) conventional testing with all 53 items; (b) tailored testing with 15 items; (c) conventional testing with 15 items whose difficulty parameters followed a peaked distribution; (d) conventional testing with 15 items whose difficulty parameters followed an equal distribution; (e_1) and (e_2) branched testing according to Figure 6.2 with 15 items ([e_1] corresponds to the left starting cluster – due to prior information about the examinee's ability level – and [e_2] corresponds to the right).

in cases of extreme abilities, where the observed differences are smallest). However, in contrast to conventional tests with the same number of items, tailored testing is clearly superior; especially the item difficulty parameters following a peaked distribution lead to substantially higher standard errors of estimation when extreme abilities are under consideration. As indicated, branched testing is slightly inferior to tailored testing as concerns accuracy of measurement – if the same number of items are used. In comparison with both conventional tests with the same number of items, however, branched testing is clearly superior as long as the starting cluster has not been chosen inadequately (see the lower portions of the [e] curves in Figure 6.3); an exception applies only for a medium ξ_v and the conventional test with item difficulty parameters following a peaked distribution.

Although formerly a general rule of thumb was sometimes posited (see Hornke, 2001) stating that an item pool of about 60 items suffices for appropriate accuracy of measurement when 15 items are adaptively (tailored) used, today we have to admit that there is no general rule. The number of necessary items does not primarily depend on the degree of accuracy that satisfies practitioners, but on the content and material of the test. Specifically, it depends on whether enough items with very low and very high difficulties can be realistically generated, and whether learning effects occur after, say, 5 to 10 items, so that the problem of item position effects comes into play (see previous section). Hence, we simply recommend that the item pool of any new psychological or educational test should be expanded until it leads to satisfactory standard errors of estimation according to a simulation study (assuming a reasonable number of administered items). Of course, this sounds odd, because each additional item would need to be tested in terms of its conformity with the IRT model in question, which is only possible after hundreds of examinees have been tested using this item and some or all of the items in the original item pool. For this reason, the approach suggested by Fischer and Pendl (1980) is to be preferred. This approach consists of applying the LLTM (see previous section) and ascertaining difficulty parameters for all basic (cognitive) item components that comprise every item; if the model (LLTM) holds, then these components establish item-generating rules, and new items containing new combinations of such components can be designed. Because the difficulties of the item components are known, the difficulty of the new items can be easily calculated without a further calibration study. Admittedly, this approach has hardly been empirically realized, but one example can be found, for instance, in Arendasy (2005). Nevertheless, it should be noted that if special content or material does not allow for the development of an item pool of, say, 100 or more items with difficulty parameters equally distributed across a very large range, making adaptive testing problematic, then conventional testing will not satisfy serious demands on accuracy of measurement, either. On the other hand, if there are actually not more than, say, 30–40 items, but these have a wide range of difficulty parameters and challenge the examinee for a rather long response time (so that not more than 7–10 items per test session are reasonable), then adaptive testing is still useful. Moreover, if the test only serves as a screening instrument for discriminating two classes of ability levels without any exact point estimation (e.g., so-called mastery tests) and the time for test application is limited, then adaptive testing is the method of choice.

To summarize, adaptive testing, whether tailored or branched, is superior for economic reasons – if the accuracy of measurement is of any practical relevance at all. If this is the case, thorough development of the item pool with equally distributed item difficulty parameters can provide equiprecise measurements, while conventional testing with items whose difficulty parameters follow a peaked distribution often fails to produce appropriate accuracy of measurement in cases of extreme ability levels. A side effect of adaptive testing is that because different examinees are most likely to be administered many different items, the item pool does not become publicly known as quickly as in the case of a conventional test. In other words, the diagnostic half-life period increases, that is, the time until some items are known in half of the relevant population (Kubinger, 2009a). A second side effect is that, in the case of repeated testing, an examinee completing an adaptive test has a very good chance of being presented with different items the second time or can even systematically be tested with other items because of the large item pool. A third claimed side effect is that, according to achievement motivation theories, the reduced number of items that are much too easy or much too difficult for an examinee makes both demotivation and frustration less likely to occur. A counterargument, however, is that examinees experience stress when completing items that are not ordered according to their difficulty. In adaptive testing, easier items sometimes follow difficult items; in other words, after failing to respond correctly to an item that was too challenging, an examinee may be confused to see a rather simple item and suspect a trick question. An early experiment of Roßmann (1992) definitely rejects this last counterargument: even 6- to 7-year-old children (as well as 12- to 15-year-old adolescents) showed no differences in mean ability parameter estimates or in mean achievement motivation scores at the beginning, middle, and end of testing, regardless of whether they were adaptively or conventionally tested. Nevertheless, the results of Ortner and Caspers (2011) emphasize that failing to inform examinees about the manner in which administered items will be selected diminishes the test performance relevantly, particularly if an examinee suffers from test anxiety.

It is important to note that presenting fewer items through adaptive testing does not automatically mean saving time. As already indicated by Wild (1989), the lack of easy items at the very beginning of a test might delay a necessary warming-up effect for moderate and difficult items that can be completed quickly only when administered after a given number of preceding items. Thus, even if there is no item position effect as concerns the item difficulty parameters, such an effect might still exist for response times. As Thissen and Mislevy (2000) pointed out, if response times and item difficulty parameters correlate, then different examinees need different test administration times, even if they are administered the same number of items.

Parameter Estimation Problems

Although Glas (1988) indicated early that pertinent Rasch model item calibration leads to biased item parameter estimations if items are administered using branched testing, test constructors may not be aware of this fact. Of course this problem does not arise if item calibration is based on samples of examinees administered with the item pool in a conventional manner. This includes the use of so-called test booklets, where a (very large) item pool is partitioned into several nondisjunctive item subpools, each of which is administered to a different (randomly allocated) group of examinees. More precisely, the different test booklets must be conceptualized according to a connected incomplete block design (see Rasch et al., 2011) in order to make item parameter estimations for the item pool as a whole possible (e.g., Kubinger et al., 2011, give an illustrative example of such an item linking strategy). On the other hand, although Eggen and Verhelst (2011) claim that parameter estimation is only problematic for branched testing when conditional maximum likelihood (CML) estimation is used instead of marginal maximum likelihood (MML) estimation, Kubinger, Steinfeld, Reif, and Yanagida (2012) show that this is only true when the stated mixture distributions of the ability parameters are actually appropriate. Their results also relativize the problem somewhat: using biased item difficulty parameter estimations like the parameters in Equations 5, they show that while ability parameter estimations within branched testing are similarly biased, the estimations' corresponding percentile ranks coincide with those of the true ability parameters. In other words, the item parameter estimation bias (due to conditional maximum likelihood estimation) that occurs if estimates are based on items administered according to a branched testing design does not have a relevant effect for case consulting. Examinees are assigned almost exactly the same percentile rank, whether biased or unbiased ability parameter estimations are used: The relative position of all the examinees within the population in question remains the same. For the present, this is true at least for the given simulation study exemplifying a specific branched testing design. However, these results also mean that analogous simulation studies must be performed by future test constructors when item calibration data are sampled in this manner.

Advancements

The fact that adaptive testing is of increasing interest in theory and practice is shown, for instance, in a recent special issue of the journal *Psychological Test and Assessment Modeling*, "Current issues in educational and psychological measurement: design, calibration, and adaptive testing," edited by Kröhne and Frey (2012, 2013).

The currently most appreciated advancement of adaptive testing is probably multidimensional adaptive testing (e.g., Frey & Seitz, 2009). This is appropriate if the items of a test measure more than a single ability dimension, but the measured dimensions correlate with each other. In this case, items are selected to be maximally informative with reference to all the vectors of ability parameters of the examinee in question. However, it is important to note that this approach regresses to correlation statistics; as a consequence, analyses depend on the concrete sample distributions. By contrast, the aforementioned Rasch model offers specific objective comparisons of examinees, meaning that measurements are independent of the population's ability parameter distribution.

For further advancements, see van der Linden (2008) and, above all, the collective volume by van der Linden and Glas (2010). These deal in particular with adaptive use of test batteries, the use of response times in adaptive testing, constraining adaptive testing representatively according to given clusters of item contents, and adaptive testing with so-called testlets (where several items refer to the same text information).

Moreover, we emphasize in this contribution that any indicated improvement of pure and original adaptive testing, either tailored or branched, would constitute an important advancement. That is:
1. Deliberately testing each item pool for actual item position effects;
2. Aiming for rule-based item generation;
3. Establishing branched testing designs with optimized accuracy of measurement based on full enumeration all the items in item clusters instead of mere intuition; and
4. Calibrating branched testing items either by first administering the items conventionally or by carrying out simulation studies in advance in order to determine the actual extent of item parameter estimation bias due to the given branched testing design.

Summary

A short introduction into the theory and practice of adaptive testing is given. All above, its embedment in item response theory (IRT) is demonstrated. The main message is that psychological and educational test construction appropriate for adaptive testing always pays when (relatively) high measurement accuracy and (relatively) short test length are of interest.

References

Arendasy, M. (2005). Automatic generation of Rasch-calibrated items: Figural matrices test GEOM and Endless-Loops Test Ec. *International Journal of Testing, 5*, 197–224. http://doi.org/10.1207/s15327574ijt0503_2

Baker, F. B., & Kim, S. H. (2004). *Item response theory: Parameter estimation techniques* (2nd ed.). New York, NY: Dekker.

Birnbaum, A. (1968). Some latent trait models and their use in inferring an examinee's ability. In F. M. Lord & M. R. Novick (Eds.), *Statistical theories of mental test scores* (pp. 395–479). Reading, MA: Addison-Wesley.

Bloxom, B. (1989). Adaptive testing: A review of recent results. *Zeitschrift für Differentielle und Diagnostische Psychologie, 10*, 1–17.

Eggen, T. J. H. M., & Verhelst, N. D. (2011). Item calibration in incomplete testing designs. *Psicológica, 32*, 107–132.

Fischer, G. H. (1973). The linear logistic test model as an instrument in educational research. *Acta Psychologica, 37*, 359–374. http://doi.org/10.1016/0001-6918(73)90003-6

Fischer, G. H. (1974). *Einführung in die Theorie psychologischer Tests* [Introduction into theory of psychological tests]. Bern, Switzerland: Huber.

Fischer, G. H., & Pendl, P. (1980). Individualized testing on the basis of the dichotomous Rasch model. In L. J. D. van der Kamp, W. F. Langerak, & D. N. M. De Gruijter (Eds.), *Psychometrics for educational debates* (pp. 171–188). New York, NY: Wiley.

Frey, A., & Seitz, N. N. (2009). Multidimensional adaptive testing in educational and psychological measurement: Current state and future challenges. *Studies in Educational Evaluation, 35*, 89–94. http://doi.org/10.1016/j.stueduc.2009.10.007

Glas, C. A. W. (1988). The Rasch model and multistage testing. *Journal of Educational Statistics, 13*, 45–52. http://doi.org/10.3102/10769986013001045

Hohensinn, C., & Kubinger, K. D. (2011). On the impact of missing values on item fit and the model validness of the Rasch model. *Psychological Test and Assessment Modeling, 53*, 380–393.

Hohensinn, C., Kubinger, K. D., Reif, M., Schleicher, E., & Khorramdel, L. (2011). Analysing item position effects due to test booklet design within large-scale assessment. *Educational Research and Evaluation, 17*, 497–509. http://doi.org/10.1080/13803611.2011.632668

Hornke, L. F. (2001). Benötigte Itemanzahlen beim mess- und entscheidungsorientierten adaptiven Testen [Necessary number of items for adaptive testing]. *Zeitschrift für Differentielle und Diagnostische Psychologie, 23*, 185–193. http://doi.org/10.1024//0170-1789.22.3.185

Kröhne, U., & Frey, A. (Eds.). (2012). Current issues in educational and psychological measurement: design, calibration, and adaptive testing; Part I. *Psychological Test and Assessment Modeling, 53*, 363–460.

Kröhne, U., & Frey, A. (Eds.). (2013). Current issues in educational and psychological measurement: design, calibration, and adaptive testing; Part II. *Psychological Test and Assessment Modeling, 54*, 79–123.

Kubinger, K. D. (1987). Adaptives Testen [Adaptive testing]. In R. Horn, K. Ingenkamp, & R. S. Jäger (Eds.), *Tests und Trends 6* [Tests and trends] (pp. 103–127). Weinheim, Germany: Beltz.

Kubinger, K. D. (2005). Psychological test calibration using the Rasch model – some critical suggestions on traditional approaches. *International Journal of Testing, 5*, 377–394. http://doi.org/10.1207/s15327574ijt0504_3

Kubinger, K. D. (2009a). *Psychologische Diagnostik – Theorie und Praxis psychologischen Diagnostizierens* (2nd ed.) [Psychological assessment – Theory and practice of psychological consulting]. Göttingen, Germany: Hogrefe.

Kubinger, K. D. (2009b). Applications of the linear logistic test model in psychometric research. *Educational and Psychological Measurement, 69*, 232–244. http://doi.org/10.1177/0013164408322021

Kubinger, K. D., & Draxler, C. (2006). A comparison of the Rasch model and constrained item response theory models for pertinent psychological test data. In M. von Davier & C. H. Carstensen (Eds.), *Multivariate and mixture distribution Rasch models – extensions and applications* (pp. 295–312). New York, NY: Springer.

Kubinger, K. D., Hohensinn, C., Hofer, S., Khorramdel, L., Frebort, M., Holocher-Ertl, S., ... Sonnleitner, P. (2011). Designing the test booklets for Rasch model calibration in a large scale assessment with reference to numerous moderator variables and several ability dimensions. *Educational Research and Evaluation, 17*, 483–495. http://doi.org/10.1080/13803611.2011.632666

Kubinger, K. D., Steinfeld, J., Reif, M., & Yanagida, T. (2012). Biased (conditional) parameter estimation of a Rasch model calibrated item pool administered according to a branched-testing design. *Psychological Test and Assessment Modeling, 54*, 450–461.

Kubinger, K. D., & Wild, B. (1989). Die Optimierung der Meßgenauigkeit beim „branched"-adaptiven Testen [Optimizing the accuracy of measurement for branched testing]. In K. D. Kubinger (Ed.), *Moderne Testtheorie – Ein Abriß samt neuesten Beiträgen* [Modern psychometrics – a brief survey with recent contributions] (2nd ed., pp. 187–218). Munich, Germany: PVU.

Lord, F. M., & Novick, M. R. (Eds.). (1968). *Statistical theories of mental test scores* (pp. 395–479). Reading, MA: Addison-Wesley.

Ortner, T. M., & Caspers, J. (2011). Consequences of test anxiety on adaptive versus fixed item testing. *European Journal of Psychological Assessment, 27*, 157–163. http://doi.org/10.1027/1015-5759/a000062

Rasch, G. (1960/1980). *Probabilistic models for some intelligence and attainment tests.* Chicago, IL: University of Chicago Press.

Rasch, D., Kubinger, K. D., & Yanagida, T. (2011). *Statistics in psychology – using R and SPSS.* Chichester, UK: Wiley. http://doi.org/10.1002/9781119979630

Reif, M. (2012). *PP: Person parameter estimation. R package (Version 0.2)* [Computer software]. Retrieved from http://cran.r-project.org

Roßmann, G. (1992). *Motivationale Effekte beim adaptiven Testen* [Achievement motivation effects at adaptive testing] (Unpublished master's thesis). University of Vienna, Austria.

Scheiblechner, H. H. (2009). Rasch and pseudo-Rasch models: suitableness for practical test applications. *Psychology Science Quarterly, 51*, 181–194.

Teresi, J. A., Ocepek-Welikson, K., Kleinman, M., Eimicke, J. P., Jones, R. N., Lai, J. S., ... Cella, D. (2009). Analysis of differential item functioning in the depression item bank from the Patient Reported Outcome Measurement Information System (PROMIS): An item response theory approach. *Psychology Science Quarterly, 51*, 148–180.

Thissen, D., & Mislevy, R. J. (2000). Testing algorithms. In H. Wainer (Ed.), *Computerized adaptive testing: A primer.* Mahwah, NJ: Lawrence Erlbaum Associates.

van der Linden, W. J. (2008). Some new developments in adaptive testing technology. *Zeitschrift für Psychologie / Journal of Psychology, 216*, 3–11. http://doi.org/10.1027/0044-3409.216.1.3

van der Linden, W. J., & Glas, C. A. W. (Eds.). (2010). *Elements of adaptive testing.* New York, NY: Springer. http://doi.org/10.1007/978-0-387-85461-8

van der Linden, W. J., & Pashley, P. J. (2010). Item selection and ability estimation in adaptive testing. In W. J. van der Linden & C. A. W. Glas (Eds.), *Elements of adaptive testing* (pp. 3–30). New York, NY: Springer.

Walter, O. B. (2010). Adaptive tests for measuring anxiety and depression. In W. J. van der Linden & C. A. W. Glas (Eds.), *Elements of adaptive testing* (pp. 123–136). New York, NY: Springer.

Warm, T. A. (1989). Weighted likelihood estimation of ability in item response theory. *Psychometrika, 54*, 427–450. http://doi.org/10.1007/BF02294627

Weiss, D. J. (1982). Improving measurement quality and efficiency with adaptive theory. *Applied Psychological Measurement, 6*, 473–492.

Wild, B. (1989). Neue Erkenntnisse zur Effizienz des „tailored"-adaptiven Testens [New results on the efficiency of tailored adaptive testing]. In K. D. Kubinger (Ed.), *Moderne Testtheorie - Ein Abriß samt neuesten Beiträgen* [Modern psychometrics – a brief survey with recent contributions] (2nd ed., pp. 179–186). Munich, Germany: PVU.

Chapter 7

Online Assessment

Siegbert Reiss[1] and Ulf-Dietrich Reips[2]

[1]Department of Psychology, Goethe University Frankfurt, Germany
[2]Department of Psychology, University of Konstanz, Germany

Introduction

Until the end of the last century, a large part of the work in the area of technology-based assessment concentrated on the administration of conventional tests by computer. Afterwards, the universal presence of the Internet has spurred current development in assessment. The Internet has opened new ways of testing by facilitating the distribution of test materials, extending the options of item presentation, enhancing the time and locations for independent collection of data, and offering increased convenience for the examinees. Because in online-testing, neither the test taker nor the testing professional needs to be on-site for test administration and scoring, analyses of results and test evaluation can usually be automated. This approach is cost-effective and leads to considerable economic advantages after initial investment. In general, it seems to be easier to compile representative norming samples for different populations, see, for example, the multiple site entry technique (e.g., Birnbaum & Reips, 2005). Test-takers can be given their results immediately after completing a test and norms can be constantly updated. Second, a large database of items offers the possibility to produce IRT-scaled items and to conduct adaptive testing. Furthermore, advantages from computer-based testing as compared to paper-and-pencil testing are inherent in Internet-based testing. A paper-and-pencil approach may limit the way some abilities, skills and competences can be measured. In contrast, computer-based testing extends the available media and allows the presentation of various scenarios and the assessment of behavior under such scenarios. It encourages the development of innovative types of tasks and items, including automatically scored essay questions, simulations of laboratory science experiments, and other forms of constructed response items that require students to produce, rather than just select, their answers (for more information on item formats, see Chapter 5, this volume). Many of these efforts have sought to incorporate the most recent information technology innovations to expand the range of activities in which students can engage. Another aspect to consider in this context is the positive reaction of test takers towards Internet assessments. Salgado and Moscoso (2003) as well as Potosky and Bobko (2004) found that Internet-based tests were more positively perceived by test-takers than the paper-and-pencil version of the same tests.

Internet-based testing, as with the other three types of Internet-based research methods (non-reactive web-based methods, web surveys, and web experiments), requires attention to various peculiarities that sometimes substantially alter a test administrator's testing routines (Reips, 2006). The various advantages of online assessment are countered by a number of disadvantages that place specific requirements on their use. First, the usability of the websites on which the test is executed must be guaranteed to ensure an unbiased and consistent performance of the test taker. Usability exceeds the requirement that the website must work without error. It is just as important to consider how easily and quickly the users can perform the tasks, how many errors users make when working on the website, and how satisfied users are with the appearance of and navigation on the website. Furthermore, data security measures are required to prevent the dissemination (and potential abuse) of confidential data.

Usually, psychometric tests are designed to be administered under controlled, standardized conditions. In contrast to traditional psychological testing that requires the presence of a test administrator, Internet-based tests are administrated to individuals outside a traditional proctored setting. An unproctored Internet test could be completed by applicants literally anywhere Internet is available. Test takers may complete assessment instruments in different locations, and under different physical and psychological conditions (e.g., Carstairs & Myors, 2009). In fact, it cannot be ruled out that any of these conditions interact with the measurement of the construct of interest. At least for personality measures, Arthur and colleagues (Arthur, Glaze, Villado, & Taylor, 2010, p. 15) demonstrated that unproctored Internet testing and proctored tests seem to reveal similar levels of cheating or response distortion as traditional testing situations. All in all, Richman, Kiesler, Weisband, and Drasgow (1999) could not find larger bias effects in their meta-analytic study of social desirability distortion in computer administered questionnaires than in traditional questionnaires (for Internet-based questionnaires, see Kaufmann & Reips, 2008). For a detailed discussion of open questions regarding unproctored Internet testing, see Tippins (2009).

However, if assessment results are to be used for an important purpose, one needs to establish that the results have not been biased by lack of standardization. While this necessity applies in general for paper-based tests in a proctored test environment as well, it should, however, be emphasized that Internet-based tests, of course, must comply with the same high psychometric quality requirements, (i.e., a sufficient level of validity), as other diagnostic instruments (Buchanan, 2001; Buchanan & Smith, 1999).

Numerous comparability studies have been conducted in the last years on a variety of psychological tests to examine whether test presentation mode – computer-based or paper-based – affects examinee performance (e.g., Davis, 1999; Texas Education Agency, 2008; Wang & Shin, 2010; Weigold, Weigold, & Russell, 2013). Whilst some studies have found benefits relating to computer administration and others have favored paper-based, the majority of recent comparability studies have indicated that computer-based and paper-based tests are comparable across delivery medium, at least in the multiple-choice format (Kingston, 2009; Mead & Drasgow, 1993; Noyes & Garland, 2008). The two methods produce similar statistical distributions (means, standard deviations, reliabilities, and standard errors of measurement) of test scores and are comparable in their predictive validity estimates. To minimize test irrelevant variance originating from an online administration, a number of documents relevant to standards and good practice for online testing have been published in the last years (e.g., Allan, Bulla & Goodman, 2003; Bailey, Schneider, & Ark, 2012; Bartram, 2006; International Test Commission, 2006; Lievens, 2006; Naglieri et al., 2004; Scheuermann & Guimarães Pereira, 2008). The objective of these guidelines is to complement the existing Standards for educational and psychological testing with a specific focus on computer-based and Internet-delivered testing. As a product of an intensive process of international collaboration and review, the International Test Commission (ITC) guidelines provides a valuable reference for best practices when conducting Internet-based testing. These guidelines are directed towards all stakeholders involved in the process of online testing such as the users, the developers and the publishers of computer-based tests (CBTs) and Internet tests. The ITC guidelines (International Test Commission, 2006) address performance characteristics and technical limitations of the Internet as a test delivery medium (i.e., network speed, integrity, bandwidth, item presentation etc.), quality issues (i.e., psychometric qualities), control issues (i.e., control over the test conditions) and security issues (e.g., keeping scoring routines confidential, controlling access to test results, legal issues relating to data protection, privacy and storage).

Item Presentation and Response Acquisition

As mentioned, a computer-based presentation extends the media available for presentation and affects response modes, stimulus materials, and the input devices of the test (Dolan, Burling, Harms, Strain-Seymour, & Way, 2013; Educational Testing Service [ETS], 2012; Rosen & Tager, 2013; Sireci & Zenisky, 2006). Aside from single and multiple-choice format, fill-in-the-blank, highlighting, inserting text, and drag and drop techniques, various graphical response modes are available. Tasks and items may include animations, interactive and static graphics, embedded audio files and video clips. Input devices include the recent information technology hardware like keyboard, mouse, touch screen, light pen, joystick, graphics tablet, voice recorder, personal digital assistant or smartphone, etc., often equipped with speech and handwriting recognition software. An example of a task with video embedded is shown in Figure 7.1. The test administrator can choose whether the video should immediately begin to be played on the webpage or provide buttons to start, pause, and stop the video.

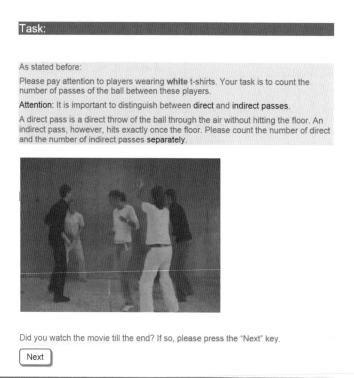

Figure 7.1. Web-based assessment task with video embedded.

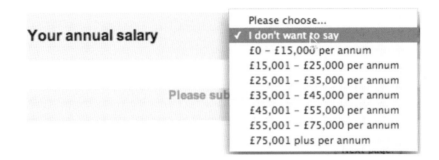

Figure 7.2.   Drop-down menu item with preselected "I don't want to say" option in second position.

In a second example, Figure 7.2 shows some of the challenges in drop-down or pop-up menus (Reips, 2002). Options only appear after the menu is clicked with the mouse arrow, then one option needs to be selected my moving the mouse arrow and releasing the mouse button. Thus, item options may differ in physical and cognitive accessibility.

Despite the availability of many new options for response presentation and functionality Buchanan and Reips (2001) observed that respondent personality is associated with technology preferences and thus, recommended a low-tech philosophy of designing Internet-based questionnaires and tests to avoid systematic errors. This principle is further supported by findings showing difficulties for individuals with lower education levels when technologically challenging response formats (e.g., slider scales) are presented (Funke, Reips, & Thomas, 2011).

Reips (2010) categorizes design and formatting issues with questionnaires and tests on the Internet into two types: (a) blatant errors and (b) design decisions made consciously, but without the designer realizing that the format makes the test less useable or, in worst case scenarios, worthless for research purposes. He cites a typical example that shows the following errors (among others) that frequently appear in Internet-based questionnaires:
• Including preselected answers in drop-down menus or radio button lists;
• Volume of text to be entered in text fields is not limited;
• Lack of options that indicate reluctance to answer (e.g., "I don't want to answer");
• All items on one run-on webpage rather than following a one-item-one-screen (OIOS) design; and
• Background information on the survey accidentally being revealed via the URL of the survey.

Online Self-Assessment

One area where Internet testing has blossomed is the area of online self-assessment. These tests are usually embedded in the context of electronic application processes or of technology-enhanced learning environments and require diagnostic self-testing by the participants.

If we examine the research about how accurately people judge themselves, the usual finding is that people have low insight to objectively assess their own skills and character. A meta-analysis by Freund and Kasten (2012) found that self-estimates of cognitive ability were positive, but moderately correlated with psychometrically measured cognitive ability at a level of roughly .33. One explanation for this weak correlation is that people do not have the knowledge and information necessary to assess their competence adequately. On the other hand, several studies suggest that integrating self-assessments improved the learning outcome and the accurate appraisal of their own performance (e.g., Chang, Liang, & Chen, 2013; Li & De Luca, 2012; Ross, 2006; Wang, 2007, 2009). So, it is not surprising that self-assessments are increasingly used in formative assessment (e.g., during the learning process) in order to improve students' attainment of the content. This area of self-assessment has benefited particularly well from the tremendous development in Internet-based assessments.

Kotter (1978, p. 7) characterizes self-assessment as "a systematic process designed to generate the type of accurate self-awareness needed to make rational job and career decisions." More recently, Frebort and Kubinger (2008) defined self-assessments as psychological relevant test batteries for the purposes of diagnostic self-testing, mostly presented via the Internet. In that sense, self-assessment is seen as one module in the process of a deliberate choice, where the test taker voluntarily engages in a diagnostic self-testing procedure and uses the feedback first and foremost to his or her own benefit. Usually the recordings are not accessible to third parties unless noted (e.g., results shared to obtain detailed psycho-diagnostic counseling). The results of a self-assessment are usually solely available to the test taker, who has a genuine desire to get veritable information about the tested content; therefore, distortion as discussed above is, under these conditions, rather unlikely. Moreover, recent research has indicated that people might be more willing to self-disclose in an online (self-)assessment than they would in person (Barak, & Gluck-Ofri, 2007; Suler, 2004). Thus, results of an online self-assessment may reflect personality aspects unfettered by normal social constraints and might lead to greater ecological validity. However, one of the implications that must be drawn from this is that normative data used in online self-assessments should be gathered from the appropriate online population.

Online self-assessment tools find their primary application in the area of career counseling, higher education institutions, and health care. All of these tools share the common goal to provide the test takers with feedback about their accordance of abilities, skills knowledge, expectations, interests and health.

Online Assessment in Career Counseling

Online assessments, and, in particular, self-assessments, are widespread in personnel consulting and personnel selection. Frequently these assessments are offered as part of electronic recruiting by internationally accessible job centers and globally active companies. Usually, it is these instruments' self-declared goal to inform job-seekers of their skills and personal suitability for a job, thus saving time and expense for the job-seekers and the company (Bartram, 2005; Psychological Testing Centre, 2006). These tests normally capture biographical information, abilities, and competencies and contain tasks that are adapted to the specific requirements and demands of the respective business sector. Additionally, intelligence tests and tests for specific cognitive abilities are mainly used in the course of recruiting trainees and job starters. In the area of personnel selection, tests primarily cover job-specific knowledge, and include personality scales, as well as scales measuring motivation, attitudes and interests to obtain information about behavior as it relates to an employees' daily professional life. Moreover, simulations of concrete daily tasks in the company are commonly applied in order to ascertain personal suitability to a job. Further, job applications may involve additional forms of electronically supported learning provided in in-company training and qualification tests.

In both cases, online self-assessments are generally used for screening and (self-)selection of suitable candidates. Nevertheless, the terms and conditions of an aptitude assessment still apply, meaning that the instruments employed should demonstrate general quality requirements for tests and demonstrate empirical evidence of the prognostic validity of the vocationally specific aptitudes measured.

Because online assessments in the employment context strive to report the test-taker's personal suitability for a job, a thorough analysis of the relevant personal conditions and requirements of the position to be filled is essential. It is good practice to have a stepwise procedure, which first covers essential information, such as possession of appropriate degrees/certifications, validated work experience and skill prescreens before finally testing abilities, competencies and personality variables. This approach reduces step-by-step the number of applicants who proceed into more time consuming parts of the assessment process (Russell, 2007).

Online Assessment in Higher Education

In the education sector, online assessments and self-assessments play a dual role. On the one hand, the assessments are used as a part of technology-enhanced learning environment; on the other hand, they are commonly embedded in the context of college and university admission.

Technology-enhanced learning environments are often used in higher education and in school education as a means of creating learning situations that require complex thinking, problem-solving and collaboration strategies. For the most part, these learning environments include self-assessment tools that are increasingly integrated into more complex and authentic problem contexts and a wider range of answer formats can be automatically scored. For example, electronic portfolios are already widely used in European schools and universities to support the formative and summative assessment of students' progress. Self- and peer-assessment can be powerful tools to assess students' learning. Additionally, immersive virtual environments, online simulations, virtual laboratories and games can recreate learning situations which require complex thinking and problem-solving, thus, allowing the development and assessment of skills and competences. For content areas such as science and technology, as well as for social and civic competencies, computer simulations and virtual laboratories provide opportunities for students to develop and apply skills and knowledge in more realistic contexts and can provide feedback in real time. Since learners' behavior in these electronic environments may be tracked, their individual learning results can be automatically assessed. Such computer-based problem-solving scenarios or *microworlds* have been successfully used to assess students' complex problem-solving behavior (Mayer et al., 2013; Sonnleitner, et al., 2012; Sonnleitner, Keller, Martin, & Brunner, 2013) and their strategies to move through the materials (Lengler & Reips, 2003). Additionally, the Internet reveals a pool of potential computer-based quizzes, games and tests which can be used for the assessment of competences in literacy, reading and text comprehension and mathematics, in the educational sector. As Redecker (2013) notes, the trends in technology-enhanced assessment is to make explicit testing obsolete:

> Learners will be continuously monitored and guided by the electronic environment which they use for their learning activities, so that diagnostic, formative and summative assessment will become embedded in the learning process. (p. 12)

Apart from technology-enhanced learning environments, online self-assessments are commonly used in the schools for issues related to student guidance and counseling. US high schools typically use career inventories in high school settings to provide feedback as to their suitability for jobs/careers as students prepare to enter higher education or the work force. In contrast to the US, in several European countries, for example in Germany and Austria, applying to colleges or universities is not linked to the participation in standardized admissions tests. In order to ensure a substantial matching between the individual competencies of the students and the specific requirements of the intended subject, many universities offer online self-assessments to inform the prospective students as to their personal suitability to that subject. On the one hand, universities expect that the profound concern with the requirements of the subject will lead to a kind of self-selection, which, in turn, may reduce the number of students leaving a major or changing the area of study. On the other hand, aptitude-related feedback opens up the opportunity to deal with strengths and weaknesses on an individual basis. This assumes that the test applied should – apart from content validity – demonstrate the empirical evidence of its prognostic validity.

While benefits to such inventories may be realized, collecting data is difficult in the context of online self-assessment and academic success as sampling bias is quite likely because of the access conditions and voluntary participation of examinees. Nevertheless, there is empirical evidence of the prognostic validity of online self-assessments in the admission to universities (e.g., Hasenberg & Schmidt-Atzert, 2013; Reiss et al., 2009).

Online Assessment in Health Care

In the last decade, the new term *eHealth* was established to describe the use of emerging interactive technologies delivered via computer and/or the Internet, to enable disease prevention and disease management. Besides the economic advantages, this approach offers an increased user and supplier control of interventions. The reduction of geographically-based, as well as time- and mobility-based barriers (Griffiths, Lindenmeyer, Powell, Lowe, & Thorogood, 2006) are the most common reasons for delivering Internet-based monitoring and interventions (Ybarra & Eaton, 2005). In accordance, a variety of computer- and web-based patient monitoring and assessment systems have been developed. As in other domains, several studies have demonstrated that computer-based assessments can rival the validity of assessments using paper-and-pencil methods or trained interviewers (e.g., Achenbach, Krukowski, Dumenci, & Ivanova, 2005; Schulenberg & Yutrzenka, 2001; Vallejo, Jordán, Díaz, Comeche, & Ortega, 2007).

A specific interactive approach in the field of eHealth is termed *expert systems*. These expert systems typically involve a collection of characteristics and generate a feedback protocol tailored to the specific needs of the user on the basis of the users input. From this perspective, expert systems attempt to model methods similar to a real-world clinical encounter. A typical example is the web-based system Systematic Treatment Selection (STS; Nguyen, Bertoni, Charvat, Gheytanchi, & Beutler, 2007). This system is a cloud-based mental health clinical platform that provides a tailored and direct assessment of the patient problem and provides a written intake report, multiple measures of intake and outcome condition, and tailored self-help resources (http://www.innerlife.com/clinician/). The system is based on empirically derived principles that define the conditions under which different types of interventions are most likely to exert positive effects. Patient characteristics that fit to these principles are identified via a web-delivered self-report measure. Research has demonstrated the therapeutic efficacy of various treatment-planning dimensions in the STS/InnerLife system (Harwood et al., 2011).

Virtual reality is another technology that appeared online in recent years to be used as a clinical component in assessment and treatment of disorders and cognitive rehabilitation. The rationale behind this approach is that real and virtual exposures elicit comparable reactions in participants. Virtual reality has been used, for instance, to develop suitable and virtual environments for areas of cognitive functions assessment and rehabilitation (Morganti, 2006), the assessment of body image (Villani, Gatti, Confalonieri, & Riva, 2012) and emotional responses (Gorini, Griez, Petrova, & Riva, 2010).

In addition, there is a growing number of online questionnaires related to clinical psychology, which stresses the importance of self-assessment in the mental health arena (e.g., Ritter, Lorig, Laurent, & Matthews, 2004). Because the assessment of adult psychopathology relies heavily on self-reports, it is important to determine how well self-reports agree with reports by informants who know the person being assessed. Achenbach and colleagues (2005) examined 51,000 articles published over 10 years in 52 peer-reviewed journals for correlations between self-reports and informants' reports about psychopathological characteristics, such as aspects of behavioral, emotional, cognitive, and personality functioning that may have been sufficiently abnormal, injurious, or troubling and warranting help from mental health professionals. They report a mean correlation of .453 across all recorded disorders. Correlations were larger for reports of substance use (.681) than for other kinds of problems (e.g., Internalizing, that included anxiety, depression, neuroticism, and suicidality, .428; Externalizing, that is, aggression, sociopathy, and antisocial behavior, .438). Achenbach et al.'s results indicate that information about adult behavior problems from self-assessment measures may differ from those reported by other informants. Accordingly, it appears reasonable to amend self-reports by including additional information for the clinical assessment of individuals.

Specifics of Constructing Online Assessments

To construct assessments online, a number of methodological specifics need to be considered. Some of these specifics are general to Internet-based research (e.g., Birnbaum & Reips, 2005; Reips, Buchanan, Krantz, & McGraw, 2016), some are specific to online assessments (Buchanan, Johnson, & Goldberg, 2005). General advice regarding the construction of online studies includes the implementation of techniques to avoid or control non-response (e.g., warm-up, seriousness check, high hurdle technique; see Reips, 2009), the use of paradata (e.g., Stieger & Reips, 2010), and measures for authentication or at least control for multiple submissions (Birnbaum & Reips, 2005).

Online assessments require specific validation as instruments that are delivered online. Buchanan (2001) writes:

> Online and offline versions of tests can be, and often are, equivalent in terms of what they measure and how well they do it. However, equivalence is not something which one may take for granted. If equivalence is considered important, it must be established for every instrument which is used. One cannot assume that an online test is reliable and valid simply because the offline test from which it was created is known to be reliable and valid. (pp. 67–68)

References

Achenbach, T. M, Krukowski, R. A., Dumenci, L., & Ivanova, M. Y. (2005). Assessment of adult psychopathology: Meta-analyses and implications of cross-informant correlations. *Psychological Bulletin, 131*, 361–382. http://doi.org/10.1037/0033-2909.131.3.361

Allan, J. M., Bulla, N., & Goodman, S. A. (2003). *Test access: Guidelines for computer administered testing.* Louisville, KY: American Printing House for the Blind. Retrieved from http://www.aph.org/tests/access/

Arthur, W., Jr., Glaze, R. M., Villado, A. J., & Taylor, J. E. (2010). The magnitude and extent of cheating and response distortion effects on unproctored Internet-based tests of cognitive ability and personality. *International Journal of Selection and Assessment, 18*, 1–16. http://doi.org/10.1111/j.1468-2389.2010.00476.x

Bailey, J., Schneider, C., & Ark, T. V. (2012). *Getting ready for online assessments. Digital learning now! Smart series.* Retrieved from http://www.digitallearningnow.com/wp-content/uploads/2013/01/Getting-Ready-for-Online-Asst.-Updated-Jan-2013.pdf

Barak, A., & Gluck-Ofri, O. (2007). Degree and reciprocity of self-disclosure in online forums. *Cyberpsychology and Behavior, 10*, 407–417. http://doi.org/10.1089/cpb.2006.9938

Bartram, D. (2005). Testing on the Internet: Issues, challenges and opportunities in the field of occupational assessment. In D. Bartram & R. K. Hambleton (Eds.), *Computer-based testing and the Internet: Issues and advances* (pp. 13–37). Hoboken, NJ: John Wiley & Sons.

Bartram, D. (2006). The internationalization of testing and new models of test delivery on the Internet. *International Journal of Testing, 6*, 121–131. http://doi.org/10.1207/s15327574ijt0602_2

Birnbaum, M. H., & Reips, U.-D. (2005). Behavioral research and data collection via the Internet. In R. W. Proctor & K.-P. L. Vu (Eds.), *The handbook of human factors in Web design* (pp. 471–492). Mahwah, NJ: Erlbaum.

Buchanan, T. (2001). Online personality assessment. In U.-D. Reips & M. Bosnjak (Eds.), *Dimensions of Internet science* (pp. 57–74). Lengerich, Germany: Pabst Science.

Buchanan, T., Johnson, J. A., & Goldberg, L. R. (2005). Implementing a five-factor personality inventory for use on the Internet. *European Journal of Psychological Assessment, 21*(2), 115–127. http://doi.org/10.1027/1015-5759.21.2.115

Buchanan, T., & Reips, U.-D. (2001). Platform-dependent biases in online research: Do Mac users really think different? In K. J. Jonas, P. Breuer, B. Schauenburg, & M. Boos (Eds.), *Perspectives on Internet research: Concepts and methods.* Retrieved from http://www.uni-konstanz.de/iscience/reips/pubs/papers/Buchanan_Reips2001.pdf

Buchanan, T., & Smith, J. L. (1999). Research on the Internet: Validation of a World-Wide Web mediated personality scale. *Behavior Research Methods Instruments & Computers, 31*(4), 565–571. http://doi.org/10.3758/BF03200736

Carstairs, J., & Myors, B. (2009). Internet testing: A natural experiment reveals test score inflation on a high-stakes, unproctored cognitive test. *Computers in Human Behavior, 25*, 738–742. http://doi.org/10.1016/j.chb.2009.01.011

Chang, C.-C., Liang, C., & Chen, Y.-H. (2013). Is learner self-assessment reliable and valid in a Web-based portfolio environment for high school students? *Computers & Education, 60*, 325–334. http://doi.org/10.1016/j.compedu.2012.05.012

Davis, R. N. (1999). Web-based administration of a personality questionnaire: Comparison with traditional methods. *Behavior Research Methods Instruments & Computers, 31*(4), 572–577. http://doi.org/10.3758/BF03200737

Dolan, R. P., Burling, K., Harms, M., Strain-Seymour, E., & Way, W. (2013). *A universal design for learning-based framework for designing accessible technology-enhanced assessments. Pearson's Research Reports.* Retrieved from http://www.pearsonassessments.com/research

Educational Testing Service. (2012). *PARCC item development (ITN 2012-31).* Retrieved from http://www.parcconline.org

Frebort, M., & Kubinger, K. D. (2008). Qualitätsansprüche an ein Self-Assessment zur Studienwahlberatung: Der Wiener Ansatz [Quality requirements to a self-assessment for study guidance: The Vienna approach]. In H. Schuler (Ed.), *Studierendenauswahl und Studienentscheidung* (pp. 95–101). Göttingen, Germany: Hogrefe.

Freund, P. A., & Kasten, N. (2012). How smart do you think you are? A meta-analysis on the validity of self-estimates of cognitive ability. *Psychological Bulletin, 138*, 296–321. http://doi.org/10.1037/a0026556

Funke, F., Reips, U.-D., & Thomas, R. K. (2011). Sliders for the smart: Type of rating scale on the Web interacts with educational level. *Social Science Computer Review, 29*, 221–231. http://doi.org/10.1177/0894439310376896

Gorini, A., Griez, E., Petrova, A., & Riva, G. (2010). Assessment of the emotional responses produced by exposure to real food, virtual food and photographs of food in patients affected by eating disorders. *Annals of General Psychiatry, 9*(30), 1–10. http://doi.org/10.1186/1744-859X-9-30

Griffiths, F., Lindenmeyer, A., Powell, J., Lowe, P., & Thorogood, M. (2006). Why are health care interventions delivered over the Internet? A systematic review of the published literature. *Journal of Medical Internet Research, 8*(2), e10. http://doi.org/10.2196/jmir.8.2.e12

Harwood, T. M., Pratt, D., Beutler, L. E., Bongar, B. M., Samarea, L., & Forrester, B. T. (2011). Technology, telehealth, treatment enhancement, and celection. *Professional Psychology: Research and Practice, 42*, 448–454. http://doi.org/10.1037/a0026214

Hasenberg, S., & Schmidt-Atzert, L. (2013). Bessere Noten und zufriedenere Studierende? Das Marburger Self-Assessment für den Studiengang Biologie [Better grades and more satisfied students? The Marburg self-assessment for the biology program]. *Wirtschaftspsychologie, 1*, 25–33.

International Test Commission. (2006). International guidelines of computer-based and Internet-delivered testing. *International Journal of Testing, 6*, 143–171. http://doi.org/10.1207/s15327574ijt0602_4

Kaufmann, E., & Reips, U.-D. (2008). *Internet-basierte Messung sozialer Erwünschtheit* [Internet-based measurement of social desirability]. Saarbrücken, Germany: VDM Verlag Dr. Müller.

Kingston, N. M. (2009). Comparability of computer- and paper-administered multiple-choice tests for K-12 populations: A synthesis. *Applied Measurement in Education, 22*, 22–37. http://doi.org/10.1080/08957340802558326

Kotter, J. P. (1978). *Self-assessment and career development*. Englewood Cliffs, NJ: Prentice-Hall.

Lengler, R. & Reips, U.-D. (2003). "Readers" and "scanners" evaluate e-learning: Same overall grading despite large differences in user behaviour and experiences. In C. Jutz, F. Flückiger, & K. Wefler (Eds.), *5th International Conference on New Educational Environments* (pp. 151–154). Bern, Switzerland: Sauerländer.

Li, J., & De Luca, R. (2012). Review of assessment feedback. *Studies in Higher Education*, 1–16.

Lievens, F. (2006). The ITC guidelines on computer-based and Internet-delivered testing: Where do we go from here? *International Journal of Testing, 6*, 189–194. http://doi.org/10.1207/s15327574ijt0602_7

Mayer, H., Hazotte, C., Djaghloul, Y., Latour, T., Sonnleitner, P., Brunner, M., … Martin, R. (2013). Using complex problem solving simulations for general cognitive ability assessment: The genetics lab framework. *International Journal of Information Science and Intelligent System, 2*, 71–88.

Mead, A. D., & Drasgow, F. (1993). Equivalence of computerized and paper-and-pencil cognitive ability tests: A meta-analysis. *Psychological Bulletin, 114*, 449–458. http://doi.org/10.1037/0033-2909.114.3.449

Morganti, F. (2006). Virtual interaction in cognitive neuropsychology. In G. Riva, C. Botella, P. Légeron, & G. Optale (Eds.), *Cybertherapy. Internet and virtual reality as assessment and rehabilitation tools for clinical psychology and neuroscience* (pp. 85–101). Amsterdam, The Netherlands: IOS Press.

Naglieri, J. A., Drasgow, F., Schmit, M., Handler, L., Prifitera, A., Margolis, A., & Velasquez, R. (2004). Psychological testing on the Internet: New problems, old issues. *American Psychologist, 59*, 150–162. http://doi.org/10.1037/0003-066X.59.3.150

Nguyen, T. T., Bertoni, M., Charvat, M., Gheytanchi, A., & Beutler, L. E. (2007). Systematic Treatment Selection (STS): A review and future directions. *International Journal of Behavioral Consultation and Therapy, 3*, 13–29. http://doi.org/10.1037/h0100178

Noyes, J. M., & Garland, K. J. (2008). Computer- vs. paper-based tasks: Are they equivalent? *Ergonomics, 51*, 1352–1375. http://doi.org/10.1080/00140130802170387

Potosky, D., & Bobko, P. (2004). Selection testing via the Internet: Practical considerations and exploratory empirical findings. *Personnel Psychology, 57*, 1003–1035. http://doi.org/10.1111/j.1744-6570.2004.00013.x

Psychological Testing Centre. (2006). *Using online assessment tools for recruitment*. Retrieved from http://www.psychtesting.org.uk

Redecker, C. (2013). *The use of ICT for the assessment of key competences. Publications Office of the European Union, JRC76971.* Retrieved from http://publications.jrc.ec.europa.eu/repository/handle/111111111/27945

Reips, U.-D. (2002). Context effects in Web surveys. In B. Batinic, U.-D. Reips, & M. Bosnjak (Eds.), *Online social sciences* (pp. 69–80). Seattle, WA: Hogrefe & Huber.

Reips, U.-D. (2006). Web-based methods. In M. Eid & E. Diener (Eds.), *Handbook of multimethod measurement in psychology* (pp. 73–85). Washington, DC: American Psychological Association. http://doi.org/10.1037/11383-006

Reips, U.-D. (2009). Internet experiments: methods, guidelines, metadata. Proceedings of SPIE: Vol. 7240. *Human Vision and Electronic Imaging XIV, 724008.* http://doi.org/10.1117/12.823416. Retrieved from http://iscience.deusto.es/wp-content/uploads/2010/03/preprintSPIE_Reips_A4_color.pdf

Reips, U.-D. (2010). Design and formatting in Internet-based research. In S. Gosling & J. Johnson (Eds.), *Advanced methods for conducting online behavioral research* (pp. 29–43). Washington, DC: American Psychological Association.

Reips, U.-D., Buchanan, T., Krantz, J. H., & McGraw, K. (2016). Methodological challenges in the use of the Internet for scientific research: Ten solutions and recommendations. *Studia Psychologica.* Advance online publication.

Reiss, S., Tillmann, A., Schreiner, M., Schweizer, K., Krömker, D., & Moosbrugger, H. (2009). Online-Self-Assessments zur Erfassung studienrelevanter Kompetenzen [Online-self-assessments to measure study-related competences]. *Zeitschrift für Hochschulentwicklung, 4,* 60–71.

Richman, W. L., Kiesler, S., Weisband, S., & Drasgow, F. (1999). A meta-analytic study of social desirability distortion in computer administered questionnaires, traditional questionnaires, and interviews. *Journal of Applied Psychology, 84,* 754–775. http://doi.org/10.1037/0021-9010.84.5.754

Ritter, P., Lorig, K., Laurent, D., & Matthews, K. (2004). Internet versus mailed questionnaires: A randomized comparison. *Journal of Medical Internet Research, 6*(3), e29 http://doi.org/10.2196/jmir.6.3.e29

Rosen, Y., & Tager, M. (2013). Computer-based assessment of collaborative problem-solving skills: Human-to-agent versus human-to-human approach. *Pearson's Research Reports.* Retrieved from http://www.pearsonassessments.com/research

Ross, J. A. (2006). The reliability, validity, and utility of self-assessment. *Practical Assessment Research & Evaluation, 11,* 1–13.

Russell, D. P. (2007). Recruiting and staffing in the electronic age: A research-based perspective. *Consulting Psychology Journal: Practice and Research, 59,* 91–101. http://doi.org/10.1037/1065-9293.59.2.91

Salgado, J. F., & Moscoso, S. (2003). Internet-based personality testing: Equivalence of measures and assessees' perceptions and reactions. *International Journal of Selection and Assessment, 11,* 194–205. http://doi.org/10.1111/1468-2389.00243

Scheuermann, F., & Guimarães Pereira, A. (Eds.). (2008). *Towards a research agenda on computer-based assessment: Challenges and needs for European educational measurement.* Luxembourg City, Luxembourg: Office for Official Publications of the European Communities. Retrieved from http://publications.jrc.ec.europa.eu/repository/bitstream/111111111/907/1/reqno_jrc44526_report%20final%20version%5B2%5D.pdf

Schulenberg, S. E., & Yutrzenka, B. A. (2001). Equivalence of computerized and conventional versions of the Beck Depression Inventory–II (BDI-II). *Current Psychology, 20,* 216–230. http://doi.org/10.1007/s12144-001-1008-1

Sireci, S., & Zenisky, A. (2006). Innovative item formats in computer-based testing: In pursuit of improved construct representation. In S. Downing & T. Haladyna (Eds.), *Handbook of test development* (pp. 329–347). Mahwah, NJ: Lawrence Erlbaum.

Sonnleitner, P., Keller, U., Martin, R., & Brunner, M. (2013). Students' complex problem-solving abilities: Their structure and relations to reasoning ability and educational success. *Intelligence, 41,* 289–305. http://doi.org/10.1016/j.intell.2013.05.002

Sonnleitner, P., Brunner, M., Greiff, S., Funke, J., Keller, U., Martin, R., … Latour, T. (2012). The genetics lab: Acceptance and psychometric characteristics of a computer-based microworld assessing complex problem solving. *Psychological Test and Assessment Modeling, 54*, 54–72.

Stieger, S., & Reips, U.-D. (2010). What are participants doing while filling in an online questionnaire: A paradata collection tool and an empirical study. *Computers in Human Behavior, 26*(6), 1488–1495. http://doi.org/10.1016/j.chb.2010.05.013

Suler, J. (2004). The online disinhibition effect. *Cyberpsychology and Behavior, 7*, 321–326. http://doi.org/10.1089/1094931041291295

Texas Education Agency. (2008). *A review of literature on the comparability of scores obtained from examinees on computer-based and paper-based tests*. Retrieved from http://www.tea.state.tx.us/WorkArea/linkit.aspx?LinkIdentifier=id&ItemID=2147494120&libID=2147494117

Tippins, N. T. (2009). Internet alternatives to traditional proctored testing: Where are we now? *Industrial and Organizational Psychology, 2*, 2–10. http://doi.org/10.1111/j.1754-9434.2008.01097.x

Vallejo, M. A., Jordán, C. M., Díaz, M. I., Comeche, M. I., & Ortega, J. (2007). Psychological assessment via the Internet: A reliability and validity study of online (vs paper-and-pencil) versions of the General Health Questionnaire-28 (GHQ-28) and the Symptoms Check-List-90-Revised (SCL-90-R). *Journal of Medical Internet Research, 9*(1), e2. http://doi.org/10.2196/jmir.9.1.e2

Villani, D., Gatti, E., Confalonieri, E., & Riva, G. (2012). Am I my avatar? A tool to investigate virtual body image representation in adolescence. *Cyberpsychology, Behavior, and Social Networking, 15*, 435–440. http://doi.org/10.1089/cyber.2012.0057

Wang, H., & Shin, C. D. (2010). Comparability of computerized adaptive and paper-pencil tests. *Pearson Test, Measurement and Research Service Bulletin, 13*, 1–7.

Wang, T. H. (2007). What strategies are effective for formative assessment in an e-learning environment? *Journal of Computer Assisted Learning, 23*, 171–186. http://doi.org/10.1111/j.1365-2729.2006.00211.x

Wang, T. H. (2009). Web-based dynamic assessment: Taking assessment as teaching and learning strategy for improving students' e-Learning effectiveness. *Computers & Education, 54*, 1157–1166. http://doi.org/10.1016/j.compedu.2009.11.001

Weigold, A., Weigold, I. K., & Russell, E. J. (2013). Examination of the equivalence of self-report survey-based paper-and-pencil and internet data collection methods. *Psychological Methods, 18*, 53–70. http://doi.org/10.1037/a0031607

Ybarra, M. L., & Eaton, W. W. (2005). Internet-based mental health interventions. *Mental Health Services Research, 7*, 75–87. http://doi.org/10.1007/s11020-005-3779-8

Part IV
Estimation of Models

Chapter 8

Overview of Estimation Methods and Preconditions for Their Application With Structural Equation Modeling

Sara J. Finney[1], Christine DiStefano[2], and Jason P. Kopp[1]

[1]Center for Assessment & Research Studies, James Madison University, Harrisonburg, VA, USA
[2]Department of Education Studies, University of South Carolina, Columbia, SC, USA

Structural equation modeling (SEM) is a useful statistical tool when developing and gathering validity evidence for tests. SEM-related techniques commonly used in scale development include assessing factor structure via confirmatory factor analysis (e.g., Brown, 2006; Worthington & Whittaker, 2006), establishing measurement invariance across groups or time (e.g., Bashkov & Finney, 2013; Vandenberg & Lance, 2000; Widaman, Ferrer, & Conger, 2010), and utilizing latent variable path models to better understand how the construct purportedly represented by the scale relates to other latent variables (e.g., Benson, 1998).

Given the prevalence of use of SEM-related techniques in test development to investigate such characteristics, it is important to recognize the assumptions associated with the estimation method. Essentially, the choice of estimation method can influence the trustworthiness of SEM results, as indices to assess model-data fit, standard errors associated with parameter estimates, and parameter estimates themselves can be biased if the incorrect estimation method is employed. If results are biased, the test developer may make faulty decisions associated with the factor structure, item quality, differential item functioning, or external validity evidence. Incorrect decisions may not only impact human and financial resources (e.g., may encourage unnecessary scale revision), but could have legal ramifications (e.g., incorrect interpretation and use of scores). Given the energy researchers expend on test development and the importance of making correct decisions during the test evaluation process, estimation methods used to analyze test data should be employed under conditions where they have been shown to produce accurate results.

Central Issues

There are several assumptions associated with SEM estimation. The two assumptions we focus on in this chapter center on the *metric* (e.g., continuous, ordered categorical) and *distribution* (e.g., normal, nonnormal) of the data being modeled. Normal theory (NT) estimators, which are employed often in scale construction studies (DiStefano & Hess, 2005), require the endogenous variables to be both continuous and multivariate normally distributed in the population. Importantly, data gathered for test development and evaluation purposes may not be continuous, and thus, not normally distributed in nature. Specifically, with respect to metric or scale of measurement, noncognitive (e.g., attitudinal or developmental) instruments often utilize ordered-categorical response items, such as a Likert scale (e.g., 1 = *strongly disagree* to 4 = *strongly agree*). Cognitive (e.g., ability or skill-based) tests often utilize multiple-choice item formats and dichotomous scoring (e.g., 1 = *correct* and 0 = *incorrect*). Thus, when modeling the item-level data, the assumption of continuous and normally distributed variables will not be met in a strict sense. Even if continuous(-like) data are available (e.g., subscale level scores), depending on the nature of the construct or population under study, the observed data may be distributionally nonnormal. To assist test developers, we explain estimation in general terms before detailing robustness studies associated with the most popular NT estimator, maximum likelihood (ML). We then describe the mechanics and performance of five strategies often used to model nonnormal and/or categorical data:

1) Satorra–Bentler (S-B) scaled χ^2 and robust standard errors utilizing a covariance matrix;
2) Weighted least squares (WLS) estimation utilizing a covariance matrix;
3) Weighted least squares (WLS) estimation utilizing a polychoric correlation matrix;
4) Robust diagonally weighted least squares (DWLS) estimation utilizing a polychoric correlation matrix; and
5) Robust ML estimation utilizing a polychoric correlation matrix.

In addition to summarizing robustness studies associated with the methods above, an example of assessing the factor structure of a scale carries through the chapter to highlight similarities and differences across the estimators. A more detailed, yet didactic, treatment of these estimators, including software implementation, is available in Finney and DiStefano (2013). Bootstrapping has been used to accommodate nonnormal continuous data. This method will not be discussed in this chapter; however, it is discussed in detail by Hancock and Liu (2012).

Conceptual Principles

Estimation in General

For instructive purposes, we utilize an example of a measurement model to elucidate the estimation of model parameters, although the principles discussed here extend to the majority of SEM techniques. We chose a confirmatory factor analysis (CFA) example because CFA is often employed during test development to determine whether a theoretically-derived factor structure aligns with (i.e., fits) the pattern of responses to a set of items. As a motivating example, a test developer believes two correlated latent factors (F1 and F2) underlie responses to an eight-item scale (y_1 to y_8). The test developer specifies simple structure, where each item is associated with only one factor (see Figure 8.1).

Making the assumption that item scores are continuous and normally distributed, ML estimation is employed to produce 17 model parameters (1 factor correlation, φ_{12}; 8 factor pattern coefficients or loadings, λ; and 8 item error variances, e; see Table 8.1). More specifically, using the covariance matrix (**S**) shown in Table 8.1, the model in Figure 8.1 is estimated from the observed item variances and covariances. In this example, 36 unique pieces of information are housed in the covariance matrix: 8 elements on the diagonal (i.e., observed item variances) and

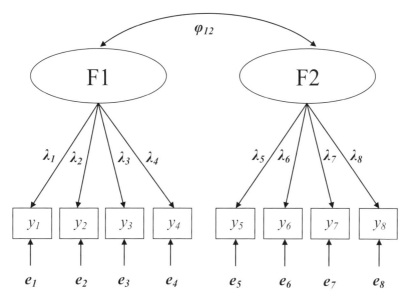

Figure 8.1. Confirmatory two-factor model fit to an eight-item test. F1 and F2 represent two continuous latent variables. A total of 17 parameters (bolded) are estimated from the 36 variances and covariances, including 1 factor correlation (φ_{12}), 8 factor pattern coefficients (λ), and 8 item error variances (e). Note that factor variances are fixed to 1. Factor pattern coefficients (i.e., loadings) quantify the influence of a factor on an item (a one unit increase in F1 results in a λ_1 change in y_1), item error variances represent the amount of variance in the item responses that is unexplained by the factor (i.e., random measurement error and systematic unique variance), and the factor correlation represents the relationships between the latent factors.

28 unique relations between items on the off-diagonal (i.e., observed item covariances). The estimated parameters (often symbolized as $\hat{\theta}$) are used to create a model-implied covariance matrix (see equations and model-implied values in Table 8.2). The parameters are estimated to minimize the difference between the model-implied and observed variances and covariances. That is, via an iterative process, different values of the parameter estimates are auditioned until the estimation process converges on the set of parameter estimates that provides the minimum discrepancy between the observed and model-implied elements. More specifically, the iterative process starts with an initial set of parameter estimates (i.e., start values provided by the software program). The initial parameter estimates are used to construct the model-implied covariance matrix, which is compared to the original sample covariance matrix, resulting in a single value that represents their discrepancy. New parameter estimate values are then auditioned and the discrepancy is recomputed. The change between the second discrepancy value and the first discrepancy value is obtained. This iterative process (iterative optimization) continues with new values of parameter estimates chosen until the model-implied covariance matrix approximates the observed covariance matrix as closely as possible, given the specified model constraints. At some point the iterations stop (i.e., converge on a solution). Convergence is dictated by the change in discrepancy values between two iterations. If the change between adjacent iterations is smaller than the chosen stopping criterion (e.g., change between discrepancy values < .0001), the model has converged on a solution. Upon convergence, this final set of parameter estimates is considered the solution for a tested model and is reported for evaluation.

Table 8.1. Input covariance matrix and unstandardized (standardized) ML parameter estimates for the two-factor model in Figure 8.1

	y_1	y_2	y_3	y_4	y_5	y_6	y_7	y_8
y_1	.4300	–	–	–	–	–	–	–
y_2	.1338	.4426	–	–	–	–	–	–
y_3	.1290	.1095	.4370	–	–	–	–	–
y_4	.1449	.1169	.1150	.4852	–	–	–	–
y_5	.0270	.0026	.0428	.0302	.4505	–	–	–
y_6	.0495	.0420	.0602	.0656	.1055	.4612	–	–
y_7	.0156	.0112	.0383	.0395	.1257	.1189	.4961	–
y_8	.0595	.0348	.0589	.0718	.1273	.1185	.1528	.5331
Parameter estimates								
Pattern coefficient	.3956	.3250	.3312	.3643	.3222	.3220	.3709	.4004
	(.603)	(.489)	(.501)	(.523)	(.480)	(.474)	(.527)	(.548)
Error variance	.2736	.3370	.3273	.3525	.3466	.3576	.3585	.3728
	(.636)	(.761)	(.749)	(.727)	(.770)	(.775)	(.723)	(.699)

Note. Covariance elements above the diagonal are identical to elements below the diagonal, and are thus not presented. The metric of the two factors were set by fixing both factor variances to a value of 1. Subtracting the number of estimated parameters (17) from the nonduplicated observed variance-covariance matrix elements (36) yields the degrees of freedom (*df*) associated with the model (36 − 17 = 19). Maximum likelihood (ML) estimation was used to produce the factor pattern coefficients, error variances, and factor correlation. Estimated factor correlation = .3185. Items y_1–y_4 represent Factor 1. Items y_5–y_8 represent Factor 2. $N = 1,000$.

Table 8.2. Model-implied covariance matrix, $\Sigma(\hat{\theta})$, for the two-factor model

	y_1	y_2	y_3	y_4	y_5	y_6	y_7	y_8
y_1	$\lambda_1^2+V(e_1)$	.1286	.1310	.1441	.0406	.0406	.0467	.0504
y_2	$\lambda_1^*\lambda_2$	$\lambda_2^2+V(e_2)$	.1076	.1184	.0334	.0333	.0384	.0414
y_3	$\lambda_1^*\lambda_3$	$\lambda_2^*\lambda_3$	$\lambda_3^2+V(e_3)$	.1206	.0340	.0340	.0391	.0422
y_4	$\lambda_1^*\lambda_4$	$\lambda_2^*\lambda_4$	$\lambda_3^*\lambda_4$	$\lambda_4^2+V(e_4)$	.0374	.0374	.0430	.0465
y_5	$\lambda_1^*\varphi_{12}^*\lambda_5$	$\lambda_2^*\varphi_{12}^*\lambda_5$	$\lambda_3^*\varphi_{12}^*\lambda_5$	$\lambda_4^*\varphi_{12}^*\lambda_5$	$\lambda_5^2+V(e_5)$	.1037	.1195	.1290
y_6	$\lambda_1^*\varphi_{12}^*\lambda_6$	$\lambda_2^*\varphi_{12}^*\lambda_6$	$\lambda_3^*\varphi_{12}^*\lambda_6$	$\lambda_4^*\varphi_{12}^*\lambda_6$	$\lambda_5^*\lambda_6$	$\lambda_6^2+V(e_6)$	.1194	.1289
y_7	$\lambda_1^*\varphi_{12}^*\lambda_7$	$\lambda_2^*\varphi_{12}^*\lambda_7$	$\lambda_3^*\varphi_{12}^*\lambda_7$	$\lambda_4^*\varphi_{12}^*\lambda_7$	$\lambda_5^*\lambda_7$	$\lambda_6^*\lambda_7$	$\lambda_7^2+V(e_7)$	.1485
y_8	$\lambda_1^*\varphi_{12}^*\lambda_8$	$\lambda_2^*\varphi_{12}^*\lambda_8$	$\lambda_3^*\varphi_{12}^*\lambda_8$	$\lambda_4^*\varphi_{12}^*\lambda_8$	$\lambda_5^*\lambda_8$	$\lambda_6^*\lambda_8$	$\lambda_7^*\lambda_8$	$\lambda_8^2+V(e_8)$

Note. The model-implied covariances above the diagonal were computed using the parameter estimates (from Table 8.1) and the formula for model-implied elements found below the diagonal. For example, the model-implied covariance between y_1 and $y_2 = \lambda_1^*\lambda_2 = .3956^*.3250 = .12857$. The model-implied variance for $y_1 = \lambda_1^2+V(e_1) = (.3956)^2 +.2735 = .4300$. Covariance residuals (i.e., indices of local misfit) are computed by subtracting corresponding elements in $\Sigma(\hat{\theta})$ from the elements in **S** (observed variances and covariances in Table 8.1). For example, the covariance residual associated with the covariance between y_1 and $y_2 = .1338 − .1286 = .0052$.

When the estimation process converges, researchers compare the corresponding elements in the observed and model-implied matrices to assess if the model is a plausible explanation for the observed item relationships. The differences between the observed and model-implied elements are termed residuals. Thus, the residuals and indices that summarize these residuals (e.g., χ^2 goodness-of-fit statistic, approximate fit indices) facilitate decisions regarding the acceptability of the model (i.e., does this two-factor model adequately represent the observed variances and covariances for these 8 items?)[1]. If the number of estimated parameters is less than the number of nonredundant elements in the observed variance/covariance matrix, the model will not perfectly reproduce the values of the observed sample covariance matrix elements in most instances (i.e., residuals will not be zero).

The estimation process, as described above, is termed *limited information estimation* because it uses a limited view of the relationships between items based on a summary of the data (e.g., sample covariance matrix). Limited information estimation is often used in SEM software programs to estimate model parameters.[2] More specifically, the estimators discussed in this chapter utilize this iterative method with limited information to produce parameter estimates that minimize the discrepancy between the observed matrix elements and the model-implied elements, which is summarized in a single value called a discrepancy function or fit function (F). All of these fit functions are variations of this general formula:

$$F = (\mathbf{s} - \boldsymbol{\sigma})'\mathbf{W}^{-1}(\mathbf{s} - \boldsymbol{\sigma}) \tag{1}$$

where $\mathbf{s}$ represents a vector of the nonduplicated elements in the sample covariance matrix ($\mathbf{S}$), $\boldsymbol{\sigma}$ represents a vector of nonduplicated elements in the model-implied (i.e., reproduced) covariance matrix [$\boldsymbol{\Sigma}(\boldsymbol{\theta})$], and $\mathbf{s} - \boldsymbol{\sigma}$ represents a residual vector of the discrepancies between the sample and model-implied values. Observed means can also be analyzed (e.g., latent mean and covariance structures analysis); however, in the interest of space, we focus our descriptions on the covariance structure. If the data are continuous, sample covariances (based on Pearson product moment methods) are an appropriate summary of the relationships. However, if ordered categorical data are present, a covariance matrix computed assuming data are continuous ignores the metric/scale of the data. Instead, when data are treated as ordered categorical, $\mathbf{s}$ and $\boldsymbol{\sigma}$ represent vectors of nonduplicated elements in the sample and model-implied *latent correlation matrix* (e.g., polychoric correlations, tetrachoric correlations).

Note in Equation 1 that the residuals are weighted by a *weight matrix*, $\mathbf{W}$. Different estimators utilize different weight matrices. Table 8.3 provides specifics regarding each estimator discussed in this chapter. The table highlights differences among the estimators; however, the table also underscores that all limited information estimators minimize the squared weighted discrepancy between the observed and model-implied matrices (i.e., minimize weighted residuals).

---

1   In addition to unstandardized covariance residuals, standardized residuals, in the form of either z-scores or correlations, are examined. That is, when modeling a covariance matrix, unstandardized covariance residuals are difficult to interpret with respect to what constitutes a large or small residual due to covariances incorporating the variables' metric. By transforming the unstandardized covariance residuals to z-scores (dividing the covariance residual by its standard error) or correlation residuals (the difference between observed and model-implied correlations), the test developer can more easily assess model-data fit. Fortunately, at least one form of standardized residuals is available in most SEM software packages.

2   Full information methods, where observed item responses are used instead of summary statistics (e.g., covariance matrix), are not discussed in this chapter. Importantly, if the data are continuous and normally distributed, the limited information methods are full information methods because all information is contained in the summary statistics—the variances, covariances, and means (the means need not be used if there are no constraints on the mean structure). See Edwards and colleagues (2012) for a discussion of full information estimators in the SEM context when data are discrete (i.e., not continuous or normally distributed).

Table 8.3. Summary of limited information estimators commonly used in SEM applications

Estimator	Commonly presented formula for estimated fit function	Weight matrix	Description
Data treated as continuous in nature			
Generalized least squares (GLS)	$$\hat{F}_{GLS} = \frac{1}{2} tr\left[\left(\mathbf{S} - \mathbf{\Sigma}(\mathbf{\theta})\right)\mathbf{W}^{-1}\right]^2$$	$\mathbf{W} = \mathbf{S}$ $\mathbf{S}$ = sample covariance matrix	GLS minimizes one-half of the trace (i.e., sum of the diagonal elements) of the matrix that represents the squared weighted discrepancies between the elements in the observed and model-implied covariance matrix. Half of the trace is necessary given the full observed and model-implied matrices are utilized and half of the elements in each matrix are redundant.
Maximum likelihood (ML)	$$\hat{F}_{ML} = \frac{1}{2} tr\left[\left(\mathbf{S} - \mathbf{\Sigma}(\mathbf{\theta})\right)\mathbf{W}^{-1}\right]^2$$ $$\hat{F}_{ML} = \log|\mathbf{\Sigma}(\mathbf{\theta})| + tr(\mathbf{\Sigma}(\mathbf{\theta})^{-1}\mathbf{S}) - \log|\mathbf{S}| - p$$	$\mathbf{W} = \mathbf{\Sigma}(\mathbf{\theta})$ $\mathbf{\Sigma}(\mathbf{\theta})$ = model-implied covariance matrix p = number of measured variables	Technically, the first formula is the *reweighted least squares fit function*, which is asymptotically equivalent to the second formula (ML's well-known formula). The term reweighted refers to updating the weight matrix at each iteration (unlike GLS, which uses the same weight matrix – $\mathbf{S}$ – throughout the estimation process).
Weighted least squares (WLS) or Asymptotically distribution free (ADF)	$$\hat{F}_{ADF} = (\mathbf{s} - \hat{\mathbf{\sigma}})'\mathbf{W}^{-1}(\mathbf{s} - \hat{\mathbf{\sigma}})$$	$\mathbf{W}$ = asymptotic covariance matrix of the observed sample covariance with elements $W_{ij,kl} = s_{ijkl} - s_{ij}s_{kl}$ where s_{ijkl} is a quantity related to multivariate kurtosis, and s_{ij} and s_{kl} are the observed covariances of x_i with x_j and x_k with x_l, respectively. $\mathbf{s}$ = vector of nonduplicated sample variances and covariances $\hat{\mathbf{\sigma}}$ = vector of nonduplicated model-implied variances and covariances	When modeling nonnormal continuous data, the WLS estimator is often termed the ADF estimator. Unlike ML and GLS, ADF does not require multivariate normality. ADF estimation is essentially GLS with a weight matrix that includes information related to kurtosis. If data are normal (i.e., no kurtosis), the ADF estimator reduces to the GLS estimator. That is, both ADF and GLS estimators employ the asymptotic covariance matrix of the sample covariance matrix as the weight matrix. However, the typical element of $\mathbf{W}$ for GLS is a function of only the covariances, as normality is assumed: $W_{ij,kl} = s_{ik}s_{jl} - s_{il}s_{jk}$. This $\mathbf{W}$, computed under the assumption of normality, paired with Equation 1, represents one form of the GLS formula. Importantly, Bollen (1989; pp. 427–429) noted that the GLS formula above, which uses $\mathbf{S}$ as the weight matrix, equals the more general form (Equation 1 paired with the asymptotic covariance matrix under the assumption of normality).

Table 8.3. continued

Estimator	Commonly presented formula for estimated fit function	Weight matrix	Description
Data treated as ordered categorical in nature			
Weighted least squares (WLS)	$\hat{F}_{WLS} = (\mathbf{r} - \hat{\boldsymbol{\rho}})'\mathbf{W}^{-1}(\mathbf{r} - \hat{\boldsymbol{\rho}})$	$\mathbf{W}$ = asymptotic covariance matrix of $\mathbf{r}$; a matrix of the variances and covariances of the sample latent correlations $\mathbf{r}$ = vector of sample latent correlations (e.g., polychoric correlations) $\hat{\boldsymbol{\rho}}$ = vector of model-implied latent correlations (e.g., model-implied polychoric correlations)	Latent correlations are analyzed to recognize the ordered categorical nature of the data. Similar to ADF, the asymptotic covariance matrix of the input data is employed as the weight matrix. This weight matrix is large, difficult to compute, and often cannot be inverted because its nonpositive definite. Thus, issues associated with nonconvergence and inadmissible solutions are common. Moreover, model-data fit, parameter estimates, and standard errors tend to become more biased as sample size decreases, model size increases, and nonnormality increases.
Robust diagonally weighted least squares (DWLS)	$\hat{F}_{DWLS} = (\mathbf{r} - \hat{\boldsymbol{\rho}})'diag\mathbf{W}^{-1}(\mathbf{r} - \hat{\boldsymbol{\rho}})$	$diag\mathbf{W}$ = asymptotic variances of the latent correlation estimates $\mathbf{r}$ = vector of sample latent correlations $\hat{\boldsymbol{\rho}}$ = vector of model-implied latent correlations	The residuals $\mathbf{r} - \hat{\boldsymbol{\rho}}$ are weighted by the asymptotic variances of the r elements. Employing only the diagonal of $\mathbf{W}$ to estimate parameters helps overcome convergence issues experienced with full WLS; however, if only the diagonal of the weight matrix is used, the standard errors and χ^2 would be biased. Information from the full $\mathbf{W}$ matrix can be incorporated into DWLS standard errors and χ^2 values in a manner akin to the S-B adjustments, resulting in robust DWLS standard errors and χ^2 values.
Robust ML applied to latent correlations (S-B scaled ML utilizing latent correlations)	$\hat{F}_{ML} = (\mathbf{r} - \hat{\boldsymbol{\rho}})'\mathbf{W}^{-1}(\mathbf{r} - \hat{\boldsymbol{\rho}})$	$\mathbf{W}$ = matrix of the model-implied latent correlations $\mathbf{r}$ = vector of sample latent correlations $\hat{\boldsymbol{\rho}}$ = vector of model-implied latent correlations	$\mathbf{W}$ employed when applying ML estimation to latent correlations is the model-implied latent correlation matrix at each iteration, which does not include information held in the asymptotic covariance matrix of the polychoric correlations. Thus, standard errors and fit indices will be biased. However, the S-B scaling method can be applied to correct ML-based standard errors and the χ^2 value. This S-B scaling involves estimating the asymptotic covariance matrix of the polychoric correlations from the data.

Normal Theory Estimators

If data are assumed to be continuous and normally distributed, then NT methods may be used for estimation. Two common NT estimators used in SEM are ML and generalized least squares (GLS). As shown in Table 8.3, GLS employs the observed sample covariance matrix, S, as the weight matrix, whereas ML employs the estimated model-implied covariance matrix, $\Sigma(\hat{\theta})$. Correct model specification will result in $\Sigma(\hat{\theta})$ that is not statistically significantly different from S, thus, the two estimators will produce similar results if the model is correctly specified. However, in cases of model misspecification, the two weight matrices will be statistically significantly different from each other, and the estimators will produce different results. GLS produces more biased parameter estimates than ML under model misspecification. Moreover, GLS-based fit indices often inaccurately indicate good model-data fit when the model is misspecified, whereas ML-based fit indices tend to be more accurate (Olsson, Foss, Troye, & Howell, 2000; Olsson, Troye, & Howell, 1999). Thus, ML is recommended over GLS. Therefore, we limit subsequent discussion of NT estimators to ML, and results from additional estimation techniques will be compared to ML results.

Estimators for Nonnormal, Continuous Data

For some instruments, subscale level data may be available and may better approximate a continuous distribution than item level data. However, this continuous data may exhibit substantial skewness and/or kurtosis due to the construct or population under study. There are three approaches commonly used to analyze nonnormal, continuous data. First, researchers often use the ML fit function (or the iteratively reweighted least squares fit function) where standard errors and fit indices are computed under the assumption of normality (i.e., the formulas presented in Table 8.3). Using this procedure ignores the actual distribution of the data (i.e., considers the nonnormal data to be normally distributed). ML-based results (i.e., standard errors and χ^2 value) have been found to be biased under particular nonnormal data conditions (discussed below). A second approach, the Satorra–Bentler scaling method, also utilizes the ML fit function, but adjusts the ML-based standard errors and χ^2 value based on the multivariate kurtosis present in the observed variables (Satorra & Bentler, 1988). Approximate fit indices based on the χ^2 value are also corrected. A third approach involves applying weighted least squares (WLS) estimation, also called the asymptotic distribution-free (ADF) estimator when modeling nonnormal continuous data. WLS/ADF estimation makes none of the distributional assumptions of ML estimation (Browne, 1984). However, this method has been shown to produce accurate results under only very restrictive data situations, as discussed below (see Muthén & Kaplan, 1992).

ML Estimation

Given the ML standard errors and χ^2 value are computed under the assumption of normality, the effects of nonnormality on these estimates depends on its extent. Although there are no cutoffs for an acceptable degree of nonnormality, research suggests ML-based results may be biased when univariate skew approaches |2| and univariate kurtosis approaches |7| (Chou & Bentler, 1995; Curran, West, & Finch, 1996; Muthén & Kaplan, 1985). Although ML estimation has been found to produce relatively accurate parameter estimates under conditions of nonnormality with continuous data (e.g., Finch, West, & MacKinnon, 1997), the resulting χ^2

statistic, approximate fit indices, and standard errors are increasingly biased as nonnormality increases (e.g., Chou, Bentler, & Satorra, 1991; Finch et al., 1997)[3]. Specifically, leptokurtic distributions (positive kurtosis) produce attenuated standard errors and an inflated χ^2 statistic, leading to an increased Type I error rate (Yuan, Bentler, & Zhang, 2005). Conversely, platykurtic distributions (negative kurtosis) result in bias in the opposite direction; standard errors are inflated and χ^2 values are attenuated, leading to increased Type II errors. Additionally, ML-based fit indices such as the Tucker-Lewis index (TLI), comparative fit index (CFI), and root-mean-square error of approximation (RMSEA) tend to be biased when data are moderately to severely nonnormal (e.g., Hu & Bentler, 1999; Yu & Muthén, 2002).

Satorra–Bentler Scaled χ^2 and Robust Standard Errors

Satorra and Bentler (1988) developed the Satorra–Bentler (S-B) scaling method to accommodate nonnormal, continuous data when employing a NT estimator. As stated above, nonnormality does not greatly affect NT-based parameter estimates, but does impact the NT-based standard errors. More specifically, when there is excess kurtosis, the ML parameter estimates remain unbiased and consistent, but they are no longer asymptotically efficient, thus the ML standard errors no longer accurately reflect their variability. The S-B robust correction allows one to utilize ML estimation by adjusting the ML-based standard errors to account for the loss in efficiency due to nonnormality (Savalei, 2014). Specifically, ML standard errors are adjusted to approximate values that would have been obtained if the data were normally distributed.

The ML-χ^2 is also biased due to nonnormality. That is, an accurate estimate of χ^2 necessitates an accurate estimate of the sampling variability of the parameter estimates (Savalei, 2014). If there is a loss in efficiency due to nonnormality and, in turn, standard errors (which are a measure of parameter estimate stability) are inaccurate, the χ^2 is no longer χ^2 distributed. More specifically, when data are normally distributed and the model is correctly specified, the expected value of χ^2 is equal to the model df. Therefore, if the two-factor model in Figure 8.1 is correctly specified, a χ^2 value of 19 would be expected. However, if data are moderately nonnormal, the ML-based χ^2 estimate will be biased upward or downward, depending upon the distribution of the data (i.e., leptokurtic or platykurtic). The S-B robust correction involves using a scaling factor to correct the χ^2 value. This correction uses the data's distributional characteristics to adjust the ML-based χ^2 to better approximate the theoretical χ^2 reference distribution:

$$\text{S-B scaled } \chi^2 = d^{-1}(\text{ML-based } \chi^2), \tag{2}$$

where d is a scaling factor that relates in part to the amount of multivariate kurtosis present in the data (Chou & Bentler, 1995; Satorra & Bentler, 1988, 1994). If no multivariate kurtosis exists, the S-B scaled χ^2 equals the ML-based χ^2. As multivariate kurtosis increases, the S-B scaled χ^2 becomes more discrepant from the ML-based χ^2.

---

3   When assumptions associated with an estimation method are met, parameter estimates are asymptotically unbiased (neither over- nor under-estimate the true population parameters in large samples), consistent (converge to population parameters as sample size increases), and efficient (have minimum sampling variability; a more efficient estimator is more stable from sample to sample). When assumptions are not met, some or all of these characteristics may not apply. For example, when modeling nonnormal continuous data using ML estimation, the parameter estimates remain unbiased and consistent, but not efficient, hence, the need to apply the robust correction to inaccurate ML standard errors and the χ^2 value when modeling nonnormal data. More specifically, the lack of efficiency (and, in turn, incorrect standard errors and χ^2 value) is due to employing the "wrong" weight matrix (Savalei, 2014).

For correctly specified models, the S-B scaled χ^2 outperforms the unadjusted ML-based χ^2, especially as nonnormality increases (Chou et al., 1991; Curran et al., 1996; Hu, Bentler, & Kano, 1992; Yu & Muthén, 2002). However, Foss, Jöreskog, and Olsson (2011) found the S-B scaled χ^2 may be insensitive to model misspecification as kurtosis increases. When the S-B scaled χ^2 is incorporated into the calculation of χ^2-based fit indices (e.g., TLI, CFI, RMSEA), these adjusted fit indices have been found to outperform the unadjusted ML indices for both correctly specified and misspecified models (Nevitt & Hancock, 2000; Yu & Muthén, 2002). Although S-B robust standard errors have been found to exhibit negative bias, the estimates outperform ML-based standard errors under conditions of nonnormality (Chou & Bentler, 1995; Chou et al., 1991). Thus, the S-B scaling adjustment to the χ^2 value, fit indices, and standard errors is recommended for nonnormal continuous data. Note that the S-B scaling complicates nested model comparisons. When employing ML estimation, the difference between ML χ^2 values for two nested models is χ^2 distributed, with df equal to the difference in df between the two models. However, the difference between two S-B scaled χ^2 values is not χ^2 distributed. Fortunately, methods have been developed for comparing S-B scaled χ^2 values across nested models (Bryant & Satorra, 2012).

Weighted Least Squares (WLS) Estimation

An alternative method for analyzing nonnormal data is to abandon NT estimators and employ an estimator that relaxes distributional assumptions. One such estimator is WLS, also called the asymptotically distribution free (ADF) estimator (Browne, 1984). WLS estimation makes no distribution assumptions, and should, theoretically, not be affected by skewed or kurtotic observed variables. WLS estimation employs the same fit function as GLS estimation and both utilize the asymptotic covariance matrix of S as the weight matrix (W); however, GLS employs the asymptotic covariance matrix computed under the assumption of normality, whereas WLS makes no such assumptions. The asymptotic covariance matrix consists of the variances and covariances of the elements of the sample covariance matrix. More specifically, the variances of the asymptotic covariance matrix (i.e., diagonal of the matrix) quantify the sampling variability associated with each element of the sample covariance matrix. The covariances of the asymptotic covariance matrix (i.e., off-diagonal of the matrix) describe the extent to which the elements of the sample covariance matrix covary. For WLS estimation, elements of the asymptotic covariance matrix, $W_{ij,kl}$, are calculated using second (i.e., variance) and fourth-order moments (i.e., kurtosis) from the observed data (Bentler & Dudgeon, 1996):

$$W_{ij,kl} = s_{ijkl} - s_{ij}s_{kl}, \tag{3}$$

where s_{ijkl} is a quantity related to multivariate kurtosis

$$s_{ijkl} = \frac{\sum_{a=1}^{N}(x_{ai}-\bar{x}_i)(x_{aj}-\bar{x}_j)(x_{ak}-\bar{x}_k)(x_{al}-\bar{x}_l)}{N} \tag{4}$$

and s_{ij} and s_{kl} are the observed covariances of x_i with x_j and x_k with x_l, respectively. $W_{ij,kl}$ is the estimated asymptotic covariance between s_{ij} and s_{kl}. Thus, the elements in W reflect both departure from normality and sampling variability. The W for WLS reduces to the W for GLS when data satisfy normality conditions (see Table 8.3).

As detailed in Equation 1, the weight matrix is inverted during the estimation process. If WLS is used, the asymptotic covariance matrix is much larger than the sample covariance matrix, and, thus, inverting this matrix becomes computationally intensive. The dimensions of W are

½(p)(p + 1) by ½(p)(p + 1), where p is the number of measured variables. In our eight-item CFA example, the weight matrix utilized by WLS estimation would be 36 by 36, much larger than the 8 by 8 weight matrix utilized with NT estimation. The dimensions of the asymptotic covariance matrix increase exponentially as the number of observed variables increases.

Although WLS estimation was created to accommodate nonnormal data (i.e., produce unbiased, consistent, and efficient parameter estimates), unfortunately, it has been found to be biased when the model is misspecified or when sample sizes are not sufficiently large (Chou et al., 1991). Similar to GLS estimation, WLS estimation produces fit indices that suggest misfitting models actually represent the data well, and this bias becomes more severe as nonnormality increases (Curran et al., 1996; Foss et al., 2011; Olsson, Foss, & Troye, 2003; Olsson et al., 2000). WLS estimation also necessitates very large sample sizes. At small sample sizes, WLS estimation produces inflated χ^2 values, and thus increased Type I errors (Curran et al., 1996). Prior research suggests sample sizes upward of 5,000 are necessary to produce Type I error rates that approach nominal rates (Hu et al., 1992). Further, small samples tend to produce negatively biased parameters and inaccurate standard errors (Hoogland & Boomsma, 1998). Fortunately, S-B scaled ML results for nonnormal continuous data have been found to be more accurate than WLS results, except at very large sample sizes (e.g., Chou & Bentler, 1995; Chou et al., 1991; Curran et al., 1996; Hu et al., 1992). Thus, WLS is not recommended when analyzing nonnormal continuous data.

Estimators for Ordered Categorical Data

Treating Ordered Categorical Data as Continuous

Estimation is further complicated when analyzing data that are categorical in nature. Commonly used test formats typically yield ordered categorical data. That is, attitudinal measures often consist of Likert-type items, and ability tests often consist of dichotomously-scored (correct/incorrect) items. These ordered categorical variables are discrete and, thus, cannot be strictly normally distributed (Kaplan, 2009). However, as the number of ordered scale points increases, the distribution of ordered categorical data may approach a coarse approximation of a normal distribution (Bollen & Barb, 1981). Therefore, strategies for analyzing ordered categorical data involve either ignoring or accounting for the categorical nature of the data.

ML Estimation

Researchers choosing to ignore the ordered categorical nature of the variables tend to treat data as continuous and thus, analyze a covariance matrix using ML estimation either unadjusted or with the S-B adjustment. Unadjusted ML estimation tends to perform well when the observed data follow a (approximately) normal distribution and there are at least five ordered categories (e.g., Babakus, Ferguson, & Jöreskog, 1987; Hutchinson & Olmos, 1998). When normally distributed ordered categorical data with five categories are analyzed as continuous, slight underestimation occurs in model fit and parameter estimates if sample size is small (e.g., Dolan, 1994; Muthén & Kaplan, 1985; Rhemtulla, Brosseau-Liard, & Savalei, 2012). Standard errors have shown greater sensitivity to categorization than parameter estimates, exhibiting negative bias when the metric of the data is ignored (Babakus et al., 1987; Muthén & Kaplan, 1985; West, Finch, & Curran, 1995).

Whereas applying ML estimation to a covariance matrix computed from approximately normally distributed five (or more) ordered categorical data does not result in severe levels of bias in parameter estimates, standard errors, or fit indices, problems emerge as the number of response options decrease or as the observed item distributions diverge from a normal distribution. More specifically, when modeling nonnormal ordered categorical data as continuous, ML-based χ^2 values are inflated and fit indices typically indicate worse fit than actually exists, leading to increased rejection of correct models (Green, Akey, Fleming, Hershberger, & Marquis, 1997; Hutchinson & Olmos, 1998; Muthén & Kaplan, 1985; West et al., 1995). Parameter estimates and standard errors are increasingly negatively biased as item-level nonnormality increases and fewer categories are present (Bababus et al., 1987; Bollen, 1989; Dolan, 1994). Thus, unadjusted ML estimation is not recommended when modeling ordered categorical variables with fewer than five categories and/or nonnormally distributed ordered categorical data.

ML Estimation With S-B Scaling

ML estimation utilizing S-B scaling to adjust the χ^2 value and standard errors has been found to empirically outperform unadjusted ML estimation when analyzing ordered categorical data (e.g., DiStefano, 2002; Green et al., 1997). The S-B scaled χ^2 has been found to be generally accurate under few category or kurtotic distribution conditions, although it is positively biased when analyzing differentially skewed data with a small number of categories (Bandalos, 2014; Green et al., 1997). S-B robust standard errors have been shown to be accurate with as few as three categories (Bandalos, 2014; DiStefano, 2003). Recall that S-B scaling methods are not applied to parameter estimates, thus, parameter estimates will exhibit negative bias, with increases in the level of bias due more to the number of ordered categories present than to the degree of nonnormality (DiStefano & Morgan, 2012).

Treating Ordered Categorical Data as Categorical

Researchers can recognize and model the categorical nature of the items by abandoning the inter-item covariances estimated from the observed data and replacing them with estimates of the latent relationships among the items. For example, tetrachoric correlations would be computed to represent the relationships between dichotomous items and polychoric correlations would be computed for items with more than two ordered categories. When estimating these latent correlations, one is making assumptions about how the observed item-level data were obtained. Researchers typically assume the observed ordered categorical responses (y) are crude categorizations of latent continuous normally distributed response variables (y^*). More specifically, when responding to an item, an examinee must convert a continuous value that represents his/her underlying latent response (y^*) into the crude category (y) that best represents y^*. To model the continuous underlying latent response variable, and, in turn, take into account the categorical nature of the data, "The goal is to 'reverse-engineer' the relationship such that we can take the observed categorical response and translate it back into the latent, continuous value corresponding to that item response" (Edwards, Wirth, Houts & Xi, 2012, p. 198).

The reverse engineering process involves computing the item-specific threshold values (τ) which determine the correspondence between the observed categorical y variable and the latent continuous y^* variable. A total of $c - 1$ thresholds are estimated, where c is the number of categories associated with y. Consider it is of interest to estimate the CFA model in Figure 8.1 using data obtained from Likert-type items. If each item used a four ordered category response scale, the observed item-level data (y) would be represented as

$$y = \begin{cases} 1 & \text{if } y^* \leq \tau_1 \\ 2 & \text{if } \tau_1 < y^* \leq \tau_2 \\ 3 & \text{if } \tau_2 < y^* \leq \tau_3 \\ 4 & y^* > \tau_3 \end{cases} \qquad (5)$$

using three item-specific threshold values. As illustrated, the threshold values specify the points along the y^* continuum for that specific item that result in a category shift (e.g., from 1 to 2) in the observed item-level data (y). Underlying response y^* variables are usually assumed to have a standard normal distribution, with a mean of zero and a standard deviation of 1. Thus, for each item, threshold values are estimated by considering the cumulative area under the normal curve up to a given point,

$$\tau_i = \Phi^{-1} \left[\sum_{k=1}^{i} \frac{N_k}{N} \right], \qquad i = 1, 2, \ldots c - 1 \qquad (6)$$

where τ_i is a particular threshold, Φ^{-1} is the inverse of the normal distribution function, N_k is the number of subjects who selected category k, N is the total sample size, and c is the total number of categories. For example, when examining responses to variable y_j, imagine we have ordered categorical data where 86% of respondents selected response category 1, 10% of respondents selected 2, 3% selected category 3, and 1% selected category 4. The z-score corresponding to the point on the standard normal curve where 86% of respondents fall at or below that point would be the first threshold value ($\tau_1 = 1.08$). The z-score corresponding to the point on the standard normal curve where 96% (i.e., 86% + 10%) of respondents scored at or below that point (the percentage who responded a 1 or 2) would be the second threshold ($\tau_2 = 1.75$). The z-score corresponding to the point on the standard normal curve where 99% (i.e., 86% + 10% + 3%) of respondents scored at or below that point (the percentage who responded a 1, 2, or 3) would be the third threshold ($\tau_3 = 2.33$).

Threshold values are then used to compute latent correlations (e.g., tetrachoric correlations, polychoric correlations) between items. More specifically, for each pair of items, a contingency table of examinees' responses to the item pair and both items' thresholds are used to estimate the latent correlation. The estimated latent correlation represents the value with the greatest likelihood of yielding the observed contingency table given the estimated thresholds. Clearly, latent correlations are conceptually and mathematically different from Pearson Product Moment correlations computed from the observed data. By estimating latent correlations (i.e., the relationships among the underlying continuous, normally distributed y^* variables), the inter-item relationships are not attenuated in the same fashion as Pearson correlations or covariances estimated from the observed ordered categorical data (y).

Figure 8.2 represents the eight-item, two-factor model applied to the continuous latent response variables (y^*). The general fit function can be utilized (Equation 1), but polychoric correlations between the items (i.e., correlations between y^* variables) are analyzed. Explicitly, the estimators described for continuous data (e.g., WLS, ML) can be applied to a polychoric correlation matrix using model specification that reflects the correlation input, thereby acknowledging the ordered categorical nature of the item responses.

WLS Estimation Utilizing Polychoric Correlations

As shown in Table 8.3, when WLS estimation is employed with latent correlation input (e.g., polychorics), the fit function minimizes the discrepancy between the observed and reproduced

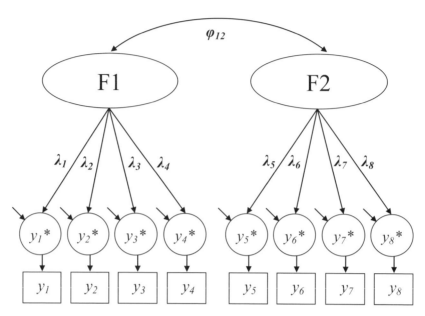

Figure 8.2. Confirmatory two-factor model fit to eight items with ordered categorical response options (i.e., scores of 1, 2, 3, 4). F1 and F2 represent two continuous latent variables. The eight observed categorical y variables, if modeled directly, would have a nonlinear relationship with F1 and F2. Instead, latent response variables, y^*, which are assumed to be continuous and normally distributed, are modeled to underlie the ordered categorical y variables. Thus, the purpose of the two-factor model is to reproduce the relationships among the continuous y^*, not categorical y, variables (allowing the application of a linear model to the latent factors and y^* variables). A total of 9 parameters (bolded) are estimated from 28 polychoric correlations, including 1 factor correlation (φ_{12}) and 8 factor pattern coefficients (λ). Note that factor variances are fixed to 1. Factor pattern coefficients (λ) indicate the unit change in y^* for every unit change in the factor (e.g., F1), which may result in a category change in y, depending on the value of y^* and threshold values. Given the analysis of a correlation matrix (i.e., polychoric matrix), the item error variances terms e_1 to e_8 (single headed arrows pointing to each y^*) are not estimated but instead are a function of the factor pattern coefficients $(e_1 = 1- \lambda_1^2)$. That is, given the variance associated with each item is fixed to 1 (i.e., 1's on the diagonal of the polychoric matrix), the error variance is simply derived by subtracting the common variance from the total variance (e.g., $e_1 = 1- \lambda_1^2$).

polychoric correlations. Thus, unlike the analysis of continuous data, which involves minimizing the discrepancy between the observed and model-implied covariances and variances (36 covariance elements for our 8-item test; [(8*9)/2] = 36), WLS estimation with latent correlation input recognizes that the diagonal elements of the correlation matrix are fixed at 1.0 (i.e., are not functions of model parameters), and thus, estimates only the parameters necessary to minimize the discrepancy between the observed and reproduced correlations included in the off-diagonal elements (28 polychoric correlations for our 8-item test; [(8*7)/2] = 28). Note that the degrees of freedom for the two-factor model applied to the 8 items is equivalent regardless if a covariance matrix (based on treating the data as continuous) is analyzed or a polychoric matrix (based on treating the data as ordered categorical) is analyzed ($df = 19$). That is, as explicated in Figure 8.1 and Figure 8.2, when reproducing the 36 variances and covariances, 17 parameters are estimated, whereas when reproducing the 28 polychorics, 9 parameters are estimated. The difference in the number of parameters stems from the error terms *not* being estimated when modeling latent correlations due to the observed variance of the 8 items being fixed at 1 (the diagonal of the polychoric correlation matrix holds values of 1.0). Thus, in situations when correlational input is analyzed with WLS, the error variances are derived, not estimated, by simply subtracting the variance explained in the item by the factor from the total item variance of 1.0. In short, software programs recognize the ordered categorical nature of the data when one couples latent correlation input with WLS estimation; thus, the typical model specification can be applied (i.e., the same syntax can be used to specify the model with only changes to the input matrix and the estimator employed; no additional syntax is needed to constrain the error terms to particular values as the software recognizes that latent correlations are included and constraints on error terms are imposed by default).

WLS estimation with polychoric correlations as input utilizes the asymptotic covariance matrix of the polychoric correlation matrix as the weight matrix in the fit function. Inverting this asymptotic covariance matrix of the polychoric correlations is computationally intensive as it consists of the variances and covariances of the sample latent correlations. Thus, WLS estimation applied to polychoric correlations has many of the same problems as WLS estimation applied to covariance matrix input. Specifically, WLS estimation with polychoric correlations often fails to reach admissible solutions at sample sizes less than 200 (Bandalos, 2014; Flora & Curran, 2004). When models do converge to an admissible solution, both WLS χ^2 and parameter estimates become increasingly inflated as model size increases or sample size decreases (DiStefano, 2002; Flora & Curran, 2004; Yang-Wallentin, Jöreskog, & Luo, 2010). Large models, nonnormal data, or small samples also result in negatively biased standard errors (Bandalos, 2014; DiStefano, 2002; Muthén & Kaplan, 1992; Potthast, 1993; Yang-Wallentin et al., 2010). Given these issues, WLS estimation utilizing polychoric correlations is not recommended.

Robust Diagonally WLS Estimation Utilizing Polychoric Correlations

Diagonally WLS (DWLS) estimation modifies traditional WLS estimation to avoid many of the computational difficulties involved in inverting the full asymptotic covariance matrix of the sample polychoric correlations during parameter estimation. DWLS estimation uses only the diagonal of the asymptotic covariance matrix (i.e., the variances associated with the polychoric correlations), and excludes the off-diagonal elements during parameter estimation. Unfortunately, excluding the off-diagonal elements of the asymptotic covariance matrix involves a loss of information, which biases standard errors and the χ^2 (Savalei, 2014). That is, DWLS estimation is not statistically efficient given it employs only the diagonal instead of the full weight matrix (i.e., the diagonal matrix is not the optimal weight matrix). Fortunately, robust DWLS estimation applies corrections akin to the S-B scaling method to the DWLS standard errors and χ^2 value to incorporate the information from the full weight matrix. Although the full asymptotic covariance matrix of the polychoric correlations is utilized when employing the robust corrections, unlike WLS estimation, the full matrix is not inverted and thus DWLS does not suffer from the convergence problems associated with WLS estimation. In this context, the robust corrections are not correcting for the loss of efficiency due to nonnormality (i.e., not adjusting for nonnormality in the underlying continuous variable), as the underlying continuous latent variables are assumed to be normally distributed, hence the use of the normal curve (e.g., threshold values) to compute the polychoric correlations. Instead, the robust corrections adjust for loss of efficiency resulting from not using the full asymptotic covariance matrix of the polychoric correlations as the weight matrix when employing DWLS estimation (Rhemtulla et al., 2012; Savalei, 2014).

Generally, robust DWLS estimation has been found to outperform WLS estimation. Importantly, robust DWLS χ^2 values are close to expected values, even with increasing model size and decreasing sample size (Bandalos, 2014; Flora & Curran, 2004; Yang-Wallentin et al., 2010). Moreover, robust DWLS χ^2 values are more accurate than unadjusted ML χ^2 values (i.e., modeling ordered categorical data as continuous) when the number of categories is small (i.e., three or less), with both robust DWLS applied to polychoric correlations and ML applied to covariances performing equally well when modeling five or six categories (Beauducel & Herzberg, 2006). However, in conditions of increasing nonnormality, robust DWLS estimation has been found to be underpowered (Bandalos, 2014; Lei, 2009), resulting in retaining models with moderate misspecification. It is unclear whether robust DWLS fit indices are accurate, as some research has found them to perform well (Yu & Muthén, 2002), whereas other research has found them to be overly optimistic (Bandalos, 2008). With respect to parameter estimates and standard errors, robust DWLS is fairly accurate (Bandalos, 2014; Flora & Curran, 2004; Oranje, 2003; Yang-Wallentin et al., 2010). Although estimates become more biased as sample size decreases and model size increases, the bias is slight and much less than WLS estimation.

The improvement over WLS estimation suggests robust DWLS estimation is a viable option for the analysis of ordered categorical data. The question remains whether robust ML estimation utilizing polychoric correlations outperforms robust DWLS estimation.

Unadjusted ML and Robust ML Estimation Utilizing Polychoric Correlations

As noted above, treating ordered categorical data as continuous and employing ML estimation with a covariance matrix can result in underestimated parameter estimates and biased standard errors and χ^2 values. Thus, one potential solution is to input latent correlations (e.g., polychoric correlations) and apply ML estimation. When analyzing ordered categorical data (from two to seven ordered response categories; Dolan, 1994), ML estimation applied to latent correlations resulted in more accurate parameter estimates than estimates obtained from ML estimation applied to a covariance matrix. Importantly, however, standard errors of parameter estimates and χ^2 values will be biased when analyzing latent correlations with ML estimation (Holgado-Tello, Chácon-Moscoso, Barbero-García, & Vila-Abad, 2008; Jöreskog, Sörbom, du Toit, & du Toit, 2000; Rigdon & Ferguson, 1991) unless two modifications are applied.

First, and as described above for DWLS estimation, the weight matrix used with ML estimation when latent correlations are analyzed is not the optimal choice for **W**. As explicated in Table 8.3, the weight matrix employed when using ML estimation with polychoric correlations is the model-implied polychoric correlation matrix updated at each iteration. Fortunately, latent correlation input paired with the S-B robust correction can potentially provide relatively unbiased standard errors and more accurate χ^2 values. As expected when utilizing the robust correction, the asymptotic covariance matrix of the input matrix (i.e., polychoric correlations) is needed to employ the adjustments to the standard errors and fit indices. Thus, when analyzing latent correlations, the asymptotic covariance matrix of the latent correlations must be estimated from the raw data to apply the corrections to the ML-based standard errors and χ^2.

Second, and unlike WLS and DWLS estimation applied to latent correlations, in some software programs, such as LISREL, ML estimation assumes an input covariance matrix. That is, the ML estimation technique assumes the data being modeled are continuous and multivariate normally distributed; hence, a covariance matrix adequately summarizes the data. Thus, when modeling latent correlations with ML estimation, model fit statistics and standard errors associated with the parameter estimates will be incorrect due to ML estimation trying to reproduce a covariance matrix instead of correlation matrix (Jöreskog et al., 2000). The standard errors may be correctly computed if the model is specified to reflect the modeling of latent correlations. In practice, this means ensuring two important specifications. First, item error variance terms should *not* be estimated. Recall, item error variances are a function of the model parameters because the variance of $y*$ is fixed to 1. Unlike WLS and DWLS estimation, which automatically constrain the item error values, ML estimation applied to latent correlations in LISREL assumes a covariance matrix is being analyzed and thus estimates item error variances. When utilizing software programs that assume a covariance matrix is being analyzed when employing ML estimation, researchers must add syntax to constrain each error term to equal the proportion of unexplained variance in the item when modeling correlations, as detailed in the LISREL syntax in the Appendix. In the current scenario, ML estimation applied to latent correlations *without* constraints on the error terms would incorrectly estimate 17 parameters (1 factor correlation, 8 factor pattern coefficients, 8 error variances) from 36 variances and covariances. Constraining the error terms results in 8 additional degrees of freedom, resulting in 27 degrees of freedom ($36 - 9 = 27$). Obviously, we are interested in testing the two-factor model specified in Figure 8.2, which has 19 degrees of freedom. The eight additional degrees of freedom (27 vs. 19) results from ML estimation assuming the input matrix is a covariance matrix, and incorrectly treating the eight 1s on the diagonal of the latent correlation matrix as observed variances. Thus, simply constraining the error terms to their correct values is insufficient to estimate the specified model from latent correlations using ML estimation.

Consequently, a second modification must be made. The *df* should be reduced by the number of observed variables (i.e., by the number of variances that equal 1 on the diagonal of the correlation matrix), resulting in the correct *df* associated with the specified model. This adjustment to the *df* is automatically completed by some software programs (e.g., EQS), but may need to be executed manually via syntax in other programs, as must be done in LISREL. In sum, care needs to be taken when employing robust ML to latent correlation input, as it may require additional programming constraints and practices to achieve correct standard errors and fit information, as well as the expected model degrees of freedom. Different software programs have different requirements when using ML with latent correlation input. The Appendix provides sample programs for LISREL. Unlike LISREL, EQS requires no additional constraints beyond specifying the robust ML estimator and that data are correlations (i.e., the appropriate constraints are invoked by default). Currently, Mplus does not allow robust ML estimation to be used with latent correlation input.

The limited research examining the robust ML-PC approach has been favorable (e.g., Lei, 2009; Lei & Wu, 2012). Parameter estimates have been found to be accurate, and χ^2 values were found to be largely accurate under correct specification and illustrated poor fit when models were misspecified (e.g., Holgado-Tello et al., 2008; Yang-Wallentin et al., 2010). However, under conditions of extreme nonnormality, the latent response variables (i.e., $y*$) can lead to biased polychoric correlations and, subsequently, biased parameter estimates (e.g., Lei & Wu, 2012). Comparatively, robust ML estimation utilizing polychoric correlations was found to be more accurate than robust DWLS at small (100) sample sizes (Lei, 2009). However, at sample sizes of 200 or greater, robust DWLS and robust ML estimation applied to polychoric correlations performed similarly with respect to parameter estimates (Lei, 2009; Lei & Wu, 2012).

Example: Performance of Different Estimators With Categorical Data

To illuminate how different estimation techniques accommodate ordered categorical data and to further examine robust ML estimation applied to latent correlations, a simulation study was conducted. LISREL and PRELIS (version 8.80, Jöreskog & Sörbom, 2006) were used to generate and analyze the data. When conducting a simulation study, a population model is specified. The population model represents the true relationships among the variables in the population; thus, all of the parameter values are known. In the current simulation study, multiple datasets were generated based on the specified population parameters and various characteristics of the data (i.e., sample size, normality, metric/scale level). The effects of changing the data characteristics on the accuracy of the parameter estimates can be assessed by comparing these estimates to the true (i.e., population) parameter values. Along these lines, a well-performing estimator should produce parameter estimates that are close in value to the population values (within sampling error) and model-data fit indices that indicate the model fits well (as the model being estimated is correctly specified).

As described earlier, Figure 8.1 represents a two-factor correlated CFA model with four items per factor and simple structure. A population model based on Figure 8.1 was specified, with the true correlation between factors equal to .3 and true factor pattern coefficients equal to .6 for all items. Continuous normally distributed item-level data were generated using these population parameters. Recall that polychoric correlations assume that a continuous normally-distributed response variable (y^*) underlies each categorical observed variable (y). Thus, the normally-distributed item-level data were partitioned to create ordered categorical data with four categories, where cut points to convert the continuous data (y^*) into nonnormal ordered categorical data (y) were based on area under the normal curve (e.g., Lei & Wu, 2012). Two different distributional conditions for the observed categorical data were created by changing the cut point values: mild nonnormality (skewness = 1.5 and kurtosis = 3) and moderate nonnormality (skewness = 3, kurtosis = 6). Samples of 250, 500, and 1,000 cases were generated for each of the two nonnormality conditions to assess the influence of sample size on the estimator performance.

The correctly specified two-factor model was estimated using four different techniques that coupled an estimator with an input data. First, a baseline condition was necessary to illustrate results under the optimal condition of modeling the (generated) continuous, normal data. This baseline condition coupled ML estimation with a covariance matrix representing the relationships between the generated continuous, normally distributed variables. This baseline provided the opportunity to contrast estimation methods appropriate for continuous, normal data (i.e., data at the y^* level) with techniques applied to the ordered categorical data (y) generated from this continuous data. Second, three techniques were examined when modeling the ordered categorical data: ML estimation with S-B robust corrections coupled with covariance matrix input (ML-R); ML estimation with S-B robust corrections with polychoric correlation input (ML-PC); and robust DWLS estimation coupled with polychoric correlation input (DWLS). Robust ML estimation was coupled with a covariance matrix calculated from the ordered categorical data to show the effects of ignoring the categorical nature of the data (i.e., the data were incorrectly treated as if continuous in nature). Alternatively, robust ML estimation coupled with polychoric correlation input (ML-PC) recognizes the metric/scale level of the (categorical) data. Robust DWLS estimation was included given it is currently the predominant approach when modeling ordered categorical data in SEM. Robust DWLS as estimated in LISREL is equivalent to the estimator termed WLSM in Mplus (i.e., mean adjusted), but not equivalent to WLSMV in Mplus (i.e., mean and variance adjusted) estimator.

In summary, the simulation study included three estimation methods applied to four-category ordered categorical data (ML-R, ML-PC, DWLS), three sample sizes (250, 500, 1,000), and two nonnormality levels (mild and moderate) producing 18 conditions (3×3×2). In addition, the baseline condition (continuous, normal) was estimated for the three samples sizes resulting in 21 total conditions. For each of the 21 conditions, 500 unique replications (i.e., 500 different datasets sampled from the population) were simulated and analyzed. Replications with implausible results (e.g., negative error variance, correlation values greater than 1) or convergence problems were removed because they do not provide an accurate interpretation of results (Flora & Curran, 2004; Forero, Maydeu-Olivares, & Gallardo-Pujol, 2009; Yang-Wallentin et al., 2010). However, the number of converged replications out of the possible 500 does provide information about situations where estimators may have difficulty arriving at a solution. Thus, information about the convergence rates were recorded and summarized by simulation condition to provide information about a given estimation technique.

Parameter estimates and model fit indices were examined for each condition.[4] Again, given the correctly specified two-factor model was fit to the data, a well-performing estimator should produce parameter estimates close in value to the population parameter values. Thus, when evaluating the accuracy of the parameter estimates, two pieces of information were calculated. First, the mean of the factor pattern coefficient and factor correlation estimates were computed and compared to the population values (i.e., .60 factor pattern coefficient, .30 factor correlation). Second, relative bias (RB) values were calculated by computing the difference between the estimated parameter value for a given replication and the true parameter value and then dividing this difference by the true parameter value. We then averaged the RB values across replications within a condition to provide an estimate of bias for each cell of the design (Flora & Curran, 2004; Hoogland & Boomsma, 1998). A positive RB value indicates overestimation of a parameter; a negative RB value indicates underestimation. Using cutoffs from prior research (e.g., Flora & Curran, 2004; Hoogland & Boomsma, 1998; Muthén & Kaplan, 1985), absolute RB values under 5% were considered a trivial level of bias, absolute values between 5% and 10% a mild level of bias, and absolute RB values greater than 10% a substantial level of bias.

Fit indices were chosen based on the results of studies involving ordered categorical data (Bandalos, 2008; Hutchinson & Olmos, 1998; Yu & Muthén, 2002). More specifically, indices found to perform well with categorical data were selected. When employing ML-R, ML-PC, and DWLS techniques, it is recommended that the S-B scaled χ^2 value is examined and reported (e.g., Jöreskog, 1994; Yang-Wallentin et al., 2010). As with similar studies examining correctly specified models, χ^2 p-values were used to track Type I errors and determine the impact of the generated conditions in terms of model rejections (Bandalos, 2008; Bandalos & Webb, 2005). That is, given the correctly specified two-factor model was fit to the data, a well-performing estimator should produce χ^2 p-values that result in a failure to reject this true model (e.g., low Type I error rates).

---

4   Previous studies have not focused much attention on standard errors of parameter estimates. Therefore, in line with previous research (e.g., Lei & Wu, 2012), the focus will be on parameter estimates and fit information.

Given their popularity in the applied literature and attention in simulation studies, four approximate fit indices were examined: CFI, TLI, RMSEA, and the standardized root mean square residual (SRMR). Recall that if robust correction procedures are used, the fit indices which rely on χ^2 in their calculations are adjusted as well (Finney & DiStefano, 2013). Thus, with the robust estimators, these approximate fit indices were adjusted (i.e., robust CFI). Approximate fit index results were summarized for each cell by computing the average value across the usable replications. Criteria used to judge poor model-data fit with categorical data have been established (Muthén, 1998–2004; Yu & Muthén, 2002) and used (Bandalos, 2008) in previous studies. More specifically, CFI, NNFI values below .95 indicated model-data misfit and RMSEA values greater than .05 indicated model-data misfit. The SRMR may be used with categorical data if sample size is at least moderate (> 250) and no covariates and no threshold structure is included (Muthén, 1998–2004). For SRMR, cutoff values under .07 have been recommended to indicate good fit when categorical data are present (Yu & Muthén, 2002).

Simulation Results

The majority of replications produced admissible solutions, with one notable exception –the smallest sample size ($N = 250$) coupled with moderately nonnormal ordered categorical data. Under this condition, the number of usable replications was 433 out of 500 for ML-PC, 447 out of 500 for DWLS, and 471 out of 500 for ML-R. All 500 replications were admissible under higher sample sizes, regardless of nonnormality level or estimator used.

Parameter Estimates

Average parameter estimates and RB results showed the effects of the combination of estimator and the ordered categorical data (see Table 8.4). Although ML-R is sometimes recommended for use with ordered categorical data when modeling four ordered categories as continuous, this technique was very sensitive to item distribution, as well as the ordinal nature of the data. That is, estimates of factor pattern loadings and factor relationship showed substantial underestimation of the true parameter value. Moreover, whereas techniques that recognized the categorical nature of the data (DWLS, ML-PC) generally showed a reduction in RB as sample size increased, ML-R did not show such improvement. Thus, aligning with previous research, although ML-R has been recommended for nonnormal continuous data, researchers should note its sensitivity to ordered categorical data and use an alternative technique that recognizes the categorical nature of the data when data have four categories. Robust estimators (DWLS, ML-PC) applied to latent correlations showed little bias in parameter estimates regardless of the level of nonnormality or sample size.

Model-Data Fit

Following previous studies investigating robust estimators with ordered categorical data (e.g., Bandalos, 2008; Bandalos & Webb, 2005; Flora & Curran, 2004), the number of model rejections based on the χ^2 beyond an $\alpha = .05$ level was recorded. Figure 8.3 illustrates the percentage of model rejections based on χ^2 values under mild and moderate nonnormality conditions. All estimation techniques exhibited rejection rates close to an expected level of .05.

Table 8.4. Average parameter estimates (relative bias) across study conditions

Estimator	N = 250		N = 500		N = 1,000	
	Factor pattern	Factor correlation	Factor pattern	Factor correlation	Factor pattern	Factor correlation
Continuous, normal data (Baseline)						
ML	.600 (0.10%)	.299 (−0.37%)	.600 (−0.06%)	.298 (−1.11%)	.600 (−0.05%)	.301 (0.53%)
Ordered category data with mild nonnormality						
ML-R	.336 (−43.94%)	.273 (−8.28%)	.336 (−44.03%)	.276 (−7.80%)	.336 (−43.89%)	.270 (−10.08%)
DWLS	.601 (0.17%)	.307 (2.60%)	.600 (0.06%)	.302 (0.82%)	.601 (0.25%)	.304 (1.49%)
ML-PC	.600 (0.54%)	.290 (−3.12%)	.600 (−0.03%)	.295 (−1.68%)	.600 (−0.05%)	.295 (−1.75%)
Ordered category data with moderate nonnormality						
ML-R	.215 (−64.13%)	.237 (−17.46%)	.213 (−64.12%)	.235 (−21.55%)	.211 (−64.70%)	.231 (−22.98%)
DWLS	.598 (−0.39%)	.320 (11.78%)	.600 (0.08%)	.309 (3.24%)	.600 (−0.03%)	.301 (0.36%)
ML-PC	.587 (−2.16%)	.254 (−8.32%)	.600 (−0.03%)	.295 (−1.68%)	.600 (−0.05%)	.295 (−1.75%)

Note. Maximum likelihood with covariance input (ML), robust maximum likelihood with covariance input (ML-R), diagonal weighted least squares with polychoric correlation input (DWLS), and robust maximum likelihood with polychoric correlation input (ML-PC). Data was generated to fit a two-factor model with factor pattern coefficients equal to .60 and a factor correlation equal to .3. Relative Bias of parameter estimates in parenthesis for Factor Pattern and Factor Correlation columns. RB values under 5% were considered trivial, values between 5% and 10% were considered mild, and values greater than 10% were considered substantial. For example, when analyzing continuous normally distributed data using ML estimation with $N = 250$, the average estimated pattern coefficient (.600) and factor correlation coefficient (.299) in this condition was associated with less than trivial bias (.10% and -.37%, respectively). This minimal bias is expected as the data being modeled in this condition are optimal (i.e., continuous, normally distributed data that align with the specified model).

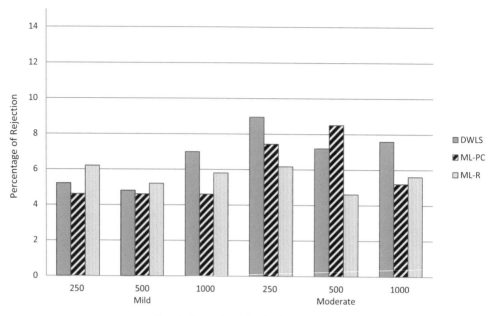

Figure 8.3. Percentage of rejections of robust chi-square values across estimators. DWLS = diagonal weighted least squares with polychoric correlation input. ML-PC = robust maximum likelihood with polychoric correlation input. ML-R = robust maximum likelihood with covariance input. Figure illustrates the percentage of model rejections based on the robust χ^2 value across estimators. Given the model was correctly specified, one would expect rejection rates of approximately 5% (i.e., Type I error). For example, under mild nonnormality, DWLS (gray bar) reported approximately 5% of the cells yielded a significant χ^2 value (i.e., indicating poor model-data fit), ML-PC (black–white striped) reported roughly 4% of the cells with significant χ^2 values, and ML-R (dotted bar) reported approximately 6% of the cells with significant χ^2 values.

Table 8.5 reports average fit information across all estimation techniques. Robust χ^2 values were close to the expected degrees of freedom for most conditions (aligning with Figure 8.3) and average approximate fit indices suggested good fit of the correctly specified model. Only the SRMR showed values above the .07 cutoff under one condition – when the smallest sample size ($N = 250$) was used with moderate nonnormality with DWLS or ML-PC as the estimation technique; however, these results align with the caveat given by Yu and Muthén (2002) regarding the sensitivity of the SRMR with categorical data and smaller sample sizes. Standard deviation values for fit indices were low, suggesting the majority of replications indicate the data fit the specified model. Thus, with respect to fit, when analyzing ordered categorical data with mild or moderate nonnormality, the fit indices would suggest good model-data fit regardless of estimator. Although the results regarding fit look promising, this simulation did not assess the indices ability to identify model misspecification, but instead only investigated the indices' ability to *not* reject a correctly specified model.

Table 8.5. Average model fit indices across study conditions

	N = 250					N = 500					N = 1,000				
	χ^2	CFI	TLI	RMSEA	SRMR	χ^2	CFI	TLI	RMSEA	SRMR	χ^2	CFI	TLI	RMSEA	SRMR
Continuous normal data (baseline)															
ML	19.52 (6.27)	.994 (.01)	.994 (<.01)	.014 (.019)	.037 (.01)	19.36 (6.46)	.999 (<.01)	.999 (<.01)	.010 (.01)	.037 (.01)	19.02 (6.47)	.999 (<.01)	1.00 (.01)	.007 (<.01)	.018 (<.01)
Ordered category data with mild nonnormality															
ML-R	19.61 (6.32)	.987 (.02)	.997 (.05)	.012 (<.01)	.044 (.01)	19.04 (6.00)	.994 (.01)	1.000 (.02)	.001 (.01)	.044 (.01)	19.30 (6.47)	.999 (<.01)	1.00 (.01)	.007 (<.01)	.022 (<.01)
DWLS	19.36 (6.43)	.993 (.01)	.999 (.02)	.012 (.01)	.060 (.01)	18.81 (6.26)	.997 (.01)	1.000 (.01)	.010 (.01)	.060 (.01)	19.19 (6.43)	.998 (<.01)	1.00 (.01)	.008 (.01)	.030 (.01)
ML-PC	19.22 (6.19)	.999 (.01)	1.019 (.02)	.002 (.01)	.060 (.01)	19.12 (6.03)	.999 (<.01)	1.000 (.01)	.002 (.01)	.060 (.01)	19.34 (6.32)	1.000 (.01)	1.00 (.01)	.007 (<.01)	.030 (.01)
Ordered category data with moderate nonnormality															
ML-R	19.58 (6.41)	.980 (.19)	1.000 (.02)	.001 (<.01)	.050 (.01)	19.54 (5.87)	.989 (.01)	.998 (<.01)	.010 (.01)	.050 (.01)	19.10 (6.41)	.995 (<.01)	1.00 (.02)	.007 (.01)	.025 (<.01)
DWLS	19.62 (6.98)	.994 (.01)	.999 (<.01)	.016 (.02)	.100 (.03)	19.85 (6.69)	.999 (<.01)	.999 (.01)	.001 (.01)	.067 (.01)	19.14 (6.72)	.998 (<.01)	.999 (.01)	.007 (<.01)	.046 (.01)
ML-PC	22.37 (11.67)	.973 (.15)	1.000 (<.01)	.001 (<.01)	.099 (.02)	20.29 (6.58)	.999 (<.01)	1.001 (.001)	.004 (<.01)	.069 (.01)	19.28 (6.37)	.999 (<.01)	1.00 (<.01)	.002 (.01)	.047 (.01)

Note. Average standard deviation of the fit indices shown in parenthesis. The baseline condition employed ML estimation using the generated variances and covariances (prior to their categorization). Satorra–Bentler robust χ^2 values are presented for conditions other than the baseline. Expected χ^2 (and model *df*) is 19 for the baseline modeling employing maximum likelihood with covariance input (ML), robust maximum likelihood with covariance input (ML-R), diagonal weighted least squares with polychoric correlation input (DWLS), and maximum likelihood with polychoric correlation input (ML-PC). CFI = comparative fit index; TLI = Tucker Lewis index; RMSEA = root mean squared error of approximation; SRMR = standardized root mean square residual.

Advice for Users

Given the current state of research regarding estimation, general recommendations can be made regarding choice of estimator when test developers encounter observed data of varying metric/scale levels and distributions. Table 8.6 summarizes our recommendations across an array of data scenarios. First, under conditions of normally distributed, continuous data, unadjusted ML estimation should be employed. Under conditions of continuous, nonnormal data, S-B scaling applied to ML-based χ^2 values and standard errors is recommended. When conditions result in data of slight to moderate nonnormality, unadjusted ML results are relatively robust. However, given the S-B scaling method will adjust for nonnormality, it is the more conservative choice in this data situation. Of course, the test developer could estimate models using both methods (ML adjusted and unadjusted) and report both sets of results. Given computational difficulties and biased results, WLS estimation is not recommended.

Table 8.6. Recommendations for choosing estimation method

Type of data	Suggestions	Caveats/notes
Continuous data		
Approximately normally distributed	• Use ML estimation	• The assumptions of ML are met and estimates should be unbiased, efficient, and consistent
Moderately nonnormal (skew < 2, kurtosis < 7)	• Use S-B/robust method to correct χ^2 and standard errors for slight nonnormality • Use ML estimation, as it is fairly robust to these conditions	• Given the availability of S-B/robust methods in the software packages, one could employ and report findings from both ML estimation and S-B/robust method
Severely nonnormal (skew > 2, kurtosis > 7)	• Use S-B/robust method	• S-B performs best, although may suffer from loss of χ^2 power
Ordered categorical data		
Number of ordered categories is 6 or more	• Treat data as continuous and use S-B scaling methods with ML estimation • Treat data as categorical and use robust DWLS estimator	• Parameter estimates from S-B/robust approach equal ML-based estimates implying that they will be attenuated to some extent • Robust DWLS will adjust the parameter estimates, standard errors, and fit indices for the categorical nature of the data • One could employ and report findings from both estimation methods
Number of ordered categories is 5 or less	• Treat data as categorical and use robust DWLS estimator	• Robust DWLS will adjust the parameter estimates, standard errors, and fit indices for the categorical nature of the data

Previous research, as well as the results from our small simulation study, may guide researchers in their choice of an estimator when ordered categorical data are analyzed. If there are six or more ordered categories (e.g., a large number of points on a Likert scale), one could treat the data as continuous (covariance input instead of latent correlation input) and apply the S-B scaling to ML-based standard errors and fit indices. Of course, in this situation, the test developer could analyze the data twice: once treating it as continuous in nature and once treating it as categorical in nature. If the results of the two analyses differ, the results from treating the data as categorical should be reported.

When modeling a small number of ordered categories, applying the S-B scaling to ML estimates derived from a covariance matrix of ordered categorical data (ML-R) is likely to have few convergence problems; however, treating the ordered categorical data as if it were continuous results in an underestimation of the parameter estimates. Both S-B scaled ML utilizing polychoric input (ML-PC) with appropriate modeling strategies and robust DWLS may be used with ordered categorical data. Both methods produce relatively unbiased estimates of the parameters and model-data fit. Based on the current results and prior recommendations, robust DWLS is recommended based on the ease of programming and accuracy of parameter estimates and fit indices. Although robust ML with latent correlation input (ML-PC) appears promising, further examination is required before we can recommend its use, as is discussed below.

Future Directions

Given the body of research examining estimation methods used when employing SEM, particularly when distribution and metric assumptions are of interest, an appropriate question is where we go from here. Below we note two avenues for future research.

There is still much uncertainty regarding the performance of the estimators for ordered categorical variables. Although research on robust DWLS and robust ML estimation using polychoric correlations is promising, there is little research establishing the range of conditions under which these estimators function well. Particularly, although some research has compared robust DWLS and robust ML estimation with respect to convergence rates, χ^2 values, and parameter bias (e.g., Lei, 2009; Yang-Wallentin et al., 2010), more research should be conducted under varied data situations (e.g., size of model, distribution of scores). Moreover, studies focused on the accuracy of standard errors when employing robust ML with latent correlation input should be undertaken. That is, the standard errors will be biased if one utilizes robust ML with latent correlation without applying the appropriate constraints to the error terms. Studies examining the amount of bias reduction with respect to the standard errors when employing both S-B scaling and the correct constraints when employing ML with latent correlations would be informative. Although our recommendations reflect the current state of research in the area, test developers should be cautious when using these methods given the need for further research.

There also remain questions regarding how to interpret the magnitude of robust DWLS-based approximate fit indices and S-B scaled ML approximate fit indices. That is, when employing robust DWLS estimation, does a CFI value of .90 suggest adequate model-data fit? In general, interpretation of approximate fit indices has received a great deal of (sometimes colorful) discussion (e.g., Hu & Bentler, 1999; Marsh, Hau, & Grayson, 2005; Marsh, Hau, & Wen, 2004). Moreover, the generalizability of guidelines for fit assessment established using ML estimation has received some attention. Specifically, Yu and Muthén (2002) suggested similar guidelines for robust DWLS-based fit indices and ML-based fit indices. In contrast, Nye and Drasgow (2011) argued that fit index guidelines recommended for ML-based fit indices were not applicable to robust DWLS-based indices. In fact, they claimed that rules of thumb cannot be established for robust DWLS-based fit indices. Finally, it is difficult to find any discussion of the best way to couple approximate fit indices with correlation residuals when assessing model-data fit across the various estimators. That is, it is not uncommon for approximate fit indices to suggest global fit, whereas correlation residuals indicate many areas of local misfit. When employing various estimators under particular data conditions, it is unclear which indices (approximate global fit indices or correlation residuals indicating local misfit) are the most accurate or how they should best be used in combination. Given the limited study of both robust DWLS and S-B ML fit indices, more attention is needed exploring this issue.

In conclusion, researchers should be aware that the choice of estimation method can impact SEM results. Namely, research has demonstrated the differential performance of estimators under particular data conditions. As noted by Edwards and colleagues (2012), "To the extent that a researcher can maximize the correspondence between the assumptions of a model and the data, more useful information will be provided" (p. 196). Thus, it is the test developers' responsibility to understand the assumptions associated with the use of particular estimators employed with structural equation models and the extent to which data align with those assumptions.

References

Babakus, E., Ferguson, C. E., & Jöreskog, K. G. (1987). The sensitivity of confirmatory maximum likelihood factor analysis to violations of measurement scale and distributional assumptions. *Journal of Marketing Research, 24*, 222–228. http://doi.org/10.2307/3151512

Bandalos, D. L. (2014). Relative performance of categorical diagonally weighted least squares and robust maximum likelihood estimation. *Structural Equation Modeling: A Multidisciplinary Journal, 21*, 102–116. http://doi.org/10.1080/10705511.2014.859510

Bandalos, D. L. (2008). Is parceling really necessary? A comparison of results from item parceling and categorical variable methodology. *Structural Equation Modeling: A Multidisciplinary Journal, 15*, 211–240. http://doi.org/10.1080/10705510801922340

Bandalos, D. L., & Webb, M. (2005, April). *Efficacy of the WLSMV estimator for coarsely categorized and nonnormally distributed data*. Paper presented at the annual meeting of the American Educational Research Association, Montreal, Canada.

Bashkov, B. & Finney, S. J. (2013). Applying Longitudinal Mean and Covariance Structures (LMACS) analysis to assess construct stability over two time points: An example using psychological entitlement. *Measurement and Evaluation in Counseling and Development, 46*, 289–314. http://doi.org/10.1177/0748175613497038

Beauducel, A., & Herzberg, P. Y. (2006). On the performance of maximum likelihood versus mean and variance adjusted weighted least squares estimation in CFA. *Structural Equation Modeling: A Multidisciplinary Journal, 13*, 186–203. http://doi.org/10.1207/s15328007sem1302_2

Benson, J. (1998). Developing a strong program of construct validation: A test anxiety example. *Educational Measurement: Issues and Practice, 17*(1), 10–17. http://doi.org/10.1111/j.1745-3992.1998.tb00616.x

Bentler, P. M., & Dudgeon, P. (1996). Covariance structure analysis: Statistical practice, theory, and directions. *Annual Review of Psychology, 47*, 563–592. http://doi.org/10.1146/annurev.psych.47.1.563

Bollen, K. A. (1989). *Structural equations with latent variables*. New York, NY: Wiley.

Bollen, K. A., & Barb, K. H. (1981). Pearson's R and coarsely categorized measures. *American Sociological Review, 46*, 232–239. http://doi.org/10.2307/2094981

Brown, T. A. (2006). *Confirmatory factor analysis for applied research*. New York, NY: Guilford Press.

Browne, M. W. (1984). Asymptotically distribution-free methods for the analysis of covariance structures. *British Journal of Mathematical and Statistical Psychology, 37*, 62–83. http://doi.org/10.1111/j.2044-8317.1984.tb00789.x

Bryant, F. B., & Satorra, S. (2012). Principles and practice of scaled difference chi-square testing. *Structural Equation Modeling: A Multidisciplinary Journal, 19*, 372–398. http://doi.org/10.1080/10705511.2012.687671

Chou, C., & Bentler, P. M. (1995). Estimates and tests in structural equation modeling. In R. H. Hoyle (Ed.), *Structural equation modeling: Concepts, issues, and applications* (pp. 37–55). Thousand Oaks, CA: Sage.

Chou, C., Bentler, P. M., & Satorra, A. (1991). Scaled test statistics and robust standard errors for non-normal data in covariance structure analysis: A Monte Carlo study. *British Journal of Mathematical and Statistical Psychology, 44*, 347–357. http://doi.org/10.1111/j.2044-8317.1991.tb00966.x

Curran, P. J., West, S. G., & Finch, J. F. (1996). The robustness of test statistics to nonnormality and specification error in confirmatory factor analysis. *Psychological Methods, 1*, 16–29. http://doi.org/10.1037/1082-989X.1.1.16

DiStefano, C. (2002). The impact of categorization with confirmatory factor analysis. *Structural Equation Modeling: A Multidisciplinary Journal, 9*, 327–346. http://doi.org/10.1207/S15328007SEM0903_2

DiStefano, C. (2003, April). *Considering the number of categories and item saturation levels with structural equation modeling.* Paper presented at the annual conference of the American Educational Research Association, New Orleans, LA.

DiStefano, C., & Hess, B. (2005). Using confirmatory factor analysis for construct validation: An empirical review. *Journal of Psychoeducational Assessment, 23*, 225–241. http://doi.org/10.1177/073428290502300303

DiStefano, C., & Morgan, G. B. (2012, April). *Examining alternative strategies to accommodate categorical data.* Paper presented at the annual meeting of the American Educational Research Association, Vancouver, BC, Canada.

Dolan, C. V. (1994). Factor analysis of variables with 2, 3, 5, and 7 response categories: A comparison of categorical variable estimators using simulated data. *British Journal of Mathematical and Statistical Psychology, 47*, 309–326. http://doi.org/10.1111/j.2044-8317.1994.tb01039.x

Edwards, M. C., Wirth, R. J., Houts, C. R., & Xi, N. (2012). Categorical data in the structural equation modeling framework. In R. Hoyle (Ed.), *Handbook of structural equation modeling* (pp. 195–208). New York, NY: Guilford Press.

Finch, J. F., West, S. G., & MacKinnon, D. P. (1997). Effects of sample size and nonnormality on the estimation of mediated effects in latent variable models. *Structural Equation Modeling: A Multidisciplinary Journal, 4*, 87–107. http://doi.org/10.1080/10705519709540063

Finney, S. J., & DiStefano, C. (2013). Nonnormal and categorical data in structural equation modeling. In G. R. Hancock & R. O. Mueller (Eds.), *A second course in structural equation modeling* (2nd ed., pp. 439–492). Charlotte, NC: Information Age.

Flora, D. B., & Curran, P. J. (2004). An empirical evaluation of alternative methods of estimation for confirmatory factor analysis with ordinal data. *Psychological Methods, 9*, 466–491. http://doi.org/10.1037/1082-989X.9.4.466

Forero, C. G., Maydeu-Olivares, A., & Gallardo-Pujol, D. (2009). Factor analysis with ordinal indicators: A Monte Carlo study comparing DWLS and ULS estimation. *Structural Equation Modeling: A Multidisciplinary Journal, 16*, 625–641. http://doi.org/10.1080/10705510903203573

Foss, T., Jöreskog, K. G., & Olsson, U. H. (2011). Testing structural equation models: The effect of kurtosis. *Computational Statistics and Data Analysis, 55*, 2263–2275. http://doi.org/10.1016/j.csda.2011.01.012

Green, S. B., Akey, T. M., Fleming, K. K., Hershberger, S. L., & Marquis, J. G. (1997). Effect of the number of scale points on chi-square fit indices in confirmatory factor analysis. *Structural Equation Modeling: A Multidisciplinary Journal, 4*, 108–120. http://doi.org/10.1080/10705519709540064

Hancock, G. R., & Liu, M. (2012). Bootstrapping standard errors and data-model fit statistics. In R. Hoyle (Ed.), *Handbook of structural equation modeling* (pp. 296–306). New York, NY: Guilford Press.

Holgado-Tello, F. P., Chácon-Moscoso, S., Barbero-García, I., & Vila-Abad, E. (2008). Polychoric correlations in exploratory and confirmatory factor analysis of ordinal variables. *Quality & Quantity, 44*, 153–166. http://doi.org/10.1007/s11135-008-9190-y

Hoogland, J. J., & Boomsma, A. (1998). Robustness studies in covariance structure modeling: An overview and a meta-analysis. *Sociological Methods & Research, 26*, 329–367. http://doi.org/10.1177/0049124198026003003

Hu, L., & Bentler, P. M. (1999). Cutoff criteria for fit indexes in covariance structure analysis: Conventional criteria versus new alternatives. *Structural Equation Modeling: A Multidisciplinary Journal, 6*, 1–55. http://doi.org/10.1080/10705519909540118

Hu, L., Bentler, P. M., & Kano, Y. (1992). Can test statistics in covariance structure analysis be trusted? *Psychological Bulletin, 112*, 351–362. http://doi.org/10.1037/0033-2909.112.2.351

Hutchinson, S. R., & Olmos, A. (1998). Behavior of descriptive fit indexes in confirmatory factor analysis using ordered categorical data. *Structural Equation Modeling: A Multidisciplinary Journal, 5*, 344–364. http://doi.org/10.1080/10705519809540111

Jöreskog, K. (1994). On the estimation of polychoric correlations and their asymptotic covariance matrix. *Psychometrika, 59*, 381–389. http://doi.org/10.1007/BF02296131

Jöreskog, K., & Sörbom, D. (2006). *LISREL 8.80 for Windows* [Computer software]. Lincolnwood, IL: Scientific Software International.

Jöreskog, K., Sörbom, D., du Toit, S., & du Toit, M. (2000). *LISREL 8: New statistical features*. Chicago, IL: Scientific Software International.

Kaplan, D. (2009). *Structural equation modeling: Foundations and extensions* (2nd ed.). Thousand Oaks, CA: Sage.

Lei, P-W. (2009). Evaluating estimation methods for ordinal data in structural equation modeling. *Quality & Quantity, 43*, 495–507. http://doi.org/10.1007/s11135-007-9133-z

Lei, P-W., & Wu, Q. (2012). Estimation in structural equation modeling. In R. H. Hoyle (Ed.), *Handbook of structural equation modeling* (pp. 164–179). New York, NY: Guilford Press.

Marsh, H. W., Hau, K-T., & Grayson, D. (2005). Goodness of fit in structural equation models. In A. Maydeu Olivares & J. McArdle (Eds.), *Contemporary psychometrics: A festschrift for Roderick P. McDonald* (pp. 275–340). Mahwah, NJ: Lawrence Erlbaum.

Marsh, H. W., Hau, K-T., & Wen, Z. (2004). In search of golden rules: Comment on hypothesis-testing approaches to setting cutoff values for fit indexes and dangers to overgeneralizing Hu and Bentler's (1999) findings. *Structural Equation Modeling: A Multidisciplinary Journal, 11*, 320–341. http://doi.org/10.1207/s15328007sem1103_2

Muthén, B. O. (1998–2004). *Mplus technical appendices*. Los Angeles, CA: Muthén & Muthén.

Muthén, B. O., & Kaplan, D. (1985). A comparison of some methodologies for the factor analysis of nonnormal Likert variables. *British Journal of Mathematical and Statistical Psychology, 38*, 171–189. http://doi.org/10.1111/j.2044-8317.1985.tb00832.x

Muthén, B. O., & Kaplan, D. (1992). A comparison of some methodologies for the factor analysis of nonnormal Likert variables: A note on the size of the model. *British Journal of Mathematical and Statistical Psychology, 45*, 19–30. http://doi.org/10.1111/j.2044-8317.1992.tb00975.x

Nevitt, J., & Hancock, G. R. (2000). Improving the root mean square error of approximation for nonnormal conditions in structural equation modeling. *Journal of Experimental Education, 68*, 251–268. http://doi.org/10.1080/00220970009600095

Nye, C. D., & Drasgow, F. (2011). Assessing goodness of fit: Simple rules of thumb simply do not work. *Organizational Research Methods, 14*, 548–570. http://doi.org/10.1177/1094428110368562

Olsson, U. H., Foss, T., & Troye, S. V. (2003). Does the ADF fit function decrease when the kurtosis increases? *British Journal of Mathematical and Statistical Psychology, 56*, 289–303. http://doi.org/10.1348/000711003770480057

Olsson, U. H., Foss, T., Troye, S. V., & Howell, R. D. (2000). The performance of ML, GLS, and WLS estimation in structural equation modeling under conditions of misspecification and nonnormality. *Structural Equation Modeling: A Multidisciplinary Journal, 7*, 557–595. http://doi.org/10.1207/S15328007SEM0704_3

Olsson, U. H., Troye, S. V., & Howell, R. D. (1999). Theoretic fit and empirical fit: The performance of maximum likelihood versus generalized least squares estimation in structural equation models. *Multivariate Behavioral Research, 34*, 31–58. http://doi.org/10.1207/s15327906mbr3401_2

Oranje, A. (2003, April). *Comparison of estimation methods in factor analysis with categorized variables: Applications to NAEP data*. Paper presented at the annual conference of the American Educational Research Association, Chicago, IL.

Potthast, M. J. (1993). Confirmatory factor analysis of ordered categorical variables with large models. *British Journal of Mathematical and Statistical Psychology, 46*, 273–286. http://doi.org/10.1111/j.2044-8317.1993.tb01016.x

Rhemtulla, M., Brosseau-Liard, P., & Savalei, V. (2012). When can categorical variables be treated as continuous? A comparison of robust continuous and categorical SEM estimation methods under suboptimal conditions. *Psychological Methods, 17*, 354–373. http://doi.org/10.1037/a0029315

Rigdon, E. E., & Ferguson, C. E. (1991). The performance of the polychoric correlation coefficient and selected fitting functions in confirmatory factor analysis with ordinal data. *Journal of Marketing Research, 28*, 491–497. http://doi.org/10.2307/3172790

Satorra, A., & Bentler, P. M. (1988). Scaling corrections for chi-square statistics in covariance structure analysis. *Proceedings of the Business and Economic Statistics Section of the American Statistical Association*, 308–313.

Satorra, A., & Bentler, P. M. (1994). Corrections to test statistics and standard errors in covariance structure analysis. In A. von Eye & C. C. Clogg (Eds.), *Latent variables analysis: Applications for developmental research* (pp. 399–419). Thousand Oaks, CA: Sage.

Savalei, V. (2014). Understanding robust corrections in structural equation modeling. *Structural Equation Modeling: A Multidisciplinary Journal, 21*(1), 149–160. http://doi.org/10.1080/10705511.2013.824793

Vandenberg, R. J., & Lance, C. E. (2000). A review and synthesis of the measurement invariance literature: Suggestions, practices, and recommendations for organizational research. *Organizational Research Methods, 3*, 4–70. http://doi.org/10.1177/109442810031002

West, S. G., Finch, J. F., & Curran, P. J. (1995). Structural equation models with nonnormal variables: Problems and remedies. In R. H. Hoyle (Ed.) *Structural equation modeling: Concepts, issues, and applications* (pp. 56–75). Thousand Oaks, CA: Sage Publications.

Widaman, K. F., Ferrer, E., & Conger, R. D. (2010). Factorial invariance within longitudinal structural equation models: Measuring the same construct across time. *Child Development Perspectives, 4*, 10–18. http://doi.org/10.1111/j.1750-8606.2009.00110.x

Worthington, R. L., & Whittaker, T. A. (2006). Scale development research: A content analysis and recommendations for best practices. *The Counseling Psychologist, 34*, 806–838. http://doi.org/10.1177/0011000006288127

Yang-Wallentin, F., Jöreskog, K. G., & Luo, H. (2010). Confirmatory factor analysis of ordinal variables with misspecified models. *Structural Equation Modeling: A Multidisciplinary Journal, 17*, 392–423. http://doi.org/10.1080/10705511.2010.489003

Yu, C., & Muthén, B. (2002, April). *Evaluation of model fit indices for latent variable models with categorical and continuous outcomes*. Paper presented at the annual meeting of the American Educational Research Association, New Orleans, LA.

Yuan, K-H., Bentler, P. M., & Zhang, W. (2005). The effect of skewness and kurtosis on mean and covariance structure analysis: The univariate case and its multivariate implication. *Sociological Methods & Research, 34*, 240–258. http://doi.org/10.1177/0049124105280200

Appendix

A. LISREL syntax for the two-factor model in Figure 8.1 when treating data as continuous and normally distributed (i.e., ML estimation applied to covariance matrix).

```
!TITLE: CONTINUOUS, NORMAL DATA WITH ML
DA NI=8 NO=500 MA=CM
CM=FIG1.CM
MO NX=8 NK=2 LX=FU,FI PH=SY,FI TD=SY
VA 1 PH(1,1) PH(2,2)
FR PH(1,2)
FR LX(1,1) LX(2,1) LX(3,1) LX(4,1)
FR LX(5,2) LX(6,2) LX(7,2) LX(8,2)
OU SC ME=ML
```

This LISREL syntax specifies eight indicators (NI=8), 500 cases (NO=500), and that a covariance matrix will be read in as input (MA=CM; the covariance matrix can be found in the file CM=FIG1.CM generated by PRELIS). The CFA model that is estimated (MO line) has eight indicators (NX=8), two latent factors (NK=2), with simple structure (LX are the elements of "lambda-X" freely estimated with items 1–4 as indictors for factor 1 and 5–8 as indictors for factor 2). The estimation method is specified on the output line (OU) as Maximum Likelihood (ME=ML) and the output also requests the completely standardized solution (SC).

B. LISREL syntax for the two-factor model in Figure 8.1 when treating data as continuous and nonnormally distributed (i.e., robust ML estimation applied to covariance matrix).

```
!TITLE: CONTINUOUS, NONNORMAL DATA WITH ROBUST ML
DA NI=8 NO=500 MA=CM
CM=FIG1.CM
AC=FIG1.ACM
MO NX=8 NK=2 LX=FU,FI PH=SY,FI TD=SY
VA 1 PH(1,1) PH(2,2)
FR PH(1,2)
FR LX(1,1) LX(2,1) LX(3,1) LX(4,1)
FR LX(5,2) LX(6,2) LX(7,2) LX(8,2)
OU SC ME=ML
```

Using the same model as specified in Figure 8.1, a covariance matrix is used as input (MA=CM; the covariance matrix can be found in the file CM=FIG1.CM). To adjust the standard errors and fit indices for nonnormality, the asymptotic covariance matrix of the observed covariances and variances is estimated by PRELIS and read into the LISREL program (AC=FIG1.ACM). The estimation method is specified as ML (ME=ML) to produce robust ML estimation.

C. LISREL syntax for the two-factor model in Figure 8.2 when treating data as categorical and employing robust DWLS with polychoric correlations

```
!TITLE: CATEGORICAL DATA WITH DWLS
DA NI=8 NO=500 MA=PM
PM=FIG2.PM
AC=FIG2.ACM
MO NX=8 NK=2 LX=FU,FI PH=SY,FI TD=SY
VA 1 PH(1,1) PH(2,2)
FR PH(1,2)
FR LX(1,1) LX(2,1) LX(3,1) LX(4,1)
FR LX(5,2) LX(6,2) LX(7,2) LX(8,2)
OU SC ME=DWLS
```

This syntax is used to estimate the structure specified in Figure 8.2. Using PRELIS, a polychoric correlation matrix is computed and this matrix is analyzed (MA=PM; PM=FIG2.PM). An accompanying asymptotic covariance matrix of the polychoric correlations is estimated by PRELIS and read into the program (AC=FIG2.ACM). The estimation method is specified as DWLS (ME=DWLS) to invoke diagonal weighted least squares estimation. Note that no additional constraints are needed, as the input (i.e., correlation matrix) is recognized by the estimator.

D. LISREL syntax for the two-factor model in Figure 8.2 when treating data as categorical and employing ML estimation with robust correlations when analyzing polychoric correlations

```
!TITLE: CATEGORICAL DATA WITH POLYCHORICS,MLR, AND CONSTRAINTS
DA NI=8 NO=500 MA=PM
MO NY=8 NE=8 NK=2 LY=DI,FR GA=FI PS=DI TE=ZE
```

```
PM=FIG2.PM
AC=FIG2.ACM
FR GA(1,1)  GA(2,1)  GA(3,1)  GA(4,1)
FR GA(5,2)  GA(6,2)  GA(7,2)  GA(8,2)

CO PS(1,1)= 1-GA(1,1)**2
CO PS(2,2)= 1-GA(2,1)**2
CO PS(3,3)= 1-GA(3,1)**2
CO PS(4,4)= 1-GA(4,1)**2
CO PS(5,5)= 1-GA(5,2)**2
CO PS(6,6)= 1-GA(6,2)**2
CO PS(7,7)= 1-GA(7,2)**2
CO PS(8,8)= 1-GA(8,2)**2
OU SC ME=ML
```

This syntax also estimates the structure specified in Figure 8.2. Similar to DWLS, a polychoric correlation matrix (MA=PM) is computed (PM=FIG2.PM) along with the asymptotic covariance matrix of the polychoric correlations (AC=FIG2.ACM). However, when employing robust ML with polychoric correlations, additional model specifications are required to produce correct standard errors. First, the syntax specifies the eight observed indicators, y, (number of "Lambda-Y's"; NY=8) are linked to their latent counterpart (y^*), Eta, (NE=8). These links between y and y^* are estimated (LY =DI,FR), but the value of the estimated LY elements are 1. Because we are modeling y^*, the factor pattern loading values are now found in the Gamma matrix (GA). Second, the error terms are not estimated but instead computed (CO) as one minus the squared factor pattern loading value (1-GA**2). The error terms are housed on the diagonal of the Psi (PS =DI) error matrix. Thus, the theta-epsilon (TE) matrix, which refers to the variances and covariances of the y variables, is set to zero (TE=ZE). The estimation method is specified as ML (ME=ML) and when paired with the asymptotic covariance matrix of the polychorics (AC=FIG2.ACM) produces robust standard errors and fit indices.

Chapter 9

Examining Fit With Structural Equation Models

Christine DiStefano

Department of Educational Studies, University of South Carolina, Columbia, SC, USA

Introduction

Following sound testing practices, instruments are constructed according to a strong theoretical perspective, and latent variable modeling techniques are used to provide evidence that the model aligns with the underlying theory (Benson, 1998). Structural equation modeling (SEM) procedures are often used with test construction to provide validity evidence. Advantages of SEM over other latent variable methods (e.g., exploratory factor analysis) include the ability to test different (and often, complex) conceptualizations of a theory and to provide a wealth of information which can be used to evaluate, and ultimately, choose a model which best represents the theory (Raykov & Marcoulides, 2011; West, Taylor, &Wu, 2012). Broadly, fit indices as well as information from the results (e.g., parameter estimates) are used for describing the fit of a model, along with providing support for other decisions, such as altering the relationships (i.e., paths) estimated in a model or to support dropping nonperforming items.

Given the popularity for using SEM in test development, it is important to have an understanding of the information and indices which may be used to assess model fit and model selection. Providing evidence of model fit involves collecting information from multiple sources (e.g., parameter estimates, fit indices, residual information, etc.) and using the set of information to support the decisions regarding the underlying theory (Kline, 2005). If information is overlooked, ignored, or misinterpreted, a test developer risks making an incorrect decision about the match between an instrument and the theoretical model. These incorrect decisions could be relatively mild, such as excluding an instrument which actually works acceptably to measure a construct of interest. On the other hand, consequences could be serious, such as adopting an instrument which does not actually measure the construct of interest and using the flawed results to make important decisions, such as student placement, admission to higher education, or hiring of an employee. Given the amount of time which it takes to develop a sound measure and the importance of making correct decisions with the test information, it is essential that researchers are informed of how to evaluate, interpret, and use information regarding model fit.

In this chapter, issues of fit are explored. First, central issues related to the development history, and limitations of fit indices, and in particular, the chi-squared (χ^2) test of model fit, are discussed. Second, information used for decision making, such as various types of fit indices and model information are presented with guidelines for interpretation. This is followed by an example of using fit information for decision making. Lastly, areas of future research are described.

Central Issues

As a methodology, SEM is a statistical procedure which focuses on testing hypothesized relationships between theoretical constructs (Jöreskog, 1993). Very briefly, the procedures generally involve identifying (or devising) appropriate ways to measure latent constructs, including finding or creating appropriate tests or surveys where items are measurable indicators of latent constructs and establishing, a priori, a model of relationships among variables. The relationships may be denoted by measurement models (relations between observed items and latent constructs) and/or structural models (relations among networks of latent variables). After the hypothesized relations are carefully constructed, researchers collect empirical data to test the fit between the model and data. In short, this is termed *model-data* fit as the model (i.e., theorized network of relations) comes first and the objective is to determine how well the data collected from the target population fit to a hypothesized model. Typically, researchers do not have just one model to evaluate (termed by Jöreskog [1993] as a *strictly confirming* situation); most situations examine alternative conceptualizations of a theory and choose an optimal model based on a combination of statistical criteria and substantive knowledge about the theory being tested.

Whereas SEM has distinct features from other more traditional statistical tests (e.g., multiple regression, analysis of variance), it also shares many commonalities with such tests. To begin the comparison, SEM is distinct from other statistical tests in that many of the more widely accepted criteria, such as *p* values, effect sizes, and power, play a minor role – or are largely absent – when evaluating fit of latent variable models (Barrett, 2007). Additionally, many of the criteria used to evaluate a model are subjective in nature or do not follow known statistical distributions (Hayduk, Cummings, Boadu, Pazderka-Robinson, & Bolianne, 2007). Thus, probability statements cannot be made for the majority of indices used with SEM model testing.

However, there are many noted similarities. Like other statistical tests, SEM requires that assumptions are met prior to testing a hypothesized structure, and failure to consider the tenability of assumptions may result in invalid conclusions (Kline, 2005; Tabachnick & Fidell, 2006). These assumptions should be tested prior to model estimation, with appropriate concessions made if the assumptions do not hold (Finney & DiStefano, 2013). Coupled with the need to evaluate required assumptions is the choice of estimator (or fit function; Bollen, 1989) as the estimator is responsible for producing the fit indices, parameter estimates, and standard errors of parameter estimates used in model interpretation (Bollen, 1989; Jöreskog, 1993). As a general assumption, this chapter will focus on using the maximum likelihood estimator for model testing and will assume that necessary assumptions involved in the use of this estimator (e.g., linearity, independent observations, sufficiently large sample size, multivariate normality of indicators, and a correctly specified model; Bentler & Dudgeon, 1996; Bollen, 1989; Tabachnick & Fidell, 2006) have been met. For additional information on SEM assumptions or consideration of fit when assumptions may be violated, see Chapter 8, by Finney, DiStefano, and Kopp, this volume.

As with other statistical tests, SEM can be thought of as testing an *omnibus* hypothesis test. With SEM, it is hypothesized that there are *true* relations among variables in the population contained in a variance-covariance matrix, Σ, and a variance-covariance matrix of relationships reproduced from the tested model, $\Sigma(\Theta)$, where Θ is a vector of the fixed (i.e., non-estimated paths) and freed parameters (i.e., estimated paths), as specified in the tested model. Under the assumption that the model is specified correctly, the (omnibus) null hypothesis (H_o) tested is:

$$H_0: \Sigma = \Sigma(\Theta), \tag{1}$$

meaning that the population covariance matrix (Σ) equals the reproduced covariance matrix ($\Sigma(\Theta)$) calculated from the population model parameters, within sampling error. However, unlike many statistical tests where the objective is to report evidence leading to rejection of the H_o, in SEM, the goal is to provide evidence in support of the H_o, which would mean that the tested model is able to adequately represent the relations between variables (Kline, 2005). Models in which the H_o is rejected require additional investigation, such as respecification of model paths or evaluation of an alternative model. It is noted that in general, measurement models should demonstrate acceptable fit before structural relations are tested (Anderson & Gerbing, 1988).

As relationships among elements in the population are not known, the observed sample co-variance matrix, S, serves as an estimate of Σ. Population parameters are estimated with the goal of minimizing the discrepancy between the elements in S and $\Sigma(\Theta)$. The overall goal of SEM is to reproduce the relations between the observed sample covariance matrix, S, and the reproduced or model-implied covariance matrix calculated from the estimated model parameters [$\Sigma(\hat{\theta})$]. To accomplish this goal, a fit function, F is minimized with respect to the free parameters in the vector, Θ. Under ML, the fit function minimized is:

$$F_{ML} = \log|\Sigma(\theta)| + tr[\Sigma(\theta)^{-1}S] - \log|S| - p, \tag{2}$$

where tr is the trace of the multiplied matrices and p is the number of observed variables (Bollen, 1989). Note that different estimation methods minimize different fit functions (e.g., see Bollen, 1989, or Tabachnick & Fidell, 2006, for fit functions under different estimation techniques). The minimization of the fit function provides for the maximization of parameter estimates, which are the parameter values that produce the least amount of discrepancy (i.e., smallest residuals) between the input matrix and the estimated variance-covariance matrix (Jöreskog, 1973). Also note that the fit function, F, will equal zero if the model perfectly reproduces the elements in the sample covariance matrix. Thus, F (as well as the estimation method selected), plays an important role in SEM as it is the mechanism used to obtain information regarding model-data fit.

Limitations of SEM Fit Indices

The assessment of model-data fit is an essential component of SEM model testing, and a crucial part of this process is how to interpret the various fit indices and information for decision making. Before evaluating fit indices, it may be helpful to recognize what information would be desirable and to recognize limitations of model assessment. As stated by Gerbing and Anderson (1993, p. 41), for many researchers, a fit index for SEM would ideally include the following characteristics:

1) Have known boundaries to (e.g., 0 to 1), where values at the lowest level denote a complete lack of fit and values at the highest level denote perfect fit or vice versa;
2) Be independent of fluctuations in sample size (i.e., fit would not be affected by substantially increasing or decreasing the number of cases); and,
3) Follow a known distribution, so critical values and probability statements could be used to assist evaluation and interpretation and confidence intervals may be constructed.

However, these ideals are just that, as no fit index (yet) exists in SEM that encompasses all of these suggestions (Kline, 2005; Revelle, 2015). Gerbing and Anderson (1993) further note that all of the above suggestions may not be acceptable to some researchers. Instead, researchers are reminded to consider the sum of the information –from fit indices as well as from multiple other sources – when judging model-data fit in SEM. Prior to discussing individual fit indices, Kline (2005) and other researchers suggest researchers are aware of the limitations of fit indices in SEM, among them:

1) Many fit indices collapse information from many model components into one index (e.g., see Steiger, 2007). Thus, it is possible that a fit index may show favorable fit overall when some portions of a tested model do not actually fit the data.

2) The H_0 is tested under the assumption of a correctly specified model. Some researchers question if this is viable assumption (e.g., Barrett, 2007) as all models are misspecified to some degree.

3) Fit indices provide an evaluation of how well the tested model fits the data. If the fit is poor, this suggests that the model may need to be respecified; however, no guidance is provided regarding *where* the model modifications may be needed (Millsap, 2007).

4) There is no one number summary that can be used to state if a tested model fits the data; instead, a variety of indices/information should be examined.

5) Good fit is not a substitute for results that are not plausible or are nonsensical given the theory being tested. The theoretical meaningfulness of the results is an important aspect to describe above the values of a specific index.

The Chi-Square Test of Model Fit

In the history of the SEM field, Jöreskog (1970) is credited as one of the landmark figures, attributed to his development of a general methodology to analyzing covariance structures (see Bollen, 1989, or Matsueda, 2012, for more on the history of SEM). Jöreskog (1973) presented his maximum likelihood framework for estimating SEMs, demonstrating that the maximum likelihood estimates may be obtained by solving Equation (1) above. Accompanying this framework was a global test for model-data fit.

Overall fit between the data and the model can be expressed as a test statistic: $T = (N - 1)$ **F**, where N is the size of the sample. The test statistic, T, is asymptotically distributed as a (central) χ^2 distribution with $(p + q) - r$ degrees of freedom, where p is the number of observed exogenous variables, q is the number of observed endogenous variables, and r is the number of parameters estimated in the model (Bollen, 1989). T is referred to as the model χ^2 value (Kline, 2005) where the degrees of freedom for the model (i.e., $(p + q) - r$) is the expected mean value of the χ^2 fit statistic. Thus, on its own, the model chi-square is a fit statistic, but, as discussed later, it is also used in the calculation of many other fit indices.

If the assumptions underlying SEM hold, then the χ^2 distribution that the test statistic T follows is called a central chi-squared distribution. This is important given that the chi-squared distribution has known probability values associated with test statistics and, thus, a formal hypothesis test can be conducted to determine if the tested model adequately fits the data (i.e., the implied covariance matrix reproduces the elements of the sample covariance matrix with little residual difference). If this central distribution can be followed, test statistics may be compared to a table of χ^2 critical values to evaluate the H_0 stated earlier. If the value of T is not significant, then a researcher may conclude that the estimated parameters identified with the tested model provides an acceptable fit to the data.

However, if the assumptions underlying SEM are not met, then the model test statistic, T, follows a noncentral χ^2 distribution instead of the central χ^2 distribution. The noncentral χ^2 distribution is defined by the degrees of freedom (calculated as stated earlier), but also includes a noncentrality parameter. This noncentrality parameter, λ, provides a measure of how discrepant the noncentral distribution is from the central χ^2 distribution. In such cases it is likely that the null hypothesis stating the population covariance matrix (Σ) equals the reproduced covariance matrix calculated from the population model parameters [$\Sigma(\Theta)$] will be rejected.

The χ^2 test of model fit is termed a test of exact fit, meaning that it is testing that there is no discrepancy between the model and the model reproduced by the data. The test relies on the assumptions being met for accurate calculation of critical test statistics and probability values (Hayduk et al., 2007). Given the view of χ^2 as an exact fit test, reviewing common rules for statistical hypothesis testing is warranted. As with other statistical tests (e.g., regression), if the (omnibus) SEM test of model-data fit is not rejected, it does not mean that the identified model should be considered the correct model. Failing to reject a null hypothesis means that the identified solution is one possible representation of the data; there may exist other models (i.e., alternative models) or, models which have not yet been identified, that show acceptable fit to the data. Information from additional fit indices as well as testing alternative models helps provide additional support when selecting a solution.

Drawbacks of the Chi-Square Test of Model Fit

While the χ^2 test is among the oldest fit index in SEM, it has some severe limitations which have led to many discussions and controversies surrounding its utility as a measure of fit. First, it is well documented that the χ^2 test is sensitive to sample size. As large sample sizes are often used with SEM, small discrepancies between the sample and model-implied covariance matrix can be found significant with a large enough sample. This led to many researchers effectively acknowledging that the χ^2 test will be significant, and, in effect, ignoring the information from a significant test when the index may be providing important information about model misfit (Hayduk et al., 2007). Further, one of the key assumptions in SEM is that the model is correctly specified, and, even with careful consideration of the underlying theory, it is likely that a model includes some degree of misspecification and reliance on the central χ^2 distribution for evaluating fit may not be warranted in most cases (Barrett, 2007; Curran, Bollen, Paxton, Kirby, & Chen, 2002). In such situations, the noncentrality parameter, λ, provides important information about the degree of model misfit.

Second, the χ^2 test has been noted to be overly liberal, suggesting that a correctly specified model does not fit (i.e., high Type I error rate) when data have nonnormal distributions, especially when kurtosis is present (e.g., DiStefano, 2002). This reinforces the need to consider the estimator prior to interpreting fit, as such decisions may impact the overall assessment of one's theory (Finney & DiStefano, 2013).

Finally, the χ^2 test of model fit is an exact test striving for perfect fit between model and estimated covariance matricies (Steiger, 2007). However, Steiger (2007) reminds researchers that there is no perfect model, and that even a small misfit (e.g., omitting a path with a low factor loading) is technically incorrect, but not likely to be rejected. Hayduk et al. (2007) emphasize this sentiment by stating that the goal when examining fit is to test the underlying *theory* represented by the model and to focus on the broader picture, where fit information is just one piece of the overall puzzle.

Conceptual Principles

Categorizing Fit Indices

Problems arising from the use of the χ^2 test led researchers to develop additional fit indices to assess model-data fit. The χ^2 test of model fit was constructed to be a global fit index, that is, to provide information about the fit of the entire model to the data, rather than any one specific component of the model. Some researchers have argued that the test of global fit does not provide much information (e.g., Barrett, 2007) as this test is often rejected. Given the limitations of the χ^2 test of model fit, researchers began to develop additional fit indices for use with SEM. Thus, on its own, the model chi-square is a fit statistic, but it is also used in the calculation of many other fit indices. Many SEM indices were developed, some of which have stood the test of time and are included in research studies and some indices which have lost popularity and fallen to the wayside.

There are many ways to categorize fit indices. Tanaka (1993, p. 16) describes six different dimensions along which fit indices can vary, including: "(1) population vs. sample based; (2) simplicity vs. complexity; (3) normed vs. nonnormed; (4) absolute vs. relative; (5) estimation method free vs. estimation method specific; and (6) sample size independent vs. sample size dependent." Researchers have recognized additional aspects, such as indices which reflect model parsimony (i.e., indices which reflect a *penalty* for estimating a greater number of parameters, as models which include more paths will generally fit better than models with fewer paths) and indices used for model comparison (i.e., indices which compare a tested model to a baseline model or which can be used for comparing across alternative models). And, as with previous researchers, it is noted that fit indices can fall into more than one category simultaneously. Following other researchers (e.g., McDonald & Ho, 2002; West et al., 2012) select fit indices will be discussed in terms of two broad categories: absolute fit and comparative (or incremental) indices. Many excellent SEM textbooks (e.g., Bollen, 1989; Kline, 2005; Schumaker & Lomax, 2012) and review articles/chapters concerning fit (e.g.; Tanaka, 1993; West et al., 2012) are available for details and discussion about additional fit indices.

Evaluating Fit

Prior to introducing fit indices, general evaluation criteria are presented. As noted earlier, the χ^2 test of model fit follows a known distribution – that is, the central χ^2, with model degrees of freedom $= (p + q) - r$ – when necessary assumptions are met. Adherence to distributional characteristics allows for the use of tabled critical values and probability statements to be used when evaluating a test statistic. However, most other fit indices used in SEM do not follow known statistical distributions; instead, other criteria are used to evaluate fit in more of a descriptive manner. To do this, researchers need knowledge of the values which may be expected and if larger or smaller values are preferred. The range of a fit index denotes the span of possible values that could be observed for a fit index. Normed values generally have a range from 0 to 1 to facilitate interpretation; however, not all fit indices used in SEM are normed. In addition, fit indices may be interpreted as goodness- or badness-of-fit indices. Generally, larger values of goodness-of-fit indices represent better model-data fit, while smaller values of badness-of-fit indices represent improved fit.

Absolute Fit Indices

Absolute fit indices describe the fit of the tested model, which compute a value by comparing among different models, and may also be referred to in the literature as *stand-alone indexes* (e.g., Marsh, Balla, & McDonald, 1988). In calculations, absolute fit indices are functions of the test statistic, T, or of the residuals (i.e., discrepancy between $\mathbf{S}$ and $\mathbf{\Sigma(\Theta)}$; Yuan, 2005). When interpreting absolute fit indices, it may help to remember that these indices focus on the discrepancy between the model input and model implied covariance matrices; thus, absolute fit indices are evaluating if there is a substantial discrepancy between the two matrices. Also, keep in mind that there is no explicit baseline used in calculations. While there are many absolute indices as well as variants of these indices (e.g., parsimony adjusted indices), six indices will be discussed: goodness of fit index (GFI), standardized root mean square residual (SRMR), root mean squared error of approximation (RMSEA), Akaike information criterion (AIC), Bayesian information criterion (BIC), and the expected cross-validation index (ECVI). These absolute fit indices were selected as they are commonly reported. Results of studies using these fit indices are noted; however, echoing West et al. (2012), many of these values were studied using confirmatory factor analysis models; little is known about performance of indices with more complex modeling situations. Table 9.1 includes a summary of fit indices discussed, formulas, and related information useful for interpreting fit with the selected absolute fit indices.

Goodness-of-Fit Index (GFI)

GFI was one of the earliest fit indices developed by Jöreskog and Sörbom in the 1980s. The value is comparable to the R^2 used in multiple regression; in SEM, the value indicates the amount of variance/covariance in the observed matrix, $\mathbf{S}$, predicted by the reproduced matrix, $\mathbf{\Sigma(\Theta)}$. The formula for GFI is presented in Table 9.1, where the $SS_{residual}$ is amount of variability related to the sum of the squared covariance residuals and the SS_{total} the total sum of squares in the data matrix. Considering $\mathbf{s}$ as a vector of nonredundant elements from the input covariance matrix and $\mathbf{e}$ as a vector of residual elements, the $SS_{residual}$ may be found by multiplying the residuals ($\mathbf{e}$, the differences between the input covariances and model-implied covariances) by a weight matrix ($\mathbf{W}$) included as part of the estimator calculations (i.e., $\mathbf{e^T W e}$). The SS_{total} is similar, but uses the values from the input matrix, s (i.e., $\mathbf{s^T W s}$) to calculate total variability (West et al., 2012).

Values of the GFI typically range between 0 and 1. The value is a goodness-of-fit index, where higher values denote a better fitting model. To evaluate an acceptable model, values over .95 are recommended (e.g., Schumaker & Lomax, 2012). However, due to the weight matrix included in the calculations of GFI, this index is dependent on the estimator used. Further, the GFI is not sensitive to model misspecification and is sensitive to sample size, where larger sample sizes will produce larger GFI values (Hooper, Coughlan, & Mullen, 2008; Hu & Bentler, 1998). Because of such limitations, some researchers recommend omitting GFI from model evaluation (e.g., Hu & Bentler, 1998); however, this value is still widely reported today, partly due to its historical significance related to being one of the early fit indices available in SEM.

Table 9.1. Selected absolute fit indices

Fit index and primary reference	Formula	What does the index measure?	Higher or lower values preferred?	Generally accepted guidelines for interpretation
GFI: goodness of fit index (Jöreskog & Sörbom, 1982)	$1 - \dfrac{SS_{residual}}{SS_{total}}$	Amount of variance/covariance in the observed matrix, S, predicted by the reproduced matrix, $\Sigma(\hat{\theta})$	Higher	Values over .95 (Schumaker & Lomax, 2012)
SRMR: standardized root mean residual (Jöreskog & Sörbom, 1982)	$\sqrt{\dfrac{\left[\sum_i^p \sum_j^i (s_{ij} - \hat{\sigma}_{ij})/s_i s_j\right]^2}{k(k+1)/2}}$	Square root of the average standardized squared residual	Lower	Values less than .08 (Hu & Bentler, 1998)
RMSEA: root mean squared error of approximation (Steiger & Lind, 1980)	$\sqrt{\dfrac{[\chi^2_{model} - df_{model}]}{[(N-1)df_{model}]}}$	Measure of approximate, or close, fit between proposed model and population	Lower	Values of .05–.08 indicate close fit and values of .10 or greater indicate poor fit (Browne & Cudeck, 1993); Hu & Bentler (1999) recommend a cutoff close to .06 If included with the software, report RMSEA 90% Confidence Interval (CI) to see if close fit values are captured (Kline, 2005)
AIC: Akaike information criterion (Akaike, 1987)	$\chi^2_{model} + 2df_{model}$,	Used when comparing competing nonnested models calculated from the same set of data	Lower	Smaller values preferred; smallest value among set of AIC values suggests best fitting model (Schumaker & Lomax, 2012)
BIC: Bayesian information criterion (Schwartz, 1978)	$\chi^2 + \ln(N)[k(k+1)/2 - df]$	Used when comparing competing nonnested models calculated from the same set of data	Lower	Smaller values preferred; smallest value among set of BIC values suggests best fitting model (Schumaker & Lomax, 2012)
ECVI: expected cross-validation index (Browne & Cudeck, 1993)	$\dfrac{\chi^2}{n-1} + 2[\dfrac{t}{n-1}]$, where t = number of estimated parameters	Measure of the discrepancy between the fitted covariance matrix in the current sample and the expected covariance matrix obtained from another sample of the same size	Lower	Smaller values preferred; smallest value among set of values suggests best fitting model. Confidence intervals (CI) for ECVI may also be reported; overlapping CIs suggest no statistical difference among models.

Note. s_{ij} = Sample covariance; $\hat{\sigma}_{ij}$ = reproduced covariance; s_i = standard deviation for variable i; s_j = standard deviation for variable j; and k is the total number of variables (i.e., endogenous and exogenous, or, $p + q$).

Standardized Root Mean Square Residual (SRMR)

The SRMR is a variant of the root mean residual (RMR), illustrating the square root of the residual elements between the sample covariance matrix and the model-implied covariance matrix. The difference between RMR and SRMR is analogous to interpreting a covariance versus a correlation between two variables. For example, by itself, the covariance value is difficult to interpret because it is reported in the scale of the variables used in its calculation. Instead, correlation values are more readily interpreted because they are scale and metric free and bound by 0 and |1|.

Considering first, the RMR, this value provides an average of the remaining residuals in a model, but is of limited value because the difference between input and estimated parameters is computed in the scale of the variables. The SRMR standardizes the RMR to be on a cor-relation metric, and is thus, not sensitive to scale of the variables (Kline, 2005). The SRMR is summarized as one value which provides an average of the (correlation) residual estimates across the entire model.

As SRMR values are correlations, the values range from 0 (no discrepancy) to 1 (high level of discrepancy). The SRMR is a badness-of-fit index, where higher values are worse, as this shows that more residual error is present – in other words, higher values illustrate a greater dis-crepancy between the elements in $\mathbf{S}$ and the model implied estimates in $\mathbf{\Sigma(\Theta)}$. Hu and Bentler (1999) recommend a cutoff of .08 or less to indicate acceptable fit; however, other sources recommend a .05 cutoff for SRMR (e.g., Byrne, 1998; Schumaker & Lomax, 2012). Also, the value is sensitive to misspecification (i.e., correctly indicating worse fit with a misspecified model). Based on these strengths, Hu and Bentler (1998) recommend to always include the SRMR when reporting model-data fit.

Root Mean Squared Error of Approximation (RMSEA)

As discussed, the χ^2 test of model fit is noted to be sensitive to large values, where large val-ues generally result in rejection of the (omnibus) null hypothesis. The RMSEA recognizes that all models are an approximation of the true population relations, and instead, focuses on the notion of "close fit" (Steiger & Lind, 1980). The index estimates the lack of fit between the population data and the model estimates, that is, the discrepancy between $\mathbf{\Sigma}$ and $\mathbf{\Sigma(\Theta)}$. The discrepancy between the two matrices is referred to as a measure of error approximation (Browne & Cudeck, 1993).

RMSEA also includes the estimated noncentrality parameter in calculations. Recall when the null hypothesis is true, the test statistic, T, follows a central χ^2 distribution. If the null hypoth-esis is *not* assumed to be true, the distribution of T does not follow the central χ^2 distribution, but instead follows a noncentral χ^2 distribution. The discrepancy between the central χ^2 and noncentral χ^2 distributions is expressed in the noncentrality parameter. Inclusion of the noncen-trality parameter in calculation is expressed as the discrepancy due to the error approximation (Browne & Cudeck, 1993).

The RMSEA is a badness-of-fit index, where higher values illustrate poorer fit. The index has a lower bound of 0, where a value of 0 would illustrate perfect fit. The greater the model misspecification (i.e., the discrepancy between $\mathbf{\Sigma}$ and $\mathbf{\Sigma(\Theta)}$) the larger the values of RMSEA will be. Cutoff values illustrating good fit by the RMSEA have become increasingly stringent (Hooper et al., 2008). General rules of thumb considered RMSEA values under .05 to illus-trate close fit, values between .05 and .08 to indicate adequate fit, and values from .08 – .10

to indicate fair fit, and values above .10 indicating an unacceptable model (e.g., Browne & Cudeck, 1993; MacCallum, Browne, & Sugawara, 1996). More recently, values close to .06 are indicative of good fitting models (Hu & Bentler, 1998).

The RMSEA has become regarded as one of the most useful fit indices because it is sensitive to the number of estimated parameters included in the model (Diamantopoulos & Siguaw, 2000). In other words, the value favors parsimonious models, as over-parameterized models will yield (misleading) good fit. Other strengths noted is that the RMSEA is moderately sensitive to simple model misspecification, very sensitive to complex model misspecification, and not overly sensitive to nonnormal distributions of the observed variables (Hu & Bentler, 1998). With sufficient sample sizes, the RMSEA is not overly sensitive to the estimation method used; however, at small sample sizes, the effect of estimator becomes more pronounced and values may vary based on the estimator used. Finally, one of the most beneficial aspects of the RMSEA is the ability to create a confidence interval (typically 90%) about the value, thus eliminating using one point-estimate to judge fit of the model (MacCallum et al., 1996). If present as part of the output, the RMSEA and associated confidence interval should both be reported. When examining the RMSEA confidence interval, a researcher can examine the interval boundaries to see if it captures values denoting good fit (e.g., .05) within the interval.

Akaike Information Criterion (AIC)

Even though the AIC is classified as an absolute index based on the formula used (i.e., no comparative model is used in calculations), by itself, an AIC index does not provide useful information. The index is used to compare competing (nonnested) models tested on the same set of data and thus, is only useful if alternative models are estimated. When evaluating lower AIC values reflect better model-data fit, and the model with the lowest AIC value is preferred.

The AIC is not limited in terms of range as it does not have an upper bound (Kenny, 2014). Strengths of the AIC are that it reflects both model-data fit and parsimony. In terms of model-data fit, the formula directly incorporates the model χ^2 value (measuring global fit) into the calculations. In addition, more parsimonious models will have lower AIC values; in other words, researchers are penalized by a factor of 2 (i.e., $2*df$) for including additional paths in a tested model (Kenny, 2014).

Bayesian Information Criterion (BIC)

The BIC (Schwartz, 1978) is similar to the AIC as it is used to compare alternative (nonnested) models, where the lowest BIC value among the set suggests the optimal model. The BIC differs from the AIC in that it places a more stringent penalty on the number of parameters estimated in the model. This helps to correct for the fact that models that estimate many parameters generally display a more positive fit than more parsimonious models. The BIC also recognizes that larger sample sizes may adversely impact fit, and thus, the index includes a correction for sample size as well as for model parsimony.

While AIC and BIC are similar, there are differences between the two indices. The goal of the AIC is asymptotic efficiency. In other words, the AIC's objective is to minimize prediction error and, as such, to maximize the predictive accuracy (Aho, Derryberry, & Peterson, 2014). The BIC is a consistent index, meaning that as sample size increases, the correct model, from any group of models, will be selected (Aho et al., 2014).

Within the structural modeling field, relatively few studies have conducted a direct comparison of these two information indices. Using a latent class scenario (where a researcher is using a covariance modeling framework to identify the optimal number of groups underlying a dataset), Morgan (2014) found that BIC tended to identify the correct solution with higher frequency than AIC when there were more continuous than categorical indicators, or when rare classes were omitted (e.g., a misspecified model situation). However, studies involving BIC and AIC comparisons for models more prevalent with test development (e.g., CFA or structural models) are sparse. Other researchers have suggested that the context under study must be considered when deciding between the indices (Aho et al., 2014). Using a simulation example, Aho and colleagues (2014) state that if a researcher can never find the true model, then the goal of the simulation would be selection of an optimal model (through minimizing error), suggesting that AIC would be preferred. However, if a researcher expects to identify the correct model, as sample size increases, then BIC may be the most appropriate index to use. In empirical research, the choice of AIC or BIC would be the one in which the situation most closely matches the descriptions above (Aho et al., 2014). Relatedly, Barrett (2007) noted that when researchers examine models which include "real world" criterion classes or outcomes, then using AIC and BIC to determine model parsimony "might prove most effective" (p. 822).

Expected Cross-Validation Index (ECVI)

The ECVI is another absolute fit index classified into this category based on how it is calculated, but, like AIC and BIC, ECVI is only useful when comparing across competing models. The ECVI is typically used when comparing competing nonnested models computed from the same set of data. The index is a measure of the discrepancy between the fitted covariance matrix in the current sample and the expected covariance matrix that would be obtained in another sample of the same size (Browne & Cudeck, 1993). In other words, ECVI can be thought of as an indication of which model will cross-validate best if another sample of the same size is selected.

The ECVI does not have an upper bound to use in interpretation; instead, when comparing values across models, smaller values are preferred. The ECVI is not sensitive to the estimation method used or to the distributional nature of the data. However, Hu and Bentler (1998) do not recommend using ECVI because the index is not sensitive to model misspecification (i.e., cannot detect a misspecified model) and is affected by large sample sizes, given the direct use of the χ^2 model test in its calculation.

Comparative Fit Indices

Comparative or, incremental, fit indices assess model fit through comparison of the χ^2 fit statistic fit from two models – the tested model and a baseline model. The idea when interpreting these fit indices is that the value provides the proportional improvement of a tested model relative to a baseline model (Widaman & Thompson, 2003). The baseline model most often used with comparative fit indices is the independence model (or null model), which is thought of as the worst case scenario – a model where there are *no* relationships among variables. That is, all the variables are modeled to be independent and all covariances among variables are set to zero. These comparisons may be conducted because the more restricted model (i.e., null model) is *nested* within the tested model. Nested models occur in situations where one model is a subset of another model; in other words, one model may be converted to the other by adding (or removing) paths (Kline, 2005).

Incremental fit indices typically use the χ^2 values from the hypothesized model and the null model in calculations. While there are many comparative fit indices, three popular incremental indices are presented: the normed fit index (NFI), the nonnormed fit index (NNFI), and the comparative fit index (CFI). These three fit indices also represent different categorization or types of comparative fit indices (e.g., Type 1, Type 2, or Type 3 indices), where the different types refer to whether or not centrality is assumed with the χ^2 test (Marsh et al., 1988). The comparative fit indices discussed here are goodness-of-fit indices, where higher values denote better fit. Again, research results from investigations using these fit indices are noted and Table 9.2 presents the formulas, relevant articles, definitions, and rules of thumb for interpretation of the selected fit indices.

Nonnormed Fit Index (NNFI)

In 1973, Tucker and Lewis developed the Tucker–Lewis index for use with exploratory factor analysis to determine the degree to which an estimated (exploratory) factor model was an improvement above a zero-factor model (Hoelter, 1983). The index was extended to the structural modeling context by Bentler and Bonnet in 1980 (West et al., 2012) to judge the improvement in a tested model above a baseline (null) model. While named the NNFI, the index may also be referred to as the Tucker–Lewis index (TLI) based on its origination. This value is similar to the NFI (see next section), but uses the χ^2/df instead of just χ^2 values in the calculation of the index. Thus, by including the degrees of freedom, the NNFI considers the expected values of the χ^2 under the central chi-square distribution. Recall that to follow the central χ^2 distribution, the underlying assumptions necessary for testing are thought to hold. This means the distribution of T will be χ^2 distributed when the assumption that the model holds exactly in the population is met [i.e., $\Sigma = \Sigma(\Theta)$]. The NNFI is often referred to as a Type 2 index because of the inclusion of the central distribution and degrees of freedom in calculations (e.g., Marsh et al., 1988).

The NNFI compares the fit of the independence model and the proposed model divided by the difference in fit of the independence model and the expected fit of the proposed model. The value can be interpreted as the relative improvement of fit per degree of freedom of the proposed model over the independence model using a mean square metric, given that the χ^2 values are divided by their degrees of freedom (Widaman & Thompson, 2003). The NNFI is not bounded by 0 –1; however, values usually fall within this range. The index penalized models that estimate many parameters (i.e., rewards parsimony) and is not overly impacted by sample size. For a cutoff, researchers recommend using recommend using a value of .95 or above for acceptable fit (e.g., Hu & Bentler, 1999).

Normed Fit Index (NFI)

The NFI was developed from the NNFI in an attempt to create an index with known bounds of 0 and 1. As shown in Table 9.2, the NFI compares the tested model χ^2 to the null model χ^2 and indicates the proportion of improvement in fit for the tested model as a proportion of covariance explained by the hypothesized model when the independence model is used as the baseline (Bentler & Bonett, 1980). In other words, the NFI indicates if using the proposed model is better than using a model with no relations between the variables (i.e., the worst model that is theoretically plausible; Bentler & Bonett, 1980). This index is sometimes called a Type 1 Index because it simply represents the proportion of increased fit gained by using the hypothesized model.

Table 9.2. Selected incremental fit indices

Fit index and primary reference	Formula	What does the index measure?	Higher or lower values preferred?	Generally accepted guidelines for interpretation
NFI: normed fit index Bentler & Bonett (1980)	$\dfrac{\chi^2_{independence} - \chi^2_{model}}{\chi^2_{independence}}$	Proportion of total observed covariance explained by the hypothesized model as compared to the independence model as a baseline Indication if proposed model is better than no model	Higher	Cutoff of .95 recommended (Schumaker & Lomax, 2012)
NNFI: nonnormed fit index (Bentler & Bonett, 1980) also called Tucker–Lewis index (TLI; Tucker–Lewis, 1973)	$\left[\dfrac{\dfrac{\chi^2_{independence}}{df_{independence}} - \dfrac{\chi^2_{model}}{df_{model}}}{\dfrac{\chi^2_{independence}}{df_{independence}} - 1}\right]$	Relative improvement of fit per degree of freedom of the proposed model over the independence model	Higher	Hu & Bentler (1998, 1999) recommend .95 or above
CFI: comparative fit index (Bentler, 1990)	$1 - \left[\dfrac{(\chi^2_{model} - df_{model})}{(\chi^2_{independence} - df_{independence})}\right]$	Relative improvement of a model over that of the independence model as a baseline	Higher	Hu & Bentler (1998, 1999) recommend .95 or above

The NFI is normed to range between 0 and 1. As shown by the formula for the NFI, if the χ^2 or fit function for the hypothesized model were zero (perfect fit), the NFI would equal 1.00 and, the value of the index would be 0 when the proposed and independence model equal. The recommended cutoff used with the NFI is .95 (Schumaker & Lomax, 2012). The NFI, generally, is not recommended (e.g., Marsh et al., 1988; Mulaik, James, Van Alstine, Bennett, Lind, & Stilwell, 1989) because it is sensitive to sample size and insensitive to model specification (Hu & Bentler, 1998).

Comparative Fit Index (CFI)

The CFI is a very popular index of incremental fit developed by Bentler (1990). This index may be considered a revised form of the NFI, where the sample size is taken into account (Widaman & Thompson, 2003). The index also considers an estimate of noncentrality in the calculations. Noncentrality arises when the model is misfitting in the population [i.e., $\Sigma \neq \Sigma(\Theta)$]. As such, the assumptions underlying SEM are violated, and the χ^2 model test statistic is not centrally distributed but instead follows a noncentral χ^2 distribution. The noncentrality parameter measures the discrepancy between the population and the tested model to determine the amount of the lack of fit, expressed as one number. The value may be estimated by taking the difference between the observed χ^2 and its degrees of freedom, as the expected χ^2 for models following the central χ^2 distribution is equal to the model degrees of freedom. The larger the discrepancy between the χ^2 and the degrees of freedom, the greater the evidence that the hypothesized model does not fit, and that an alternative model will better represent the relationships underlying the data. The noncentrality parameter is referred to as a measure of error of approximation – or, the same error of approximation that was used with the RMSEA.

The CFI can be interpreted as the relative reduction in the noncentrality parameter between the proposed model and the independence model. The difference is expressed as a proportion of the lack of fit due to the independence model (Widaman & Thompson, 2003). The CFI may be referred to as a Type 3 index, as it uses the expected values of the χ^2 under the *noncentral* χ^2 distribution (expressed as: $\chi^2 - df$) in calculations. The RMSEA is similar to the Type 3 indices in that both are noncentrality based; however, the important difference is that RMSEA is an absolute index, whereas the CFI assesses fit of the tested model relative to a baseline model.

When interpreting the CFI, values are bounded between 0 and 1. Researchers have recommended using values of .95 or higher to denote good model-data fit (e.g., Schumaker & Lomax, 2012; Hu & Bentler, 1998). The CFI has not been found to be overly sensitive to small sample sizes (Hu & Bentler, 1998); but has been found to be sensitive to estimation method and model misspecification. With incremental indices, Type 2 and 3 indices outperformed both Type 1 (e.g., NFI) and absolute fit indices; and are recommended for researchers to include when reporting (Hu & Bentler, 1998, 1999).

The majority of the comparative fit indices calculated in software packages, and, thus, reported in the literature, use the null model for comparison. However, researchers can create their own baseline model to use with comparisons to determine how much better a tested model fits from a base that is more plausible than a model with no relations among variables (i.e., independence or null model; Bentler, 1990; Schreiber, 2008). As a simple example with a multifactor model, a researcher may be interested in examining the improvement in fit between a model with correlated factors versus an orthogonal model as a baseline. In such situations, comparative fit indices may be calculated by hand. In addition, other researchers have argued that the null model comparison does not make sense in some situations as it is not nested within some models, such as when models with means are tested (e.g., growth models), multiple sample models, and models with specialized constraints (e.g., tau-equivalent models, Kenny, 2014; Widaman & Thompson, 2003). In such situations, specifying a different null model may be of interest by constraining mean parameters and residual variance parameters rather than use of the standard null model, which typically constrains only residual variances (Widaman & Thompson, 2003). Before using incremental fit indices, researchers may want to ensure that the typical null model makes sense to include as the most restrictive model for comparison.

Additional Indices/Information to Assess Model Fit

As one method of measuring model fit centers on use of fit indices, researchers have noted that the indices, in general, describe a global description of how well the model can reproduce the relationships among the data (e.g., Brown, 2014). Relying on this information alone does not provide a complete picture of fit, as the model may be acceptable overall, but some relationships are not accurately reproduced. Additional information is needed to provide a full picture of the hypothesized model's fit to the data.

Parameter Values and Standard Errors of Parameters

Information about parameter estimates size, direction, and interpretability may be examined to ensure that the estimates make substantive sense, given the theory under study. Parameter estimates should be examined to ensure that paths are of the appropriate direction and magnitude as suggested by theory or prior research (Benson, 1998). Typically, software programs provide unstandardized and (completely) standardized parameter estimates for interpretation. Unstandardized estimates base parameters in the original metric of the indicators where completely standardized parameters are standardized relative to the metric of the factor as well as to the metric of the items included on the factor (see Brown, 2014, for additional information). In addition, the squared multiple correlation values can be interpreted to determine the proportion of variance in an indicator explained by the factor (and other sources, if the indicator is cross loading or an endogenous variable). Indicators with low squared multiple correlation values may be targeted for further examination or even deletion.

T-values (or Z-values) associated with parameters may be examined to ensure that the relationships are important (i.e., statistically significant) in the model. Standard errors associated with individual parameter estimates can be examined to alert researchers to potential problems with measurement of a variable or to situations in which a construct is not precisely measured. In addition, using both the parameter estimates and standard errors, a researcher may construct confidence intervals to determine if parameter estimates are statistically similar to other parameter estimates within the same model (e.g., Raykov & Marcoulides, 2011).

Amount of Variance

The amount of variance accounted for in a dependent variable has been used in other statistical testing situations (e.g., ANOVA, regression) to demonstrate the strength of the relationship between the independent and dependent variables. In SEM, the amount of variance provided is also examined and maybe used to identify dependent variables that do not have a strong relationship to latent variables within a model. With item-level dependent variables (e.g., CFA), squared multiple correlation (SMC) values report the amount of variance in an item that is attributed to the latent variable(s). With structural models, endogenous (dependent) latent variables will produce R^2 values that show the variance which may be attributed to the exogenous (independent) latent variables within the model. Items with low SMCs or endogenous variables with low R^2 values suggest that there is a lot of unaccounted variability attributed to the dependent variable in question. Items with low SMC values (e.g., < .20) do not illustrate a strong relation with the latent variable(s) and may be considered for removal or to restructure relations in the tested model. However, the situation is more complex for latent variables with low R^2 values, as removal may involve changes to the underlying theory being examined. In such cases, the structure of the model may be reexamined to determine if there are omitted or unmeasured variables that may contribute to the measurement of the endogenous variable with low R^2 values or restructuring the paths of the existing variables to provide more precise measurement of the latent variable in question.

Residuals

Residual values (i.e., differences between the model implied parameter estimate (i.e., elements in $\Sigma(\Theta)$) and the input (i.e., corresponding element in S) can be examined to provide information about individual areas of the model which are unable to be estimated precisely. Considering the variance/covariance matrix, residual elements are produced for each variable (i.e., variance) and each pair of indicators (e.g., covariance elements) to provide information about how well the hypothesized model can reproduce the modeled relationships. Fitted residuals [e.g., elements of $S - \Sigma(\Theta)$] provide information about how close, or how small, the differences are between input values and estimated parameters. Fitted residuals are often difficult to interpret as they are in the raw metric of the variables (Kline, 2005) and are sensitive to the amount of variability in a variable's distribution. Instead, standardized residual values may be interpreted. These are computed by dividing fitted residuals by their estimated standard errors to produce a standard score, which may be interpreted as a Z-score (Brown, 2014). As with Z-scores, standardized residual values show the number of standard deviations difference between the estimated and input parameters, where larger values represent greater difference in standard deviation units, and, hence, a larger discrepancy. As with Z-values, the sign of the standardized residuals are also interpreted. Positive residuals show elements which are *underestimated* [i.e., $S > \Sigma(\Theta)$] and negative standardized residual elements identify relationships which are *overestimated* [i.e., $S < \Sigma(\Theta)$]. Because standardized residuals may be interpreted on a Z-metric, critical values associated with probability (e.g., Z-critical values associated with $p < .05$ or $p < .01$) can be used to flag excessively large residuals. In addition, values may be examined to identify standardized residual values that are discrepant from the set. Also, researchers may want to note specific variables which are consistently associated with large standardized residuals, as this may indicate a problem with the item(s) in question.

Modification Indices

Modification indices are typically computed as part of software program output. These values are computed for every fixed parameter to show what the approximate drop in the model χ^2 fit test would be if the fixed (or restrained) parameter was freely estimated. Thus, these tests may be considered as nested models, where the two models differ by the one parameter that is fixed in one model and freed in the other. Modification indices are thought to follow a χ^2 distribution and may be considered as *1 degree of freedom* tests, as the two models in question differ by only one parameter (Brown, 2014). To determine if the modification indices are significant, (approximate) drops in the χ^2 can be compared to a χ^2 table of critical values to determine if freeing the parameter in question would result in a significant drop in the χ^2 test of model fit. When using modification indices to judge the model-data fit, large values may be examined to see if the paths should be added into a hypothesized model. The additional paths must align with the theory being tested, and, should be tested on an independent sample of data rather than just retested with the same sample (e.g., Kline, 2005).

Research Issues

Tanaka (1993) recommended that a variety of fit indices from different families of fit be used for researchers to specify fit of a structural model across multiple domains. Building off of this recommendation, Hu and Bentler (1998, 1999) conducted comprehensive simulation studies of many different fit indices under differing situations and have made some recommendations to the field of SEM as to what indices should be reported (based on optimal performance) and what cutoff levels should be used. While many fit indices were examined in their simulation studies, the discussion here focuses on the fit indices reviewed within this chapter. In addition, it is recognized that the recommendations for use of indices and cutoff guidelines presented by Hu and Bentler (1998, 1999) provide the most well-known advice in the field, but are not without controversy (e.g., Barrett, 2007; Fan & Sivo, 2005; Marsh, Hau, & Wen, 2004).

In general, Hu and Bentler (1998, 1999) recommended a *two-index presentation strategy* which consists of pairing a residual-based index (such as SRMR) with an incremental fit index (e.g., NNFI or CFI) or with RMSEA. Cutoff values of .95 for NNFI and CFI, .06 for RMSEA, and .08 for SRMR were generally recommended based on sufficient sample size and with the ML-estimator. However, in these works Hu and Bentler (1998, 1999) detail how the recommendations provided are general guidelines and cutoff values used to examine model-data fit may change slightly depending on various conditions of the research situations, such as smaller sample sizes, nonnormality, and estimation technique used.

Considering what researchers in the field are reporting with SEM studies, a few authors have conducted in-depth reviews of articles in different social science fields (e.g., social work, psychology, counseling, educational research) to determine what researchers are reporting with SEM-studies and to determine how the practices have been influenced by recommendations from Tanaka (1993), Hu and Bentler (1998, 1999) and others. The review articles have largely examined confirmatory factor analysis studies (DiStefano & Hess, 2005; Guo, Perron, & Gillespie, 2009; Jackson, Gillaspy, & Purc-Stephenson, 2009; Schreiber, Nora, Stage, Barlow, & King, 2006; Worthington & Whittaker, 2006); however, confirmatory factor analysis is of interest here, as many test construction situations are providing evidence that a test works appropriately and in line with a given theoretical perspective.

Researchers have largely found that SEM-researchers are reporting more frequently recommended values, such as CFI, NNFI, RMSEA (e.g., DiStefano & Hess, 2005; Jackson et al., 2009) with fit index values using higher cutoffs in more recent years. In addition, researchers are reporting multiple indices to provide information from different classes of fit indices (DiStefano & Hess, 2005). While fit indices are providing information about global model fit, some information was lacking. For example, information concerning loading values (standardized or unstandardized) were not consistently presented by researchers (e.g., Jackson et al.,

2009) and competing or alternative models were not consistently presented (Guo et al., 2009). Researchers are recommended to provide more information about residual information to ensure that localized model misfit is not overshadowed by an emphasis on global fit (Jackson et al., 2009; Kline, 2005). Finally, the two-step strategy suggested by Hu and Bentler (1998, 1999) is the most widely-used set of guidelines for evaluating model fit in SEM (Fan & Sivo, 2005).

Previous research provides support that applied researchers are including information about multiple aspects of fit when evaluating models; however, some researchers have raised questions about the use of fit index guidelines when evaluating model-data fit. Researchers have noted that fit indices also reflect aspects such as the sample size, the distribution of the data, the strength of loading values, and estimator used (Fan & Sivo, 2005; Heene, Hilbert, Draxler, Ziegler, & Bühner, 2011; Sivo, Fan, Witta, & Willse, 2006; Yuan, 2005). Thus, the cutoff values used may depend upon the specified model as well the testing conditions. For example, higher cutoff values for goodness of fit indices (lower for badness of fit indices) may be warranted with larger sample sizes and lower (higher) cutoff values with smaller (larger) sample sizes (Sivo et al., 2006). Similarly, if the guidelines presented by Hu and Bentler (1998, 1999) are interpreted as fixed values, researchers are likely to make errors as parameters used in empirical research are often lower than the values used with Hu and Bentler's studies (.7–.8) resulting in the adoption of a misspecified or nonfitting model (Heene et al., 2011). Thus, the guidelines provided by Hu and Bentler (1998, 1999) may be overly stringent and could be relaxed in many situations (Marsh et al., 2004).

The performance of fit indices under misspecified models is a concern, given that researchers are unlikely to correctly specify a model under most empirical research situations and are reliant on fit indices (e.g., Heene et al., 2011; Sivo et al., 2006; Marsh et al., 2004). Marsh et al. (2004) noted that many conditions examined by Hu and Bentler (1998, 1999) would result in assessments of good model-data fit under the misspecified conditions. These *acceptable – misspecified models* (Marsh et al., 2004) may be appropriate alternative models to consider. Also, the level of error (i.e., large uniqueness terms), the severity of the model misspecification, and the power associated with the model can adversely impact fit (Heene et al., 2011; Sivo et al., 2006).

Although problems were noted with absolute guidelines, researchers were able to offer some guidance regarding the performance of various fit indices under alternative situations. The SRMR and RMSEA values were cited as optimal for distinguishing between correctly specified and incorrectly specified models (Heene et al., 2011; Sivo et al., 2006) and were recommended if major misspecification was not present along with lower loading levels (Heene et al., 2011). Also, CFI was shown to accept misfitting models if lower sample sizes were used or lower loadings were used; under such situations, a loss of power resulted in lower CFI (and χ^2) values (Heene et al., 2011). In summary, SRMR, RMSEA, and CFI were shown to work as expected if sample sizes were 500 or higher and loading values were .5 or higher. The maximum likelihood based χ^2 was recommended if the majority of the data were symmetric (Yuan, 2005). In sum, while rules of thumb are commonly used with fit indices in SEM, the issue of what constitutes appropriate fit is still under debate.

Illustrative Example

To illustrate decision making and evaluation of fit indices in SEM, an empirical example is provided. The Behavioral and Emotional Screening System (BESS; Kamphaus & Reynolds,

2007) is employed in many US schools as part of social/emotional Response to Intervention (RtI) procedures to identify problems (e.g., academic, behavioral) and intervene early through special services and classroom-devised interventions. Generally, a RtI approaches include three tiers for prevention and intervention services (Glover & Albers, 2007). Tier 1, the foundational level, consists of universal screening and implementation of an evidence-based curriculum for all children. Tier 2 consists of targeted interventions for those children who have emerging learning and behavioral difficulties (i.e., exhibiting higher risk). Finally, Tier 3, for a small number of children includes the most intensive and individualized level of assessments and interventions. To date, RtI has been primarily implemented and evaluated with older students, most often older than kindergarten or even first grade (e.g., Coleman, Buysse, & Neitzel, 2006; Jimerson, Burns, & VanDerHeyden, 2007). However, RtI programs for such competencies may be especially appreciated in preschools as behavioral and social-emotional development is a core part of the preschool curriculum standards (National Association for the Education of Young Children, 2008).

Given that Tier 1 RtI procedures are implemented with all children, the importance of a psychometrically sound screening instrument is essential. One available instrument for school-based screening with young children is the BESS Teacher Rating Scale-Preschool form (BESS TRS-P; Kamphaus & Reynolds, 2007). The BESS TRS-P screener was developed by reducing items from a 185-item pool (published and nonpublished items) used in the norming of the related, longer behavioral instrument (i.e., Behavioral Assessment System for Children-2nd edition; Reynolds & Kamphaus, 2004). The longer version measures three interrelated dimensions in preschoolers, using 11 multi-item subscales. Externalizing Problems measures children's tendencies to display aggressive or hyperactive behaviors in the classroom. Internalizing Problems includes children's tendencies to show feelings of anxiety, worry, or sadness. This dimension includes behaviors, which are not marked by acting out behaviors but, instead, are associated with dysregulated emotions. Finally, the Adaptive Skills dimension measures how students develop socially and interact with peers and authority figures. These skills represent positive and resiliency behaviors and social skills of young children.

The BESS TRS-P screener is thought to measure one construct, maladaptive behavior, characterized as the "behavioral and emotional strengths and weaknesses" of young children (Kamphaus & Reynolds, 2007, p. 1); however, there is debate as to the underlying structure of the instrument. The unidimensional model aligns with the scoring procedures (an overall score), but a three-factor model may also be warranted, given that the items were selected from three different constructs. Further, selected items measuring Attention Problems in preschoolers are included with the Externalizing Problems subscale with preschoolers, but with a new dimension, School Problems, for the child form (ages 6–18). Even with the preschool form, these items may be better suited as their own factor, measuring a (Emerging) School Problems component, which reports students' tendency to attend and process information in a classroom environment. Finally, given that overall scores and dimensional information is considered, a bifactor model or higher order factor model may fit well with theory and also align with the BESS TRS-P's scoring mechanism (DiStefano, Greer, & Kamphaus, 2013). Initially, the four dimensions were thought to be unrelated, with the variance between factors related to the higher order factor or the general factor. Thus, this example will compare the fit of different theoretical structures underlying the BESS TRS-P based on the different perspectives noted above.

Public school teachers provided ratings of preschool aged students as part of a nationally funded grant project investigating the validity of the BESS TRS-P scale. Data were collected in the fall of an academic year over a 3-year period from 2012 to 2014. The sample included 67 teachers who rated a total of 3,206 children attending public preschool.

The following five confirmatory factor analysis models were analyzed: unidimensional, three-factor, four-factor, bifactor, and higher-order using Mplus software with the rescaled maximum likelihood estimator (v. 7.2; Muthén & Muthén, 1998–2010). Six fit indices were examined: global χ^2, CFI, NNFI, AIC, RMSEA, and SRMR along with standardized fit indices, squared multiple correlation values, predicted residuals, and modification indices.

Table 9.3 reports fit indices for the set of tested models. As shown, all models reported significant global χ^2 values, suggesting that the data did not show good alignment with the tested model. However, some of the other fit indices showed a more positive view of model-data fit. Beginning with the unidimensional model, this model exhibited poor fit to model, all fit indices were outside of acceptable bounds (as reported in Table 9.1 and Table 9.2), the AIC value was highest across the set of models, and the largest global χ^2 value was reported. Due to the unacceptable fit values, the unidimensional model was not considered further.

Table 9.3. Robust maximum likelihood based fit indices – alternative models for the BESS TRS-P (N = 3,206)

Model	χ^2	df	AIC	RMSEA (p)	RMSEA 90% CI	CFI	NNFI	SRMR
Unidimensional	19,505.72	275	161,034.65	.148 (< .001)	.146–.148	.570	.531	.134
3-Factor	8,120.49	272	145,705.59	.095 (< .001)	.093–.097	.825	.806	.089
4-Factor	5,983.13	269	142,952.64	.081 (< .001)	.080–.083	.872	.858	.091
4-Factor higher-order model	7,037.96	272	144304.77	.088 (< .001)	.086–.090	.849	.833	.197
4-Factor bifactor	4,298.60	250	140,738.73	.071 (< .001)	.069–.073	.909	.891	.064
Revised 4-factor bifactor model[a]	2,322.59	222	133,341.54	.054 (< .001)	.052–.056	.950	.938	.030

Note. [a] = Final model selected. AIC = Akaike information criterion; RMSEA = root mean squared error of approximation; CFI = comparative fit index; NNFI = Nonnormed fit index; SRMR = standardized root mean residual.

Next, the two multifactor models were considered to find a general structure to test the more complex bifactor model and higher order model. The three-factor model yielded less than optimal fit, with CFI and NNFI below recommended bounds, a high SRMR value, and a RMSEA value and confidence interval suggesting poor model-data fit. While the four-factor model also presented fit indices outside of recommended cutoff values, the fit of the four-factor model was better than the three-factor model, as shown by lower values of AIC and RMSEA and higher CFI and NNFI values. Interestingly, the SRMR value for the four-factor model was higher than the value in the three-factor model, illustrating a problem with some portion(s) of the model to accurately reproduce select elements in the input covariance matrix. Based on the comparison, the four-factor model was chosen as the base for the more complex models. In terms of interpretation, the four-factor model suggests that the Attention Problems items are a separate factor, representing (Emerging) School Problems; this structure for the preschool sample aligns with the BESS at the elementary level (e.g., DiStefano et al., 2013; Kamphaus & Reynolds, 2007).

The bifactor and higher order models were modeled using an underlying four-factor solution. Considering the two complex models, the fit indices associated with the higher order model illustrated worse fit than with the free standing four-factor model. The bifactor model reported the best fit of the set of models. This representation of the data illustrated the lowest AIC of the set of models and a SRMR at the recommended level (i.e., .06; Hu & Bentler, 1999), but the RMSEA was just above the recommended value. However, the RMSEA value still illustrated adequate fit and the CFI and NNFI were close to the .90 level. The bifactor model is consistent with prior research using the BESS teacher rating norm sample (DiStefano et al., 2013) and aligns with the instrument's scoring; thus, this model made conceptual and theoretical sense as well.

Given that the bifactor model represented optimal fit among the set of models, additional fit information was examined. The squared multiple correlation values were all high (> .45), showing that the latent factors were accounting for a substantial portion of variability associated with each item. However, considering the standardized loading values, not all values were significant. Two items from the Adaptive Skills factor (Item 2 – "Is a 'good sport' " – and Item 24 – "Shares toys or possessions") yielded nonsignificant relations to the Adaptive Skills factor. Further, examination of residual values showed that there were high standardized residuals associated with Item 22, showing that the model was having difficulty in reproducing relationships between this item and other items. Based on the information above, Item 22 was considered a candidate for deletion. Item 24 was kept to see how the fit information was changed after Item 22 was removed.

Model modifications were also examined. There were three large item variance (i.e., uniqueness) terms suggesting a relationship between three pairs of items beyond what was accounted for by the latent variable. An investigation of the item content showed that the items had similar words in common and were associated with the same latent factor (e.g., "Bothers the play of other children" and "Disrupts other children" from the Externalizing Problems factor). While there may be some theoretical support for allowing the item residuals to correlate, these paths were not freed. However, the largest gain was to be seen by allowing the four BESS factors to correlate. While correlations with the general factor are not permitted, prior CFA models have allowed the four dimensions of the BESS to be related (e.g., Kamphaus & Reynolds, 2007). Thus, these modifications were included.

The revised four-factor bifactor model is provided in Table 9.3. As shown, this model shows acceptable fit to the data. The AIC value is the lowest of the entire set of models considered. Further, the CFI value is at the more stringent recommended .950 cutoff value (Schumaker & Lomax, 2012) and the NNFI is close to this level too, at .938. The RMSEA value showed close model-data fit, with a value of .054; finally, the model had an easier time reproducing relationships in the input covariance matrix, as seen by an SRMR of .028. Investigation of additional indices showed that Item 24 ("Shares toys or possessions with other children") was now significant after Item 22 was removed. This also illustrates the advantage of making changes in an iterative pattern, as one item which is removed affects the relationships with the other variables and the system of relationships. There were no outlying standardized residual values and no modification indices to be included that were aligned with theory. In sum, with an independent sample of teacher ratings, the revised four-factor bifactor model is thought to represent the theoretical underpinning of the preschool BESS form.

Future Directions

As discussed, there are many decisions that researchers must undertake when examining model-data fit in SEM. While many fit indices have been developed and various recommendations have been proposed, there is still much to learn in this area. If a theorized model is correctly specified and the input variables do follow a multivariate normal distribution, then the choice of estimator is arbitrary, as all estimators used will converge upon the same maximum and produce equivalent fit (Schermelleh-Engel, Moosbrugger, & Müller, 2003). However, a more realistic perspective is that empirical models are not correctly specified and that data are not multivariate normally distributed. Thus, use of different estimators may produce differences in fit – even with the same data. Fit indices have been found to be influenced by characteristics of the testing situation, such as sample size, estimation method, and model misspecification (Fan, Thompson, & Wang, 1999; Schermelleh-Engel et al., 2003). For example, under comparisons of the Generalized Least Squares (GLS) estimator and Maximum Likelihood (ML) with misspecified models, GLS has been found to produce overly optimistic fit indices than ML (e.g., Fan et al., 1999; Olsson, Troye, & Howell, 1999; Olsson, Foss, Troye, & Howell, 2000). While this difference may be attributed to differences in the final weight matrix (**W**) used at the final iteration, most researchers do not actually know the degree to which the model is misspecified. Ideally, fit indices should be able to detect misspecification and provide estimates which suggest researchers reject a tested model. It is problematic when fit indices are not able to provide such suggestions, as, with test construction, these errors may lead a researcher to retain a misspecified test structure, possibly leading to erroneous decisions made from the test results.

In structural modeling, the use of robust estimators that accommodate nonnormal and/or categorical data is increasingly popular. Robust estimators involve adjusting the χ^2, fit indices, and standard errors by a factor based on the amount of nonnormality in the data. Such corrections are needed as models which include nonnormality are likely to have large χ^2 model fit values, which would lead to rejection of the tested model, even if the model was correctly specified (Finney & DiStefano, 2013). Robust corrections use the observed data's distributional characteristics to adjust the χ^2 model fit index downward in order to better approximate the theoretical χ^2 reference distribution (i.e., central χ^2 distribution, with expected χ^2 value equal to the model degrees of freedom). Under robust estimation, a scaling factor is multiplied with the obtained χ^2 to produce a new, robust χ^2 estimate of model-data fit. (Note that a similar process is used for correcting standard errors for attenuation; however, because standard errors are not directly used in calculation of fit indices, these will not be discussed further. See Finney & DiStefano, 2013, for additional information). Various corrections currently exist including the Satorra–Bentler scaling procedure (which is typically applied to the ML-estimator), diagonal weighted least squares estimation (DWLS) for use with ordered categorical data, and even robust adjustments that correct the χ^2.value for mean and variance anomalies, such as the weighted least squares mean and variance estimator via the Mplus software package.

Given that the model χ^2 is impacted under robust estimation, it follows that the robust χ^2 would be incorporated into the computation of fit indices that rely upon the model χ^2 value as part of its calculation (e.g., NNFI, CFI) in order to gain benefits of the scaling procedure and, in turn, provide more accurate reflections of model-data fit. Nevitt and Hancock (2000) found that the Satorra–Bentler scaled RMSEA outperformed the unadjusted index. Yu and Muthén (2002) also examined this index in addition to the Satorra–Bentler scaled NNFI and CFI and found that, under conditions of moderate to severe nonnormality coupled with small sample size ($N \leq 250$), the Satorra–Bentler scaled versions of these three indices were preferred over the ML-based estimates. Yu and Muthén (2002) suggested that values at or below .05 for the Satorra–Bentler scaled RMSEA and at or above .95 for the Satorra–Bentler scaled CFI indicate adequate fit, which are quite similar to the cutoff values recommended by Hu and Bentler (1999) for the unadjusted indices. The robust χ^2 corrections also apply to estimators which accommodate ordered categorical data (e.g., DWLS estimation). Such corrections have been found to produce χ^2 fit indices to be close to expected values, even with increasing model size and decreasing sample size (Bandalos, 2008, 2014; Flora & Curran, 2004; Yang-Wallentin, Jöreskog, & Luo, 2010). See Chapter 8 of this volume for additional information concerning fit with robust estimators.

However, fit indices, and the rules of thumb used with fit indices to evaluate model-data fit, were developed under ML, estimation and not much is known about the performance of fit indices under robust estimation (Nye & Drasgow, 2011). When robust estimators are used, questions remain including what values should be used with fit indices and which fit indices perform best? Researchers have continued to generally use existing rules with robust estimation and/or categorical data (e.g., Schreiber, Nora, Stage, Barlow, & King, 2006; Yu & Muthén, 2002). However, as robust estimators are increasingly evaluated, differences in fit are emerging. In a study of nonnormal dichotomous data with misspecified CFA models, Nye and Drasgow showed that DWLS-based fit largely surpassed existing rules of thumb for TLI, CFI, RMSEA, and SRMR. For example, most values of TLI and CFI were above .99 for all study conditions. To avoid a misleading view of model-data fit, more stringent criteria were suggested when DWLS estimation was used (Nye & Drasgow, 2011). Fit under robust estimation is an area well-suited for future research to gain greater insight about the performance of fit indices under these methods and examination of criteria to use for model evaluation.

In addition, researchers have proposed additional corrections for CFI, NNFI (Brosseau-Liard & Savalei, 2014) and RMSEA (Brosseau-Liard, Savalei, & Li, 2012) under robust estimation to correct for nonnormality. These corrections include the scaling correction used to correct both the baseline and the hypothesized model in the calculations to provide a measure of the degree of nonnormality. While limited research using these new corrections has been conducted, simulation results using the ML-estimator and nonnormally distributed continuous data showed that these scaling-corrected estimates of fit produce values that more closely approximate the population values of these indices, even under model misspecification and smaller sample size conditions (Brosseau-Liard et al., 2012; Brosseau-Liard & Savalei, 2014). Further, the typically used robust corrected fit indices were not as accurate as the newer versions, suggesting that researchers may be adversely reporting the robust-fit of their models. Currently, these corrections must be computed by hand. With these newer corrections, limited study of their performance has been conducted; future study may consider different models and estimators to determine effects of incorporating scaling corrections into the view of model-data fit.

Conclusion

In conclusion, there are a few final pointers for researchers to remember when using fit information to evaluate structural equation modeling results. First, be aware that different software programs may use slightly different formulas for calculating indices or, even slightly different formulas for estimators and calculation of weight matrices or robust corrections. Such differences may impact the calculation of fit indices or even additional information used to evaluate model-data fit, such as parameter estimates or standard errors used in parameter tests. For example, the popular LISREL program (Jöreskog & Sörbom, 2007) calculates fit indices based on the reweighted least squares χ^2 fit index (starting with version 8.52) rather than the maximum likelihood based χ^2 fit index used by other popular software programs (e.g., EQS; Bentler, 1985–2010; Mplus; Muthén & Muthén, 1998–2010) This change not only may result in different software programs reporting different fit indices for the same data tested, but the comparative fit indices under LISREL report a much larger null model χ^2 value than would be reported under the maximum likelihood based χ^2 null value (Schmukle & Hardt, 2005). The RMSEA, SRMR, and parameter indices were not greatly impacted; however, the comparative fit indices were impacted. Thus, under LISREL the fit of some models may be misleading, as a larger null χ^2 fit value would produce higher incremental fit values and a more positive view of model-data fit than would be obtained with the same data under other programs. Further, the typical fit index cutoff recommendations were built from simulation studies based upon maximum likelihood χ^2 fit values; thus, different fit index recommendations may apply under situations using the reweighted least squares χ^2 fit values. With LISREL, researchers do have an option to produce a separate file of fit information with up to four different χ^2 values noted (specifying FT on the Options line within the LISREL program) to obtain ML-based χ^2 values, however, this file must be requested as part of the LISREL program (Schmukle & Hardt, 2005).

In addition, when using robust estimators, it is important to note that LISREL currently does not adjust all fit indices for nonnormality. In fact, no incremental indices are adjusted (e.g., CFI, NNFI). Adjustments to these indices must be calculated by hand. This is done by first specifying and estimating the independence model under a particular robust procedure and then using the independence model's χ^2 along with the hypothesized model's χ^2 in the corresponding fit index formula (see, e.g., Hu & Bentler, 1998, for fit index formulas). Other popular structural modeling software (e.g., EQS and Mplus) adjust all relevant fit indices and report adjusted values when the robust scaling methods are used. These examples suggest that researchers should closely examine the choice of software to determine how fit index calculations are conducted and exactly what information is reported to ensure that correct information is used in model evaluation.

While testing alternative models has long been recommended in structural equation modeling (e.g., Jöreskog, 1993), the problem of equivalent models is recognized. Equivalent models are models which differ in the structure and interpretation; however, are identical in terms of model-data fit (Hersberger & Marcoulides, 2013). For example, a structural model which proposes different causal paths with the same variables would be an example of how equivalent models may arise. When evaluating equivalent models, the role of theory is paramount to ensure that a model may be eliminated based on substantive grounds, as no differences in fit will be apparent (Schermelleh-Engel et al., 2003). To provide greater support for the selected model, equivalent models are recommended for investigation and inclusion in a researcher's discussion of model data fit (Hersberger & Marcoulides, 2013).

Finally, it is re-emphasized that model fit in structural equation modeling does differ substantially from evaluating model fit with more traditional hypothesis testing situations due to the many indices which may be reported, the different views of model-data fit, and the subjective nature of fit interpretation. Thus, staying abreast of current practices and new developments in fit is essential. The question "What is good model-data fit?" has troubled structural equation researchers for decades; thus, the practice of model evaluation is under constant study and development. Researchers are encouraged to read, use, and report current research regarding model fit (i.e., within the past 5–10 years) because new information, indices, and performance strategies are continually evolving, and informing the field of best practices (Heene et al., 2011). As the test development process encompasses many steps to produce a sound instrument, evaluating model fit is also a multistep process, to document the evaluation, interpretation, and use of information. Attention to the myriad of decision points regarding model fit can only help test developers feel confident that the actions will result in the creation of the best possible instrument.

Acknowledgments

The research reported here was partly supported by the Institute of Education Sciences, US Department of Education, through Grant R324A100104 to the South Carolina Research Foundation. The opinions expressed are those of the author and do not necessarily represent views of the Institute of Education Sciences or the US Department of Education.

References

Aho, K., Derryberry, D., & Peterson, T. (2014). Model selection for ecologists: The worldviews of AIC and BIC. *Ecology, 95*(3), 631–636.

Akaike, H. (1987). Factor analysis and AIC. *Psychometrika, 52*(3), 317–332.

Anderson, J. C., & Gerbing, D. W. (1988). Structural equation modeling in practice: A review and recommended two-step approach. *Psychological Bulletin, 103*(3), 411.

Bandalos, D. L. (2008). Is parceling really necessary? A comparison of results from item parceling and categorical variable methodology. *Structural Equation Modeling: A Multidisciplinary Journal, 15*, 211–240. http://doi.org/10.1080/10705510801922340

Bandalos, D. L. (2014). Relative performance of categorical diagonally weighted least squares and robust maximum likelihood estimation. *Structural Equation Modeling: A Multidisciplinary Journal, 21*(1), 102–116.

Barrett, P. (2007). Structural equation modelling: Adjudging model fit. *Personality and Individual Differences, 42*(5), 815–824.

Benson, J. (1998). Developing a strong program of construct validation: A test anxiety example. *Educational Measurement: Issues and Practice, 17*(1), 10–17.

Bentler, P. M. (1985–2010). *EQS for Windows (Version 6.1)* [Computer software]. Encino, CA: Multivariate Software, Inc.

Bentler, P. M. (1990). Comparative fit indexes in structural models. *Psychological Bulletin, 107*(2), 238–246. http://doi.org/10.1037/0033-2909.107.2.238

Bentler, P. M., & Bonett, D. G. (1980). Significance tests and goodness of fit in the analysis of covariance structures. *Psychological Bulletin, 88*(3), 588–606. http://dx.doi.org/10.1037/0033-2909.88.3.588.

Bentler, P. M., & Dudgeon, P. (1996). Covariance structure analysis: Statistical practice, theory, and directions. *Annual Review of Psychology, 47*(1), 563–592.

Bollen, K. A. (1989). *Structural equation modeling with latent variables*. New York, NY: Wiley.

Brosseau-Liard, P. E., & Savalei, V. (2014). Adjusting incremental fit indices for nonnormality. *Multivariate Behavioral Research, 49*, 460–470. http://dx.doi.org/10.1080/00273171.2014.933697

Brosseau-Liard, P. E., Savalei, V., & Li, L. (2012). An investigation of the sample performance of two nonnormality corrections for RMSEA. *Multivariate Behavioral Research, 47*, 904–930. http://doi.org/10.1080/00273171.2012.715252

Brown, T. A. (2014). *Confirmatory factor analysis for applied research*. New York, NY: Guilford Press.

Browne, M. W., & Cudeck, R. (1993). Alternative ways of assessing model fit. In K. A. Bollen & S. Long (Eds.), *Testing structural equation models*. (pp. 136–154) Thousand Oaks, CA: Sage Publishers.

Byrne, B. M. (1998). *Structural equation modelling with LISREL, PRELIS and SIMPLIS: Basic concepts, applications and programming*. Mahwah, NJ: Lawrence Erlbaum Associates.

Coleman, M. R., Buysse, V., & Neitzel, J. (2006). *Recognition and response: An early intervening system for young children at-risk for learning disabilities*. Chapel Hill, NC: UNC, FPG Child Development Institute.

Curran, P. J., Bollen, K. A., Paxton, P., Kirby, J., & Chen, F. (2002). The noncentral chi-square distribution in misspecified structural equation models: Finite sample results from a Monte Carlo simulation. *Multivariate Behavioral Research, 37*(1), 1–36.

Diamantopoulos, A., & Siguaw, J.A. (2000). *Introducing LISREL*. London, UK: Sage Publications.

Distefano, C. (2002). The impact of categorization with confirmatory factor analysis. *Structural Equation Modeling: A Multidisciplinary Journal, 9*, 327–346. http://doi.org/10.1207/S15328007SEM0903_2

DiStefano, C., Greer, F. W., & Kamphaus, R. W. (2013). Multifactor modeling of emotional and behavioral risk of preschool-age children. *Psychological Assessment, 25*(2), 467–476.

DiStefano, C., & Hess, B. (2005). Using confirmatory factor analysis for construct validation: An empirical review. *Journal of Psychoeducational Assessment, 23*(3), 225–241. http://doi.org/10.1177/073428290502300303

Fan, X., & Sivo, S. A. (2005). Sensitivity of fit indexes to misspecified structural or measurement model components: Rationale of two-index strategy revisited. *Structural Equation Modeling: A Multidisciplinary Journal, 12*(3), 343–367. http://doi.org/10.1207/s15328007sem1203_1

Fan, X., Thompson, B., & Wang, L. (1999). Effects of sample size, estimation methods, and model specification on structural equation modeling fit indexes. *Structural Equation Modeling: A Multidisciplinary Journal, 6*(1), 56–83. http://doi.org/10.1080/10705519909540119

Finney, S. J., & DiStefano, C. (2013). Nonnormal and categorical data in structural equation modeling. In G. R. Hancock & R. O. Mueller (Eds.), *Structural equation modeling: A second course* (pp. 439–392). Charlotte, NC: Information Age Publishers.

Flora, D. B., & Curran, P. J. (2004). An empirical evaluation of alternative methods of estimation for confirmatory factor analysis with ordinal data. *Psychological Methods, 9*, 466–491. http://doi.org/10.1037/1082-989X.9.4.466

Gerbing, D. W., & Anderson, J. C. (1993). Monte Carlo evaluations of goodness-of-fit indexes for structural equation models. In K. A. Bollen & J. S. Long (Eds.), *Testing structural equation models* (pp. 40–65). London, UK: Sage.

Glover, T. A., & Albers, C. A. (2007). Considerations for evaluating universal screening assessments. *Journal of School Psychology, 45*(2), 117–135. http://doi.org/10.1016/j.jsp.2006.05.005

Guo, B., Perron, B. E., & Gillespie, D. F. (2009). A systematic review of structural equation modelling in social work research. *British Journal of Social Work, 39*(8), 1556–1574. http://doi.org/10.1093/bjsw/bcn101

Hayduk, L., Cummings, G. G., Boadu, K., Pazderka-Robinson, H., & Boulianne, S. (2007). Testing! Testing! One, two, three – testing the theory in structural equation models! *Personality and Individual Differences, 42*(2), 841–850. http://doi.org/10.1016/j.paid.2006.10.001

Heene, M., Hilbert, S., Draxler, C., Ziegler, M., & Bühner, M. (2011). Masking misfit in confirmatory factor analysis by increasing unique variances: A cautionary note on the usefulness of cutoff values of fit indices. *Psychological Methods, 16*(3), 319. http://doi.org/10.1037/a0024917

Hersberger, S. L., & Marcoulides, G. A. (2013). The problem of equivalent structural models. In G. R. Hancock & R. O. Mueller (Eds.), *Structural equation modeling: A second course* (pp. 3–40). Charlotte, NC: Information Age Publishers.

Hoelter, J. W. (1983). The analysis of covariance structures goodness-of-fit indices. *Sociological Methods & Research, 11*(3), 325–344.

Hooper, D., Coughlan, J., &, Mullen, M. (2008). Structural equation modelling: Guidelines for determining model fit. *Electronic Journal of Business Research Methods, 6*(1), 53–60.

Hu, L., & Bentler, P. M. (1998). Fit indices in covariance structure modeling: Sensitivity to underparameterized model misspecification. *Psychological Methods, 3*, 424–453. http://doi.org/10.1037/1082-989X.3.4.424

Hu, L., & Bentler, P. M. (1999). Cutoff criteria for fit indexes in covariance structure analysis: Conventional criteria versus new alternatives. *Structural Equation Modeling: A Multidisciplinary Journal, 6*, 1–55. http://doi.org/10.1080/10705519909540118

Jackson, D. L., Gillaspy, J. A., Jr., & Purc-Stephenson, R. (2009). Reporting practices in confirmatory factor analysis: An overview and some recommendations. *Psychological Methods, 14*(1), 6–23. http://doi.org/10.1037/a0014694

Jimerson, S. R., Burns, M. K., & VanDerHeyden, A. M. (2007). Response to intervention at school: The science and practice of assessment and intervention. In S. R. Jimerson, M. K. Burns, & A. M. VanDerHeyden (Eds.), *Handbook of response to intervention* (pp. 3–9). New York, NY: Springer Publishers. http://doi.org/10.1007/978-0-387-49053-3

Jöreskog, K. G. (1970). A general method for analysis of covariance structures. *Biometrika, 57*(2), 239–251.

Jöreskog, K. G. (1973). A general method for estimating a linear structural equation system. In A. S. Gold-berger & O. D. Duncan (Eds.), *Structural equation models in the social sciences* (pp. 85–112). New York, NY: Seminar Press.

Jöreskog, K. G. (1993). Testing structural equation models. In K. A. Bollen & S. Long (Eds.), *Testing structural equation models* (pp. 136–154). Thousand Oaks, CA: Sage Publishers.

Jöreskog, K. G., & Sörbom, D. (1982). Recent developments in structural equation modeling. *Journal of Marketing Research, 19*, 404–416.

Jöreskog, K. G., & Sörbom, D. (2007). *LISREL 8.80 for Windows* [Computer software]. Lincolnwood, IL: Scientific Software International, Inc.

Kamphaus, R. W., & Reynolds, C. R. (2007). *BASC-2 behavior and emotional screening system (BASC-2 BESS)*. Bloomington, MN: Pearson.

Kenny, D. Q. (2014). *Measuring model fit*. Retrieved from http://davidakenny.net/cm/fit.htm

Kline, R. B. (2005). *Principles and practice of structural equation modeling* (2nd ed.). New York, NY: Guilford Press.

MacCallum, R. C., Browne, M. W., & Sugawara, H. M. (1996). Power analysis and determination of sample size for covariance structure modeling. *Psychological Methods, 1*(2), 130–149. http://doi.org/10.1037/1082-989X.1.2.130

Marsh, H. W., Balla, J. R., & McDonald, R. P. (1988). Goodness-of-fit indexes in confirmatory factor analysis: The effect of sample size. *Psychological Bulletin, 103*(3), 391–410. http://doi.org/10.1037/0033-2909.103.3.391

Marsh, H. W., Hau, K. T., & Wen, Z. (2004). In search of golden rules: Comment on hypothesis-testing approaches to setting cutoff values for fit indexes and dangers in overgeneralizing Hu and Bentler's (1999) findings. *Structural Equation Modeling: A Multidisciplinary Journal, 11*, 320–341. http://doi.org/10.1207/s15328007sem1103_2

Matsueda, R. L. (2012). Key advances in the history of structural equation modeling. In R. H. Hoyle (Ed.), *Handbook of structural equation modeling* (pp.17–42). New York, NY: Guilford Press.

McDonald, R. P., & Ho, M.-H.R. (2002). Principles and practice in reporting statistical equation analyses. *Psychological Methods, 7*(1), 64–82. http://doi.org/10.1037/1082-989X.7.1.64

Millsap, R. E. (2007). Structural equation modeling made difficult. *Personality and Individual Differences, 42*(5), 875–881. http://doi.org/10.1016/j.paid.2006.09.021

Morgan, G. B. (2014). Mixed mode latent class analysis: An examination of fit index performance for classification. *Structural Equation Modeling: A Multidisciplinary Journal*, http://dx.doi.org/10.1080/10705511.2014.935751

Mulaik, S. A., James, L. R., Van Alstine, J., Bennett, N., Lind, S., & Stilwell, C. D. (1989). Evaluation of goodness-of-fit indices for structural equation models. *Psychological Bulletin, 105*(3), 430–445.

Muthén, L. K., & Muthén, B. O. (1998–2010). *Mplus user's guide* (6th ed.). Los Angeles, CA: Muthén & Muthén.

National Association for the Education of Young Children [NAYCE]. (2008). *Overview of the NAEYC Early Childhood Program Standards*. Retrieved from http://www.naeyc.org/academy

Nevitt, J., & Hancock, G. R. (2000). Improving the root mean square error of approximation for nonnormal conditions in structural equation modeling. *The Journal of Experimental Education, 68*(3), 251–268.

Nye, C. D., & Drasgow, F. (2011). Assessing goodness of fit: Simple rules of thumb simply do not work. *Organizational Research Methods, 14*, 548–570. http://doi.org/10.1177/1094428110368562

Olsson, U. H., Troye, S. V., & Howell, R. D. (1999). Theoretical fit and empirical fit: The performance of maximum likelihood versus generalized least squares estimation in structural equation models. *Multivariate Behavioral Research, 34*, 31–58. http://doi.org/10.1207/s15327906mbr3401_2

Olsson, U. H., Foss, T., Troye, S. V., & Howell, R. D. (2000). The performance of ML, GLS, and WLS estimation in structural equation modeling under conditions of misspecification and nonnormality. *Structural Equation Modeling: A Multidisciplinary Journal, 7*, 557–595. http://doi.org/10.1207/S15328007SEM0704_3

Raykov, T., & Marcoulides, G. A. (2011). *Introduction to psychometric theory*. New York, NY: Routledge Publishers.

Revelle, W. (2015). *An introduction to psychometric theory with applications in R*. Retrieved from http://www.personality-project.org/r/book/

Reynolds, C. R., & Kamphaus, R. W. (2004). *BASC-2: Behavior assessment system for children*. Bloomington, MN: Pearson.

Schermelleh-Engel, K., Moosbrugger, H., & Müller, H. (2003). Evaluating the fit of structural equation models: Tests of significance and descriptive goodness-of-fit measures. *Methods of Psychological Research Online, 8*(2), 23–74. Retrieved from http://www.dgps.de/fachgruppen/methoden/mpr-online/issue20/art2/mpr130_13.pdf

Schmukle, S. C., & Hardt, J. (2005). A cautionary note on incremental fit indices reported by LISREL. *Methodology: European Journal of Research Methods for the Behavioral and Social Sciences, 1*(2), 81–85. http://doi.org/10.1027/1614-1881.1.2.81

Schreiber, J. B. (2008). Core reporting practices in structural equation modeling. *Research in Social and Administrative Pharmacy, 4*(2), 83–97. http://doi.org/10.1016/j.sapharm.2007.04.003

Schreiber, J. B., Nora, A., Stage, F. K., Barlow, E. A., & King, J. (2006). Reporting structural equation modeling and confirmatory factor analysis results: A review. *The Journal of Educational Research, 99*(6), 323–338. http://doi.org/10.3200/JOER.99.6.323-338

Schumacker, R. E., & Lomax, R. G. (2012). *A beginner's guide to structural equation modeling*. New York, NY: Routledge Academic.

Schwartz, G. (1978). Estimating the dimensions of a model. *Annals of Statistics, 6*, 451–464.

Sivo, S. A., Fan, X., Witta, E. L., & Willse, J. T. (2006). The search for "optimal" cutoff properties: Fit index criteria in structural equation modeling. *The Journal of Experimental Education, 74*(3), 267–288. http://doi.org/10.3200/JEXE.74.3.267-288

Steiger, J. H. (2007). Understanding the limitations of global fit assessment in structural equation modeling. *Personality and Individual Differences, 42*(5), 893–898. http://doi.org/10.1016/j.paid.2006.09.017

Steiger, J. H., & Lind, J. C. (1980, May). *Statistically based tests for the number of common factors*. Paper presented at the Annual Spring Meeting of the Psychometric Society, Iowa City, IA.

Tabachnick, B. G., & Fidell, L. S. (2006). *Using multivariate statistics* (5th ed.). New York, NY: Allyn and Bacon.

Tanaka, J. S. (1993). Multifaceted conceptions of fit in structural equation models. In K. A. Bollen & J. S. Long (Eds.), *Testing structural equation models*, (pp. 10–40). Thousand Oaks, CA: Sage.

Tucker, L. R., & Lewis, C. (1973). The reliability coefficient for maximum likelihood factor analysis. *Psychometrika, 38*, 1–10. http://doi.org/10.1007/BF02291170

West, S. G., Taylor, A. B., & Wu, W. (2012). Model fit and model selection in structural equation modeling. In R. H. Hoyle (Ed.), *Handbook of structural equation modeling* (pp. 209–231). New York, NY: Guilford.

Widaman, K. F., & Thompson, J. S. (2003). On specifying the null model for incremental fit indices in structural equation modeling. *Psychological Methods, 8*(1), 16. http://doi.org/10.1037/1082-989X.8.1.16

Worthington, R. L., & Whittaker, T. A. (2006). Scale development research a content analysis and recommendations for best practices. *The Counseling Psychologist, 34*(6), 806–838. http://doi.org/10.1177/0011000006288127

Yang-Wallentin, F., Jöreskog, K. G., & Luo, H. (2010). Confirmatory factor analysis with ordinal variables with misspecified models. *Structural Equation Modeling: A Multidisciplinary Journal, 17*, 392–423. http://doi.org/10.1080/10705511.2010.489003

Yu, C., & Muthén, B. (2002, April). *Evaluation of model fit indices for latent variable models with categorical and continuous outcomes*. Paper presented at the annual meeting of the American Educational Research Association, New Orleans, LA.

Yuan, K. H. (2005). Fit indices versus test statistics. *Multivariate Behavioral Research, 40*(1), 115–148. http://doi.org/10.1207/s15327906mbr4001_5

Part V

Group-Based Analysis

Chapter 10

Detecting Differential Item Functioning

Brian F. French[1] and W. Holmes Finch[2]

[1]Educational Leadership, Sports Studies, Educational/Counseling Psychology,
Washington State University, Pullman, WA, USA
[2]Educational Psychology, Ball State University, Muncie, IN, USA

Introduction and Central Issues

To understand the place of differential item functioning (DIF) detection in test construction, the ubiquity of test score use in many areas of society and the concomitant importance of test fairness in that context must first be understood. Test scores are used in areas as diverse as education, clinical psychology, health care, and management, to name just a few. For instruments developed for making decisions about individuals, the validity of scores must be demonstrated, in the context to which these scores would be used. Demonstrating such validity involves the use of a wide range of statistical analyses, with a focus on a wide range of questions targeting the theoretically meaningful use of the scores. With respect to the issue of DIF in particular, Messick (1989) suggested that in order to avoid unfavorable social consequences of test use, the measurement process must minimize construct irrelevant variance in scores. Construct irrelevant variance can come from many sources, including differential behavior of an instrument across subgroups in the population tested. To state Messick's point more clearly, merely providing evidence of construct validation for the majority group is insufficient, but rather the measurement process must be fair and equal across identified subgroups in the population. Evidence also must be provided to demonstrate that test scores have equal meaning across groups within the broader population. When construct validity is not invariant (i.e., the same) across groups, inferences based on scores from such measures cannot be taken as the same. Equitable instrument performance across groups lies at the heart of DIF investigations.

This issue of fairness and bias in test construction is essential as evidenced by the attention received from the legal system, policy makers, test consumers, educational and psychological researchers, test developers, and the general public. This attention is well deserved because the essence of the issue is that test use be ethical for all individuals to which it is applied. We note here that for convenience sake, throughout this chapter we use the word test to indicate any psychological measure, whether it is a test, such as in the context of educational assessments, or some other tool that is not a test in the educational sense. As an example of the ethical issues surrounding psychological and educational assessments, many regulations that concern the misuse of psychological tests, especially in employment decisions, were developed in part, as a result of Title VII of the Civil Rights Act of 1964. Title VII provided government regulations to ensure that employment decisions were not based on a person's ethnicity, race, sex, color, or religion. The United States Supreme Court required employers to show that the measurement process used was an indication of job performance and not an indication of a group characteristic (Wigdor & Garner, 1982).

Educational testing received legal attention around the same time in the United States. The outcome of *Brown v. Board of Education* in 1954 began the attempt to achieve equality in education. The court ruled that segregated school systems were to end; yet equality was not obtained. Students were placed into academically tracked classes based on measures of ability, which some persons argued were unfair to some ethnic groups. Improper and unfair classroom placement was brought to the court's attention in *Larry P. v. Riles* in California. The case centered on the misuse of intelligence test scores to place African American students in special education classes. The plaintiffs in this case argued that the tests were biased against African Americans. This was the first case at the federal level to demand validity evidence of tests used to place students in certain classes (Wigdor & Garner, 1982). The court ruled that tests without such validation were not to be used. The same issue ended with a different legal outcome in 1980, in Illinois. A judge ruled that certain intelligence tests were free of cultural bias and therefore could be used for placement of African American students in special education classes. However, the decision that the test was bias-free in the case of *Parents in Action on Special Education v. Hannon* was based on a subjective review of the items by the judge (Wigdor & Garner). This method of validating an instrument simply by reviewing item content, especially by a nonexpert in the field of intelligence tests, cannot provide sufficient evidence to claim that the test is unbiased (Plake, 1980; Sandoval & Whelan-Miille, 1980). The legal fights over test fairness continue today, and the move to provide evidence based on DIF detection methods was set.

The issue of proper use of tests and their inferences continues to be an important topic at the center of test validation. Whether the tests are developed and used for employment or education decisions, the question remains the same: Is the score from the test truly a measure only of the construct that it was designed to assess (e.g., intelligence, aptitude for specific types of employment), or does it also measure, at least in part, an individual's race, religion, cultural background, ethnicity, gender, or disability? With tests being used to guide policy and law, the use of state-of-the-art measures that minimizes construct irrelevant variance in the test development process is imperative in order to develop the best test possible with the necessary supporting evidence. If this is not the case, educational, psychological, and employment decisions will be based on invalid information, potentially resulting in serious negative impacts on the educational opportunities and life outcomes of individuals against whom the measurements are skewed. Organizations, such as the American Educational Research Association, the National Council on Measurement in Education and International Test commission are taking steps to assist researchers and practitioners in ensuring a fair testing process through, for instance, the dissemination of guidelines that specify fair practices to which everyone involved in the testing process should adhere.

The *Standards for Educational and Psychological Testing* (American Educational Research Association [AERA], American Psychological Association [APA], & National Council on Measurement in Education [NCME], 2014), for example, addresses the ethical issues involved in fair and unbiased testing. All persons must have comparable and equitable treatment in the entire testing process, including inferences and decisions based on test scores. Although this appears to be straightforward and relatively easy to achieve, the process of testing has many steps as outlined in this book (e.g., development of the test items, gathering reliability and validity evidence). An important component of this work is to ensure items function similarly across groups. This is where DIF assessment enters the process.

Bias

There are many forms of a lack of measurement invariance that would be necessary but insufficient to claim there is bias present in an assessment and scores. Bias in tests or items generally refers to some systematic process unrelated to the construct being measured that either inflates or attenuates the information one is using, typically scores, to make decisions about groups or individuals. There is also debate about if it should be called bias, which implies knowing a reason for why the difference is occurring. Pinpointing the reason we observe statistical differences between groups, methods, etc. is difficult! Millsap (2011) provides an in-depth examination of measurement bias mostly related to examinees membership in a group. In contrast, Podsakoff, MacKenzie, and Podsakoff (2012) have recently discussed, for example, the complex nature of method bias, and remedies to control and minimize it in social sciences research. They call on the definition offered by Campbell and Fiske (1959), which is centered on irrelevant method variance that would render scores invalid if said scores are influenced by such variance. Their review of this issue is suggested reading for those interested in current views of method bias, and differing opinions on what it entails. We do not focus on such differences in this chapter. This same idea of bias as *irrelevant information* is also captured in Messick's (1989) writings about construct validity. The measurement process should aim to minimize construct irrelevant variance. If not, the risk increases of having inaccurate scores due to having scores comprised of variance that not only reflects the intended construct but also additional unwanted information. The main point about bias to remember is that it can influence covariation between latent constructs, psychometric properties of scores, and item quality. We turn our attention to the item level quality and how DIF detection can be used to take a step toward identifying bias.

DIF as Item Bias

The presence of DIF is a necessary but insufficient condition to support a claim of item bias. Item bias and DIF have generally been defined somewhat differently by psychometricians and measurement specialists. The term item bias was in use before the term DIF, with the latter developed in order to differentiate between broader societal and more technical statistical issues. See Angoff (1993) and Cole (1993) for the evolution of the terminology. The important point to understand is that DIF refers to a statistical difference in the probabilities of a specific (e.g., correct) item response between persons of different groups but with equal levels of the construct being measured. In contrast, item bias refers not only to the difference in these item response probabilities, but also to the determination as to why an item functions differentially. In other words, DIF refers only to the results of a statistical analysis of item responses, whereas bias refers to the broader combination of statistical results, and an explanation as to the source of groups' differential performance on an item (Angoff 1993; Camilli & Shepard, 1994). Thus, the reader should understand that the possibility exists for a DIF item (i.e., a statistically significant difference in item performance between groups after individuals in the groups are matched on the construct being measured) to not be biased (i.e., the source of this performance difference cannot be attributed to wording or content that is clearly discriminatory against one of the groups).

Because of the increased interest in ensuring fair educational and psychological assessments that emerged in the 1960s as the result of the aforementioned legal cases, DIF analysis has become the method of choice for the detection of potential item bias (McAllister, 1993). Simply stated, DIF analyses provide important validity evidence, through an examination of the extent to which items measure what they are intended to measure in an equitable manner across groups. DIF analysis should be a key element in the test development process in order to ensure that the instrument can be ethically used with all potential consumers. Indeed, we argue that the test developer has the responsibility to provide evidence of the extent to which the test is equally valid for various groups intended to use the assessment. This evidence will serve as a key piece of evidence in demonstrating that the test is fair and unbiased. In addition to supporting the fairness argument, DIF studies must be conducted in order to: (a) identify problematic items during test development, and (b) identify and eliminate DIF items to assist in guarding against differences in test score meaning (Berk, 1982).

Types of DIF

DIF is typically described as being one of two types. The first type (uniform DIF) occurs when there is a difference in the probability of providing a particular item response (e.g., correct) between groups, and this difference is consistent across levels of the trait being measured. For example, in Figure 10.1, Panel A, Group 1 has a higher probability of a correct response com-

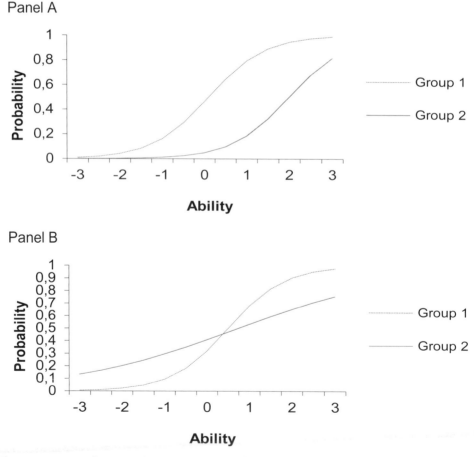

Figure 10.1. Panel A contains an example of uniform DIF where the item is easier for Group 1. Panel B contains an example of nonuniform DIF where the item is easier of Group 2 at the lower end of ability yet harder at the high end of ability for the same group.

pared to Group 2 across all ability levels. This difference indicates that a lower ability level was required for Group 1 compared to Group 2 to respond correctly. In other words, the item was easier for Group 1, even though individuals in the two groups were matched on the trait being measured.

The second type of DIF (nonuniform DIF) occurs when there is a difference in the probability of a particular item response, but this difference is not consistent across ability levels between the groups. For example, in Figure 10.1, Panel B, persons in group 2 with lower ability levels have a higher probability of a correct response compared to persons from Group 1 with the same ability. However, the situation reverses as ability increases. Persons with higher ability levels from Group 1 have a greater probability of a correct response compared to persons from Group 2 of the same ability. In other words, with nonuniform DIF, the item is easier for Group 1 at certain ability levels and for Group 2 at other ability levels. Consider, for example, the item that assesses social-emotional skills written as, "Does [name of child] come to you for guidance when he/she needs help?" This item appears to be a nonuniform DIF item as seen in Figure 10.2, Panel B where the item characteristic curves of boys and girls cross at approximately 0 along the latent trait continuum. What we see is that boys (solid line) are more likely to be rated a yes compared to girls at the low end of ability (i.e., social-emotional skills), and are less likely to be rated as a *yes* at the higher end of the social-emotional skills trait.

Conceptual Principles and/or Statistical Assumptions

A large number of statistical methods have been suggested, empirically tested, and adequacies and inadequacies documented over the past 30 years for DIF detection. A comprehensive review of all such methods is not feasible here. Instead, we highlight one of the classical and proven techniques in order to provide the general idea of how DIF detection works. All methods, despite their differences, share two components in the DIF detection process. First, all approaches to DIF detection focus in some way on differential item performance (i.e., difficulty and/or ability to differentiate among individuals with different levels of the latent trait, or discrimination). There is an attempt to determine if persons from different groups who are matched on the construct being measured have an equal chance of providing the same item response (e.g., correct). Second, the methods are all limited by a reliance on an internal criterion for estimating the level of the latent trait that an individual possesses. The actual nature of this criterion differs across methods. For example, some use the group mean test score, while others use the individuals' total observed test scores (e.g., sum of number of correct item responses), and still others use estimates of the latent trait based upon item response theory. This reliance on some internal (to the data) criterion for estimating the construct can result in an inability to detect pervasive or constant bias in a test (Camilli & Shepard, 1994). Despite this potential shortcoming, the internal criterion is often the best choice for matching because (a) the total test scores most likely have high reliability, (b) validity evidence often has been provided for the scores, and (c) the scores are obtained under similar, if not standardized conditions, for all persons (Dorans & Holland, 1993). However, identifying the optimal matching criterion remains a problematic issue, in part because high reliability does not ensure validity, and because validity evidence may not have been provided for each group. Thus, in some cases the matching criterion cannot be assumed to be valid for both groups.

For a review of many DIF detection methods see Camilli and Shepard (1994), Millsap and Everson (1993), and Millsap (2011). DIF approaches can be separated into two broad categories. The first category includes methods that do not take into account the latent trait (e.g.,

Panel A

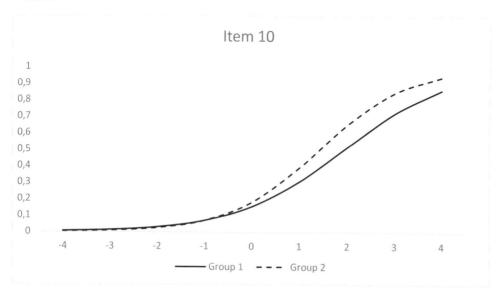

Panel B

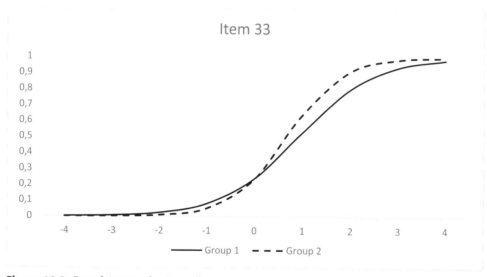

Figure 10.2. Panel A was the item "Does ___ exercise control and constraint so others will not be hurt during play?" that was identified as a DIF item favoring females. Panel B was the item "Does ___ come to you for guidance when he/she needs help?" that was identified as a DIF item favoring primarily females.

transformed item index, Angoff & Ford, 1973; ANOVA). Given that a key part of the DIF definition involves matching individuals in different groups on the latent trait of interest, these methods are no longer recommended for use. The second and preferred category includes methods that do account for the latent trait. Thus, for historical purposes we explain one of the first DIF detection methods that accounted for, or conditioned on, ability. Table 10.1 contains a sample of methods used for DIF detection that represent accounting for and not accounting for ability. This list is not comprehensive but provides the reader with a general sense of the methods that are available. Again, many other methods do exist (e.g., latent mixture models, confirmatory factor analysis, generalized linear models) but our purpose is not to review these here. Additionally, once the general DIF process is understood in the context of less complex methods, it is quite easy to understand more complex DIF modeling strategies.

Table 10.1. Example of methods to detect DIF

Method	Reference
Nonstatistical methods	
Judgmental/sensitivity review	Engelhard, 1989; Sandoval & Whelan-Miille,1980
Statistical methods	
Do not account for ability	
Transformed item index	Angoff & Ford, 1973; Angoff, 1982
Discrimination index	Ironson & Subkoviak, 1979
Rank order correlation of p–values	Reynolds, 1982
Analysis of variance	Camilli & Shepard, 1987
Do account for ability	
SCHEUN/full chi-square	Scheuneman, 1979; Holland & Thayer, 1988
Mantel–Haenszel	Holland & Thayer, 1988
Standardization procedure	Dorans & Kulick, 1986; Dorans, 1989; Dorans & Holland, 1993
SIBTEST	Shealy & Stout, 1993;
Logistic regression	Swaminathan & Rogers, 1990
IRT – differences between a and b parameters (Difference Test)	Lord, 1980; Thissen, Steinberg, & Wainer, 1993
IRT – various models (1PL, 2PL, 3PL, graded response model [GR])	(Thissen et al., 1988, 1993)

One of the most tested, empirically supported, effective, and widely used DIF detection procedure is the Mantel–Haenszel (MH; Narayanan & Swaminathan, 1994). Holland and Thayer (1988) applied the Mantel–Haenszel procedure (MH), first used in medical research to match patients for comparison to DIF detection. This technique is an extension of the chi-square test of association, allowing for comparison of item responses between the focal and reference groups conditioning on a matching subtest score. In DIF detection involving two groups, which is by far the most common, one group is referred to as the reference and the other the focal. Most typically, the focal group is the one to which special attention is paid, such as ethnic minority, while the reference is the majority group. Three statistics are typically computed with the implementation of the MH procedure. First is the MHχ^2 statistic given by the equation (Holland & Thayer, 1988):

$$\frac{\{|\sum_{j=1}^{S}[A_j - E(A_j)]| - .5\}^2}{\sum_{j=1}^{S} Var(A_j)}, \tag{1}$$

where

$$Var(A_j) = \frac{n_{Rj}n_{Fj}m_{1j}m_{0j}}{T^2_j(T_j-1)}, \tag{2}$$

where $A_j - E(A_j)$ is the difference between the observed and expected (under the null hypothesis of no DIF) number of correct responses (in the educational testing context) by the reference group on the item being studied for DIF across S scores levels. The values n_{Rj} and n_{Fj} are the sample sizes for the reference and focal group respectively at score j of the matching subtest, m_{1j} and m_{0j} represent the number of correct and incorrect responses, respectively at j matching subtest score, and T represents total sample size for a given matching subtest score. The matching score is typically the sum of the items on the unidimensional set of items which includes the studied item. This statistic is distributed as chi-square with one degree of freedom and tests the null hypothesis of no uniform DIF.

A second statistic that is also typically used with the MH is the common odds ratio (α). This value represents the ratio of the odds that a person from the reference group will respond correctly to an item as compared to a matched (on the matching subtest) person from the focal group. An α equal to 1 supports the null hypothesis that the odds of responding correctly to an item are the same for the groups when individuals are matched on the latent trait being measured. This value is calculated using the following formula given in Holland and Thayer (1988):

$$\alpha_{MH} = \frac{\sum A_j D_j / T_j}{\sum B_j C_j / T_j} \qquad (3)$$

Where T_j is as defined above, A_j and D_j represent correct and incorrect responses for the reference and focal groups, respectively, given the jth score level, and B_j and C_j represent incorrect and correct responses for the reference and focal groups, respectively, given the jth score level. Values from zero to one would indicate that the item favors the focal group and values from one to infinity indicate that the item favors the reference group. Holland and Thayer (1988) suggested that practitioners and others use the log of α_{MH} in order for zero, not 1.0, to be the indication that the null hypothesis of no DIF holds. This transformation makes the reported value symmetric around zero and thus easier to interpret. Furthermore, Holland and Thayer suggested that the ln (α_{MH}) be multiplied by –2.35 resulting in Δ_{MH}, yielding the third value associated with the MH in DIF detection. This statistic, known as the Educational Testing Service's (ETS) *delta*, provides another indication as to the amount of DIF present for a particular item. Values from negative infinity to zero indicate that the item favored the reference group, whereas items with values from zero to infinity favored the focal group. In terms of classifying the magnitude of DIF, ETS advocates use of a three level classification system with Δ_{MH} as an effect size measure of the extent to which an item exhibits DIF. An item would be considered DIF level A if its Δ_{MH} had an absolute value of less than 1.0, and/or it did not have a significant chi-square value. Such items would be considered free of DIF and may be included in tests. At the other extreme, an item placed in level C would have an absolute value of Δ_{MH} greater than 1.5, and a statistically significant chi-square test. Such items would most likely not be included in an assessment, unless a content expert deemed them essential to the measurement of the construct (Clauser & Mazor, 1998). Items that do not fit into DIF level A or C are placed in the middle DIF level, B. These items are included in an assessment only if there is a lack of appropriate level A items to meet the test content specifications.

In addition to MH, a number of other statistical procedures are available for ascertaining the presence of DIF. Some methods, such as SIBTEST (Li & Stout, 1996; Shealy & Stout, 1993) and the Item Response Theory Likelihood Ratio (IRTLR) test (Thissen, 2001; Thissen, Steinberg, & Wainer, 1988) were developed specifically for this purpose, while others, including Logistic Regression (LR), MH, and confirmatory factor analysis are general statistical techniques employed for DIF detection (e.g., Naryanan & Swaminathan, 1994, 1996). Each method applied to DIF is associated with its unique strengths and weaknesses, and no one approach has been found to be universally optimal. Thus, researchers interested in investigating DIF are encouraged to first learn about these major methods, and then apply the one that prior literature would suggest is optimal for data similar to their own.

Research Issues

More than 20 years ago six practical questions concerning the use of DIF in test development were offered to the testing community (Zieky, 1993). These questions focused on issues ranging from what the matching criteria should be, whether DIF items should be eliminated automatically, and when and how should DIF data be used in the test development process. Although great strides have been made over the time since Zieky first posed these questions, some of these questions are still fundamental to DIF assessment in test construction and will likely remain areas of work for some time as research continues to inform DIF detection and how DIF items influence test properties and test construction. In our own work, there seem to be four questions that continually arise as we conduct DIF analysis on applied data, review such work, and establish conditions for studying DIF methods. We offer some brief insights to each issue to help guide practice in conducting DIF analyses related to test construction.

First, the necessary sample size for successful identification of DIF is one of the first questions asked by persons wanting to carry out such studies, especially when working with low incidence populations or small testing programs. The answer to this question depends on the statistical DIF method employed. Different methods rely upon different assumptions, estimation methods, and model specification requirements. Based upon the research literature, and practical experience, we can offer two suggestions in determining the adequacy of the sample size. First, the user can refer to simulation work with the method of choice to examine what has been found related to the sample size to power ratio. Research in this area provides recommendations for minimum sample sizes which range from small (e.g., 50 per group with MH) to rather large (e.g., > 1,000 with IRT DIF detection methods for polytomous items). The best advice we can offer is to search the literature for the method you select and rely on that work to inform your decision. That said, for most methods, sample sizes per group lower than 250 or 300 can result in lower statistical power (e.g., French & Maller, 2007; Finch & French, 2007). The second approach for determining optimal sample size is to conduct an a priori power analysis as you would with any other planned statistical analysis. Once assumptions are made (e.g., average effect size, alpha) various standalone programs, power tables, or even simulations (e.g., CFA DIF approach; Hancock & French, 2013) can be used to aid in determining the optimal size of the sample.

A second question in DIF research that has a direct influence on sample size, centers on the groups that should be compared. Quite often the answer to this question is that DIF detection should be conducted for all major groups for which demographic information is collected. Certainly, major grouping variables (e.g., sex, race/ethnicity) are the primary focus of test developers in term of ensuring equal item functioning. Beyond simply using such easily identified and major population subgroups, the test developer would also want to carefully consider how scores from the assessment will be used and then compare groups where major decisions will be made about groups or individuals. For example, if the measure is designed to screen for developmental delays, assessment of item invariance would want to occur for those groups compared to aid in ensuring that the mean differences are most likely a result of ability differences and not a lack of item invariance or DIF.

A third key question in planning for and conducting a DIF detection study concerns deciding on the matching criterion, which continues to be a problematic area in DIF detection. We provide some detail on this topic due to its central role in the statistical analyses for assessing DIF. Ideally, the matching variable would be external to the assessment under study but is rarely practical (i.e., persons complete another assessment of the same content known to be free of DIF just for DIF detection). Matching persons on this internal criterion of ability can become problematic when the ability estimate is comprised of items that themselves contain DIF. If persons from different groups have unequal chances of responding correctly to some items, even when they have the same level of the latent trait in actuality, the resulting criterion estimates can be inaccurate or what is often termed unpurified. The use of such a contaminated estimate of ability can in turn lead to inaccurate identification of DIF (Clauser, Mazor, & Hambleton, 1993; Narayanan & Swaminathan, 1996). See Ackerman (1992) for a visual representation of the issue.

In recognition of the internal criterion problem, Lord (1980) outlined a detailed approach to test purification before detection of item bias with IRT methods. The purification process involves the following multistep process: (a) analysis of all items for bias, (b) removal of items with significantly different response patterns, (c) estimation of ability for both groups while ability is held constant, (d) for all items, estimation of discrimination (a) and difficulty (b) parameters for each group separately, and (e) comparison of estimated parameters. Holland and Thayer (1988) suggested a two-step process for use with the MH procedure as a way to control ability contamination and refine or purify the ability scale. This purification process involves conducting DIF analyses twice. The first analysis involves the use of the total score as the ability estimate to match persons and in the identification of DIF items. In the second analysis, identified DIF items are removed except for the item under study and a new score (i.e., a purified score) is calculated and used in the identification process.

The purification process when used with various DIF procedures has resulted in higher rates of correct identifications for certain types of DIF compared to the use of unpurified ability (Clauser et al., 1993; French & Maller, 2007; Woods, 2009). The process has been suggested for use with other DIF methods including item response theory (Camilli & Shepard, 1994; Lord, 1980). Detection rates are improved when using such methods (Candell & Drasgow, 1988). The general recommendation for the test developer is to use some form of scale purification or refinement to ensure that the matching of persons across groups is completed in an accurate manner so DIF detection is as accurate as possible.

The fourth question that arises in DIF application is what to do with an identified item. The first reaction for many people is to claim that it is biased and thus should be eliminated. This seems reasonable until we recall that the presence of DIF does not necessarily mean the presence of bias. A statistically significant DIF result only provides evidence that the item is functioning differentially from a statistical point of view. If an effect size, such as Δ_{MH} was used in addition to the hypothesis test, we may also possess some information about the magnitude of the difference as describe above and can follow rules such as those following the ETS classification. It is important to keep in mind that group differences based on statistical criteria alone could be the result of a Type I error, high statistical power leading to detection of very small actual differences, or some other artifact of the process (e.g., ignoring multilevel data; Finch & French, 2010).

Without further investigation into the item content, it is not possible to determine whether bias is present, and even with such investigation the bias question is not always easily answered. The determination of what to do with such an item will ultimately rely on a judgment process that will review the item to see if it has characteristics that can be identified as being a source of unfairness for a certain group. This process typically relies on the literature in the area under question. For example, DIF results suggested that multiple choice mathematics items tended to favor males whereas free response mathematics items favored females (Zhang & French, 2010). In such items, if DIF is identified there may be reasons to eliminate the item. On the other hand, if no obvious causes for the presence of DIF can be identified the item may be placed on reserve to be tried again later with another sample. Also, the DIF detection process when multiple groups are involved becomes a multidimensional comparison situation where certain items may be identified for some groups and not others. This certainly complicates the review process with no clear answer for how to look across all groups and items. In the "Future Directions" section, we offer some suggestions to confirmatory approaches to handle some of these issues.

Two Examples for Users

Example 1: Multilevel Data and DIF

This first example employs the MH method as described above in this chapter with one small modification. We have adjusted the statistic to account for multilevel data. We explain why we have done this so the reader is aware of the issue of inconsistency between statistical models and data structures. That said, please think about the MH procedure as described above. For more technical information on this adjustment please see French and Finch (2013). Our recent work in DIF detection has involved adjusting popular DIF methods, such as MH, to account for multilevel data. This type of data structure is common in educational research where, for example, students are nested in classrooms. The methodological issue to be dealt with in such situations is that statistical tests may be biased due to the influence of correlated item responses among lower level units (i.e., examinees) within the same higher level units (i.e., schools) on the standard errors. Essentially, standard errors are biased downward when a multilevel data structure is ignored, which in turn inflates Type I error. This issue is not restricted to DIF detection, of course, but the rate of Type I error does increase in DIF detection as well (e.g., Finch & French, 2010; French & Finch, 2010). In order to account for this issue, we have adjusted popular DIF methods to account for this problem and provide an example here.

We applied the Begg adjustment for the MH procedure that is effective for DIF detection in the presence of multilevel data (French & Finch, 2013). Briefly, the Begg MH adjustment involves estimating the variance in the MH statistic due to clustering of examinees and the naïve variance assuming no such clustering (Begg, 1999; BMH). This can be thought of as in multilevel modeling where both within and between variance is estimated. This BMH approach first estimates the underestimation bias in the standard error of the MH test using generalized estimating equations. The adjusted MH statistic then uses a correction to the MH statistic. When there is no correlation in scores among examinees (no clustering) from the same school, then the adjusted MH (MH_B) is equal to MH. Details and SAS code to implement the BMH are available (French & Finch, 2013).

In this example, data are from a US standardization sample ($N = 684$; 49% female; age range 3–7 years 11 months) for the *Brigance Inventory of Early Development III Standardized* (IED III; French, 2013). Sample demographics closely match the US student demographics. The IED III is an individually administered screening measure designed for children ages birth through 7 years 11 months old to help determine school readiness and eligibility for special services and allow comparisons of children's skills across multiple developmental domains. For this example, MH_B was applied to the *IED III* Social-emotional developmental skills, which consist of 50 items that were rated by the caregiver or examiner where students were nested in childcare centers or schools. Items assess prosocial and regulation skills, motivation and confidence skills, peers and play skills and adult relationship skills.

Analysis

DIF analysis using the MH_B procedure was conducted in SAS version 9.1. We employed an iterative purification procedure (e.g., French & Maller, 2007) to purify or refine the matching score. However, the studied item was included in the total score. To classify DIF items, the ETS classification system mentioned in the section "Conceptual Principles and/or Statistical Assumption" of the chapter was employed. For results, we provide a brief report as an example of what was found. Intraclass correlations (ICC) were first computed for each subscale to assess the presence of multilevel data. Findings indicate that between 7% and 11% of the variance in the social-emotional domain item responses can be accounted for by site (i.e., prosocial and regulation = .11, motivation and confidence= .07, peers and play = .08, and adult relationships = .10). This confirms that the adjustment is needed. No DIF items were identified in the peers and play subdomain or the motivation and confidence subdomain. Across the prosocial and regulation subdomain, 19% of items exhibited DIF based on stated criteria (33.3% of these favoring females). As an example, Figure 10.2, Panel A contains the item response curves (ICCs) for boys and girls for the DIF item, "Does ____ exercise control and constraint so others with not be hurt during play?" The dotted line in panel A (ICC for girls) illustrates this item favored girls (Δ_{MH} =1.90) over boys. Across the adult relationships subdomain, 1 of 12 items was identified as a DIF item (Δ_{MH} = 1.31). This item, as a second example, asked: "Does ____ come to you for guidance when he/she needs help." Panel B of Figure 10.2 contains the ICCs for this item between boys and girls. Table 10.2 contains the items and the statistical test information.

Table 10.2.   Large DIF items identified in the Social Emotional Scale of the IED III Standardized

Item	χ^2	p	Δ_{MH}
Does ____ exercise control and constraint so others will not be hurt during play?	7.214	0.007	1.90
If supervised by an adult, does ____ take turns without undue objection?	8.127	0.004	1.65
Does ____ react to a disappointment or failure in an acceptable manner by being a good sport and refraining from shouting or getting upset?	6.732	0.009	1.51
Does ____ come to you for guidance when he/she needs help?	6.705	0.009	1.32

Only 4 items out of 50 items were classified as displaying large DIF, and these appeared on the prosocial and regulation, and the adult relationships subdomains. Given these findings, the test developer may conclude that raters do have some differences in rating social-emotional skill items following sex role expectations (males favored on play and regulation items, females favored on adult relationship items). However, because only 8% of items across domains exhibited DIF, these findings suggest there is not a major concern of DIF effecting *IED III* scores related to making individual decisions. Regardless of the amount of DIF, test developers need to be aware of sex role stereotypes when rating children on such items and how DIF can help identify such problems.

Example 2: Measurement Sensitivity and DIF

When conducting educational and psychological research, a key choice that researchers must make that will directly impact the observed effect of interest in an intervention study is the measurement tool for assessing the outcome of interest. Indeed, research suggests that decisions regarding the operationalization or measurement of the outcome appear to be associated with at least as much variance in observed effects as do other features of the design (e.g., random vs. nonrandom assignment; Wilson & Lipsey, 2001). In other words, the instrument that is selected for measuring the outcome of interest can, in some cases, have as much impact on the final decision as to the effectiveness of an intervention as the impact of the intervention itself. Measurement, therefore, is a nontrivial aspect of efficacy and effectiveness research, regardless of the field of study, including assessments of teacher effectiveness. This impact of the measurement tool on the size of the observed effect comes from its sensitivity, or its ability to detect changes in the construct of interest due to the intervention. The challenge in such cases is to develop instruments using items that are most sensitive to the outcome.

Most standardized measures commonly used in intervention studies, particularly in educational contexts, are designed to measure general constructs (e.g., reading proficiency) primarily for accountability purposes, and therefore may not be particularly sensitive to specific abilities that are influenced by fairly discrete changes in instruction (Popham, 2007; Popham & Ryan, 2012). As such, they are not optimized to detect hypothesized changes in achievement that result from a specific intervention (e.g., Hevey, McGee, & Horgan, 2004) such as a new instructional technique, which may be designed to influence a small number of very specific skills, rather than the more global abilities measured by standardized instruments. On the other hand, researchers developed measures for the particular intervention are typically well aligned with and more sensitive to an intervention's hypothesized effects, but they can suffer from poor psychometric properties such as reliability and validity (e.g., Belland, French, & Ertmer, 2009). To address the problem of obtaining measures that are both sensitive to the outcomes of interest, and psychometrically sound, we propose the use of DIF in a two-step process to evaluate measurement sensitivity, in accord with suggestions of such invariance method use (Millsap, 2011; Popham & Ryan, 2012).

Although traditionally the presence of DIF is seen as a threat to score validity and is therefore undesirable, in the context of measurement sensitivity assessment DIF would indicate a difference in the way experimental and control group individuals, matched on an overall proficiency in the area of interest, respond to an item that has been hypothesized to directly measure the treatment effect. In other words, when considering sensitivity of a scale to an intervention, the presence of DIF would not represent potentially problematic item bias, but rather hypothesized treatment effects (e.g., Millsap, 2011). A strength of this approach to examining intervention effectiveness is that a priori hypotheses are specified regarding which items should exhibit DIF due to the intervention, based upon their content alignment with expected intervention outcomes. To be clear, we are not suggesting that this method be used post facto to identify and use only those items that are sensitive to an intervention's effect. Such an approach could lead to erroneous conclusions regarding an intervention's effectiveness because apparent group differences may not be tied to hypotheses grounded in the literature. Instead, we demonstrate the following methods *only* to evaluate sensitivity during the instrument development and item selection stage of a project.

The current example consisted of two overarching steps. Step 1 involved engaging experts in the intervention to conduct a content analysis to align items with the intervention. Step 2 employed DIF analysis to test the sensitivity of items identified in step 1 for detecting effects related to the intervention. Content analysis provided a priori hypotheses regarding each item's sensitivity to the intervention. The two-step process is also in accord with suggestions to use judgmental and empirical strategies to evaluate measurement and instructional sensitivity and treatment effects (Millsap, 2011; Popham & Ryan, 2012).

Data from a randomized cluster field trial that implements the Science Writing Heuristic (SWH) approach, an immersive approach to teaching on the scientific argument, were used. Participants ($n = 2,181$ treatment, $n = 1,004$ control) were a representative sample of students taken from 48 schools in the Midwestern United States in Grades 3 through 5 who completed the Cornell Critical Thinking Test (Ennis, Millman, & Tomko, 2005). The author of the SWH involved in the RCT and graduate students assisted with item-level content review and hypothesis development. The Cornell Critical Thinking Tests (CCTT; Ennis et al., 2005) assesses general critical thinking ability across four factors including Induction, Deduction, Observation/Credibility, and Assumptions. The CCTT requires approximately 50 min for 71 items. There are three response options per item in a multiple-choice format, and the items are scored dichotomously (i.e., correct or incorrect).

Analysis

Alignment

The alignment process involved a review of items by content experts who were trained to match items to specific skills to be targeted by the intervention. The process for identifying the relevant items was similar to the manner in which content experts are used in item bias reviews (Tittle, 1982). The alignment process sought to identify the items that were aligned to the intervention content and therefore likely candidates for detecting the intervention's effects. Experts matched items with the targeted intervention skills, rating items on a scale of 1 to 5 with 5 representing an exact match of the item to the targeted skill and 1 representing no match. The items with a rating of 4 or higher were those that were hypothesized to be sensitive to the intervention and thus show significant DIF between the treatment and control groups.

Multilevel Mantel–Haenszel for Estimating Sensitivity

The data for this study were collected in a multilevel framework (students nested in classrooms). Therefore, we employed MH_B discussed above to detect DIF. Again, recall the logic of the analysis is the same as with the standard MH expect the MH_B is adjusted to account for multilevel structured data. We report the percentage of total items analyzed that were identified by (a) both content and DIF analysis, (b) only content analysis, and (c) only DIF analysis. Results assist to determine the degree to which the DIF analyses are capable of detecting treatment effects in items less aligned to the intervention.

Results

Content Analysis

Several items within the four domains were rated as matching to the intervention. However, no items were rated as a perfect match (e.g., 5). In the domain of Induction, 100% percent of the items were rated a 4 across the raters. Recall that a rating of 4 indicates that the item should be impacted by the intervention and thus show DIF between the treatment and control groups. In the domain of Deduction, 100% of the items were rated as a 4 across raters. In the domain of Observation and Credibility, 0% of items were rated as aligned with the intervention. Finally, in the domain of Assumptions, 100% percent of the items were rated a 4 across raters. From the content ratings, it would appear treatment and comparison groups should differ on scores on the Induction, Deduction, and Assumptions scores.

To assess differences first at the total score level for each domain, independent t-tests were conducted on each domain. There were no differences between the groups on the Induction domain, $t(2263) = 0.42$, $p = 0.67$; $d = 0.02$; Deduction domain, $t(2263) = 0.59$, $p = 0.55$; $d = 0.02$, or the Observation domain, $t(2263) = 0.52$, $p = 0.60$; $d = 0.02$. However, there was a significant difference on the scores between groups in the Assumptions domain, $t(2263) = 4.89$, $p = < 0.01$, $d = 0.21$.

DIF Analysis

In the domain of Induction, there were 4 items that were identified statistically as DIF items. The associated effect sizes ranged from 1.80 to 3.34 indicating C DIF items (i.e., large magnitude of DIF) on the ETS classification. This outcome reflects 16% of the items rated as aligned with the intervention being identified as DIF items. We also note that although not significant, the remaining items had delta values ranging from 1.8 to 2.9, and favored the treatment group. In the Deduction domain, 20% were identified statistically as DIF items out of the items that were rated as aligned with the intervention. The associated effect size of these items ranged from 1.8 to 3.2, again reflecting C DIF items on the ETS classification scale and thus reflecting a large magnitude of difference. Similarly, the nonsignificant DIF items also had delta values above 1.8, and favored the treatment group. In the Observation/Credibility domain, no items were identified as DIF items. This was in accord with the content analysis where no items were rated as aligned with the intervention. In the Assumptions domain, 20% of items were identified statistically as DIF items out of the items that were rated as aligned with the intervention. The associated effect size of these items ranged from 2.5 to 2.6, again reflecting C DIF items on the ETS classification scale and thus a large magnitude of difference. Similarly, the nonsignificant DIF items had Delta values above 1.9, and favored the treatment group.

Conclusion

This example suggests an innovative solution to a common challenge in educational effectiveness research in terms of test development. A new paradigm is illustrated through the implementation of an instructionally sensitive invariance framework for developing more sensitive items and hence measures. The lack of group mean score differences for three of the domains demonstrates the problem with currently used approaches in intervention research, whereby effects of the intervention are not detectable at the mean total score level. Our findings suggest that although mean differences were not observed across all domains between treatment and comparison groups, we were able to find effects associated with the professional development administered to the teachers in the treatment on specific items that were rated as being aligned with the intervention that can inform test development for assessing critical thinking skills. In each of three domains rated to be targeted by the intervention there was a rate of DIF that ranged from 16% to 20% as well as DIF items that were large in magnitude.

This example is motivated by evaluation in the social, behavioral, and medical sciences where the lack of sensitive outcome measures renders limited assessment of intervention effects but could be addressed through invariance methods in the test development process. Increasing instrument sensitivity through creative test construction is relevant to the research community because it improves accuracy of conclusions regarding effectiveness of interventions or instruction. Detecting items that are sensitive to the intervention can be particularly informative to researchers because it provides detailed evidence regarding the specific subdomains and skills where the intervention is most effective in producing change, rather than simply reporting mean differences on some global measure. Developing instruments that are sensitive to program effects at the subdomain level may reveal benefits that go undetected when only total scores are used. We hope this work is a start to a sustainable line of work in the use of DIF detection with a twist to assist test developers in addressing concerns that measures are not sensitive. Such a change widens our use of DIF methodology.

Future Directions

The argument has been made by some individuals that "DIF is DEAD." In other words, we know all that we need to know about item invariance. There may be some truth to this if we are satisfied with mere detection of DIF. There exists a plethora of methods and evidence to support the accuracy of DIF detection. Yes, we, as a field, do this well in the test development process. However, there remains a great deal of room for conversations and research focused on the area of DIF if we expand the horizon beyond only its detection. In this chapter, we highlight two areas that could be fruitful for researchers to continue to explore in relation to test development. The first area ripe for further research attention is confirmatory DIF. Such a call is not new (e.g., Roussos & Stout, 2004) but there has not been sustained and prolonged engagement with this topic in DIF detection. This may be because DIF detection, in part, is inherently exploratory in its application. That is, the majority of DIF analysis occurring at the try-out stage of items is implemented to be a screening procedure that hopefully stops an item with a statistical difference and large magnitude of difference between groups from passing into an operational testing program. This same screening procedure is used ex post facto in many instances to assess how items are functioning across various groups of interest. In both cases, results are not based on hypothesis about which items will favor one group or another based on theory. This is most likely due to the fact that content judges have a difficult time specifying why an item is functioning differently between two groups (e.g., Berk 1982; Engelhard, 1989; Sandoval & Whelan-Miille, 1980). Indeed, the development of DIF hypotheses between groups can be a tremendous challenge. As the *Standards for Educational and Psychological Testing* (AERA et al., 2014) discuss, although DIF procedures may hold some promise for improving test quality, there has been little progress in identifying the causes or substantive themes that characterize items exhibiting DIF.

This difficulty should not stop us from using past work to inform the development of hypotheses regarding for which items DIF between specific subgroups is most likely to occur. In examining gender-related DIF on mathematics assessments, for example, attempts to identify item features such as item format, mathematical content, item context, and their interaction with differential performance by males and females has had some success (e.g., O'Neil & Mcpeek, 1993; Ryan & Chiu, 1996). In fact, females performed better on algebra and on more abstract mathematics items compared to males (Garner & Engelhard, 1999; O'Neil & McPeek, 1993), and worse on geometry, measurement, and data analyses. Moreover, in examining results from 14 tests and over 700 mathematics items, DIF results suggest that multiple choice mathematics items tend to favor males whereas free response mathematics items favor females (Zhang & French, 2010). Such trends are supported by continued work in this area (e.g., Taylor & Lee, 2012) and give convincing evidence to begin to develop hypotheses for screening procedures in test construction to confirm these trends.

In accord with an increased focus on identifying sources of DIF, work such as that suggested by Samuelson (2008) should be encouraged. Samuelson presents a convincing argument for the use of latent mixture models in the process of identifying the cause of DIF. Such methods begin to overcome the inherent flaws of observed score variable approaches, in particular the identification of a matching criterion. We would also encourage continued efforts such as those of Penfield (2010), and Gattamorta and Penfield (2012) that also provide insight to the sources of DIF in polytomous items through differential step functioning analysis. Of course, as is often the case when comparing more complicated approaches to DIF detection (e.g., IRT DIF) versus less complicated methods (MH), the application of such advancements in test construction and operational testing programs is delayed because it is simply more complicated and requires more resources (e.g., time, training, advanced software) to conduct DIF analysis. To overcome these issues, we encourage the continued development of ways to make these more-informative methods also more user-friendly in order to increase the likelihood of their use in test construction.

The last area of DIF investigation that remains largely unexplored is the influence of DIF on score differences and psychometric properties of tests. We know, for instance, that DIF may not influence the psychometric properties of long tests (Burton & Burton, 1993), where coefficient alpha is not seriously degraded in the presence of some DIF items (Roznowski & Reith, 1999) yet alpha can differ significantly across groups when certain types and magnitudes of DIF are present (French & Maller, 2006). We have seen with applied data that the mean differences cannot be influenced to a great extent in the presence of small amounts of DIF (e.g., Park & French, 2011, 2013) yet differences about groups can change when a lack of invariance is accounted for in models of group differences (French & Mantzicopoulos, 2007). Some of our simulation work in invariance in general shows that observed score variances across groups are influenced in the presence of some types of invariance (e.g., Finch & French, in press). Others have observed the inflation of Type I errors on group mean differences in the presence of a lack of invariance (Li & Zumbo, 2009). Thus, more work is needed to understand when DIF influencing score interpretation and conclusions about individuals to assist the test develop process. In the end, careful attention in the test development process to how items function across groups should lead to better scores and ultimately decisions about individuals.

Acknowledgments

The multilevel DIF example was a component of the research supported by the Institute of Education Sciences, U.S. Department of Education, through Grant R305D110014 to Washington State University. The opinions expressed are those of the authors and do not represent views of the Institute or the U.S. Department of Education.

References

Ackerman, T. A. (1992). A didactic explanation of item bias, item impact, and item validity from a multidimensional perspective. *Journal of Educational Measurement, 29*, 67–91. http://doi.org/10.1111/j.1745-3984.1992.tb00368.x

American Educational Research Association, American Psychological Association, & National Council on Measurement in Education. (2014). *Standards for educational and psychological testing.* Washington, DC: American Educational Research Association.

Angoff, W. H. (1982). Use of difficulty and discrimination indices for detecting item bias. In R. Berk (Ed.), *Handbook of methods for detecting test bias* (pp. 96–116). Baltimore, MD: The Johns Hopkins University Press.

Angoff, W. H. (1993). Perspectives on differential item functioning methodology. In P. W. Holland & H. Wainer (Eds.), *Differential item functioning* (pp. 3–23). Hillsdale, NJ: Lawrence Erlbaum Associates.

Angoff, W. H., & Ford, S. F. (1973). Item-race interaction on test of scholastic aptitude. *Journal of Educational Measurement, 10*, 95–105. http://doi.org/10.1111/j.1745-3984.1973.tb00787.x

Belland, B., French, B. F., & Ertmer, P. (2009). *Validity and problem-based learning research: A review of instruments used to assess intended learning outcomes, Interdisciplinary Journal of Problem-Based Learning, 3*, 59–89.

Begg, C. (1999). Analyzing k (2x2) tables under cluster sampling. *Biometrics, 55*, 302–307. http://doi.org/10.1111/j.0006-341X.1999.00302.x

Berk, R. A. (1982). *Handbook of methods for detecting test bias.* Baltimore, MD: Johns Hopkins University Press.

Burton, E., & Burton, N. W. (1993). The effect of item screening on test scores and test characteristics. In P. W. Holand & H. Wainer, (Eds.), *Differential item functioning* (pp. 321–335). Hillsdale, NJ: Lawrence Erlbaum.

Camilli, G., & Shepard, L. A. (1987). The inadequacy of ANOVA for detecting test bias. *Journal of Educational and Behavioral Statistics, 12*(1), 87–99.

Camilli, G., & Shepard, L. A. (1994). *Methods for identifying biased test items.* Thousand Oakes, CA: Sage.

Campbell, D. T., & Fiske, D. (1959). Convergent and discriminant validation by the multitrait-multimethod matrix. *Psychological Bulletin, 56*, 81–105 http://doi.org/10.1037/h0046016

Candell, G. L., & Drasgow, F. (1988). An iterative procedure for linking metrics and assessing item bias in item response theory. *Applied Psychological Measurement, 12*, 253–260. http://doi.org/10.1177/014662168801200304

Clauser, B. E., & Mazor, K. M. (1998). Using statistical procedures to identify differentially functioning test items. *Educational Measurement: Issues & Practice, 17*, 31–44. http://doi.org/10.1111/j.1745-3992.1998.tb00619.x

Clauser, B., Mazor, K., & Hambleton, R. K. (1993). The effects of purification of the matching criterion on the identification of DIF using the Mantel-Haenszel procedure. *Applied Measurement in Education, 6*, 269–279. http://doi.org/10.1207/s15324818ame0604_2

Cole, N. S. (1993). History and development of DIF. In P. W. Holland & H. Wainer (Eds.), *Differential item functioning* (pp. 25–30). Hillsdale, NJ: Erlbaum.

Dorans, N. J. (1989). Two new approaches to assessing differential item functioning: Standardization and the Mantel–Haenszel method. *Applied Measurement in Education, 2*(3), 217–233.

Dorans, N. J., & Holland, P. W. (1993). DIF detection and description: Mantel-Haenszel and standardization. In P. W. Holland & H. Wainer (Eds.), *Differential item functioning* (pp. 35–66). Hillsdale, NJ: Erlbaum.

Dorans, N. J., & Kulick, E. (1986). Demonstrating the utility of the standardization approach to assessing unexpected differential item performance on the Scholastic Aptitude Test. *Journal of educational measurement*, 355–368.

Engelhard, G. (1989). Accuracy of bias review judges in identifying teacher certification tests. *Applied Measurement in Education, 3*, 347–360. http://doi.org/10.1207/s15324818ame0304_4

Ennis, R. H., Millman, J., & Tomko, T. N. (2005). *Cornell critical thinking tests.* Seaside, CA: The Critical Thinking Co.

Finch, W. H., & French, B. F. (2007). Detection of crossing differential item functioning: A comparison of four methods. *Educational and Psychological Measurement, 67*, 565–582. http://doi.org/10.1177/0013164406296975

Finch, W. H., & French, B. F. (2010). Detecting differential item functioning of a course satisfaction instrument in the presence of multilevel data. *Journal of the First Year and Students in Transition, 22*(1), 27–48.

Finch, W. H., & French, B. F. (in press). The impact of factor noninvariance on observed composite score variances. *International Journal of Research and Reviews in Applied Sciences*.

French, B. F. (2013). *Brigance Inventory of Early Development (IED III): IED III Standardization and validation manual*. North Billerica, MA: Curriculum Associates, Inc.

French, B. F., & Finch, W. H. (2010). Hierarchical logistic regression: Accounting for multilevel data in DIF detection. *Journal of Educational Measurement, 47*, 299–317. http://doi.org/10.1111/j.1745-3984.2010.00115.x

French, B. F., & Finch, W. H. (2013). Extensions of Mantel-Haenszel for multilevel DIF detection. *Educational and Psychological Measurement, 73*, 648–671. http://doi.org/10.1177/0013164412472341

French, B. F., & Maller, S. J. (2006, April). *The influence of differential item functioning on internal consistency reliability*. Paper presented at the American Educational Research Association, San Francisco, CA.

French, B. F., & Maller, S. J. (2007). Iterative purification and effect size use with logistic regression for DIF detection. *Educational and Psychological Measurement, 67*, 373–393. http://doi.org/10.1177/0013164406294781

French, B. F., & Mantzicopoulos, P. (2007) A first- to second- grade examination of the factor structure and stability of the Pictorial Scale of Perceived Competence and Social Acceptance with a group of economically disadvantaged children. *Journal of School Psychology, 45*, 311–331.

Garner, M., & Engelhard, G. (1999). Gender differences in performance on multiple-choice and constructed response mathematics items. *Applied Measurement in Education, 12*, 29–51. http://doi.org/10.1207/s15324818ame1201_3

Gattamorta, K. A., & Penfield, R. D. (2012). A comparison of adjacent categories and cumulative differential step functioning effect estimators. *Applied Measurement in Education, 25*, 142–161. http://doi.org/10.1080/08957347.2012.660387

Hancock, G. R., & French, B. F. (2013). Power analysis in structural equation modeling. In G. R. Hancock & R. O. Muller (Eds.), *Structural equation modeling: A second course* (2nd ed., pp. 117–159). Charlotte, NC: Information Age Publishing.

Hevey, D., McGee, H. M., & Horgan, J. (2004). Responsiveness of health-related quality of life outcome measures in cardiac rehabilitation: Comparison of cardiac rehabilitation outcome measures. *Journal of Consulting and Clinical Psychology, 72*, 1175–1180. http://doi.org/10.1037/0022-006X.72.6.1175

Holland, P. W., & Thayer, D. T. (1988). Differential item performance and the Mantel-Haenszel procedure. In H. Holland & H. I. Braun (Eds.), *Test validity* (pp. 129–145). Hillsdale, NJ: Erlbaum.

Ironson, G. H., & Subkoviak, M. J. (1979). A comparison of several methods of assessing item bias. *Journal of Educational Measurement, 16*(4), 209–225.

Li, H-H., & Stout, W. (1996). A new procedure for detection of crossing DIF. *Psychometrika, 61* (4), 647–677. http://doi.org/10.1007/BF02294041

Li, Z., & Zumbo, B. D. (2009). Impact of differential item functioning on subsequent statistical conclusions based on observed test score data. *Psicologica, 30*, 343–370.

Lord, F. M. (1980). *Applications of item response theory to practical testing problems*. Hillsdale, NJ: Erlbaum.

McAllister, P. H. (1993). Testing, DIF, and public policy. In P. W. Holland & H. Wainer (Eds.), *Differential item functioning* (pp. 389–396). Hillsdale, NJ: Erlbaum.

Messick, S. (1989). Validity. In R. L. Linn (Ed.), *Educational measurement* (3rd ed., pp. 13–103). New York, NY: Macmillan.

Millsap, R. E. (2011). *Statistical approaches to measurement invariance*. New York, NY: Routledge.

Millsap, R. E., & Everson, H. T. (1993). Methodology review: Statistical approaches for assessing measurement bias. *Applied Psychological Measurement, 17*, 297–334. http://doi.org/10.1177/014662169301700401

Narayanan, P., & Swaminathan, H. (1994). Performance of the Mantel-Haenszel and simultaneous item bias procedures for detecting differential item functioning. *Applied Psychological Measurement, 18*, 315–328. http://doi.org/10.1177/014662169401800403

Narayanan, P., & Swaminathan, H. (1996). Identification of items that show nonuniform DIF. *Applied Psychological Measurement, 20*, 257–274. http://doi.org/10.1177/014662169602000306

O'Neill, K. A., & McPeek, W. M. (1993). Item and test characteristics that are associated with differential item functioning. In P. W. Holland & H. Wainer (Eds.), *Differential item functioning* (pp. 255–276). Hillsdale, NJ: Erlbaum.

Park, G-P., & French, B. F., (2013). Gender differences in the foreign language classroom anxiety scale. *System, 41*, 462–471. http://doi.org/10.1016/j.system.2013.04.001

Park, G.-P., & French, B. F. (2011). Beyond the mean differences of the SILL by gender: Differential item functioning. *The Journal of Asia TEFL, 8*, 201–229.

Penfield, R. D. (2010). Explaining crossing DIF in polytomous items using differential step functioning analysis. *Applied Psychological Measurement, 34*, 563–579. http://doi.org/10.1177/0146621610377083

Plake, B. S. (1980). A comparison of a statistical and subjective procedure to ascertain item validity: One step in the test validation process. *Educational and Psychological Measurement, 40*, 397–404. http://doi.org/10.1177/001316448004000217

Podsakoff, P. M., MacKenzie, S. B., & Podsakoff, N. P. (2012). Sources of method bias in social science research and recommendations on how to control it. *Annual Review of Psychology, 63*, 539–569. http://doi.org/10.1146/annurev-psych-120710-100452

Popham, W. J. (2007). Instructional sensitivity of test: Accountability's dire drawback. *Phi Delta Kappa, 89*(2), 146–150. http://doi.org/10.1177/003172170708900211

Popham, J. W., & Ryan, J. M. (2012, April). *Determining a high-stakes test's instructional sensitivity*. Paper presented at the National Council on Measurement in Education, Vancouver, BC.Reynolds, C. R. (1982). Methods for detecting construct and predictive bias. In R. Berk (Ed.), *Handbook of methods for detecting test bias* (pp. 199–227). Baltimore, MD: The Johns Hopkins University Press.

Reynolds, C. R. (1982). Methods for detecting construct and predictive bias. In R. Berk (Ed.), *Handbook of methods for detecting test bias* (pp. 199–227). Baltimore, MD: The Johns Hopkins University Press.

Roznowski, M., & Reith, J. (1999). Examining the measurement quality of tests containing differentially functioning items: Do biased items result in poor measurement? *Educational and psychological Measurement*, 59(2), 248–269.

Roussos, L. A., & Stout, W. F. (2004). Differential item functioning analysis: Detecting DIF items and testing DIF hypotheses. In D. Kaplan (Ed.), *The SAGE handbook of quantitative methodology for the social sciences* (pp. 107–115). Thousand Oaks, CA: SAGE.

Ryan, K. E., & Chiu, S. (1996, April). *Detecting DIF on mathematics items: The case for gender and calculator sensitivity*. Paper presented at the annual meeting of the American Educational Research Association, New York, NY.

Samuelson, K. M. (2008). Examining differential item functioning from a latent mixture perspective. In G. R. Hancock & K. M. Samuelsen (Eds.), *Latent variable mixture modeling* (pp. 177–197). Charlotte, NC: IAP.

Sandoval, J., & Whelan-Miille, M. P., (1980). Accuracy of judgments of WISC-R item difficulty for minority groups. *Journal of Consulting and Clinical Psychology, 48*, 249–253. http://doi.org/10.1037/0022-006X.48.2.249

Scheuneman, J. (1979). A method of assessing bias in test items. *Journal of Educational Measurement, 16*(3), 143–152.

Shealy, R., & Stout, W. F. (1993). A model-based standardization approach that separates true bias/DIF from group differences and detects test bias/DTF as well as item bias/DIF. *Psychometrika, 58*, 159–194. http://doi.org/10.1007/BF02294572

Swaminathan, H., & Rogers, H. J. (1990). Detecting differential item functioning using logistic regression procedures. *Journal of Educational Measurement, 27*(4),361–370.

Taylor, C., & Lee, Y. (2012). Gender DIF in reading and mathematics tests with mixed item formats. *Applied Measurement in Education, 25*, 246–280. http://doi.org/10.1080/08957347.2012.687650

Tittle, C. K. (1982). Use of judgmental methods in item bias studies. In R. A. Berk (Ed.), *Handbook of methods for detecting item bias*. Baltimore, MD: The Johns Hopkins University Press.

Thissen, D. (2001). *IRTLRDIF v.2.0b: Software for the computation of the statistics involved in item response theory likelihood ratio tests for differential item functioning*. Unpublished manual, L. L. Thurstone Psychometric Laboratory, University of North Carolina at Chapel Hill.

Thissen, D., Steinberg, L., & Wainer, H. (1988). Use of item response theory in the study of group differences in trace lines. In H. Wainer & P. W. Holland (Eds.), *Test validity* (pp. 147–169). Hillsdale, NJ: Erlbaum.

Thissen, D., Steinberg, L., & Wainer, H. (1993). Detection of differential item functioning using the parameters of item response models. In P. W. Holland & H. Wainer (Eds.), *Differential item functioning*. Hillsdale, NJ: Lawrence Erlbaum Associates.

Wilson, D. B., & Lipsey, M. W. (2001). The role of method in treatment effectiveness research: Evidence from meta-analysis. *Psychological Methods, 6*, 413–429.

Wigdor, A. K., & Garner, W. R. (Eds.). (1982). *Ability testing: Uses, consequences, and controversies, Part 1*. Washington, DC: National Academy Press.

Woods, C. (2009). *Empirical selection of anchors for tests of differential item functioning, Applied Psychological Measurement, 33*, 42–57.

Zhang, M., & French, B. F. (2010, May). *Gender related differential item functioning in mathematics tests: A meta-analysis*. Paper presented at the National Council on Measurement in Education conference, Denver, CO.

Zieky, M. (1993). Practical questions in the use of DIF statistics in test development. In P. W. Holland & H. Wainer (Eds.), *Differential item functioning* (pp. 337–347). Hillsdale, NJ: Erlbaum.

Chapter 11

Assessing Measurement Invariance of Scales Using Multiple-Group Structural Equation Modeling

Marilyn S. Thompson

T. Denny Sanford School of Social and Family Dynamics, Arizona State University, Tempe, AZ, USA

Introduction and Central Issues

After developing and validating a newly constructed scale or system of indicators devised to measure one or more traits, researchers frequently seek to evaluate whether the specified measurement model holds across multiple populations or multiple occasions (Schmitt & Kuljanin, 2008; Vandenberg & Lance, 2000). Scales developed in the social sciences are often used in populations that may be distinguished with respect to language, ethnicity, gender, age, clinical status, or other characteristics. For example, researchers might ask whether the factor structure of an ethnic identity scale is consistent across populations with different ethnic backgrounds, or whether a parental bonding scale assesses parenting constructs the same way across male and female respondents. If the measurement model underlying a scale varies between the focal populations, then the instrument does not measure the same construct in a consistent manner across these groups, calling into question the use of the scale and its resulting scale scores to compare or make decisions about these populations.

Testing of measurement invariance between populations or across repeated measurement occasions is a necessary step for addressing several types of research questions. Knowing which parameters vary may be inherently interesting, such as when culturally or linguistically relevant phenomena can explain these differences, or, alternatively, identification of noninvariant parameters can provide guidance in revising the instrument to adapt or remove measures (e.g., items) that do not perform consistently between groups as measures of a focal construct (Cheung & Rensvold, 1999). Depending on the nature and degree of noninvariance, caution may be advised when proceeding to use the measurement model as a basis for comparing latent means (Thompson & Green, 2013), for making selection decisions (Millsap & Kwok, 2004), or for computing and interpreting subscale composite scores for purposes such as evaluating growth over time (Motl, McAuley, & Mullen, 2011).

Measurement Invariance Defined

Measurement models may be broadly defined as models expressing the relationships between latent variables and measured (i.e., observed or manifest) variables. The motivating question for this chapter is whether a measure or set of measures functions in relation to the latent variable in an equivalent – or invariant – manner between populations. Although measurement invariance can also be applied for repeated measures of a construct, key definitions are cast here in terms of a between-population framework. *Measurement invariance* implies that, for respondents with a given level on the latent variable, the probability of achieving any particular score on a measure does not differ as a function of membership in different focal populations. This definition can be expressed mathematically in terms of conditional probabilities (e.g., see Millsap, 2011, for an extensive development). Suppose, for example, we are interested in examining the measurement invariance of a test purported to measure linguistic processing in both English- and Spanish-speaking populations. If the probabilities of obtaining a specific score, X, on the test, given a particular level, W, on the linguistic processing construct are equivalent across English- and Spanish-speaking populations, we have:

$$P(\mathbf{X} \mid \mathbf{W}, \text{English}) = P(\mathbf{X} \mid \mathbf{W}, \text{Spanish}) \tag{1}$$

That is, measurement invariance holds for this linguistic processing test if the conditional probability functions are equal across English- and Spanish-speaking populations, noting that this equality must be true for all values of X and W. According to this definition, any differences between English- and Spanish-speaking populations on X are attributable to differences between these populations on the linguistic processing construct W. Although Equation 1 was introduced here to express the probability of obtaining a particular test score given a single latent variable, this equation comprises a more general framework for measurement invariance. That is, $\mathbf{X}$ is defined as a vector of scores that may include multiple observed measures (e.g., items on a test or scale) and $\mathbf{W}$ is a vector of unobserved scores on one or more latent variables. Accordingly, Equation 1 generalizes to describe measurement invariance for sets of measures (i.e., equality of conditional probability functions for tests or scales with multiple items) as well as for individual measures (i.e., equality of item response functions) on one or more latent variables.

Failure of measurement invariance to hold implies that *measurement bias* exists. A measure is biased if observed between-group differences in scores on the measure are not fully accounted for by differences in levels on the underlying construct(s). An alternative phrasing is that a scale including one or more noninvariant indicators does not measure the construct in the same way in the compared populations. If Equation 1 does not hold, test X evidences measurement bias as a measure of linguistic processing for English- and Spanish-speaking populations in that the latent level of linguistic processing alone does not fully explain score differences between these groups on test X.

It is critical to note that measurement invariance does not require scores on a measure to be equivalent across groups. If groups differ with respect to their proficiency level on the construct, for example, scores on measures of that construct would be expected to differ between groups. Problems arise, however, if the reason for score differences between groups is differential functioning of the measure between the focal populations. Suppose, for example, that one of the indicators purported to be a measure of linguistic processing draws upon linguistic patterns that are inherent in English, but are less prevalent in Spanish. Such a measure may be a valid indicator of linguistic processing in English, but may fail to be a valid measure of linguistic processing in a Spanish-language version of the same test. In this case, English-

and Spanish-speaking individuals with identical levels on the construct may exhibit different scores on this indicator, owing to the greater familiarity of English-language participants with linguistic patterns used in this particular measure.

The focus of this chapter is on understanding the critical role of assessing measurement invariance in the context of scale construction and validation, and to address some of the key decisions and challenges researchers face in applying these techniques. Although the conceptual development of the analysis of measurement invariance is on multiple-group applications as approached within a structural equation modeling (SEM) framework, the concepts and methods presented here are readily extended to several other contexts. First, in a manner analogous to that used for evaluating measurement invariance between groups, measurement invariance may also be examined between repeated measurement occasions in longitudinal contexts, thereby addressing the stability of a latent variable model over time (Little, 2013; Widaman, Ferrer, & Conger, 2010). Second, questions of measurement invariance, particularly for tests, can also be addressed in the framework of item response theory (IRT). In the IRT framework, bias is typically defined and examined by identifying differential item functioning (DIF) between groups. For measurement models involving dichotomous measures, IRT models can be parameterized such that they yield results equivalent to CFA-based specifications (Kamata & Bauer, 2008), and comparable procedures for evaluating measurement invariance have been described across these frameworks (Meade & Lautenschlager, 2004; Raju, Laffitte, & Byrne, 2002; Reise, Widaman, & Pugh, 1993; Stark, Chernyshenko, & Drasgow, 2006). Measurement invariance in this chapter, however, is presented in the context of the common factor model. Accordingly, a semantic note is that the term *factorial invariance* is sometimes used in the literature to denote measurement invariance considered specifically in factor analytic contexts (Widaman & Reise, 1997).

An attempt is made in this chapter to elucidate the concepts and methods for assessing measurement invariance for readers differing widely in their substantive interests and background in psychometrics. Interested readers can find more technical treatments of measurement invariance available in the literature (e.g., Meredith, 1993; Millsap, 2011).

In What Types of Studies Should We Evaluate Measurement Invariance?

To aid in understanding why measurement invariance is important to consider in various research contexts, it is useful to consider some examples from published studies drawn from different disciplines. Perhaps some of the most common applications involve checking for evidence of measurement bias in scales administered in different languages or to different cultural populations, examining stability of a measurement model over time, and testing measurement invariance prior to evaluating differences in latent means. In addition, lists of published studies employing measurement invariance analyses can be found in the reviews by Schmitt and Kuljanin (2008) and Vandenberg and Lance (2000).

Invariance of Scales Across Different Languages and/or Cultures

Sousa, West, Moser, Harris, and Cook (2012) examined measurement invariance between the English and Spanish versions of the Paediatric Asthma Quality of Life Questionnaire (PAQLQ; Juniper et al., 1996). They found that measurement invariance held across the English and

Spanish versions of the PAQLQ (i.e., invariance of factor loadings, measurement intercepts, residual variances and covariances); the article also provided a clear illustration of how measurement invariance can be evaluated and presented using multiple-group confirmatory factor analysis. A unique feature of this study was the use of both qualitative and quantitative item analysis to inform factor structure modifications.

Snow, Ward, Becker, and Raval (2013) employed multiple-group confirmatory factor analysis to validate the use of the Difficulties in Emotion Regulation Scale (DERS; Gratz & Roemer, 2004) in college students from India, who completed the survey in the Gujarati language, and students from the United States, who took the survey in English. A modified five-factor model was tested for measurement invariance and the hypothesized configuration of the factor structure of the DERS was found to differ across these two populations. They offered culturally-based insights from the literature on why emotion dysregulation constructs might hold different meaning across these groups, and also noted that translation of the scale into Gujarati may also contribute to the lack of invariance.

Byrne and Watkins (2003) examined the equivalence of nonacademic subscales of the Self-Description Questionnaire I (SDQ-I; (Marsh, 1992) across Australian and Nigerian adolescents in English. They conducted extensive analyses to elucidate context-specific determinants of the observed noninvariance of particular parameters. They found seven noninvariant SDQ-I items, four of which showed significant bias as evidenced by ANOVA-based analyses showing significant main effects for culture. They also examined the utility of graphical displays of item response and distribution patterns for exploring differences between the Australian and Nigerian adolescents. Byrne and Watkins' manuscript includes clear discussions of how focal constructs, methodological procedures, and item content can contribute to bias in cross-cultural research.

Stability of Measurement Models Over Time

If researchers seek to model growth on a latent variable or assess change based on a composite score for a scale, it is desirable to ensure that the measurement model itself is stable over the repeated measurement occasions (Little, 2013; Widaman et al., 2010). Motl et al. (2011) investigated measurement invariance for the Multiple Sclerosis Walking Survey-12 (MSWS-12), which measures the walking ability of individuals diagnosed with multiple sclerosis. The 12-item rating scale was administered at baseline, 6-month, and 12-month intervals and measurement invariance was tested across the three administrations. Results supported invariance of factor loadings, measurement intercepts, and item residual variances from baseline to the 6-month administration and from baseline to the 12-month administration. They concluded that evidence of longitudinal measurement invariance supports use of composite MSWS-12 scores in evaluating change in perceived walking impairment over time, and, further, they noted the strong coefficient of stability indicated little change had occurred in the rank ordering of individuals over the 12-month period.

As a Precursor to Testing Differences in Latent Means

Evaluation of measurement invariance is an essential step in assessing differences in factor means given that incorrect between-group constraints on model parameters can distort comparisons of factor means. Tragant, Thompson, and Victori (2013) showed that a two-factor model of a scale constructed to assess foreign language learning strategies was appropriate for both middle- and upper-grade populations of students whose primary language was Catalan. After establishing a satisfactory degree of measurement invariance in factor loadings and measurement intercepts, they compared the latent means and found that upper-grade students were more likely to use the more advanced skills-based deep processing strategies and less likely to use language study strategies than middle-grade students.

Conceptual Principles and Statistical Assumptions

Although different approaches to testing for measurement invariance exist, the typical method involves testing a series of progressively restrictive between-group constraints on sets of model parameters. This section describes procedures commonly used in evaluating what Meredith (1993) termed weak, strong, and strict factorial invariance – that is, the between-population invariance of sequentially constrained factor loadings, measurement intercepts, and residual variances, respectively. First, however, it is necessary to develop a clear understanding of the common factor model with both a mean and covariance structure.

To provide a realistic context for describing the process of evaluating measurement invariance, suppose we are interested in evaluating a new scale for measuring academic engagement of undergraduate students who have declared a major. An academic engagement construct is hypothesized to underlie four self-reported indicators of engagement that are assessed on a 7-point, Likert-type scale (1 = *not at all strong* to 7 = *extremely strong*): school liking (V1), in-class participation (V2), strength of identity with declared major (V3), and strength of connections with faculty (V4). Evidence for the validity of this scale should include support for the invariance of the academic engagement measurement model across the populations for which it is intended to be used. In the context of academic engagement, populations could be defined as varying, for example, as a function of gender, ethnicity, age (e.g., traditional vs. nontraditional college-aged students), domain of discipline (e.g., behavioral sciences, natural sciences, business, the arts), or type of institutional setting. For this example, let's consider whether the scale measures academic engagement in the same manner across populations of students who attend state universities and those who attend private, liberal arts colleges. In other words, is the academic engagement measurement model invariant between these populations?

A Multiple-Group Confirmatory Factor Analytic Model With Mean Structure

The measurement model applied throughout this chapter is a multiple-group CFA model that allows for the inclusion of means in addition to variances and covariances among measured variables (Sörbom, 1974). This model is referred to as a structured means model (SMM), or alternatively as a mean and covariance structure (MACS) model, because it incorporates a mean structure as well as a covariance structure; the term SMM is used here. Incorporating means into the model requires the use of intercepts as model parameters, along with path coefficients and variances and covariances of independent variables. Many researchers do not include means in their single-group, factor analytic studies because inclusion of a mean structure does not provide fit information beyond that offered by analyzing only the covariance structure. Inclusion of means is necessary, however, for identifying differential functioning of measures between groups. Further, if a reasonable degree of measurement invariance holds, the SMM allows for the comparison of means on the latent variables between groups, which is often of substantive interest.

In an attempt to provide a transparent, didactic treatment of measurement invariance, I illustrate a prototypical SMM using figures and narrative rather than employing a matrix equation presentation. The model specification and notation system used throughout this chapter is based on the Bentler–Weeks VFED (i.e., Variable, Factor, Error, Disturbance) symbols for measured and latent variables, along with the *a-b-c* system for notating parameters as advanced in Hancock and Mueller 2006, 2013; see also Thompson and Green's (2013) equation-based presentation of SMM parameters using this system, extended to a two-factor model). Figure 11.1 depicts a two-group SMM for academic engagement example. The single academic engagement factor, F1, is indicated by the four measures of engagement, V1–V4. The observed variables V1–V4 are considered to be imperfect measures of academic engagement and thus are modeled to include measurement errors E1–E4, respectively, which are assumed to be independent and normally distributed around a mean of zero. The panel on the left depicts the model for state university students, denoted as Group 1 (G1), and the panel on the right is for liberal arts college students, denoted as Group 2 (G2). Pre-subscripts of G1 and G2 are used to indicate parameters that are estimated uniquely for each group (i.e., no between-group constraints on the parameter), whereas the absence of these pre-subscripts indicates that a single parameter value is estimated for both groups due to either identification constraints or equality constraints. The data consist of means, variances, and covariances among the four measures for samples drawn from each population.

Understanding a Single-Group CFA With Mean Structure

Before considering the SMM for two populations, let us first consider a single-group CFA model with mean structure for state university students (i.e., G1), as shown in the left panel of Figure 11.1. In discussing this single-group model, the G1 pre-subscripts on parameters can be ignored.

Within the *a-b-c* notation system, the symbol *b* denotes a direct effect. For a CFA model, the factor loadings are specified as direct effects, and therefore each estimated factor loading is designated by a subscripted *b*. Subscripts on the factor loadings identify the direct effect to a measured variable from a factor; for example, factor loading b_{V3F1} is the regression of measure

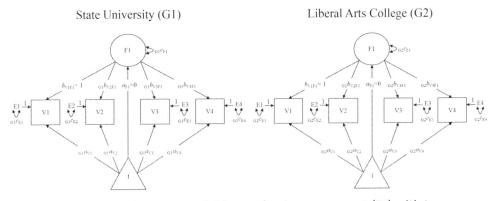

Figure 11.1. Structured means model for academic engagement (F1) with two groups. Model specified is configurally invariant (i.e., Model 2 in Table 11.2). G1 = Group 1; G2 = Group 2.

V3 on F1. In accordance with regression models, the b factor loadings may be regarded as slopes, such that b_{V3F1} estimates the change in V3 resulting from a one-unit change in F1.

As in any CFA model, we must scale the factor in order for the model to be mathematically identified. As shown in Figure 11.1, the referent indicator approach is used here to scale the factor by fixing the loading for the first measure to 1; that is, $b_{V1F1} = 1$. I discuss later some methodological issues related to the choice of a referent indicator.

Intercepts are used to incorporate information about means into the model. A unit predictor, sometimes called a pseudovariable, is included in the model. This unit predictor is a constant, such that the value equals one for all subjects. When depicted in a model diagram, the unit predictor is represented by a *1* enclosed in a triangle (see Figure 11.1). Parameters associated with paths from this unit predictor to the measures or factors are intercepts, which, akin to intercepts in a regression equation, are additive constants in their respective prediction equations. As shown in Figure 11.1, each intercept parameter is symbolized by an a, followed by a subscript that designates the particular measure or factor with which the intercept is associated (e.g., a_{V3} is the intercept for the regression of measured variable V3 on F1).

In the present model, there is a single factor, F1, and its intercept is a_{F1}. The intercept a_{F1} is equal to the mean of factor F1. However, given that F1 is a latent variable, it does not have an inherent mean and, as such, the mean must be defined to identify the model. This can be done by fixing the factor intercept a_{F1} equal to zero, which conveniently defines the factor mean of academic engagement to be zero.

By examining the paths leading into each measure, we see that each measure is a function of three components: the factor (F1), the unit predictor, and the respective measurement error. The structural equations for the four measures of academic engagement are as follows:

$$
\begin{aligned}
V1 &= a_{V1} 1 + \phantom{b_{V2F1}} 1 \ F1 + 1E1 \\
V2 &= a_{V2} 1 + b_{V2F1} \ F1 + 1E2 \\
V3 &= a_{V3} 1 + b_{V3F1} \ F1 + 1E3 \\
V4 &= a_{V4} 1 + b_{V4F1} \ F1 + 1E4 .
\end{aligned}
\tag{2}
$$

Viewing these as regression equations, each intercept is the predicted score on a particular measure V given a value of zero on the latent variable F1. With the inclusion of freely-estimated intercepts in a single-group CFA, the means of the measured variables can be perfectly reproduced and, in fact, are equal to the respective intercepts in the equations for each measure. For example, given we have set the mean of F1 equal to zero (by setting $a_{F1} = 0$) and we assume the mean of E3 to be equal to zero, the mean of V3 is equal to its intercept a_{V3}.

In accordance with the a-b-c notation system, the symbol c followed by a subscript is used in this model to designate parameters that are variances and covariances of the exogenous (i.e., independent) variables. In Figure 11.1, these are the residual variances c_{E1} to c_{E4}, as well as the factor variance, c_{F1}.

When examining Figure 11.1, there may be some confusion given that Factor 1 is predicted by the unit predictor and, accordingly, Factor 1 could be regarded as a dependent variable in the model. Assigning Factor 1 status as a dependent (i.e., endogenous) factor would require the factor to also be predicted by an error term that is designated in the Bentler–Weeks model as disturbance D1 with variance c_{D1}; accordingly, the factor variance c_{F1} would not formally be a model parameter. This would be consistent with the alternative specification of the SMM presented by Bentler (1995), which models the factor as having disturbance D1 with a disturbance variance parameter that is parameterized to be equivalent to the factor variance. Further, in a model with two or more factors, the covariances between factors would be parameterized as covariances between disturbance variances. To summarize, the parameters specified in this chapter as the factor means, factor variances, and factor covariances could be equivalently parameterized as factor intercepts, disturbance variances, and disturbance covariances, respectively (e.g., see Bentler, 1995; Thompson & Green, 2013).

Specifying a Two-Group Structured Means Model

In the previous section, a single-group CFA model with mean structure was specified, which could be fitted separately to data from each of the two types of educational settings. The next step is to combine the models for the two groups into a multiple-group SMM and proceed to evaluate measurement invariance across the two groups. Figure 11.1, when viewed in its entirety, depicts the two-group SMM and shows the specification of analogous parameters for each of the two groups. Recall that the pre-subscripts G1 and G2 are used in this model to specify parameters that are allowed to be freely estimated for both the state university (G1) and liberal arts college (G2) groups; parameters without a group-specific prefix are either constrained to be equal between groups or fixed to a specified value for identification purposes.

The model shown in Figure 11.1 specifies the least constrained version of this two-group SMM that is mathematically identified. It comprises a model with identically specified patterns of free and fixed parameters for the two groups. As in the single-group model, the variances for factors (c_{F1}) and errors (c_{E1} to c_{E4}) are freely estimated in both groups (and thus have G1 or G2 pre-subscripts); although not hypothesized in the present model, any specified covariances among factors or errors would also be freely estimated in both groups. For both groups, the academic engagement factor is scaled by fixing to 1 the loading of V1 in both groups (i.e., $b_{V1F1} = 1$); all other factor loadings are freely estimated (e.g., the loading of V3 is allowed to vary between groups, so these are designated $_{G1}b_{V3F1}$ and $_{G2}b_{V3F1}$, respectively). The intercepts for regressions of the measures on F1 are freely estimated in both groups (e.g., intercepts in the structural equations for V3 are $_{G1}a_{V3}$ and $_{G2}a_{V3}$). To identify this multiple-group model, the factor means are also set to zero in both groups by fixing the factor intercepts $a_{F1} = 0$ for both groups. Note that other options for identification constraints exist; for example, the intercepts for V1 could be constrained to zero for both groups instead of fixing the factor means to zero.

Given that the same configuration of the model is specified in both groups, but without constraining any parameters to be equal between groups (i.e., beyond parameters fixed to identify the model), this model is commonly regarded as a configurally invariant model. As the least constrained multiple-group specification, the configurally invariant model may be regarded as a baseline model for evaluating measurement invariance.

Procedures for Evaluating Measurement Invariance
With the Structured Means Model

Although different approaches to testing for measurement invariance exist, most often researchers test a series of progressively restrictive constraints on sets of model parameters. Strictly interpreted, complete factorial invariance may be regarded as requiring equivalence across the focal populations with respect to all model parameters – factor loadings, intercepts for measures, error variances and covariances, factor variances and covariances, and factor means. However, the research goals of most multiple-group applications do not require this degree of invariance. For example, researchers seeking to examine differences in latent means can proceed to test differences in latent means under partial invariance of factor loadings and intercepts for measures (Byrne, Shavelson, & Muthén, 1989), although caution is warranted when the degree of invariance is limited (Millsap & Kwok, 2004; Thompson & Green, 2013). Additionally, as indicated earlier, the emphasis in this chapter is on invariance of the measurement components of the common factor model – that is, whether measures function in relation to the latent variable in an equivalent manner between populations. Factor variances, factor covariances, and factor means are parameters associated with the structural component of the model and, as such, invariance of these parameters is not requisite for measurement invariance. Because these parameters may be of interest for specific research purposes, I discuss briefly invariance tests of these structural parameters as well.

As in any application of SEM, judging the fit of a model can be complicated and is typically approached by evaluating the model χ^2 statistic and goodness-of-fit indices such as the comparative fit index (CFI), standardized root mean square residual (SRMR), and root mean square error of approximation (RMSEA). The fit of the model at each step should be satisfactory before proceeding to test further constraints. Beyond evaluating the fit of the model specified at a step, model comparisons are central to assessing measurement invariance. The series of models most often used to evaluate measurement invariance is defined by applying sets of between-group constraints on less constrained models, yielding pairings of more-constrained models that are nested within less-constrained models. Accordingly, the χ^2 difference tests (i.e., likelihood ratio tests) can be used to test the null hypothesis that an added set of constraints does not produce a decrement in fit. Researchers typically maintain these constraints if they fail to reject this null hypothesis, whereas rejecting it implies that the tested set of parameters is not invariant across populations. A caveat is that with large samples and/or complex models, the χ^2 difference test, like the model χ^2 test, can lead to rejection of the null hypothesis even for trivial differences in parameters between groups. As discussed later in this chapter, some methodologists have advocated using incremental differences in goodness-of-fit indices – such as ΔCFI, ΔRMSEA, and ΔSRMR – to aid in identifying misfit due to incorrect between-group constraints (e.g., Chen, 2007; Cheung & Rensvold, 2002).

It is worth noting that many different nomenclatures have been used to describe the types or levels of invariance, and in some cases even the same term has been used by different methodologists to describe different degrees of invariance (see Vandenberg & Lance, 2000, for discussion of nomenclature problems in the MI literature). To avoid confusion, I use headings that describe the constraints applied at a step and mention other common designations.

Configural Invariance

Prior to specifying a multiple-group model, researchers typically fit the same model specification to each group separately to ensure that the model fits adequately in both groups. Then, as described in the previous section, the first multiple-group model is specified to reflect *configural invariance*, in which the same configuration of the model is specified in both groups, but no between-group parameter constraints are imposed other than those fixed to a value to identify the model. Adequate fit of this model supports that the same form of the factor model holds in both populations. In our example, the one-factor, four-indicator specification of the academic engagement model is tenable for students in state universities and liberal arts colleges. For models with two or more factors, the configurally invariant model would support that the same measures load on the same factors across groups (i.e., the models have the same pattern of fixed and free loadings).

Note that the test of configural invariance would yield the same result regardless of whether the mean structure was included in the model, as no constraints are imposed on the measurement intercepts at this stage. The models specified at subsequent steps are derived by applying between-group constraints on specific sets of model parameters and, accordingly, are nested within this baseline configural invariance model.

Invariance of Factor Loadings

The next step in evaluating measurement invariance typically involves testing the equality of factor loadings between groups. The condition in which all factor loadings are equal between groups has also been referred to as *metric invariance* (Horn & McArdle, 1992) or *weak factorial invariance* (Meredith, 1993; Widaman & Reise, 1997). Using the configurally invariant specification as the baseline model, between-group constraints are imposed on all factor loadings, except for the loadings of the referent indicator(s) in each group which are already set to 1 to scale the factors. Accordingly, the metric invariance model is nested within the configural invariance model. If the loading constraints are tenable, the linear relationships (i.e., regression slopes) between the factors and measures are invariant across populations. In the context of our example, invariance of factor loadings would imply that the unit of measurement for the academic engagement factor is identical for students at state universities and liberal arts colleges; that is, a one-unit increase in the level of academic engagement produces the same change for both populations on any particular measure.

Several caveats are important at this point. First, as in the configurally invariant model, we could test invariance of factor loadings with or without including the mean structure in the model with the same result. Second, although we have included the mean structure for transparency in testing a series of nested models, the measurement intercepts are still free to vary even though the slopes are fixed between groups. Accordingly, we cannot yet attribute any differences in means for the measures to differences on the underlying factors or proceed to compare factor means between groups, as the origin of the scale may vary between groups. Third, because the unit of measurement for the factor is equal across groups under invariance of loading constraints, researchers could choose at this point to examine relationships between the factors (in models with multiple factors). These could include invariance tests for factor variances and covariances or examination of relationships with external variables, for example, if seeking evidence of construct validity. Finally, we should also recognize that if the set of loading constraints produces a significant decrement in fit, some subset of the between-group loading constraints may need to be released; procedures for identifying partial invariance of parameters is discussed in a later section.

Invariance of Measurement Intercepts

At this step, the mean structure finally comes into play. Invariance constraints on intercepts in the regression equations for measures regressed on latent factors are imposed on the model from the previous step with noninvariant factor loadings. At this point, it is not necessary to maintain the identification constraints on the factor means in both groups (i.e., previously, a_{F1} = 0 for both groups); at this step, the factor mean remains fixed to zero in the first group (i.e., $_{G1}a_{F1}$ = 0) but is allowed to be freely estimated in the second group (i.e., estimate $_{G2}a_{F1}$). With this specification, the estimate of the factor mean for the second group is the between-group difference in factor means.

Between-group constraints jointly applied on both factor loadings and measurement intercepts specify *scalar invariance* (Steenkamp & Baumgartner, 1998), or, alternatively, *strong factorial invariance* based on Meredith's (1993) framework. When scalar invariance holds, differences between population means on the measures, or between means for composites or scale scores of these measures, can be attributed to mean differences on their respective factors. Achieving scalar invariance also supports evaluation of between-group differences in factor means, as will be discussed soon. Failure of scalar invariance to hold is regarded as evidence of measurement bias, or differential item functioning. In our example, suppose we find that measurement intercepts vary between state university and liberal arts college groups for our measure of strength of connections with faculty (V4). This would imply, for example, that given equivalent levels of academic engagement, the mean strength of connection with faculty differs between the college groups. In other words, this mean difference on strength of connection with faculty may be attributable to something other than differences in academic engagement.

Invariance of Error Variances

Between-group constraints on measurement error variances (i.e., also termed unique variances or residual variances) are applied to the scalar invariance model to yield *strict factorial invariance* (Meredith, 1993). The condition of strict factorial invariance involves between-group constraints on factor loadings, measurement intercepts, and measurement error variances – a specification that implies all group differences in covariances, means, and variances of the measures are due to differences between groups on the common factors. The expectation that between-group differences in variances of measured variables are explained fully by between-group differences in factor variances is quite restrictive and, as such, may be difficult to achieve in some applications. As described in the previous paragraph, invariance of error variances is not typically regarded as necessary for comparing differences in means of measures or factors, although some cautions are noted in the following paragraphs. Nonetheless, achieving strict factorial invariance may be a worthwhile goal in many studies, even when the interest is in evaluating mean differences on measures or factors, because ambiguity due to unmodeled, systematic effects is eliminated.

As observed in the extensive literature reviews of measurement invariance practices conducted by Vandenberg and Lance (2000) and by Schmitt and Kuljanin (2008), some confusion persists regarding both the need for evaluating invariance of error variances and the potential implications of lack of invariance in these parameters. In some cases, this was apparent from the inclusion or omission of this step in evaluating measurement invariance without any accompanying explanation, whereas in others, improper inferences were made based on results of a test of strict factorial invariance (e.g., inferences regarding reliabilities of measures). I discuss here a few issues that, in part, may be sources of this confusion, and also direct interested readers to recent literature on this topic. First, a somewhat common misconception is that equality of reliabilities of measured variables can be inferred based on invariance of the residual variances. The reliability of a measure is defined in the context of the common factor model as the proportion of the total variance of a measure explained by the common factors. The total variance of a measure is the sum of the variance explained by the common factors and the variance due to measurement error. In the CFA model specification, measurement error includes both random error and specific, reliable error unique to that measure, but these components cannot be distinguished in the common factor model (see Lubke & Dolan, 2003, for further discussion). Strict factorial invariance does not include between-group constraints on the variances or covariances of the common factors, so a finding that the set of invariance constraints on error variances is tenable is not sufficient to support the claim of invariant reliabilities of measures.

Second, as Widaman and Reise (1997) noted, there are conditions in which the variances of measures, and therefore the variances of the residuals of these measures, are expected to vary over time. As an example, they described how growth over time on developmental constructs yields not only increasing means but also often increasing variances over time. If the reliability of a measure of such a construct remains consistent over time, then the increasing variance on the construct would necessarily produce increasing variances of the measure over time. Under these conditions, strict invariance would not hold, yet researchers could proceed based on invariance of loadings and measurement intercepts to test differences over time in factor means and factor variances.

Finally, some of the confusion regarding the decision about whether to evaluate and/or maintain constraints on error variances likely results because the implications of this choice are not yet well understood and are likely to be context specific. Little (1997) expressed concern about introducing bias into other model parameters when constraining error variances that vary minimally due to differences in either the random error component or the reliable component of the measurement errors (e.g., systematic bias due to translation effects). On the other hand, several recent discussions have promoted the importance of homogeneity of error variances for achieving unambiguous interpretations of between-group comparisons of scale means, variances, and covariances (DeShon, 2004; Lubke & Dolan, 2003; Wu, Li, & Zumbo, 2007). In summary, strict factorial invariance is desirable for many research contexts and thoughtful consideration is urged in making decisions about the specification and testing of between-group equality of error variances.

Partial Invariance

It is possible that invariance constraints on some subset of parameters within a set are appropriate, whereas other constraints do not hold. Suppose, for example, that we reject the omnibus null hypothesis that the measurement intercepts are equal between groups by finding that the fit of this model with intercept and loading constraints is significantly worse than the model with only loading constraints applied. We might then seek to identify which of the measurement intercepts are noninvariant, and then specify the model such that those parameters are freely estimated between groups. A model in which one or more measurement model parameters are noninvariant between-groups indicates a condition of *partial invariance* (Byrne et al., 1989). If a priori hypotheses or information based on previous studies suggest that parameters for a particular measure may vary between groups, the tenability of constraints on these parameters should first be considered. In the absence of such information, however, empirically-based specification searches are frequently employed to aid in identifying noninvariant parameters.

As with specification searches in general, there are multiple ways in which a search for noninvariant parameters can be conducted; for example, constraints can be applied progressively on a minimally-constrained model until no further constraints hold, or constraints can be relaxed sequentially from a more-constrained model until improvements in fit are minimal. The most common approach is to identify the between-group constraints within a set (e.g., factor loadings) that contribute most to the decrement in fit. Modification indices, also called Lagrange multiplier (LM) tests, frequently are used to identify the between-group parameter constraint that, if freed, would most improve model fit according to the estimated change in the model chi-square statistic. Examination of residuals and expected parameter change statistics may also be useful. The model is respecified by freeing the indicated constraint and the model fit is re-evaluated; MIs based on the new model can again be examined to suggest any further constraints that should be freed. This process continues until there is no other constraint that appears to contribute significant misfit. The resulting model specification with a partially invariant set of parameters is typically retained as the analyst progresses through subsequent steps in testing the multiple-group hypotheses.

Two caveats should be noted regarding specification of models with partial invariance. First, if a loading is determined to be noninvariant and its constraint is relaxed, then the intercept for that loading should also be freely estimated between groups. Recall that a factor loading is the slope of the regression of a measure on the factor. If the slopes vary (i.e., slopes for regressions in the multiple groups are not parallel), it is highly unlikely that the intercepts for these regressions would be equal, as this would imply the point of intersection is exactly at the origin of the factor. Second, to be mathematically identified, a model with partial measurement invariance must maintain between-group equivalence for the factor loading and intercept of at least one measure for each factor. Of course mathematical identification is a minimum criterion, and, as discussed later, researchers should be wary of the potentially adverse implications of proceeding to evaluate substantive hypotheses with such a minimal degree of measurement invariance.

Let us consider an example of partial invariance in terms of our academic engagement model. Suppose that in conducting the test of metric invariance, we rejected the null hypothesis for the set of constraints on factor loadings. Based on an examination of the MIs for these loading constraints, the factor loading for strength of identity with declared major (V3) was freed between groups and then all other constraints held. When proceeding to test scalar invariance (i.e., intercept invariance), the factor loading for V3 would remain freely estimated between groups and all other loading constraints would be maintained (i.e., partial metric invariance); we would also then freely estimate the intercept for V3. At this step, it is possible that at one or more additional intercepts are not equivalent between groups, and modification indices could similarly be used to suggest, for example, that the intercept for strength of connections with faculty (V4) should also be relaxed. Subsequent tests on equality of error variances or of differences in factor means would proceed with the partially invariant model specification (i.e., with the factor loading and intercept for V3 and the intercept for V4 freely estimated between groups).

Beyond Measurement Invariance: Factor Variances, Covariances, and Means

Researchers' substantive hypotheses may include theoretical questions about population differences involving the constructs themselves. These may be addressed by tests of between-group invariance of variances, covariances, and/or means of the latent variables. Because these parameters are not part of the measurement component of the model that relates measures to the underlying factors, they are regarded as structural model parameters. In their review of measurement invariance applications published between 2000 and 2007, Schmitt and Kuljanin (2008) found that invariance of factor variances and covariances was tested in 47% of the included studies, and 41% evaluated differences in factor means. Equality constraints on these parameters are often examined following a finding of invariance of factor loadings and measurement intercepts (or at least of partial invariance of these parameters), although as discussed elsewhere in this chapter, the implications of proceeding to test equality of these parameters under partial invariance or without assessing strict factorial invariance are unclear.

Substantively, tests of equality of factor variances evaluate whether the variance of the construct is consistent between populations or between waves of measurement. We may, for example, wish to test whether students attending state universities versus liberal arts colleges are similarly variable with respect to academic engagement. Regarding factor covariance parameters, researchers seeking evidence for a scale's validity may wish to examine correlations of a focal scale's factors with those from established external scales; strong correlations with highly similar constructs provide evidence of convergent validity, whereas near-zero correlations with dissimilar constructs support discriminant validity. Accordingly, if the scale is intended for use in multiple populations, the correlational patterns that support the scale's validity should be equivalent between populations.

Researchers are frequently interested in evaluating mean differences on measures or constructs between groups. The SEM framework allows researchers to first evaluate invariance of the measurement model and then to estimate group differences in construct means, which provide the advantage of being theoretically error-free representations of the constructs. As indicated earlier, this test of equality of latent means may be conducted following a finding of at least partial invariance of factor loadings and intercepts (Byrne et al., 1989; Meredith, 1993). In our example, after finding invariance of factor loadings and intercepts, we could test whether state university and liberal arts college groups differ on academic engagement. Recall we had set the factor mean equal to zero in the first group (i.e., $_{G1}a_{F1} = 0$), but allowed the factor mean to be freely estimated in the second group such that the estimate of the factor mean for the second group's model (i.e., $_{G2}a_{F1}$) equals the between-group difference in factor means. An effect size for the difference in latent means can also be computed to aid in judging magnitude of the difference (Hancock, 2001). Researchers should be aware, however, that estimates of factor mean differences may be biased if equality constraints on model parameters are misspecified. Additionally, if too few indicators for a factor exhibit invariant parameters between groups, construct validity – and hence the conceptual meaning of estimated differences in factor means – may be compromised (e.g., see Thompson & Green, 2013).

Assumptions and Caveats for Evaluating Measurement Invariance Using the SMM

Thus far, I have based the discussion of procedures for evaluating measurement invariance on several assumptions. First, the focus here is on the common factor model, which assumes a latent variable system in which the measured variables are effect indicators that are presumed to be correlated because they share common causes – the same underlying factors. In the example we have considered, academic engagement is a latent variable that explains means, variances, and covariances among a set of measures of academic engagement. Alternatively, researchers might find that the most appropriate measurement model is an emergent variable system. In emergent variable systems (also called formative systems), effects flow from indicators that combine additively to form either: (a) emergent latent variables that have causal indicators, with a disturbance on each latent variable, or (b) composite variables that are linear combinations of the indicators, with no disturbance on the composite variable (Bollen & Bauldry, 2011; see also Bollen & Lennox, 1991; MacKenzie, Podsakoff, & Jarvis, 2005; Treiblmaier, Bentler, & Mair, 2011). Before undertaking a measurement invariance study, researchers are encouraged to consider carefully the form of the measurement model that is most consistent with theory being examined. Methods discussed in this chapter apply only to measurement systems based on the common factor model.

A second assumption made thus far in this chapter is that the analyst has specified a factor model that at a minimum represents the correct number of latent variables. As discussed by Millsap and Olivera-Aguilar (2012), omission of key constructs in models for one or more groups implicitly violates measurement invariance, and inclusion of factors beyond the focal constructs we intend to measure may lead researchers to find invariance in parameters due to the impact of these extraneous factors on the measures. Further, even if the correct factors are included in the model, the pattern of nonzero loadings that is typically used to define a CFA model in which each measure loads on only one factor may be incorrect. Less restrictive configurations for the factor structure are also possible. For example, a factor model in which measures are allowed to load on all factors (i.e., with the only restrictions being those necessary for identification) can be used to evaluate whether a model with a fixed number of common factors is tenable across populations (Millsap, 2011).

Third, the methods described in the chapter thus far have been based on the use of maximum likelihood (ML) estimation. ML is a large-sample estimator with several assumptions: (a) random and independent sampling from the population, (b) correct specification of the model, and (c) multivariate normal distributions of the dependent variables in the population. Sampling of multiple participants within clusters – such as children within classrooms or clients within therapists – violates the independence assumption; multilevel SEM approaches can be used to account for this type of dependency in the data but are beyond the scope of this chapter. I discuss in the next section some alternative estimation procedures that address the concern of nonnormality.

Research Issues: Some Practical Considerations for Evaluating Measurement Invariance

There are several methodological decisions researchers should be aware of in evaluating measurement invariance. These include, but are not limited to, selection of an estimation procedure that is appropriate for the distributions of the observed variables in a study, approaches for identifying noninvariant parameters, selection of referent indicators, and software options for multiple group analyses. Although I discuss each of these issues only briefly in this chapter, it is critical for data analysts to consider carefully their methodological choices in these domains and how they may impact the findings of a study.

Estimation With Nonnormal Measured Variables

Data collected in the behavioral sciences frequently violate the multivariate normality assumption due either to marked skew and/or kurtosis of the measures (Micceri, 1989) or to categorization of response scales (e.g., Likert-type scales). The problem of nonnormality is not unique to the measurement invariance context, but applies more generally to many SEM applications. For a thorough review of the literature on estimation procedures for conducting SEM with nonnormal data, I direct readers to a chapter by Finney and DiStefano (2013) as well as to Chapter 8 in the current volume (Finney, DiStefano, & Kopp, 2016).

Continuous, Nonnormal Data

When distributions of measured variables are continuously scaled but moderately to severely nonnormal due to skewness and/or kurtosis, the use of robust ML estimators is recommended

(Finney & DiStefano, 2013). The Satorra–Bentler (S-B) scaling method can be applied to yield the S-B scaled χ^2 statistic and other corrected fit indices, as well as robust standard errors (Satorra & Bentler, 1988) and test statistics based on these standard errors. Measurement invariance analyses can be conducted using this estimation procedure, but with an important caveat regarding tests of differences in fit between nested models, such as those conducted when evaluating sets of between-group parameter constraints. The difference between robust S-B scaled χ^2 statistics for nested models does not follow a χ^2 distribution and should not be used for hypothesis testing. Rather, a corrected version of the χ^2 difference test for nested models that involves the scaling factor must be used when comparing these models based on S-B scaled χ^2 statistics (Bryant & Satorra, 2012; Satorra & Bentler, 2001; Satorra & Bentler, 2010).

Ordered Categorical Data

If the response scale for one or more measured variables in a study offers respondents a choice between multiple discrete, ordered categories (e.g., Likert-type items), the resulting data are coarsely categorized and implicitly violate the multivariate normality assumption. Although the linear common factor model is technically inappropriate for such data, some research has indicated that it provides a reasonable approximation when used in conjunction with a robust ML estimator such as the Satorra–Bentler scaling method if the response scale comprises at least five or six ordered categories (see Finney & DiStefano, 2013, for a review and discussion of the literature); others have argued that this approximation may be inadequate in several ways (e.g., Lubke & Muthén, 2004). When the number of response categories is small – perhaps fewer than five or six – categorical variable methodology (CVM; Muthén, 1984) with a robust diagonally-weighted least squares (DWLS) estimator is generally recommended. In the following paragraphs, I discuss CVM and its implications for measurement invariance analyses in a brief and conceptually-oriented manner; accordingly, I have kept mathematical notation to a minimum (e.g., no subscripts are used to designate participants, measures, and populations) and have referenced more comprehensive and technical treatments of this topic available in the literature.

In CVM, an ordered categorical variable, X, is conceptualized to have underlying it a continuous, latent response scale, X^*, that is assumed to be normally distributed. A participant's response category on X is determined by the location of this participant on the continuous latent response variable X^* relative to one or more threshold parameters that define the divisions between the response categories. To illustrate this, consider the simplest case of a dichotomous measure for which there are two possible observed score values such as 0 and 1. These two response options may be used to designate, for example, an incorrect versus correct response on a test item measuring understanding of a p value, or perhaps a *disagree* versus *agree* response on a scale item assessing perceived usefulness of hypothesis testing. A continuous latent response scale, X^*, underlies this dichotomy; in the examples above, the latent response scale underlying the dichotomy refers to the gradations of understanding a p value or the perceived usefulness of hypothesis testing. The participant's categorical response depends on the location of the individual's score on the underlying latent response variable in comparison with the threshold parameter value. More specifically, if the score on X^* is greater than the threshold, then the score on X is 1; otherwise, the score on X is 0. The case with a two-category response generalizes to items with greater numbers of response categories, such that C thresholds are required to define $C + 1$ response categories for an item.

In the context of common factor analysis, CVM is employed to model the relationships between the factors and the latent response variables (X^*) rather than the observed variables (X).

CVM proceeds by first estimating threshold parameters from the sample data for each ordered categorical variable X by assuming multivariate normality in X^*. These threshold parameters are then used to estimate polychoric correlations among the latent response variables, X^*; special cases of these include tetrachoric correlations if the two observed variables are dichotomous or polyserial correlations if one variable is ordinal and one is continuous. Finally, the model is estimated based on these polychoric correlations, preferably using a DWLS estimator such as WLSMV within Mplus (Muthén & Muthén, 2012; see Finney & DiStefano, 2013, for a comparative discussion of WLSMV and other estimators).

Measurement invariance in the context of CVM requires that given particular levels on the underlying common factors, the conditional probabilities of response categories for all measures (X) are equal across populations. This would be true if, assuming multivariate normality for X^* and given particular levels on the common factors, the conditional distribution of X^* is invariant across populations. Methods for assessing factorial invariance that consider the metric of ordered categorical data via use of CVM have been described and involve evaluation of parameters including factor loadings, thresholds, and residual variances (Millsap, 2011; Millsap & Yun-Tein, 2004). Somewhat in parallel to the recommended procedure for evaluating invariance with continuously scaled measures, a series of progressively constrained factor models are estimated. These include a configurally invariant baseline model, followed by models with sets of between-group constraints added on factor loadings, thresholds, and error variances, respectively. A finding of noninvariant thresholds between groups suggests that given equivalent levels on the underlying constructs, participants in the two groups endorse one or more items with differential frequencies across the $C+1$ categories. The details are beyond the scope of this chapter, but additional identification constraints are required to identify these multiple-group models for ordered categorical variables. Further, approaches for applying CVM and imposing constraints on thresholds differ across software packages. Interested readers are encouraged to read Millsap and Yun-Tein (2004) and Millsap (2011) for more extensive presentations of these issues.

Challenges in Achieving Proper Specification of Between-Group Constraints

At any step in the process of evaluating measurement invariance, decisions are made that could yield a misspecified model. For example, the empirical specification search procedures typically used to identify sources of partial invariance are subject to the problem of capitalizing on the chance characteristics of a sample. Further, model misspecification in general is known to reduce the accuracy of specification search processes (e.g., Green, Thompson, & Poirier, 1999; MacCallum, Roznowski, & Necowitz, 1992), which may complicate the process of locating noninvariant parameters correctly in the assessment of partial invariance. This section addresses two challenges researchers face that may impact proper model specification: (1) uncertainties regarding how empirical criteria should be used to identify noninvariance, and (2) the problem of selecting an invariant reference indicator for scaling factors.

Criteria for Judging Noninvariance

Complexities inherent in using the model χ^2 test and other goodness-of-fit indices (GFIs, e.g., CFI) to evaluate the fit of any one model become even more arduous in the context of model comparisons to evaluate the between-group equivalence of one or more parameters. A particular challenge facing researchers is how to locate noninvariant parameters that should be freely estimated between groups. As noted earlier, the traditional χ^2 difference statistic used to test between-group constraints can lead to rejection of the null hypothesis even for trivial differences in parameters between groups when samples are large; nonnormality can also lead to inappropriate rejection of the null hypothesis. A handful of studies have been conducted in recent years to evaluate whether changes in goodness-of-fit indices that result when between-group invariance constraints are applied may aid researchers in judging the tenability of these constraints. Optimal characteristics for these change criteria include sensitivity to noninvariance and lack of sensitivity to sample size and the numbers of items and factors.

Cheung and Rensvold (2002) examined the utility of changes in 20 GFIs for evaluating between-group invariance of parameters in CFA models when the null hypothesis of invariance was true; ΔGFIs were computed by subtracting the CFI for a less-constrained model (i.e., without imposing the focal between-group constraints) from the CFI for a more-constrained model (i.e., with the focal between-group constraints imposed). They suggested that the hypothesis of measurement invariance for a set of parameters was tenable if the decrement in fit resulting from the imposition of between-group constraints these parameters was less than or equal to .01 for the CFI, .02 for McDonald's noncentrality index (Mc), and .001 for gamma hat. Given adequate sample sizes (total $N > 300$) that were equal between groups, Chen (2007) corroborated the .01 criterion for the ΔCFI, accompanied by a ΔRMSEA that did not worsen (i.e., increase) by more than .015 or ΔSRMR that did not worsen (i.e., increase) by more than .030 (or .010 for constraints on intercepts and residual variances); Chen also offered more nuanced criteria for different total and within-group sample sizes and patterns of noninvariance. Meade, Johnson, and Braddy (2008) offered markedly different guidelines than Cheung and Rensvold for two indices, suggesting that the decrement in fit resulting from the between-group constraints should be less than or equal to .002 for the CFI and, depending on the conditions of a study, .0041 to .0228 for McDonald's noncentrality index. Noting that GFIs were developed to evaluate fit of the model to the covariance structure, Fan and Sivo (2009) did not find that incremental changes on any of the nine fit indices they evaluated were satisfactory for judging invariance constraints in the mean structure, largely due to their sensitivity to model size. In summary, it is difficult at the present time to recommend specific cutoffs for changes in goodness-of-fit indices for evaluating measurement invariance, but some evidence suggests at least descriptively considering the ΔCFI, assuming a proper baseline is used in computation of the CFI for multiple-groups models (Widaman & Thompson, 2003).

If a parameter is found to differ statistically between groups, it may be useful to consider whether the degree of noninvariance is meaningful from a practical perspective. One approach for gauging the practical importance of a noninvariant parameter might be to compute an effect size for the between-group difference in the parameter. Millsap and Olivera-Aguilar (2012) illustrated how effect sizes can be computed for differences in factor loadings, intercepts, and error variances. From a practical perspective, decisions about whether to maintain between-group constraints on one or more parameters based on fit indices, incremental changes in these indices, and/or effect sizes are subjective; researchers may reach different conclusions based on the same model results.

Selecting Referent Indicators

Another decision that must always be made in applications of CFA is the approach used to scale the common factors. A popular choice is to fix the loading of one measure on each factor to 1.0. Although the default option in several software packages is to consider the first measure named for each factor as the reference variable, this choice is entirely arbitrary and is made in the absence of empirical information about the measure. In a multiple-group SMM, each factor must be scaled in all groups. If the factor loading for a reference measure is set to 1.0 (or any other value) in each group to scale the factor, this identification constraint is also implicitly an invariance constraint because the parameter is fixed to the same value across groups. If the loading of the chosen reference variable is noninvariant in the population, this misspecification can affect the estimates and tests of other parameters (Cheung & Rensvold, 1999; Johnson, Meade, & DuVernet, 2009).

A measure should be considered a good candidate for serving as a reference variable if prior information exists that parameters associated with this measure are invariant across populations. In the absence of such information, it is not straightforward to empirically choose a reference variable given that estimating any model requires an initial choice of identification constraints, and this choice may be incorrect. Several alternative solutions to the problem of choosing identification constraints have been suggested in the literature. For example, Rensvold and Cheung (2001) delineated an approach for identifying the most invariant loadings in which each measure takes a turn as the referent variable while the invariance of all possible pairs of loadings are evaluated (see also Cheung & Rensvold, 1999). Based on a simulation study, French and Finch (2008) found Rensvold and Cheung's approach to perform reasonably well, but the practical utility of this approach becomes limited as the number of measures increases, at least until a software-based automation is implemented. Other approaches have been suggested that involve alternative methods for applying identification constraints (e.g., see Little, Slegers, & Card, 2006). Yoon and Millsap (2007) proposed and evaluated a less computationally-demanding approach that involves first evaluating metric invariance by imposing between-group constraints on all factor loadings, while scaling the factor by fixing factor variances in one group to 1.0. Thus, no identification constraints are initially placed on loadings. LM statistics are then utilized in a stepwise, backward elimination of constraints to identify noninvariant parameters. To date, these various approaches have not been compared empirically, so defining reference indicators remains an ongoing challenge for researchers conducting measurement invariance studies.

Software Implementation

Most of the statistical software packages designed for conducting structural equation modeling analyses can be used for evaluating measurement invariance between groups. For example, commercially available software packages such as Mplus (Muthén & Muthén, 2012), EQS (Bentler, 1989), LISREL (Jöreskog & Sörbom, 2006), and AMOS (Arbuckle, 2006; now marketed as an SPSS add-on) can all be used for multiple-groups analyses, as can more recently developed R-based packages such as lavaan (Rosseel, 2012). The methods for specifying models with between-group constraints vary across these packages, but those already familiar with a particular software package likely will be able to specify the desired models following a reading of content related to multiple-groups analysis in the relevant user's manual or online documentation. Additionally, users of one the four commercial packages named above will find several chapters on multiple group analyses in Byrne's books that provide detailed chapters on particular types of SEM-based applications as conducted in a particular software package (see Byrne, 2011, for the Mplus version; see also similar books for EQS, LISREL, and AMOS users). The choice of software for measurement invariance analyses is largely one of user preference, but analysts should pay careful attention to default specifications employed, such as how identification constraints are set to scale the factors, which baseline model is used in the computation of comparative fit indices, and which between-group parameter constraints are assumed.

Example: Measurement Invariance of an Academic Engagement Scale Between State University Students and Liberal Arts College Students

Now that we have discussed the fundamentals of evaluating measurement invariance, I present an empirical evaluation of the measurement invariance of the academic engagement scale. Recall that the focal question of our illustrative example is whether the academic engagement measurement model is invariant between two populations of undergraduate students who have declared a major: those who attend state universities and those who attend private liberal arts colleges. Our hypothetical sample consists of 300 state university students and 262 liberal arts college students who rated on a 7-point, Likert-type scale (1 = *not at all strong* to 7 = *extremely strong*) their agreement with four academic engagement items: school liking (V1), in-class participation (V2), strength of identity with declared major (V3), and strength of connections with faculty (V4). Summary data are shown in Table 11.1 in the form of correlation matrices, means, and standard deviations for each group.

Table 11.1. Correlations, means, and standard deviations for academic engagement measures for the state university and liberal arts college samples

Measure	V1	V2	V3	M	SD
Group 1 – State university students (N_1 = 300)					
V1	1			4.343	1.527
V2	.600	1		4.167	1.590
V3	.464	.417	1	4.070	1.621
V4	.536	.506	.454	4.023	1.726
Group 2 – Liberal arts college students (N_2 = 262)					
V1	1			4.354	1.713
V2	.602	1		4.073	1.710
V3	.636	.566	1	4.282	1.982
V4	.559	.584	.631	3.973	1.950

Note. M = mean; *SD* = standard deviation; V1 = school liking; V2 = in-class participation; V3 = strength of identity with declared major; V4 = strength of connections with faculty.

Mplus 7.11 (Muthén & Muthén, 2012) was used to estimate all single- and multiple-group CFA models. As discussed earlier, the robust Satorra–Bentler maximum likelihood estimation procedure has been recommended for analyzing ordered, categorical data collected using at least six scale points. Accordingly, the robust maximum likelihood estimator with mean adjusted chi square statistic (MLM) was used within Mplus to obtain the S-B scaled χ^2 statistic (Satorra & Bentler, 1988) and corrected fit indices, as well as robust standard errors and test statistics. Corrected χ^2 difference tests based on the S-B χ^2 statistics were used to compare nested models for evaluating invariance constraints (Bryant & Satorra, 2012; Satorra & Bentler, 2001, 2010).

Model fit indices and statistics for progressively constrained models are presented in Table 11.2. As shown in Models 1a and 1b, the two-factor CFA model fit very well in both the state university sample and the liberal arts college sample, although confidence intervals for the RMSEA were larger than desired. The configurally invariant multiple-groups model, Model 2, fit both samples simultaneously using the same factor model specification, but without constraining parameters to be equal between the groups. The configural invariance model fit the data well, $\chi^2(4) = 7.938$, $p = .094$, RMSEA = .059, CFI = .995, SRMR = .015, and is consistent with the hypothesis that the one-factor, four-indicator specification of the academic engagement model holds across students in state universities and liberal arts colleges. The configural invariance model serves as a baseline for the more rigorous invariance tests that follow.

Table 11.2. Fit indices for analysis of measurement invariance of the academic engagement model across state university and liberal arts college students

Model		S-B scaled χ^2 (df)	RMSEA [90% CI]	CFI[a]	SRMR	Models compared	S-B scaled $\Delta\chi^2$ (Δdf)[b]
1a	CFA for state university	2.574 (2)	.031 [.000, .123]	.999	.014	–	–
1b	CFA for liberal arts	5.298 (2)	.079 [.000, .165]	.994	.016	–	–
2	Configural invariance	7.938 (4)	.059 [.000, .120]	.995	.015	–	–
3	Loadings invariant	21.355 (7)*	.085 [.046, .128]	.983	.049	3 vs. 2	14.987 (3)*
3a	Loadings invariant except Item 3	10.105 (6)	.049 [.000, .100]	.995	.020	3a vs. 2	1.700 (2)
4	Model 3a plus intercepts invariant except Item 3; factor means free in liberal arts group	10.822 (8)	.035 [.000, .083]	.997	.021	4 vs. 3a	.904 (2)
5	Model 4 plus error variances invariant	15.179 (12)	.031 [.000, .072]	.996	.024	5 vs. 4	4.311 (4)

Note. df = Degrees of freedom; RMSEA = root mean square error of approximation; CFI = comparative fit index; SRMR = standardized root mean residual; CI = confidence interval.
[a]CFIs were computed using an appropriate baseline model for the SMM in which intercepts as well as covariances among measures are constrained to be equal between groups (see Thompson & Green, 2013).
[b]The Satorra–Bentler scaled chi-square difference test was used to test differences between nested models.
*$p < .05$.

Models 3 and 3a were estimated to evaluate invariance of factor loadings. First, in Model 3, all factor loadings were constrained to be equal between groups. The null hypothesis of perfect model-data fit was rejected for this model, $\chi^2(7) = 21.355$, $p = .003$, although other indices suggest that the overall fit of this model was at least moderate, RMSEA = .085, CFI = .983, SRMR = .049. A Satorra–Bentler (2001) scaled chi-square difference test was used to compare the fit of the configurally invariant model (Model 2) with Model 3 to test whether the factor loadings are equivalent between groups. The decrement in fit was statistically significant, $\Delta\chi^2(3) = 14.990$, $p = .002$, and further, the CFI decreased by .012. Based on examination of modification indices, the loading for Item 3 was allowed to vary between groups in Model 3a; this model fit the data well, $\chi^2(4) = 10.105$, $p = .120$, RMSEA = .049, CFI = .995, SRMR = .020, and did not differ significantly in fit from the configurally invariant model, $\Delta\chi^2(3) = 1.700$, $p = .427$. Accordingly, the factor loading for Item 3, "strength of identity with declared major," was freely estimated for both groups in all subsequent models. This model denotes partial metric invariance. With the exception of the factor loading for Item 3, the pattern and strength of relationships between the academic engagement factor and its measures were quite consistent between the two groups.

At the next step, invariance of intercepts for measures was evaluated to examine whether differences in means on the academic engagement measures result exclusively from between-group differences in the population factor mean. Because the factor loading of Item 3 was found to differ in the previous step, the intercept for Item 3 was allowed to differ in Model 4 and subsequent models. Model 4, with all loadings and intercepts except those for Item 3 constrained to be equal between groups, fit the data well, $\chi^2(8) = 10.822$, $p = .212$, RMSEA = .035, CFI = .997, SRMR = .021, and its fit did not differ significantly with that of Model 3a, $\Delta\chi^2(2) = .904$, $p = .636$.

In the final step, Model 5 was specified by imposing on Model 4 between-group constraints on all error variances. Model 5 fit the data well, $\chi^2(12) = 15.179$, $p = .232$, RMSEA = .031, CFI = .996, SRMR = .024, and its fit did not differ significantly with that of Model 4, $\Delta\chi^2(4) = 4.311$, $p = .366$. Figure 11.2 shows unstandardized parameter estimates for Model 5; parameters that are constrained to be equal between groups vs. those that are freely estimated can be distinguished by examining the symbols and estimated parameters in this figure. The academic engagement measurement model is relatively invariant between undergraduate students who attend state universities and those who attend private liberal arts colleges. The only parameters found to be noninvariant were the factor loading and intercept parameters for Item 3, "strength of identity with declared major," with liberal arts college students exhibiting a stronger relationship with the academic engagement factor than state university students on this item.

Future Directions

In this chapter, I have introduced concepts and procedures for examining measurement invariance in the context of multiple-groups CFA using the structured means model. I have attempted to draw from the recent measurement invariance literature in discussing methodological choices and caveats researchers should consider, while also pointing out a number of unresolved issues are in need of further research. More work is needed to hone methods for optimizing success in locating noninvariant parameters, and, relatedly, for addressing the challenge of applying proper identification constraints, such that the risk of introducing misspecification with these constraints is minimized. This is critical because incorrect equality constraints can

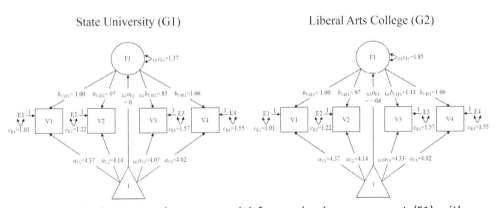

Figure 11.2. Final structured means model for academic engagement (F1) with unstandardized parameter estimates (i.e., Model 5 in Table 11.2). G1 = Group 1; G2 = Group 2.

distort parameter estimates and lead to faulty conclusions about measurement invariance and other hypotheses involving the specified model. Simulation research has indicated that correct identification of noninvariant parameters diminishes with decreases in sample size, the magnitude of factor loadings, the magnitude of differences in parameter values, and the proportion of invariant parameters (Johnson et al., 2009; Lo & Thompson, 2009; Yoon & Millsap, 2007).

Relatively few measurement invariance studies have been published that have involved alternative measurement models in the context of CFA, which is an area ripe for growth in both the methodological and applied literature. As discussed earlier, methodologists have argued for the importance of considering the discrete nature of ordered categorical measures when conducting factor analyses (e.g., Lubke & Muthén, 2004; Millsap & Yun-Tein, 2004). Recent work has also aimed to extend the application of measurement invariance to more complex multiple-group factor models. Such applications include second-order factor models (e.g., Chen, Sousa, & West, 2005), bifactor models (e.g., Chen, West, & Sousa, 2006), and models with latent subgroups (Merkle & Zeileis, 2013).

Finally, one of the most important dilemmas researchers conducting a measurement invariance study might face is how to proceed when a model is found to exhibit partial invariance. For example, what if only half of the measures on a scale are found to have invariant loadings and intercepts? Should these measures be retained or dropped? Should the scale be deemed unsuitable for use across multiple populations? Further, partial invariance may be described not only in the context of the number and proportion of measures with noninvariant parameters, but also by the effect size of differences and the pattern of differences (e.g., are loadings or intercepts always higher in one group, or is the pattern mixed?). The implications of partial invariance are not well understood in general and depend on the intended use of a scale. A level of partial invariance that is acceptable if the researcher's goal is to compare latent means between males and females on an empathy construct may not be suitable for making high-stakes selection decisions in an educational context. Millsap and Kwok (2004) argued for the necessity of evaluating the impact of partial invariance in relation to the intended purpose of the scale and offered an approach for evaluating the impact of partial invariance on selection decisions. More research of this type is needed to develop approaches for evaluating the potential impact of partial invariance in a context-specific manner.

References

Arbuckle, J. L. (2006). *AMOS (Version 7.0)*. Chicago, IL: SPSS.

Bentler, P. (1995). *EQS structural equations program manual*. Encino, CA: Multivariate Software.

Bentler, P. M. (1989). *EQS (Version 6.1)*. Encino, CA: Multivariate Software.

Bollen, K. A., & Bauldry, S. (2011). Three Cs in measurement models: Causal indicators, composite indicators, and covariates. *Psychological Methods, 16*(3), 265–284. http://doi.org/10.1037/a0024448

Bollen, K., & Lennox, R. (1991). Conventional wisdom on measurement: A structural equation perspective. *Psychological Bulletin, 110*(2), 305–314. http://doi.org/10.1037/0033-2909.110.2.305

Bryant, F. B., & Satorra, A. (2012). Principles and practice of scaled difference chi-square testing. *Structural Equation Modeling: A Multidisciplinary Journal, 19*(3), 372. http://doi.org/10.1080/10705511. 2012.687671

Byrne, B. M. (2011). *Structural equation modeling with Mplus: Basic concepts, applications, and programming*. New York, NY: Routledge Academic.

Byrne, B. M., Shavelson, R. J., & Muthén, B. (1989). Testing for the equivalence of factor covariance and mean structures: The issue of partial measurement invariance. *Psychological Bulletin, 105*(3), 456–466. http://doi.org/10.1037/0033-2909.105.3.456

Byrne, B. M., & Watkins, D. (2003). The issue of measurement invariance revisited. *Journal of Cross-Cultural Psychology, 34*(2), 155–175. http://doi.org/10.1177/0022022102250225

Chen, F. F. (2007). Sensitivity of goodness of fit indexes to lack of measurement invariance. *Structural Equation Modeling: A Multidisciplinary Journal, 14*(3), 464. http://doi.org/10.1080/10705510701301834

Chen, F. F., Sousa, K. H., & West, S. G. (2005). Testing measurement invariance of second-order factor models. *Structural Equation Modeling: A Multidisciplinary Journal, 12*(3), 471–492. http://doi.org/10.1207/s15328007sem1203_7

Chen, F. F., West, S. G., & Sousa, K. H. (2006). A comparison of bifactor and second-order models of quality of life. *Multivariate Behavioral Research, 41*(2), 189. http://doi.org/10.1207/s15327906mbr4102_5

Cheung, G. W., & Rensvold, R. B. (1999). Testing factorial invariance across groups: A reconceptualization and proposed new method. *Journal of Management, 25*(1), 1–27. http://doi.org/10.1177/014920639902500101

Cheung, G. W., & Rensvold, R. B. (2002). Evaluating goodness-of-fit indexes for testing measurement invariance. *Structural Equation Modeling: A Multidisciplinary Journal, 9*(2), 233–255. http://doi.org/10.1207/S15328007SEM0902_5

DeShon, R. P. (2004). Measures are not invariant across groups without error variance homogeneity. *Psychology Science, 46*, 137–149.

Fan, X. T., & Sivo, S. A. (2009). Using goodness-of-fit indexes in assessing mean structure invariance. *Structural Equation Modeling: A Multidisciplinary Journal, 16*(1), 54–69. http://doi.org/10.1080/10705510802561311

Finney, S. J., & DiStefano, C. (2013). Nonnormal and categorical data in structural equation modeling. In G. R. Hancock & R. O. Mueller (Eds.), *Structural equation modeling: A second course* (2nd ed., pp. 439–492). Charlotte, NC: Information Age Publishing.

Finney, S. F., DiStefano, C., & Kopp, J. P. (2016). Overview of estimation methods and preconditions for their application with structural equation modeling. In K. Schweizer and C. Distefano (Eds.), *Principles and methods of test construction* (pp. 135–165). Göttingen, Germany: Hogrefe Publishing.

French, B. F., & Finch, W. H. (2008). Multigroup confirmatory factor analysis: Locating the invariant referent sets. *Structural Equation Modeling: A Multidisciplinary Journal, 15*(1), 96–113. http://doi.org/10.1080/10705510701758349

Gratz, K. L., & Roemer, L. (2004). Multidimensional assessment of emotion regulation and dysregulation: Development, factor structure, and initial validation of the difficulties in emotion regulation scale. *Journal of Psychopathology and Behavioral Assessment, 26*(1), 41–54. http://doi.org/10.1023/B:JOBA.0000007455.08539.94

Green, S. B., Thompson, M. S., & Poirier, J. (1999). Exploratory analyses to improve model fit: Errors due to misspecification and a strategy to reduce their occurrence. *Structural Equation Modeling: A Multidisciplinary Journal, 6*(1), 113–126. http://doi.org/10.1080/10705519909540122

Hancock, G. R. (2001). Effect size, power, and sample size determination for structured means modeling and mimic approaches to between-groups hypothesis testing of means on a single latent construct. *Psychometrika, 66*(3), 373–388. http://doi.org/10.1007/BF02294440

Hancock, G. R., & Mueller, R. O. (Eds.). (2006). *Structural equation modeling: A second course*. Charlotte, NC: Information Age Publishing, Inc.

Hancock, G. R., & Mueller, R. O. (Eds.). (2013). *Structural equation modeling: A second course* (2nd ed.). Charlotte, NC: Information Age Publishing.

Horn, J. L., & McArdle, J. J. (1992). A practical and theoretical guide to measurement invariance in aging research. *Experimental Aging Research, 18*(3), 117–144. http://doi.org/10.1080/03610739208253916

Johnson, E. C., Meade, A. W., & DuVernet, A. M. (2009). The role of referent indicators in tests of measurement invariance. *Structural Equation Modeling: A Multidisciplinary Journal, 16*(4), 642. http://doi.org/10.1080/10705510903206014

Jöreskog, K. G., & Sörbom, D. (2006). *LISREL 8.8 for Windows (Version 8.8)*. Skokie, IL: Scientific Software International.

Juniper, E. F., Guyatt, G. H., Feeny, D. H., Ferrie, P. J., Griffith, L. E., & Townsend, M. (1996). Measuring quality of life in children with asthma. *Quality of Life Research: An International Journal of Qual-*

ity of Life Aspects of Treatment, Care and Rehabilitation, 5(1), 35–46. http://doi.org/10.1007/BF00435967

Kamata, A., & Bauer, D. J. (2008). A note on the relation between factor analytic and item response theory models. *Structural Equation Modeling: A Multidisciplinary Journal, 15*(1), 136–153. http://doi.org/10.1080/10705510701758406

Little, T. D. (1997). Mean and covariance structures (MACS) analyses of cross-cultural data: Practical and theoretical issues. *Multivariate Behavioral Research, 32*(1), 53–76. http://doi.org/10.1207/s15327906mbr3201_3

Little, T. D. (2013). *Longitudinal structural equation modeling*. New York, NY: Guilford Press.

Little, T. D., Slegers, D. W., & Card, N. A. (2006). A non-arbitrary method of identifying and scaling latent variables in SEM and MACS models. *Structural Equation Modeling: A Multidisciplinary Journal, 13*(1), 59. http://doi.org/10.1207/s15328007sem1301_3

Lo, W.-J., & Thompson, M. S. (2009, April). *Using goodness-of-fit indices and alternative search procedures for identifying partial measurement invariance*. Paper presented at the Annual meeting of the American Educational Research Association, San Diego, CA.

Lubke, G. H., & Dolan, C. V. (2003). Can unequal residual variances across groups mask differences in residual means in the common factor model? *Structural Equation Modeling: A Multidisciplinary Journal, 10*(2), 175–192. http://doi.org/10.1207/S15328007SEM1002_1

Lubke, G. H., & Muthén, B. O. (2004). Applying multigroup confirmatory factor models for continuous outcomes to Likert scale data complicates meaningful group comparisons. *Structural Equation Modeling: A Multidisciplinary Journal, 11*(4), 514–534. http://doi.org/10.1207/s15328007sem1104_2

MacCallum, R. C., Roznowski, M., & Necowitz, L. B. (1992). Model modifications in covariance structure analysis: The problem of capitalization on chance. *Psychological Bulletin, 111*(3), 490–504. http://doi.org/10.1037/0033-2909.111.3.490

MacKenzie, S. B., Podsakoff, P. M., & Jarvis, C. B. (2005). The problem of measurement model misspecification in behavioral and organizational research and some recommended solutions. *Journal of Applied Psychology, 90*(4), 710–730. http://doi.org/10.1037/0021-9010.90.4.710

Marsh, H. W. (1992). *Self Description Questionnaire (SDQ) I: A theoretical and empirical basis for the measurement of multiple dimensions of preadolescent self-concept: A test manual and research monograph*. Macarthur, New South Wales, Australia: University of Western Sydney, Faculty of Education.

Meade, A. W., Johnson, E. C., & Braddy, P. W. (2008). Power and sensitivity of alternative fit indices in tests of measurement invariance. *Journal of Applied Psychology, 93*(3), 568–592. http://doi.org/10.1037/0021-9010.93.3.568

Meade, A. W., & Lautenschlager, G. J. (2004). A comparison of item response theory and confirmatory factor analytic methodologies for establishing measurement equivalence/invariance. *Organizational Research Methods, 7*(4), 361–388. http://doi.org/10.1177/1094428104268027

Meredith, W. (1993). Measurement invariance, factor analysis and factorial invariance. *Psychometrika, 58*(4), 525–543. http://doi.org/10.1007/BF02294825

Merkle, E. C., & Zeileis, A. (2013). Tests of measurement invariance without subgroups: A generalization of classical methods. *Psychometrika, 78*(1), 59–82. http://doi.org/10.1007/s11336-012-9302-4

Micceri, T. (1989). The unicorn, the normal curve, and other improbable creatures. *Psychological Bulletin, 105*(1), 156–166. http://doi.org/10.1037/0033-2909.105.1.156

Millsap, R. E. (2011). *Statistical approaches to measurement invariance*. New York, NY: Routledge.

Millsap, R. E., & Kwok, O.-M. (2004). Evaluating the impact of partial factorial invariance on selection in two populations. *Psychological Methods, 9*(1), 93–115. http://doi.org/10.1037/1082-989X.9.1.93

Millsap, R. E., & Olivera-Aguilar, M. (2012). Investigating measurement invariance using confirmatory factor analysis. In R. H. Hoyle (Ed.), *Handbook of structural equation modeling* (pp. 380–392). New York, NY: The Guilford Press.

Millsap, R. E., & Yun-Tein, J. (2004). Assessing factorial invariance in ordered-categorical measures. *Multivariate Behavioral Research, 39*(3), 479–515. http://doi.org/10.1207/S15327906MBR3903_4

Motl, R. W., McAuley, E., & Mullen, S. (2011). Longitudinal measurement invariance of the Multiple Sclerosis Walking Scale-12. *Journal of the Neurological Sciences, 305*(1–2), 75–79. http://doi.org/10.1016/j.jns.2011.03.008

Muthén, B. (1984). A general structural equation model with dichotomous, ordered categorical, and continuous latent variable indicators. *Psychometrika, 49*(1), 115–132. http://doi.org/10.1007/BF02294210

Muthén, L. K., & Muthén, B. O. (2012). *Mplus (Version 7)*. Los Angeles, CA: Muthén & Muthén.

Raju, N. S., Laffitte, L. J., & Byrne, B. M. (2002). Measurement equivalence: A comparison of methods based on confirmatory factor analysis and item response theory. *Journal of Applied Psychology, 87*(3), 517–529. http://doi.org/10.1037/0021-9010.87.3.517

Reise, S. P., Widaman, K. F., & Pugh, R. H. (1993). Confirmatory factor analysis and item response theory: Two approaches for exploring measurement invariance. *Psychological Bulletin, 114*(3), 552–566. http://doi.org/10.1037/0033-2909.114.3.552

Rensvold, R. B., & Cheung, G. W. (2001). Testing for metric invariance using structural equation models: Solving the standardization problem. In C. A. Schriesheim & L. L. Neider (Eds.), *Research in management* (Vol. 1, pp. 25–50). Greenwich, CT: Information Age Publishing.

Rosseel, Y. (2012). lavaan: An R package for structural equation modeling. *Journal of Statistical Software, 48*(2), 1–36. http://doi.org/10.18637/jss.v048.i02

Satorra, A., & Bentler, P. M. (1988). Scaling corrections for chi-square statistics in covariance structure analysis. *Proceedings of the American Statistical Association, 1*, 308–313.

Satorra, A., & Bentler, P. M. (2001). A scaled difference chi-square test statistic for moment structure analysis. *Psychometrika, 66*(4), 507–514. http://doi.org/10.1007/BF02296192

Satorra, A., & Bentler, P. M. (2010). Ensuring positiveness of the scaled difference chi-square test statistic. *Psychometrika, 75*(2), 243. http://doi.org/10.1007/s11336-009-9135-y

Schmitt, N., & Kuljanin, G. (2008). Measurement invariance: Review of practice and implications. *Human Resource Management Review, 18*(4), 210–222. http://doi.org/10.1016/j.hrmr.2008.03.003

Snow, N. L., Ward, R. M., Becker, S. P., & Raval, V. V. (2013). Measurement invariance of the difficulties in emotion regulation scale in India and the United States. *Journal of Educational and Developmental Psychology, 3*(1), p147. http://doi.org/10.5539/jedp.v3n1p147

Sörbom, D. (1974). A general method for studying differences in factor means and factor structure between groups. *British Journal of Mathematical and Statistical Psychology, 27*(2), 229–239. http://doi.org/10.1111/j.2044-8317.1974.tb00543.x

Sousa, K. H., West, S. G., Moser, S. E., Harris, J. A., & Cook, S. W. (2012). Establishing measurement invariance: English and Spanish Paediatric Asthma Quality of Life Questionnaire. *Nursing Research, 61*(3), 171–180. http://doi.org/10.1097/NNR.0b013e3182544750

Stark, S., Chernyshenko, O. S., & Drasgow, F. (2006). Detecting differential item functioning with confirmatory factor analysis and item response theory: Toward a unified strategy. *Journal of Applied Psychology, 91*(6), 1292–1306. http://doi.org/10.1037/0021-9010.91.6.1292

Steenkamp, J.-B. E. M., & Baumgartner, H. (1998). Assessing measurement invariance in cross-national consumer research. *Journal of Consumer Research, 25*(1), 78–90. http://doi.org/10.1086/209528

Thompson, M. S., & Green, S. B. (2013). Evaluating between-group differences in latent variable means. In G. R. Hancock & R. O. Mueller (Eds.), *Structural equation modeling: A second course* (2nd ed., pp. 163–218). Charlotte, NC: Information Age Publishing.

Tragant, E., Thompson, M. S., & Victori, M. (2013). Understanding foreign language learning strategies: A validation study. *System, 41*(1), 95–108. http://doi.org/10.1016/j.system.2013.01.007

Treiblmaier, H., Bentler, P. M., & Mair, P. (2011). Formative constructs implemented via common factors. *Structural Equation Modeling: A Multidisciplinary Journal, 18*(1), 1–17. http://doi.org/10.1080/10705511.2011.532693

Vandenberg, R. J., & Lance, C. E. (2000). A review and synthesis of the measurement invariance literature: Suggestions, practices, and recommendations for organizational research. *Organizational Research Methods, 3*(1), 4–70. http://doi.org/10.1177/109442810031002

Widaman, K. F., Ferrer, E., & Conger, R. D. (2010). Factorial invariance within longitudinal structural equation models: Measuring the same construct across time. *Child Development Perspectives, 4*(1), 10–18. http://doi.org/10.1111/j.1750-8606.2009.00110.x

Widaman, K. F., & Reise, S. P. (1997). Exploring the measurement invariance of psychological instruments: Applications in the substance use domain. In K. J. Bryant & S. G. West (Eds.), *The science of prevention: Methodological advances from alcohol and substance abuse research* (pp. 281–324). Washington, DC: American Psychological Association.

Widaman, K. F., & Thompson, J. S. (2003). On specifying the null model for incremental fit indices in structural equation modeling. *Psychological Methods, 8*(1), 16. http://doi.org/10.1037/1082-989X. 8.1.16

Wu, A. D., Li, Z., & Zumbo, B. D. (2007). Decoding the meaning of factorial invariance and updating the practice of multi-group confirmatory factor analysis: A demonstration with TIMSS data. *Practical Assessment, Research and Evaluation, 12*(3), 1–26.

Yoon, M., & Millsap, R. E. (2007). Detecting violations of factorial invariance using data-based specification searches: A Monte Carlo study. *Structural Equation Modeling: A Multidisciplinary Journal, 14*(3), 435–463. http://doi.org/10.1080/10705510701301677

Part VI

Topics of Special Relevance

Chapter 12

Bifactor Modeling in Construct Validation of Multifactored Tests: Implications for Understanding Multidimensional Constructs and Test Interpretation

Gary L. Canivez

Department of Psychology, Eastern Illinois University, Charleston, IL, USA

Factor analytic methods (exploratory [EFA] and confirmatory [CFA]) are integral parts of test development in both construction and later construct validation. Some examinations of test structure may originate at the item level, examining interrelationships or covariance among a set of items. Some examinations of test structure may originate at the subtest level, examining the interrelationships or covariance among a set of subtests. Yet another means of examination would be to examine interrelationships or covariance among items or subtests gathered from multiple different measures thought to measure the same or related latent constructs. Determining item or subtest retention and assignment to latent dimensions is a first step in test construction but understanding the latent dimensions captured by a psychological test and evaluating their psychometric characteristics is critical for application (interpretation) once the test is constructed. Interpretation of a test score from a unidimensional measure is rather straight forward as there will be only one score to report, but interpretation of *scores* produced by a multidimensional measure is more complicated and requires thorough examination and understanding of the reliability and validity of *each* of the provided scores as well as any comparisons between scores. The purpose and focus of this chapter is to present and illustrate use of the bifactor model, which is a model that is increasingly used for understanding the structure of multifactor tests and assisting in determining which scores can be appropriately interpreted. While bifactor modeling can also be applied to item level indicators, this was recently well illustrated with relationships to item response theory applications by Reise (2012) and thus, not included as part of this chapter. The bifactor model has important implications for both understanding the structure of a test as well as interpretation of various scores. To facilitate understanding and application of the bifactor model, comparisons are made to various alternate models used to explain the interrelationships among a set of subtest indicators. Finally, a research example is used to illustrate exploratory *and* confirmatory bifactor modeling with one of the most popular and frequently used intelligence tests for children, the Wechsler Intelligence Scale for Children-Fourth Edition (WISC-IV; Wechsler, 2003). While bifactor modeling has primarily been applied to intelligence tests (see Canivez, 2011, 2014a; Canivez & Watkins, 2010a, 2010b; Chen, Hayes, Carver, Laurenceau, & Zhang, 2012; Gignac, 2005, 2006, 2008; Gignac & Watkins, 2013; Holzinger & Harman, 1938; Holzinger & Swineford, 1937; Watkins, 2006, 2010), it has been applied to personality tests (see Ackerman, Donnellan, & Robins, 2012; Chen et al., 2012) and psychopathology tests (see Brouwer, Meijer, & Zevalkink, 2013), but too few researchers and many fewer clinicians are familiar with its use even with intelligence tests.

Introduction/Central Issues

Constructs and the tests designed to measure them may be unidimensional or multidimensional and various factor analytic methods will assist in determining whether a collection of indicators (items or subtests) are unidimensional or multidimensional. When a test is unidimensional (see Figure 12.1) the covariance among the group of indicators is associated with one latent factor or dimension. Essentially all indicators will be correlated with one another and converge on one factor.

Multidimensional constructs and tests that reflect multiple factors allow for different ways of explaining relationships among the indicators and the factors or dimensions extracted (EFA) or specified (CFA). When multiple factors are uncorrelated or reasonably uncorrelated ($r < .33$; Tabachnick & Fidell, 2007) in oblique rotation of extracted factors, then an orthogonal rotation may be justified and the latent factors will be independent (uncorrelated). Interpretation of such orthogonal dimensions is uncomplicated, as each factor may be considered distinct from all the others. Figure 12.2 illustrates a structural measurement model for a hypothetical multidimensional test structure where the multiple latent factors are uncorrelated (orthogonal). However, when multiple factors *are* correlated ($r \geq .33$; Tabachnick & Fidell, 2007) in oblique rotations then the latent dimensions are not independent and the correlations between the multiple factors must be accommodated. In this situation there are three competing measurement models that could represent the test structure. Model 1 in Figure 12.3 presents the measurement model corresponding to a correlated factors or oblique measurement model. This illustrates the relationship between the latent factors and the indicators as well as the correlations *between* the latent factors. Interpretation of correlated factors is more complicated due to the shared variance among the factors. While some might like to use this structure to guide inter-

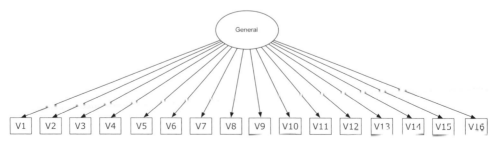

Figure 12.1. Unidimensional measurement model for a hypothetical test with 16 observed variables (indicators V1–V16).

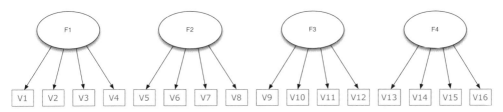

Figure 12.2. Orthogonal (uncorrelated) multidimensional measurement model for a hypothetical test with 16 observed variables (indicators V1–V16) and four uncorrelated latent first-order factors.

pretations of factor score patterns or profiles, the correlated factors obfuscate common variance (Reise, 2012). However, the correlated factors (oblique) model is considered insufficient because correlated factors imply a higher-order or hierarchical factor or factors that must be explicated (Gorsuch, 1983; Thompson, 1990, 2004).

One way to address correlated (oblique) factors is to subject the oblique factor correlation matrix to a higher-order factor analysis. In EFA, one may factor analyze the first-order factor correlation matrix and generate a higher-order factor (or factors). In CFA this higher-order structure is specified as part of the modeling process. Model 2 in Figure 12.3 illustrates the higher-order CFA structure. This measurement model has paths specified from a second-order factor to the first-order factors, which in turn have paths leading to the observed indicators. In the higher-order model the influence of the second-order factor on the observed indicators is indirect. McDonald (1999) referred to this model as the *indirect hierarchical model*, which is terminology that has subsequently been used by others (e.g., Canivez, 2014a; Gignac, 2008; Watkins, 2010). The second-order factor influence on observed indicators is fully mediated by the first-order factors (Yung, Thissen, & McLeod, 1999). How much influence the second-order factor has on the observed indicators is obscured and an important question regarding higher-order models is whether influences of a higher-order factor *should be* fully mediated by first-order factors (Gignac, 2005, 2006, 2008).

Model 3 in Figure 12.3 illustrates the bifactor measurement model. This model is a rival to the higher-order model and has a general factor (analogous to the second-order factor in the higher-order model), which has direct paths to all the observed indicators and has specific group factors with direct paths to the observed indicators related to that specific factor. In the bifactor model both the general factor (broad) and the specific group factors/subscales (narrow) have direct influences on the observed indicators and the specific group factors *do not* mediate the influence of the broad, general factor. In contrast to the higher-order model where the higher-order factor is a superordinate dimension, the bifactor model establishes the general dimension as a breadth dimension (Gignac, 2008; Humphreys, 1981) and can be considered more parsimonious (Gignac, 2006).

In tests of intelligence such as the Wechsler Intelligence Scale for Children-Fourth Edition (WISC-IV, Wechsler, 2003) there are subtest scores, factor (index) scores, and an omnibus, Full Scale score that represent different levels of the test. When CFA procedures are applied the subtests are the observed indicators while the first-order factors are correlated latent dimensions (see Figure 12.5) and the general factor implied by correlated first-order factors can be modeled as a higher-order latent dimension (see Figure 12.6) or as a parallel broad general dimension to the narrow, specific group factors (see Figure 12.7). When one concentrates interpretation on the individual scores (subtests or first-order factors) the influence of broad/

Model 1

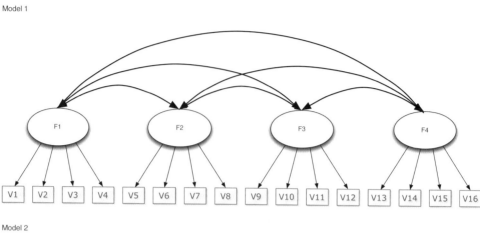

Model 2

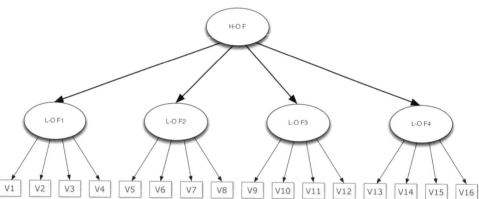

Model 3

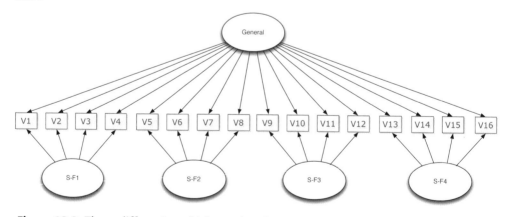

Figure 12.3. Three different multidimensional measurement models for a hypothetical test with 16 observed variables (indicators V1–V16) and four latent first-order factors. Model 1 is the oblique (correlated) factor model, Model 2 is the higher-order (indirect hierarchical) factor model with one higher-order (H O) and four lower-order (L-O) factors, and Model 3 is the bifactor (nested factor/direct hierarchical) model with one general and four specific (S) factors.

general construct is conflated while concentration of interpretation on an omnibus, total score may miss important unique contributions provided by specific facets (Chen et al., 2012). For individuals it is not possible to disentangle the two sources of common variance (general and specific group factor). The bifactor model is less ambiguous than a higher-order model because it simultaneously discloses effects provided by a broad, general dimension while also disclosing effects of narrow, specific dimensions (Chen et al., 2012; Reise, 2012).

Conceptual Principles

The Bifactor Model

The bifactor model was first proposed and illustrated by Holzinger and Swineford (1937) and Holzinger and Harman (1938), although their method is no longer used (Jennrich & Bentler, 2011). There are both exploratory *and* confirmatory approaches to bifactor modeling. Alternate names for the bifactor model that appear in the literature include the nested factors model (Gustafsson & Balke, 1993) and the direct hierarchical model (e.g., Canivez, 2014a; Gignac, 2008, McDonald, 1999; Watkins, 2010). Gignac's original use of the term *direct hierarchical* was influenced by McDonald and relates to the direct influence of the general factor on subtest indicators in a bifactor model as opposed to the *indirect hierarchical* influence of the general factor on subtests mediated by first-order factors (Gignac, 2008; McDonald, 1999).

The bifactor model offers a number of key advantages including:
1. The general factor is easy to interpret with direct influences on indicators as this implies inferences directly from the subtest indicators rather than inferences from inferences (factors) (or interpretations based on other interpretations) present in the higher-order model, which Gorsuch (1983) noted was ambiguous;
2. Both general *and* specific influences on indicators (subtests) can be examined *simultaneously*, which allows for judgments of general and specific group scale importance (Gorsuch, 1983; Reise, 2012; Reise, More, & Haviland, 2010);
3. The psychometric properties necessary for determining scoring and interpretation of the general dimension and subscales may be examined (i.e., model based reliability using Omega-hierarchical and Omega-subscale [Reise, 2012; Zinbarg, Yovel, Revelle, & McDonald, 2006]); and
4. Unique contributions of the general and specific group factors in predicting external criteria or variables may be assessed (Chen et al., 2012; Chen, West, & Sousa, 2006; Gignac, 2006, 2008; Reise et al., 2010).

Exploratory Bifactor Model

The exploratory bifactor model has historically and most frequently been estimated by the Schmid and Leiman (1957) orthogonalization procedure (Jennrich & Bentler, 2011; Reise, 2012). The Schmid–Leiman (SL) procedure transforms "an oblique factor analysis solution containing a hierarchy of higher-order factors into an orthogonal solution which not only preserves the desired interpretation characteristics of the oblique solution, but also discloses the hierarchical structuring of the variables" (Schmid & Leiman, 1957, p. 53). It is a reparameterization of a higher-order model (Reise, 2012). Thus, subtest or indicator common variance is apportioned first to the higher-order factor and the residual common variance is then apportioned to the lower-order factors. This solution, "not only preserves the desired interpretation characteristics of the oblique solution, but also discloses the hierarchical structuring of the variables" (Schmid & Leiman, 1957, p. 53). It is this feature that led Carroll (1995) to insist on SL orthogonalization of higher-order models:

> I argue, as many have done, that from the standpoint of analysis and ready interpretation, results should be shown on the basis of orthogonal factors, rather than oblique, correlated factors. I insist, however, that the orthogonal factors should be those produced by the Schmid-Leiman (1957) orthogonalization procedure, and thus include second-stratum and possibly third-stratum factors. (p. 437)

Procedurally the first step in the traditional method of exploratory bifactor modeling is conducting an exploratory factor analysis (principal factors) of the subtests or indicators using an oblique rotation. Following the oblique rotation a second-order exploratory factor analysis of the first-order factor correlation matrix would be conducted. Next the Schmid–Leiman transformation would be applied to apportion subtest or indicator variance to the higher-order dimension and the lower-order specific group factors. The MacOrtho program produced by Watkins (2004) is available for Mac and Windows OS and is perhaps the easiest to use and is based on the instructions provided by Thompson (2004). MacOrtho is available as freeware from http://www.edpsychassociates.com. Thompson (1990) also described this procedure and SPSS syntax is also provided in Thompson (2004). Wolff and Preising (2005) also provided SPSS and SAS syntax code for the SL procedure. From the MacOrtho results, which provide orthogonal standardized coefficients of subtest or indicator loadings with the higher-order and lower-order factors, one may square the loadings to yield variance estimates (see Table 12.3). Results then disclose the portions of subtest or indicator variance associated with the general higher-order factor and the variance associated with the specific first-order factor. In this exploratory bifactor solution subtest variance attributable to alternate first-order factors will also be disclosed (i.e., cross-loadings).

While the SL procedure is the most commonly used method for estimating an exploratory bifactor model it is not without some potential limitations. As pointed out by Yung et al. (1999) and others (Chen et al., 2006; Reise, 2012) the SL transformation of a higher-order model includes a proportionality constraint of general and specific variance ratios. Reise (2012) also noted that nonzero cross-loadings are problematic and the larger the cross-loadings the greater the distortion of overestimating general factor loadings and underestimating specific group factor loadings. Such cross-loadings might suggest problems with the scale content, however. As stated by Brunner, Nagy, and Wilhelm (2012):

> The proportionality constraint limits the value of the higher order factor model in providing insights into the relationship between general and specific abilities, on the one hand, and other psychological constructs, sociodemographic characteristics, or life outcomes, on the other. (p. 811)

However, how prevalent this is with real data is as yet unknown (Jennrich & Bentler, 2011) and it is possible that this issue may be more theoretical than real. Bifactor models, however, do not suffer from such proportionality constraints.

Recently, several exploratory bifactor modeling alternatives have been developed. Jennrich and Bentler (2011) reported on the development of an exploratory bifactor analysis using an orthogonal bifactor rotation criterion and related it to the SL procedure while Jennrich and Bentler (2012) reported on the development of an exploratory bifactor analysis using an oblique bifactor rotation criterion. These will likely be the topic of comparative research in the coming years and may offer useful alternatives to the SL procedure. Finally, Reise, Moore, and Maydeu-Oliveres (2011) developed and evaluated a target bifactor rotation method. These three exploratory bifactor methods avoid the proportionality constraints of the SL procedure applied to higher-order models. Dombrowski (2014b) compared EFA results from the SL procedure and the exploratory bifactor analysis (Jennrich & Bentler, 2012) and found similar results suggesting Reise et al. (2010) may be correct that proportionality constraint may be inconsequential with real data.

Confirmatory Bifactor Model

To provide evaluation of competing structural models in explaining the latent dimensions of an instrument, CFA procedures are used. In CFA, specific plausible theoretical structural models are examined to evaluate fit to data. When specifying a bifactor model, paths or associations from the broad general dimension are included to all subtest indicators *and* paths or associations from specific group dimensions are included to theoretically related subtest indicators. Thus, each subtest indicator will have one path from its specific group factor and one path from the broad general factor (see Model 3, Figure 12.3 and Figure 12.7). This is in contrast to the higher-order model where the specified model has specific group factor paths to related subtest indicators while the higher-order general factor has paths to each of the specific group factors (see Model 2, Figure 12.3 and Figure 12.6). Chen et al. (2012) also noted an advantage of the bifactor model in that when there were only two indicators a bifactor model may be applied but higher-order models require at least three indicators. Yung et al. (1999) noted that differences between the bifactor model and the higher-order model have a qualitative distinction that may also be quantitatively evaluated using a χ^2 difference test. Thus it is possible to evaluate which model provides the better explanation and determine whether the latent structure should illustrate the broad general dimension as a breadth factor (Humphreys, 1981) or as a superordinate factor.

Standardized coefficients produced by the CFA that are estimated for the paths from the general dimension to the subtest indicators and those estimated for the paths from the specific group factors to the subtest indicators are analogous to the similar coefficients produced by the SL transformation (see Table 12.5). However, in the case of CFA, the absence of paths from alternate specific group factors to subtest indicators not associated with that factor means they are fixed to zero even though in reality they may be small (and possibly moderate) nonzero values. Procedures such as Bayesian SEM (Golay, Reverte, Rossier, Favez, & Lecerf, 2013) or exploratory SEM (Asparouhov & Muthen, 2009) may assist with this issue by estimating small, nonzero path coefficients. The standardized path coefficients from the CFA bifactor model may be illustrated as in Table 12.5, which is similar to those in Table 12.3 produced by the SL transformation, but as illustrated in Table 12.5 there are no coefficients for subtests on rival or alternate specific group factors (these are set to zero). Similar to Table 12.3 the standardized coefficients may be squared to provide variance estimates for the broad general factor and the specific group factors.

Model-Based Reliability Estimates

In psychometrics is it common for reliability to be estimated by coefficient alpha, KR-20, or Spearman-Brown corrected split-half correlations. Chen et al. (2012) however, noted that "for multidimensional constructs, the alpha coefficient is complexly determined, and McDonald's omega-hierarchical (ω_h; 1999) provides a better estimate for the composite score and thus should be used" (p. 228). Bifactor (nested, direct hierarchical) models are prime examples where the variance of each observed measure is complexly determined and "omega hierarchical is an appropriate model-based reliability index when item response data are consistent with a bifactor structure" (Reise, 2012, p. 689). The same may be applied when subtests are the indicators. A prerequisite to using omega is a well-fitting, completely orthogonal bifactor model. While calculating decomposed variance estimates for SL transformed higher-order structures or bifactor models is common, calculation of omega is not, but is increasing (see Canivez, 2014a; Canivez & Watkins, 2010a, 2010b; Dombrowski, 2014a).

The value of omega is that it may assist in helping determine which composite scales possess sufficient reliable variance to be interpreted. As originally created, omega (ω) is a model based reliability estimate that combines higher-order and lower-order factors (Brunner et al., 2012; Zinbarg, Revelle, Yovel, & Li, 2005; Zinbarg et al., 2006). However, in the case of a bifactor model it is necessary to separately estimate the reliability of the broad general dimension as well as the specific group dimensions with the influences of the others removed. Omega-hierarchical (ω_h) is the model based reliability estimate of one target construct with others removed (Brunner et al., 2012; McDonald, 1999; Zinbarg et al., 2005; Zinbarg et al., 2006). Reise (2012) used this same approach, but in order to provide greater specificity, provided a slightly different name when applied to the specific group factors.

Omega-subscale (ω_s) is the model based reliability estimate of one specific group factor with all other group *and* general factors removed (Reise, 2012). Omega estimates (ω_h and ω_s) may be obtained from either CFA-based bifactor solutions or EFA SL-based bifactor solutions. Watkins (2013) created the Omega program to easily calculate these estimates (freeware available for Mac and Windows OS at http://www.edpsychassociates.com). Examination and evaluation of ω_h and ω_s will assist the researcher and clinician in determining if there is sufficient reliable variance associated with the broad general dimension and the specific group factors. It is possible that a multidimensional instrument could have a very high ω_h coefficient but low ω_s coefficients that would indicate primary unidimensionality, but it is also possible that an instrument might have a somewhat lower ω_h coefficient and much larger ω_s coefficients that would indicate greater importance of the specific group factors. It has been suggested that omega coefficients should exceed .50 at a minimum, but .75 would be preferred (Reise, 2012; Reise, Bonifay, & Haviland, 2013).

Research Examples

To illustrate the use of bifactor modeling in comparison to other models using exploratory and confirmatory approaches, a data set that was the basis for a recently published study utilizing bifactor modeling (Canivez, 2014a) was used. This data set includes Wechsler Intelligence Scale for Children-Fourth Edition (WISC-IV; Wechsler, 2003) scores from clinical evaluations of children referred for learning difficulties in one medium size public school district. The sample of 345 children between the ages of 6 and 16 years had complete data for all 10 WISC-IV core subtests necessary for producing the global FSIQ and the four factor index scores (Verbal Comprehension [VC], Perceptual Reasoning [PR], Working Memory [WM], Processing Speed [PS]). Pearson product-moment correlations and descriptive statistics are presented in Table 12.1 to illustrate the subtest interrelationships and that subtest scores were normally distributed. EFA is a method of extracting latent factors from the correlation matrix of the indicators and allow "the data to speak for themselves" (Carroll, 1995, p. 436) while CFA is a method of proposing various theoretical measurement models and empirically testing which fits data best. Gorsuch (1983) noted greater confidence in the latent structure of a test when both EFA and CFA were in agreement. Carroll (1995) and Reise (2012) noted that EFA procedures are particularly useful in suggesting possible models to be tested in CFA. What follows are EFA and CFA illustrating application of bifactor solutions in understanding the latent structure of the WISC-IV with the referred sample of 345 children.

Table 12.1. Pearson correlations and descriptive statistics for Wechsler Intelligence Scale for Children-Fourth Edition (WISC-IV) core subtests with a referred sample (*N* = 345)

Subtest	BD	SI	DS	PCn	CD	VO	LN	MR	CO	SS
Block Design (BD)										
Similarities (SI)	.539									
Digit Span (DS)	.397	.386								
Picture Concepts (PCn)	.501	.489	.368							
Coding (CD)	.257	.242	.217	.313						
Vocabulary (VO)	.503	.732	.417	.467	.267					
Letter-Number Sequencing (LN)	.462	.439	.459	.470	.291	.560				
Matrix Reasoning (MR)	.701	.517	.393	.507	.295	.555	.511			
Comprehension (CO)	.426	.643	.404	.484	.342	.723	.499	.462		
Symbol Search (SS)	.518	.423	.383	.399	.511	.472	.428	.515	.428	
M	7.660	7.840	7.590	9.080	7.550	7.380	7.310	8.320	8.090	7.850
SD	3.251	2.928	2.909	3.203	2.724	2.969	3.221	3.090	2.812	3.271
Sk	0.270	0.513	0.310	−0.279	0.123	0.453	−0.211	0.188	−0.180	−0.269
K	−0.389	0.255	0.295	−0.256	−0.081	0.517	−0.520	0.037	0.079	−0.551

Note. Sk = skewness; *K* = kurtosis. Mardia's (1970) multivariate kurtosis estimate was 1.17.

Example 1: Exploratory Bifactor Analysis With the SL Method

Principal axis (principal factors) EFA (SPSS v. 21) produced a Kaiser–Meyer–Olkin measure of sampling adequacy coefficient of .894 (exceeding the .60 criterion; Tabachnick & Fidell, 2007) and Bartlett's Test of Sphericity was 1,663.05, $p < .0001$, indicating that the correlation matrix was not random. Communality estimates ranged from .337 to .994 (*Mdn* = .666). Given the communality estimates, number of variables, and factors, the sample size was judged adequate for factor analytic procedures (Fabrigar, Wegener, MacCallum, & Strahan, 1999; Floyd & Widaman, 1995; MacCallum, Widaman, Zhang, & Hong, 1999). Multiple criteria as recommended by Gorsuch (1983) were examined and included eigenvalues > 1 (Guttman, 1954), visual scree test (Cattell, 1966), standard error of scree (SE_{Scree}; Zoski & Jurs, 1996) as recommended by Nasser, Benson, and Wisenbaker (2002) and programmed by Watkins (2007), Horn's parallel analysis (HPA; Horn, 1965) as programmed by Watkins (2000) with 100 replications (see Figure 12.4), and minimum average partials (MAP; Velicer, 1976) using the SPSS code supplied by O'Connor (2000). *All* criteria indicated only one factor *should* be

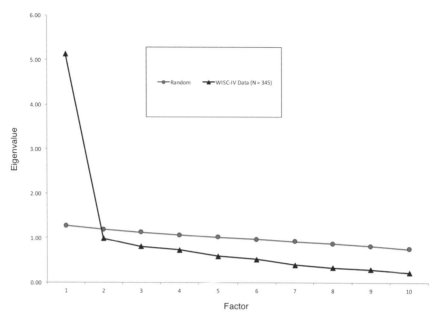

Figure 12.4. Scree plots for Horn's parallel analysis for the 10 WISC-IV core subtests with a referred sample (*N* = 345).

extracted (illustrating the dominance of the general intelligence dimension) but theory suggested four latent first-order factors (VC, PR, WM, PS).

To explore and illustrate the WISC-IV *multidimensional* structure, four factors were extracted and obliquely rotated with promax (*k* = 4; Gorsuch, 2003). Results are presented in Table 12.2 and show that when four factors were extracted to be consistent with the underlying theory, 9 of the 10 WISC-IV core subtests demonstrated salient factor pattern coefficients (≥ .30; Child, 2006) on the theoretically consistent factor but one salient cross-loading on an alternate factor was observed (Symbol Search). The Picture Concepts subtest did not have a salient coefficient on any of the four factors although its highest factor pattern coefficient was on the theoretically consistent factor (PR). Symbol Search, however, had its highest pattern coefficient on a theoretically inconsistent factor (PR) that was slightly higher than the pattern coefficient on its theoretically consistent factor (PS). These anomalies are likely due to sampling error as such findings are rarely obtained. Of greater importance, however, are the correlations between the four extracted factors (see Table 12.2). The moderate to high factor correlations (.398 to .729) imply a higher-order or hierarchical factor that requires explication (Gorsuch, 1983; Thompson, 1990, 2004) and thus ending analyses at this point is premature for full understanding of the WISC-IV structure.

The four first-order factors were then orthogonalized using the Schmid and Leiman (SL, 1957) procedure as programmed in the MacOrtho computer program (Watkins, 2004), which uses the procedure described in Thompson (1990). Carroll (1995) insisted that correlated factors be orthogonalized by the SL procedure and, as stated by Schmid & Leiman (1957), this transforms:

> An oblique factor analysis solution containing a hierarchy of higher-order factors into an orthogonal solution which not only preserves the desired interpretation characteristics of the oblique solution, but also discloses the hierarchical structuring of the variables. (p. 53)

Table 12.2. Factor pattern and structure coefficients from principal axis extraction of four WISC-IV factors with promax ($k = 4$) rotation and factor correlations

Subtest	g[a]	Factor pattern coefficients				Factor structure coefficients			
		VC	PR	WM	PS	VC	PR	WM	PS
Similarities	.757	**.839**	.183	-.169	-.042	.826	.625	.552	.291
Vocabulary	.812	**.852**	-.021	.093	-.049	.886	.611	.676	.325
Comprehension	.746	**.784**	-.133	.120	.076	.810	.524	.634	.388
Block Design	.747	-.028	**.972**	-.062	-.056	.575	.886	.573	.315
Picture Concepts	.643	.192	.281	.216	.055	.566	.589	.579	.352
Matrix Reasoning	.748	.042	**.690**	.123	-.013	.602	.800	.631	.353
Digit Span	.548	.084	.123	**.428**	-.015	.474	.474	.568	.270
Letter–Number Sequencing	.695	-.002	-.005	**.839**	-.049	.587	.562	.812	.341
Coding	.507	-.014	-.040	-.046	**1.037**	.339	.357	.401	.994
Symbol Search	.655	.061	***.356***	.120	**.315**	.520	.615	.561	.546
Eigenvalue		5.134	.990	.727	.806				
variance %		47.889	8.826	2.936	5.387				
Factor correlation matrix									
VC		1							
PR		.689	1						
WM		.729	.701	1					
PS		.398	.422	.467	1				

Note. WISC-IV = Wechsler Intelligence Scale for Children–Fourth Edition; g = General Intelligence; VC = Verbal Comprehension; PR = Perceptual Reasoning; WM = Working Memory; PS = Processing Speed. WISC-IV factors listed in order most commonly presented although the PS factor accounted for somewhat greater variance than the WM factor in this sample. Salient factor pattern coefficients presented in bold. Factor pattern coefficients in italics denote salient loading on alternate factor than theoretically proposed.
[a]Factor structure coefficients from first unrotated factor (g-loadings) are correlations between the subtest and the general factor.

In order to enter appropriate data into the program it was necessary to first perform a second-order factor analysis of the four WISC-IV factors correlation matrix (presented in Table 12.2). The extraction of one factor from the four factors correlation matrix produced communalities from the second-order solution and factor structure coefficients for the second-order solution. The Schmid–Leiman (SL) procedure uses the first-order factor pattern coefficients matrix, second-order communalities, and second-order coefficients to apportion subtest variance to the higher-order, first-order, or to the subtest (specific and error variance). The resulting set of SL coefficients (b) and their variance (Var) estimates (b^2) from the present WISC-IV analyses are presented in Table 12.3. Thus, *both* the multidimensionality of subtests (associations with the four latent dimensions) *and* the huge influence of the general dimension are illustrated. In this specific case, as frequently observed in measurement of intelligence, most reliable common subtest variance is apportioned to or associated with the broad, general dimension (general intelligence [g]) and substantially less apportioned to the narrow, specific (group) dimensions (Bodin, Pardini, Burns, & Stevens, 2009; Canivez, 2008, 2011, 2014a; Canivez, Konold, Collins, & Wilson, 2009; Canivez & Watkins, 2010a, 2010b; Dombrowski, 2013, 2014a, 2014b; Dombrowski & Watkins, 2013; Dombrowski, Watkins, & Brogan, 2009; Gignac, 2005, 2006; Gignac & Watkins, 2013; Golay & Lecerf, 2011; Golay et al., 2013; Nelson & Canivez, 2012; Nelson, Canivez, Lindstrom, & Hatt, 2007; Nelson, Canivez, & Watkins, 2013; Niilekssela, Reynolds, & Kaufman, 2013; Watkins, 2006; Watkins, 2010, Watkins & Beaujean, 2014; Watkins, Canivez, James, Good, & James, 2013; Watkins, Wilson, Kotz, Carbone, & Babula, 2006). Without applying a method such as the SL procedure to apportion subtest variance there is no way to know how much subtest variance is associated with the first-order group factor and how much is really associated with a more general, hierarchical/higher-order factor.

Another interesting difference between results from the first-order oblique solution and the SL results in the present data analyses relates to the two subtests that failed to conform to theoretical expectations in the oblique four-factor model. With regard to Picture Concepts, the SL apportionment of 36.7% of its reliable variance to the general dimension was reasonable and the largest portion of residual reliable variance, albeit small at 2.6%, was with its theoretically consistent factor (PR). With regard to the Symbol Search subtest, after apportioning 37% of its reliable variance to the general dimension it no longer had its highest coefficient on the PR factor. Symbol Search had a higher portion of residual reliable variance apportioned to its theoretically consistent specific group factor (PS).

One final important analysis relates to the estimates of reliability of latent factors and the extent to which specific group factors are interpretable. In order for scales to be interpretable they must have appreciable true score variance. Most tests report coefficients alpha or other similar methods (split-half) for estimating the internal consistency of scores but there has been significant criticism of this index in multidimensional measures and alternative model based reliability estimates have been promoted (Chen et al., 2012; Schweizer, 2011; Sijtsma, 2009; Yang & Green, 2011). Omega-hierarchical (ω_h) and omega-subscale (ω_s) are more appropriate indicators of proportion of reliable variance attributable to the latent construct (Zinbarg et al., 2006). Table 12.3 also presents ω_h and ω_s estimates for the present WISC-IV data set based on the SL coefficients.

Omega hierarchical (ω_h) coefficient presented in Table 12.3 provided an estimate of the reliability of the latent general intelligence construct with the effects of other constructs removed as programmed by Watkins (2013) based on the tutorial by Brunner et al. (2012) who used formulae provided by Zinbarg et al. (2006). The ω_h coefficient for general intelligence (.827) was high and sufficient for interpretation. Omega subscale (ω_s) coefficients for the four WISC-IV indexes presented in Table 12.3 estimated the scale reliabilities with the effects of the general factor and other group factors removed and ranged from .128 (WM) to .428 (PS). These results

Table 12.3. Sources of variance in the Wechsler Intelligence Scale for Children-Fourth Edition for the referred sample (N = 345) according to an orthogonalized (Schmid & Leiman, 1957) higher-order factor model

Subtest	General		VC		PR		WM		PS		h^2	u^2
	b	Var	b	Var	b	Var	b	Var	b	Var		
Similarities	.676	.457	**.469**	.220	.106	.011	-.082	.007	-.036	.001	.696	.304
Vocabulary	.746	.557	**.477**	.228	-.012	.000	.045	.002	-.042	.002	.788	.212
Comprehension	.685	.469	**.439**	.193	-.077	.006	.058	.003	.065	.004	.675	.325
Block Design	.688	.473	-.016	.000	**.561**	.315	-.030	.001	-.048	.002	.792	.208
Picture Concepts	.606	.367	.107	.011	**.162**	.026	.104	.011	.047	.002	.418	.582
Matrix Reasoning	.700	.490	.023	.001	**.398**	.158	.059	.003	-.011	.000	.653	.347
Digit Span	.537	.288	.047	.002	.071	.005	**.207**	.043	-.013	.000	.339	.661
Letter–Number Sequencing	.704	.496	-.001	.000	-.003	.000	**.405**	.164	-.042	.002	.661	.339
Coding	.426	.181	-.008	.000	-.023	.001	-.022	.000	**.859**	.738	.920	.080
Symbol Search	.608	.370	.034	.001	.205	.042	.058	.003	**.271**	.073	.490	.510
% Total Variance	41.5		6.6		5.6		2.4		8.3		64.3	35.7
% Common Variance	64.5		10.2		8.8		3.7		12.8		100	
	ω_h = .827		ω_s = .265		ω_s = .196		ω_s = .128		ω_s = .428			

Note. b = Standardized loading of subtest on factor; Var = variance (b^2) explained in the subtest; h^2 = communality; u^2 = uniqueness; VC = Verbal Comprehension; PR = Perceptual Reasoning; WM = Working Memory; PS = Processing Speed; ω_h = Omega Hierarchical; ω_s = Omega Subscale. Largest first-order factor coefficients presented in bold.

indicated that in the present sample the four specific WISC-IV group factors possessed too little reliable variance for clinicians to confidently interpret (Reise, 2012; Reise et al., 2013).

Example 2: Confirmatory Bifactor Analysis

The present data set was used in the CFA study recently published (Canivez, 2014a). In the CFA approach various measurement models that are theoretically possible explanations for the covariance among indicators are specified and compared. With respect to the WISC-IV, theoretical and historical structures that have evolved have included a unidimensional (general intelligence) model, a two-factor model (verbal and performance), three-factor model (verbal comprehension, perceptual organization, freedom from distractibility), and a four-factor model (verbal comprehension, perceptual reasoning, working memory, processing speed). The two-, three-, and four-factor models all have correlated factors so examination of higher-order and bifactor models that account for the correlated first-order dimensions are also needed.

Table 12.4 presents results of 6 different hypothesized measurement models for the 10 core WISC-IV subtests as estimated in EQS, Version 6.2 (Bentler & Wu, 2012), using maximum likelihood estimation. Because the WM and PS factors are estimated by only two indicators (i.e., just identified) the two subtests were constrained to be equal in the bifactor model to ensure specification. Results showed increasingly better fit from one to four factors but the one-, two-, and three-factor models did not achieve good fit (CFI > .95 and/or RMSEA < .06) to these data and were judged inadequate. Of the four first-order models the four oblique factor model was the best fitting and is illustrated in Figure 12.5. Because these four factors are highly correlated, a higher-order or hierarchical structure is implied and must be explicated (Gorsuch, 1983, 2003; Thompson, 1990, 2004). While chi-square difference tests found the bifactor model to be a statistically better fit to these data than the four oblique factor model ($\Delta\chi^2 = 10.72$, $\Delta df = 2$, $p < .01$) and the higher-order model ($\Delta\chi^2 = 14.33$, $\Delta df = 4$, $p < .01$), meaningful differences in fit statistics based on criteria from Cheung and Rensvold (2002; ΔCFI > .01) and Chen (2007; ΔRMSEA > −.015) were not observed. AIC estimates also indicated the bifactor model to be best of all tested models. Based on Hu and Bentler's (1998, 1999) dual criteria, both the bifactor model and the higher-order model were well-fitting models.

Table 12.4. CFA fit statistics for the Wechsler Intelligence Scale for Children-Fourth Edition among 345 children

Model	χ^2	df	CFI	RMSEA	RMSEA 90% CI	AIC
One factor	256.47	35	.865	.136	[.120, .151]	186.47
Two oblique factors (V & NV)	159.16*	34	.924	.103	[.087, .120]	91.16
Three oblique factors (VC, PR, [WM+PS])	111.91*	32	.951	.085	[.068, .102]	47.91
Four oblique factors (VC, PR, WM, PS)	65.30*	29	.978	.060	[.041, .080]	7.30
Higher-Order (Indirect hierarchical)	68.91	31	.977	.060	[.041, .079]	6.91
Bifactor (Direct hierarchical)[a]	54.58**	27	.983	.054	[.033, .075]	.58

Note. V = Verbal; NV = Nonverbal; VC = Verbal Comprehension; PR = Perceptual Reasoning; WM = Working Memory; PS = Processing Speed; CFI = comparative fit index; RMSEA = root mean square error of approximation; AIC = Akaike information criterion.
[a]Two indicators of WM and PS factors were constrained to be equal to ensure identification.
*Statistically different (p < .001) from previous model. **Statistically different (p < .001) from previous two models. In the Wechsler four factor first-order model, correlation between: VC and PR = .75, VC and WM = .79, VC and PS = .57, PR and WM = .81, PR and PS = .67, and WM and PS = .64.

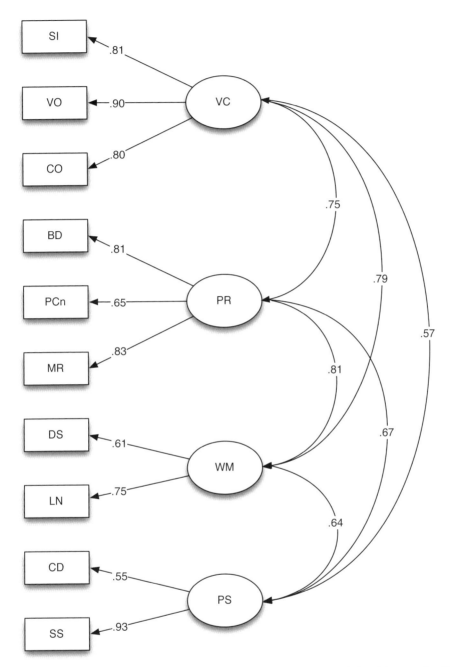

Figure 12.5. Oblique (correlated) four-factor measurement model, with standardized coefficients, for the Wechsler Intelligence Scale for Children-Fourth Edition (Wechsler, 2003) for 345 referred children; SI = Similarities, VO = Vocabulary, CO = Comprehension, BD = Block Design, PCn = Picture Concepts, MR = Matrix Reasoning, DS = Digit Span, LN = Letter-Number Sequencing, CD = Coding, and SS = Symbol Search, VC = Verbal Comprehension factor, PR = Perceptual Reasoning factor, WM = Working Memory factor, PS = Processing Speed factor.

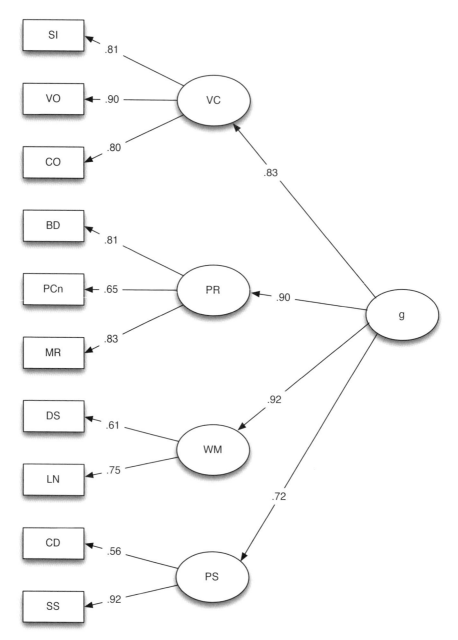

Figure 12.6. Higher-order (indirect hierarchical) measurement model, with standard-
ized coefficients, for the Wechsler Intelligence Scale for Children-Fourth
Edition (Wechsler, 2003) for 345 referred children; SI = Similarities, VO = Vo-
cabulary, CO = Comprehension, BD = Block Design, PCn = Picture Concepts,
MR = Matrix Reasoning, DS = Digit Span, LN = Letter-Number Sequencing,
CD = Coding, and SS = Symbol Search, VC = Verbal Comprehension factor,
PR = Perceptual Reasoning factor, WM = Working Memory factor, PS = Pro-
cessing Speed factor, g = General Intelligence.

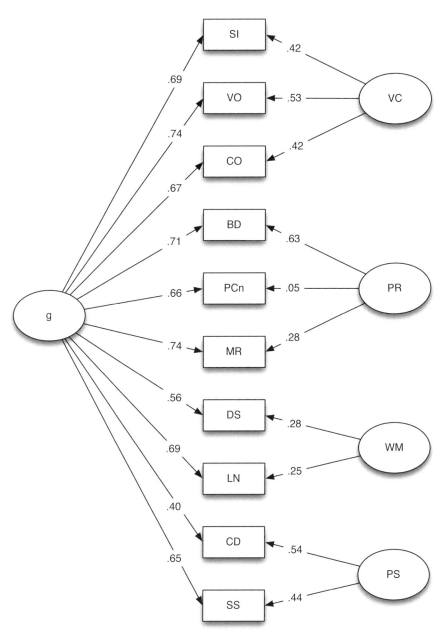

Figure 12.7. Bifactor (nested factors/direct hierarchical) measurement model, with standardized coefficients, for the Wechsler Intelligence Scale for Children-Fourth Edition (Wechsler, 2003) for 345 referred children; SI = Similarities, VO = Vocabulary, CO = Comprehension, BD = Block Design, PCn = Picture Concepts, MR = Matrix Reasoning, DS = Digit Span, LN = Letter-Number Sequencing, CD = Coding, and SS = Symbol Search, VC = Verbal Comprehension factor, PR = Perceptual Reasoning factor, WM = Working Memory factor, PS = Processing Speed factor, g = General Intelligence.

Table 12.5. Sources of variance in the Wechsler Intelligence Scale for Children-Fourth Edition for the referred sample (N = 345) according to the bifactor (nested factor/direct hierarchical) model

Subtest	General		VC		PR		WM		PS		h^2	u^2
	b	Var	b	Var	b	Var	b	Var	b	Var		
Similarities	.691	.477	.417	.174							.651	.349
Vocabulary	.742	.551	.525	.276							.826	.174
Comprehension	.675	.456	.423	.179							.635	.365
Block Design	.708	.501			.605	.366					.867	.133
Picture Concepts	.663	.440			.052	.003					.442	.558
Matrix Reasoning	.741	.549			.290	.084					.633	.367
Digit Span	.561	.315					.281	.079			.394	.606
Letter–Number Sequencing	.692	.479					.254	.065			.543	.457
Coding	.405	.164							.545	.297	.461	.539
Symbol Search	.652	.425							.454	.206	.631	.369
% Total variance	43.6		6.3		4.5		1.4		5.0		60.8	39.2
% Common variance	71.6		10.3		7.4		2.4		8.3		100	
	$\omega_h = .843$		$\omega_s = .259$		$\omega_s = .140$		$\omega_s = .098$		$\omega_s = .330$			

Note. b = Standardized loading of subtest on factor; Var = variance (b^2) explained in the subtest; h^2 = communality; u^2 = uniqueness; VC = Verbal Comprehension; PR = Perceptual Reasoning; WM = Working Memory; PS = Processing Speed; ω_h = Omega Hierarchical; ω_s = Omega Subscale.

To understand differences between the higher-order model (Figure 12.6) and the bifactor model (Figure 12.7) it is useful to compare the two rival measurement models. The standardized measurement model for the higher-order model in Figure 12.6 illustrates high standardized path coefficients from the first-order factors to their subtest indicators as well as the high standardized path coefficients from the higher-order general factor to each of the four first-order factors. In this model the general factor has no direct effects on the subtest indicators. Rather, influence of the general factor on the subtests is fully mediated through the first-order factors and thus its influence on subtest indicators obfuscated. The standardized path coefficients form the first-order factors to the subtests include both the direct influence from the first-order factor *and* mediated influences from the second-order factor. Another conceptualization for this model is that the subtest indicators are observed variables while the first-order factors are inferred from them. First-order factors are, in a sense, abstractions from the observed variables. The same may be said about the second-order factor in that it is an abstraction from the first-order factors due to their correlated nature. Thus, the second-order factor is an abstraction from abstractions (Thompson, 2004)! As such it is difficult to know just what a second-order factor is or means.

The standardized measurement model for the bifactor model (Figure 12.7), however, has high standardized path coefficients from the general factor to the 10 subtest indicators but significantly lower standardized path coefficients from the four specific group factors to their subtest indicators than observed in the higher-order model. Thus, both the general factor *and* the specific group factors independently directly influence subtest performance. Standardized path coefficients in Figure 12.7 show that in most instances the general factor has greater influence on subtest performance and the specific group factors generally have less influence. In contrast to the higher-order model above, both the general factor and the specific group factors are inferred from the subtest indicators.

To fully understand the psychometric properties of the bifactor model for this data set, Table 12.5 presents the sources of variance for the referred sample in the WISC-IV. Table 12.5 illustrates that the proportions of variance from the subtests accounted for by the general factor and the specific factors. The general factor accounted for 71.6% of the common variance while the specific VC, PR, WM, and PS factors accounted for 10.3%, 7.4%, 2.4%, and 8.3% of the common variance, respectively. The general factor accounted for 43.6% of the total variance while the specific VC, PR, WM, and PS factors accounted for 6.3%, 4.5%, 1.4%, and 5.0% of the total variance, respectively. Thus, as observed in the exploratory bifactor model prescribed by the SL transformation, the general factor accounted for substantially greater portions of WISC-IV common and total variance relative to the specific group factors.

One final important analysis relates to the reliability estimates of latent factors and the extent to which specific group factors are interpretable. In order for scales to be interpretable they must have appreciable true score variance. Most tests report coefficients alpha for estimating the internal consistency of scores but significant criticism of this index was previously noted. Omega-hierarchical (ω_h) and omega-subscale (ω_s) are more appropriate indicators of proportion of reliable variance attributable to the latent construct. Table 12.5 also presents ω_h and ω_s estimates for the present WISC-IV data set CFA bifactor solution.

Omega hierarchical (ω_h) coefficients presented in Table 12.5 provided estimates of the reliability of the latent constructs with the effects of other constructs removed. In the case of the four WISC-IV factor indexes, ω_s coefficients estimated the scale reliabilities with the effects of the general and other group factors removed and ranged from .098 (WM) to .330 (PS) which were lower but similar to those obtained from the EFA based SL procedure. These results indicate that in the present sample the general factor possessed sufficient reliable variance for interpretation but the four specific WISC-IV factors possessed too little reliable variance to interpret (Gignac & Watkins, 2013; Reise, 2012; Reise et al., 2013).

Taken together both EFA and CFA based bifactor models provided substantial support for the WISC-IV general intelligence dimension and while the WISC-IV reflects a multidimensional structure for its subtests it is nevertheless dominated by the general factor. The bifactor model provides a more parsimonious explanation (Gignac, 2006) and this structure seems more consistent with Spearman's (1904, 1927) conceptualization of general intelligence, which is also at the core of Wechsler's (1939, 1958) definition of intelligence (global capacity). Further, the dominance of the general intelligence dimension and low portions of reliable specific group factor variance provided by the four WISC-IV specific group factors (VC, PR, WM, PS) is a likely cause for the substantial predictive validity of the WISC-IV FSIQ or general intelligence dimension in accounting for academic achievement variance and the poor *incremental* validity of WISC-IV factor index scores beyond the FSIQ or general factor when using either hierarchical multiple regression analysis or structural equation modeling (Glutting, Watkins, Konold, & McDermott, 2006).

Future Directions

As pointed out in the present chapter there are important advantages to using bifactor models in evaluating psychological measurements whether one originates at an item level (Chen et al., 2012; Reise, 2012) or at the subtest level. While correlated first-order factor structures and higher-order structures have most commonly been reported in the literature their limitations are noteworthy and rival bifactor models should be routinely examined and tested against oblique first-order and higher-order structures to fully understand the dimensionality of an instrument. Understanding where item or subtest variance resides is critical in order for researchers and clinicians to adequately judge the value of various scores (global composite versus specific group). Further, estimation of model-based reliabilities (ω_h and ω_s) should also be routinely reported in order for researchers and clinicians to judge the merits of the various composite or factor based scores. Bifactor models (EFA and CFA) and omega estimates need to be reported in studies in the peer-reviewed literature as well as in test technical manuals where such indices and analyses are conspicuously absent even when explicitly and repeatedly implored (see Canivez, 2010; Canivez, 2014b; Canivez & Kush, 2013; Canivez & Watkins, 2016).

As noted earlier the SL procedure contains a potential problem of proportionality constraints that may limit its accuracy or utility (Brunner et al., 2012; Chen, West, & Sousa, 2006; Jennrich & Bentler, 2011; Reise, 2012; Yung et al., 1999). Reise (2012) described alternative exploratory bifactor methods (e.g., target bifactor rotations [Reise et al., 2011] and analytic bifactor rotations [Jennrich & Bentler, 2011, 2012]) that avoid the proportionality constraints of the SL procedure and these will likely be further examined in comparison to the most often used SL transformation procedure. It is hoped that these alternatives become integrated in standard statistical software to facilitate use.

One problem that has been documented in standard CFA procedures is that paths from latent constructs to subtests or indicators that are not theoretically associated are set to zero while it is understood that such paths are typically *not* zero but may be small. It was shown by Asparouhov and Muthen (2009) that when such paths are not zero such as when tests have complex (not simple) structure, setting such paths to zero has significant consequences for inaccurate parameter estimates that have consequences for decisions regarding latent models (see Canivez, 2011; Kranzler & Keith, 1999). Distortions produced by CFA when test subtests substantially cross-load may benefit from methods such as Exploratory Structural Equation Modeling (E-SEM; Asparouhov & Muthen, 2009) or Bayesian structural equation modeling (Golay et al., 2013) where such paths are not set to zero. Further examination of E-SEM and Bayesian SEM with bifactor models will also be instructive.

Within the test development community it is imperative that test authors and publishers examine and report rival bifactor models in comparison to oblique first-order and higher-order structures in test technical manuals as a matter of routine to provide clinicians ample evidence supporting recommended interpretations of scores. While Carroll (1995) insisted on explication of the SL orthogonalization in consideration of the multidimensionality of intelligence tests and resulting explication of subtest variance estimates associated with broad general and specific group factors, test publishers have ignored this admonition. Reporting ω_h and ω_s should also be routinely reported to provide more appropriate estimates of composite score reliabilities that would further assist in researcher and clinician judgments as to which scores were adequately supported for interpretation.

Acknowledgments

The author would like to thank to Dr. Stefan Dombrowski for very helpful comments and suggestions concerning an earlier version of this chapter.

References

Ackerman, R. A., Donnellan, M. B., & Robins, R. W. (2012). An item response theory analysis of the narcissistic personality inventory. *Journal of Personality Assessment, 94*, 141–15. http://doi.org/10.1080/00223891.2011.645934

Asparouhov, T., & Muthen, B. (2009). Exploratory structural equation modeling. *Structural Equation Modeling, 16*, 397–438. http://doi.org/10.1080/10705510903008204

Bentler, P. M., & Wu, E. J. C. (2012). *EQS for Windows*. Encino CA: Multivariate Software.

Bodin, D., Pardini, D. A., Burns, T. G., & Stevens, A. B. (2009). Higher order factor structure of the WISC-IV in a clinical neuropsychological sample. *Child Neuropsychology, 15*, 417–424. http://doi.org/10.1080/09297040802603661

Brouwer, D., Meijer, R. R., & Zevalkink, J. (2013). On the factor structure of the Beck Depression Inventory–II: G is the key. *Psychological Assessment, 25*, 136–145. http://doi.org/10.1037/a0029228

Brunner, M., Nagy, G., & Wilhelm, O. (2012). A tutorial on hierarchically structured constructs. *Journal of Personality, 80*, 796–846. http://doi.org/10.1111/j.1467-6494.2011.00749.x

Canivez, G. L. (2008). Hierarchical factor structure of the Stanford-Binet Intelligence Scales-Fifth Edition. *School Psychology Quarterly, 23*, 533–541. http://doi.org/10.1037/a0012884

Canivez, G. L. (2010). Review of the Wechsler Adult Intelligence Test–Fourth Edition. In R. A. Spies, J. F. Carlson, & K. F. Geisinger (Eds.), *The eighteenth mental measurements yearbook* (pp. 684–688). Lincoln, NE: Buros Institute of Mental Measurements.

Canivez, G. L. (2011). Hierarchical factor structure of the Cognitive Assessment System: Variance partitions from the Schmid–Leiman (1957) procedure. *School Psychology Quarterly, 26*, 305–317. http://doi.org/10.1037/a0025973

Canivez, G. L. (2014a). Construct validity of the WISC–IV with a referred sample: Direct versus indirect hierarchical structures. *School Psychology Quarterly, 29*, 38–51. http://doi.org/10.1037/spq0000032

Canivez, G. L. (2014b). Review of the Wechsler Preschool and Primary Scale of Intelligence–Fourth Edition. In J. F. Carlson, K. F. Geisinger, & J. L. Jonson (Eds.), *The nineteenth mental measurements yearbook* (pp. 732–737). Lincoln, NE: Buros Institute of Mental Measurements.

Canivez, G. L., Konold, T. R., Collins, J. M., & Wilson, G. (2009). Construct validity of the Wechsler Abbreviated Scale of Intelligence and Wide Range Intelligence Test: Convergent and structural validity. *School Psychology Quarterly, 24*, 252–265. http://doi.org/10.1037/a0018030

Canivez, G. L., & Kush, J. C. (2013). WISC–IV and WAIS–IV structural validity: Alternate methods, alternate results. Commentary on Weiss et al. (2013a) and Weiss et al. (2013b). *Journal of Psychoeducational Assessment, 31*, 157–169. http://doi.org/10.1177/0734282913478036

Canivez, G. L., & Watkins, M. W. (2010a). Investigation of the factor structure of the Wechsler Adult Intelligence Scale–Fourth Edition (WAIS-IV): Exploratory and higher order factor analyses. *Psychological Assessment, 22*, 827–836. http://doi.org/10.1037/a0020429

Canivez, G. L., & Watkins, M. W. (2010b). Exploratory and higher-order factor analyses of the Wechsler Adult Intelligence Scale-Fourth Edition (WAIS-IV) adolescent subsample. *School Psychology Quarterly, 25*, 223–235. http://doi.org/10.1037/a0022046

Canivez, G. L., & Watkins, M. W. (2016). Review of the Wechsler Intelligence Scale for Children-Fifth Edition: Critique, commentary, and independent analyses. In A. S. Kaufman, S. E. Raiford, & D. L. Coalson, *Intelligent testing with the WISC-V* (pp. 683–702). Hoboken, NJ: Wiley.

Carroll, J. B. (1995). On methodology in the study of cognitive abilities. *Multivariate Behavioral Research, 30*, 429–452. http://doi.org/10.1207/s15327906mbr3003_6

Cattell, R. B. (1966). The Scree test for the number of factors. *Multivariate Behavioral Research, 1*, 245–276. http://doi.org/10.1207/s15327906mbr0102_10

Chen, F. F. (2007). Sensitivity of goodness of fit indexes to lack of measurement invariance. *Structural Equation Modeling, 14*, 464–504. http://doi.org/10.1080/10705510701301834

Chen, F. F., Hayes, A., Carver, C. S., Laurenceau, J.-P., & Zhang, Z. (2012). Modeling general and specific variance in multifaceted constructs: A comparison of the bifactor model to other approaches. *Journal of Personality, 80*, 219–251. http://doi.org/10.1111/j.1467-6494.2011.00739.x

Chen, F. F., West, S. G., & Sousa, K. H. (2006). A comparison of bifactor and second-order models of quality of life. *Multivariate Behavioral Research, 41*, 189–225. http://doi.org/10.1207/s15327906 mbr4102_5

Cheung, G. W., & Rensvold, R. B. (2002). Evaluating goodness-of-fit indexes for testing measurement invariance. *Structural Equation Modeling, 9*, 233–255. http://doi.org/10.1207/S15328007SEM0902_5

Child, D. (2006). *The essentials of factor analysis* (3rd ed.). New York, NY: Continuum.

Dombrowski, S. C. (2013). Investigating the structure of the WJ-III Cognitive at school age. *School Psychology Quarterly, 28*, 154–169. http://doi.org/10.1037/spq0000010

Dombrowski, S. C. (2014a). Exploratory bifactor analysis of the WJ–III Cognitive in adulthood via the Schmid–Leiman procedure. *Journal of Psychoeducational Assessment, 32*, 330–341. http://doi.org/10.1177/0734282913508243

Dombrowski, S. C. (2014b). Investigating the structure of the WJ-III Cognitive in early school age through two exploratory bifactor analysis procedures. *Journal of Psychoeducational Assessment, 32*, 483–494. http://doi.org/10.1177/0734282914530838

Dombrowski, S. C., & Watkins, M. W. (2013). Exploratory and higher order factor analysis of the WJ-III full test battery: A school aged analysis. *Psychological Assessment, 25*, 442–455. http://doi.org/10.1037/a0031335

Dombrowski, S. C., Watkins, M. W., & Brogan, M. J. (2009). An exploratory investigation of the factor structure of the Reynolds Intellectual Assessment Scales (RIAS). *Journal of Psychoeducational Assessment, 27*, 494–507. http://doi.org/10.1177/0734282909333179

Fabrigar, L. R., Wegener, D. T., MacCallum, R. C., & Strahan, E. J. (1999). Evaluating the use of exploratory factor analysis in psychological research. *Psychological Methods, 4*, 272–299. http://doi.org/10.1037/1082-989X.4.3.272

Floyd, F. J., & Widaman, K. F. (1995). Factor analysis in the development and refinement of clinical assessment instruments. *Psychological Assessment, 7*, 286–299. http://doi.org/10.1037/1040-3590.7.3.286

Gignac, G. E. (2005). Revisiting the factor structure of the WAIS-R: Insights through nested factor modeling. *Assessment, 12*, 320–329. http://doi.org/10.1177/1073191105278118

Gignac, G. E. (2006). The WAIS-III as a nested factors model: A useful alternative to the more conventional oblique and higher-order models. *Journal of Individual Differences, 27*, 73–86. http://doi.org/10.1027/1614-0001.27.2.73

Gignac, G. E. (2008). Higher-order models versus direct hierarchical models: g as superordinate or breadth factor? *Psychology Science Quarterly, 50*, 21–43.

Gignac, G. E., & Watkins, M. W. (2013). Bifactor modeling and the estimation of model-based reliability in the WAIS-IV. *Multivariate Behavioral Research, 48*, 639–662. http://doi.org/10.1080/00273171.2013.804398

Glutting, J. J., Watkins, M. W., Konold, T. R., & McDermott, P. A. (2006). Distinctions without a difference: The utility of observed versus latent factors from the WISC–IV in estimating reading and math achievement on the WIAT–II. *Journal of Special Education, 40*, 103–114. http://doi.org/10.1177/00224669060400020101

Golay, P., & Lecerf, T. (2011). Orthogonal higher order structure and confirmatory factor analysis of the French Wechsler Adult Intelligence Scale (WAIS-III). *Psychological Assessment, 23*, 143–152. http://doi.org/10.1037/a0021230

Golay, P., Reverte, I., Rossier, J., Favez, N., & Lecerf, T. (2013). Further insights on the French WISC-IV factor structure through Bayesian structural equation modeling (BSEM). *Psychological Assessment, 25*, 496–508. http://doi.org/10.1037/a0030676

Gorsuch, R. L. (1983). *Factor analysis* (2nd ed.). Hillsdale, NJ: Lawrence Erlbaum Associates.

Gorsuch, R. L. (2003). Factor analysis. In J. A. Schinka & W. F. Velicer (Eds.), *Handbook of psychology: Vol. 2. Research methods in psychology* (pp. 143–164). Hoboken, NJ: John Wiley.

Gustafsson, J.-E., & Balke, G. (1993). General and specific abilities as predictors of school achievement. *Multivariate Behavioral Research, 28*, 407–434. http://doi.org/10.1207/s15327906mbr2804_2

Guttman, L. (1954). Some necessary conditions for common-factor analysis. *Psychometrika, 19*, 149–161. http://doi.org/10.1007/BF02289162

Holzinger, K. J., & Harman, H. H. (1938). Comparison of two factorial analyses. *Psychometrika, 3*, 45–60. http://doi.org/10.1007/BF02287919

Holzinger, K. J., & Swineford, F. (1937). The bi-factor method. *Psychometrika, 2*, 41–54. http://doi.org/10.1007/BF02287965

Horn, J. L. (1965). A rationale and test for the number of factors in factor analysis. *Psychometrika, 30*, 179–185. http://doi.org/10.1007/BF02289447

Hu, L.-T., & Bentler, P. M. (1998). Fit indices in covariance structure modeling: Sensitivity to under parameterized model misspecification. *Psychological Methods, 3*, 424–453. http://doi.org/10.1037/1082-989X.3.4.424

Hu, L.-T., & Bentler, P. M. (1999). Cutoff criteria for fit indexes in covariance structure analysis: Conventional criteria versus new alternatives. *Structural Equation Modeling: A Multidisciplinary Journal, 5*, 1–55. http://doi.org/10.1080/10705519909540118

Humphreys, L. G. (1981). The primary mental ability. In M. P. Friedman, J. P. Das, & N. O'Connor (Eds.), *Intelligence and learning* (pp. 87–102). New York, NY: Plenum.

Jennrich, R. I., & Bentler, P. M. (2011). Exploratory bi-factor analysis. *Psychometrika, 76*, 537–549. http://doi.org/10.1007/s11336-011-9218-4

Jennrich, R. I., & Bentler, P. M. (2012). Exploratory bi-factor analysis: The oblique case. *Psychometrika, 77*, 442–454. http://doi.org/10.1007/s11336-012-9269-1

Kranzler, J. H., & Keith, T. Z. (1999). Independent confirmatory factor analysis of the Cognitive Assessment System: What does the CAS measure? *School Psychology Review, 28*, 117–144.

MacCallum, R. C., Widaman, K. F., Zhang, S., & Hong, S. (1999). Sample size in factor analysis. *Psychological Methods, 4*, 84–99. http://doi.org/10.1037/1082-989X.4.1.84

Mardia, K. V. (1970). Measures of multivariate skewness and kurtosis with applications. *Biometrika, 57*, 519–530. http://doi.org/10.1093/biomet/57.3.519

McDonald, R. (1999). *Test theory: A unified treatment*. Mahwah, NJ: Lawrence ErlbaumAssociates.

Nasser, F., Benson, J., & Wisenbaker, J. (2002). The performance of regression-based variations of the visual scree for determining the number of common factors. *Educational and Psychological Measurement, 62*, 397–419. http://doi.org/10.1177/0016440206200300

Nelson, J. M., & Canivez, G. L. (2012). Examination of the structural, convergent, and incremental validity of the Reynolds Intellectual Assessment Scales (RIAS) with a clinical sample. *Psychological Assessment, 24*, 129–140. http://doi.org/10.1037/a0024878

Nelson, J. M., Canivez, G. L., Lindstrom, W., & Hatt, C. (2007). Higher-order exploratory factor analysis of the Reynolds Intellectual Assessment Scales with a referred sample. *Journal of School Psychology, 45*, 439–456. http://doi.org/10.1016/j.jsp.2007.03.003

Nelson, J. M., Canivez, G. L., & Watkins, M. W. (2013). Structural and incremental validity of the Wechsler Adult Intelligence Scale–Fourth Edition (WAIS–IV) with a clinical sample. *Psychological Assessment, 25*, 618–630. http://doi.org/10.1037/a0032086

Niileksela, C. R., Reynolds, M. R., & Kaufman, A. S. (2013). An alternative Cattell–Horn–Carroll (CHC) factor structure of the WAIS-IV: Age invariance of an alternative model for ages 70–90. *Psychological Assessment, 25*, 391–404. http://doi.org/10.1037/a0031175

O'Connor, B. P. (2000). SPSS and SAS programs for determining the number of components using parallel analysis and Velicer's MAP test. *Behavior Research Methods, Instruments, & Computers, 32*, 396–402. http://doi.org/10.3758/BF03200807

Reise, S. P. (2012). The rediscovery of bifactor measurement models. *Multivariate Behavioral Research, 47*, 667–696. http://doi.org/10.1080/00273171.2012.715555

Reise, S. P., Bonifay, W. E., & Haviland, M. G. (2013). Scoring and modeling psychological measures in the presence of multidimensionality. *Journal of Personality Assessment, 95*, 129–140. http://doi.org/10.1080/00223891.2012.725437

Reise, S. P., Moore, T. M., & Haviland, M. G. (2010). Bifactor models and rotations: Exploring the extent to which multidimensional data yield univocal scale scores. *Journal of Personality Assessment, 92*, 544–559. http://doi.org/10.1080/00223891.2010.496477

Reise, S. P., Moore, T. M., & Maydeu-Olivares, A. (2011). Targeted bifactor rotations and assessing the impact of model violations on the parameters of unidimensional and bifactor models. *Educational and Psychological Measurement, 71*, 684–711. http://doi.org/10.1177/0013164410378690

Schmid, J., & Leiman, J. M. (1957). The development of hierarchical factor solutions. *Psychometrika, 22*, 53–61. http://doi.org/10.1007/BF02289209

Schweizer, K. (2011). On the changing role of Cronbach's alpha in the evaluation of the quality of a measure. *European Journal of Psychological Assessment, 27*, 143–144. http://doi.org/10.1027/1015-5759/a000069

Sijtsma, K. (2009). On the use, misuse, and the very limited usefulness of Cronbach's alpha. *Psychometrika, 74*, 107–120. http://doi.org/10.1007/s11336-008-9101-0

Spearman, C. (1904). General intelligence, objectively determined and measured. *American Journal of Psychology, 15*, 201–293.

Spearman, C. (1927). *The abilities of man.* New York, NY: Macmillan.

Tabachnick, B. G., & Fidell, L. S. (2007). *Using multivariate statistics* (5th ed.). Boston, MA: Pearson Education.

Thompson, B. (1990). SECONDOR: A program that computes a second-order principal components analysis and various interpretation aids. *Educational and Psychological Measurement, 50*, 575–580. http://doi.org/10.1177/0013164490503011

Thompson, B. (2004). *Exploratory and confirmatory factor analysis: Understanding concepts and applications.* Washington, DC: American Psychological Association. http://doi.org/10.1037/10694-000

Velicer, W. F. (1976). Determining the number of components form the matrix of partial correlations. *Psychometrika, 31*, 321–327. http://doi.org/10.1007/BF02293557

Watkins, M. W. (2000). *Monte Carlo PCA for Parallel Analysis* [Computer software]. State College, PA: Ed & Psych Associates.

Watkins, M. W. (2004). *MacOrtho* [Computer software]. State College, PA: Ed & Psych Associates.

Watkins, M. W. (2007). *SEscree* [Computer software]. State College, PA: Ed & Psych Associates.

Watkins, M. W. (2006). Orthogonal higher order structure of the Wechsler Intelligence Scale for Children-Fourth Edition. *Psychological Assessment, 18*, 123–125. http://doi.org/10.1037/1040-3590.18.1.123

Watkins, M. W. (2010). Structure of the Wechsler Intelligence Scale for Children–Fourth Edition among a national sample of referred students. *Psychological Assessment, 22*, 782–787. http://doi.org/10.1037/a0020043

Watkins, M. W. (2013). *Omega* [Computer software]. Phoenix, AZ: Ed & Psych Associates.

Watkins, M. W., & Beaujean, A. A. (2014). Bifactor structure of the Wechsler Preschool and Primary Scale of Intelligence–fourth edition. *School Psychology Quarterly, 29*, 52–63. http://doi.org/10.1037/spq0000038

Watkins, M. W., Canivez, G. L., James, T., Good, R., & James, K. (2013). Construct validity of the WISC–IV^UK with a large referred Irish sample. *International Journal of School and Educational Psychology, 1*, 102–111. http://doi.org/10.1080/21683603.2013.794439

Watkins, M. W., Wilson, S. M., Kotz, K. M., Carbone, M. C., & Babula, T. (2006). Factor structure of the Wechsler Intelligence Scale for Children-Fourth Edition among referred students. *Educational and Psychological Measurement, 66*, 975–983. http://doi.org/10.1177/0013164406288168

Wechsler, D. (1939). *The measurement of adult intelligence*. Baltimore, MD: Williams & Wilkins. http://doi.org/10.1037/10020-000

Wechsler, D. (1958). *The measurement and appraisal of adult intelligence* (4th ed.). Baltimore, MD: Williams & Wilkins. http://doi.org/10.1037/11167-000

Wechsler, D. (2003). *Wechsler Intelligence Scale for Children–Fourth Edition*. San Antonio, TX: Psychological Corporation.

Wolff, H.-G., & Preising, K. (2005). Exploring item and higher order factor structure with the Schmid–Leiman solution: Syntax codes for SPSS and SAS. *Behavior Research Methods, 37*, 48–58. http://doi.org/10.3758/BF03206397

Yang, Y., & Green, S. B. (2011). Coefficient alpha: A reliability coefficient for the 21st century? *Journal of Psychoeducational Assessment, 29*, 377–392. http://doi.org/10.1177/0734282911406668

Yung, Y.-F., Thissen, D., & McLeod, L. (1999). On the relationship between the higher-order factor model and the hierarchical factor model. *Psychometrika, 64*, 113–128. http://doi.org/10.1007/BF02294531

Zinbarg, R. E., Revelle, W., Yovel, I., & Li, W. (2005). Cronbach's alpha, Revelle's beta, and McDonald's omega h: Their relations with each other and two alternative conceptualizations of reliability. *Psychometrika, 70*, 123–133. http://doi.org/10.1007/s11336-003-0974-7

Zinbarg, R. E., Yovel, I., Revelle, W., & McDonald, R. P. (2006). Estimating generalizability to a latent variable common to all of a scale's indicators: A comparison of estimators for ωh. *Applied Psychological Measurement, 30*, 121–144. http://doi.org/10.1177/0146621605278814

Zoski, K. W., & Jurs, S. (1996). An objective counterpart to the visual scree test for factor analysis: The standard error scree. *Educational and Psychological Measurement, 56*, 443–451. http://doi.org/10.1177/0013164496056003006

Chapter 13

Creating Short Forms and Screening Measures

Fred Greer and Jin Liu

Department of Educational Studies, University of South Carolina, Columbia, SC, USA

Introduction

Identification of individual needs among large populations is an important goal in the fields of education, medicine, and mental health. The ability to systematically and efficiently distinguish behaviors, features, performance levels, or other attributes of examinees, can improve decisions on direction of services to those who most require them, and avoid dilution of resources and efforts. Often, long comprehensive tests are constructed to collect a wealth of information about the examinees, but such instruments can be costly to produce, administer, and score. Additionally, the nature of such tests themselves may adversely impact the data collected. Measures that are overly long can cause respondent fatigue and exasperate those with attentional deficits, leading to unreliable or missing data. Readability levels or wording, too, may protract assessment duration among those with reading difficulties, or whose first language is not that of the test. Time expenditure may be a particular concern for respondents that have multiple instruments to complete in addition to the demands of their numerous daily tasks (e.g., teachers rating student behaviors). Most importantly, if in-depth information is needed on many subjects, and it is not feasible to administer instruments on a wide scale, then there is less chance to act early so as to reduce risk, prevent onset, or minimize the effect of a behavior disorder, to resolve deficits in academic functioning, or address delays in development of critical skills.

For many test construction situations, short forms and screening instruments may be developed to help collect information through a quick, inexpensive, initial investigation of an issue or characteristic (Pagano, Cassidy, Little, Murphy, & Jellinek, 2000; Reise, Waller, Comrey, 2000; Smith, McCarthy, & Anderson, 2000). While a shorter instrument provides benefits in terms of time, cost, effort, and readability, there is a challenge in the creation of such an instrument with acceptable psychometric reliability and validity (Smith, Conrad, Chang, & Piazza, 2002). This chapter will discuss the approaches to the design of short forms and screening instruments as presented in the literature. For simplicity, the term *short form* will be used unless specifically discussing screening measures.

Differentiating Between Short Forms and Screeners

While the terms *short form* and *screener* are often used interchangeably, there are differences between the two measures (Smith et al., 2000). These differences extend to the design of the instruments, situations in which the instruments are used, and the scores produced.

Short Forms

Short forms are abbreviated measures, derived from full-length tests by reducing the number of administered items. The most commonly found examples of short forms in the psychoeducational literature have been created from comprehensive tests designed for intensive assessment and diagnostic purposes (e.g., intelligence: Wechsler Adult Intelligence Scale – Third Edition [Girard, Axelrod, & Wilkins, 2010]; personality: Minnesota Mulitphasic Personality Inventory [Butcher et al., 1992]; affective: Children's Behavior Questionnaire [Putnam & Rothbart, 2006]). Approaches to the selection of items to be retained from the original test vary. Developers may choose to include items from all areas of a multidimensional full test (Gameroff, Wickramaratne, & Weissman, 2012), while others opt for focus on scales that considered key to the domain covered by the full instrument (Silverstein, 1990).

The goal of reducing the time-burden of assessment necessitates that short form developers weigh brevity against reliability. Therefore, short forms often have lower reliability than the full measure, due primarily to the number of items included on the abbreviated form. While this balancing challenge (content coverage and reliability versus the time savings of brevity) is shared in screening test creation, short form developers often face the additional choice of retaining enough items from the full test to preserve the ability to derive scores for some, or all, of the scales available on the original instrument. This potential feature of short forms contrasts with the single scale score reported by most screeners (Smith et al., 2000).

In addition, it is important to estimate validity evidence for short forms (Smith et al., 2000). Most often, however, the validity of short forms has been evaluated on the basis of their relationship to the full test version (Silverstein, 1990), with the magnitude of correlation being the primary indicator of quality, followed by matters such as ease of administration and scoring (Prewett, 1995). Short forms are similar to screeners in their utility within time-limited situations to indicate the merit of additional, in-depth, assessment. Whereas screening tests are most often designed to indicate overall functioning, short forms can signal functioning across the areas measured by a comprehensive instrument. Short forms may be used within the role for which screeners are specifically designed, but care should be taken in such situations, as the two forms do have different roles and functions (Smith et al., 2000).

Screeners

Screening tests are very brief measures, usually containing fewer than 30 items. While they usually range from one to two dozen items, screeners may consist of still fewer items; for example, ultra-brief version of Penn State Worry Questionnaire: three items (Berle et al., 2011); Mini-Social Phobia Inventory: three items (Weeks, Spokas, & Heimberg, 2007); Brief Screen for Depression: four items (Hakstian & McLean, 1989). In addition to their brevity, screening tests ordinarily yield results on a single latent factor. The highly limited number of items included on screeners preclude their reliably measuring multiple constructs. With this in-built aspect of screeners in mind, test constructors must set cut scores appropriate to the construct being measured, the setting in which it will be administered, and the frequency with which it will be administered.

In contrast to short forms, screening instruments are generally relatively short and broad in scope. For example, comprehensive emotional-behavioral assessment for diagnostic purposes often utilizes broad-band instruments measuring a range of related constructs (e.g., aggression, hyperactivity, depression, anxiety, withdrawal, sociability, etc.), through administration of items contributing to one or more of the test scales. By their nature, such measures are composed of many – sometimes hundreds – of items and, thus, require substantial time to administer.

Screeners, by contrast, are often developed for the measurement of broad, upper tier skills (e.g., school readiness, motor development, etc.) or global ratings of functioning (physical condition, mental health). With this design, screeners are useful as an initial view to detect possible need of more thorough assessment. This is not always the only application for purpose-built screeners, however. Screening tests can fulfill a role in circumstances where assessment is part of a frequent routine, and here may be designed with a tighter scope. For example, in settings wherein patient progress is routinely monitored as part of ongoing treatment (e.g., programs for chronic psychological conditions, substance dependency, etc.), screeners may measure a relatively narrow construct (depression, alcohol abuse) to guide decisions intervention modification or need. In such situations, it should be noted, though the results of recurrent screenings can contribute to a collectively stable presentation of functioning/performance supportive of a diagnosis, they would not be diagnostic in themselves. This is because screeners are not constructed to provide comprehensive information under multiple situations or with multiple (typically long) instruments, as is needed to make a diagnosis.

Professionals responsible for delivery of services must assess needs as quickly and accurately as practicable. Doing so demands balancing several competing issues. Early childhood educators, for example, must consider not only the monetary cost of cognitive/physical/language screening of incoming preschoolers, but also the time and effort necessary for to individually assess these children. Ordinarily, neither a comprehensive broad-band instrument nor a shorter narrow-band instrument would meet this need: the first being too expensive in time and other resources and the other too constricted in its scope of detection. The *wide net* quality of the screener, paired with its relative speed of administration, offset its lower reliability within the conditions for which it is designed. Similar considerations bolster the application of screening instruments for other concerns, such as physical health (e.g., hearing, vision, and fitness) and mental health (e.g., mood, anxiety, suicide risk), and substance abuse.

The conditions for use of screening instruments are sometimes formalized. The rise of multilevel systems of support such as that of the response-to-intervention (RtI) framework offers one such example. An approach toward identification of academic and behavioral difficulties and timely interventions of appropriate intensity and duration, RtI is founded on assessment of all students' needs. The concept of universal screening integrates well with the idea of monitoring the functioning of students for signals of unidentified needs in order to provide early intervention. Education professionals' competency in screening tool selection, use, and interpretation is essential to this process (Christ & Nelson, 2014).

Glover and Albers (2007) identified several criteria that must be met for screening instruments to be useful. First, the psychometric characteristics of the instrument must be sound, including acceptable reliability and validity evidence for score inferences. Second, the instrument should meet the needs of the users, meaning that it is feasible for raters (e.g., parents, clinicians, teachers, children) to complete the measure quickly, without additional training, and that is consistent of content that identifies examinees at-risk for the targeted problem. Finally, the instrument should be as accurate as possible in its identification of students at risk, simultaneously minimizing the number of students who are erroneously selected for additional assessment (i.e., false-positive) and those who are in need of intervention yet missed by the instrument (i.e., false-negative).

Conceptual Principles

Various methods exist to create short forms and screening forms. While different methods exist, we take the perspective that a longer instrument or item pool is used as a base and a shorter form (for use as a short form or screener) may be constructed from selecting items from the set of items and, for simplicity, use the term short form throughout. It is recognized that the same methods may be used, but the perspective and the final form created will differ if the focus is to make a short form (covering a wider array of areas) or a screener (selecting specific items to target a disorder or risk). Four different methods are presented – selection of items based on: empirical or theoretical considerations, classical test theory methods, factor analytic methods, and item response theory.

Different Methods for Short Form Creation

Theoretical/Empirical

A natural approach to begin creating short forms is to eliminate items subsequent to a theoretical review of a full test and its items. Obtaining an understanding of the hypotheses of the measure and how its authors operationalize the measure of its scale constructs in its items may initiate this process. Next, developers can examine items grouped according to the scales to which they contribute. For developers with the objective of a short form that yields a single overall score, they may choose to eliminate subtests or scales deemed unessential or secondary to the central construct of interest. Further prioritization would follow if the parent test yields multiple scales that developers wish to preserve. Item purging choices may then be made, often beginning for any items seeming redundant, ambiguously worded, or unclear in their relationship to the factor(s) being measured. Empirical study of the remaining candidate items follows the theory-based processes of development. Even so, evaluation of statistics provided by analysis of item contributions and relationships to measurement factors should continue to reference the theory relating to the intended construct so that item inclusion choices demonstrate proportionality to the parent scale (Smith et al., 2000). In reference to the short test hazard of narrowing the scope of the target construct (Loevinger, 1954), Schipolowski, Schroeders, & Wilhelm (2014) note:

> Content considerations are still relevant in the sense that the rationale for item generation has to be grounded in substantive theory. (p. 191)

The literature offers examples of test abbreviation that include a theoretical approach (Thompson, 2007; Schipolowski et al., 2014). Thompson (2007), for example, describes a qualitative process during development of a short form wherein focus groups identified items with language perceived as vague or easily misinterpreted. Items flagged as problematic can then be used by short form developers to "examine statistically the wisdom and psychometric feasibility" (Thompson, 2007, 232) of ultimately purging them from the parent test item set. In another instance, developers Putnam and Rothbart's (2006) use of content analysis altered item choices suggested by statistical processes in order to preserve breadth of the target construct. While incorporating statistical characteristics into their item culling decisions, some developers have also balanced these factors with commitment to the parent test structure (Arthur & Day, 1994).

Classical Test Theory Methods

Classical test theory (CTT) methods are often used to select optimal items from a larger pool of candidates. These methods include a consideration of reliability, validity, and item analysis techniques. Overall scale reliability is often computed to provide a measure of the replicability of scores produced by a form or a set of examinees. Typically, Cronbach's alpha or Kuder–Richardson (KR)-20 or KR-21 are computed (Kehoe, 1995). Additionally, the well-known Spearman–Brown prophecy formula to estimate reliability can also be used to estimate the reliability of a test that is a fraction of the length of a total test. In other words, if a shorter version of a test is desired, where the shorter form is 1/N as long as the full form of size N, the following formula can be used to estimate reliability of the shorter form:

$$\rho_{YY'} = \frac{\frac{1}{N}\rho_{XX'}}{1+\left(\frac{1}{N}-1\right)\rho_{XX'}} \tag{1}$$

is the estimated reliability of the shorter form and is the reliability of the existing measure (Allen & Yen, 1979). Of course, this formula only estimates the reliability of the shorter form, and the actual reliability will need calculated. In addition, the Spearman–Brown formula also assumes that the items are parallel (i.e., all items measure the latent score equally well with equal error terms); if the items included are not parallel, the calculated reliability may differ from the estimated reliability.

Another well-known technique to select items is through a CTT-based item analysis. Item analysis uses many different CTT-based statistics to examine the quality of a set of items and allows the researcher to select the best items for a shorter form. To choose the best items, the following statistics are usually evaluated (e.g., Allen & Yen, 1979; Crocker & Algina, 1986; Kehoe, 1995): item difficulty, item-total correlation, alpha if item deleted. The item difficulty (p), represents the percentage of examinees providing a correct response to the item. Item difficulty values may be examined for the purpose of the form. For example, a short form may select items from a wide range of difficulty values to measure examinees along the latent trait continuum, while a screener may have p values in a much more narrow range. The item-total correlation (or, alternatively, point-biserial correlation) provides the relationship between an item and the remaining items on the scale. The value measures discrimination of an item, illustrating how well the item distinguishes between those examinees high on the latent trait and those low on the measured trait. In an item analysis, these values are examined to eliminate nonperforming items, where higher values are desired. Item-total correlation values under .20 show that an item is not discriminating well among examinees, values between .20 and .39 show acceptable discrimination, and item values above .40 show items that are performing well to discriminate among examinees (Field, 2005). Any item with a negative discrimination value should be deleted as the item may indicate a mistake, such as a miskeyed correct option with scoring, poor distractors, or confusing wording. Finally, the alpha if-item-deleted may be computed for each item. The value provides a measure of the scale's overall Cronbach's alpha reliability estimate if an item in question is deleted from the scale (Field, 2005). Values that lower the overall reliability for the scale are items that may be considered important to the latent construct; items for which the reliability improves or stays the same if deleted are not contributing to the measurement of the targeted trait.

Allen and Yen (1979, p. 124) suggest that four indices are needed to choose the best items from a larger set of N items to create a smaller test of size k: item difficulty (p_i), the item standard deviation ($s_i = \sqrt{p_i(1-p_i)}$), the item-reliability index ($s_i r_{iX*}$, where r_{iX*} is the point biserial correlation defined above), and the item validity index $s_i r_{iY}$, where r_{iY} is the point biserial correlation between an item score and an external criterion.) From these four values, Allen and Yen (1979) state that the mean, standard deviation, reliability ($r_{xx'}$), and validity (r_{XY}) of a test score, X, can be computed for a smaller test (k) as follows:

$$\bar{X} = \Sigma_i^k p_i \, ,$$

$$\hat{s}_X = \Sigma_i^k s_i \, r_{iX} \, ,$$

$$\hat{r}_{XX'} = \frac{k}{k-1}\left[1 - \frac{\Sigma_i^k s_i^2}{\left(\Sigma_i^k s_i \, r_{iX}\right)^2}\right], \tag{2}$$

$$\hat{r}_{XY} = \frac{\Sigma_i^k s_i r_{iY}}{\Sigma_i^k s_i r_{iX}}$$

If all items are kept, $N = k$; however, if a subset of items (k) is selected, estimated statistics for the smaller scale can be computed. These formulas can provide estimates for different subsets of items, allowing researchers to try out different combinations of items to maximize reliability and/or validity estimates.

Factor Analysis

Selecting items from a full test for the purpose of creating a short form may be guided by factor analytic methods. The initial step in this approach should be the examination of descriptive statistics for the items composing the original measure. This procedure may allow developers to note any irregularities in the distribution of item responses. For example, some items may exhibit a low incidence of endorsement relative to other items (i.e., exhibiting skewness and/or kurtosis). Although such difficult to endorse items will have more limited application among the broader population of interest, individuals to whom the items relate may constitute a group with a shared, distinguishable behavioral profile. Without consideration of such matters in the item elimination process, developers risk undue constriction of a short form's scope from that of the parent test.

The results of a principal components factor analysis can further inform decisions on culling items for short forms (Comrey & Lee, 1992; Gorsuch, 1983). A shortcoming of this method, however, must be noted in its not accounting for measurement error in responses. This is indicated by the fixed diagonal of the correlation matrix at a true 1.0. The effect of this artificial relationship between off-diagonal elements and the matrix diagonal is mitigated by an increasing inclusion of items (Comrey & Lee, 1992). For more detailed information on exploratory factor analysis, many texts are available (e.g., Comrey & Lee, 1992; Gorsuch, 1983).

Different methods of factor analysis exist to extract the underlying factors. Principal axis factoring (PAF) is commonly used when the researcher is interested in uncovering the latent dimensions underlying an instrument while principal components analysis (PCA) is used for item reduction (Benson & Nasser, 1998). The method fitting the objective of the scale development may be selected. For example, PAF may be useful when creating a short form to ensure that all underlying dimensions are included while PCA may be useful when creating a screener is the goal.

Item Response Theory

One of the main purposes of IRT is to evaluate item parameters used to measuring a unidimensional construct (Smith et al., 2002). The goal in IRT is to relate the probability of a person's response to each item given the latent ability level of the person and the item characteristics. The latent score for an individual, θ, is linked with a person's test score or defined construct score. There are different types of IRT models (Baker, 2001), for example, the Rasch model is a one-parameter (1PL) model IRT model that estimates item difficulty. Item difficulty is analogous to the item difficulty in CTT, which is the probability of answering the item correctly. The higher the item difficulty, the higher the latent ability level is need to endorse the item. The two-parameter IRT model (2PL) includes an estimate of item discrimination along with item difficulty. Item discrimination, which is analogous to item-total correlation in CTT (Lord, 1980), indicates how strongly one item is able to separate the subjects which are at different latent ability levels. Another commonly used IRT model includes an additional parameter – guessing – besides item difficulty and item discrimination. Inclusion of guessing showed us how the low ability subjects may still have a probability to endorse an item. Where CTT measures are sample specific, one advantage using IRT models is that they are thought to be at the latent level and not as reliant on scores from one sample (Bond & Fox, 2007). The following procedures can be used to check the performance of items and the instrument after the data is fit to the selected IRT model; however, it just provides an overview of the methods. For more detailed information on IRT, there are many excellent texts available (e.g., Baker, 2001; Embretson & Reise, 2000; Hambleton, Swaminathan, & Rogers, 1991).

Item Characteristics

Selection of items can be conducted through item analysis in the IRT framework. The process includes: determining the item parameters using the selected models and utilizing IRT model fit criteria or analysis of residuals (i.e., the difference between the actual value and the estimate of a correct or incorrect response, based on the number parameters estimated) to detect items that do not fit the IRT model (Hambleton & Jones, 1993). For instance, with the Rasch model (1PL) two fit indices, Outfit and Infit, may be used to detect unexpected response patterns. Outfit statistics place greater emphasis on responses to items far from a subject's (or item's) average latent score and Infit statistics place greater emphasis on unexpected responses targeted on a person's (or item's) latent score measure (Bond & Fox, 2007). These fit indices are based on the squared standardized residual between what is observed (i.e., actual response) and expected (or predicted) given the Rasch model. The expected item Infit and Outfit mean square value is 1.0, with an acceptable range within .5 to 1.5 (Linacre, 2006). Values outside of this range may suggest a lack of fit between the item and model and these items may be deleted in the final form.

In general, items may be deleted if difficulty indices are too low or too high (i.e., too easy or too hard) and/or the discrimination indices are low positive or negative values. In the three-parameter models, items may be removed if low ability subjects have a relatively high probability to endorse the item. In addition, the form may target items across a range of the difficulty levels and items that have the same difficulty level may be eliminated to produce information across a range of latent scores (θ; Bond & Fox, 2007).

For IRT models, the goodness of fit test provides a measure of overall fit. The test produces a chi-squared index and results show the difference between observed frequencies and expected frequencies (based on the tested model). This value may be used to compare the difference between models (e.g., 1PL vs. 2PL). One caveat is that the chi-squared test statistic is sensitive to sample size, and may denote a significant difference between models due to large sample size in practice.

Differential Item Functioning

Differential item functioning (DIF) or item bias occurs when people from different demographic subgroups, but with similar levels of the latent trait (θ), have different probability of correctly endorsing an item. DIF can be assessed through examination of the Item Characteristic Curve calculated in concert with the number of parameters in the IRT model. Items exhibiting DIF are considered biased and should be deleted to develop a fair instrument. Normally, gender and ethnicity are considered in the DIF detecting process for many achievement and psychological tests. For more on DIF, see Chapter 10 by French and Finch in this volume.

Note that one caveat to using IRT models is that model assumptions need to be checked for accurate estimation. These include testing that (1) unidimensionality (that the test measures one latent construct), (2) monotonic scale (higher scores refer to a higher amount of the construct), and local independence (scores to the items are dependent on the score). Additional assumptions may need to be evaluated depending upon the IRT model chosen (e.g., Rasch model or graded response model).

Methods for Creating a Cut Score

Creating cut scores are essential for instruments that are used for decision making. The goal is to identify a score such that examinees are above this score are selected for a treatment, program, intervention, etc. However, different cut score methods will lead to different cut scores for the same screening form (DiStefano & Morgan, 2011). Practitioners need to decide which method is the best one in their test by considering the importance of a correct classification versus making an incorrect classification. While we recognize there are many different methods, three popular methods are discussed: receiver operating characteristic curve analysis (ROCC), Rasch analyses and test information from item response theory methodology, are presented.

ROCC Analysis

ROCC analysis is a popular method for creating optimal cut scores with health and psychological instruments (Bricker & Squires, 1999; Swets, 1996). ROCC modeling attempts to minimize the number of classification errors by balancing the probability of correctly identifying true positive cases (e.g., children at risk for a disorder) and true negative cases (i.e., children who are developing normally). Therefore, this method requires a previously diagnosed group to use in evaluations of possible cut scores. That is, individuals need to be independently classified at the time of the study. ROCCs provide a two-dimensional plot of the true positive rate (i.e, sensitivity) against the false positive rate (i.e., specificity) to provide different possible cut scores for a diagnostic test (Altman, 1991; Metz, 1978). An advantage of ROCC is that many different cut points can be examined within one analysis.

The ROCC curves demonstrate the tradeoff between sensitivity and specificity associated with different cut scores, where increases in sensitivity are accompanied by decreases in specificity. A measure that is ineffective to distinguish between diagnosed and undiagnosed cases would be represented by a diagonal line with a positive slope; here the cut point is not functioning better than chance to classify diagnosed cases. An effective cut point would be represented by a curve that shows an inverted U above the diagonal line. Here, the effectiveness of an instrument is assessed by evaluating the accuracy of discrimination between children at risk for emotional/behavioral problems and those without risk. An area under the curve of 1 defines a perfect test, whereas an area of 0.5 represents a relatively inefficient measure; areas of 0.80–0.90 are considered good discriminators, and curves of 0.90–1 are considered excellent (Swets, 1996).

Rasch Modeling

For many psychological instruments, summing item-level data to create a total score may not be appropriate, given that many instruments use Likert scales to collect data. Likert data are ordinal by definition, and ordinal data do not often possess the needed property of equal intervals, making procedures relying on sum scores or sum score transformations questionable for use in statistical analyses (Smith et al., 2002). An alternative to methods using sum scores to identify cut scores is to use item response theory (IRT) modeling techniques (Smith et al., 2002). These models limit the amount of measurement error associated with different cut points for an instrument.

A special case of IRT, Rasch methods refer to a family of mathematical models that compute the probability that an individual will respond favorably to an item, given the amount of the latent construct the individual possesses (typically *ability* in Rasch terminology) and the hardness of the item (i.e., item difficulty). The basic model allows a researcher to predict how likely it is that a respondent will answer an item in a certain manner, given his or her level of the construct. The Rasch model produces scores for each person and each item on a common, interval-level scale, called a logit (i.e., log-odds) scale (Linacre, 2004). The logit scale is unique in that both sets of scores are on a common level of measurement. Another distinguishing feature of the Rasch model is that it provides *sample-free measurement* estimates, making it possible to estimate a person's level of the latent construct free of the distribution of the individual items and to estimate an item's difficulty level free from the distribution of people used in the sample (Schumaker, 2004). Finally, the models are probability based; no diagnosed group is needed for a researcher to decide upon a cutoff score.

Test Information

IRT methods estimate item parameters and also an examinee's placement on the latent variable. Under this method, information theory can be described as the amount of information an individual item is providing for examinees at a certain latent trait level (θ). For example, under the Rasch model with dichotomous items, the information function is stated as the probability of a correct response [$p(\theta)$] multiplied by the probability of an incorrect response [$q(\theta)$] at a given level of the latent trait:

$$I(\theta) = \frac{1}{p_i(\theta) * q_i(\theta)} \tag{3}$$

The number of item parameters estimated with the IRT model impacts the amount of information computed. In other words, the amount of information calculated will be different if a two-parameter IRT model or a three-parameter model are used.

The information function also provides a standard error of estimation at each latent trait level, θ, defined as the reciprocal of the test information at given trait level. Therefore, if there is more information known at a given level of θ, there will be a smaller standard error of measurement. In general, item information functions create a bell-shaped curve. An item is said to provide maximum amount of information for examinees at the center of the curve (i.e., mean of the bell-shaped curve). Based on the assumption of local independence, item information functions are additive to produce a test information curve. The test information curve is also bell-shaped and shows the degree of precision for the test at measuring different levels of the latent scale, θ. The test information function (TIF) may be used to create an optimal cutoff level based on the amount of information the test provides. For example, items may be selected to maximize information about a given level of θ by selecting the peak of the distribution as the cutoff score.

Evaluating Cut Scores

The goal of an instrument is to be useful in correctly classifying subjects in different performance levels; that is, to minimize error rates. Using forms of identifying children's behavioral and emotional problem as an example, researchers hope to minimize errors where a student who is developing is flagged as *at risk* as well as minimizing errors where children with behavior problems are not identified. There are multiple indices that can be used to judge the accuracy of a cutoff score in balancing errors. Kessel and Zimmerman (1993) recommended that researchers summarize classification results in a contingency table as well as provide a summary of classification statistics definitions. A summary of classification definitions adapted from DiStefano and Morgan (2011) is provided in Table 13.1. The elements in the table illustrate different decisions made as a result of the short form in rows and the true statement in columns. All subjects were identified as at risk (c + d) by the short form. As seen in the table, it was assumed that subjects' true conditions were included to test the accuracy of cutoff scores. Also, elements on the diagonal (a, d) represent correct decisions, and elements on the off diagonal (b, c) represent incorrect decisions.

Table 13.1. Contingency table for assessing cut scores

Decision made	True state		Row totals
	Developing normally	Functionally impaired	
Not at-risk	a (True negative)	b (False negative)	a + b
At-risk	c (False positive)	d (True positive)	c + d
	a + c	b + d	N = a + b + c + d

Adapted from DiStefano & Morgan (2011).

Using information in the different cells, one may calculate seven statistics to evaluate accuracy of a cut point. Two commonly used errors are the false-positive rate and the false-negative rate. The false-positive rate identifies the proportion of students developing normally who are misclassified as at risk c/(a + c) and the false-negative rate provides the proportion of students who are actually functionally impaired but are misidentified as on track developmentally b/(b + d). Table 13.1 provides a summary contingency table that may be used to assess the accuracy of a cut-point.

Two other widely known statistics used to evaluate effectiveness include sensitivity and specificity, both of which relay a correct decision. As discussed previously, the sensitivity rate shows the adequacy of an instrument to identify the proportion of functionally impaired children correctly identified from the set of children referred for treatment (d/b + d). The specificity rate (a/a + c) provides information on the screener's ability to correctly identify children who are developing normally. Other indices computed to judge the accuracy of the classifications include the (a) true-positive hit rate, or positive predictive power (PPP; d/d + c); (b) true-negative hit rate, or negative predictive power (NPP; a/a + b); and (c) proportion correct overall (a + d)/N. These summary statistics are provided in Table 13.2. In addition, guidelines have been suggested to evaluate the effectiveness of a cut score (Glascoe, 2005). The following evaluation guidelines will be used in identifying cut scores: Sensitivity between 70 and 80%, specificity close to 80%, and NPV of 30–50% (Glascoe, 2005). For false-positive and false-negative errors, values under .10 and will be preferred. Further, hit rate values of .80 or higher will be considered acceptable. Researchers are reminded that after choosing a method, and setting a cut score, validity needs to be considered carefully (Pant, Rupp, Tiffin-Richards, & Köller, 2009). Only on the basis of validity evidence will suggest that the method – and the screener – are performing as intended.

Table 13.2. Summary of seven indices commonly used to evaluate cut scores

Indices	Statement	Formula
Sensitivity / true positive rate	The proportion of functionally impaired children correctly identified from the set of children referred for treatment	d / (b + d)
Specificity / true negative rate	The probability to correctly identify children who are developing normally	a / (a + c)
Positive predictive value (PPV)	The proportion of positive test results that are true positives	d / (d + c)
Negative predictive value (NPV)	The proportion of subjects with a negative test result who are correctly diagnosed	a/ (a +b)
False-positive (FP) error rate	The proportion of children who are developing normally but are misclassified as at risk	c / (a + c)
False-negative (FN) error rate	The proportion of children who are functionally impaired but are misidentified as on track developmentally	b / (b + d)
Total hit rate	Proportion correct overall	(a + d) / N

Adapted from DiStefano & Morgan (2011).

Example

The Pediatric Symptom Checklist (PSC; Jellinek & Murphy, 1988) is a 35-item form designed to screen children for behavioral and emotional risk. It was originally developed for use in clinical settings for parents or doctors to rate the frequency of a child's maladaptive behavior, but is gaining attention for use by teachers in the school environment (Liu & DiStefano, 2014). The full form is freely available on the Internet (http://www.massgeneral.org/psychiatry/assets/PSC-35.pdf).

The scale measures three factors: internalizing problems, externalizing problems and attention problems. PSC items are rated on a three-point scale, using anchors of *often, sometimes,* or *never* with scored values of 2, 1, or 0, respectively. Raw item scores are summed to a total score by adding all item scores together (score range: 0–70), with higher scores denoting risk. Scores exceeding a cutoff score of 28 for children from 6 to 18 denote risk (note: the cutoff score is 24 for children from 3 to 5, as four items dealing with school are ignored for younger children).

From the PSC, a shorter form was developed by researchers, the PSC-17, with only 17 items (Gardner et al., 1999). The same three factors were included, just with fewer items per dimension (i.e., Externalizing Problems – 7 items, Internalizing Problems – 5 items, Attention Problems – 5 items). The PSC-17 was developed based on the exploratory factor analysis results from the PSC; however, few details were provided for the short form development (Gardner et al., 1999). In addition, different items may emerge as optimal if the short form is to be used in the schools or with young children.

To investigate this possibility, similar procedures were repeated using an independent sample of preschool children's PSC ratings ($N = 875$) to determine if similar procedures applied to the full PSC (35-item) would produce a similar shorter form. The principal axis factor (PAF) exploratory factor analysis method was chosen to reduce the scale, as it can be used when the assumption of normality for the data is violated (Costello & Osborne, 2005). Since there are only three response categories for the data, PAF may be the most appropriate method. Also, the PAF is less likely than other exploratory factor analysis methods to produce improper solutions (e.g., negative variance estimates).

The promax rotation method was selected to allow factors to correlate and raise the statistical power. Given that the goal with short forms is often to ensure that the same dimensions are demonstrated in the shorter instrument, a three-factor solution was extracted to choose the items that were the best marker variables from each factor. The three-factor solution was used based on prior theory; however, other factor solutions (e.g., two-, four-factor) were examined to allow for the possibility of a different underlying factor solution.

The following criteria were used with PAF to find the optimal solution for the underlying factor structure: (1) Item loadings that are higher than .6 were considered as marker variables of the given factor. These items were examined to select only those which were the most representative of the factor, where the loading values were examined to see where there were large gaps between loading values; (2) Simple structure, meaning that most items should have a substantial loading on one factor but low loadings on other factors. (3) The factor solution makes sense based upon interpretability and match to theory. In addition, each factor should be defined by at least three items, and (4) Internal reliability estimate (Cronbach's alpha) of each factor should be higher than .80.

As with the PSC-17 creation, exploratory factor analysis was applied to the set of 35 items. A three-factor solution was shown to be optimal, for which the definitions of the three factors (and items included per factor) aligned with the structure measured by the PSC. Loading values on each factor were examined to identify the best markers of each factor that loaded highly (above .6). Items that cross-loaded or with lower loading values were excluded. Based on the criteria above, 14 items were retained. This solution was rerun using PAF to identify final loading values. The final solution is presented in Table 13.3 and is compared with PSC-17 identified by Gardner et al. (1999). To facilitate interpretation, the item number used is the same as noted with the original PSC-35.

The overall three-factor structure was conceptually consistent with the PSC-17 developed by Gardner et al. (1999) in that the same factors were identified: Internalizing Problems, Externalizing Problems, and Attention Problems. However, only 14 items were identified for the PSC in the preschool environment. The internal consistencies meet the cutoff score of greater than .80. This held even for the Attention Problems factor, which only has 3 items. Overall, in the short form the current analysis showed slightly different results compared with the PSC-17.

Table 13.3. PSC Preschool Short Form creation: factor loadings of the final solution of preschooler ratings (*N* = 875)

	Factor 1	Factor 2	Factor 3	Internal consistency
Internalizing problems				
Q10 Is afraid of new situations	.693	−.091	−.008	
Q11 Feels sad, unhappy	.711	.066	.003	
Q13 Feels hopeless	.633	.222	−.137	.834
Q15 Less interested in friends	.620	−.131	.192	
Q22 Worries a lot	.724	−.017	−.115	
Q27 Seems to be having less fun	.736	−.097	.056	
Externalizing problems				
Q16 Fights with other children	−.136	.747	.128	.859
Q32 Teases others	−.075	.732	.048	
Q33 Blames others for his or her troubles	.042	.652	.051	
Q34 Takes things that do not belong to him or her	−.109	.672	.099	
Q35 Refuses to share	−.034	.622	.202	
Attention problems				
Q4 Fidgety, unable to sit still	−.151	.172	.767	.879
Q9 Distracted easily	.003	−.006	.816	
Q14 Has trouble concentrating	−.021	−.061	.858	

Note. Marker items for each factor are noted in bold.

The Internalizing Problems factor consisted of six items, of which four of the same items selected with the PSC-17 were chosen. Two new items were selected: "Is afraid of new situations" (Q10) and "Is less interested in friends" (Q11). These items may be noted by a teacher as he/she has a peer group for which to compare a young child. One item was selected with the PSC-17, but was not selected here, as it was below the loading cutoff at .595.

Five items measuring externalizing problems formed Factor 2. All the items in the preschool short form factors were also included in the PSC-17. The two items that were not selected exhibited low loadings and were cross loading on more than one factor.

Items under Factor 3 measured children's attention level in classrooms. As with the Externalizing Problems factor, all items selected for the Attention Problems factor were also included in the PSC-17. The factor selected here only had three items, instead of the five noted on the PSC-17; the two excluded items had low loadings and cross loadings on more than one factor.

The newly developed short form is even shorter than PSC-17; however, results may differ given that the sample used here were teacher ratings of preschoolers, instead of parents or clinicians. Given that the setting and the situation are different than those used with the original analyses (e.g., Gardener et al., 1999), the PSC 14 for the preschool environment is in need of replication and validation to ensure it works as intended.

Future Research

The increasing recognition of the value of early intervention, the right to equitable access to services, and a rising responsibility to survey populations for emerging deficits in performance or functioning signal likely opportunities for the implementation of short forms and screeners (Kettler, Glover, Albers, & Feeney-Kettler, 2014). For example, with screening, any consequent success in the identification of intervention needs also introduces a requirement for effective treatment monitoring. The activities assessment and intervention, whether in the sphere of public or private institutions, are affected by the real constraints of time and other resources, both of service providers as well as those they serve. All of these factors demand instruments that produce scores that are both reliable and valid for their intended application.

While research in the construction of short forms and screening instruments has expanded knowledge on the development of such measures, the means for widespread, practical use of such forms are not yet clear. Future investigations will need to examine the use of technology for more quickly gathering data and directing use of results. Information on the timely and effective usage of results – the "what next?" practicalities – of short forms and screening tests also require research. Greater distribution of technologies (computers, tablets, high-speed wireless Internet, etc.) and the capacities of these tools suggest coming opportunities for real world use of screening tests and short forms at their maximum potential.

Acknowledgments

The research reported here was partly supported by the Institute of Education Sciences, U.S. Department of Education, through Grant R324A100104 to the South Carolina Research Foundation. The opinions expressed are those of the author and do not necessarily represent views of the Institute of Education Sciences or the U.S. Department of Education.

References

Allen, M. J., & Yen, W. M. (1979). *Introduction to measurement theory*. Monterey, CA: Brooks/Cole.

Altman, D. G. (1991). *Practical statistics for medical research*. London, UK: Chapman & Hall.

Arthur, W., & Day, D. V. (1994). Development of a short form for the Raven Advanced Progressive Matrices Test. *Educational and Psychological Measurement*, *54*(2), 394–403. http://doi.org/10.1177/0013164494054002013

Baker, F. (2001). *The basics of item response theory*. ERIC Clearinghouse on Assessment and Evaluation, University of Maryland, College Park, MD.

Bricker, D., & Squires, J. (1999). *Ages and stages questionnaires: A parent-completed child-monitoring system* (2nd ed.). Baltimore, MD: Brookes.

Benson, J., & Nasser, F. (1998). On the use of factor analysis as a research tool. *Journal of Vocational Education Research*, *23*, 13–33.

Berle, D., Starcevic, V., Moses, K., Hannan, A., Milicevic, D., & Sammut, P. (2011). Preliminary validation of an ultra-brief version of the Penn State Worry Questionnaire. *Clinical Psychology & Psychotherapy*, *18*(4), 339–346. http://doi.org/10.1002/cpp.724

Bond, T. G., & Fox, C. M. (2007). *Applying the Rasch Model: Fundamental measurement in the human sciences* (2nd ed.). Mahwah, NJ: Erlbaum.

Butcher, J. N., Williams, C. L., Graham, J. R., Archer, R. P., Tellegen, A., Ben-Porath, Y. S., & Kaemmer, B. (1992). *MMPI–A: Manual for administration, scoring, and interpretation*. Minneapolis, MN: University of Minnesota Press.

Christ, T. J., & Nelson, P. M. (2014). Developing and evaluation screening systems: Practical and psychometric considerations. In R. J. Kettler, T. A. Glover, C. A. Albers, & K. A. Feeney-Kettler (Eds.), *Universal screening in educational settings: Evidence-based decision making for schools* (pp. 79–110). Washington, DC: American Psychological Association.

Costello, A. B., & Osborne, J. W. (2005). Best practices in exploratory factor analysis: Four recommendations for getting the most from your analysis. *Practical Assessment, Research & Evaluation, 10*(7). Retrieved from http://pareonline.net/getvn.asp?v=10&n=7

Comrey, A. L., & Lee, H. B. (1992). *A first course in factor analysis*. Hillsdale, NJ: Erlbaum.

Crocker, L., & Algina, J. (1986). *Introduction to classical and modern test theory*. Fort Worth, TX: Harcourt Brace Jovanovich College Publishers.

DiStefano, C., & Morgan, G. B. (2011). Examining classification criteria: A comparison of three cut score methods. *Psychological Assessment, 23*(2), 354–363. http://doi.org/10.1037/a0021745

Embretson, S. E., & Reise, S. P. (2000). *Item response theory for psychologists*. Mahwah, NJ: Lawrence Erlbaum.

Field, A. P. (2005). *Discovering statistics using SPSS* (2nd ed.). London, UK: Sage.

Gameroff, M. J., Wickramaratne, P., & Weissman, M. M. (2012). Testing the short and screener versions of the Social Adjustment Scale – Self-Report (SAS-SR). *International Journal of Methods in Psychiatric Research, 21*(1), 52–65. http://doi.org/10.1002/mpr.358

Gardner, W., Murphy, J. M., Childs, G., Kelleher, K., Pagano, M., Jellinek, M., … Chiappetta, L. (1999). The PSC-17: A brief Pediatric Symptom Checklist with psychosocial problem subscales. A report from PROS and ASPN. *Ambulatory Child Health, 5*, 225–236.

Girard, T. A., Axelrod, B. N., & Wilkins, L. K. (2010). Comparison of WAIS-III short forms for measuring index and full-scale scores. *Assessment, 17*(3), 400–405. http://doi.org/10.1177/1073191110369763

Gorsuch, R. L. (1983). *Factor analysis* (2nd ed.). Hillsdale, NJ: Erlbaum.

Glascoe, F. P. (2005). Screening for developmental and behavioral problems. *Mental Retardation and Developmental Disabilities Research Reviews, 11*, 173–179. http://doi.org/10.1002/mrdd.20068

Glover, T. A., & Albers, C. A. (2007). Considerations for evaluating universal screening assessments. *Journal of School Psychology, 45*(2), 117–135. http://doi.org/10.1016/j.jsp.2006.05.005

Hakstian, A. R., & McLean, P. D. (1989). Brief screen for depression. *Psychological Assessment: A Journal of Consulting and Clinical Psychology, 1*(2), 139–141. http://doi.org/10.1037/1040-3590.1.2.139

Hambleton, R. K., & Jones, R. W. (1993). Comparison of classical test theory and item response theory and their applications to test development. *Educational Measurement: Issues and Practice, 12*(3), 3847.

Hambleton, R. K., Swaminathan, H., & Rogers, H. J. (1991). *Fundamentals of item response theory*. Newbury Park, CA: Sage.

Jellinek, M. S., & Murphy, J. M. (1988). Screening for psychosocial disorders in pediatric practice. *American Journal of Diseases of Children, 112*, 1153–1157.

Kessel, J. B., & Zimmerman, M. (1993). Reporting errors in studies of the diagnostic performance of self-administered questionnaires: Extent of the problem, recommendations for standardized presentation of results, and implications for the peer review process. *Psychological Assessment, 5*, 395–399. http://doi.org/10.1037/1040-3590.5.4.395

Kettler, R. J., Glover, T. A., Albers, C. A., & Feeney-Kettler, K. A. (2014). An introduction to universal screening in educational settings. In R. J. Kettler, T. A. Glover, C. A. Albers, & K. A. Feeney-Kettler (Eds.), *Universal screening in educational settings: Evidence-based decision making for schools* (pp. 3–16). Washington, DC: American Psychological Association. http://doi.org/10.1037/14316-000

Kehoe, J. (1995). Basic item analysis for multiple-choice tests. *Practical Assessment, Research & Evaluation, 4*(10). Retrieved from http://PAREonline.net/getvn.asp?v=4&n=10

Linacre, J. M. (2004). Optimizing rating scale category effectiveness: Rasch measurement. The dichotomous model. In E. V. Smith & R. M. Smith (Eds.), *Introduction to Rasch measurement* (pp. 258–278). Maple Grove, MN: JAM Press. http://doi.org/10.1891/jnum.10.3.189.52562

Linacre, J. M. (2006). *WINSTEPS: Rasch Measurement software*. Retrieved from http://www.winsteps.com/winsteps.htm

Liu, J., & DiStefano, C. (2014, May). *Analysis of the factor structure of the Pediatric Symptoms Checklist (PSC-17)*. Paper presented at the Modern Modeling Methods Conference, Storrs, Connecticut.

Loevinger, J. (1954). The attenuation paradox in test theory. *Psychological Bulletin, 51*(5), 493–504. http://doi.org/10.1037/h0058543

Lord, F. M. (1980). *Applications of item response theory to practical testing problems.* Hillsdale, NJ: Erlbaum.

Metz, C. E. (1978). Basic principles of ROC analysis. *Seminars in Nuclear Medicine, 8*, 283–298. http://doi.org/10.1016/S0001-2998(78)80014-2

Pant, H. A., Rupp, A. A., Tiffin-Richards, S. P., & Köller, O. (2009). Validity issues in standard-setting studies. *Studies in Educational Evaluation, 35*(2-3), 95–101. http://doi.org/10.1016/j.stueduc.2009.10.008

Pagano, M. E., Cassidy, L. J., Little, M., Murphy, J. M., & Jellinek, M. S. (2000). Identifying psychosocial dysfunction in school-age children: The Pediatric Symptom Checklist as a self-report measure. *Psychology in the Schools, 37*(2), 91–106. http://doi.org/10.1002/(SICI)1520-6807(200003)37:2<91::AID-PITS1>3.3.CO;2-V

Prewett, P. N. (1995). A comparison of two screening tests (the Matrix Analogies Test–Short Form and the Kaufman Brief Intelligence Test) with the WISC-III. *Psychological Assessment, 7*(1), 69. http://doi.org/10.1037/1040-3590.7.1.69

Putnam, S. P., & Rothbart, M. K. (2006). Development of short and very short forms of the Children's Behavior Questionnaire. *Journal of Personality Assessment, 87*(1), 102–112. http://doi.org/10.1207/s15327752jpa8701_09

Reise, S. P., Waller, N. G., & Comrey, A. L. (2000). Factor analysis and scale revision. *Psychological Assessment, 12*, 287–297.

Schipolowski, S., Schroeders, U., & Wilhelm, O. (2014). Pitfalls and challenges in constructing short forms of cognitive ability measures. *Journal of Individual Differences, 35*(4), 190–200. http://doi.org/10.1027/1614-0001/a000134

Schumaker, R. E. (2004). Rasch measurement: The dichotomous model. In E. V. Smith & R. M. Smith (Eds.), *Introduction to Rasch measurement* (pp. 226–257). Maple Grove, MN: JAM Press. http://doi.org/10.1891/jnum.10.3.189.52562

Silverstein, A. B. (1990). Short forms of individual intelligence tests. *Psychological Assessment, 2*, 3–11. http://doi.org/10.1037/1040-3590.2.1.3

Smith, E. V., Conrad, K. M., Chang, K., & Piazza, J. (2002). An introduction to Rasch measurement for scale development and person assessment. *Journal of Nursing Measurement, 10*, 189–206. http://doi.org/10.1891/jnum.10.3.189.52562

Smith, G. T., McCarthy, D. M., & Anderson, K. G. (2000). On the sins of short-form development. *Psychological Assessment, 12*, 102–111. http://doi.org/10.1037/1040-3590.12.1.102

Swets, J. A. (1996). *Signal detection theory and ROC analysis in psychology and diagnosis: Collected papers.* Mahwah, NJ: Erlbaum.

Thompson, E. R. (2007). Development and validation of an internationally reliable short-form of the positive and negative affect schedule (PANAS). *Journal of Cross-Cultural Psychology, 38*(2), 227–242. http://doi.org/10.1177/0022022106297301

Weeks, J. W., Spokas, M. E., & Heimberg, R. G. (2007). Psychometric evaluation of the Mini-Social Phobia Inventory (Mini-SPIN) in a treatment-seeking sample. *Depression and Anxiety, 24*(6), 382–391. http://doi.org/10.1002/da.20250

Chapter 14

Using Multitrait–Multimethod Analyses in Testing for Evidence of Construct Validity

Barbara M. Byrne

School of Psychology, University of Ottawa, Canada

Construct validity encompasses two modes of inquiry: (a) validation of a construct (i.e., trait), and (b) validation of a measuring instrument. Although the terms *construct* and *trait* bear different connotations depending on one's theoretical/philosophical perspective (see Messick, 1981), these terms are used interchangeably here in the interest of simplicity. In validating a construct, the researcher seeks empirical evidence in support of hypothesized relations among dimensions of the same construct (termed within-network relations), and among the construct of interest and other dissimilar constructs (termed between-network relations). In their seminal investigative research addressing the issue of construct validity, Cronbach and Meehl (1955) viewed these theoretical linkages as representing a construct's *nomological network*. In contrast to a construct, validation of a measuring instrument, demands empirical evidence that the construct purportedly measured by the instrument is, in fact, the one actually measured. In the case of an instrument having several subscales (i.e., each representing one facet or dimension of the construct measured), evidence of construct validity is demonstrated if the subscales exhibit a well-defined factor structure that is consistent with the underlying theory. Considered as a whole, then, construct validation involves the interplay of theory construction and test development, the two processes being complementary, rather than concurrent (see Anastasi, 1986). That is to say, given an adequate theory, researchers can test a measuring instrument. Alternatively, given an adequate instrument, researchers can test a theory.

For over 50 years now (Eid & Nussbeck, 2009), the multitrait–multimethod (MTMM) matrix has been a favored methodological strategy in testing for evidence of construct validity. Across this timespan, it seems evident that researchers have never lost their fascination in searching for solutions to its various limitations. As a result, construct validity researchers can now choose from several different approaches to the analysis of MTMM data. My intent in this chapter is to provide you with an overview of MTMM approaches that have received the most attention in the literature, either through their comparison with other MTMM strategies, or through their application to example data. I present this overview in four sections. I begin by examining the basic criteria considered to constitute evidence of construct validity. In the next section, I outline the original MTMM approach to measurement of construct validity as proposed by Campbell and Fiske (1959) and then summarize the many weaknesses associated with this approach as brought to light via subsequent construct validity research. The following section presents an overview of four alternate approaches to the analysis of MTMM data, along with the perceived advantages and disadvantages of each. Finally, in the last section, I present an illustrated application to real data based on one of the most prominent confirmatory factor analytic (CFA) models used in testing for construct validity.

Criteria in Support of Construct Validity

In essence, construct validity is an umbrella term encompassing two crucially important concepts – *convergent validity* and *discriminant validity*. Convergent validity refers to the extent to which constructs known to be theoretically related are in fact found to be related based on observed data; that is, a measure should correlate highly with other measures to which it is theoretically linked. In sharp contrast, discriminant validity refers to the extent to which constructs known *not* to be theoretically related are found, empirically, not to be related; that is, a measure should correlate negligibly with others to which it is theoretically unrelated. As such, convergent and discriminant validity represent two sides of the same coin. Importantly, any claim of construct validity must be accompanied by evidence of both types of validity (Campbell & Fiske, 1959; Messick, 1981).

Cronbach and Meehl's (1955) proposed nomological network represented a seminal roadmap to establishment of construct validity. They believed that by developing a nomological network for their construct(s) of interest, researchers would ultimately establish both its theoretical framework (relations among the constructs) and its empirical framework (linkages between the observed variables and their underlying constructs), as well as specification of the linkages between these two frameworks. However, despite its theoretical usefulness as a means to determining construct validity, a major limitation of this work was the failure to provide any methodological strategy capable of quantifying the extent to which construct validity had been attained.

The Multitrait–Multimethod (MTMM) Matrix

Addressing this methodological problem in determining construct validity, Campbell and Fiske (1959) proposed that such evidence could be empirically achieved through a structured matrix of zero-order correlations between multiple traits assessed by multiple methods. As such, assessment of construct validity would focus on four blocks of correlations: (a) scores on the same traits measured by the same methods (termed monotrait–monomethod [MTMM] values), (b) scores on the same traits measured by different methods (monotrait–heteromethod [MTHM] values), (c) scores on different traits measured by different methods (heterotrait–heteromethod [HTHM] values), and (d) scores on different traits measured by the same method (heterotrait–monomethod [HTMM] values). Whereas the first comparison reflects on the reliability of each trait measured by each method, the second set of values reflects on convergent validity for the same traits measured by different methods. The latter two comparisons focus on discriminant validity. However, in contrast to the third comparison whereby the extent to which independent assessment methods diverge in their measurement of different traits is of interest, the fourth comparison focuses on method effects, an extension of the discriminant validity issue. Method effects represent bias that can derive from use of the same method in the assessment of different traits. An example MTMM matrix is shown in Figure 14.1.

Campbell and Fiske (1959) proposed four criteria for evaluating convergent and discriminant validity: (1) convergent validities should be statistically significantly different from zero and sufficiently large to warrant further investigation of validity, (2) monotrait–heteromethod values should be higher than correlations between different traits assessed by different methods values, (3) monotrait–heteromethod values should be higher than correlations between different traits assessed by the same method, and (4) the pattern of correlations between different traits should be the same in both the heteromethod and monomethod blocks, and consistent with relevant theories.

In the years subsequent to Campbell and Fiske's introduction of the MTMM design, there has been a growing body of research reporting on the many limitations of its basic analytic schema (see, e.g., Bagozzi & Yi, 1993; Marsh, 1988; Schmitt & Stults, 1986; Widaman, 1985). At least five such limitations are worthy of note. First, the criteria function as rules of thumb,

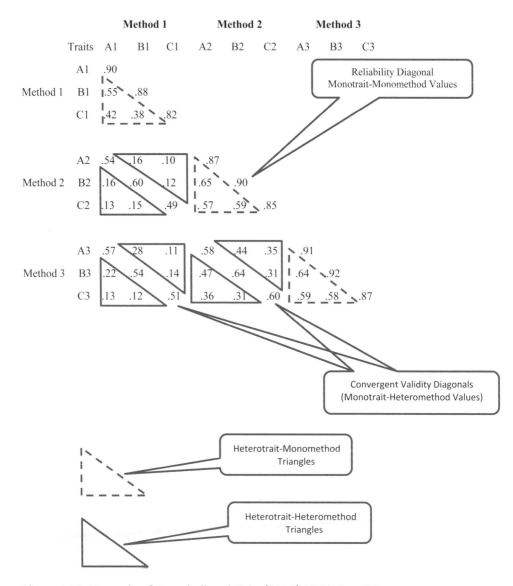

Figure 14.1. Example of Campbell and Fiske (1959) MTMM matrix.

rather than as precise quantitative measurements in determining evidence of construct validity. Second, with each addition of traits or methods to the model, the number of nonindependent comparisons increases dramatically; these two factors in combination make it difficult, if not impossible to determine the extent to which the Campbell and Fiske (C-F) criteria have been met. Third, although based only on visible inspection of observed correlations, findings derived from the C-F criteria are used to make inferences regarding the underlying (i.e., latent) traits and methods. Fourth, the provision of separate estimates of variance due to traits, methods, and error, as well as estimated relations among the latent trait and method factors is not possible. Fifth, hypotheses bearing on construct validity cannot be tested statistically.

Alternative Approaches to Implementing MTMM Analyses

As realization of these weaknesses in the C-F approach to MTMM analyses have come to light over the years, construct validity researchers have sought to develop different approaches that can not only address these limitations, but are more quantitatively based. Throughout this pursuit of a more effective and problem-free approach to the analysis of MTMM data, each proposed model has built upon the foundations of its predecessor while concomitantly mending any known limitations. This ongoing methodological research has resulted in several alternative strategies (for an overview, see Conway, Lievens, Scullen, & Lance, 2004; Lance, Noble, & Scullen, 2002; Marsh & Grayson, 1995; Millsap, 1995). Of these, the use of structural equation modeling (SEM) within the framework of confirmatory factor analytic (CFA) models has gained the most prominence and has been the most widely implemented (e.g., Eid, Lischetzke, Nussbeck, & Trierweiler, 2003; Kenny & Kashy, 1992; Marsh & Grayson, 1995; Widaman, 1985).

There are now at least four well-recognized variants of CFA MTMM models; these include the so-called *general CFA model* (GCFA; Widaman, 1985), the *correlated uniquenesses model* (CUCFA; Kenny, 1979; Marsh, 1988, 1989), the *composite direct product model* (CDPCFA; Browne, 1984)[1], and the more recent correlated trait-correlated method minus one model (CT-C[M-1]; Eid, 2000). Of these, the GCFA and CUCFA models have received the most attention in the literature with some arguing for the superiority of the former (e.g., Conway et al., 2004; Lance et al., 2002), and others supporting the latter (Kenny, 1976, 1979; Kenny & Kashy, 1992; Marsh, 1989; Marsh & Bailey, 1991). This popularity notwithstanding, it is important to note the surge of interest in, and application of the more recently developed CT-C(M-1) model (see, e.g., Maydeu-Olivares & Coffman, 2006; Nussbeck, Eid, & Lischetzke, 2006). In sharp contrast, although the CDPCFA model has been included in studies where interest focuses on its comparison with other CFA models (see, e.g., Bagozzi & Yi, 1993; Byrne & Goffin, 1993; Goffin & Jackson, 1992), its use as a sole MTMM analytic strategy is scarce and likely due to the specificity of the software needed in performing the analyses. (For assorted MTMM model comparisons, readers are referred to Coenders & Saris, 2000; Corten et al., 2002; Eid et al., 2003; Hernández & González-Romá, 2002; Lance et al., 2002; Marsh & Bailey, 1991; Marsh et al., 1992; Marsh & Grayson, 1995; Tomás, Hontangas, & Oliver, 2000; Wothke, 1996) On the basis of both comparability and popular usage, the MTMM models reviewed in this chapter will focus on only the GCFA, CUCFA, and CT-C(M-1) models; they are now presented in this same order. Based on the same data for ease of comparison, the GCFA model is presented in Figure 14.2 and the CUCFA and CT-C(M-1) models in Figure 14.3.

---

1   The MUTMUM software program (Browne, 1990) was specifically designed for fitting CDP models to MTMM data as, unlike the other models noted here, this model assumes that trait and method effects are multiplicative, rather than additive.

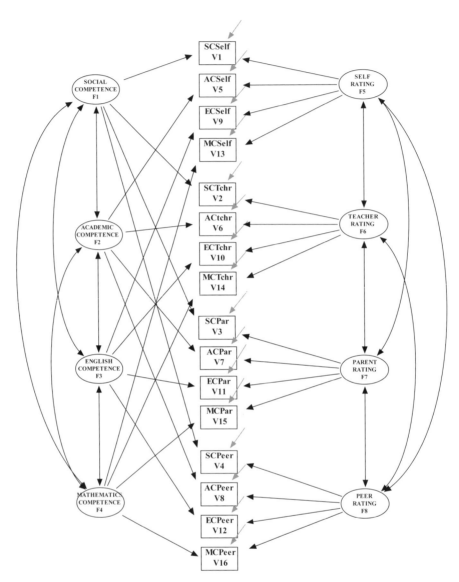

Figure 14.2. Hypothesized MTMM general CFA model (Model 1).
© 2012 From *Structural equation modeling with Mplus: Basic concepts, applications, and programming* by B. M. Byrne. Reproduced by permission of Taylor and Francis Group, LLC, a division of Informa plc.

The General Confirmatory Factor Analytic (GCFA) Model

Confirmatory factor analytic models have evolved from the early work of Jöreskog (1969) in developing statistical software capable of testing such models. However, the popularity of the GCFA model as a means to formulating an MTMM approach for testing construct validity is considered to have stemmed from Widaman's (1985) proposed taxonomy of nested model comparisons in the analysis of data that lend themselves to this type of research design. Indeed, a particularly appealing feature of this model was its perceived capability to overcome

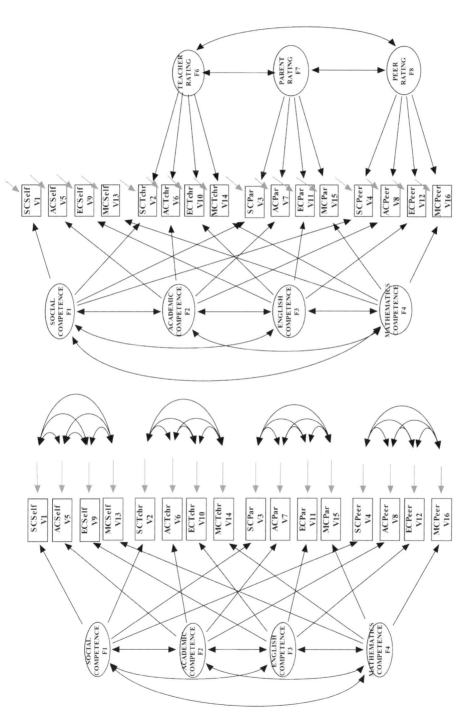

Figure 14.3. Correlated uniquenesses (CUCFA) model (left). Correlated traits-correlated methods minus one (CT-C[M-1]) model (right).

weaknesses indigenous to the original Campbell–Fiske approach, which is based on zero-order correlations. In particular, the GCFA model provides for: (a) an explanation of the MTMM matrix in terms of underlying latent constructs, rather than observed variables, (b) the evaluation of convergent and discriminant validity at the matrix, as well as at the parameter level, (c) the testing of hypotheses related to convergent and discriminant validity, and (d) separate estimates of variance due to traits, methods, and error, in addition to estimated correlations among trait and among method factors. Of particular note with respect to the latter is assumed nonrelatedness between trait and method factors.

These positive features notwithstanding, the GCFA model too is not without its own shortcomings. Indeed, at least six limitations of this MTMM approach have been noted. First, perhaps the most notable limitation of the GCFA model is its tendency to yield ill-defined solutions that typically result in negative variances. Such findings are purported to arise as a consequence of two issues: (a) the requirement that each assessment method be specified as a separate method (Marsh, 1989; Marsh & Bailey 1991), and (b) empirical underidentificaton[2] (Eid et al., 2003; Kenny & Kashy, 1992; Lance et al., 2002). Second, the assumption that method factors are truly indicative of method effects has been seriously challenged. In particular, Marsh (1989; Marsh & Bailey, 1991) has argued that method factors can also represent trait variance, and if found to be the case, the nested model comparisons as suggested by Widaman (1985), may not be justified. Third, a related limitation occurs when, in fact, the method factors are intercorrelated. In such instances, Marsh (1989) cautions that because the method factor structure then explains a portion of the variance pertinent to all observed variables, it more realistically represents a general trait influence, rather than a method specific influence. Fourth, due to problems related to statistical identification, the GCFA model is limited in its ability to yield estimates of trait/method correlations (Schmitt & Stults, 1986; Widaman, 1985). Fifth, as noted earlier, the GCFA model assumes that trait and method factors are uncorrelated. However, given that this assumption appears to lack a substantive rationale (Marsh & Grayson, 1995) and in light of the nature of psychological data, Eid et al. (2003) question under what circumstances this condition would be considered reasonable. Finally, as noted by Eid et al. (2003, p. 39), the GCFA model "assumes that the method effect due to one method generalizes homogeneously across all applications of this method." Given that all observed variable indicators of a particular method factor load on the same common factor, the existence of any trait-specific method factor is made impossible. Again, Eid et al. (2003) question the rationality of this restriction, particularly when applied to psychological data.

The Correlated Uniqueness Confirmatory Factor Analytic (CUCFA) Model

Building upon the early work of Kenny (1976, 1979) in addressing the problem of ill-defined solutions in the GCFA model, Marsh (1988, 1989) proposed an alternative CFA approach to MTMM analyses that allows method effects to be represented by correlated error/uniqueness terms, labeling this parameterization the *correlated uniqueness model*. (The term uniqueness is used in the factor analytic sense to mean a composite of random and specific measurement error associated with a particular measure; subscale scores in the present application.)

---

2   The issue of model identification in SEM is a complex topic for which a comprehensive explanation goes beyond the scope of this chapter. In simple terms, however, model identification is evidenced if all unknown parameters can be uniquely estimated. Empirical underidentification can occur in MTMM analyses based on the GCFA parameterization if, for example, two or more factor loadings have the same value (see Kenny & Kashy, 1992).

Marsh argued that problematic fit in the GCFA model derives in part from the assumption that method effects are unidimensional and have a congeneric structure such that the magnitude of method factor loadings presumably represents the method's influence on each of the measured variables. Addressing this limitation (noted earlier), the CUCFA model specifies correlations among the error terms (i.e., residuals) of observed indicator variables measuring the same method factor in lieu of correlations among the method factors. Based on extensive testing of both empirical and simulated data, Marsh (1988, 1989; Marsh & Bailey, 1991) has reported consistently satisfactory performance pertinent to the CUCFA model. He posited two major advantages of this model over the GCFA model. First, in contrast to the GCFA model, the CUCFA model typically results in well-defined and proper solutions. Second, when the effects of a particular method are not unidimensional (i.e., method factors are correlated), the data are more accurately represented by the CUCFA model.

Unquestionably, a major improvement of the CUCFA model over the GCFA model is its high consistency in yielding convergent and admissible solutions. Given the critical importance of this criterion, Lance et al. (2002) caution against any tendency to conclude that the CUCFA approach to MTMM analyses is superior to that of the GCFA approach as the drawing of such a conclusion would be erroneous. In an extensive critique of the CUCFA model, Lance and colleagues (2002) cited numerous limitations of this model that occur as a consequence of serious theoretical issues; these are as follows: First, due to the confounding of systematic, nonsystematic, and method variance, direct measurement of method variance components is made impossible. Second, despite evidence to the contrary (see, e.g., Conway et al., 2004; Kenny & Kashy, 1992), the CUCFA model assumes the method factors to be uncorrelated. Given the nature of social psychological data, Conway et al. (2004) consider this assumption to represent a major weakness of the CUCFA model. Third, compared with the GCFA model, the CUCFA model has been found to be less efficient in its estimation of method effects. Fourth, findings reported by several authors support those of Lance and colleagues in suggesting that trait estimates tend to exhibit an upward biasing trend (see, e.g., Byrne & Goffin, 1993; Kenny & Kashy, 1992; Marsh & Bailey, 1991). Furthermore, in a test of this hypothesized upward biasing effect, Conway et al. (2004) found the prediction to hold particularly when the method factor loadings are substantial and the method factors highly correlated. As a result of the bias trend, these estimates may be biased toward stronger evidence of convergent validity, and weaker evidence of discriminant validity. Finally, citing an empirical example in which relations between the latent trait variables comprising a MTMM CFA model and other trait variables external to the model might be of interest, Lance et al. (2002) note that although the testing of such hypothesized relations are possible with the GCFA model, they are not so with the CUCFA model. (For more detailed explanation in support of these cited limitations, readers are referred to Lance et al., 2002.)

The Correlated Trait-Correlated Method Minus One (CT-C[M-1]) Model

In an effort to resolve the frequently found problems of nonconvergence associated with the GCFA model, Eid (2000) proposed an alternate approach to the analysis of MTMM data which he termed the CT-C(M-1) model. In essence, this model represents a modified form of the GCFA model, albeit with the specification of one method factor less than the actual number of methods included in the MTMM analyses (Eid et al., 2003). The philosophical underpinning of the CT-C(M-1) model contends that because each observed variable represents a trait-method unit (see Campbell & Fiske, 1959), it is not possible for a trait to be measured independently of the method (Geiser, Eid, & Nussbeck, 2008). Nonetheless, it allows for an assessment of method convergent validity by contrasting one method against another. This procedure is made possible by selecting one of the methods to serve as a *comparison method standard*. Eid et al. (2003) explain that for each trait, the true score variance of the observed indicator variable measured by the comparison standard "is taken as a regressor in a regression analysis" (p. 41). A method factor can then be defined as a residual factor that is common to all observed variables measured by the same factor. Thus, it can be said that "a method factor, represents that part of a trait measured by a method k that cannot be predicted by the true-score variable of the indicator measured by the method taken as the comparison standard" (Eid et al., 2003, p. 41). (For a walk-through of steps involved in practical applications of the CT-C(M-1) model, readers are referred to Eid et al., 2003 when data represent interval scale, and to Nussbeck, Eid, & Lischetzke, 2006 when they represent ordinal scale.)

As with all previously proposed MTMM models, the CT-C(M-1) model is not without limitations and Lance et al. (2002) have noted at least three: (a) Given that trait factors are defined in reference to a comparison method, estimates of method effects are precluded, (b) because the trait and method factors are unrelated, the comparison method must necessarily be orthogonal to the remaining M-1 method factors, and (c) it represents a less straightforward method than either the GCFA or CUCFA models. Furthermore, Eid et al. (2003) note that in order to specify trait specific method effects, trait-method units require multiple and homogeneous indicators.

An Illustrated CFA MTMM Application

To provide readers with a sense of how MTMM analyses are conducted within the framework of CFA, I now present an illustrated application based on the GCFA model and includes Widaman's (1985) nested model comparisons. The selection of this CFA MTMM model was made for two reasons: (a) the strong recommendations by Lance et al. (2002), following their through comparison of the GCFA and CUCFA models, that the GCFA model is the more preferable of the two; and (b) for readers who may not be familiar with the conduct of MMTM analyses within the CFA framework, the GCFA model is likely the most straightforward of the three discussed in this chapter. Furthermore, Widaman's suggested model comparisons are easy to follow in testing for evidence in support of convergent and discriminant validity, as well as method effects. What follows now are details related to the sample data, model estimation, criteria used in judging model goodness-of-fit to the sample data, the model under study, tests for evidence of construct and discriminant validities and finally, interpretation of the results.

The Sample Data

The GCFA model under study here is based on data taken from a study by Byrne and Bazana (1996) in which the primary intent was to test for evidence of convergent validity, discriminant validity, and method effects related to four facets of perceived competence (social, academic, English, mathematics) as measured by self, teacher, parent, and peer ratings for early/late preadolescents and adolescents in grades 3, 7, and 11, respectively. For our purposes here, however, we focus only on data for late preadolescents (grade 7; $n = 193$). Failure of parents to return their ratings was the primary reason for severe reduction in the original sample size ($n = 290$) Although the final sample size can be considered slightly less than optimal for the analysis of SEM models (approximately 200 and greater), it is nonetheless substantially larger than the typical MTMM sample of 125 (see Conway et al., 2004). (For further elaboration of the substantive topic, the sample, and/or the instrumentation, readers are referred to the original paper.)

Mode of Statistical Estimation

All SEM analyses were conducted using Version 6 of the Mplus program (Muthén & Muthén, 2007–2010). Given that the data were found to be normally distributed, analyses were based on maximum likelihood (ML) estimation. Thus, chi-square difference values reported for various analytic comparisons required no scaling correction. For detailed explanation and annotated walk-through of the specification and testing of the MTMM model described and illustrated here, readers are referred to Byrne (2012).

Goodness-of-Fit Criteria

Judgment of model fit to the sample data was based on the comparative fit index (CFI; Bentler, 1990), the root mean-square error of approximation (RMSEA; Steiger & Lind, 1980; Browne & Cudeck, 1993), the RMSEA 90% confidence interval (CI; Steiger, 1990), and the standardized root mean square residual (SRMR). The CFI ranges in value from 0 to 1.00, with a value of .95 and greater considered indicative of well-fitting models (Hu & Bentler, 1999). The RMSEA takes into account the error of approximation in the population and is expressed per degree of freedom, thus making it sensitive to model complexity; values less than .05 indicate good fit and values as high as .08 represent reasonable errors of approximation in the population. The accompanying 90% CI indicates the precision of the RMSEA value. A narrow interval argues for good precision of the RMSEA value in reflecting model fit in the population (MacCallum, Browne, & Sugawara, 1996). Finally, the SRMR represents the average discrepancy between the sample and hypothesized correlation matrices; ideally, values should be less than .10. (For detailed, yet nonmathematical explanation of SEM model testing procedures and goodness-of-fit criteria based on the Mplus, EQS, and Amos programs, readers are referred to Byrne, 2012, 2006, and 2009, respectively.)

The Analytic Strategy

In testing for evidence of construct validity based on the GCFA model, it has become customary to follow guidelines set forth by Widaman (1985). As such, the hypothesized MTMM model is compared with a nested series of more restrictive models in which specific parameters are either eliminated, or constrained equal to 0 or 1.0. The difference in χ^2 ($\Delta\chi^2$) provides the yardstick by which to judge evidence of convergent and discriminant validity. Although these evaluative comparisons are made solely at the matrix (or variance-covariance) level, the CFA format allows also for an assessment of construct validity at the individual parameter level. A review of the literature bearing on the CFA approach to MTMM analyses indicates that assessment is typically formulated at both the matrix and the individual parameter levels; we examine both in the present application.

The model portrayed in Figure 14.2 represents the hypothesized GCFA model under study and serves as the baseline against which three alternatively specified, albeit nested models are compared in the process of assessing evidence of construct validity. In the lexicon of MTMM design, the model is composed of four traits (social competence, academic competence, English competence, mathematics competence), and four methods (self-ratings, teacher ratings, parent ratings, peer ratings), with each observed variable representing a subscale score. Clearly, this model represents a much more complex structure than the usual multifaceted CFA model. This complexity arises primarily from the loading of each subscale score onto both a trait and a method factor. In addition, the model postulates that, although the traits and methods are correlated among themselves, any correlations between traits and methods are assumed to be zero. We proceed first in testing for evidence of construct validity at the matrix level, and then move on to an examination of the individual parameters. The four nested models described and tested in this application (Models 1–4) represent those most commonly included in the GCFA approach to MTMM analyses.

Testing for Construct Validity at the Matrix Level

Prerequisite to any comparison of models, it is necessary to establish the goodness-of-fit of each model (i.e., Models 1–4) to the MTMM data. The first model to be tested (Model 1) represents the hypothesized model shown in Figure 14.1 and, as noted earlier, embodies the baseline against which all other models are compared. Because its specification includes both trait and method factors and allows for correlations among traits and among methods, this model represents the least restrictive of the four models. The Mplus input file for Model 1 is shown in the Appendix.

Consistent with the known propensity of the GCFA model to yield improper solutions, this problem was encountered in the testing of Model 1. As noted earlier, when these inappropriate solutions occur, the offending parameter typically represents a negative variance associated with either a residual or a factor. In this case, the variance of the residual term associated with ACSELF (self-reported academic competence) was found to be negative. One possible resolution of this problem is to impose an equality constraint between the offending parameter and another parameter from the same matrix having a similarly estimated value (Marsh et al., 1992). Heeding this recommendation, Model 1 was respecified with the residual variance of ACSELF constrained equal to the residual variance of ECSELF. Unfortunately, this model also resulted in an error message indicative of an improper solution and the yielding of a negative residual variance thus requiring that a different approach be taken in resolving the problem. Negative variances typically represent *boundary parameters*, meaning their estimated values are so close to zero that they can bounce back and forth on each side of zero. Thus, a second approach to resolving this difficulty is to constrain the offending parameter to zero. Addition of this constraint for the ACSELF residual resulted in a proper solution and thus remained intact for Models 1, 3, and 4 (see footnote in Table 14.1). Goodness-of-fit statistics for this initial model are shown in Table 14.1.

We turn now to the other MTMM models against which Model 1 is compared. The first of these (Model 2) differs from Model 1 only in that it specifies no trait factors; specification of freely correlated method factors remains the same as for Model 1. As indicated by the goodness-of-fit statistics shown in Table 14.1, this model exhibited an extremely poor fit to the data.

The next model (Model 3) postulates a structure having perfectly correlated traits (i.e., trait factor covariances are fixed to a value of 1.0); again, specification of the method factors as freely estimated is consistent with Models 1 and 2. Model fit statistics for this model, as shown in Table 14.1, indicated barely a marginally good fit to the data.

Finally, Model 4 argues for freely correlated traits, albeit methods that are completely independent (i.e., method covariances are fixed to 0.0). Results from the testing of this model yielded an exceptionally good fit to the data as indicated in Table 14.1.

Table 14.1.   Summary of goodness-of-fit statistics for GCFA models

Model	χ^2	df	SRMR	CFI	RMSEA	90% CI
1 Freely correlated traits;[a] Freely correlated methods	77.164	77	.042	1.00	.003	.000 .041
2 No traits; Freely correlated methods	335.635	99	.084	.829	.111	.098 .124
3 Perfectly correlated traits;[a] Freely correlated methods	216.164	83	071	.904	.091	.076 .106
4 Freely correlated traits;[a] Uncorrelated methods	111.117	83	.067	.980	.042	.017 .061

Note. [a]Represents respecified model with residual variance for ACSELF fixed to 0.0.
© 2012 From *Structural equation modeling with Mplus: Basic concepts, applications, and programming* by B. M. Byrne. Reproduced by permission of Taylor and Francis Group, LLC, a division of Informa plc.

Comparison of Models

We turn now to a comparison of particular pairs of models in determining evidence of construct validity consistent with procedures recommended by Widaman (1985). These results are reported in Table 14.2.

Table 14.2.   Goodness-of-fit indices for MTMM nested model comparisons

Model comparisons	χ^2	Difference in df	Difference in CFI	p
Test of Convergent Validity				
Model 1 vs. Model 2 (traits)	258.471[a]	22	.171	<.001
Test of Discriminant Validity				
Model 1 vs. Model 3 (traits)	139.000[b]	6	.096	<.001
Model 1 vs. Model 4 (methods)	33.953[c]	6	.020	<.001

Note. [a](335.635 − 77.164); [b](216.164 − 77.164); [c](111.117 − 77.164).
© 2012 From *Structural equation modeling with Mplus: Basic concepts, applications, and programming* by B. M. Byrne. Reproduced by permission of Taylor and Francis Group, LLC, a division of Informa plc.

Assessment of Convergent Validity

As noted earlier, one criterion of construct validity bears on the issue of convergent validity, the extent to which *independent measures* of the *same trait* are correlated (e.g., teacher and self-ratings of social competence); these values should be substantial and statistically significant (Campbell & Fiske, 1959). Using Widaman's (1985) paradigm, evidence of convergent validity can be tested by comparing a model in which traits are specified (Model 1), with one in which they are not (Model 2). This comparison serves to evaluate the impact of the trait factors in providing evidence of convergent validity. Here, the difference in χ^2 between the two models ($\Delta\chi^2$) provides the basis for judgment, with a statistically significant difference in χ^2 supporting evidence of convergent validity. In an effort to base model comparisons on a more realistic criterion than the, χ^2 difference test, some researchers (e.g., Bagaozzi & Yi, 1993; Widaman, 1985) have examined differences in CFI (ΔCFI) values. However, until the work of Cheung and Rensvold (2002), these ΔCFI values have served as an evaluative tool only in a heuristic sense. Following examination of 20 goodness-of-fit indexes and working within the context of tests for measurement invariance, Cheung and Rensvold (2002) arbitrarily recommended that for evidence of invariance to hold, the ΔCFI should not exceed a value of .01. That is to say, from a practical perspective, there are no differences between the groups. This same principle can be applied to MTMM model comparisons. As shown in Table 14.2, the $\Delta\chi^2$ was highly significant ($\chi^2_{(22)} = 258.471$, p < .001), and the difference in practical fit very substantial (ΔCFI = .171), thereby arguing for strong evidence of convergent validity. Within the context of the current example data, these results reveal a convergence of self, teacher, parent, and peer ratings in the measurement of social, academic, English, and mathematics competence.

Assessment of Discriminant Validity

Discriminant validity is typically assessed in terms of both traits, and methods. In testing for evidence of trait discriminant validity, one is interested in the extent to which independent measures of *different traits* are correlated; these values should be negligible. When the independent measures represent *different methods*, correlations bear on the discriminant validity of methods; when they represent the same method, correlations bear on the presence of method effects, another aspect of discriminant validity.

In testing for evidence of discriminant validity among traits, we compare a model in which traits correlate freely (Model 1), with one in which they are constrained to a value of 1.00 (Model 3). When evaluating results, the larger the discrepancy between the χ^2, and the CFI values, the stronger the evidence in support of discriminant validity. In other words, a large discrepancy between these two models provides evidence that the traits are uncorrelated, or at the very least, minimally correlated. This comparison yielded a $\Delta\chi^2$ value that was statistically significant ($\chi^2_{(6)} = 139.000, p < .001$), and the difference in practical fit moderately large (ΔCFI = .096), thereby suggesting only modest evidence of discriminant validity. These results are consistent with the theory in showing that although the four facets of perceived competence can be measured as separate constructs, they nonetheless are minimally intercorrelated.

Based on the same logic, albeit in reverse, evidence of discriminant validity related to method effects can be tested by comparing a model in which method factors are freely correlated (Model 1), with one in which the method factors are specified as zero (Model 4). In this case, a large $\Delta\chi^2$ (or substantial ΔCFI) argues for the lack of discriminant validity and thus, for common method bias across methods of measurement. That is, a large discrepancy between these two comparative models indicates some degree of overlap across the methods and is considered to represent a method effect. On the strength of both statistical ($\Delta\chi^2_{(6)} = 33.953$) and nonstatistical ($\Delta$CFI = .020) criteria, as shown in Table 14.2, it seems reasonable to conclude that evidence of discriminant validity for the methods was substantially stronger than it was for the traits. In other words, these findings indicate that, despite the fact that the four methods were all rating scales, there was little evidence of overlap across ratings by self, teachers, parents, and peers thereby indicating minimal method effects.

Testing for Construct Validity at the Parameter Level

Examination of Parameters

A more precise assessment of trait- and method-related variance, compared with assessment at the matrix level, can be ascertained by examining individual parameter estimates. Specifically, the factor loadings and factor correlations of the hypothesized model (Model 1) provide the focus here. Factor loading estimates are summarized in Table 14.3 and factor correlations in Table 14.4. (For a more extensive discussion of these MTMM findings, see Byrne & Bazana, 1996.)

Table 14.3. Trait and method loadings for MTMM Model 1 (correlated traits; correlated methods)[a]

	Trait Factors				Method Factors			
	SC	AC	EC	MC	SR	TR	PAR	PER
Self-Ratings (SR)								
Social competence	.806				.265			
Academic competence		.472[b]			.882			
English competence			.726		.382[b]			
Mathematics competence				.674	.479			
Teacher Ratings (TR)								
Social competence	.408					.283		
Academic competence		.176[b]				.939		
English competence			.250			.776		
Mathematics competence				.450		.609		
Parent Ratings (PAR)								
Social competence	.584						.387	
Academic competence		.483[b]					.663	
English competence			.646				.468	
Mathematics competence				.730			.529	
Peer Ratings (PER)								
Social competence	.311							.416
Academic competence		.151[b]						.931
English competence			.210[b]					.674
Mathematics competence				.298				.700

Note. [a]Standardized estimates; [b]not statistically significant.
© 2012 From *Structural equation modeling with Mplus: Basic concepts, applications, and programming* by B. M. Byrne. Reproduced by permission of Taylor and Francis Group, LLC, a division of Informa plc.

Table 14.4. Trait and method correlations for MTMM Model 1 (correlated traits; correlated methods)[a]

	Traits				Methods			
Measures	SC	AC	EC	MC	SR	TR	PAR	PER
Social Competence (SC)	1.000							
Academic Competence (AC)	.213[b]	1.000						
English Competence (EC)	.087[b]	.770	1.000					
Mathematics Competence (MC)	.157[b]	.786	.337[b]	1.000				
Self Ratings (SR)					1.000			
Teacher Ratings (TR)					.423	1.000		
Parent Ratings (PAR)					.432[b]	.626	1.000	
Peer Ratings (PER)					.396	.439	.252	1.000

Note. [a]Standardized estimates; [b]not statistically significant.
© 2012 From *Structural equation modeling with Mplus: Basic concepts, applications, and programming* by B. M. Byrne. Reproduced by permission of Taylor and Francis Group, LLC, a division of Informa plc.

Assessment of Convergent Validity

In examining individual parameters, convergent validity is reflected in the magnitude of the trait loadings. As indicated in Table 14.3, all trait loadings, with the exception of those for self, teacher, parent and peer ratings of Academic Competence, along with peer ratings of English Competence were found to be statistically significant. However, in a comparison of factor loading values across traits and methods, we see that the method variance exceeds trait variance in a little over a half (9 of 16) ratings. Specifically, these include self-ratings of Academic Competence (e.g., .882 as compared to .472), teacher ratings of Academic, English, and Mathematics Competence (e.g., .939 vs. .176; .776 vs. .250; .609 vs. .450), parent ratings of Academic Competence (.663 vs. .483), and peer ratings of all four Competence traits (.416 vs. .311; .931 vs. .151; .674 vs. .210; .700 vs. .298). (Trait and method variance, within the context of the GCFA model, equals the factor loading squared.) Values compared in assessing convergent validity are bolded in Table 14.3. Thus, although at first blush, evidence of convergent validity appeared to be very strong when evaluated at the matrix level, a more in-depth examination at the individual parameter level reveals some attenuation of the traits from method effects related mainly to teacher and peer ratings, thereby tempering evidence of convergent validity (see also, Byrne & Goffin, 1993 with respect to adolescents).

Assessment of Discriminant Validity

Discriminant validity bearing on particular traits and methods is ascertained by examining their factor correlation matrices as reported in Table 14.4. That is to say, we separately examine correlations among the traits and correlations among the methods. Although, conceptually, correlations among traits should be negligible to satisfy evidence of discriminant validity, such findings are highly unlikely in general, and with respect to psychological data in particular. For example, whereas the correlation between social competence and academic, English, and mathematics competencies (.213; .087; .157, respectively; see bolded in Table 14.4) could be considered to meet this requirement, correlations among the remaining trait pairs are more problematic. The problem here, of course, is how to establish a criterion cut-point against which to judge evidence of discriminant validity. In this regard, Marsh and Hocevar (1983) suggested that with attitudinal constructs, only correlations approaching unity should be of concern, Widaman (1985) suggested the measurement of two standard errors from 1.00, and Goffin and Jackson (1992) recommended values > .71 in that trait correlations exceeding this value are indicative of more than 50% shared variance thereby rendering their distinctiveness somewhat dubious.

Based on the latter two criteria, with the exception of the correlation between Academic and English Competence ($r = .770$), and between Academic and Math Competence ($r = .786$), discriminant validity for the traits was considered to be moderately attained. Although these findings, at face value, suggest that relations between Academic Competence and the specific subject areas of English and Math were most detrimental to the attainment of trait discriminant validity, a review of construct validity research in this area reveals their intercorrelations to reflect appropriate levels of discriminant validity within the context of related theory (see, e.g., Byrne, 1990; Byrne & Shavelson, 1986; Byrne & Worth Gavin, 1996; Marsh, 1990; Marsh, Byrne, & Shavelson, 1988).

Finally, an examination of method factor correlations in Table 14.4 reflects on their discriminability, and thus on the extent to which the methods are maximally dissimilar, an important underlying assumption of the MTMM strategy (see Campbell & Fiske, 1959). Given the obvious dissimilarity of self, teacher, parent, and peer ratings, it is somewhat surprising to find a correlation of .626 between teacher and parent ratings of perceived competence. One possible explanation of this finding is that, except for minor editorial changes necessary in tailoring the instrument to teacher, parent, and peer respondents, the substantive content of all comparable items in these rating scales was identically worded in order to maximize consistent internalization of item content by different raters of the same student.

Conclusion

This chapter has provided an overview of the primary issues addressed in testing for evidence of construct validity as it relates to the measurement of a theoretical construct, reviewed the benefits and limitations of three CFA MTMM approaches to these tests (GCFA, CUCFA, CT-C[M-1]), and presented an illustrated empirical application based on the model considered to be the one most closely aligned with the original theoretical thrust of MTMM analyses as portrayed in the Campbell and Fiske (1959) matrix (GCFA model; see Lance et al., 2002; Becker & Cote, 1994). In closing out this chapter, I now wish to spotlight research that has sought to both improve and expand these three modeling approaches to MTMM analyses within the framework of CFA.

Turning first to the GCFA model, Lance et al. (2002) and Conway et al. (2004) have recommended that this model be the one of choice, albeit with two important caveats: (a) that the size of the MTMM matrix be expanded to include more than the usual three traits and three methods (see, e.g., Conway et al. 2004; Marsh & Bailey, 1991), and (b) that sample sizes be substantially larger than the average sample size of 125 typically reported in the MTMM literature (Conway et al., 2004; Millsap, 1995). Of course, it is now well known that sample sizes larger than 200 are highly recommended whenever analyses are based on SEM analyses (Boomsma & Hoogland, 2001). Adherence to these cautionary measures has been shown empirically to minimize the risk of inadmissible solutions.

Recent research involving the CUCFA model has focused on comparisons between results derived from its original parameterization and those from alternative specifications of the model. For example, in contrast to most comparisons of additive and multiplicative models, which typically have involved individual tests of the GCFA, CUCFA, and CDPCFA models, Coenders and Saris (2000) conducted these comparisons on alternative parameterizations of the CUCFA model that simulate these additive and multiplicative characteristics. Importantly, this research revealed that for designs with three methods, the CUCFA model with multiplicative constraints is equivalent to the CDPCFA model. In a subsequent study, these same respecifications of the CUCFA model were tested on 87 data sets collected in the United States, Austria, and The Netherlands. Goodness-of-fit results were found to be most optimal for models that assumed additive method effects (see Corten et al., 2002). Finally, in an attempt to clarify the substance of correlated uniquenesses in the CUCFA model, Saris and Aalberts (2003) tested several alternative models and determined that these parameters are best explained by a model that assumes unequal method effects.

Another area of growing interest in MTMM research is the extent to which both the GCFA and CUCFA models can be improved if multiple, rather than single indicator variables are used and higher-order structures are specified (see, e.g., Marsh, 1993; Marsh & Hocevar, 1988). Based on a Monte Carlo manipulated study in which single-indicator models were compared with multiple-indicator models, Tomás et al. (2000) found the GCFA model to work well and even better than the CUCFA model when more than two indicators were specified.

Finally, Hox and Kleiboer (2007) present a very unique parameterization of MTMM data structured as a multilevel model in which daily measurement occasions are nested within subjects. Modeling the data in this way allows for the assessment of reliability and validity of measurements at both the subject and occasion levels.

It is now well over a decade since Marsh and Grayson (1995) asserted that, due to an inherently complicated structure that may not be fully described by any modeling approach, there appears to be "no right way to analyse MTMM data that works in all situations", (p. 198). Indeed, this claim would appear to be as valid today as it was 18 years ago! Thus, it seems evident that development of novel modeling approaches to MTMM analysis will continue well into the future as researchers strive to meet its many frustrating, yet intriguing, challenges.

References

Anastasi, A. (1986). Evolving concepts of test validation. *Annual Review of Psychology, 37*, 1–15. http://doi.org/10.1146/annurev.ps.37.020186.000245

Bagozzi, R. P., & Yi, Y. (1993). Multitrait-multimethod matrices in consumer research: Critique and new developments. *Journal of Consumer Psychology, 2*, 143–170. http://doi.org/10.1016/S1057-7408(08)80022-8

Becker, T. E., & Cote, J.A. (1994). Additive and multiplicative effects in applied psychological research: An empirical assessment of three models. *Journal of Management, 20*, 625–641. http://doi.org/10.1177/014920639402000306

Bentler, P. M. (1990). Comparative fit indexes in structural models. *Psychological Bulletin, 107*, 238–246. http://doi.org/10.1037/0033-2909.107.2.238

Boomsma, A., & Hoogland, J. J. (2001). The robustness of LISREL modelling revisited. In R. Cudeck, S. du Toit, & D. Sörbom (Eds.), *Structural equation modeling: Present and future* (pp. 139–168). Lincolnwood, IL: Scientific Software International.

Browne, M. W. (1984). The decomposition of multitrait–multimethod matrices. *The British Journal of Mathematical and Statistical Psychology, 37*, 1–21. http://dx.doi.org/10.1111/j.2044-8317.1984.tb00785.x

Browne, M. W. (1990). *MUTMUM PC user's guide*. Unpublished manuscript. Department of Statistics, University of South Africa, Pretoria.

Browne, M. W., & Cudeck, R. (1993). Alternative ways of assessing model fit. In K. A. Bollen & J. S. Long (Eds.), *Testing structural equation models* (pp. 445–455). Newbury Park CA: Sage.

Byrne, B. M. (1990). Methodological approaches to the validation of academic self-concept: The construct and its measures. *Applied Measurement in Education, 3*, 185–207. http://doi.org/10.1207/s15324818ame0302_4

Byrne, B. M. (2006). *Structural equation modeling with EQS: Basic concepts, applications programming* (2nd ed.). Mahwah, NJ: Erlbaum.

Byrne, B. M. (2009). *Structural equation modeling with AMOS: Basic concepts, applications programming* (2nd ed.). New York, NY: Taylor & Francis/Routledge.

Byrne, B. M. (2012). *Structural equation modeling with Mplus: Basic concepts, applications, and programming*. New York, NY: Taylor & Francis/Routledge.

Byrne, B. M., & Bazana, P. G. (1996). Investigating the measurement of social and academic competencies for early/late preadolescents and adolescents. A multitrait-multimethod analysis. *Applied Measurement in Education, 9*, 113–132. http://doi.org/10.1207/s15324818ame0902_2

Byrne, B. M., & Goffin, R. D. (1993). Modeling MTMM data from additive and multiplicative covariance structures: An audit of construct validity concordance. *Multivariate Behavioral Research, 28*, 67–96. http://doi.org/10.1207/s15327906mbr2801_5

Byrne, B. M., & Shavelson, R. J. (1986). On the structure of adolescent self-concept. *Journal of Educational Psychology, 78*, 474–481. http://doi.org/10.1037/0022-0663.78.6.474

Byrne, B. M., & Worth Gavin, D. A. (1996). The Shavelson model revisited: Testing for the structure of academic self-concept across pre-, early, and late adolescents. *Journal of Educational Psychology, 88*, 215–228. http://doi.org/10.1037/0022-0663.88.2.215

Campbell, D. T., & Fiske, D. W. (1959). Convergent and discriminant validation by the multitrait-multimethod matrix. *Psychological Bulletin, 56*, 81–105. http://doi.org/10.1037/h0046016

Cheung, G. W., & Rensvold, R. B. (2002). Evaluating goodness-of-fit indexes for testing measurement invariance. *Structural Equation Modeling: A Multidisciplinary Journal*, 9, 233–255. http://dx.doi.org/10.1207/S15328007SEM0902_5

Coenders, G., & Saris, W. E. (2000). Testing nested additive, multiplicative, and general multitrait-multimethod models. *Structural Equation Modeling, 7*, 219–250. http://doi.org/10.1207/S15328007SEM0702_5

Conway, J. M., Lievens, F., Scullen, S. E., & Lance, C. E. (2004). Bias in the correlated uniqueness model for MTMM data. *Structural Equation Modeling, 11*, 535–559. http://doi.org/10.1207/s15328007sem1104_3

Corten, I. W., Saris, W., Coenders, G., van der Veld, W., Aalberts, C. E., & Kornelis, C. (2002). Fit of different models for multitrait-multimethod experiments. *Structural Equation Modeling, 9*, 213–232. http://doi.org/10.1207/S15328007SEM0902_4

Cronbach, L. J., & Meehl, P. E. (1955). Construct validity in psychological tests. *Psychological Bulletin, 52*, 281–302. http://doi.org/10.1037/h0040957

Eid, M. (2000). A multitrait-multimethod model with minimal assumptions. *Psychometrika, 65*, 241–261. http://doi.org/10.1007/BF02294377

Eid, M., Lischetzke, T., Nussbeck, F. W., & Trierweiler, L. I. (2003). Separating trait effects from trait-specific method effects in multitrait-multimethod models: A multiple-indicator CT-C(M-1) model. *Psychological Methods, 8*, 38–60. http://doi.org/10.1037/1082-989X.8.1.38

Eid, M., & Nussbeck, F. W. (2009). The multitrait-multimethod matrix at 50! *Methodology: European Journal of Research methods for Behavioral and Social Sciences, 5*, 71. http://doi.org/10.1027/1614-2241.5.3.71

Geiser, C., Eid, M., & Nussbeck, F. W. (2008). On the meaning of the latent variables in the CT-C(M-1) model: A comment on Maydeu-Olivares and Coffman (2006). *Psychological methods, 13*, 49–57. http://doi.org/10.1037/1082-989X.13.1.49

Goffin, R. D., & Jackson, D. N. (1992). Analysis of multitrait-multirater performance appraisal data: Composite direct product method versus confirmatory factor analysis. *Multivariate Behavioral Research, 27*, 363–385. http://doi.org/10.1207/s15327906mbr2703_4

Hernández, A., & González-Romá, V. (2002). Analysis of multitrait-multioccasion data: Additive versus multiplicative models. *Multivariate Behavioral Research, 37*, 59–87. http://doi.org/10.1207/S15327906MBR3701_03

Hox, J. J., & Kleiboer, A. M. (2007). Retrospective questions or a diary method? A two-level multitrait-multimethod analysis. *Structural Equation Modeling, 14*, 311–325. http://doi.org/10.1080/10705510709336748

Hu, L-T., & Bentler, P. M. (1999). Cutoff criteria for fit indexes in covariance structure analysis: Conventional criteria versus new alternatives. *Structural Equation Modeling, 6*, 1–55. http://doi.org/10.1080/10705519909540118

Jöreskog, K. G. (1969). A general approach to confirmatory maximum likelihood factor analysis. *Psychometrika, 34*, 183–202. http://dx.doi.org/10.1007/BF02289343

Kenny, D. A. (1976). An empirical application of confirmatory factor analysis to the multitrait-multimethod matrix. *Journal of Experimental Social Psychology, 12*, 247–252. http://doi.org/10.1016/0022-1031(76)90055-X

Kenny, D. A. (1979). *Correlation and causality*. New York, NY: Wiley.

Kenny, D. A., & Kashy, D. A. (1992). Analysis of the multitrait-multimethod matrix by confirmatory factor analysis. *Psychological Bulletin, 112*, 165–172. http://doi.org/10.1037/0033-2909.112.1.165

Lance, C. E., Noble, C. L., & Scullen, S. E. (2002). A critique of the correlated trait-correlated method and correlated uniqueness models for multitrait-multimethod data. *Psychological Methods, 7*, 228–244. http://doi.org/10.1037/1082-989X.7.2.228

MacCallum, R. C., Browne, M. W., & Sugawara, H. M. (1996). Power analysis and determination of sample size for covariance structure modeling. *Psychological Methods, 1*, 130–149. http://doi.org/10.1037/1082-989X.1.2.130

Marsh, H. W. (1988). Multitrait-multimethod analysis. In J. P. Keeves (Ed.), *Educational research methodology, measurement, and evaluation: An international handbook* (pp. 570–578). Oxford, UK: Pergamon.

Marsh, H. W. (1989). Confirmatory factor analyses of multitrait-multimethod data: Many problems and a few solutions. *Applied Psychological Measurement, 15*, 47–70. http://doi.org/10.1177/014662169101500106

Marsh, H. W. (1990). A multidimensional, hierarchical model of self-concept: Theoretical and empirical justification. *Educational Psychology Review, 2*, 77–172. http://doi.org/10.1007/BF01322177

Marsh, H. W. (1993). Multitrait-multimethod analyses: Inferring each trait/method combination with multiple indicators. *Applied Measurement in Education, 6*, 49–81. http://doi.org/10.1207/s15324818ame0601_4

Marsh, H. W., & Bailey, M. (1991). Confirmatory factor analyses of multitrait-multimethod data: A comparison of alternative models. *Applied Psychological Measurement, 15*, 47–70. http://doi.org/10.1177/014662169101500106

Marsh, H. W., Byrne, B. M., & Craven, R. (1992). Overcoming problems in confirmatory factor analyses of MTMM data: The correlated uniqueness model and factorial invariance. *Multivariate Behavioral Research, 27*, 489–507. http://doi.org/10.1207/s15327906mbr2704_1

Marsh, H. W., Byrne, B. M., & Shavelson, R. J. (1988). A multifaceted academic self-concept: Its hierarchical structure and its relation to academic achievement. *Journal of Educational Psychology, 80*, 366–380. http://doi.org/10.1037/0022-0663.80.3.366

Marsh, H. W., & Grayson, D. (1995). Latent variable models of multitrait-multimethod data. In R. H. Hoyle (Ed.), *Structural equation modeling: Concepts, issues, and applications* (pp. 177–198). Thousand Oaks, CA: Sage.

Marsh, H. W., & Hocevar, D. (1983). Confirmatory factor analysis of multitrait-multimethod matrices. *Journal of Educational Measurement, 20*, 231–248. http://doi.org/10.1111/j.1745-3984.1983.tb00202.x

Marsh, H. W. & Hocevar, D. (1988). A new, more powerful approach to multitrait–multimethod analyses: Application of second-order confirmatory factor analysis. *Journal of Applied Psychology, 72*, 107–117. http://dx.doi.org/10.1037/0021-9010.73.1.107

Maydeu-Olivares, A., & Coffman, D. L. (2006). Random intercept item factor analysis. *Psychological Methods, 11*, 344–362. http://doi.org/10.1037/1082-989X.11.4.344

Messick, S. (1981). Constructs and their vicissitudes in educational and psychological measurement. *Psychological Bulletin, 89*, 575–588. http://doi.org/10.1037/0033-2909.89.3.575

Millsap, R. E. (1995). The statistical analysis of method effects in multitrait-multimethod data: A review. In P. E. Shrout & S. T. Fiske (Eds.), *Personality research, method, and theory: A festschrift honoring D.W. Fiske* (pp. 93–109). Hillsdale, NJ: Erlbaum.

Muthén, L. K., & Muthén, B. O. (2007–2010). *Mplus user's guide* (6th ed.) Los Angeles, CA: Muthén & Muthén.

Nussbeck, F. W., Eid, M., & Lischetzke, T. (2006). Analysing multitrait-multimethod data with structural equation models for ordinal variables applying the WLSMV estimator: What sample size is needed for valid results? *British Journal of Mathematical and Statistical Psychology, 59*, 195–213. http://doi.org/10.1348/000711005X67490

Saris, W.E. & Aalberts, C. (2003). Different explanations for correlated disturbance terms in MTMM studies. *Structural Equation Modeling, 10*, 193–213. http://doi.org/10.1207/S15328007SEM1002_2

Schmitt, N., & Stults, D. N. (1986). Methodology review: Analysis of multitrait-multimethod matrices. *Applied Psychological Measurement, 10*, 1–22. http://doi.org/10.1177/014662168601000101

Steiger, J. H. (1990). Structural model evaluation and modification: An interval estimation approach. *Multivariate Behavioral Research, 25*, 173–180. http://doi.org/10.1207/s15327906mbr2502_4

Steiger, J. H., & Lind, J. C. (1980, June). *Statistically based tests for the number of common factors*. Paper presented at the Psychometric Society Annual Meeting, Iowa City, IA.

Tomás, J. M., Hontangas, P. M., & Oliver, A. (2000). Linear confirmatory factor models to evaluate multitrait-multimethod matrices: The effects of number of indicators and correlation among methods. *Multivariate Behavioral Research, 35*, 469–499. http://doi.org/10.1207/S15327906MBR3504_03

Widaman, K. F. (1985). Hierarchically nested covariance structure models for multitrait-multimethod data. *Applied Psychological Measurement, 9,* 1–26. http://doi.org/10.1177/014662168500900101

Wothke, W. (1996). Models for multitrait–multimethod matrix analysis. In G. A. Marcoulides & R. E. Schumacker (Eds.), *Advanced structural equation modeling: Issues and techniques* (pp. 7–56). Mahwah, NJ: Erlbaum.

Appendix

TITLE: MTMM Test for Construct Validity

Correlated Traits; Correlated Methods

DATA:

FILE IS "C:\Mplus\Files\ind7mt.DAT";

VARIABLE:

NAMES ARE SCSELF SCTCH SCPAR SCPEER ACSELF ACTCH ACPAR ACPEER EC-SELF ECTCH
ECPAR ECPEER MCSELF MCTCH MCPAR MCPEER;
USEVARIABLES ARE SCSELF - MCPEER;

MODEL:

F1 by SCSELF* SCTCH SCPAR SCPEER;
F2 by ACSELF* ACTCH ACPAR ACPEER;
F3 by ECSELF* ECTCH ECPAR ECPEER;
F4 by MCSELF* MCTCH MCPAR MCPEER;
F5 by SCSELF* ACSELF ECSELF MCSELF;
F6 by SCTCH* ACTCH ECTCH MCTCH;
F7 by SCPAR* ACPAR ECPAR MCPAR;
F8 by SCPEER* ACPEER ECPEER MCPEER;

F1 - F8@1;

F1 with F5@0;
F1 with F6@0;
F1 with F7@0;
F1 with F8@0;
F2 with F5@0;
F2 with F6@0;
F2 with F7@0;
F2 with F8@0;
F3 with F5@0;
F3 with F6@0;
F3 with F7@0;
F3 with F8@0;
F4 with F5@0;
F4 with F6@0;
F4 with F7@0;
F4 with F8@0;

OUTPUT: STDYX TECH1;

Chapter 15

Method Effects in Psychological Assessment Due to Item Wording and Item Position

Karl Schweizer[1] and Stefan Troche[2]

[1]Department of Psychology, Goethe University Frankfurt, Germany
[2]Department of Psychology and Psychotherapy, University of Witten/Herdecke, Germany

The purpose of this chapter is to introduce method effects in psychological measures due to item position and item wording as well as to the handling of such effects. Both item position and item wording are possible sources of lack of the structural validity of psychological measures with crucial consequences to conclusions regarding the quality of the scales and also the constructs the scales intend to measure. This chapter implicitly discusses the appropriateness of some assumptions of measurement models that are basic to major theories of psychological tests. These measurement models assume that each measurement is composed of true and error components (Gulliksen, 1950; Novick, 1966) or that item responses can be described by a function of the person's attribute and characteristics of the items (Rasch, 1960/1980). Further assumptions are, for example, that true scores are expected values and that the responses to different items are independent of each other. Such assumptions are challenged by an increasing body of studies demonstrating that the response behavior is influenced by method effects such as item positioning and wording. For a time these sources of influence were hard to identify due to the lack of appropriate statistical methods. Advancements during the last decades, however, have opened up new possibilities to handle such method effects.

Many method effects are associated with a specific assessment method. For example, if participants complete a questionnaire, some of them may tend to check response options signifying agreement independent of content whereas some other participants may prefer the contrary. As a consequence of such response tendencies, items are likely to be spuriously correlated with each other. These correlations lead to an overestimation of the consistency of the scale composed of these items and an overestimation of correlations between conceptually different scales.

It was the seminal work by Campbell and Fiske (1959) that revealed the problems resulting from method effects in a very convincing way. They emphasized that the psychometric quality of scales can be misjudged due to the assessment methods applied in data collection. In order to gain insight into the impact of such effects on measurements, Campbell and Fiske (1959) proposed the multitrait–multimethod (MTMM) design. This design has been complemented by a number of confirmatory factor models for separating trait and method variance (Marsh, 1989; Marsh & Bailey, 1991).

The effects due to item wording and item position are two other effects that result from specific characteristics of assessment methods as compared to method effects reflecting response tendencies, such as acquiescence or social desirability. Both effects are associated with additional systematic variance that is to be characterized as method variance following the terminology proposed by Campbell and Fiske. This additional method variance is likely to transform the originally unidimensional structure into a two-dimensional structure in investigations by factor analysis. In the case of the effect due to the item position the additional factor is not to be confused with the so-called difficulty factor (e.g., McDonald, 1974). If the source is the item position, the factor reflects the additional method variance whereas the difficulty factor is defined to be due to a broad range of different degrees of difficulty.

Method effects inflict damage on research work that is conducted in the frameworks of all theories of test construction. Selecting a specific framework for demonstrations does not mean that this framework is especially prone to method effects as compared to other frameworks. It is the factor-analytic approach that is selected for this chapter.

The Effect Due to Item Position

Historically, research on the effect of the item position can be traced back to Ebbinghaus (1885), the founder of memory research. In his famous studies leading to the discovery of the forgetting curves, participants had to memorize a series of artificial words. One forgetting curve describes the probability to remember a word as a function of the position at which it was presented in the series. Another type of position effect was found in repeated-measures studies when the same participants were exposed to different treatments in a fixed order. In this case the position in the sequence was observed to influence the size of the effect. Counterbalancing has been recommended to control for this effect (Tabachnick & Fidell, 2007).

Furthermore, there is growing evidence for a position effect in items of psychological scales. This effect unfolds as the responses to just-completed items exert an influence on the responses to the next items. It is this effect that is addressed as item-position effect in the following sections. The first report on such an item-position effect appears to have been published by Campbell and Mohr (1950) who investigated the positions of the items of a checklist. They found that the variability of the responses to the initially presented items referring to the same construct turns into consistency in completing the last items.

Since then, a number of studies on the item-position effect have been conducted, and evidence has accumulated in favor of the assumption of an item-position effect in psychological scales. Most notable are studies by Knowles (1988; Knowles & Byers, 1996) who related the item reliabilities to the item positions in an attitude scale and demonstrated an increase in item reliability from the first to the last items. Thus, the proportion of true variance increased while participants completed the items of the scale.

Furthermore, quite a number of other studies on the item-position effect were conducted within the framework of item response theory (IRT; e.g., Embretson, 1991; Gittler & Wild, 1989; Kubinger, 2003; Verguts & DeBoeck, 2000). Some of them used multidimensional Rasch models, others linear logistic test models. More recent studies employed factor-analytic methods for investigating the item-position effect (Hartig, Hölzl, & Moosbrugger, 2007; Schweizer, 2012; Schweizer & Ren, 2013; Schweizer, Schreiner, & Gold, 2009; Schweizer, Troche, & Rammsayer, 2011).

The item-position effect has been observed in measures representing quite different human attributes. It was observed in data achieved by personality and attitude measures (Hartig et al.,

2007; Knowles, 1988) as well as by ability measures (Embretson, 1991; Schweizer, et al., 2009; Verguts & DeBoeck, 2000). Despite the generality of the effect, it is not clear whether it is always due to the same source, and, there are different hypotheses concerning the origination of the effect. Hamilton and Shuminsky (1990) argue that self-perception plays a major role in the occurrence of the item-position effect. Self-perception may actually be important if the item-position effect is observed in personality data, as self-perception may be associated with the tendency to respond in a consistent way. However, the consistency explanation does presumably not apply to ability data, since, in this case, the focus is on a correct response. The learning hypothesis has been proposed to explain the item-position effect in ability data (Embretson, 1991; Verguts & DeBoeck, 2000). This hypothesis is quite appealing as completing a series of rather similar items can lead to an increasing insight into the construction rules of the items, or the automation of basic processing.

An important issue is the coincidence of the gradually increasing item-position effect and the arrangement of items according to item difficulty that characterizes many reasoning scales such as Raven's Advanced Progressive Matrices (APM; Raven, Raven, & Court, 1997). It was argued that the item-position effect simply reflects the increasing item difficulty or a special difficulty factor. This argument stimulated research work and the results appear to disprove it. First, Knowles (1988) constructed versions of the original item list that differed according to the ordering of items. The comparison of the data obtained by the various versions of the lists indicated that the item-position effect and item difficulty were independent of each other. Unfortunately, Knowles did not investigate reasoning items but personality items. Second, there are IRT investigations using the linear logistic test model (LLTM). An investigation by means of this model requires that different sequences of the list of items are generated and used in data collection so that data referring to different sequences of items are available (Kubinger, 2003). The change of the sequence of items can be expected to highlight the dependency on the item difficulty, if such dependency exists. Consequently, the evidence in favor of the item-position effect achieved by means of LLTM supports the assumption that the item-position effect and the item difficulties are independent of each other.

Models for Investigating the Item-Position Effect

The item-position effect can influence the structural validity of a scale and, thereby, the outcome of confirmatory factor analyses of the items of this scale. This effect is especially obvious when the items are arranged in the same fixed sequence for all participants. If the participants complete different sequences of the same items, the effect may be no longer apparent but can still be expected to exert an influence on responding.

The standard model of confirmatory factor analysis is the congeneric model of measurement (Jöreskog, 1971). The congeneric model is not well suited for representing the item-position effect as it proceeds from the assumption of only one systematic source of variance that exerts its influence relatively evenly on the performance regarding all items of a homogeneous scale. Considering the item-position effect, however, means considering another source that gradually builds up in its influence on performance. Therefore, a variant of the bifactor model (Chen, West, & Sousa, 2006) is more appropriate than the congeneric model to represent the trait intended to be measured as a first latent variable as well as the item-position effect as a second latent variable. Figure 15.1 provides a graphical representation of such a model.

Under this framework there are two latent variables, one for representing the basic ability or trait and the other one for illustrating the item-position effect. Furthermore, there are p mani-

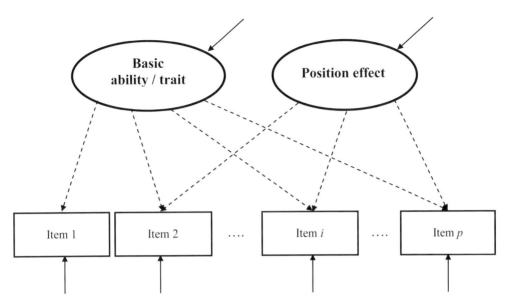

Figure 15.1. Illustration of the bifactor model for representing the effect of the item position in combination with the representation of an ability or trait.

fest variables (i.e., items) of which four are depicted in Figure 15.1. The arrows showing solid lines signify parameters that are to be estimated whereas dashed lines represent constrained parameters. Obviously, the first item loads only on the latent variable denoted basic ability/ trait whereas the other items load on both latent variables. The missing loading is due to the fact that the first item cannot be influenced by previous items. Furthermore, there are arrows pointing to the ellipses illustrating the latent variables and representing their variances.

Since the gradual increase of factor loadings cannot be appropriately represented and evaluated by the congeneric measurement model, models with fixed factor loadings are necessary for this purpose. Such factor loadings characterize models for investigating growth (McArdle, 1986, 1989, 2009; Choi, Harring, & Hancock, 2009), latent change (Tisak & Tisak, 1996) or the hypothesis-guided decomposition of variance (Schweizer, 2006, 2008). Models including fixed factor loadings enable the representation of specific expectations concerning the change of the sizes of factor loadings. This feature enables the selection of a specific course of increase in the size of factor loadings. In previous research, either a linear increase or a quadratic increase was successfully applied to represent the item-position effect (Schweizer, 2012). Furthermore, it is necessary to represent the ability or trait of interest. Assuming that this source of responding contributes to each item equally, a constant value larger than 0 (e.g., 1) is usually selected for this purpose.

In order to avoid very large numbers, the constraints for the factor loadings are divided by the largest number that is to be considered so that the constraints vary between 0 and 1. Thus, the linear function f_l is defined as

$$f_l(i) = (i-1)/(p-1) \qquad (1)$$

where i ($i = 1, \ldots, p$) corresponds to the position of the individual item in the sequence of p items of the scale. In the case of the quadratic function f_q the numerator and denominator are squared so that

$$f_q(i) = (i-1)^2 / (p-1)^2 . \tag{2}$$

Both functions predict no item-position effect for the first item and a gradually increasing effect for the following items. The factor loading of the last item is 1.

The numbers achieved this way are inserted into the $p{\times}q$ matrix of the factor loadings Λ. In the case of a linear increase and five items it is a $5{\times}2$ matrix, and the procedure leads to the following matrix of factor loadings:

$$\Lambda = \begin{bmatrix} 0 & 1 \\ 0.25 & 1 \\ 0.50 & 1 \\ 0.75 & 1 \\ 1 & 1 \end{bmatrix} . \tag{3}$$

The first column of the matrix represents the linear increase due to the item-position effect and the second column the constant contribution of the ability or trait of interest.

Additionally a link transformation is necessary if the data are binary in order to establish relationships between the distributions of the various variables of the model (Schweizer, 2013; Schweizer & Reiss, 2014; Schweizer, Ren, & Wang, 2015). If σ_s is the true variance associated with $p_s = .5$ and σ_i another variance associated with $p_i \ne .5$, the function v is assumed to establish the following relationship:

$$\sigma_i = v(\sigma_s, p_i) . \tag{4}$$

Under the assumption that the data show a binomial distribution and that the constraints reflect the differences between the variances, linked constraints $f_L(i)$ can be obtained as follows:

$$f_L(i) = \left[\frac{p_i(1-p_i)}{p_s(1-p_s)} \right]^{1/2} \times f(i) . \tag{5}$$

Furthermore, it is necessary to specify the $q{\times}q$ matrix of the covariances of the latent variables Φ and to estimate the variances of the latent variables. Because it is the aim to separate the item-position effect from the ability or trait, the covariance of the latent variables is set equal to zero:

$$\Phi = \begin{bmatrix} \phi_{increase} & 0 \\ 0 & \phi_{constant} \end{bmatrix} \tag{6}$$

Finally, the appropriateness of Λ and ϕ as part of the model of the covariance matrix with respect to the empirical covariance matrix of items is investigated. The goodness of fit statistics must show whether the consideration of the item-position effect improves the model-data fit compared to a model representing the ability or trait only.

Demonstration

The investigation used here describes university students' responses to Raven's APM. APM is a measure of fluid intelligence and has been used in a large number of studies. It includes two sets of 12 and 36 items; however, since the items of Set I are generally too easy for university students, researchers usually apply Set II only. The data were collected from 400 students.

The following models of measurement are considered in this investigation of the data. First, there is the *congeneric model* that does not take into consideration the item-position effect. It includes one latent variable, and the factor loadings are estimated. Second, there is the model with representations of ability and item-position effect as two independent latent variables. While the ability is represented by a latent variable with constant factor loadings, the factor loadings on the latent variable representing the item-position effect are fixed to show a linear increase. This model is referred to as *linear-effect model*. The third model also considers two independent latent variables associated with the ability and the item-position effect but in this case the factor loadings on the latent variable representing the position-effect increase quadratically. This model is denoted *quadratic-effect model*.

The chi-square, normed chi-square, RMSEA, SRMR, CFI, TLI and AIC were used as fit indices and are reported in Table 15.1 for the three models.

Table 15.1.   Fit results of investigating the items of APM by means of models with and without representations of the position effect ($N = 400$)

Model	χ^2	df	normed χ^2	RMSEA	SRMR	CFI	TLI	AIC
Linear increase	959	628	1.52	.036	.073	0.80	0.80	1,035
Quadratic increase	868	628	1.38	.031	.067	0.84	0.83	944
Congeneric	1,189	594	2.00	.050	.059	0.72	0.71	1,333

Note. AIC = Akaike's information criterion; CFI = comparative fit index; RMSEA = root mean square error of approximation; SRMR = standardized root mean square residual; TLI = Tucker Lewis index.

Suggestions for good model-fit include normed chi-square ≤ 2, RMSEA $\leq .06$, SRMR $\leq .08$, CFI $\geq .95$, and TLI $\geq .95$ (Bollen, 1989; Hu & Bentler, 1999). From Table 15.1, all three models yielded a good model-data fit according to normed chi-square, RMSEA and SRMR. According to CFI and TLI the results are less favorable. To some degree, these statistics reflect the large range of item difficulty and the heterogeneity that occasionally characterizes a large set of items. According to the AIC results for comparing nonnested models, the quadratic-effect model shows the best degree of model fit. This model is also characterized by the best results according to the chi-square, normed chi-square, RMSEA, CFI and TLI results. It is apparent that the representation of the item-position effect as a latent variable substantially improved the model-data fit – especially if a quadratic increase was chosen.

As the factor loadings in the quadratic-effect model were fixed, the variances of the two latent variables were estimated. The variances were 0.11 ($t = 10.22$, $p < .05$) and 0.30 ($t = 8.48$, $p < .05$) for the latent variables representing the ability and the item-position effect in the quadratic-effect model. In order to learn about the relationship of the variances, it was necessary to scale them (Schweizer, 2011). In assuming that the size of the average factor loadings was .5 the scaled variances of the latent variables are 0.066 and 0.052 in corresponding order. The original scaling procedure assumed an average factor loading of 1.0 that considerably deviated from what was normally observed in empirical data. According to these numbers the basic ability accounted for 55.9 % of the variance at the latent level and the item-position effect for 44.1%.

Conclusion

The item-position effect can considerably impact the fit of a confirmatory factor model. This is seen from the improvement in model fit due to the inclusion of an additional latent variable und also from the comparison of the variances of the latent variables. It is also obvious that the item-position effect can impair a demonstration of the structural validity of a scale. In the face of poor model fit when investigating structural validity, the researcher should consider an item-position effect as a possible reason.

Additionally, it should be noted that the item-position effect is not simply an effect associated with an observational method. Recent research found that the latent variable representing the item-position effect in APM was related to executive attention (Ren, Wang, Altmeyer, & Schweizer, 2014). Furthermore, Schweizer, Reiss, Schreiner, and Altmeyer (2012) analyzed two reasoning scales. For both scales, two latent variables were identified, respectively, representing reasoning and the item-position effect. The two latent variables representing reasoning were substantially correlated with each other. The same was found for the two latent variables representing the item-position effects. But none of the correlations between reasoning and the item-position effect from different scales reached the level of statistical significance (Schweizer et al., 2012).

The Effect Due to Item Wording

Self-report surveys are a preferred means for collecting data about traits, emotions, attitudes, preferences, beliefs and other aspects of human behavior. In such a survey, the language plays a major role because it stimulates the cognitive processes generating the responses. Unfortunately, cognitive processing can imply a kind of distortion that becomes apparent as a method effect respectively a response bias, as for example, the acquiescence bias which is the tendency to generally agree with the statements of a questionnaire. Because similar phrases and similar wordings seem to promote the occurrence of biased responses, it has been recommended to vary the wording of items, that is, the direction of the item (e.g., DeVellis, 1991; Nunnally, 1978; Spector, 1992). Thus, some items are worded positively (e.g., "I like parties.") and others are worded negatively (e.g., "I am not outgoing.") so that sometimes agreement and sometimes disagreement is characteristic for a given trait. In the case of a change in the item wording direction, a more thorough cognitive processing is stimulated than if all items are in the same direction. Suppressing the influence of a potential response bias this way is considered as a provision that has no effect on the relationship between item and corresponding construct (Marsh, 1996). As a consequence, many scales are composed of a combination of positively and negatively worded items on the same scale.

The variation of the item wording, however, reduces the homogeneity of survey scales (e.g., DiStefano & Motl, 2006; Quilty, Oakman, & Risko, 2006; Rauch, Schweizer, & Moosbrugger, 2007; Vautier, Steyer, Jmel, & Raufaste, 2005). The item-wording effect appears to be especially prominent if the scale is composed of equal numbers of positively and negatively worded items. A lot of research work on the effect of item wording concentrated on the Rosenberg Self-Esteem Scale (Rosenberg, 1989) and the Life Orientation Test (Scheier, Carver, & Bridges, 1994); each one of these scales comprises equal numbers of positively and negatively worded items.

The heterogeneity among items has led to doubts concerning the assumed unidimensional structure of scales. Some researchers interpret this observation as an indication of two dimensions underlying the items of the scale, that is, the responses result from two latent variables instead of only one (e.g., Herzberg, Glaesmer, & Hoyer, 2006). However, this interpretation might be premature since there is usually a considerable dependency of the two dimensions, suggesting a hierarchical structure or overlap among the constructs. Thus, there are two alternative interpretations that should be considered: the low degree of homogeneity may be perceived as a method effect, or alternatively as the outcome of the contributions of two related but distinguishable traits.

In a series of six studies DiStefano and Motl (2006) investigated the effect of different item wordings on the structure of the Rosenberg Self-Esteem Scale and the Social Physique Anxiety Scale. Their analyses revealed that the effect due to item-wording can best be depicted by a latent variable.

Models for Investigating the Effect of Item Wording

The confirmatory factor models considering an effect due to item wording originate from the models proposed for investigating multitrait–multimethod matrices (Marsh, 1989; Marsh & Bailey, 1991; see also Chapter 14 of this volume). The MTMM design is quite complex because of the systematic combination of several traits and several methods, and it is necessary to allow each manifest variable to load on two latent variables – one trait variable and one method variable. Several MTMM models have been proposed for investigating such data. Two of them have become especially important for the investigation of the method effect due to item wording. There is the type of models characterized by correlated traits and correlated methods with one group of correlated latent variables representing the traits and another group of correlated latent variables associated with the methods. It is known as general CFA model (GCFA; Widaman, 1985) and also addressed as the correlated trait-correlated method (CTCM) model. In case that the influence of the assessment method on the measurement is inconsistent, the representation of a method by a factor is insufficient. Instead, the method factors are replaced by correlated uniqueness to remove variance (Marsh, 1988, 1989). This model is labeled correlated uniqueness CFA model (CUCFA) or correlated trait-correlated uniqueness (CTCU) model. The appropriateness of the CTCU model depends on the number of manifest variables. This model may be appropriate for small numbers of manifest variables, as it may cause an inflation of parameter estimates when there are many manifest variables that load on the same method factor.

The controversy about the structure of scales composed of positively and negatively worded items in combination with attempts to model method effects led to a set of specific models to investigate questionnaire data for the presence of an item-wording effect. These models are based on the following hypotheses.

Hypothesis 1

The responses to the positively and negatively worded items of the item list are due to the same trait. Thus, the congeneric model that assumes one latent variable describes appropriately the participants' responses to the questionnaire. This hypothesis is tested by Model 1 in Figure 15.2, which provides a graphical representation of a scale composed of three positively worded and three negatively worded items.

Hypothesis 1a$^{p/n}$

The responses to the positively and negatively worded items are due to the same trait in combination with the *consistent* influence of the method used with data collection. The consistent influence of the method can be expected to give rise to systematic variance that provides the

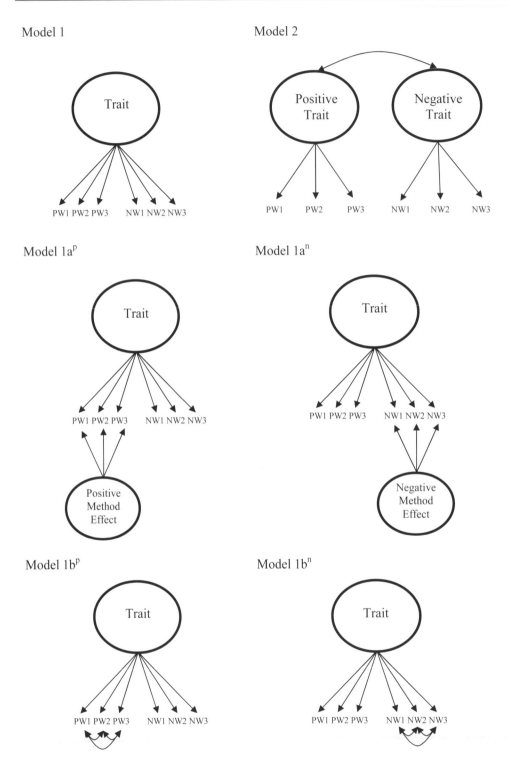

Figure 15.2. Illustrations of the models for representing scales composed of equal numbers of positively and negatively worded items.
Note. [n]negative wording; [p]positive wording.

basis for an additional latent variable. Proceeding from this hypothesis, a latent variable can be derived from all items to represent the trait. Additionally, an item-wording effect can be depicted by a second latent variable derived either from the negative items (Hypothesis $1a^n$) or from the positive items (Hypothesis $1a^p$) due to the consistent influence of the wording direction. This hypothesis is tested by Models $1a^n$ and $1a^p$ in Figure 15.2.

Hypothesis $1b^{p/n}$

The responses to the positively and negatively worded items of the item list are due to the same trait in combination with an *inconsistent* influence originating from the assessment method. As the influence of the method is not consistent, a latent variable cannot describe the method effect. Nevertheless, its influence is reflected by correlated residuals of the positively (see Model $1b^p$ in Figure 15.2) or negatively worded items (see Model $1b^n$ in Figure 15.2).

Hypothesis 2

The responses to the positively and negatively worded items of the item list are attributed to different traits as represented by Model 2 in Figure 15.2.

From the hypotheses, it is apparent that either one (Models 1, 1a, and 1b) or two traits (Model 2) are to be represented in investigating the effect of item wording. Furthermore, there are usually two different assessment methods, for example positively and negatively worded items. However, only one of them is considered at a time in order to avoid identification problems. This restriction is especially useful if the number of items is small. As a consequence of this restriction, there is the question whether positive wording or negative wording needs to be considered. According to DiStefano and Motl (2006) a method effect has primarily been found in negatively worded items. Various reasons have been considered as the source of this effect, such as social desirability and the avoidance of unfavorable feedback. According to a recent study the positive wording of items is associated with the acquiescence style of responding (DiStefano, Morgan, & Motl, 2012a, 2012b). Although presently the major bulk of evidence regarding this issue suggests the consideration of the method effect due to negatively worded items, all this evidence does not exclude the possibility of a method effect resulting from positively worded items. Nevertheless, it is the modeling of this effect that is helpful in achieving a good degree of model fit (Rauch, Schweizer, & Moosbrugger, 2007).

Demonstration

The Personal Optimism Scale measures the generalized expectation of a positive outcome concerning oneself (Schweizer & Koch, 2001). Thereby, the emphasis is on one's personal optimism as distinguished from optimism regarding other people or objects. The expectations concerning one's own optimism level are usually much more positive than expectations for optimism regarding other sources. This scale comprised four positively and four negatively worded items. With a balanced combination of items, it is likely that there is an effect due to item wording.

The models of Figure 15.2 provide the outset to investigate the structure of the Personal Optimism Scale. The differences of the models are especially apparent when specifying the matrices of factor loadings to be estimated, since each model must be specified differently. Assuming that there are eight manifest variables, Table 15.2 includes the columns associated with the specification of parameters to be estimated for each of the models outlined in Figure 15.2.

Table 15.2. The lambda matrices for the models proposed for investigating the effect of item wording

Number of the model					
1	2	1a^n	1b^n	1a^p	1b^p
$\begin{bmatrix} \lambda_{11} \\ \lambda_{21} \\ \lambda_{31} \\ \lambda_{41} \\ \lambda_{51} \\ \lambda_{61} \\ \lambda_{71} \\ \lambda_{81} \end{bmatrix}$	$\begin{bmatrix} \lambda_{11} & 0 \\ \lambda_{21} & 0 \\ \lambda_{31} & 0 \\ \lambda_{41} & 0 \\ 0 & \lambda_{52} \\ 0 & \lambda_{62} \\ 0 & \lambda_{72} \\ 0 & \lambda_{82} \end{bmatrix}$	$\begin{bmatrix} \lambda_{11} & 0 \\ \lambda_{21} & 0 \\ \lambda_{31} & 0 \\ \lambda_{41} & 0 \\ \lambda_{51} & \lambda_{52} \\ \lambda_{61} & \lambda_{62} \\ \lambda_{71} & \lambda_{72} \\ \lambda_{81} & \lambda_{82} \end{bmatrix}$	$\begin{bmatrix} \lambda_{11} \\ \lambda_{21} \\ \lambda_{31} \\ \lambda_{41} \\ \lambda_{51} \\ \lambda_{61} \\ \lambda_{71} \\ \lambda_{81} \end{bmatrix}$	$\begin{bmatrix} \lambda_{11} & \lambda_{12} \\ \lambda_{21} & \lambda_{22} \\ \lambda_{31} & \lambda_{32} \\ \lambda_{41} & \lambda_{42} \\ \lambda_{51} & 0 \\ \lambda_{61} & 0 \\ \lambda_{71} & 0 \\ \lambda_{81} & 0 \end{bmatrix}$	$\begin{bmatrix} \lambda_{11} \\ \lambda_{21} \\ \lambda_{31} \\ \lambda_{41} \\ \lambda_{51} \\ \lambda_{61} \\ \lambda_{71} \\ \lambda_{81} \end{bmatrix}$

Note. ^{n}negative wording; ^{p}positive wording.

Furthermore, it is necessary to specify the $q \times q$ covariance matrices of latent variables (i.e., $\boldsymbol{\Phi}$). For model identification the variances of the factors are set equal to one or, alternatively, need to be scaled, by setting one factor loading equal to one. Since it is a basic assumption that traits and methods should not overlap, the covariance between the two latent variables is set equal to zero. Only in the case of Model 2 the relationship between the latent variables is allowed. Moreover, the matrix that includes the error variances and error covariances (i.e., $\boldsymbol{\Theta}$) plays a crucial role. In the Models 1, 2, 1a^n and 1a^p the error covariance matrix is a diagonal matrix. In contrast, Models 1b^n and 1b^p set some of the covariances free for estimation (see Table 15.3).

Table 15.3. The theta ($\boldsymbol{\Theta}$) matrices for the Models 1b^n and 1b^p

Type of model	
1b^n	1b^p
$\begin{bmatrix} \theta_{11} & 0 & 0 & 0 & 0 & 0 & 0 & 0 \\ 0 & \theta_{22} & 0 & 0 & 0 & 0 & 0 & 0 \\ 0 & 0 & \theta_{33} & 0 & 0 & 0 & 0 & 0 \\ 0 & 0 & 0 & \theta_{44} & 0 & 0 & 0 & 0 \\ 0 & 0 & 0 & 0 & \theta_{55} & \theta_{56} & \theta_{57} & \theta_{58} \\ 0 & 0 & 0 & 0 & \theta_{65} & \theta_{66} & \theta_{67} & \theta_{68} \\ 0 & 0 & 0 & 0 & \theta_{75} & \theta_{76} & \theta_{77} & \theta_{78} \\ 0 & 0 & 0 & 0 & \theta_{85} & \theta_{86} & \theta_{87} & \theta_{88} \end{bmatrix}$	$\begin{bmatrix} \theta_{11} & \theta_{12} & \theta_{13} & \theta_{14} & 0 & 0 & 0 & 0 \\ \theta_{21} & \theta_{22} & \theta_{23} & \theta_{24} & 0 & 0 & 0 & 0 \\ \theta_{31} & 0\theta_{32} & \theta_{33} & \theta_{34} & 0 & 0 & 0 & 0 \\ \theta_{41} & 0\theta_{42} & \theta_{43} & \theta_{44} & 0 & 0 & 0 & 0 \\ 0 & 0 & 0 & 0 & \theta_{55} & 0 & 0 & 0 \\ 0 & 0 & 0 & 0 & 0 & \theta_{66} & 0 & 0 \\ 0 & 0 & 0 & 0 & 0 & 0 & \theta_{77} & 0 \\ 0 & 0 & 0 & 0 & 0 & 0 & 0 & \theta_{88} \end{bmatrix}$

Note. ^{n}negative wording; ^{p}positive wording.

To demonstrate the analysis of the item-wording effect, the Personal Optimism Scale (Schweizer & Koch, 2001) was applied to a sample of university students ($N = 248$). The four positively worded items and the four negatively worded items of the scale were interspersed among the items of other scales. The models presented in Figure 15.2 were investigated by using LISREL and evaluated by the following model fit indices: normed chi-squares, RMSEA, SRMR, CFI, TLI. Table 15.4 gives the results for the set of models.

Table 15.4. Fit results of investigating the Personal Optimism Scale (N = 248)

Model	χ^2	df	normed χ^2	RMSEA	SRMR	CFI	TLI	AIC
1	72.51	20	3.62	.097	.056	0.91	0.88	104
2	38.47	19	2.02	.061	.041	0.97	0.95	72
1a[n]	27.54	16	1.72	.051	.044	0.98	0.96	67
1b[n]	27.15	14	1.94	.058	.034	0.97	0.95	72
1a[p]	33.95	16	2.12	.064	.053	0.97	0.94	73
1b[p]	29.60	14	2.11	.063	.037	0.97	0.94	73

Note. [n]negative wording; [p]positive wording. AIC = Akaike's information criterion; CFI = comparative fit index; RMSEA = root mean square error of approximation; SRMR = standardized root mean square residual; TLI = Tucker Lewis index.

As can be seen from Table 15.4, only Model 1a[n] and Model 1b[n] showed a good model-data fit assuming a general optimism latent variable in combination with a method factor for the negatively worded items (Model 1a[n]) or correlated error components of the negatively worded items. According to the AIC results that enable the comparison of nonnested models, Model 1a[n] including a method latent variable appears to be superior to Model 1b[n]. Furthermore, Model 1 (the unidimensional model) is clearly inappropriate to account for the observed variances and covariances of the items, whereas Model 2 shows good model-data fit according to selected fit statistics. However, the latent variables of Model 2 are closely related to each other; the standardized correlation coefficient of r = .77 suggests substantial overlap between the two traits – personal optimism and personal pessimism – and additionally the existence of a common source of responding, which could be interpreted as personal optimism.

Conclusion

The effect due to item wording can be a problem when investigating the structural validity of a scale. Although the variation of item wording is motivated by the expectation to avoid response biases and, thus, to improve the validity of measurement, it is usually not achievable without negative consequences. One problem results from the increased homogeneity among the items phrased in the same direction. Having two subsets of items showing similarity due to the direction of item wording leads to two subsets of items showing increased homogeneity. This, in turn, means that the overall degree of homogeneity for the scale is likely to be decreased. If two large subsets of items with different wording directions are included in the same scale, it is unlikely that the scale will exhibit unidimensionality. Models including one method factor are most appropriate for taking this construct relevant variance into consideration. With the help of such models, it can be demonstrated that there is one underlying content dimension.

Concluding Remarks

Psychometric data may exhibit method effects, such as effects due to the item wording direction or item position. Such effects appear to be more the norm than the exception (Micceri, 1989). They indicate that there is distortion in measurement. In some cases the effect can easily be detected, but not so easily in other cases. The detection of such an effect is important because it can influence the evaluation of the quality of a scale and, consequently, affect research results on the construct the scale intends to measure. The likelihood of the detection of such an effect depends on the sensitivity of the statistical methods applied for investigating the structure of the data. The more sophisticated the statistical methods, the larger the likelihood of the detection of such an effect and of disturbance in data analysis.

For a while researchers coped with such effects or disturbance by modeling correlated errors. However, allowing errors to correlate with each other is not appropriate because correlated errors usually improve model fit without providing an account for the misfit. Frequently it is not clear whether a disturbance is really due to the method applied in data collection. It may also result from a specificity of the sample, the context of data collection or a specific facet of the trait that is over-represented by the items of the scale. Furthermore, it is possible that there is another important source of responding that was neglected in constructing the model. Allowing for correlated errors is not helpful in identifying such sources of misfit. Therefore, whenever possible the method effect should be explicitly modeled in order to separate it from the trait that the scale is intended to measure. In sum, the modeling of method effects leads to a better account of the data than otherwise and to clarification concerning the acceptability of the sources influencing model misfit.

References

Bollen, K. A. (1989). *Structural equations with latent variables*. New York, NY: Wiley.

Campbell, D. T., & Fiske, D. (1959). Convergent and discriminant validation by the multitrait-multi-method matrix. *Psychological Bulletin, 56*, 81–105. http://doi.org/10.1037/h0046016

Campbell, D. T., & Mohr, P. J. (1950). The effect of ordinal position upon responses to items in a check list. *Journal of Applied Psychology, 34*, 62–67. http://doi.org/10.1037/h0061818

Chen, F. F., West, S. G., & Sousa, K. H. (2006). A comparison of bifactor and second-order model of quality of life. *Multivariate Behavioral Research, 41*, 189–225. http://doi.org/10.1207/s15327906mbr4102_5

Choi, J., Harring, J. R., & Hancock, G. R. (2009). Latent growth modeling for logistic response functions. *Multivariate Behavioral Research, 44*, 620–645. http://doi.org/10.1080/00273170903187657

DeVellis, R. F. (1991). *Scale development: theory and application*. Newbury Park, CA: Sage.

DiStefano, C., & Motl, R. (2006). Further investigating method effects associated with negatively worded items on self-report surveys. *Structural Equation Modeling, 13*, 440–464. http://doi.org/10.1207/s15328007sem1303_6

DiStefano, C., Morgan, G. B., & Motl, R. (2012a). An examination of personality characteristics related to acquiescence. *Journal of Applied Measurement, 13*, 1–16.

DiStefano, C., Morgan, G. B., & Motl, R. (2012b). Detecting acquiescence underlying Rosenberg's Self Esteem Scale using the Rasch partial credit model. In S. De Wals & K. Meszaros (Eds.), *Handbook of self esteem*. Hauppauge, NY: Nova Science Publishers.

Ebbinghaus, H. (1885). *Memory: A contribution to experimental psychology*. New York, NY: Dover.

Embretson, S. E. (1991). A multidimensional latent trait model for measuring learning and change. *Psychometrika, 56*, 495–515. http://doi.org/10.1007/BF02294487

Gittler, G., & Wild, B. (1989). Der Einsatz des LLTM bei der Konstruktion des Itempools für das adaptive Testen [The use of LLTM for the construction of an item pool for adaptive testing]. In K. D. Kubinger (Ed.), *Moderne Testtheorie – Ein Abriss samt neuesten Beiträgen* (pp. 115–139). Munich, Germany: PVU.

Gulliksen, H. (1950). *Theory of mental tests*. New York, NY: Wiley & Sons. http://doi.org/10.1037/13240-000

Hamilton, J. C., & Shuminsky, T. R. (1990). Self-awareness mediates the relationship between serial position and item reliability. *Journal of Personality and Social Psychology, 59*, 1301–1307. http://doi.org/10.1037/0022-3514.59.6.1301

Hartig, J., Hölzel, B., & Moosbrugger, H. (2007). A confirmatory analysis of item reliability trends (CAIRT): differentiating true score and error variance in the analysis of item context effects. *Multivariate Behavioral Research, 42*, 157–183. http://doi.org/10.1080/00273170701341266

Herzberg, P. Y., Glaesmer, G., & Hoyer, J. (2006). Separating optimism and pessimism: a robust psychometric analysis of the Revised Life Orientation Test (LOT-R). *Psychological Assessment, 18*, 433–438. http://doi.org/10.1037/1040-3590.18.4.433

Hu, L., & Bentler, P. M. (1999). Cutoff criteria for fit indexes in covariance structure analysis: conventional criteria versus new alternatives. *Structural Equation Modeling, 6*, 1–55. http://doi.org/10.1080/10705519909540118

Jöreskog, K. G. (1971). Statistical analysis of sets of congeneric tests. *Psychometrika, 36*, 109–133. http://doi.org/10.1007/BF02291393

Knowles, E. S. (1988). Item context effects on personality scales: Measuring changes the measure. *Journal of Personality and Social Psychology, 55*, 312–320. http://doi.org/10.1037/0022-3514.55.2.312

Knowles, E. S., & Byers, B. (1996). Reliability shifts in measurement reactivity: Driven by content engagement or self-engagement? *Journal of Personality and Social Psychology, 70*, 1080–1090. http://doi.org/10.1037/0022-3514.70.5.1080

Kubinger, K. D. (2003). On artificial results due to using factor analysis for dichotomous variables. *Psychology Science, 45*, 106–110.

Marsh, H. W. (1988). Multitrait-multimethod analysis. In J. P. Keeves (Ed.), *Educational research methodology, measurement, and evaluation: An international handbook* (pp. 570–578). Oxford, UK: Pergamon.

Marsh, H. W. (1989). Confirmatory factor analysis of multitrait-multimethod data: Many problems and a few solutions. *Applied Psychological Measurement, 13*, 335–361. http://doi.org/10.1177/014662168901300402

Marsh, H. W. (1996). Positive and negative global self-esteem: A substantively meaningful distinction or artifactors? *Journal of Personality and Social Psychology, 70*, 810–819. http://doi.org/10.1037/0022-3514.70.4.810

Marsh, H. W., & Bailey, M. (1991). Confirmatory factor analyses of multitrait-multimethod data: A comparison of alternative models. *Applied Psychological Measurement, 15*, 47–70. http://doi.org/10.1177/014662169101500106

McArdle, J. J. (1986). Latent variable growth within behavior genetic models. *Behavior Genetics, 16*, 163–200. http://doi.org/10.1007/BF01065485

McArdle, J. J. (1989). Structural modeling experiments using multiple growth functions. In P. Ackerman, R. Kanfer, & R. Cudeck (Eds.), *Learning and individual differences: Ability, motivation and methodology* (pp. 71–117). Hillsdale, NJ: Erlbaum.

McArdle, J. J. (2009). Latent variable modeling of differences and change with longitudinal data. *Annual Review of Psychology, 60*, 577–605. http://doi.org/10.1146/annurev.psych.60.110707.163612

McDonald, R. P. (1974). Difficulty factors in binary data. *British Journal of Mathematical and Statistical Psychology, 27*, 82–99. http://doi.org/10.1111/j.2044-8317.1974.tb00530.x

Micceri, T. (1989). The unicorn, the normal curve, and other improbable creatures. *Psychological Bulletin, 105*, 156–166. http://doi.org/10.1037/0033-2909.105.1.156

Novick, M. R. (1966). The axioms and principal results of classical test theory. *Journal of Mathematical Psychology, 3*, 1–18. http://doi.org/10.1016/0022-2496(66)90002-2

Nunnally, J. M. (1978). *Psychometric theory*. New York, NY: McGraw-Hill.

Quilty, L.C., Oakman, J. M., & Risko, E. (2006). Correlates of the Rosenberg self-esteem scale method effects. *Structural Equation Modeling, 13*, 99–117. http://doi.org/10.1207/s15328007sem1301_5

Rasch, G. (1980). *Probabilistic models for some intelligence and attainment tests* (Copenhagen, Danish Institute for Educational Research, expanded edition, with foreword and afterword by B. D. Wright). Chicago, IL: The University of Chicago Press. (Original work published 1960)

Rauch, W., Schweizer, K., & Moosbrugger, H. (2007). Method effects due to social desirability as a parsimonious explanation of the deviation from unidimensionality in LOT-R scores. *Personality and Individual Differences, 42*, 1597–1607. http://doi.org/10.1016/j.paid.2006.10.035

Raven, J. C., Raven, J., & Court, J. H. (1997). *Raven's progressive matrices and vocabulary scales*. Edinburgh, UK: J. C. Raven.

Ren, X., Wang, T., Altmeyer, M., & Schweizer, K. (2014). A learning-based account of fluid intelligence from the perspective of the position effect. *Learning and Individual Differences, 31*, 30–35.

Rosenberg, M. (1989). *Society and adolescent self-image* (revised ed.). Middletown, CT: Wesleyan University Press.

Scheier, I. H., Carver, C. S., & Bridges, M. W. (1994). Distinguishing optimism from neuroticism (and trait anxiety, self-mastery, and self-esteem): A re-evaluation of the Life Orientation Test. *Journal of Personality and Social Psychology, 67*, 1063–1078. http://doi.org/10.1037/0022-3514.67.6.1063

Schweizer, K. (2006). The fixed-links model in combination with the polynomial function as tool for investigating choice reaction time data. *Structural Equation Modeling, 13*, 403–419. http://doi.org/10.1207/s15328007sem1303_4

Schweizer, K. (2008). Investigating experimental effects within the framework of structural equation modeling: An example with effects on both error scores and reaction times. *Structural Equation Modeling, 15*, 327–345. http://doi.org/10.1080/10705510801922621

Schweizer, K. (2011). Scaling variances of latent variables by standardizing loadings: applications to working memory and the position effect. *Multivariate Behavioral Research, 46*, 938–955. http://doi.org/10.1080/00273171.2011.625312

Schweizer, K. (2012). The position effect in reasoning items considered from the CFA perspective. *International Journal of Educational and Psychological Assessment, 11*, 44–58.

Schweizer, K. (2013). A threshold-free approach to the study of the structure of binary data. *International Journal of Statistics and Probability, 2*, 67–75. http://doi.org/10.5539/ijsp.v2n2p67

Schweizer, K. & Koch, W. (2001). The assessment of components of optimism by POSO-E. *Personality and Individual Differences, 31*, 563–574. http://doi.org/10.1016/S0191-8869(00)00161-6

Schweizer, K., & Reiss, S. (2014). The structural validity of the FPI Neuroticism Scale revisited in the framework of the generalized linear model. *Psychological Test and Assessment Modeling, 56*, 320–335.

Schweizer, K., Reiss, S., Schreiner, M., & Altmeyer, M. (2012). Validity improvement in two reasoning measures due to the elimination of the position effect. *Journal of Individual Differences, 33*, 54–61. http://doi.org/10.1027/1614-0001/a000062

Schweizer, K., & Ren, X. (2013). The position effect in tests with a time limit: the consideration of interruption and working speed. *Psychological Test and Assessment Modeling, 55*, 62–78.

Schweizer, K., Ren, X., & Wang, T. (2015). A comparison of confirmatory factor analysis of binary data on the basis of tetrachoric correlations and of probability-based covariances: a simulation study. In R. E. Millsap, D. M. Bolt, L. A. van der Ark, & W.-C. Wang (Eds.), *Quantitative psychology research* (pp. 273–292). Heidelberg, Germany: Springer.

Schweizer, K., Schreiner, M., & Gold, A. (2009). The confirmatory investigation of APM items with loadings as a function of the position and easiness of items: A two-dimensional model of APM. *Psychology Science Quarterly, 51*, 47–64.

Schweizer, K., Troche, S., & Rammsayer, T. (2011). On the special relationship between fluid and general intelligence: New evidence obtained by considering the position effect. *Personality and Individual Differences, 50*, 1249–1254. http://doi.org/10.1016/j.paid.2011.02.019

Spector, P. E. (1992). *Summated rating scale construction: An introduction.* Newbury Park, CA: Sage. http://doi.org/10.4135/9781412986038

Tabachnick, B. G., & Fidell, L. S. (2007). *Using multivariate statistics* (5th ed.). Boston, MA: Allyn & Bacon.

Tisak, J., & Tisak, M. S. (1996). Longitudinal models of reliability and validity: A latent curve approach. *Applied Psychological Measurement, 20*, 275–288. http://doi.org/10.1177/014662169602000307

Vautier, S., Steyer, R., Jmel, S., & Raufaste, E. (2005). Imperfect or perfect dynamic bipolarity? The case of antonymous affective judgements. *Structural Equation Modeling, 12*, 391–410. http://doi.org/10.1207/s15328007sem1203_3

Verguts, T., & De Boeck, P. (2000). A Rasch model for detecting learning while solving an intelligence test. *Applied Psychological Measurement, 24*, 151–162. http://doi.org/10.1177/01466210022031589

Widaman, K. F. (1985). Hierarchically nested covariance structure models for multitrait-multimethod data. *Applied Psychological Measurement, 9*, 1–26. http://doi.org/10.1177/014662168500900101

Contributors

Deborah Bandalos
Assessment and Measurement PhD Program
James Madison University
821 S. Main Street
Harrisonburg, VA 22801
USA
Tel. +1 (540) 568-7132 (office)
E-mail bandaldl@jmu.edu

Barbara M. Byrne
School of Psychology
University of Ottawa
Ottawa, Ontario KIN 6N5
Canada
E-mail bmbch@uottawa.ca

Gary L. Canivez
Eastern Illinois University
600 Lincoln Avenue
Charleston, IL 61920
USA
E-mail glcanivez@eiu.edu
http://www.ux1.eiu.edu/~glcanivez

Christine DiStefano
138 Wardlaw Hall
Department of Educational Studies
University of South Carolina
Columbia, SC 29208
USA
E-mail distefan@mailbox.sc.edu

W. Holmes Finch
Office of the Dean
Teachers College (TC), Room 1005
Ball State University
Muncie, IN 47306-0625
USA
E-mail whfinch@bsu.edu

Sara J. Finney
Center for Assessment & Research Studies
James Madison University--MSC 6806
Harrisonburg, VA 22807
USA
E-mail finneysj@jmu.edu

Brian French
100 Dairy Street
College of Education
Washington State University
Pullman, WA 99164
USA
E-mail frenchb@wsu.edu

Jerusha J. Gerstner
Talent Management Analytics and Solutions
Marriott Corporation
Washington, DC
USA
E-mail jerusha.gerstner@marriott.com

Fred Greer
143 Wardlaw Hall
Department of Educational Studies
University of South Carolina
Columbia, SC 29208
USA
E-mail greerf@mailbox.sc.edu

Robert L. Johnson
131 Wardlaw Hall
Department of Educational Studies
University of South Carolina
Columbia, SC 29208
USA
E-mail rjohnson@mailbox.sc.edu

Lale Khorramdel
Educational Testing Service/Research &
Development
Center for Global Assessment
660 Rosedale Road, E-215
Princeton, NJ 08541
USA
E-mail lkhorramdel@ets.org

Jason P. Kopp
American Board of Surgery
1617 John F. Kennedy Boulevard, Suite 860
Philadelphia, PA 19103
USA

Klaus D. Kubinger
Division of Psychological Assessment and
Applied Psychometrics
Faculty of Psychology
University of Vienna
Liebiggasse 5
1010 Vienna
Austria
E-mail klaus.kubinger@univie.ac.at

Jin Liu
115B Wardlaw Hall
Department of Educational Studies
University of South Carolina
Columbia, SC 29208
USA
E-mail jinliu091128@hotmail.com

Grant B. Morgan
Department of Educational Psychology
Baylor University
One Bear Place #97301
Waco, TX 76798-7301
USA
E-mail grant_morgan@baylor.edu

Ulf-Dietrich Reips
Psychological Methods, Assessment, and
iScience
Department of Psychology Box 31
78457 Konstanz
Germany
http://iscience.uni.konstanz.de

Siegbert Reiss
Department of Psychology
Goethe University Frankfurt
Theodor-W.-Adorno-Platz 6
60323 Frankfurt am Main
Germany
E-mail reiss@psych.uni-frankfurt.de

Karl Schweizer
Department of Psychology
Goethe University Frankfurt
Theodor-W.-Adorno-Platz 6
60323 Frankfurt am Main
Germany
E-mail k.schweizer@psych.uni-frankfurt.de

Marilyn S. Thompson
T. Denny Sanford School of Social and
Family Dynamics
Arizona State University
Tempe, AZ 85287-3701
Tel. +1 (480) 727-6924
E-mail m.thompson@asu.edu

Stefan Troche
Department of Psychology and Psychotherapy
University of Witten/Herdecke
Alfred-Herrhausen-Str. 44
58455 Witten
Germany
E-mail stefan.troche@uni-wh.de

Fons J. R. van de Vijver
Department of Culture Studies
Room D258
Tilburg University
P.O. Box 90153
5000 LE Tilburg
The Netherlands
E-mail fons.vandevijver@uvt.nl

Matthias von Davier
Educational Testing Service/
Research & Development
Center for Global Assessment
660 Rosedale Road, E-201
Princeton, NJ 08541
USA
E-mail mvondavier@ets.org

Subject Index

Also available in the series
Psychological Assessment – Science and Practice

Vol. 1
Tuulia M. Ortner, Fons J. R. van de Vijver (Eds.)
Behavior-Based Assessment in Psychology
Going Beyond Self-Report in the Personality, Affective, Motivation, and Social Domains
2015 (July), vi + 232 pages
ISBN 978-0-88937-437-9
US $63.00 / £36.00 / €44.95

Vol. 2
Yael Benyamini, Marie Johnston, Evangelos C. Karademas (Eds.)
Assessment in Health Psychology
2016 (February), vi + 345 pages
ISBN 978-0-88937-452-2
US $69.00 / £39.00 / €49.95

For more information and further volumes, please see www.hogrefe.com
Prices subject to change.